EXAMPLES & EXPLANATIONS

Secured
Transactions

ASPEN PUBLISHERS

EXAMPLES&EXPLANATIONS

Secured Transactions

Fourth Edition

James Brook
Professor of Law
New York Law School

Wolters Kluwer
Law & Business

AUSTIN   BOSTON   CHICAGO   NEW YORK   THE NETHERLANDS

Aspen Publishers
Attn: Permissions Department
76 Ninth Avenue, 7th Floor
New York, NY 10011-5201

To contact Customer Care, e-mail customer.care@aspenpublishers.com, call 1-800-234-1660, fax 1-800-901-9075, or mail correspondence to:

Aspen Publishers
Attn: Order Department
PO Box 990
Frederick, MD 21705

Printed in the United States of America.

1 2 3 4 5 6 7 8 9 0

ISBN 978-0-7355-6797-9

Library of Congress Cataloging-in-Publication Data

Brook, James, 1946-
Secured transactions : examples and explanations / James Brook. — 4th ed.
     p. cm.
Includes index.
ISBN-13: 978-0-7355-6797-9
1. Chattel mortgages — United States. 2. Security (Law) — United States.
3. Personal property — United States. 4. Personal property — United States. I. Title.
     KF1053.Z9B76 2008
     346.7307′4 — dc22

                                                                    2007035696

About Wolters Kluwer Law & Business

Wolters Kluwer Law & Business is a leading provider of research information and workflow solutions in key specialty areas. The strengths of the individual brands of Aspen Publishers, CCH, Kluwer Law International and Loislaw are aligned within Wolters Kluwer Law & Business to provide comprehensive, in-depth solutions and expert-authored content for the legal, professional and education markets.

CCH was founded in 1913 and has served more than four generations of business professionals and their clients. The CCH products in the Wolters Kluwer Law & Business group are highly regarded electronic and print resources for legal, securities, antitrust and trade regulation, government contracting, banking, pension, payroll, employment and labor, and health-care reimbursement and compliance professionals.

Aspen Publishers is a leading information provider for attorneys, business professionals and law students. Written by preeminent authorities, Aspen products offer analytical and practical information in a range of specialty practice areas from securities law and intellectual property to mergers and acquisitions and pension/benefits. Aspen's trusted legal education resources provide professors and students with high-quality, up-to-date and effective resources for successful instruction and study in all areas of the law.

Kluwer Law International supplies the global business community with comprehensive English-language international legal information. Legal practitioners, corporate counsel and business executives around the world rely on the Kluwer Law International journals, loose-leafs, books and electronic products for authoritative information in many areas of international legal practice.

Loislaw is a premier provider of digitized legal content to small law firm practitioners of various specializations. Loislaw provides attorneys with the ability to quickly and efficiently find the necessary legal information they need, when and where they need it, by facilitating access to primary law as well as state-specific law, records, forms and treatises.

Wolters Kluwer Law & Business, a unit of Wolters Kluwer, is headquartered in New York and Riverwoods, Illinois. Wolters Kluwer is a leading multinational publisher and information services company.

For Johanna and Andrew

Contents

PART IV. DEFAULT AND ENFORCEMENT

Preface

I start with a simple assumption. You come to this book because for one reason or another you want to learn the basic law relating to secured transactions involving personal property collateral as such transactions are governed by Article 9 of the Uniform Commercial Code. You may be trying to pick this up on your own, but more likely you are in a course — either a course devoted distinctly to the topic or a more expansive survey course in Commercial Law that will necessarily devote a great deal of time to the subject. The book may have been assigned or recommended as additional reading by the professor teaching the course, or you may have come upon it on your own as means of review. Whatever the circumstances, I hope this book is of help. If it is, it will not be simply because you bought it or even because of the considerable energy I put into writing it, but because of the time, energy, and thought you put into using it. Here are a few basic points you should understand from the outset if you are to make the best use of what I have written and what you have bought:

- This is not a review text. You may find it helpful to think of it as a kind of workbook, giving you an organized way of *working through* the various sections, definitions, concepts, and controversies that make up the modern law of secured transactions as rendered in Article 9 of the Uniform Commercial Code.
- This volume is not a substitute for your own copy of the Uniform Commercial Code (including Official Comments). I will be quoting snippets of the Code from time to time. At other points I may simply suggest that you "recall the rule of §9-322(a)(1)" or "look to §9-609(c)." What you have here should not distract you, however, from the fundamental proposition that the law you are learning is found in, not merely suggested by or illustrated through, the exact language of the Code as it has been enacted into law in the several states. I assume throughout that as you work through the material you will always have at your side and at the ready the primary text for the study of secured transactions, the Code itself.
- The general organization and sequence of chapters follows what is a fairly standard order in which the various topics are taken up in courses on Secured Transactions. You should certainly start with Chapter 1 and move on from there. If this book has been assigned or

recommended by your professor you will of course follow his or her instructions as to which chapters to look to when and even as to which Examples to do and which to leave for another day. If you are working through the book on your own and trying to coordinate it with your course, you should be able to determine fairly easily which chapters to take up just by the chapter headings, but if you are having any trouble finding where to turn there is help available by Topic in the Index and a Table showing which Uniform Commercial Code (U.C.C.) sections are dealt with, both at the back of the book.

- Each chapter is structured in the same way: an introductory text, a set of Examples for you to ponder, followed finally by my own Explanations of the questions asked and issues raised by the Examples. It is very important that you appreciate that the introductory text does not purport to outline or give a full account of the chapter's topic. This is not the type of book where you are given all the law up front and then asked to apply the rules and principles to the questions that follow. The law you are going to have to apply is to be found in the Uniform Commercial Code which you have right there with you. In some chapters the introductory text can be very brief. In others it goes on for a while. But in any event the introductory text is meant only to set the stage; its purpose is to put you on the best possible course for learning *through the Examples*. In other words, if you aren't prepared to go through the Examples thoroughly on your own — if not writing down a carefully constructed answer to each one then at least jotting down an idea or two on how you see the situation and how you expect the Code would deal with it — then there's really not much point in your starting the chapter to begin with.

One final note on the Examples: It will not surprise you if when you get to my analysis in the Explanations you find I cannot always offer a simple yes or no in many cases. I am, after all, a law professor and this subject, like any other you have already studied, has its unresolvable questions, places where the statute seems to be of little or no help, and "subtle" difficulties. On the other hand, don't think just because this is the study of law that the answer to even the most simple question must necessarily be open to argument or subject to competing analyses. Sometimes, perhaps most of the time, a question can and should be answered in a word or two, directly and without any hedging. If the answer is "Yes," you should say "Yes." If "No," say "No." Beyond that, of course, you should go on to say why — citing the Code, chapter and verse — you respond as you do. I always give my students in Commercial Transactions courses some rules of thumb to follow, which are in general good advice when dealing with this material, in writing their examination answers:

- Where an answer is given or suggested by a specific section of the Code, make reference to that section.
- Where a particular subsection is relevant, cite the subsection.
- Where a particular word or phrase in the section or subsection is of importance to your answer, identify exactly what that word or phrase is.
- Where an Official Comment answers — or seems to answer — the question, refer to it, reporting as you do whether you have any qualms or questions about the position taken in the Comment.
- Where the answer appears to be dictated by a single fact or a set of facts, make clear what facts those are.

If, as will sometimes be the case, the answer has to be "that depends," say *on what* you see the outcome depending. If you need to know other facts to better analyze the situation, say *whom* you would ask and *what* you would want to know. If the answer seems to depend on how a court would interpret a particular provision or how it would settle a seeming conflict between two provisions, what are the various possible interpretations or resolutions? What argues for one resolution over the other?

As I have said, I hope and expect this book will be helpful. If at the same time you find it stimulating and even mildly entertaining, then so much the better.

James Brook
November 2007

Acknowledgments

I would like to thank Dean Rick Matasar and Associate Deans Steve Ellmann and Jethro Lieberman, who have shown their support in a variety of ways for this project and for my other endeavors at New York Law School. I also wish to acknowledge the continuing contribution of my staff assistant, Silvy Singh, without whom my workdays would be much more difficult and certainly a lot less pleasant. Thanks as well to my colleagues at New York Law School and to the large numbers of students over the past few years with whom I first got a chance to work over and test out so many of the Examples that form the core of this book. The feedback that I have been given by them, in ways subtle and not so subtle, has been of enormous help even if I have not always said as much at the time.

Special thanks go to the people of Aspen Publishers, and in particular to Carol McGeehan, Melody Davies, Kathy Yoon, Taylor Kearns, Peter Skagestad, Annie Sloniker, and Richard Mixter. Their consistent encouragement, gentle nudging when nudging was called for, and good-natured support make them a pleasure to work with and to know.

Portions of the Official Text and Comments to the Uniform Commercial Code reproduced and quoted herein are copyright © 2007 by The American Law Institute and the National Conference of Commissioners on Uniform State Laws and are reprinted with the permission of the Permanent Editorial Board for the Uniform Commercial Code.

A Note on Revised Article I

In 2001, the National Conference of Commissioners on Uniform State Law (NCCUSL) and the American Law Institute (ALI), the two bodies responsible for upkeep of the Uniform Commercial Code, promulgated and sent to the states for adoption a revised version of Article 1. This article, comprising the General Provision of the Code including an important set of definitions and general principles, inevitably ends up coming into play and being cited in any work dealing with any aspect of commercial law. This "new Article 1" did not, at least initially, attract much attention, being adopted only in the U.S. Virgin Islands. Things on the Article 1 revision front were fairly moribund for a while. In the past few years, however, a goodly number of state legislatures have begun to consider and actually adopt this revised version of Article 1. In fact, by the summer of 2007 a slight majority of states, 29 of the 50, had adopted the new version and other states may be doing so in time.

For your purposes in using this book, it generally doesn't matter which version of Article 1 — the original or the revised — you refer to. Just to keep us on our toes, however, I have found that some statutory supplements used in such courses have begun putting the new version of Article 1 at the front of the book, while others have kept the original Article 1 at the front of the book and put the revised version in an appendix. As a practical matter there is no great difference in substance between the original and the new versions of this article, at least as far as we will be using it here, but the definitions have been renumbered and other important passages moved around, which can easily enough lead to confusion or at the least exasperation.

The references to Article 1 in this volume are few enough that I have followed the path of least resistance and given parallel cites to both official versions. So, for example, Original §1-201(39) is for all intents and purposes the same as Revised §1-201(b)(37) [or, as I'll end up abbreviating it, §1-201(39) = §1R-201(b)(37)]. You should be able to use this edition regardless of which version of Article 1 your professor, or your own predilection, has you following.

For the record, however, it should be noted that *none* of the states which have as of this writing adopted revised Article 1 has accepted the substantially and substantively changed new section on choice of law that

NCCUSL and the ALI put into §1R-301 of the Official Version of Revised Article 1. All of the adopting jurisdictions (other than the U.S. Virgin Islands) have retained the prior choice of law provision found in "old" §1-105 even if they have moved it to fit in with the new numbering scheme of the revised version. In addition, and just to keep things more interesting, something like ten of the states that have adopted the revised version have not followed the drafter's lead in changing the Article 1 definition of "good faith" in §1-201(19) — which has since the Code's initial adoption carried the so-called "subjective" definition of that term — with the broader definition proposed for §1R-201(b)(20) in 2001, which adds to this subjective test an objective "commercial reasonableness" component. For the latest information on whether the revised Article 1 has been adopted in any particular jurisdiction, and if so with what, if any, modifications, you will have to do a bit of research. A convenient place to start is at NCCUSL's Web site, http://www.nccusl.org.

Secured
Transactions

PART I

The Article 9 Security Interest and Its Attachment

CHAPTER 1

The Scope of Article 9

BY WAY OF INTRODUCTION

Let's start at the very beginning. Look at §9-101. Nothing terribly interesting or surprising there. Do read, however, the first two sentences of Official Comment 1 to this section:

> This Article supercedes former Uniform Commercial Code (UCC) Article 9. As did its predecessor, it provides a comprehensive scheme for the regulation of security interests in personal property and fixtures.

The former Article 9 to which the comment alludes — which you will also find referred to at times as the "old" or "prerevision" version of the article — was initially promulgated by those bodies that have taken upon themselves responsibility for drafting and upkeep of the Uniform Commercial Code in the early 1960s.* The drafters of that initial version of Article 9 had been confronted with a particularly difficult task. Over the

---

* The Uniform Commercial Code is a joint project of the American Law Institute (ALI) and the National Conference of Commissioners on Uniform State Laws (NCCUSL). Any given part of this project, whether it be the creation of the initial version or a subsequent amendment or wholesale revision of any article, entails a long and complex process involving large numbers of individuals, a drafting committee, numerous advisors and consultants, and so on. The final written product (conventionally referred to as being the work and conveying the intention of a vaguely defined group known as "the drafters" of this or that article or revision) must then be approved by both the sponsoring entities, the ALI and NCCUSL, who then send it out to the states for their individual adoption of the proposal as part of their state statutory law.

years there had arisen a great variety of devices, each with its own intriguing if not terribly illuminating name — for starters, I could mention the pledge, chattel mortgage, conditional sales agreement, trust receipt, and factor's lien — intended to give one party a security interest in another's personal property. The individual states tried to keep up with these developments, each newly devised form of transaction accompanied by its own terminology, arcane rules, and procedures, and in many instances requiring filings covering that one particular type of transaction at some office or offices somewhere in the state, by enacting statutes meant to regulate each type of transaction in turn. The result in any given state was typically something like a jigsaw puzzle of commercial practices, law office procedures, and legislative enactments in which the pieces didn't fit together well at all. Add to this the fact that there was no guarantee that the puzzle, however the ill-fitting pieces were to be jammed together, would look the same in any two states. The complexities and mysteries of the multiplicity of "standard" security devices within any one state were intricate enough. Transactions that had to contend with the laws of more than one state were that much more difficult to carry out with any degree of confidence that things were done as they should be and would not later fall victim to a challenge based on some technical ground or another. This crazy quilt of sundry forms of transactions and nonuniform state laws governing their use and effect resulted in a whole burgeoning area of commercial transactions burdened by a large degree of uncertainty, even for the most careful and conscientious transacting party and his or her lawyer.

The drafters of the original Article 9 met the problem head-on. The article they fashioned — adopted by virtually all of the states with little modification in short order as part of the original adoption of the Uniform Commercial Code — was written on a clean slate. Article 9 explicitly superceded in the state of its adoption all prior legislation dealing with what had up until then been a series of traditional devices piling up over the years, each intended in some way to create a security interest in personal property. With adoption of the initial Article 9, a state would now have in place a *single comprehensive scheme* for the regulation of security interests in personal property. A transaction that in the past may have been denominated a pledge, a chattel mortgage, or a what-have-you could be referred to by the parties involved by the old, traditional term if they so chose. The heading at the top of whatever document the parties drew up, however, was now beside the point. The result of their labors would be, from the law's perspective, one thing and one thing only — an Article 9 security interest. And the rules governing that interest's creation and effect were those set out in Article 9 and nowhere else.

The initial Article was, as I have said, adopted by virtually all of the states by the end of the 1960s, and a generation of lawyers has learned to plan, practice, and — hopefully rarely — litigate under its provisions. Minor amendments were made to the text in later years, but on the whole the text remained as it had been written originally. Then, in 1990, the bodies responsible for upkeep of the Code set up a Study Committee, and following that a Drafting Committee to prepare an entirely new version of Article 9. These committees labored mightily, and not without controversy, but the end result was a totally revised version of Article 9 adopted by the sponsoring bodies in 1998. This version, what will be referred to for at least some years to come as the "new" or "revised" Article 9, was sent to each of the states with the recommendation that it be adopted as a replacement for the state's then-existing prerevision version of the article. Furthermore, to avoid problems that were foreseen if some states were operating under the old version of the article while others were operating under the new, the sponsors recommended that any state enacting the new version adopt it with an effective date of July 1, 2001. If all went according to plan and all the states adopted the new version in time, the entire country would switch over to the new, revised version of Article 9 on this one date.*

It is this revised version of Article 9 that we will be considering in our study of secured transactions in this volume.† I will do my best to keep to a minimum references to how a particular problem was dealt with in prerevision Article 9 or how the revision process retained or changed a particular result. As a matter of fact, the core principles and directives of Article 9 remain fairly well intact following the revision. The drafters of Revised Article 9 did not set out to reinvent, nor even reconfigure, the wheel. There are, to be sure, some changes of substance in the new article from what was true under the old, and we will be sure to note them. What can't be denied is that the new Article 9 *looks* a lot different from the old one. The revision rearranged things into what was thought to be a more logical and "user-friendly" form; the result is that with only rare accidental exception, the section numbers in the new version bear no relationship to the numbers of the section or sections of the old version that dealt with the same matter. This should pose no particular problem if you are looking at this material for the first time and sticking with the revised version, as we will here. You should be aware, however, that if as part of your studies you find yourself reading cases decided under or other materials written with reference to the old Article 9, don't be surprised if the section numbers (much less the exact language quoted from the article) don't match up with what you have in your copy of the Code or with what you are seeing in this book.

---

* Sometimes, to the surprise of us skeptics, things actually *do* go according to plan. It was a bit of a near thing, but by the last day of June 2001, the revised version of Article 9 had been enacted in each of the 50 states and the District of Columbia.

† If for some reason you need to review an aspect of secured transactions as it was dealt with by the "old" version of Article 9, as that version will continue to govern still outstanding controversies for some time — hopefully not long — the best suggestion I can offer is to find a copy of the first edition of this book, which dealt with the topic under that version.

As a practical matter, practicing attorneys will not be able to immediately discard all they know about the prerevision version of Article 9. Questions will come up for some time in which reference to the law as it was prior to a state's adoption of the revised Article 9 will be needed. The revised Article 9, in fact, devotes a large number of sections to what was to become of security interests created under the old regime after the magical date of July 1, 2001. You may want to take note of — but please do not consider now delving into — the so-called transition rules starting at §9-702. These sections are probably the most maddeningly complex and intricate part of the new Article 9. Fortunately, we will not be covering them in this introductory survey of the law of secured transactions. The topic has, as you can see, a past as well as a future, and as this is being written has only recently completed a period of transition between the two. (The transition period should have ended for all intents and purposes five years after the effective date of the revision, that is, on June 30, 2006, but it is only reasonable to anticipate continuing litigation and concern about whether actions taken during that period and purportedly according to the special transition rules worked out as the actors intended.)

We will be concerning ourselves strictly with the present, with the advent of the newly created Revised version of Article 9, and on the future. Our goal in all that follows is to take that Revised Article 9 as it has been given to us and learn, through a series of Examples and Explanations, how that article is to be read and understood and what it means for the practice of law in this area.

So let's see what the drafters of Revised Article 9 have given us to work with. We have already looked at §9-101. We can skip over for the moment §§9-102 through 9-108, which set forth a whole slew of definitions and special rules of interpretation that apply in general to the workings of Article 9. You can be sure we will come back to particular parts of these sections, again and again, as the need arises. Our introduction to Article 9 and the modern law of secured transactions starts in this chapter with careful consideration of what is to be found in §9-109, the section dealing with the scope of the article itself. What transactions are governed by Article 9? The general scope of the article is, as you can see, set forth in subsection (a). While this subsection lists a number of items to consider, by far the most important — and the one on which we will necessarily focus in this book — comes first. Stripped to its essentials, §9-109(a)(1) reads:

> [T]his article applies to . . . a transaction, regardless of its form, that creates a security interest in personal property or fixtures by contract.*

---

* For now I ask you simply to ignore the reference in this and many of the sections you will later be reading to "fixtures." We will deal with fixtures, what they are, and the special treatment they are afforded by Article 9, in Chapter 15.

Whatever may have once been the chattel mortgage, the conditional sales agreement, or the factor's lien is now, "regardless of its form," one and one thing only — the *Article 9 security interest*. It is a transaction, a contract between two parties, that is intended by those parties to create a security interest in the personal property of one running in favor of the other. Stepping back for a second, we consult the U.C.C.'s general definition of *security interest* as found in either §1-207(37) of the original version of Article 1 (which I will cite from here on out as simply "§1-201(37)") or §1-201(b)(35) of Revised Article 1 ("§1R-201(b)(35)"). Read the first sentence *only* of that definition:

> "Security interest" means an interest in personal property or fixtures which secures payment or performance of an obligation.

Our story, the quest for the Article 9 security interest, necessarily starts with an obligation.

Obligations come in all forms and sizes. A principal form of obligation, although by no means the only one, is the obligation to pay money at some time in the future. The obligor, who in such an instance we tend to refer to as the "Debtor," owes some money to another, the obligee (or the "Creditor"). The money may be owed because of a loan made by Creditor, which is of course eventually to be repaid, or because of some goods delivered to or some service done by Creditor for Debtor. Whatever the background, the central truth remains: Debtor has received some value from Creditor and is for that reason obliged to make specified payment to Creditor as and when that payment becomes due. A simple (and admittedly not terribly original) diagram of the situation would look like this:

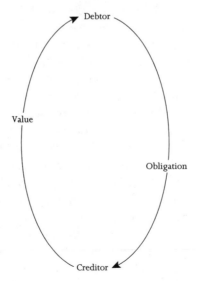

What assures Creditor that the obligation will be met? Any number of pressures will be on Debtor to do as he or she is obliged. For one thing, we may assume that Debtor is a being with a sense of moral obligation, and for that reason alone will normally do what is expected of him or her, what he or she has promised. Also working in Creditor's favor are the various social pressures, most particularly fear of loss of reputation in the commercial community in which he or she must operate, with which Debtor has to be concerned. People tend not to like, and business people tend not to want to deal with, debtors who do not pay their debts.

Beyond all of these forces, the law, you will not be surprised to learn, plays a part in making debtors meet their obligations. At least you shouldn't be surprised if you think back to your study of the law of contracts. Debtor's obligation is typically in the form of a promise and, more to the point, a promise of the type deemed enforceable by the law of the land. I will assume that you are familiar with contract law and the enforcement of contract promises. (If nothing else, the little diagram above should have put you in mind of the doctrine of consideration.) People keep their contractually binding promises, because, for example, their failure to do so will only land them in more hot water. As a legal matter they can be made to make compensation for their failure to perform.

There is, however, a limit to what the threat of a contract action can do. Not to disparage our majestic law of contract (in fact it's a subject I have taught often enough and for which I feel great affection), but as you studied that subject you were undoubtedly confronted time and time again with some of its practical limitations. Creditor may have all the right in the world to sue Debtor on an obligation, but it does Creditor no good if Debtor is broke or has fled the jurisdiction, or if the costs of bringing the suit would quickly outweigh anything that Creditor could recover.

There are other means by which Creditor could raise the probability of Debtor's meeting the obligation. Through the long history of debtors and creditors various arrangements have been developed to put some extra backing behind the promise. Debtor could ask a friend or relative to become a co-signer on the obligation or to put up a guarantee that the promise will be kept. Creditor now has the assurance that if Debtor doesn't do as he or she has promised there will be at least one other party contractually bound to carry through with the obligation. Of course there will still be all the difficulties attendant to enforcing a contractual obligation even if there is now one more potential defendant. Getting a co-signer or a guarantee is certainly not a bad idea. There still remains the possibility, however, that when the time comes for payment there will be no one around worth pursuing through the complexities of a contract action, in the hope of being able to obtain (and even less likely to get substantial recovery on) a judgment. As a matter of fact, the primary value to Creditor in Debtor's getting another person's personal guarantee that the obligation will be met may be not the right to sue this other person (although there is that) but the knowledge that this other person will ordinarily monitor Debtor's performance and can apply the necessary pressure if Debtor's resolve to do what's required seems to waver. No one — and this has to include any guarantor as much as Debtor or Creditor — wants to end up in court only to see a large percentage of any amount involved eaten up in attorneys' fees.

Another method developed in the commercial community by which Creditor can be given greater assurance of payment is the use by Debtor of some of his or her present wealth as collateral to secure, as we would say, the promise to perform. A particular piece of Debtor's property is put at risk to increase the pressure on Debtor to pay the debt. Debtor agrees with Creditor that should the obligation not be met this specific property will become directly available to Creditor and that Creditor can take whatever steps are necessary to seize the property, sell it if need be to realize its value, and then get what is coming to him or her out of that value.

When the property in question is so-called real property — land and the buildings on it — the legal device used to create this relationship and the resultant interest given to Creditor are traditionally referred to as a mortgage (for the law of which you will have to look elsewhere). If the parties agree that a piece of Debtor's *personal property* is to serve as collateral, then the law traditionally referred to the mechanism involved as, well, a pledge or a chattel mortgage or a factor's lien or one of that whole list of cleverly dubbed devices that, as we've seen, Article 9 was meant to replace. We now as a matter of custom might still use one of those terms colloquially, but as far as the involved parties' legal rights and responsibilities are concerned we would simply say that Debtor has granted an Article 9 security interest in the piece of property in favor of Creditor.

Allow me to expand my initial diagram to reflect this added part of the relationship:

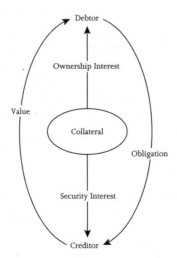

You'll notice that I have labeled Debtor's relationship to the Collateral as the "Ownership Interest." This is, I admit, a term of my own invention. It just means that Debtor is, and remains, the rightful owner of the property. I could have, I suppose, referred to Debtor's "title" in the collateral, but that word has such historical baggage and has caused enough confusion in the past that I'd just as soon do without it.*

Let's reconfigure, or rather slim down, our basic diagram one last time:

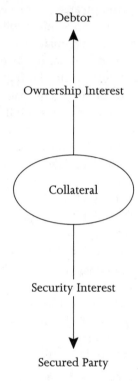

Debtor

Ownership Interest

Collateral

Security Interest

Secured Party

Basically what I've done here is drop the Value given by Creditor to Debtor and the Obligation owed by Debtor to Creditor. This is not, I hasten to add, because these elements of the overall scheme are not important. Quite the contrary. The very fact of a security interest presupposes two parties, a debtor and a creditor, and an obligation running from one to the other. I feel comfortable in leaving off the two arrows representing the underlying transaction just because we can always assume them to be lurking, not at all mysteriously, in the background. You should always in analyzing any secured transactions make sure that you have clearly in mind just what obligation is being secured and how that obligation initially arose.

---

* While it's getting a bit ahead of where we need to be, you can note that the drafters of Article 9 had no great love of the five-letter "t" word either. See §9-202, captioned with no great subtlety "Title to Collateral Immaterial." If you have studied Article 2 of the U.C.C. at all, you should be aware how the drafters of that Article expressed a similar aversion to reliance on the concept of "title" to personal property.

No doubt you noticed one other change made in the diagram. Creditor has been transformed into the "Secured Party." Well, that is the idea after all behind the grant of the security interest. More to the point, the diagram now features a set of terms defined by and consistently used in Article 9. Look at the introductory sentence to §9-102(a)(12) on *collateral* and (a)(72)(A) on *secured party*. The definition of "debtor" in subsection (a)(28) must, for reasons not important here, add some complexities, but the basic idea certainly fits in with what we've been saying so far.

So this much is clear: Each and every time you claim to have spotted an Article 9 security interest you should be able to identify each of the following: the debtor, the secured party, the underlying obligation, and the collateral. If you can't clearly identify each of these constituent parts of the whole, then chances are something is wrong (either with the situation or with your understanding of it). If you are tempted as you move through this material to get right into further and deeper analysis without doing the basic spadework, without first going through these fundamentals, then rest assured you're bound for a fairly confusing and frustrating time of it. If the basic diagram above looks terribly simple to you, just flip through some of the later pages in this book to see what's in store.

One final point before we move on. You may be concerned that I have not defined the term "security interest," which so prominently figures in our diagram. We do have the Article 1 definition to which we have already referred, but can we say any more? The answer is of course that we can say a lot more. In fact it will take all of Article 9, and all of this book, to say it in all its full and lusty detail. The security interest in the diagram above, the Article 9 security interest, is a very special thing. It is, to be sure, not a physical thing, not something you can bat around or store in a file cabinet. It is a legal interest in a particular piece of property, what we have termed the collateral. To fully understand the legal interest involved, to define it if you will, we have to be able to lay out the full set of rights and responsibilities conferred on the secured party by virtue of his, her, or its holding of this interest. We have to consider these rights and responsibilities not just in relation to the debtor but also as they affect and are affected by the claims in the collateral of a whole variety of third parties as they might come into the picture over time. In other words, to "define" the Article 9 security interest we have to study in all of its various aspects the law of Article 9. And that, of course, is what brought you to this book to begin with. We have a long, and I think you will find, interesting road to travel together.

The Examples and Explanations of this chapter will give you a chance to explore the fundamental defined scope of Article 9 as we have seen it laid out in subsection (a)(1) of §9-109. We will also take a brief look at some other situations that do not fit within this model but the drafters saw fit to place within the scope of Article 9 (in other parts of subsection (a)) as well as some, but by no means all, of the exceptions provided for in subsections (c) and (d).

Examples

In each example the question will be the same: Has an Article 9 security interest been created by the actions of the parties? If you determine the answer to be yes, you should go on to identify who is the debtor, who is the secured party, what is the obligation secured, and what is the collateral.

1. It is now August. Deborah, an artist, believes she can make some extra money by producing a large number of intricate handmade Christmas tree ornaments and selling them at a local crafts fair to be held in November. Her problem is that she does not have the cash necessary to buy all the materials she will need. A friend, Sam, agrees to lend her $8,000 until the end of the year at a reasonable rate of interest, provided she can come up with some collateral for the loan. Deborah has only a large ruby ring that has been in her family for years. The ring has an appraised value of something over $12,000. Deborah hands the ring over to Sam on the understanding that he will return it to her when she repays the loan. It is agreed that should she not repay the loan by December 31 he may sell the ring and retain from the proceeds of the sale the amount due him, turning over to her what is then left of the proceeds. Sam gives Deborah the $8,000. Deborah and Sam, being friends, do not bother themselves with any legal formalities. They have never even heard of the Uniform Commercial Code. But the question remains: Does Sam have an Article 9 security interest in Deborah's ring?

2. Dan buys a used motorcycle from Speedy Pete's World of Wheels. He agrees to pay for his purchase over the next three years in monthly installments of $110 each. He signs a purchase agreement provided by Speedy Pete to this effect.
   a. Does Speedy Pete have an Article 9 security interest in the motorcycle? That is, should Dan fall behind in his payments can Speedy Pete repossess the bike?
   b. Would your answer be any different if Dan had given Speedy Pete a note (a negotiable instrument under Article 3) as payment?
   c. What if the purchase agreement Dan signed also contained a clause stating, "Buyer hereby grants Seller a security interest in all items purchased as security for Buyer's obligation to pay any amounts due under this Agreement?"
   d. What if instead the purchase agreement had included the following provision: "It is agreed by Buyer and Seller that title to any item sold pursuant to this Agreement shall remain in Seller until such time as Buyer has made full and final payment of any amounts due hereunder?" See either the final sentence of the first paragraph of §1-201(37) or the second to last sentence of §1R-201(b)(35).

3. Arnold Moneybucks has agreed to buy a diamond pinkie ring from Selma the jeweler for the cash price of $3,000. He comes into Selma's store to pick up the ring carrying with him a cashier's check made out to Selma in the amount of $3,000. As Selma is polishing the ring one last time prior to handing it over, Arnold spots a pair of sapphire earrings on display. They bear a price tag of $1,350. Arnold tells Selma he would like to buy the earrings as well so that he could give them to his mother on her birthday, but that he doesn't have the ready cash. Selma suggests that he buy the earrings on credit. She writes up and has Arnold sign a contract calling for him to pay $1,350 with interest over a term of one year. The contract also states that Arnold is granting to Selma an interest in his new diamond ring "for the purpose of securing his obligation to pay" for the earrings. Arnold gives Selma the cashier's check. He walks out of the store with the ring and the earrings. Does Selma end up with an Article 9 security interest here?

4. In the middle of the summer Farmer White arranges a loan from the Planters and Growers State Bank, the proceeds of which she will use to continue paying her farmhands needed to finish out the growing season. Among the various papers she signs at the Bank is one declaring that she is granting the Bank a security interest in "all crops now growing on her land, Whiteacre." Does this transaction create an Article 9 security interest in favor of the Bank? See §9-102(a)(44)(iv).

5. At the beginning of the growing season, Farmer White of the previous example bought a large quantity of seed from Heartland Supplies, an agricultural supply company. The purchase and sale agreement she entered into with Heartland provided that she would pay for her purchases after the growing season was complete, her intention being to make the payment out of what she anticipates being paid when she eventually sells off the harvested crops. A statute in the state in which her farm, Whiteacre, is located provides in relevant part that "any supplier who furnishes crop production inputs [defined to include such things as the seed] has an agricultural input lien for the unpaid retail cost of inputs provided, which lien attaches to any crops grown using furnished seed or other inputs." Later Heartland Supplies asserts an interest in the crops grown on Whiteacre basing its claim on the state statute.
   a. Is Heartland's interest in the crops a security interest within the scope of §9-109(a)(1)?
   b. What term does Article 9 use to characterize Heartland's interest? See §9-102(a)(5).
   c. Is Heartland's interest in the crop governed by Article 9? See §9-109(a)(2).

6. Acme Corporation, a manufacturer of a variety of household appliances, sells its products to major retailers under a standard agreement calling for the buyer to pay within 60 days of receipt for any goods delivered. Once a shipment is sent out pursuant to such an arrangement, Acme records the amount due it as an account receivable.

   a. In order to take advantage of a chance to buy a large shipment of one of its more expensive raw materials at a very desirable price, Acme needs a quick infusion of cash. It is able to obtain a $2 million loan from the Mechanical National Bank by agreeing to give that bank a security interest in "all of its accounts receivable now held or hereafter acquired." Has the Bank obtained an Article 9 security interest?

   b. Suppose that instead of taking out this loan Acme had sold its accounts receivable outright to a firm called Factors Unlimited for the sum of $1.85 million. How, other than the substitution of the Factors firm for the Bank, does this transaction differ from the loan set out in part (a)? Is this transaction — the sale of the accounts to Factors — governed by Article 9? Look to §9-109(a)(3).

7. Jules has, for a number of years, been designing and handcrafting pieces of expensive jewelry out of precious metals and gems. He sells individual items out of his workshop to clients who have sought him out (based on word-of-mouth about his exquisite work) and commissioned individual pieces. Jules feels he is now in a position to sell more of his work to a larger clientele. He contacts Selma, who owns a fashionable jewelry store, and suggests that he create and sell to her a collection of his jewelry so she could sell the pieces in her shop. Selma says she is not willing to purchase any of his work because she has found it best to purchase her stock of jewelry from only a limited number of major makers. Selma, however, makes the following proposition: She suggests that she will display a collection of Jules's work in her store and, should any customer want to buy one, she will act as his agent in selling the piece. She will take a percentage of the price paid as a commission and turn over the remainder to him. Jules agrees to this arrangement and soon delivers to Selma's store an assortment of pieces, which Selma puts on display.

   a. Does Selma have any interest in these pieces of jewelry made by Jules, now resting in her store, of the type that would be considered an Article 9 security interest under §9-109(a)(1)?

   b. What term does Article 9 use to describe the transaction that Jules and Selma have entered into? See §9-102(a)(20).

   c. Is this transaction governed by Article 9? See §9-109(a)(4).

8. Homer, the long-time owner of a pleasant house at 789 Widget Lane, has been offered a job in another city. He would like to make the move

but is having trouble finding a buyer for his house. He finally is able to sell the house to one Newby, on the condition that he, Homer, will finance the sale. Newby gives Homer a down payment in cash, but the rest of the purchase price is represented by a note signed by Newby along with an accompanying mortgage covering the Widget Lane property.

   a. Is this a transaction within the scope of Article 9?

   b. Assume that Homer then goes and borrows money (to set up house-keeping at his new location) from the Second City National Bank. Among the collateral that he uses to obtain the loan is the note he has been given by Newby. Is Second City's interest in the note an Article 9 security interest? See §9-109(b).

9. Daniel finds that he has inherited a fine old violin from a distant relative. He takes it to the shop of one Stella, who is an expert in the repair and restoration of such instruments, and contracts to have the violin refurbished for a price of $500. Stella promises to have the work done within two months. Two months later Daniel goes to Stella's shop and asks to be given the violin. Stella tells him that she is willing to turn over the instrument but only upon payment of her fee. Stella points out to Daniel that under a state statute she is entitled to "a lien" on the instrument to assure payment of any amounts due as a result of the work she has done on it. Assuming Stella does have this statutory right, is the interest she claims in the violin an Article 9 security interest? See §9-109(d)(2).

10. Sky Masterson Airlines has arranged to buy a new plane to add to its fleet. The money with which to buy this plane is to be borrowed from Detroit National Bank. As part of the loan transaction, the airline is to grant the bank a security interest in the new plane. You should be aware that under the Federal Aviation Act the Administrator of the FAA is commanded to, and has, established a system of recording "any conveyance which affects the title to, or any interest in, any civil aircraft of the United States," and that it is undisputed that a security interest is covered by this provision and notice of such an interest needs to be recorded with the FAA to be effective. Is the security interest to be granted by the airline to Detroit National Bank governed by Article 9? See §9-109(c)(1).

11. Hartford Cogs and Widgets, a manufacturer of an assortment of mechanical devices, has recently been issued a patent by the United States Patent Office covering a new type of digital widget. In order to put the new widget into production it will have to expand its plant, so the company arranges for a $1.45 million loan from the Metalgrinders Bank of New England. The principal collateral for this loan is to be "all of Hartford's rights in and title to" the recently acquired patent.

The loan officer from Metalgrinders Bank comes to you for advice: Does Article 9 cover the granting and enforcement of a security interest in this sort of thing? What type of research would you need to do before you could answer this question with any confidence?

Explanations

1. Yes. Sam has an Article 9 security interest. Their transaction, whether or not they had the U.C.C. in mind at the time or knew the precise legal lingo, was a contract entered into by them that created a security interest in the ring, a nice bit of personal property. No particular formalities were required. Deborah is the debtor, Sam is the secured party, the ring is the collateral, and the obligation secured is Deborah's obligation to repay Sam the $8,000 plus agreed interest by the end of the year.

2a. No. Speedy Pete has no security interest in the motorcycle since none was granted to him by Dan in this transaction. It makes no difference that Pete is the seller. An Article 9 security interest can be created only by contractual language intended by them to do so. If Dan doesn't make all necessary payments as due, Pete will have every right to sue him for a contract debt unpaid but will have no special right to repossess the motorcycle. Speedy Pete is merely an unsecured creditor of Dan.

2b. No. The note may change Dan's obligation somewhat, but Speedy Pete is still only an unsecured creditor. Should Dan not pay on the note under its terms, Pete (or whoever holds the note at the time) can sue on the note which (as another part of your studies in Commercial Law will help you understand) may give the plaintiff an easier case against Dan. But the fact remains: Dan did not consent in the sales transactions to Speedy Pete's having a security interest in the motorcycle, so none was created.

2c. Here we do find, because the parties did create, an Article 9 security interest. There's nothing magical about it. The Article 9 security interest is always, as it was here, created by contract. The motorcycle is the collateral, Dan is the debtor, and Speedy Pete is the secured party. The obligation is Dan's duty, whether a mere contract obligation or one on a negotiable instrument like a note, to pay what is owed when due.

2d. As that cited sentence in §1-201(37) or §1R-201(b)(35) makes clear, this arrangement — what is sometimes referred to colloquially as a "conditional sale" or a "title retention" agreement — is for U.C.C. purposes just a sale with the seller retaining a security interest in the goods. The substance of the transaction is identical to that in (c) above, even if the language used to obtain the result is different. And remember, under

§9-109(a)(1) it is substance, not form, that counts in determining the scope of Article 9.

3. Yes. Selma has a security interest. The principal reason for my including this hypothetical is to make sure you can correctly characterize the component parts of the interest. Obviously Arnold is the debtor and Selma the secured party. It should be equally clear to you that the collateral is the diamond ring (for which Arnold has fully paid) and the obligation is Arnold's duty to pay the $1,350 due on the sapphire earrings. It just happened to work out this way because that's what the parties agreed to, what they in the individual instance intended.

4. Yes. Planters and Growers has an Article 9 security interest in the crops, as growing crops are considered to be "goods" under the cited definition. So we're confronted with a transaction between White and the Bank intended to create a security interest in goods, a form of personal property, and Article 9 applies.

5a. No. Heartland's interest in the crops was not created by a contract between the two parties. That is, Farmer White never contractually granted an interest in the crops to the supplier. Heartland's interest is in the nature of a lien created by the state statute.

5b. Article 9 uses the term "agricultural lien" to characterize the type of interest that Heartland has acquired. You should check for yourself that Heartland's interest meets the criteria found in the definition set out in §9-102(a)(5).

5c. Yes. The prerevision version of Article 9 did not cover the agricultural lien, such as we have here. As you can see in §9-109(a)(2), the revised version does. The existence and creation of an agricultural lien is, of course, governed by whatever state statute is relied on by the supplier or lessor who wishes to assert such a lien. The effect of the lien, how it will stack up, for example, against other interests claimed in Farmer White's crops and how it may be enforced, will be governed by rules laid out in Article 9. Notice, by the way, that while an agricultural lien is not considered a "security interest" for Article 9 purposes, many of the definitions we have already looked at do lump the two together. For instance, "collateral" is defined in §9-102(a)(12) to include property "subject to a security interest or agricultural lien." In §9-102(a)(72)(B), the secured party is defined to include "a person that holds an agricultural lien."

6a. There is no trick about it. This is a security interest governed by Article 9. The two-word phrase "accounts receivable" is a term of art in the business world and in accounting but is not defined for Code purposes. As we will see in more detail in a later chapter, however, under §9-102(a)(2) such amounts owed Acme for goods sold are characterized simply as "accounts," and as such are personal property in which a security interest can be taken.

6b. This transaction is also governed by Article 9, in spite of the fact that it actually is — in substance and not just in form — an outright sale and not the granting of a security interest. Under §9-109(a)(3), Article 9 is expressly made to apply to "a sale of accounts, chattel paper, payment intangibles, or promissory notes." (There is no reason to worry for the moment what chattel paper, payment intangibles, or promissory notes are; we'll get to them soon enough. For now we'll just concentrate on the sale of accounts.)

How do the transactions in (a) and (b) differ? Well, for one thing in the case of the loan the Bank will find value in the transaction by its right to receive repayment, with interest of course, on some set schedule. That's the amount it is due. Acme may well be planning to find the money to make the loan payments by collecting on its accounts, but collection on the accounts and exactly what is realized from them is not the Bank's concern. If many of Acme's customers don't pay for one reason or another or start falling behind in their payments it could create problems for Acme, but its debt to the Bank is unchanged. If, on the other hand, Acme's customers pay regularly, and there are fewer unpaid accounts than Acme might have been expecting, then that's all to the manufacturer's benefit. Only if Acme fails to pay the Bank amounts owed as and when due may it, probably much to its annoyance, have to get involved with the accounts receivable. If it has no other choice it may have to foreclose on this collateral. It could then either collect on the accounts from Acme's customers over time or perhaps try to sell off the accounts for some reasonable value. (There's a market for accounts just like there's a market for just about everything.) To the extent it eventually received on this collateral less than the outstanding value of Acme's loan, it would still have an action against Acme for that amount, what we will call the *deficiency*. If by some chance it was able to wring more value out of the accounts than it was still owed by Acme, adding in its expenses for going through all this hassle, the *surplus* of value would be due to Acme.

This is all, of course, getting way ahead of ourselves as far as Article 9 goes. It does, however, allow us to compare the loan situation to the outright sale of accounts to Factors in (b). Factors gives up the money right away, just like any buyer would, and gets not just a security interest but an ownership interest in the accounts. From now on Acme's customers will be paying Factors (whether they know it or not), and whether Factors makes a profit or loss on the transaction will depend on how much it ultimately collects. Should Factors wish to get out of the collection business, it could naturally sell off these accounts just as it has now bought them, but in that case the difference in sale price from Factors' purchase price of $1.85 million, either a net gain or a net loss, will all be to Factors' benefit or detriment. Acme has no further interest, either legally, psychologically, or economically, in the accounts once it sells them off.

If the transaction in (b) is a sale and not the archetypal granting of a secured transaction, why is it included in Article 9 at all? Look at Official Comment 4 to §9-109:

> Under subsection (a)(3), as under former Section 9-102, this Article applies to sales of accounts. . . . This approach generally has been successful in avoiding difficult problems of distinguishing between transactions in which a receivable secures an obligation and those in which the receivable has been sold outright. In many commercial financing transactions the distinction is blurred.

Finally, note that the definitional scheme we've been using is perfectly able to take in this situation. The Article 1 definition of "security interest," in either version, is clear that this term includes "any interest of a . . . buyer of accounts . . . that is subject to Article 9." By looking at the relevant parts of §9-102(a), you should be able to assure yourself that, assuming the outright sale of accounts by Acme to Factors, Acme is well within the definition of "debtor," Factors is a "secured party," and the accounts that were sold are true "collateral."

7a. No. Jules has not granted any interest in the jewelry to Selma. He is under no obligation to Selma that would need securing in any fashion.

7b. The arrangement between Jules and Selma is defined as a *consignment* under §9-102(a)(20). Jules is referred to as the consignor (§9-102(a)(21)) and Selma the consignee (§9-102(a)(19)).

7c. Yes. Prior to its revision, Article 9 did not deal with consignments directly, but as you can see, Revised Section 9-109(a)(4) explicitly brings consignments within the scope of Article 9. You can check that the consignee comes within the Article 9 definition of "debtor" and the consignor is a "secured party." The goods that are the subject of the assignment, here the jewelry collection prepared by Jules and on display at Selma's place of business, are "collateral." The transaction is, like the agricultural lien and the outright sale of certain forms of receivables that we have seen in earlier examples, a type of commercial dealing that is governed by Article 9, even if it is not the classic secured transaction of §9-109(a)(1), a security interest in personal property granted by the debtor to the secured party under contract to secure an obligation owed by the debtor to the secured party.

In the chapters to follow I will focus almost exclusively on those aspects of Article 9 that govern the classic security interest granted by contract to secure an obligation — those transactions falling within the scope of Article 9 by virtue of part (a)(1) of §9-109. You should keep in mind, however, that Article 9 does govern some additional forms of commercial dealing as well (in particular the agricultural lien and the consignment), and that should you later find yourself having to sort out how that lien or consignment is to be dealt with, reference to Article 9, at least after July 1, 2001, is called for.

8a. No. The Homer–Newby transaction was the creation of a real estate mortgage, which is a mechanism for giving a creditor an interest in real not personal property as collateral. It is not a "security interest" within the Article 1 definition. It does not come within the scope of Article 9 as set forth in §9-109(a)(1).

8b. Yes. Second City has an Article 9 security interest in the note, which is a kind of personal property (what we'll learn to call an "instrument" under Article 9). Look at §9-109(b):

> The application of this article to a security interest in a secured obligation is not affected by the fact that the obligation is itself secured by a transaction or interest to which this article does not apply.

In our example, the "secured obligation" is Newby's obligation to pay on his note. It is secured by a transaction, a real estate mortgage, to which Article 9 does not apply. The Article 9 transaction here is the one between Homer (as debtor) and the Second City National Bank (as secured party) in which an interest in Newby's note (the collateral) is granted. See also Comment 7 to §9-109, which contains an illustration to the same effect.

9. No. Stella's right under what is traditionally referred to as a mechanics lien statute is not an Article 9 interest. In some states mechanics liens are not the subject of any statute but are found to arise under the common law. In either event, you should be able to convince yourself that Article 9 does not govern by reference to the essential principle that its authority extends to *consensual* arrangements and consensual arrangements only. Stella's interest here is created not by the intention of the parties but by the automatic operation of a statute acting on the parties regardless of their individual intentions or consent. Section 9-109(d)(2) just makes the case against Stella's interest coming within Article 9 all the more airtight.

Be careful here: We're not saying that Stella's interest is not valid or that it isn't valuable, only that the rules that govern it are to be found elsewhere than in Article 9. More specifically, this interest is governed by the mechanics lien statute that creates it. There is one minor exception or qualification to this last statement. Look again at §9-109(d)(2). The relative priority of liens obtained under the mechanics lien statute as they stack up against Article 9 interests is to be determined under §9-333. We don't have to worry about any issue of priority here, but compare part (d)(2) of §9-109 with, say, part (d)(1). A landlord's lien (whatever that is, but you can guess) is not subject to Article 9 nor apparently is there anything in Article 9 that would determine the relative priority of such a creature in competition with Article 9 interests. A court faced with such a priority issue will perforce have to make a determination based on some principle of law outside of Article 9 itself. As we proceed in these materials our study will be principally focused on the relative priority of different Article 9 players, but we can't forget that there can be others lurking just beyond our U.C.C. horizon claiming some kind of legally valid interest in a given piece of property whose claims arise in other ways altogether. We ignore such interests at our peril.

10. This security interest will not be governed by Article 9, but rather by the Federal Aviation Act and the regulations pertaining to that act which have been promulgated by the FAA Administrator. It has long been acknowledged that the Act's establishment of a central recording system for recording not only sales of but also security interests in aircraft (as well as certain aircraft engines, propellers, and stores of spare parts) effectively preempts any state law on the subject. As you see in §9-109(c)(1), Article 9 acknowledges the possibility of such federal preemption and explicitly removes from its scope any transaction which it could not in any event govern under the doctrine of federal preemption. For a recent case discussing and testing the limits of this preemption, see In re AvCentral, Inc., 289 Bankr. 170, 49 U.C.C.2d 1336 (D. Kansas 2003).

11. Under §9-109(c)(1), the issue that needs investigation is whether the federal statute that regulates the grant and enforcement of patents so covers the field as to bar, under the constitutional doctrine of preemption, any state from passing legislation at all relevant to patents, or at least relevant to security interests that might be granted in patents. If so, that is if patent law is strictly a federal matter, then Article 9 acknowledges as much and defers to that federal law. Any attempt to take a security interest in a federally registered patent would then necessarily have to comply with any federal rules or regulations (if any) governing the taking of such an interest and Article 9 would not be relevant. If, on the other hand, federal patent law does not preempt the field, then Article 9 can and does govern the granting and consequences of any attempt to create a security interest in this one particular type of personal

property, which just happens to be a patent issued by the United States Patent Office.

Federal preemption by statutes such as the Federal Aviation Act, which we saw in the previous example, dealing with certain types of tangible property in which the federal government has taken a particular interest, has long been recognized and is not at all controversial. Only in recent years, however, have the courts had to deal with the increasingly important question of sorting out which federal statutes relating to what is generally termed *intellectual property* do themselves regulate security interests in the specific type of property, and which therefore will result in an exclusion of Article 9 through preclusion from those that do not. Each federal statute has had to be viewed and analyzed on its own terms, and about the only thing they have in common is that it soon becomes clear that they weren't written with this particular problem — their relationship with state statutory Article 9 — in mind.

You would not even try to answer a question of this type without doing a good deal more research into the particular federal enactment and how it has been interpreted by the courts. In researching the Metalgrinders problem, on the applicability of Article 9 to an interest to be taken in a federally issued patent, you would I hope become acquainted with a pair of notable cases even if neither deals directly with the patent situation. In the case of In re Peregrine Entertainment, Ltd., 116 Bankr. 194, 11 U.C.C.2d 1025 (C.D. Cal. 1990), the United States District court held that, as the federal Copyright Act specifically provides for recordation in the Copyright Office of an agreement granting a security interest in a registered copyright and further establishes its own scheme of priorities that differs in certain respects from that of Article 9, such an interest would be regulated under the federal act and not Article 9. The court held that "any state recordation system pertaining to interests in copyrights would be preempted by this Copyright Act." A second case, coming out of the Bankruptcy Court in the same federal district only a couple of years later, concluded that as far as security interests in federally protected trademarks are concerned there is no federal preemption by the Lanham Act and that Article 9 governed. In re 199Z, Inc., 137 Bankr. 778, 17 U.C.C.2d 598 (Bankr. C.D. Cal. 1992). The court, acknowledging the result in *Peregrine*, found dispositive the fact that

> one critical distinction exists between the federal legislation at issue in Peregrine [the Copyright Act] and the Lanham Act trademark legislation. The Copyright Act provides expressly for the filing of any "mortgage" or "hypothecation" of a copyright, including a pledge of the copyright as security or collateral as a debt. [Citing *Peregrine*]. The Lanham Act, however,

provides only for the filing of any assignment of a trademark, and the definition of "assignment" does not include pledges, mortgages or hypothecations of trademarks.

Hence, the court concluded, it could not find as a matter of law that the federal preemption found in *Peregrine* applies equally to the perfection of security interests in federally registered trademarks.

Just to make things even more interesting, the Ninth Circuit has recently ruled that Article 9 does apply, and is not preempted by federal law, when the subject matter is an *unregistered* copyright. See *Aerocon Engineering, Inc. v. Silicon Valley Bank*, 303 F.3d 1120, 48 U.C.C.2d 447 (9th Cir. 2002), *cert. denied*, 537 U.S. 1146 (2003).

We are obviously dealing with some pretty fine distinctions here, and we would be wise to refrain from even attempting a generalization. Just to make matters more complex, if we should conclude with respect to any particular federal statute that it does not act to remove totally Article 9 from consideration, that does not mean we can simply ignore that federal regime altogether. It just means that we have two statutory schemes, one federal and one state (including the potential for filing under either, both, or neither) to worry about.

These two cases are interesting and informative, but they do not, of course, answer the question directly relevant to the Metalgrinders situation: Does Article 9 apply to a security interest taken in a patent granted by the federal government, or is that article preempted by the federal law in the field? As it turns out, a case decided by the Ninth Circuit in 2001 does (as you would discover in your research) deal with the question head-on. *In re Cybernetic Services, Inc.*, 252 F.3d 1039, 44 U.C.C.2d 639 (9th Cir. 2001), *cert. denied*, 534 U.S. 1130 (2002). The circuit court held after a lengthy discussion of the issue, and recognizing that commentators have had differing views on the question, that "the Patent Act does not preempt Article 9." This result has recently been cited with approval in several other cases. See, for example, *In re Tower Tech, Inc.*, 67 Fed. Appx. 521, 50 U.C.C.2d 923 (10th Cir. 2003), and *In re Pasteurized Eggs Corp.*, 296 Bankr. 283, 51 U.C.C.2d 274 (D.N.H. 2003). So the *Cybernetics* case may seem to be a definitive answer to our question on how to deal with a patent as collateral, but is it really? Its conclusion is gaining support, but it is certainly possible that other courts might see the matter differently. Should Metalgrinders Bank of New England proceed in its dealings with Hartford Cogs and Widgets as it would any other Article 9 transaction, treating the valuable patent as just one more type of Article 9 collateral? There still exists the possibility that how it handles the situation could later be challenged on the grounds of federal preemption.

All commentators are quick to point out that the exact interplay between federal statutes governing intellectual property — such as the Copyright Act, the Lanham Act, and the Patent Act — and Article 9 is a particularly tricky bit of business. Those Acts were definitely not written with the needs of the commercial lawyer, like one advising Metalgrinders National Bank, in mind, and a good deal of uncertainty remains on the preemption question even after the decision of the three recent cases that we just had a look at.

It may turn out that this is one of those instances where the best job we could do would be to acknowledge from the outset that there is a measure of uncertainty about exactly what the rules are in the situation and proceed accordingly, doing what we can to minimize if not totally eliminate the risks involved. Even if it is not apparent at the moment, as you work through later parts of these materials you will see again and again how the lawyer's task in dealing with this type of transaction is often best handled by exploring and then planning for a set of possible alternatives. Rarely will it be necessary to respond to an iffy situation by picking one road to go and staking all on the outcome. As we will see, practice in the area of secured transactions is not for the sloppy or the seat-of-the-pants type of operator; it requires that we get used to dotting every i and crossing every t. When in doubt about what to do, however ("Am I supposed to spell it with one t or two?"), it will often be possible and perfectly respectable merely to cover all the options ("I'll spell it out both ways just to be safe.") and move beyond the question entirely.

In advising Metalgrinders Bank of New England, the prudent and perfectly respectable course will likely be that, while a good argument can be made that the bank should treat its transaction with Hartford Cogs and Widgets as it would any other Article 9 transaction, it should play it safe and take a little extra effort in order to protect itself should this conclusion later be the subject of serious dispute or even prove to be wrong. In particular this would mean that Metalgrinders would be well-advised to file a notice of its security interest not only under the Article 9 filing system (that we will explore in sufficient detail in chapters to come), but also to make a separate filing giving notice of its interest with the United States Patent Office, as is allowed although perhaps (but it is just this "perhaps" we are worried about) not necessarily required. There is no way that the lender can be hurt or faulted for taking this cautious approach, even if it does involve some arguable redundancy and a bit of extra expense. Any such redundancy and expense seems well-warranted in light of the lingering questions that still surround the issue of federal preemption in the patent area. The people at the bank, and you as their legal advisor, can sleep more easily knowing they've covered all the bases.

Leases of Goods and Article 9

WHEN IS A LEASE NOT REALLY A LEASE?

Having worked through the previous chapter, you should be comfortable with the notion that Article 9 of the Uniform Commercial Code governs any transaction *regardless of its form*, which is intended to and hence does create a security interest in personal property. We now note that another article entirely, Article 2A introduced into the Code in its present form in 1990 and by now adopted in each of the states, deals with what would seem to be a different matter altogether, the lease of goods.* Section 2A-102, the scope provision of Article 2A, neatly parallels what we have seen in §9-109(a)(1). It declares that Article 2A "applies to any transaction, *regardless of form*, that creates a lease in goods." In theory at least it should not be difficult to tell the difference between these two prototypical commercial transactions, the secured transaction and the lease, and after having observed the distinction to apply the correct law to the facts of the situation. A secured transaction is one kind of commercial arrangement, a lease is another. We follow the Code by applying Article 9 in the case of a secured transaction and Article 2A where a lease of goods is involved. Unfortunately, things in the real world do not always work out as easily as we might hope. In particular, as we will

---

* Note that we are dealing here with a lease of goods, one distinct kind of personal property. The lease of real property is a whole other subject, perfectly fascinating I'm sure, but for whatever reasons not considered a topic within the bounds of "commercial law" as is the lease of goods. For the lease of real property look to "property law" or "land transactions" or "landlord and tenant" law.

discover, the commercial lawyer may find himself or herself confronted with a transaction that in form has all the appearance of a lease but that may upon further analysis really be intended by the parties to work in *substance* as a secured transaction. The answer from the Code's perspective is still perfectly clear. Since Article 9 is to apply to any legal contrivance that in substance is a secured transaction irrespective of the form in which it is initially presented to the world, Article 9 applies here. So a transaction that looks like a lease but acts like a secured transaction comes within the scope of Article 9 without any question. At the same time of course, the lease of goods, which really is a lease of goods in substance and not just in form, does not fall within the scope of Article 9. It is governed by Article 2A. The problem then becomes naturally enough being able to distinguish between the two — the lease, which really is a lease, and the "lease," which is in reality a secured transaction even if dressed up in a lease's clothing. Making this distinction is what this chapter is about.*

We start out by looking at the definition of "lease" given in §2A-103(1)(j):

> "Lease" means a transfer of rights to possession and use of goods for a term in return for consideration. . . .

Yes, that sounds like what we think of as a lease, whether it be the common and relatively prosaic transaction by which you or I contract for the short-term use of a rental car or the more complex undertaking that a large industrial firm might enter into in the form of a so-called "equipment lease" to obtain some expensive piece of machinery to use in its enterprise over a more protracted period of time. What characterizes a commercial transaction as a lease is that one party (whom we would term the "lessor") owns some goods in which it has no interest or intention of giving up "title" or ultimate ownership, only in generating some present cash by letting the other party (the "lessee") have possession and the use of the goods for a period of time. At the end of that time (the "lease term") it is expected that the goods will be returned to the lessor, the rightful and continuing owner. The lessee has gotten the use of the goods for some specified term, and the

---

* It should be noted that an analogous issue can arise when the parties to a transaction have set it out in form and designated it to be a "consignment," but where in substance it does not meet the criteria for being a consignment but is rather a security interest. See the third paragraph of Comment 6 to §9-109. If a transaction purporting to be a consignment is indeed what we may call a "true consignment" within the definition of §9-102(a)(20), then it comes within the scope of Article 9 via §9-109(a)(4) and the governing principles are those set out in the article with respect to consignments. If what purports to be a consignment is in reality and "regardless of form" a security interest, then it is still within the scope of Article 9, but now by virtue of §9-109(a)(1) and the rules applicable to the transaction are those which Article 9 applies whenever a security interest is involved.

lessor has gotten payment in exchange for allowing their use. Compare this situation to a *sale* of goods as defined in §2-106(1):

> A "sale" consists in the passing of title from the seller to the buyer for a price [citing the Article 2 section on passage of title to goods.]

At least making the distinction between the lease of goods and the sale of goods looks like it should be straightforward and easy enough.

Things get a bit more interesting when we read further into §2A-103(1)(j), the 2A definition of a lease:

> "Lease" means a transfer of rights to possession and use of goods for a term in return for consideration, but a sale, including a sale on approval or a sale on return, or retention or creation of a security interest is not a lease.

Don't worry about the sale on approval or sale on return; they are relatively minor matters. But pay close attention to what follows: "the retention or creation of a security interest" is not a lease. This should pique your interest, if for no other reason than that it makes reference to the security interest, which is after all what our study is supposedly all about.

The problem recognized by the drafters of Article 2A is that just as you can't always judge a book by its cover you can't always tell a lease by its documentation. For reasons that have to do with matters best left to those familiar with the intricacies of federal income tax law and principles of corporate accounting, many business concerns will find it advantageous in obtaining new equipment to do so through a lease transaction. Nothing unusual there. Leasing will often be an efficient and effective way of getting the use of goods for some particular period of time during which you need them. But there has also been motivation — again driven by tax and accounting rules and complexities — for these concerns to structure what would be in actuality their permanent acquisition of such equipment through a direct purchase on long-term credit in a form that is *made to appear* a lease transaction or that *could pass* for a lease. Documents are drafted in terms not of a "seller" to whom the "buyer" makes "installment payments" of the "price" but of a "lessee" paying "rent" to the owner of the goods denoted the "lessor." Slap the title of "Lease" on the top of the document, and there you have it.

Does the ruse succeed? Fortunately we need not concern ourselves here with whether it does or doesn't, whether the transaction can legitimately be treated as a lease for accounting purposes or when the tax authorities come calling. In the field of commercial law, and under the U.C.C., one general principle always stands at the forefront. Whether a given transaction is a lease is not a matter of the apparent form the transaction followed. It can't be resolved simply by checking the heading of the principal documents signed. Whether a given transaction characterized by the parties and their attorneys as a lease is *really* a lease has to be determined by looking at the underlying business and economic reality of the transaction. Substance governs, not mere form.

We refer back to the Code definitions of "sale" and "lease" quoted earlier. The sale of goods and the lease of goods are fundamentally different transactions as conceived by the commercial law. In the sale the seller turns the goods, title and all, over to the buyer in exchange for the price. If the sale transaction is successful in meeting its goals, if it goes through as expected, the seller is saying goodbye to the goods forever. The seller does not expect to get, indeed does not have any interest in getting, return of the goods at any time in the future. Should the seller have to reassert authority over the goods, that is, go through the trouble of repossessing them, or should the buyer want to return them, this will be an indication of something amiss in the buyer/seller relationship.

Compare this to the lease paradigm. The lessor, in exchange for some consideration, is parting with the goods and allowing the lessee their use for *some term*, some limited time. The successful completion of the lease is marked by the return of the goods to the lessor's possession. And, we have to assume, the return of the goods is of some economic consequence to the lessor. There is some value left in the goods, there is still some use to be made out of them, which it is for the lessor to exploit.

How could we even confuse the two or could one (a sale) be made to appear, even by the craftiest of lawyers, as if it were the other (a lease)? The line begins to blur when the purchase of goods is carried out not by payment of the price in one lump sum at the time of purchase but with the seller's extension of long-term credit to the buyer. One party, denoted the "lessor," conveys the goods to the other, termed the "lessee." The lessee is given the right to possess and make use of the goods for a period of years, in exchange for which lessee will make monthly payments (termed "rental payments") during that term. This could, of course, truly be a lease, in which case we would expect that a significant part of the lessor's business calculation at the time of entering into the transaction would involve its right to the return of the goods at the end of the term and its expectation that those goods would still have some economic value left to them when they are recovered. If this is in actuality the situation — the transaction is a lease not just as the documents are drafted and as it is reported by the accountants and to the IRS, but as the transaction is in some objective fashion actually understood in economic terms — then this lease *really* is a lease. Believe it or not, the convention has arisen of calling such a transaction a *true lease*. It's a bit of a funny phrase, something like "true fact" or "real cheese," but it's one you'll hear often. And it does help to distinguish the lease, the true lease, from whatever else it is that a lease may be when a lease isn't truly a lease.

And what would that be? Consider the sale of equipment where the buyer is not able to come up with the cash purchase price right away.

In order to make the sale, the seller is willing to deliver the goods immediately and to extend to the buyer long-term credit, with payments (reflecting both the purchase price and some reasonable rate of interest) to be made periodically. In this situation, however, there is no expectation by the seller that it will get return of the goods once the last payment is made. Once it has received all of the payments promised, it has gotten out of the transaction all that it has bargained for and could legitimately expect. Or it may be that the time for payments has extended so long that once the last payment has been made there would be no real reason for the seller to want return of the goods — they have been figuratively if not literally used up by the time the last payment has been made and would be of no real economic value, would indeed only be a burden, if the buyer were to dump them back on the seller. There is, of course, the possibility that the credit seller might have to repossess the goods when there is still some value to them, that is, if the buyer should stop making the installment purchase payments. The seller makes sure it has the right to do this by obtaining as part of the total agreement a security interest in the goods themselves, securing the obligation which the buyer has undertaken to pay for them over time.

So now we have come to some sort of answer to the question with which we started: When is a lease not really a lease? A transaction that purports to be a lease of goods is not a true lease when it is in reality and in substance an installment sale of goods coupled with the seller's retention of a security interest in the goods sold to secure the buyer's obligation to make the installment payments as they become due. The transaction that purports to be a lease but really isn't is sometimes referred to in the literature as a "disguised sale" or as a "lease intended as security." I find it better, if a bit wordier, to refer to it as what it is in all its glory — a sale of goods on credit in which the seller retains a security interest in the goods securing the buyer's payment obligation. The party referred to as the "lessor" in the documents is in reality a seller under Article 2 and a secured party under Article 9. The "lessee" is an Article 2 buyer and an Article 9 debtor. Any issues which may arise between them having to do with the sale aspect of their relationship are governed by Article 2. Issues involving the security interest are resolved under Article 9.

The difference between the true lease coming within the scope of Article 2A and the, well, untrue one is, as you would expect after all this build-up, more than just a matter of semantics. As we will see time and time again as we make our way through the Article 9 material, there will be a lot riding on whether an Article 9 security interest — which will be determined to be such an interest based not on what the parties hoped it to be taken for, or what they thought it would be, but by what it really is — is what we will term "perfected." The secured party's rights against a host of potential third parties making claims to the collateral, and particularly in the case of a bankruptcy proceeding, will rise or fall depending on whether perfection has been obtained. Perfection in many cases, and certainly in the kind that we're dealing with here, will almost always have to be accomplished by an appropriate filing in the public records. After some initial debate, the drafters of Article 2A determined not to include in their handiwork any filing requirement for true leases. The comment to the definition of lease in Article 2A, §2A-103(1)(j) includes the following:

> It is necessary to define lease in order to determine whether a transaction creates a lease or a security interest disguised as a lease. If the transaction creates a security interest disguised as a lease, the transaction will be governed by the Article on Secured Transactions (Article 9) and the lessor [Don't they mean the secured party masquerading as a "lessor"?] will be required to file a financing statement or take other action to perfect its interest in the goods against third parties. There is no such requirement with respect to leases under the common law and [with one minor exception], this Article imposes no such requirement.

You can fool some of the people some of the time, and, for all we care, you can fool (or at least satisfy) the accounting profession and the IRS as you may. But when it comes to the substantive law of commercial transactions and the Uniform Commercial Code, if you think you are creating a lease transaction but are in reality doing something else, you will only be fooling yourself, and the repercussions could be potentially devastating.

The comment to §2A-103(1)(j) just quoted, stressing the importance of being able to tell when a lease really is a lease, continues,

> Yet the distinction between a lease and a security interest disguised as a lease is not clear from the case law at the time of the promulgation of this Article [which would have been the late '80s].

It then goes on, at the end of the next paragraph, to assure us that "an amendment to [Article 1] has been promulgated with this Article to create a sharper distinction." The next paragraph then begins with the injunction that "This section as well as [the relevant Article 1 provision] must be examined to determine whether the transaction in question creates a lease or a security interest." We've already looked at §2A-103(1)(j). It's brief and to the point, but doesn't offer much in the way of a solution to the problem. We'd be fools not to turn to Article 1. We are not fools. Where you should (cleverly) now look in Article 1 depends, however, on which version of that article you are using.

If you are studying from the Original Version of Article 1, turn to §1-201(37). This subsection of the original Article 1, as amended with the adoption of Article 2A, serves as the Code's all-purpose definition of the term "security interest." We've looked at it, or at least parts of the initial paragraph, already.

Now drift down to the second paragraph, the one starting "Whether a transaction creates a lease or a security interest . . . ." From there on — running about a page or so in length up to where the puny definition of "send" commences — is what we seek. The riddle with which we started — When is a lease not a lease? — is short; the resolution of the riddle is anything but. True, we are deep within the definition section of Article 1, but it simply doesn't work to think of this as a definition. This page or so of text — complete with a set of factors (a) through (d), a second set of factors conveniently also labeled starting with (a), and three imbedded definitions now sporting (x), (y), and (z) — all of this material added to the Code in 1990 and now adopted by each of the states, this is not mere definition. We have come across the Code's substantive rule for determining when a transaction characterized by the parties as a lease is indeed a lease as opposed to a sale on credit accompanied by the seller's retention of a security interest in the goods sold.

If you are studying from the *Revised Version* of Article 1, look first at §1R-201(b)(35). Here you will find a one paragraph (granted, a long paragraph) definition of "security interest" that is applicable wherever that term is used in the Code. The substantive rules used for distinguishing between a security interest and a lease are now to be found in §1R-203. Note the first paragraph of the comment to this section. This section of Revised Article 1 is "substantially identical" to what your colleagues who are still using Original Article 1 find in its §1-201(37).

In what follows I will continue to give cites in terms of the Original Article 1 followed by the parallel cite in Revised Article 1. You should feel free to consistently use one or the other set of cites. You'll gain nothing, other than perhaps even more of a headache, by looking at both.

The real problem we now face is to get acquainted with how this gangling bit of statutory prose — as found in either §1-201(37) or §1R-203 — works in practice. And that, as you by now will have guessed, is where the soon to follow Examples and Explanations come in. Just a few points before we begin. First of all, note that the second paragraph of §1-201(37) (or its equivalent, §1R-203(a)) starts out with the injunction that whether a lease is created in fact "is determined by the facts of each case." That makes sense. Prior to the amendment to this subsection, there wasn't much more said than this, leading courts to ferret out "the intent" of the parties to the transaction. If you look about halfway through the long Comment 37 to this section, you'll see a paragraph commencing with the rather understated observation that "Reference to the intent of the parties . . . has led to unfortunate results." Read that paragraph and note its conclusion that the revised version of §1-201(37) (§1R-203) "deletes all reference to the parties' intent." What then replaces reference to intent? The comment doesn't lay out the big picture as well as it might, but what follows makes clear that the focus is on the *economics* of the transaction, by which is meant presumably not something to do with the international balance of payments or the gold standard but rather the *business economics* of the transaction as it affects the parties. A true lease is distinguished, in a phrase you see recurring in the cases, by the true lessor's having by intention retained from the outset "an economically meaningful reversionary interest" in the property. This is explained to mean that at the time the transaction is entered into, each party, the lessor and the lessee, in making its business calculation as to the deal's worth and acceptability on the terms concluded, takes into account the fact that the goods will at the end of the lease be returned to the lessor, and furthermore that the goods as returned can reasonably be anticipated to have some economic value left to them at that time. Since the goods will ultimately arrive back into the hands of the lessor, it is the lessor who bears the risk that this "reversionary interest" will be more or less valuable, dependant on factors like future demand for this type of property, changing economic conditions and so forth. The lessor truly, not just on paper, retains what we think of as the ownership interest in the goods and hence has the ultimate stake in their value at the end of the day—meaning the end of the lease.

A diagram may come in handy at this point to bring together the various elements of the discussion and to focus us on the problem that we face:

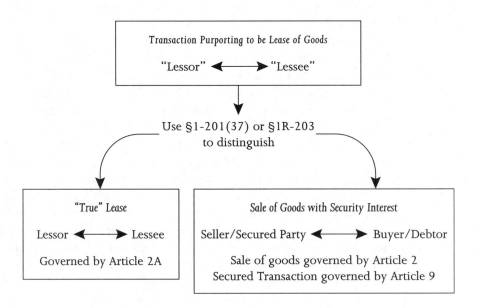

That's the big picture. To see how it is brought to life by the various snippets that come together in §1-201(37) (§1R-203), we turn to some examples.

Examples

1. Professor Brock, exhausted after a hard year of dedicated law teaching, decides to take a vacation. He goes to Arrow Rent-a-Car and arranges for a month-long rental of a fairly new luxury sedan, for which he agrees to pay $1,000. Is the arrangement between Brock and Arrow a lease of the car?

2. Returning from his well-deserved vacation, Professor Brock decides that he is getting too old to continue commuting to his office by bicycle and that he really needs a gas-guzzling automobile of his own. Dazed by all of the options open to him (the last car he owned having been a VW Beetle during the '60s), and on the advice of a number of know-it-all colleagues on his faculty, he decides to lease rather than buy a car. He enters into an agreement with Smiling Sam of Sam's Autorama for a brand new Cadillac Coupe. The agreement, denoted a "Lease" in all the paperwork, is to run for four years. Brock pays $616.26 at the time he picks up the car, which includes a "Security Deposit" of $300. He further agrees to pay $275.26 per month for each of the next 48 months. He agrees to return the vehicle to Smiling Sam "upon expiration of the agreement."
   a. Does the transaction between the good professor and Smiling Sam result in law in a true lease or something else?
   b. Would your answer be any different if the agreement also included a provision that gave Brock the option of purchasing the Cadillac at the expiration of the four-year term for "$3,458.36 or 95 percent of the value of the vehicle as determined by the National Auto Dealer's Association Official Used Car Trade-In Guide, whichever is less?"
   c. How would you analyze the situation if the provision in the agreement *required* Brock to purchase the car after four years at the price so determined?

3. Tom Toner's Office Equipment has a thriving business catering primarily to the city's large legal community. In 2008 Toner arranges for the purchase from their manufacturer, for $1,000 each, of several hundred of the latest-model copying machines. He advertises widely that these machines are available "For Sale or Rent." Lydia Lawyer, whose practice is growing, needs an additional copy machine. Toner offers to sell her one of the new models and to have it delivered directly to her office for $2,450. Or, if she prefers, she can rent the same machine for $100 a month. Lydia decides to rent. She signs an agreement committing her to a minimum six-month term and to continuation of the lease thereafter on a month-to-month basis subject to her giving termination notice two weeks prior to the end of any month. Is this transaction a lease?

4. Barry Barmember, another lawyer just setting up his practice and in need of a copy machine, also responds to Toner's advertisement. He signs an

agreement denoted a "Long-Term Office Equipment Lease" under which he agrees to "lease" one of the machines for $100 a month. The agreement provides that Barry will pay this amount for 60 months, at which time he will either return the machine to Toner or "at his option purchase full title and right to the machine" for the sum of $10.

   a. Is this transaction between Toner and Barry a lease or something else?

   b. Would your answer be any different if the agreement signed did not contain any reference to what would happen at the end of the five-year period? All it said was that Barry was obligated to make monthly payments for 60 months, and left it at that.

   c. What if, instead, the agreement was drafted on the basis of a three-year "initial term" and a further obligation on the part of Barry to renew on the same terms and conditions for at least two additional years?

5. The Cinderblock Corporation has long been one of the area's largest construction contractors, and at any one time may be involved in a variety of large building projects. While the contractor owns some construction equipment of its own, the project manager will determine, when a particular project is undertaken, if any special equipment is necessary for that job and for how long. When the contractor is awarded the contract to construct a large downtown office park ("Moneybucks Plaza"), the manager of the project estimates that for the better part of two years the work will require a specific type of 50-foot crane. With the approval of the President of the corporation, Cinderblock's Vice President for Equipment and Supply enters into a lease for the use of such a crane with a firm called Industrial Resources Incorporated. The transaction is characterized in the documentation as a lease for a term of two years. Cinderblock, which is to make monthly payments of $2,356.80 to Industrial Resources, is also obligated under the lease to carry adequate insurance covering the crane and its use during the two-year period and to assume all responsibility for its maintenance and repair. Do you see any reason, under the facts as you now know them, to doubt that this is a "true lease" of the crane by Cinderblock? How does it affect your view of the situation to learn that Industrial Resources operates out of a small suite of offices in a downtown office building, which while it is well-equipped with a phone, a fax, and a goodly number of file cabinets, is hardly the kind of place you could store a 50-foot crane? You can't even get it up the elevator.

6. Cosmo Grafix runs a small business specializing in the burgeoning field of computer graphic design. He is contacted by a representative of the H.A.L. Computer corporation, which has just come out with a powerful new computer system intended for use by just such a business. Grafix takes a look at the new system and is impressed. At the same time he finds

it expensive and is concerned that it might not fit in well over time with the direction his business (and indeed the entire industry) will take. On one hand, this system might really represent "the wave of the future," as the company's representative keeps insisting, in which case Grafix would do really well for himself by being one of the first to acquire one. On the other hand, however, it's possible that within a year or two it could prove to be superseded by a whole new level of technology, and Grafix could be left with an expensive white elephant on his hands. Seeing his concern, the H.A.L. representative suggests the following: Grafix will lease the computer system for an initial term of one year for $2,300 a month. He will then have, for each of the four following years, the option, at his discretion, to renew for successive one-year periods on the same terms. If he chooses to renew each time, and keeps up with his payments for the full five years, he will then have the option at the end of the fifth year to buy the system outright for $1. Grafix agrees to this arrangement.

a. Should this transaction be characterized as a lease or as a security interest in disguise under the rules of Article 1?

b. Should there be doubt as to how the transaction should or will later be correctly characterized, what can the parties do other than fret about the problem? See §9-505 and the second comment to that section.

Explanations

1. Yes, this is a lease of goods. After all of the buildup in the introduction, I thought it worthwhile to begin with an example to leave no doubt that when you or I rent a car for a weekend out or a month in the country it truly is a lease of goods under the Code and nothing else. To prove the point, look again at the second paragraph of §1-201(37) (§1R-203(a)). The issue is to be decided by the facts of each case. Fine, we are always willing to consider the facts. That paragraph goes on, however, beginning with the word "however" (or we move on to §1R-203(b)), to set forth a set of four instances where we're told in no uncertain terms how to read the facts. If the lessee's obligation is for a term "not subject to termination by" that lessee *and* if in addition at least one of the four criteria listed is established, then the transaction is to be deemed, on these facts alone, one creating a security interest and not a true lease at all. This second paragraph of §1-201(37) (§1R-203(b)) sets out what the courts have begun to refer to as the "bright-line" test for determining whether the transaction created a security interest rather than a true lease. See, for example, *In re Sankey*, 307 Bankr. 674, 2004 U.S. Dist. LEXIS 5791 (D. Alaska 2004), which states, "Under this test, a security interest is conclusively found to exist if the lease [meaning, I assume, the transaction purporting to be a lease]

is not subject to termination by the lessee and any one of the four enumerated conditions is found to exist."

So we start by asking whether in our particular instance Professor Brock's obligation is to last through the term of what purports to be a lease and is not terminable at his will. The answer is yes. The term is one month, and Brock is given no option to shorten it at his pleasure. So the instant transaction has at least the potential for creating a security interest under the authority of this second paragraph (§1R-203(b)). If, in another set of facts, the party denoted the "lessee" did have the right and power to terminate the "lease" at will, would this automatically rule out the possibility of a disguised sale with security interest? No, not unequivocally; it's just that the answer would not be definitively given by consideration of the four factors that immediately follow. Nor, for that matter, would we get much help from any of the rest of §1-201(37) (or §1R-203). We'd be thrown back to making the substantive determination based on "the facts of [the particular] case" as initially instructed. For the moment, however, Brock having committed himself irrevocably for a whole month, we can move on.

We now know that the transaction between Brock and Arrow, under the facts as given, must be considered to create a security interest if at least one of the factors (a) through (d), which immediately follow in this second paragraph of §1-201(37) (or §1R-203(b)(1)–(4)), is found to exist. You should be able to convince yourself fairly easily that here none of the factors fits the situation. The term of the lease, one month, is pretty clearly less than the "remaining economic life" of the car. You don't have to go through any heavy economic calculation (no supply and demand curves or anything like that) to note that a fairly new luxury sedan can be expected to retain a nonnegligible economic value after one more month of use. It might be worth a little less on the used car market, however that market is defined or its value estimated, but surely it's worth something. No one would give it up as worthless just because it had gone through one more month of wear and tear and was one month older. So the first factor isn't present.

The other factors — some of which we'll have to consider in later examples — all have to do with options or obligations on the part of the lessee, either to renew the lease or to purchase the goods, made part of the initial agreement. The simple rental agreement entered into by Brock and Arrow contains no such fancy stuff, so there's not much more to say than that none of those factors is present here.

None of the four factors being present, we cannot use the "bright-line" test as authoritative for calling this transaction anything other than a true lease. Does this mean that we have definitively established that it is a true lease? No, not exactly. You see that the language setting out this test says only that if this particular test is met — if the obligation is not terminable by the lessee and at least one of the four delineated factors is present — then a security interest has to be found. It says nothing about what the score is exactly if that particular test is not met. It certainly does *not* say that a security interest, as opposed to a true lease, must be found if *and only if* this test is satisfied. Nor does anything else in the following, the third, paragraph of §1-201(37), or the paragraph following that, (or in §1R-203(c)–(e)) give us something more on which to hang our hat.

With no "lease intended as security" having been established by the bright-line test we are thrown back to the more general language of that relevant section, the invocation at its beginning of a "facts of each case" analysis. In and of itself this wouldn't seem very helpful, but in the context of what we've already seen, from the history of this whole issue, the revision of §1-201(37) in 1990, and in the official commentary to this subsection (or §1R-203) and to §2A-103(1)(j), we are not exactly left in the dark. There should now be no doubt that in appraising the facts of any specific case the fundamental principal, the prime directive if you will, to be remembered is that what distinguishes a true lease from another type of transaction disguising itself in a lease's clothing is that in a lease the lessor retains an "economically meaningful reversionary interest" in the goods involved. As the court in the *Sankey* case, cited above, noted, if the bright-line test does not resolve the issue, it then becomes necessary "to examine all the facts to determine whether the economic realities of a particular transaction creates a security interest." This determination is commonly referred to by courts and commentators as the "economic realities" test.

The long and the short of it is that here Brock has leased a car. Is there any doubt that Arrow retains a reversionary interest in the car (that is, that it expects to get return of the car at the end of the month) or that this interest is "economically meaningful" to Arrow (that it is an interest of more than psychological or symbolic worth to the rental company)? If you have any doubt, just imagine what would happen if Brock never returned with the car after a month had passed. The good people at Arrow Rent-a-Car would, we can be sure, notice the absence of one of their vehicles and see it in their interest (not just psychologically) to chase down Brock and get their car back.

2a. The facts and figures in this example come, with only minor tinkering on my part, from the case of *In re Paz*, 179 Bankr. 743, 28 U.C.C.2d 52 (S.D. Ga. 1995). In this first part of the question, where Brock has committed himself only to a four-year lease of a new vehicle, the analysis is not really any different from the prior example. True, four years is a lot longer than a month, but it still doesn't cover the full "useful economic life" of an initially new automobile (and certainly not a new Caddy), so the situation is basically the same. You can think of it as a long-term lease, but it's a lease, in substance and not just in documentation, nevertheless.

2b. This part of the example, with Brock's having an option but not the obligation to purchase the car at the end of the initial four-year term, reflects the facts in the *Paz* case itself. Paz, the lessee, had gone into bankruptcy and was arguing (for reasons relevant to the law of bankruptcy that needn't concern us here) that the "lessor" was in reality actually a secured party. The bankruptcy court, applying the then new version of §1-201(37), which governed the transaction, concluded that the relationship was that of a true lease. (Those of you using revised Article 1 should easily be able to see how the court's analysis would be no different under §1R-203.) The court first scrutinized the agreement and found no evidence that Paz as lessee had any right to terminate the lease prior to the expiration of its four-year term. It was then in the position of having to review each of the four factors, (a) through (d). It found none to be present. Because the vehicle was new at the beginning of the term, the court could not find that at the end of four years it would be devoid of economic life, and hence (a) was not met. This is no different from our answer to the prior part of this example. Similarly there was nothing in the lease that bound Paz to renew the lease for the remaining life of the vehicle or to eventually purchase the vehicle. So (b) was not met. Factor (c) could also be easily disposed of: "The lease was silent regarding renewal. Hence this factor is inapplicable."

The remaining factor, (d), deserves a bit more consideration. Paz did have the option (which is of course different than the obligation) to become the owner of the goods at the end of the four-year term. The issue then became whether this option was available to the lessee "for no additional consideration or nominal additional consideration." In order to get the car at the end of the four years, Paz would have had to part with $3,456.36 or 95 percent of its then trade-in value, whichever was less. The court referring to the language in (x) in the final part of §1-201(37) concluded that whatever the exact figure might have been had Paz not gone bankrupt early in the relationship, the cost to him of exercising the option to buy would not have been "nominal."

The bankruptcy court, in citing to the (x) factor, makes the statement, "The Georgia Code provides that fair market value is not nominal." You could quibble by pointing out that the language of the agreement gave Paz the option of purchasing the vehicle for 95 percent, not 100 percent, of the "Official Used Car Trade-In Guide" evaluation, but it doesn't seem like a point very much worth pursuing here. Inclusion of the five percent reduction puts a little play in the price but doesn't suggest anything one would think of as a nominal figure. It probably just reflects the fact that "official trade-in" value of a used car may be normally somewhat higher than actual cash market value. A seller, trying to sell you a new car, will often inflate somewhat what he or she will "give you in trade-in" to conclude the sale of the new vehicle. Come back with the same used car and say you simply want to sell it to the dealer for cash, and you wouldn't be offered the same amount. What if the option-to-buy provision had been written in terms of "$3,458.36 or *nine* percent of the value" as determined by the official guide? Then the situation, of course, would appear different. You could argue that however it was worded, the agreement in effect provided for nominal consideration, and that hence the whole transaction was from its inception really a sale with the seller retaining a security interest. Of course, you'd also expect that the monthly payments that Paz would have had to make over the four-year term, prior to "buying" the car for a pittance, would have to have been that much higher for the seller to assure itself of making a respectable profit on the transaction.

Note that (x) initially speaks only of when additional consideration "is not nominal." As with much of this recent helpful but, you have to admit, ungainly version of §1-201(37) (or the sleeker, but really no different, §1R-203), it speaks primarily in negatives. It doesn't say much about, and certainly never comes close to defining per se, what nominal additional consideration is. The last sentence of (x) does state: "Additional consideration is nominal if it is less that the lessee's reasonably predictable cost of performing under the lease agreement if the option is not exercised." I take this sentence to mean that in a case such as the one before us we compare the lessee's cost of performance, meaning his return of the vehicle at the end of the term, with the cost to him of exercising the option. If the option price were set at the time of the initial transaction at one dollar, or even at a price so low that it would be "reasonably predictable" from the start that only a fool wouldn't take up the option, we can treat the additional consideration as nominal. Indeed, as one Bankruptcy Court judge recently noted, something like my suggested "only a fool" test has come to be widely adopted by the courts.

> The Economic Realities Test is also referred to in the case law as the "sensible person test," the "No Sensible Alternative But to Exercise the Option" Test, and the "No Lessee in its Right Mind Test."

In re *WorldCom, Inc.*, 339 Bankr. 56, 58 U.C.C.2d 913 (Bankr. S.D.N.Y. 2006) (citations omitted).

So, for instance, if the option price in *Paz* had been set initially at a flat $500, say, and it would have been reasonably predictable that a four-year-old vehicle of this type would have been worth significantly more than this, then the consideration is nominal and what we're dealing with is not a true lease, but a sale. The buyer is to make monthly payments for four years and then one single final payment — $500 in this situation — and the vehicle is his. In fact, the whole point of the U.C.C.'s substance-over-form approach here is that the sale was complete and the vehicle was his from the time the transaction was entered into. What the so-called "lessor" had during all that time was not ownership interest or "title" to the vehicle, but only a security interest securing the buyer's obligation to make the series and then the one final payment. Or, as we tend to say, the deal was such that it did not retain an "economically valuable reversionary interest" in the property itself.

Of course this is all spinning out further hypotheticals. In the facts as I gave them in part (b), and in the *Paz* case itself, the option price was not nominal and the transaction was a true lease. You certainly shouldn't get in the habit of assuming any long-term lease, either at the consumer or the commercial level, is likely to be just a disguised security interest. True leases are entered into by consumers like you or me and also commercially sophisticated parties all the time. The subject of the lease can be just about anything. See, for instance, *In re Harry & Larry Maronde Patnership*, 2002 Bankr. LEXIS 1780 (Bankr. D. Neb. 2002), where Harry and his brother Larry, being hog farmers, had entered into an agreement with American Leasing, Inc., to expand their operation by leasing from American what turned out to be a total of 331 female swine. The lease was expected to run for at least four but no more than five litters. The lessee's were to pay two isowean pigs (early-weaned pigs less than 21 days old) to American presumably per sow per litter. Evidence presented at trial indicated that there would be little or no economic life available in the sows *as breeding stock* at the end of the lease term, as after four or five litters a female sow becomes too large. Or as the judge more daintily put it, "her size becomes a factor, as she is likely to outgrow the physical facilities and is more prone to cause mortality in the litter by accidentally laying on piglets." Such more mature sows still had, however, economic value as animals held and eventually sold for slaughter. The arrangement between the Maronde brothers and American was a true lease of sows.

2c. If Brock were obligated to make the purchase, whatever the price, this is no longer a lease but a "lease intended as security." It comes under factor (b) of the by now infamous second paragraph of §1-201(37) (§1R-203 (b)(2)), Brock is obligated to continue paying on the "lease" during its term with no right on his part to terminate and in addition he is "bound to become the owner of the goods." Hence, the transaction is a present sale of the Cadillac Coupe and in addition creates a security interest in favor of Arrow with the car as collateral, securing Brock's obligation to make the 48 monthly payments and the single final payment at the end.

3. Yes, this is a lease. While Lydia does not have the right to terminate the arrangement any time during the first six months, at the end of that time the copier should still have plenty of viable "economic life." She has no obligation to renew, and while she has the right to do so on a month-to-month basis, the cost per month will never be "nominal." This seems like a lease, and it is. Notice how Toner definitely retains a meaningful reversionary interest in the particular copying machine he initially delivers to Lydia. He has to be aware from the outset that just about any time after six months he will get notice from her that she no longer wants the machine. He would then be forced to pick it up and figure out how to continue making money off of it. This example along with the one that follows track pretty closely the comment to the definition of lease in §2A-103(1)(j), which you may find helpful.

4a. This is not a lease but a sale with a security interest retained by the seller. It fits neatly under the factor (d) of that second paragraph of §1-201(37) (§1R-203(b)(4)), Barry has no right to terminate during the lease term of five years and then has the option to purchase the goods for "nominal additional consideration." From Barry's point of view he is purchasing the machine for good, but paying for it in 60 installments. These installments presumably are calculated to reflect some kind of interest charge for the credit he is being advanced by Toner. But once he makes all the monthly payments (and comes up with the additional $10) the thing is his. And then consider it from Toner's angle. No economically meaningful reversionary interest here. The only way the copier is going to come back into Toner's possession is if Barry stops paying during the five years or doesn't want to fork over the $10 at the end of that time. Toner then may be forced to repossess, as could any seller who isn't being paid the purchase price as agreed. But you (and Toner) have to assume that this would only happen if something were going wrong with the transaction, if Barry was finding it hard to pay his debts. Why else would he stop paying on something into which he has already sunk a good measure of his funds (building up what we can term in the broad sense "equity" in the machine) if after only a few more payments it would be entirely his?

4b. It may not be as immediately obvious, but this should and presumably would be treated no differently from the prior situation and hence as a "lease intended as security." True, there is no right to purchase for a nominal consideration at the end of the term, but if we assume that all else is the same, don't "the facts of the case" lead to the same conclusion? Previously we saw that Toner was willing to part for all time with one of these copiers and would consider he has received an acceptable purchase price, if the recipient gave him in exchange a promise to pay $100 each month for the next five years — OK, and one additional token $10 bill at the end. Is it so different in the economic sense if all he gets is the same income stream with no promise of the $10?

Another way of looking at this for me is that the facts as presented in (a) indicate to us that once a machine such as this is five years old and has given five years of faithful service it is virtually devoid of any further useful economic life as far as Toner is concerned. That doesn't mean that it won't make copies anymore, only that from the beginning he has evaluated the transaction on the assumption that after that period of time the machine would be sufficiently old and perhaps out-of-date that he really wouldn't have any use for it. Why else would he be willing to part with it for a paltry $10? If this is the case, of course, we assume that Toner has calculated the monthly payments of $100 taking into account that he has to wring all of its value to him out of the machine within those first five years. If, as we posited in (a), after that time he anticipates that he'd have no regrets having to part with it for $10, it seems that basically he'd be willing to part with it for nothing at all. He's sold the thing for five years' worth of payments of a specified sum. If that monthly sum is the same in this part of the example, if the product is identical and so on, then there's every reason to think that at the time of the transaction, here the original term of the lease, the five years, was "equal to or greater than the remaining economic life of the goods." Hence, under the rules of §1-201(37) (or §1R-203), this too is a lease intended as security. The facts of this particular case allow us to conclude that from the very beginning the economic nature of the transaction was a sale by Toner to Barry, which Barry would pay for over a five-year period. At the end of that time the copier would be Barry's. In fact from the very date of the transaction the copier was Barry's, albeit one on which he had to make payments and one encumbered with a security interest held by Toner.

I would not want you to take from this example the conclusion that any time a purported lease is silent as to what is to happen at the end of the term it must be a sale with a disguised security interest. Far from it. Look, for instance, at the very first example. The question becomes what the "expected economic life of the goods" is, and that would always be a question of fact for the particular case. In Example 1, we had no difficulty concluding that a new luxury sedan has an expected economic life of greater than one month, no matter how hard on it Professor Brock should turn out to be. The lessor would definitely be aggrieved, to put it mildly, should the vehicle not be returned. In the copier situation for this example, the particulars allow at least a fairly strong argument that Toner was working from the outset on the assumption that such a copier would have a useful economic life (as far as he was concerned) of approximately five years. At the end of that time, he anticipates, he really wouldn't want it back, presumably because he can conceive of no profitable use, as his business is run, for a five-year-old copier of this type. He knows that it simply isn't worth his while to have to deal with models this old or outmoded. If he hears that a potential client has on its hands a copier of this vintage, his reaction is most likely that here is someone ripe for a replacement with a new machine entirely.

This concept of "useful economic life" or "remaining economic life of the goods" is obviously important to the whole approach of Article 1's method for distinguishing a lease from a security interest, and yet we're told nothing more than the invocation in that Article, that it is something "to be determined with reference to the facts and circumstances at the time the transaction is entered into." I hope that is what I've been doing all along. Note that just because some goods are still in existence and being put to productive use by someone well beyond what was their anticipated "economic life" at the time of the initial transaction doesn't mean that there is something fishy going on or that someone made a mess of the initial evaluation. A lot of things can be perfectly fine and workable in the hands of their present owner without their having any kind of value to anyone else or generalizable market value. Anyone who bought a brand-new state-of-the-art computer printer anything like a decade ago knows what I'm talking about. If you have such a printer (a dot matrix, presumably) it still may be serving you as well as it did on the day you bought it. Should you decide to buy a new printer, however, you're not going to get any trade-in value from it. You could try selling it for at least a little cash through an ad in the paper or at the local laundromat, but good luck. Maybe, and only maybe, your favorite charity will take it off your hands, but even they may not find it worth their while. And forget trying to give it as a gift to one of your nieces or nephews; she or he will more than likely just ask what would make you think they'd want anything to do with "that old thing." In my experience, at least, old computer printers, as well as other computer components, often just get packed away in the rear of a closet or left out with the trash. They may still work perfectly well and have plenty of "useful life" left in them, but their "economic life" (except perhaps in the antique collector's world) is shot in an amazingly short amount of time.

For a good recent example of the economic-realities test in operation, you may want to look at the recent case of In re Pillowtex, Inc., 349 F.3d 711, 52 U.C.C.2d 18 (3rd Cir. 2003). In 1998 Duke Energy Royal entered into what was termed a Master Energy Services Agreement with Pillowtex under which Duke agreed to install certain energy-savings equipment valued at $10.41 million in ten different Pillowtex facilities. Duke removed the existing equipment at these Pillowtex locations and then provided and installed the new equipment. In exchange Pillowtex was to pay Duke on a monthly basis "one-twelfth of its annual energy savings" (really a set amount the parties had agreed to in advance) for the next eight years. Although the agreement was for an eight-year term, in it the parties stipulated that the "useful life" of the energy fixtures was some 20 to 25 years. The agreement further provided that at the end of the eight-year term Duke had a series of options. One was to remove the new equipment it had installed and replace that equipment "with equipment comparable to" that originally in place. Another option Duke would have would be to "abandon the Equipment in place." When Pillowtex went into bankruptcy, Duke argued that this agreement was a true lease. The district court and later the Third Circuit found otherwise. As the circuit court noted:

> The economic realities of the particular transaction in this case belie any [plausible intent on Duke's part to take back possession of the equipment at the end of the eight years rather than just abandon it]. Although the useful life of the lighting fixtures is 20-25 years, eclipsing the [agreement's] 8-year term, it would be unreasonable for Duke to incur the high costs necessary to repossess the fixtures: namely, the costs associated with removing, scrapping, and replacing the fixtures. Also, the uncontroverted evidence in this case establishes that there is little (if any) market value for used lighting fixtures. In short, it would have made no economic sense for Duke to spend large amounts of money to reclaim the fixtures, especially in the face of poor resale prospects.

The agreement was held not to be a true lease but a sale on secured credit of the energy-saving equipment with the price to be paid over eight years. At the time the agreement was entered into it would have been clear that the only economically realistic outcome at the end of the eight-year term would have been for Duke to have abandoned the equipment, giving Pillowtex full ownership.

4c. If the facts are such that the copier has an "economic life" as determined at the time of the transaction of only five years, then this too would be a sale with a reserved security interest. This comes under factor (b) of that second paragraph to §1-201(37) (§1R-203(b)(2)).

5. This seems clearly to be a lease. Even if the crane was getting pretty old as cranes go and perhaps destined for retirement from day-to-day service at the end of the two-year term, you have to assume it would have some nonnegligible value, as scrap metal if nothing else, when its time came to go wherever it is that old cranes go. Industrial Resources is not renting out disposable construction equipment or anything like that, and its intention from the inception of the deal to insist upon return of the crane at the end of the two years, its own reasonable perception of a valuable reversionary interest, can hardly be doubted.

So what's the problem? The problem is that prior to the revision of §1-201(37) in 1990 some courts, floundering around amidst the facts of individual cases, displayed a tendency to be distracted by certain aspects of lease transactions and make too much out of them. Seeing in one "factor" or another seemingly clear indication of a sale and change of ownership, as opposed to a temporary change in possession as in a lease, and not having the benefit of the revised version of §1-201(37) as we now do (or §1R-203), there were numerous examples of courts making bad or at least highly questionable calls. Part of this, to be fair, also stemmed from the earlier version of this section giving so very little guidance on how to deal with the characterization — true lease or security interest — issue, and unfortunate language in that version insinuating that the primary goal for the court was to ferret out the "intention of the parties" as to what manner of business arrangement they were creating. Not the least of the problems was that the reason this whole issue arises in the first place is that the parties themselves, even if you could read their minds, are not always that clear themselves about why they are doing what they are doing and what they want the result to be. Or their intentions may be purposefully ambiguous, the transaction carried out in a way seeking to make it a lease for at least one purpose and not a lease for another.

Notice a paragraph about halfway through the comment added along with the newer version of §1-201(37):

> Reference to the intent of the parties to create a lease or a security interest has led [under the initial version] to unfortunate results. In discovering intent, courts have relied upon factors that were thought to be more consistent with sales or loans than leases. Most of these criteria, however, are as applicable to true leases as to security interests. Examples include the provision of the typical net lease provisions, a purported lessor's lack of storage facilities or its character as a financing party rather than a dealer in goods. Accordingly, amended Section 1-201(37) deletes all reference to the parties' intent.

(This same language is found in the comment to §1R-203.) Not only was reference to the parties' intent removed from the section, but an additional paragraph — the one following the one we have been focusing on up to this point, the one with the second listing of (a) through now (e) — was added (§1R-203(c)). Reading it you see that again the section speaks in negatives, and nonconclusive ones at that: "A transaction does not create a security interest *merely because* it provides that" this or that is to be done by one party or the other. You see now the genesis for this strange bit of statutory prose; it was intended to counter a series of individual cases which relied on one or another of these five factors almost to the exclusion of any other facts about the case to come to what the revisors call their "unfortunate results." The present language does not say that these factors may never be considered, only that the determination based on "the facts of the case" has to be made on the overall situation, and recall with a focus on the "economics" of the relationship, not the "intent of the parties." It may help if you now read the three longer paragraphs of the comment following the one I've just quoted.

Returning to Cinderblock and its twenty-four month lease of a crane, you see the particular relevance here of factor (b), now of the third paragraph of the section (§1R-203(c)(3)). That the lease contains provisions calling on the lessee to provide insurance and take care of maintenance does not in and of itself give rise to the conclusion that the transaction creates a security interest. In fact, as the commentary suggests, it is fairly typical in what is often referred to as a "net lease." On the basis of all the facts, a court should hold this to be a lease.

I see no reason for the answer to change even when we introduce the fact that the lessor would have no obvious place to store the crane on its "return" at the end of the lease term. Apparently some decisions prior to the revision of this section took the "lessor's" lack of a storage facility as a strong and perhaps conclusive indication that it had no expectation of return of the goods. But this really doesn't follow. Why should Industrial Resources spend money on a great big barn of a storage facility when, at least if all is going according to plan, practically all of the equipment it owns will be leased out and hence at some construction site at any one time? When you think of it, even the typical rental car agency wouldn't have enough parking spaces if each and every one of its cars coincidentally were returned to its garage at the very same time. It counts on the fact that most of the cars are out there on the road most of the time. Is there any realistic expectation that Industrial Resources of our example would at the end of the two years (or even earlier if the lessee fell too far behind in its monthly payments) tell Cinderblock just to keep the gosh darn thing and not bother returning it, simply because it couldn't find a convenient place for the crane in its suite of offices within its filing cabinets?

Presumably there are people right in that office suite whose principal responsibility and expertise is in arranging for the acquisition, disposal, relocation, and, when necessary, the short-term storage of all kinds of massive equipment, none of which would fit neatly next to the ferns or under the window. That's why they (the people, that is, not the ferns or the windows) earn the big bucks.

The other factors in that third paragraph of §1-201(37) (§1R-203(c)) are all to the same effect. They're meant to undo some nasty business in a number of the earlier cases that, by stressing one aspect of the transaction or another, resulted in a true lease not being appreciated for what it was. The new version of the section wants all facts to go into the mix and the presence or absence of a "meaningful reversionary interest" in the lessor to be the key question.

One interesting situation that I did not put into the examples is the so-called full payout lease, at which the (a) factor (remember we're in the third paragraph of §1-201(37) now) or §1R-201(c)(1) is driving. In some instances the type of goods and their scarcity, general economic conditions, the relative bargaining positions of the parties, or probably a combination of all of these things are such that the terms of the lease create (at least initially) the impression that by the time the lessee has made the final payment it will have forked over as much or more as if it had contracted to buy the thing outright in the first place. Some courts, reasoning from this fact alone, have in the past concluded that the transaction had to be a sale in disguise and not a true lease. Yet, it may still be true, even if "the present value [on which see (z) of the final paragraph] of the consideration the lessee is obligated to pay . . . is substantially equal to or greater than the fair market value of the goods at the time the lease is entered into," that the lease is not contemplated to run over the entire anticipated useful economic life of the goods. Some goods apparently can, due to inflation alone, appreciate in value even as the lessee is paying heavily for their use on a month-to-month or year-to-year basis. When the lease term is over, the lessor will certainly want them back, and will have agreed to a lease, a true lease, only on the clear understanding that it will get them back. Once again, it's all in the facts of the particular case. Factor (a) of the third paragraph stands only for the proposition, in the words of the comment that, "[A] full payout lease does not *per se* create a security interest." The emphasis is in the original.

6a. If the idea is that a thoughtful observer, familiar with the intricacies of §1-201(37) or §1R-203, should be able to characterize the transaction as a lease or as a security interest correctly once and for all as of the time the transaction is entered into, you see the difficulty here. How this transaction plays out, indeed how it is expected to play itself out, is left hanging. Only time, and future decisions on Grafix's part on whether to renew or not, will tell. Grafix has not committed himself to a lease for anything more than a year, so he certainly hasn't entered into a lease for a period "equal to or greater than the "remaining economic life of the goods" nor has he committed himself to renew for even one more year. This transaction cannot be classified as one creating a security interest on the basis of the somewhat more precise and easily applied tests that follow from factors (a) through (d) in the second paragraph of the section or §1R-203(b). So we are left to analyze it based on all of the facts of the case, and with an eye to whether the lessor has reserved an economically significant reversionary interest.

Is there a real likelihood that H.A.L. will find itself back in possession of this particular system prior to the time all the economic life (as least as evaluated as of the inception of the lease) has been drained from its circuitry? We have to assume that the parties reasonably see the economic life extending at least five years, or why would they enter into the arrangement they have? Is there a reasonable likelihood that the system will revert to H.A.L. before five years are up? If you look at this as of the inception or the first year or two of the deal, the answer seems to be yes. Grafix could rent the system for only the first year and then be perfectly within his rights in foregoing any further renewal. The system could revert to H.A.L., the lessor, in just one year. Grafix might not want it any more, or at least not at that monthly rate, but that's not the same thing as saying it is worth nothing. Others may be very willing to take it, even if Grafix does not want or need it anymore. You could even envision a situation where Grafix chooses not to renew not because the computer system isn't doing all that it could do, but perhaps because for other reasons he is not attracting as much business as he had hoped and cannot justify the expense of the machine. His competitors, with better artistry, a more aggressive sales staff, and so on, would be more than happy to snap up such a system at a reduced but still fairly hefty price because it has gone through only one year's use. But we needn't catalog all the possibilities. Life is uncertain. That's exactly why the parties entered into the kind of agreement they did. And it's sufficient to say that the real possibility that Grafix will have and use the machine for only a year and make only twelve payments on it creates what seems to be — at least viewed in this light — a classic lease.

Things could go differently, however. It's also perfectly possible, viewed from the moment of the transaction, that Grafix will love the computer system and find the expense more than justified by what he's getting for the money. If so, and if Grafix eagerly exercises his option to renew on identical terms at the end of each of the first, second, third, and fourth years, then see what the situation has become. We are in the fifth year of the transaction. Does it seem that H.A.L. has any realistic expectation of getting return of the system? No, not under this scenario. Grafix has only to continue making the monthly payments for the rest of that year, which he's obligated to do under the terms of the agreement in any event, and then with the payment of only one more dollar it is his to keep forever and ever free and clear! Is there any real likelihood that Grafix would finish up his fifth year of payments and then balk at having to pay one dollar more, thus giving H.A.L. the right to come over and take the wonderful moneymaking machine away? Of course not. By the fifth year the situation is just as it would be in the classic outright sale on long-term credit. It has worked out that Grafix has bought the machine through five years of steady monthly payments plus a nominal dollar at the end. Now it seems that the situation all along should have been understood as a "lease intended to create security" and not a true lease after all.

No one scenario or the other is inherently more likely. Neither is "better" or more or less "honest" than the other. It's just from the inception of the agreement we can anticipate that things will look differently as time goes by and depending on what decisions the lessee, in all honesty and for whatever reason, makes. What begins looking for all the world like a true lease will become, should Grafix exercise his option to renew each and every time, a nice neat example of a purchase through the use of long-term credit where the seller retained throughout the term an Article 9 security interest but nothing more. Such transactions have been referred to as "chameleon leases" and you can see why.

In the case of *Matter of Marhoefer Packing Co., Inc.*, 674 F.2d 1139, 33 U.C.C. 370 (7th Cir. 1982), the Seventh Circuit was faced with a lease that allowed the lessee a single option to renew on terms that included the option to purchase for a nominal sum at the end of the renewal period. The court held that during the initial lease period the transaction was to be classified as a true lease. It suggested that the transaction would have become one "creating a security interest" had the option to renew ever been exercised (an opportunity that never arose because things fell apart for the lessee during the initial term and it never got to that stage). If this analysis is correct, then the particular chameleon there under consideration was to change from one color to another all at once.

As you can see, I've made the problem in my example that much more sophisticated by having a series of renewal possibilities. Even if the Grafix and H.A.L. deal looks pretty clearly one color or the other in the first, as opposed to the fifth year, the change is a slow and subtle metamorphosis, truly worthy of being identified with the chameleon and bearing the appellation. How should this transaction be treated by the parties at the time they enter into it? Must they observe the Article 9 filing requirement or wait until some time further down the pike to take the time and trouble? As we will see at any number of places in the chapters to follow, a basic tenet of practice in this area is that when in doubt, you file. In fact, if you're in doubt as to whether you are reasonably in doubt, file. Just file. But is this possible? Is it even kosher to file on a lease, chameleon-like or otherwise? If you can do it, that is, offer a filing on a lease or something that *may be* a lease, does that action itself put you at risk in some other way? May you suffer untoward consequences under the statutory dictates of Article 9 or (even worse) the wrath of the filing officer when you try it? This brings us to the next and concluding part of this example.

6b. Section 9-505 and its commentary pretty much speak for themselves, and I have gone on long enough. When in doubt, you can and you should file. Safety first.

CHAPTER 3

Attachment: The Security Agreement

AN INTEREST CREATED BY CONTRACT

As should be abundantly clear from the preceding chapters, the very nature of an Article 9 security interest is that it is created by contract; it results from an agreement between a debtor and one of his or her creditors. However much the legal interest thus created may be of concern to and possibly affect the rights of third parties, and however much we ourselves will be concerned in what is to come with third-party issues, creation of an Article 9 security interest is a two-party affair. The debtor, who has rights in some personal property,* agrees by contract to give some interest — a security interest as that term is defined in Article 1 — in that property to another, whom we can then appropriately refer to as the secured party.

It is important in studying Article 9 not to forget all you have learned in the past about the general law of contracts. A contract is necessary to make the security interest come alive, and when and how a contract arises, how it is to be interpreted should a dispute arise, and so on are all the kinds of questions to which general contract law will be applied. See, for example,

---

* I know that in the diagrams I developed in the first chapter I used the expression "ownership interest," and that I'm making a switch here. You may even wonder why I don't just drop all pretense and say "title" when that must be what I'm talking about. I've adopted the language of "rights in" the collateral here to conform to the language used in Article 9 itself. See §9-203(b)(2), the meaning of which we'll explore in the next chapter. As to "title," a term which the U.C.C. drafters tried their best to reduce to just another five-letter word not to be used in polite company, see §9-202. For Article 9 purposes, try to put out of your mind all that you may ever have known, or thought you've known, about title to personal property.

3. Attachment: The Security Agreement

Medallion Biomedical, LLC v. Rosania, 298 Bankr. 442, 51 U.C.C.2d 563 (Bankr. D. Colo. 2003), holding that the contract doctrine of reformation on the grounds of "mutual mistake" was applicable to a written security agreement.

There are, of course, some special things to be considered when it is claimed that a particular contract has given rise to a security interest valid under Article 9 and subject to its rules. We start out with the concept of attachment. Under Article 9 if a security interest has been created and become enforceable as between the two parties, the debtor and the secured party, with respect to a particular piece of property, then we say that it has *attached* to that property. See §9-203(a). Note at the outset how important it is to focus on a specific piece of property, or some well-defined assemblage of bits and pieces of property, as collateral. It makes no sense to speak about a security interest "attaching" in some abstract or metaphysical sense. There must be some real, valuable, and identifiable collateral in the picture, something that the interest attaches *to,* or the whole thing is just so much talk and of no legal much less practical significance whatsoever. Similarly, if you find yourself speaking of an "unattached security interest" as if that meant something, think again. If a security interest has not attached, if it isn't enforceable by or against anybody, then it is worthless, despite what someone once hoped it would turn out to be. An "unattached security interest" is something along the lines of an uncontract contract or a deed that transfers no interest in anything whatsoever.

So attachment of a security interest is about as fundamental as you can get. Look at §9-203(b). Subject to a few provisions that needn't concern us here, "a security interest is enforceable against the debtor and third parties with respect to the collateral only if" three criteria are met. Value must have been given by the secured party to the debtor, (b)(1); the debtor must have what we will term "rights in the collateral," (b)(2); and the debtor must have entered into a security agreement covering the collateral and giving a security interest in it to the secured party, (b)(3). We deal in this chapter with the last of these conditions, the existence of a binding security agreement entered into by the debtor. The following chapter takes up the first two parts of the package, value and rights in the collateral.*

Section 9-102(a)(73) defines a *security agreement* as "an agreement that creates or provides for a security interest." As to *agreement* as that term is used generally in the Code, see §1-201(3) or §1R-201(b)(3). It is the bargain of the parties "in fact." So, as used in Article 9, the security agreement is not a physical thing. It is a state of being for the two parties involved, the

---

* In looking over §9-203(b)(3) do not concern yourself at present with paragraphs (C) and (D). These cover some special types of collateral with which you are understandably not yet familiar. The Examples and Explanations of this chapter will deal with the general requirement of the security agreement only as it is featured in (A) and (B) of subsection (b)(3).

condition of their having come to agreement as to the creation of a particular type of interest in some specific piece or pieces of property. As a practical matter, however, speakers and writers have gotten into the habit of using the term "security agreement" to mean a concrete object, a writing that embodies the intangible but quite real legal construct of agreement. We tend to talk about what the security agreement "says" or what it "provides," when what we really mean is what language appears in a writing that was created by the parties to evidence their agreement. Under Revised Article 9, habits will have to change and we will have to expand our vocabulary and our thinking in an important respect. Prior to revision, Article 9, written as it was in the middle of the last century and before the advent of the electronic age, set out a requirement at various places that a certain agreement be in "writing" (for the definition of which see §1-201(46) or §1R-201(b)(43)) or that a particular writing be "signed" (§1-201(39) or §1R-201(b)(37)) by one person or another. For a party or parties to set out on paper the terms of an agreement, a notice, or any other communication, was thought of as not just the paradigm but virtually the only way in which the terms of the communication could be memorialized with certainty. For a person to sign a writing was conceived of the way in which that person could adopt that writing as representative of his or her intention. Times have changed — as anyone knows who has ever sent or received an e-mail. Electronic transmission and storage of information has become available, affordable, and, in many instances, the rule rather than the exception.

The drafters of the Revised Article 9 gave recognition to the new era in which we live by replacing in almost all instances the requirement that an agreement or notice be in writing with the need for a *record* of the information that the writing would otherwise contain. Look at the definition in §9-102(a)(69):

> "*Record*" . . . means information that is inscribed on a tangible medium or which is stored in an electronic medium and is retrievable in a perceivable form.

So any writing would be a record, but not all records would necessarily be in writing. Note also that in §9-102(a)(7) a definition is given of the term *authenticate* that goes beyond the notion of signing to recognize the different ways in which a person may exhibit his or her present intent to "adopt or accept a record." So, to take one simple example, if I send you an e-mail that you store on a computer disk, what you have on that disk (even if you never print it out, but retain the ability to do so) is a record of whatever I said in the e-mail authenticated by me, presumably when I hit the "send" button on my own computer's e-mail program. The drafters give us a good outline of how this new terminology — appropriate to the twenty-first century — is to be understood in Comment 9 to §9-102, which it would pay for you to look over now.

3. Attachment: The Security Agreement

The temptation to think of the piece of paper or some other more modern record of the parties' agreement in fact as if it *were* the security agreement itself as opposed to just a symptom of it is, I have to admit, virtually impossible to resist. Nor does it really do any harm in most instances. It is healthy, however, to keep the distinction in mind. Among other things, as you will soon see, it is entirely possible for a security agreement never incorporated into a record of any sort to be legally enforceable, even if in only a limited number of situations (and even if in those situations responsible legal practice or just plain common sense would suggest a well thought-out record in any event).

The Examples and Explanations in this chapter will steer us through some questions involving the security agreement, a necessary component of the attachment trilogy. When must the agreement be reduced to a writing or be otherwise evidenced by a record? If a record of agreement is required, what type of document (whether stored on paper or in some other media) will suffice? What elements or provisions *must* the security agreement, whether stored in a record or not, contain to be valid under Article 9? One element you will quickly come across is that the agreement may need to provide "a description of the collateral." On this criterion, see §9-108, which offers guidance.*

Examples

1. Dexter Moneybucks, in need of some ready cash, asks his friend Susan if she can lend him $12,000. He promises to repay that amount with interest within a year and further offers to let Susan keep a valuable ruby ring of his "as collateral for the loan." Susan agrees. She gives Dexter a check for $12,000, and in exchange he hands over the ring. Nothing is in writing.

   a. Have Dexter and Susan created a security interest that attaches to the ring under Article 9?

---

* It is of course a distinct matter to ask what terms and provisions a written or otherwise recorded security agreement *may* or *typically* will include, even if not required by the Code, but which reflect the drafting parties' special concerns, general wisdom, and lessons learned from past experience. The security agreement is, after all, a contract between two parties and like any contract has to be negotiated and drafted with attention to the particular circumstances and the needs and desires of the individuals involved. Throughout this book there will be several instances where we will have to consider what the effect is of a provision in a security agreement under which the parties provide that this or that is to be done or not to be done. Other times you will want to reflect on how the parties might have avoided some problem by better drafting of the security agreement initially. All you know about contract law, not just in theory but in practice, can be put to use in your studies of secured transactions. For the moment, however, and in this chapter we are concentrating only on the minimal requirements that apply to the security agreement as a distinct kind of contract governed by Article 9 of the Code.

b. Suppose that in fact Susan had refused to take the ring when Dexter tried to hand it over to her, saying, "I see no reason you shouldn't keep wearing it, as long as it's agreed I can get it if you don't make repayment." How does this affect your analysis?

2. Meanwhile, in another part of town, Dexter's sister, Deborah Moneybucks, is also short of cash. She borrows $4,000 from one Stella, who asks for no interest or any collateral in making the loan. It is agreed that Deborah will repay Stella within two weeks. As she is handing over the check to Deborah, Stella notices and comments on a small but obviously valuable cameo that Deborah is wearing. Deborah, in recognition of the help her friend is giving her, agrees to let Stella borrow the piece so that she, Stella, might wear it to a fancy party she is to attend the following week. A month later Deborah's fortunes are not going as well as she had anticipated. She calls Stella to assure her that one way or the other she will be repaid although she cannot say exactly when. Deborah also says that she will be coming over to pick up the cameo. Stella declares, however, that she intends to hang onto the bauble until her friend is no longer in default on the loan. Would Stella be within her rights to do so?

3. A third member of the Moneybucks clan, David, arranges to borrow money from a business acquaintance named Sandy. Before Sandy releases any funds to David, she insists that he sign two documents that she has prepared. The first is a note calling for payment by David, as the two had agreed. The second reads in its entirety:

> I, David Money Bucks, hereby grant Sandy a security interest in my 1994 Honda civic in connection with a loan being made by her to me.
>
> _____
> David Money Bucks

David signs on the dotted line and gets his loan. Has a security interest in the automobile been created? In particular, if David were to fail to make proper payment on the note and Sandy then tried to enforce what she claims to be a valid interest by repossessing the Pontiac, could David argue against the repossession on the grounds that

a. the document was not headed "Security Agreement" or anything of the sort;

b. David did not sign the document in front of any witnesses, nor was his signature notarized;

c. it is nowhere signed by Sandy;

d. it gives neither David's nor Sandy's address;

e. it gives David's name *incorrectly* (as I'm sure you immediately noticed);

f. it carries no information about the loan terms?

4. Dewey buys a new refrigerator from Selma's Appliance City, agreeing to pay for it over a period of two years under what Selma advertises as her "EZ Credit" plan. Dewey gives Selma a check for a portion of the price as a down payment. He also signs a document prepared by her headed "Retail Sales Installment Agreement." This paper makes no reference to a security interest, collateral, Article 9, or anything of the sort. It states only that Dewey is to finish paying for the refrigerator in specified monthly installments over the two years and further that "title in any appliance or appliances sold hereunder remains in Selma until full and final payment" by Dewey. One year later, when Dewey is behind in his payments, Selma threatens to repossess. Can Dewey defend on the absence of an authenticated security agreement as called for in §9-203(b)(3)(A)?

5. Dan runs a small delivery service ("Dan's Vans") using two Ford vans that he has had for some time and that he now owns outright. He decides that the volume of his business justifies his buying a third van and arranges to borrow the money he needs to purchase this vehicle, a 2008 Chevy van, from a lender, Trucker's Credit Service. The security agreement he signs gives the Credit Service an interest in "one delivery van owned by Dan and used in his business."
   a. Is this agreement sufficient to create a security interest under Article 9?
   b. Would your answer be any different if the description had read "one 2008 Chevrolet cargo van?"
   c. What if, because of a mistake by someone at the Credit Service, the description had read "one 2008 Chevrolet cargo van serial number 56Z789Q?" This serial number is incorrect; it should read "56Z798Q." Does this defeat the Credit Service's security interest?
   d. Finally, consider what the result would be if the description of the collateral in the security agreement had read only "One motor vehicle as more fully described in Schedule A attached hereto," but that, again because of a mistake, no Schedule A was to be found attached to the agreement?

6. Isabelle Inkster runs a small printing business out of a shop attached to her home. Over the years she has accumulated various pieces of equipment, a press, a binding machine, and so forth, all of which are fully paid for. She also owns outright a truck with which she makes deliveries. She finds, however, that she is sometimes not able to take on large projects from which she could profit because she doesn't have the ready cash to buy the large quantities of paper and ink that she would need. Isabelle negotiates with her local bank, Downtown Federal, for a small business line of credit on which she can draw up to a specified amount. As part of the documentation required by the bank, she signs a security agreement that describes the collateral simply as "all Inkster's equipment."

a. Does this agreement sufficiently describe the collateral in order to be effective? See §9-108(b)(3).

b. Suppose instead that the agreement's description read "all of Inkster's assets." Can the bank's interest attach to any of Inkster's property? See §9-108(c).

7. Samantha, a retired university professor, is in need of some money to meet her mounting medical bills. She approaches a firm, Local Lending Associates, and arranges for a loan. Local Lending asks her to sign a written security agreement that describes the collateral that Samantha is putting up to secure the loan as "all consumer goods held" by Samantha. Is this a valid description of the collateral, sufficient to make the security agreement Samantha signs enforceable against her should she not repay the loan? See §9-108(e)(2) and §9-102(a)(23) and (26).

Explanations

1a. Yes. Susan's security interest has attached under Article 9. She has no record of the security agreement authenticated by Dexter, but under the circumstances and in light of the language of §9-203(b)(3)(B) that isn't a problem. The ring is collateral and is in her possession "pursuant to the debtor's security agreement." As we've already noted, the Code defines *agreement* clearly in Article 1 as the agreement "in fact," not as any particular piece of paper or other physical manifestation of the agreement. Dexter and Susan may not have explicitly invoked any specific section or language from Article 9 (indeed, neither of them may have even the foggiest notion that an Article 9 exists and rides herd over their actions), but it's clear that they've agreed to something regarding the ring and that Dexter has *by agreement* given Susan some kind of interest in it. What they've agreed to is what we would know (since we at least have a deep and abiding belief in not just the existence but the efficacy and indeed the majesty of Article 9) to be a U.C.C. *security interest* as defined in Article 1. And a security interest in personal property created intentionally by the parties thereto is governed by Article 9, whether the parties are aware of this simple fact or not. Recall §9-109(a)(1) and all we saw in Chapter 1.

All of this is just a long-winded way of saying that the condition imposed by §9-203(b)(3) has been met here because "the collateral is in the possession of the secured party pursuant to the debtor's security agreement," satisfying paragraph (3)(b). We will deal with the subtleties of the other two conditions imposed by paragraphs (1) and (2) in more detail in the next chapter, but there seems to be no question that they're met here. Susan has given value, the $12,000, to Dexter. Dexter, we've assumed from the start, has "rights in" the ring. It's his. He owns it. Take my word for it. It's been in the Moneybucks family for ages. So a security interest in the ring has attached — has been created — in favor of Susan. Susan can be congratulated. But, let us not forget, congratulations go to Dexter as well. He's gotten his loan and the ready cash he so desperately needed.

1b. If Susan allows Dexter to retain possession of the ring, then her failure to get a signed copy or other authenticated record of his security agreement does most definitely make a difference. No security interest ever attaches in her favor. Look at §9-203(b)(3)(A). If the collateral is neither in the possession of the secured party nor of a special type dealt with in either paragraph (3)(C) or (3)(D), it is essential that

> the debtor has authenticated a security agreement that provides a description of the collateral and, if the security interest covers timber to be cut, a description of the land concerned.

Putting aside, as we can here, any concern about timber, what is crucial is that the debtor must generally have authenticated a security agreement meeting some (very minimal) standards.

As to the purpose underlying the general requirement of §9-203(b)(3)(A) that attachment can occur only when the debtor has authenticated in some fashion a security agreement (other than in those exceptional cases covered by paragraphs (B),(C), and (D)), see the first two sentences of Comment 3 to this section:

> Under subsection (b)(3), enforceability requires the debtor's security agreement and compliance with an evidentiary requirement in the nature of a Statute of Frauds. Paragraph (3)(A) represents the most basic of the evidentiary alternatives, under which the debtor must authenticate a security agreement that provides a description of the collateral.

Note also the possibility of attachment without an authenticated record in the case where the collateral is in the possession of the secured party "pursuant to the debtor's [wholly oral] security agreement" under paragraph (3)(B) — which is what saved Susan in the first part of this example — is explained at the beginning of Comment 4 as being appropriate since "the secured party's possession substitutes [as a means of providing evidence supporting the secured party's claim of an interest] for the debtor's authentication under paragraph (3)(A)."

2. No. Stella was lent the cameo on certain terms, and, like any other borrower of a precious trinket, has to return it as agreed. It should be clear that even though Deborah handed it to her at the same time as the loan was being made, Stella has no security interest in the cameo

as she seems to be trying to assert. The problem is not that there is no authenticated security agreement; it's much more basic than that. There is no security agreement at all under the facts. Deborah gave Stella temporary possession but never agreed that she, Stella, had any interest in the piece as collateral or in any way connected to the loan obligation. I put this example in to highlight once again an important point: The security interest can only be created by contract of the parties. The fact of possession by the secured party may obviate the need for an *authenticated* security agreement under §9-203(b)(3)(B), but crucial to everything is the need for the consent of both parties to a security agreement in fact, and nothing can substitute for that.

3.   Yes. There is a valid security agreement here. The agreement David signed may have been short, but it was to the point and meets the requisites for an authenticated security agreement under §9-203(b)(3)(A). As you can see, these requirements are not terribly elaborate. David must have authenticated the document, which he did. The document must also "provide [] a description of the collateral." If we assume that he has only one 1994 Honda Civic, then this description seems all that we could ask for. (Later examples deal with situations where the description as given is more of a problem.)

What of (d)? As a matter of how contracts are written up, depending on who is doing the drafting and what the circumstances are, the parties' addresses may or may not be included in the text. There certainly is no absolute requirement that these addresses be included in order to bind anybody. What is important is merely that the parties have sufficient information to know one another and for each to assent to the relationship with the other. Addresses could help in this regard, but they could just as easily get in the way, because people may move around without any thought that their contractual

I see no reason why any of the factors (a) through (f) would prevent Sandy from enforcing the agreement. Remember once again that for these purposes Article 9 law is just ordinary contract law. Contract law does not require that any document setting forth the contract be headed in a particular way or that it take a particular form. There certainly is no general requirement, unlike what may be true in the law of wills, for example, that any signature be made in front of witnesses or notarized. So that takes care of (a) and (b). The very nature of the security agreement and basic contract principles presumably require that Sandy agree to the creation of this security interest in her favor (Why would she not?), but there would not be any general requirement that she evidence assent by her signature. And, of course, §9-203(b)(3)(A) itself requires only the *debtor's* having to authenticate the agreement. So much for (c).

relationships will be affected. You will, of course, often see language in contract documents to the effect that notice to a party "shall be deemed given" if sent to such-and-such an address unless and until a change of address is effectively given to the other party. Such a provision makes a good deal of sense for obvious reasons, but it just as obviously has nothing to do with any requirement that the parties be identified in the writing in any one particular way for the contract to be enforceable.

So neither David's nor Sandy's address need necessarily be included for the security agreement to be effective under §9-203 (b)(3)(A). But remember, here we're concerned only with the security agreement. For the moment, simply note that when we get to considering the criteria for a second important document crucial to the Article 9 scheme of things, what we will call the financing statement, the lack of an address can be significant. Similarly, consider the mistake regarding how David's name is rendered. As we will see in Chapter 6, and consider there in no small detail, a mistake or misspelling of the debtor's name on a financing statement will turn out to be a major problem for the secured party. Even a misspelling that may seem to us terribly trivial can render the entire financing statement in effect null and void, as if it had never been filed at all. But again, that will turn out to be because of the distinct nature of the document in question, the financing statement. For the purposes of the security agreement, I would argue that a mistake in the rendering of one party's name in the documentation, as long as no one can claim he or she was actually misled or mistaken as to who was who, has no legal effect under any general principle of contract and hence is not likely to be of any real consequence here.

Finally, as to part (f), there is no requirement that any details of the obligation secured by the arrangement be spelled out in the security agreement. It is sufficient if there is the kind of generalized reference to the obligation as was made here ("the loan being made by her to me") that makes the character of the agreement unmistakable as a security agreement, which after all must by its nature be related to *some* underlying obligation of the debtor to the secured party. The impression that, should David fail to make timely payments on the note, Sandy has the right to take action involving the Honda — as sanctioned by Article 9 and as we will explore more fully in the last chapters of this book — seems clear enough from even the single sentence agreement that Sandy has come up with. To be sure, we can imagine problems that could arise and that would have been eliminated by a more detailed and lengthier document. What if, for example, over the course of time Sandy makes several loans to David? To which loan does this simple piece of paper refer? Sandy could assert that, one loan being overdue, she has the right to repossess the Honda, while David insists that the Honda was collateral for another loan entirely, one on which he has made regular payments. Still, the point here is that this is the kind of controversy that can arise in any contractual setting where the language used is open to more than one possible interpretation and the parties disagree on how the document is to be understood. A court called upon to settle the matter would presumably deal with this as just your run-of-the-mill (albeit terribly unfortunate) contract interpretation problem that would never have come up had the parties been a little more careful in their drafting. Parol evidence might be allowed in to assist the court in determining which of David's manifold obligations to Sandy was being secured by the Honda. Or the court could conclude that the document was fatally ambiguous and hence unenforceable. It's all simple and straightforward contract law. (By which I certainly don't mean to imply that contract law is all that easy, only that its complexities and perplexities are for another book in the Examples and Explanations series.)

Aside from the very limited requirements as actually spelled out in §9-203(b)(3)(A) — and in distinct contrast to what we'll see later when we turn our attention to the financing statement — the law of the security agreement is just our old friend contract law. At least in theory, and by and large in practice as well, no special rules need apply.

4. No. Whatever else Dewey may do to keep his refrigerator from being repossessed — paying Selma what's due her would be nice — he has no defense based on the lack of a written security agreement. The arrangement he entered into with Selma, while phrased in terms of retention of title by the seller, is deemed under the Code immediately to transfer the property to the buyer at the same time it reserves a security interest in the seller. See the directly applicable language in the Article 1 definition of "security interest," or for that matter the second sentence of §2-401(1). The arrangement between Dewey and Selma's Appliance City is, therefore, a security agreement under Article 9. That being so, the paper he signed is the authenticated record, here a conventional written agreement, and all Selma will need to establish her rights under §9-203.

5a. It's hard to believe the description of "one delivery van" will do, at least not when Dan is the proud owner of a fleet (albeit a fairly modest fleet) of vans. Section 9-108(a) says that for the purposes of Article 9, "a description of personal . . . property . . . is sufficient, whether or not it is specific, if it reasonably identifies what is described." This doesn't seem to do much for us, but it may help to appreciate the background against which the drafters were working when they included this provision. Read the second paragraph of Official Comment 2 to this section. Prior statutes and practice often set a very high standard for the necessary description of the property, something much more like what you'd expect to see in land transactions perhaps. Article 9 calls for a more functional approach. "The test of sufficiency of a description . . . is that the description do the job assigned to it: make possible the identification of the collateral described." Fair enough, but how does that work out in our particular situation?

We have to consider what precisely is the "job assigned" to the description of the collateral in the security agreement under §9-203(b)(3)(A). Recall that a comment to that section refers to the requirement as "in the nature of a Statute of Frauds." I take it from this, and from the very essence of the security agreement itself as a contract written up to establish rights as between the two parties, that the purpose of the description in the security agreement is rather elemental. It is to make clear, in light of the possibility of later dispute between the parties, *exactly what property* is the subject of the agreement. Imagine the kind of dispute that could arise between Dan and the Credit Service. The most obvious problem is that Dan may fail to make payment on the loan. As we will see, this can give the Trucker's Credit Service, as the secured party, the right to take action, to repossess the collateral and in this it will need no distinct official mandate such as a court order or the participation of a sheriff. In most cases all Trucker's Credit Service need do is find the collateral in which it has an interest and take it away.

So we are contemplating the possibility that Dan has fallen behind in his payments and the Credit Service comes around to repossess the collateral. Suppose further that they get their hands on and are able to drive off with one of Dan's Ford vans, perhaps because it's the only one parked outside and the most easily accessible. Dan complains to the local constabulary that as far as he is concerned, one of his vans has been stolen by someone with no rights in it. The Credit Service, he will explain to anyone who will listen, may have had every right to repossess the Chevy van, in which it had a legitimate security interest, but not one of his other vehicles. If, as we are now positing, the description in the written security agreement were only "one delivery van owned by Dan and used in his business," the writing is of no help in resolving this dispute. The sheriff who is called in to try to calm things down as the Credit Service's tow truck stands all hooked up and poised to tow away the Ford and as Dan's face gets redder and redder would get no help from looking at the paper produced by the creditor, nor would the judge who may have to be called upon to make a final determination of who did what to whom somewhere down the road.

So I conclude that this description, "one delivery van owned by Dan and used in his business," simply won't pass muster. It doesn't do the job assigned to it. Remember that the consequence of this conclusion is to hold that Trucker's Credit Service never gets an enforceable security interest of any type or in any collateral at the time it makes the loan. Even if no repossession dispute of the type I have hypothesized ever arises, indeed even if no one ever takes a look over the written security agreement after it is once signed and thrown in the files, the Credit Service may find itself out in the cold as only a general creditor should Dan's Vans descend into bankruptcy. On the other hand, the requirements that Trucker's Credit has to fulfill to get a very special privileged place in any potential bankruptcy proceeding, the attachment of a valid Article 9 security interest and its perfection, are, as we continue to see, not terribly onerous. If it fails to make the right moves, as for example by failing to adequately describe the collateral, we can argue that it has no one to blame but itself.

Other commentators and some courts would perhaps be somewhat more generous (but, we have to ponder, generous to whom and at whose expense?) than I in what they would allow as a description sufficient to satisfy §9-203(b)(3)(A), at least when there is no third party who claims that he or she actually consulted the description and was misled. I, as you can tell, can't see why the position of third parties has anything to do with it, other than that of my hypothesized third-party adjudicators, who could be brought in to settle disputes between the two parties to the security agreement — the debtor and the creditor. In any event, I doubt any court or commentator would find favor with the description here, "one delivery van owned by Dan and used in his business." Perhaps some would allow in parol evidence of which van exactly the parties intended to cover in their agreement, but this seems to me to defeat the whole requirement of a description doing the "job assigned" to it in the instrument itself.

5b. Under the circumstances I would think this description passable. True, there may be any number of "2008 Chevrolet cargo vans" out on the road, but it seems that Dan has only one (the subject of all this discussion), and if there could be no possible misunderstanding or dispute *between the two parties* as to which vehicle was meant, I see no reason for anyone else — even me — to make a fuss. I find support, of course, in the §9-108(a) instruction that any description "is sufficient, whether or not it is specific, if it reasonably identifies what is described." This reasonably identifies Dan's one 2008 Chevy van, and that is good enough for me.

5c. Perhaps I'm getting just too easygoing in my middle age, but I'm inclined to think that even this description — or to be more fastidious, this misdescription — will be acceptable and not defeat the creation of Trucker's Credit Service's security interest under Article 9. It's important to this argument, of course, that there really is only one Chevy van of this vintage in the picture. Were we talking about a whole fleet of vans, then keeping them straight might really depend on keeping track of each and every serial number, and getting even one digit incorrect might well cost the Credit Service dearly. In the circumstances here, however, it's hard to see how the minor error would even be uncovered, except perhaps by an eagle-eyed lawyer type trying to find some "technicality" with which to undermine a legitimate claim of the honest and altogether noble Credit Service. Section 9-108(a) and its Official Comment 2 again suggest, if they don't necessarily dictate, a response to this kind of minor foul-up. Perhaps a misdescription of this sort will defeat a party's interest under the highly technical and formalistic regimen of the system of land titles and mortgages; there's no reason for the same attitude to be carried over into the supposed "reasonable" Article 9 system.

5d. This mistake pretty clearly renders the security agreement insufficient for the purposes of §9-203(b)(1). And yes, it is the kind of mistake the fallout from which turns up all too often in the case reports. See, for example, In re Southern Illinois Rail Car Co., 301 Bankr. 305, 2002 Bankr. LEXIS 1433 (Bankr. S.D. Ill. 2002).

6a. Yes. Subsection 9-108(b) is intended to give examples of how the parties may "reasonably identify," for the purposes of subsection (a), collateral subject to a security agreement. One way that a description may be given, according to (b)(3) is, with some exceptions not relevant here, by "a type of collateral defined in" the Uniform Commercial Code itself. In Chapter 5 we will deal in detail with the various "types" of collateral that Article 9 contemplates and to each of which it or another article of the Code gives precise definition. For the moment it is sufficient that the term "equipment" is indeed one of the types of collateral, as you will find it defined in §9-102(a)(33). Don't worry now what exactly is or is not part of Inkster's equipment. The point here is simply that the description of the collateral required by §9-203(b)(3)(A) that the authenticated security agreement is required to provide is met by the language in the writing Inkster signed, that is, "all Inkster's equipment."

6b. No. The cited subsection specifically states that what is referred to as a "supergeneric description" such as we have here is not a reasonable, and hence not a sufficient, description of the collateral for the purposes of creating a valid and enforceable authenticated security agreement for the purposes of §9-203(b). That being so, Downtown Federal will never be able to gain a security interest that attaches to any of Inkster's property.

7. No. As you can see in §9-102(a)(23), *consumer goods* are a type
    of collateral defined in Article 9. Under the general rule of
    §9-108(b)(3), this would appear to make the description in the doc-
    ument Samantha signed one that reasonably identifies the collateral and
    hence a proper description for §9-203(b)(3)(A) purposes, similar to
    the satisfactory description we saw ("all Inkster's equipment") in
    Example 6a. Section 9-108(b)(3), however, is explicitly made subject
    to the exceptions contained in subsection (e) of the same section. Here
    we are looking at the effect of (e)(2). Samantha's arrangement with
    Local Lending is, as you can check for yourself, a *consumer transaction* under
    §9-102(a)(26). In such a transaction, a description of the collateral as
    "all consumer goods" is deemed insufficient (as would be a description
    by type of certain kinds of what we will later learn to identify as forms of
    investment properties that the consumer might be asked to put up as
    collateral by a lender).

    The rationale behind this exception to the general notion that
    identification by defined type of collateral is a proper way to describe
    collateral in a security agreement is, as the drafters tell us in Comment
    5 to §9-108, "to prevent debtors from inadvertently encumbering
    certain property." Would Samantha, even if she is a very smart
    woman, understand that in granting the lender a security interest in all
    of her "consumer goods" she had given it the right, should she fail to
    repay the loan when due, to take possession of any and all of the
    furniture in her home, the clothing in her closets, and indeed the food
    in her cupboards? All of this perfectly well qualifies as consumer
    goods held by her under the Article 9 definition of that type of
    collateral. It may be that Local Lending would not actually be that
    interested in repossessing such stuff as this, but just the threat that it
    could happen gives that firm a way of putting pressure on Samantha
    which, the drafters concluded, was not one that she as a consumer
    could be expected to have been aware of when she signed a document
    as seemingly innocuous as the one the lender had put before her.

    By and large, and not without criticism, the process leading to the
    formulation of the original version of Article 9 left it relatively free of
    what we may think of generally as "consumer protection" provisions.
    The arguments of the drafters at the time were that this was best left
    to separate legislation outside of the grand, overarching Uniform
    Commercial Code that had other things to worry about and was not
    to be cluttered with special provisions for any one particular group
    (and certainly not individual consumer debtors). By the time of the
    drafting of the Revised Article 9, the thinking had changed, not least
    because consumer advocates were brought in and had their voices
    heard as part of the drafting process in a way that had not been true
    when the original Article 9 had been created. The consumer advocates

argued strenuously on behalf of the interests they represent for various aspects of consumer protection to be made part of the revised article. These advocates did not get all that they wanted out of the revision process (no single interest group did in what necessarily was a process of drafting by compromise), but the concerns they expressed could not be ignored. The result is that Revised Article 9 pays much more attention to how individual consumer, nonbusiness debtors are affected by its workings and includes many provisions not in the original article intended to protect consumers from overreaching or unscrupulous lenders — and also from the individual consumer's understandable potential ignorance of all of the fine points of secured lending. The rule of §9-108(e)(2) is just one of the additions made to the Revised Article 9 to reflect this newfound concern for incorporating protection of consumers into the article itself and not leaving it to other law or to slip through the cracks.

Notice that if, in fact, Local Lending had made the decision to loan to Samantha on a secured basis because she did have some particular property, say a large collection of rare and valuable books built up over her years as a professor, which it saw as truly valuable collateral worthy of backing up a loan (unlike the shoes in her closet and the boxes of cereal in her kitchen), it would be able to do so. The security agreement could then have been written to describe the collateral "by category" as provided for in §9-108(b)(2) as, for example, "all books held by Samantha." This should pass muster under §9-108(b) as reasonably identifying the collateral and allow for an enforceable security agreement under §9-203(b)(3)(A). It would also more properly put Samantha on notice of exactly what property of hers she has put at risk by using it as collateral to obtain the loan.

Attachment: Further Criteria

THE HOW AND WHEN OF ATTACHMENT

As we first discovered in the preceding chapter, attachment of a security interest is dependent on three distinct conditions being satisfied. In addition to there being a security agreement entered into by the parties satisfying paragraph (3) of §9-203(b), that subsection requires that value have been given and the debtor have rights in the collateral. Comment 2 to §9-203 confirms:

> Subsection (b) states three basic prerequisites to the existence of a security interest: value (paragraph (1)), rights or power to transfer rights in the collateral (paragraph (2)), and agreement plus satisfaction of an evidentiary requirement (paragraph (3)). When all of these elements exist, a security interest becomes enforceable between the parties and attaches under subsection (a).

In the last chapter we focused on the last of the three listed criteria, the necessity that there be a security agreement entered into by the parties. In some carefully circumscribed instances it will be sufficient (if not necessarily terribly prudent) for this agreement to be oral. Most often it is a written or otherwise recorded security agreement authenticated by the debtor, which as we saw articulates in some way that the debtor is granting to the secured party a security interest in certain sufficiently well-described collateral.

This chapter adds to the mix the other two prerequisites that will have to be established whenever a security interest is claimed to have attached to a given piece or agglomeration of collateral. Beyond the existence of a security agreement, it will have to be shown that *value* has been given — that is, given by the secured party to the debtor in some form or another. No one gets a security interest in another's property just for being a nice guy, gal, corporation, or unincorporated jural entity. Section 9-203 has nothing more to say on the subject of value, and indeed the word "value" is not even defined in Article 9. Fortunately, we have a definition of the word in §1-201(44) or §1R-204 which being a general definition good for all the Code is applicable here, as the courts have rightly understood.

The remaining piece that must come into place for attachment is that the debtor have "*rights in*" or at least the power to transfer rights in the collateral. Again, this makes sense. You can't (at least normally) give an interest in something that isn't yours to begin with. Even if in most instances there can be no real argument about this part of the puzzle, its exact contours can, as we'll see in a few of the examples, cause a bit of confusion or at least leave room for argument. It doesn't help matters any that, unlike with the case of the word "value," the term "rights in" the collateral is nowhere defined or further explicated, not in Article 9 or anyplace else in the Code.

As we will see again and again in chapters to follow, often the most significant controversies in the field of secured transactions will have to do with matters of timing. So it is with attachment. It matters not merely *whether* attachment of a security interest to a given piece of collateral occurred, but *when* exactly that happened. When it comes to the moment of attachment we are given a clear enough rule by §9-203(a).

> A security interest attaches to collateral when it becomes enforceable against the debtor with respect to the collateral [that is, when all of the criteria of subsection (b)(1), (2), and (3) have been met], unless an agreement expressly postpones the time of attachment.

It is possible, I suppose, to think of reasons why the parties might agree to some postponement of the time of attachment, but the circumstances would have to be fairly unusual. Unless there is such an explicit agreement to the contrary, attachment occurs as soon as the last of the three parts of the puzzle — value, rights in the collateral, and agreement — is locked into place. Be aware that if the facts allow for any play, the secured party will have every interest in arguing for as early a moment of attachment as possible. Those with interests opposed to the secured party's may benefit from establishing even a slightly later date. With that in mind, ponder the following examples, taking into consideration not just whether attachment has occurred, but when.

Examples

1. On April 21, Dexter Moneybucks, always in need of some ready cash, gets his friend Sarah to loan him $2,000, which he promises to repay within a year. He further agrees that one of the more valuable pieces of modern art hanging on his library walls ("Composition Looking Like Hell"), which he had purchased from the artist when still an unknown (the artist that is), will stand as collateral for the loan. Dexter and Sarah shake hands on the agreement, and Sarah delivers over to Dexter a check for $2,000. A few weeks later Sarah, having related this story to a friend who is in law school, becomes concerned that she has nothing in writing signed by Dexter. She visits him on May 15 and asks that he sign a simple form security agreement, which her friend has helped her prepare. Dexter (only sightly put out that his friend would think such a formality at all necessary) whips out his expensive Mont Blanc pen and signs the agreement. Has an Article 9 security interest in favor of Sarah ever attached to the work of art? If so, when?

2. Isabelle Inkster runs a small printing business. She started small, making use of a modest amount she had saved before going into business on her own. Over the years she has done well and the business has grown. She has accumulated various pieces of printing equipment, all of which are fully paid for. She now finds, however, that she doesn't have the capital to take advantage of her success. She is sometimes not able to take on bigger projects from which she could profit because she doesn't have the ready cash to buy large supplies of paper and ink that she would have to have on hand. Furthermore, when buying supplies she is often not able to take advantage of quantity discounts because of the cash outlay it would entail, nor is she able to advertise in ways that she feels would be of benefit to her. In November she speaks to a loan officer at her local bank, Downtown Federal, about getting a small business loan. The officer has her complete a Loan Application. He also has her sign a security agreement, which he fills in with a description of the collateral as "all Inkster's equipment, now owned or hereafter acquired." This officer tells Inkster that he is "confident" that the loan committee will look favorably on her application but that the decision will take some time. A couple of weeks later he calls her to ask for a few more details about her business. He says that "everything looks in order." Inkster then hears nothing for several weeks.

   a. Has a security interest in favor of the bank covering her equipment yet attached?

   b. Finally, on January 14, Inkster hears from the bank officer, who tells her to come to his office as soon as possible. There he hands her a letter from the bank stating that her loan application has been approved and that she now has a "Small Business InstaLoan" line of credit for $80,000 with the bank. The terms of the credit line are set forth in the letter. "All you have to do," he explains, "to have the money available to you is sign this note." Inkster signs the bank's standard form note for such a loan, and the officer hands her a packet of materials explaining how she can "call on" the money now at her disposal, how she'll be billed for payments and so on. The beginning of the year is a slow time in the printing business, so Inkster does not draw a check from this credit line until some time in March. Has a security interest ever attached, and if so when?

3. Thad's a thief. While casually browsing over the merchandise at Xavier's, a fashionable jewelry store, he skillfully pockets a small emerald pin. He takes the pin to Happy Harry's, a respected neighborhood pawnshop, where he uses it to borrow $500 from Harry. The pin is in Harry's possession, and he has Thad's agreement that it will stand as collateral for the loan.

   a. Has a security interest in the pin with Harry as secured party ever attached?

   b. What if Thad, instead of pawning the pin, had sold it to one Emily, a complete innocent who had no knowledge of the theft and who paid a fair market value for it? Later Emily is the one to leave it with Harry as security for a loan. Would Harry's security interest — now granted by Emily — attach under this scenario?

   c. Would your answer to either (a) or (b) of this question be different if it turned out Thad was not a thief but just a nogoodnik? To be more specific, suppose he did not steal the pin from Xavier's but instead paid for it with a personal check that later bounced, leaving Xavier's unpaid. Can attachment in Harry's favor ever occur here? Look at §2-403(1).

   d. Here's one more way that Thad may show his true colors: Suppose he asks a friend, Bill, if he can borrow Bill's saxophone so that he, Thad, can have a try at playing the thing. Bill agrees to lend the sax to Thad for a few months. Thad quickly discovers that he has no aptitude for the instrument, but also discovers he is in need of some cash to pursue other lines of endeavor. He takes the saxophone to Happy Harry's, pawning it and walking out with a loan of $325. Does a security interest in favor of Harry ever attach to the sax?

4. Christopher Heath is the major investor in two separate corporations, First Vertica Corporation and Second Vertica Corporation. Other than having Heath as president, the two corporations have distinct directors and officers and keep their business affairs carefully segragated. The two corporations are run out of a single suite of offices with the name and logo of "Vertica Solutions" displayed prominently on the door and share a Web site Heath has specially created for "Vertica Solutions."

In July 2000 First Vertica Corporation purchased a large amount of computer products from Comark for $2.8 million. In July of the same year, Tyrone Owens, the treasurer of Second Vertica Corporation, arranged to borrow $25,000 from Fifth Third Bank and signed a security agreement granting that bank a security interest in all of the Comark computer equipment located in the Vertica Solutions offices. Owens never had any official position with First Vertica. No one with any authority concerning the affairs of First Vertica had authorized, or was even aware of, this loan from Fifth Third. Did that bank's security interest ever attach to the computer equipment?

5. Selma's Appliance City is a retail store. In February Selma negotiates a loan from Credit Associates. On March 1 she signs a security agreement granting Credit Associates a security interest in all of her inventory, "now held or hereafter acquired." On March 3 she picks up a check from Credit Associates for the amount of the loan.
   a. Does a security interest in favor of Credit Associates ever attach to the inventory on Selma's showroom floor and in her warehouse as of the beginning of March? If so, when?
   b. In April Selma receives an order of toasters from one of her principal suppliers, Bakewell America. She immediately puts some of the toasters out on her store shelves; others she puts in her warehouse. Does the Credit Associates security interest ever attach to these toasters? See §9-204(a). Does it make any difference that Credit Associates extends no additional funds to Selma in April? What about the fact that Selma has purchased the toasters from Bakewell on open trade credit — that is, she has agreed to pay Bakewell the price charged her within 90 days of their delivery to her store and has given Bakewell no security for this payment, only her contractual promise that she will pay?
   c. Assuming that the security interest does attach to this particular shipment of toasters, when is the exact moment of attachment? To be more precise: What is the earliest date that Credit Associates can claim for attachment? Assume that she placed the order on April 1, that Bakewell packaged the toasters in a crate marked for delivery to her store on April 6, and that this crate was put in the hands of a shipping company on April 7. The crate is delivered to Selma's store on April 15. Consult §2-501.
   d. Finally, assume that sometime in May Selma puts in a call to Bakewell with the intent of ordering more of Bakewell's products for immediate delivery. Someone at that company informs her that (for whatever reason) they have become concerned about selling to her on open credit with no security to ensure their eventually being paid. Selma works out an agreement under which they will send her more of their wares to be paid for within 90 days of delivery, but only after

she has signed a security agreement prepared by Bakewell under which she grants that company a security interest in "all Bakewell products that have been or are to be supplied by that company to Selma and held by her as inventory." Selma receives such a form. She signs it on May 20 and returns it to Bakewell. Does a security interest in *favor of Bakewell* ever attach to those toasters delivered in April that haven't yet been sold and are still in Selma's possession? If so, when?

6. Samantha, a retired university professor faced with some large medical bills, gets a loan from Local Lending Associates. The lender is willing to give her the loan based on her putting up as collateral the impressive collection of books in her field of study that she has accumulated over the years, including a number of rare and valuable volumes. She grants to Local Lending a security interest in "all books now held or hereafter acquired" by her. Six months after obtaining the loan, Samantha inherits from a distant relative a Bible which has been in her family for generations. She feels honored now to be the custodian of this important record of her family's long history and, while she recognizes that it would have a significant market value due to the age and rarity of the edition, would never think of parting with it for any amount of money. She has every intention of passing it on to a member of the next generation in her will. A question remains: Did Local Lending's security interest attach to this Bible at the time it came into Samantha's possession? See §9-204(b)(1).

Explanations

1. Yes. A security interest attached on May 15. You should satisfy yourself that each of the criteria of §9-203(b) has been met and on what date. Because the collateral was neither in the possession of Sarah, the secured party, nor of a type dealt with in §9-203(b)(3)(C) or (D), it was necessary that there be an authenticated security agreement describing the collateral. There eventually was such an agreement, but only on May 15. Value was given — that is, given by the secured party to the debtor — when Sarah gave Dexter the check on April 21. I doubt you'd have much difficulty accepting the idea that the check is value, but just to be sure look at the Article 1 definition of "value." A person gives value for rights if the person "acquires them . . . in return for any consideration sufficient to support a simple contract." A check for $2,000 will do. Lastly, Dexter had rights in the artwork from some time prior to April 21. So the mighty triumvirate has been established. The last event to occur was the preparation and signing of the written security agreement on May 15, and so that is the moment that attachment occurred.

   There is, of course, no reason why the requirement of §9-203(b)(3) will necessarily be the last to fall into place and to mark the moment of attachment. The three pieces of the puzzle — the giving of value, the debtor's rights in the collateral, and the agreement — can occur in any order. There's nothing for it but to check out each one under the facts of the particular situation. If ever an issue in law called for a checklist approach, albeit a pretty modest one, it is the question of attachment of an Article 9 security interest. As an exercise you might want to try your hand at rearranging the facts of this example so that the giving of value is the last event and hence determines the moment of attachment, then rearranging things once again so that it is the time at which Dexter actually attains "rights in" (and not just bragging rights about) the painting hanging on his wall.

2a. No security interest has attached as of this moment. Inkster, the hopeful borrower, has signed a security agreement, and she presumably has rights in her equipment, but no value has been given. There's nothing inherently unusual about this situation, and certainly nothing for Inkster to be embarrassed about. A lender will understandably often need some time to investigate the borrower's credit history, get some independent evaluation of the worth of the collateral, and so on. The period between making the loan application and eventually getting a response from the lender can be a very frustrating one for the potential borrower, but there is not much she can do but wait — and cooperate with any reasonable request from the lender that will help move the application process along towards a successful conclusion.

2b. Yes. Attachment occurs on January 14. The bank, by approving her loan application and making a line of credit available, has given value as of that date. This is so even though Inkster may not actually draw on the credit for some time. Look now at either §1-201(44)(a) or §1R-204(1). It says it all.

3a. No security interest in Harry's favor ever attaches since Thad, as a thief, can never have any type of "rights in" the property he has stolen nor does he have any power to transfer rights in it. That term "rights in," as it occurs in §9-203(b)(2), is nowhere defined, and might in some instances leave some room for argument, but not here. Even if you won't find it anywhere in the Uniform Commercial Code, it's just your most basic common law of property as it relates to goods. A thief of personal property gets possession of the goods, but that's about it; he or she can never gain title, or an interest, or any kind of rights in the goods no matter how you were to define any of those terms. The thief gets nothing even approaching "right in" or power over what he or she has stolen.

3b. Emily, even if she may be a complete innocent in the situation (and I assure you there's no reason to doubt it), can never gain any rights to the pin if she bought it from a thief. Under the common law, and under the Article 2 law of sales, the thief can transfer even to the so-called "good faith purchaser for value" only what interest he or she (the thief that is) has to begin within. We see this in the introductory language to §2-403(1): "A purchaser of goods acquires all title which his transferor had or had power to transfer . . . ." In this case what Thad legitimately had to transfer was nothing, so Emily ends up with nothing beyond mere possession of something to which she has no right. Should Xavier's, the true owner of the pin, be able to track it down and find it in her hands, she'd have no rights against that firm and no choice but to give it back. So Emily, being like Thad in having no "rights in" the item, or any power to transfer any such rights, is never able to grant a security interest in the pin to another, no matter how much she wants to, how innocent she is, or how hard she tries.

3c. Whatever we may think about Thad's behavior as the example has now been transmogrified, at least he's no thief. And he gets different treatment under Article 2 — or at least someone who qualifies as a "good faith purchaser for value" from him does. Read on in §2-403(1). A person with what the section terms "voidable title" does have the power to transfer "good title" to the good faith purchaser for value. Without getting into all the hairy details of this distinction between truly void and merely voidable title, which §2-403(1) sets forth, it is clear from (b) of this subsection that Thad got such voidable title, and hence the power to pass on true title to the right kind of person, when he purchased the pin from Xavier's in exchange for a check that was later dishonored.

There's no single definition of "good faith purchaser for value" in the Code, but you can piece it together from the definitions of "good faith," "purchaser," and "value," the citations for which are given at the end of §2-403. Emily, being naive, and having given value for the trinket (as opposed to having gotten it as a gift from Thad the nogoodnik), clearly must qualify as one who gets "good title" to the pin when she buys it from Thad. And having what Article 2 calls "good title" to the item must mean she has "rights in" it for Article 9 purposes. So if Emily does buy it from Thad, who's obtained it in this way, and then later tries to use it as collateral at Happy Harry's, there's no reason a security interest in favor of Harry couldn't or wouldn't attach under §9-203.

What's more interesting is the result if Thad himself, having bought the pin with a bum check and still in possession of it, tries to use it at Harry's to obtain some ready cash by way of loan. Is it possible that Harry can get a valid attached security interest from a fellow such as Thad? The answer seems to be yes. Remember that under the circumstances Thad was able to transfer "a good title" to any good faith purchaser for value. And the terms "purchase" and, through it, "purchaser" have a decidedly broad range under the Code. Look at §1-201(32) or §1R-201(b)(29). "Purchase" includes

> taking by sale, lease, discount, negotiation, mortgage, pledge, lien, security interest, issue or reissue, gift, or any other voluntary transaction creating an interest in property.

This certainly includes Harry, who has taken, by way of what has historically been referred to as a pledge, a type of security interest. Certainly what he has gotten is an interest in the property — not a full ownership interest, I grant you, but to him a not insignificant security interest — and it was an interest coming out of a voluntary transaction between him and Thad. Harry, assuming he has given value (And if he hasn't, how's he possibly claiming attachment?) and that he acted in good faith (on which see the standard of §1-201(19) or §1R-201(b)(20)) qualifies as a good faith purchaser for value. Thad, whether or not he acquired for himself any "rights in" the pin when he got it under the circumstances here, did pick up the *power* if not the *right* to transfer rights of the pin to Harry. And this is enough to meet the requirement of §9-203(b)(2). The debtor need have either rights in the collateral "or the power to transfer rights in the collateral to a secured party." This phrase concluding §9-203(b)(2) was added to Article 9 in the recent revision and makes this situation easier to deal with than it was under the prerevision version, which required that the debtor have "rights in" the collateral and did not offer the alternative way of meeting the criterion now found in (b)(2). For a case that came to the conclusion that a pawnbroker such as Harry could obtain a security interest in goods obtained in such a fashion as Thad has obtained the pin here, decided under the old Article 9 but that only gains support from the "power to transfer rights" language now in §9-203(b)(2), see *National Pawn Brokers Unlimited v. Osterman,* 176 Wisc. 2d 418, 500 N.W.2d 407, 21 U.C.C.2d 1176 (1993).

3d. Thad here is not a thief; he's a bailee. Bill gave him the right to possession of the instrument, but not the right to sell it, to give it away, or anything like that. There's no reason to think that he has the right to use it as collateral. Cases refer to Thad as a "bailee for a limited purpose," and at least if the purpose is as it seems to be here, he would not have any "rights in" the sax that would allow him to grant a security interest in favor of Harry. Nor would he have ever acquired any power to transfer any rights in the instrument to a secured party. The *Osterman* case, cited above, has a good discussion of this situation if you care to pursue it any further.

All of Happy Harry's potential dealings with the likes of Thad should teach him a valuable lesson. Indeed, it's a lesson important to all lenders who make decisions on whether and how much to lend influenced by the value of particular collateral in which they intend to take a security interest. It's usually not that hard (or at least it shouldn't be) for the lender to determine whether it has a valid and sufficient security agreement to satisfy criterion (b)(3). Likewise, a lender should know when it gives value to meet the requirement of (b)(2). But how do you know — really know for sure — that the debtor has the requisite "rights in" the collateral or the power to deal in such rights? One thing's for certain, you can't just ask the debtor. In any of these situations Thad (or the innocent Emily in part (b) for that matter) will say, "Yeah, no doubt about it. It's mine all right." Would it help any to ask the potential borrower to sign a statement, attested to every which way and under oath, to the effect that the property he or she is about to use as collateral is truly his or hers to do with exactly as he or she wishes? When you get right down to it, such contractual covenants, promises, or what have you are about as valuable as the paper they are written on.

This is not to suggest that most people are crooks or out to pull a fast one. It's just that some people are, and the careful lender has to be looking out for himself or herself. Even beyond that, many totally honest and forthright people will end up for one reason or another being confused as to exactly what stuff they own and what strings might already be attached to their property. The lender, if he or she is truly interested in having an attached security interest that will be of help should push come to shove, has to do what is possible under the circumstances to determine *independent of what the borrower is willing to attest to* that the collateral and the borrower's interest in it are really what the borrower says is so.

In the instant case Harry will at the very least have to satisfy himself, either through his own expertise or by getting an outside appraisal, that the emerald in the pin is really an emerald and not just a bit of green glass. What should Harry do to content himself that the person pawning it has rights to the thing? He could ask for proof of ownership, something that has at least some chance of not being fake. Notice that if Thad really was a thief, as we started out postulating, he would not be able (unless he wanted to spend some time forging papers as well) to come up with a bill of sale showing that he had ever purchased and paid for such a bauble. Compare this to the situation in part (c), where Harry bought the pin with a bum check. If Xavier was willing to part with a valuable piece of jewelry in exchange for a personal check and to give a bill of sale marked "Paid in Full" as well, then Harry will have something to rely on and, as we saw, will triumph over Xavier. This does go some way toward explaining why the situations in parts (a) and (c), while they may look so similar from the jeweler's point of view, come out differently under Articles 2 and 9 of the Code, as we saw.

The point more generally — and in truth and for obvious reasons pawnbrokers are probably among the most casual about this — is that any lender taking an Article 9 interest has to do what it can to satisfy itself not just of the true value but of what I sometimes refer to as the provenance of the collateral in question. How did it come to be in this potential borrower's hands and does he or she have the right to encumber it with this kind of interest? When it comes to questions like this, it's very much the lender's duty to itself to ask the right questions and make an appropriate investigation. Article 9 will not be very forgiving towards the casual, the sloppy, or the too readily trusting lender.

4.   Obviously it isn't only pawnbrokers who have to be concerned about the provenance and ownership of what is being offered up as collateral. This example is inspired, if that is the word, by *Fifth Third Bank v. Comark, Inc.*, 794 N.E.2d 433, 51 U.C.C.2d 533 (Ind. App. 2003), with the names of the parties only slightly altered for convenience. Fifth Third Bank (that is its real name) was held not to have any security interest in the computers as its debtor, Second Vertica, had no rights in the computers owned by another distinct entity, First Vertica. The court took note of the age-old general principle that "one cannot encumber another man's property in the absence of consent, estoppel or some other special rule." No consent, no estoppel, and certainly no special rule was found under the circumstances to help out Fifth Third, which could have protected itself by doing a careful investigation of who actually owned all that computer equipment. There's a rule of thumb in the secured lending business: Know Who Your Debtor Is. For two other recent cases leading to the same moral, see *Preferred Funding, Inc. v. Jackson*, 185 Ore. App. 693, 61 P.3d 939, 49 U.C.C.2d 620 (Ore. App. 2003), and *In re Ace Sports Management, LLC*, 271 Bankr. 134, 47 U.C.C.2d 790 (Bankr. E.D. Ark. 2001).

5a. Yes. A security interest covering all of Selma's presently held inventory attaches as of March 3. It's just a matter of going through the three criteria of §9-203(b) one more time. She signed a security interest on March 1. She got value in the form of a check on March 3, and as of that date she had rights in all the stuff in her possession. So as of March 3 all parts are in place and the interest attaches to all of that present inventory.

5b. Yes. The Credit Associates' security interest attaches to the toasters as soon as she gets "rights in" them. We can argue about the exact moment when that happens — as we will in the next part — but no doubt she has rights in these particular appliances by the time she receives delivery and has them in her possession. As I suggested, we first note §9-204(a). Putting aside for a moment the one exception which need not detain us here,

> a security agreement may create or provide for a security interest in after-acquired collateral.

So the provision in the security agreement Selma signed is perfectly permissible and has just the effect we're seeing here. As of the date of their delivery a security interest in the toasters arises, it attaches, in favor of Credit Associates. Going back one more time to §9-203(b) we can see that Selma already signed an agreement covering this collateral and has already received value. So as soon as she gains "rights in" some more collateral of the type covered, the interest attaches to that collateral as well. There is no requirement that additional value be given to allow for the attachment to these new bits of collateral. And even if Selma bought the toasters on credit and still owes Bakewell for them, that doesn't prevent her having rights in them for the purposes of §9-203 and attachment.

Take note of the very first sentence of Comment 2 to §9-204: "Subsection (a) makes clear that a security interest arising by virtue of an after-acquired property clause is no less valid than a security interest in collateral in which the debtor has rights at the time value is given." The security interest that Credit Associates can now claim in the new toasters that have more recently shown up is, apart from a later moment of attachment, otherwise no different, no less in favor, or no lower in status, than the security interest that earlier attached in the older inventory. There's no second class citizenship here, just a different date of birth. The rest of Comment 2 might be hard for you to fully appreciate (if that's the word with respect to Uniform Commercial Code commentary) before you've gotten further into this material, but you should read it now.

Do notice how valuable, practical, and efficient this so-called "after-acquired property" provision and from it the working concept of the "continuing general lien" or "floating lien" turn out to be. Selma is able to work out a comprehensive long-term lending relationship with Credit Associates putting all of her inventory on the line. As new pieces come into that inventory, there is no need for any new paperwork on her part or on the lender's. There will be no need for additional or amended public filings when we get to talk about those, much less anything like a closing or any formal and hard to arrange meeting of the parties. Nor is there any need for Credit Associates to hand over in dribs and drabs the money it's lending as each shipment of toasters, microwave ovens, pasta makers, and the like come to her delivery dock and into her possession.

5c. You may wonder why the day in April on which the moment of attachment occurred could be that important, but as we will see in much of what is to come if Selma's business position starts to sour and the going gets rough, it all of a sudden becomes every man, woman, and lending institution for himself, herself, or itself, respectively, and a matter of a day here or there can make all the difference in the world. We've seen that the moment of attachment will occur when the last of the three prerequisites to attachment has fallen into place, and in this situation it's clearly the time when Selma first could claim "rights in" those toasters. By the time they're in her possession under the contract for sale, on April 15, this criterion is surely met. But can Credit Associates argue successfully for any earlier moment? One possibility, as suggested by my referring you to §2-501, is to try to drag in the Article 2 concept of "identification" of goods to a contract for sale. Notice that §2-501(1) says that the buyer, here Selma, obtains "a special property interest" in the goods by identification. Nobody knows for sure exactly what this term is supposed to mean, but it certainly can be argued that whatever it is having "a special [!] property interest" in a particular identifiable conglomeration of toasters is sufficient to give the person involved "rights in" those very toasters.

This is neither the time nor the place to go into all the nitty-gritty about identification under Article 2. Suffice it to say that here identification would seemingly occur, by virtue of part (b) of §2-501(1), when the toasters were "shipped, marked, or otherwise designated by the seller as goods to which the contract refers," on April 6. For a case that does use this Article 2 identification analysis to set the moment of attachment for Article 9 purposes, see *Trust Company Bank v. Gloucester Corp.*, 419 Mass. 48, 643 N.E.2d 16, 25 U.C.C.2d 62 (1994). But then, for a case that finds identification under Article 2 not enough in and of itself to establish "rights in" the collateral for Article 9 purposes, see *First Tennessee Bank, N.A. v. Graphic Arts Centre, Inc.*, 859 S.W.2d 858, 23 U.C.C.2d 269 (Mo. App. 1993). Perhaps the two cases can be reconciled; perhaps they cannot. It is a fairly minor point in any event, and given the vagueness of the "rights in" language of §9-203(b)(2), it's probably too much to ask for or to expect some bright-line definitive test. On the edges of the concept, at least, you would not be surprised to learn that the courts appear to engage in a kind of case-by-case, you-know-it-when-you-see-it, approach.

5d. Yes. Bakewell does acquire a security interest in the toasters still on hand, and that interest attaches as of May 20 when Selma signs the Security Agreement granting such an interest. No doubt that as of that date she has rights in those toasters. What about the value requirement? Look back to the Article 1 definition of "value." Value is given for

79

rights — here Bakewell's security interest — if Bakewell acquired those rights "as security for . . . a pre-existing claim." Bakewell had from the very outset a claim to be paid for the merchandise it delivered. Originally this claim was unsecured. In May, Selma agrees to give Bakewell this security interest in these toasters as "security for" this pre-existing right on Bakewell's part that it be paid. So Bakewell has an Article 9 security interest, which attaches just like any other.

A couple of points need to be made in wrapping up this tale of the toasters. First of all, as the last part of the example should have made clear, it is perfectly possible for two, or even more than two, distinct parties to have Article 9 security interests in — that is attached to — the same piece of collateral. By the end of part (d) each one of these simple appliances was subject to one security interest held by Credit Associates and another held by Bakewell America. I would not say the more the merrier — not by a long shot — but the Article 9 scheme as a general matter creates no impediment to this kind of multiple interests and in fact spends a lot of time and energy (as we ourselves will in Part III of this book not coincidentally labeled "Priorities") sorting out the players and their relative positions should things get dicey.

A second general point, or rather a question, may have occurred to you: If Article 9 security interests keep attaching to collateral, attaching often to more collateral as time goes on, and sometimes attaching to items to which other interests have already attached — well, doesn't the whole process threaten eventually to overwhelm if not the collateral itself then at the very least our meager powers of comprehension? A toaster is, after all, just a toaster. How much of a burden as a piece of collateral in this exciting, ever-changing world of Article 9 interests can it be expected to take on? From what we've seen so far, security interests keep attaching and attaching, clasping onto the collateral for dear life, but seemingly never letting go. Have no fear, at least on this score. In material to follow we will learn how interests may and do fall away either at the happening of a specific event or by the passage of time. While the drafters of Article 9 (mercifully) have spared us from having to speak of an interest "detaching" or "unattaching," we will learn in chapters to follow of how an interest may "terminate" or become "no longer effective" against particular parties. There stands the simple toaster, apparently unaffected by all the activity swirling around it. Article 9 security interests come and go like, well, so many slices of bread.

6. No. All of Samantha's books, the family Bible included, constitute consumer goods. There's no reason to worry about "accessions" here (if ever), so it is clear from §9-204(b)(1) that Local Lending's security interest will not attach to the Bible, no matter how valuable, in spite of

the after-acquired property clause that firm wrote into the security agreement that Samantha was asked to and did sign. She acquired rights in the Bible more than ten days after the lender gave value. Comment 3 to §9-204, which deals with this exception to the general enforceability of after-acquired property clauses, doesn't do much more than restate the conclusion as we found it in the Code text, but the reason for the exception should be obvious. It is another example (like the rule of §9-108(e)(2), which we looked at in the last example of the previous chapter), of a bit of consumer protection finding its way into Article 9. When Samantha originally took out the loan she had to know that she was putting at risk — should she not be able to repay Local Lending — her collection of scholarly books. She may not have been happy to do so, but we have to assume that had she not been willing to put that collection up as collateral she could not have obtained the loan. At the same time, Local Lending would have been making its decision to lend on this basis based on what it estimated to be the worth of the scholarly book collection at the time she applied for the loan. It could not have been relying on the possibility that her collection of books would grow, especially not in the way that it has here by her unforeseen inheritance of a family treasure. There is no valid reason for allowing Local Lending's interest to extend to this later-acquired piece of Samantha's personal property, and Samantha is protected by §9-204(b)(1) from inadvertently encumbering it with a security interest just because there was some language, which she might well not have fully understood, about "now held or hereafter acquired" in the document she signed. The Bible stays free of Local Lending's security interest.

PART

II

Perfection of the Interest

CHAPTER 5

Introduction to Perfection and Classification of Collateral

INTRODUCTION TO PERFECTION

A security interest granted by the debtor in favor of the secured party having attached to any specific piece of collateral, the interest is as of the moment of attachment effective as between those two parties. That's what attachment is all about. In particular the secured party will have the right, should the debtor fail to meet its underlying obligation, of "going against" the collateral; the creditor will have an opportunity to get paid (hopefully all, but in most cases at least some of) what it is owed by taking control of the collateral through repossession if necessary, reselling or otherwise disposing of it for gain, retention of the proceeds of the disposition, and so on. If this were all the secured party cared about, attachment would be not just necessary but sufficient for the creditor's purposes. Being able to assure the secured party that its security interest had indeed attached would be the end of our story and the moment of attachment the culmination of the secured party's dreams. If, that is, this were sufficient for the secured party's, the creditor's, purposes. And if any lender *were* to trust in a belief that attachment of a valid interest is all that can ever be hoped for or might ever be needed, then that lender would almost assuredly be brought rather quickly to the realization that he, she, or it has in fact been living in a world of dreams and not facing some fairly basic if dispiriting realities of everyday commercial life.

The secured party needs more than attachment to protect its interests to as great an extent as Article 9 will allow. It needs to be sure that the security interest has not only attached, but that it has been *perfected* as well. Perfection is the mechanism through which the secured party asserts its rights in the collateral, should push come to shove, *against third parties* who might come into the picture and make some claim of their own against that particular bit of the debtor's property. As we will see, among the most important of third parties with whom the secured party may later have to tangle is the all-important trustee in bankruptcy, who appears on the scene in the event a bankruptcy petition is filed by or against the debtor and whose obligation is to represent the rights of the whole class of unsecured creditors.

Look at the second comment to §9-317. The first sentence says that the section "lists the classes of persons who take priority over, or take free of, an unperfected security interest." Without going into all the details of this section here, the fact that there are parties who can have priority over an *unperfected* interest, indeed a whole list of them, suggests quite strongly that for the secured creditor holding a security interest which is attached but unperfected is far from ideal. Compare the language that concludes the first paragraph of Comment 2 to §9-308:

> [I]n general, after perfection the secured party is protected against creditors and transferees of the debtor and, in particular, against any representative of creditors in insolvency proceedings instituted by or against the debtor.

Perfection is not perfect. The extent to which a *perfected security interest* will give the secured party a favored position should the debtor go into bankruptcy, should others claim security interests in the same collateral, should the collateral be sold or otherwise transferred — these and a whole slew of other gripping questions are to be dealt with in the next part of this volume. For the moment it is sufficient that you appreciate how all-important it is for the secured party that its interest have not just attached to the collateral, as we have already discussed, but that it be perfected in each individual case. The chapters that follow in this part are about the means by which perfection of an Article 9 security interest is achieved. We deal with the how, the where, and the when of perfection. Part III can then focus in greater depth on the consequences of perfection, and of course on the consequences, often pretty appalling, should the secured party have failed initially to attain or to have later lost perfected status for one reason or another. The secured party will not, indeed should not, sleep easy at night unless it can rest assured its interest has been and continues to be perfected.

Before we can get into exploring exactly how the secured party attains perfection of its security interest, we need to do one exceptionally important bit of preparatory work. What means of perfection will be necessary or even possible and the exact steps for carrying them out come to depend in Article 9 on what is referred to as the *classification of the collateral* by type. Article 9 is structured around a system of definitions under which any piece or pieces of collateral that could possibly be subject to a security interest under the article will have to come within exactly one type of collateral or another. Sometimes it is simple to correctly classify a certain bit of collateral; other times it is not, and a good deal can be riding on whether one party or the other has made a mistake in the classification. We start, therefore, as we must, in this chapter with a thorough grounding in the Article 9 scheme for classification of collateral.

CLASSIFICATION OF THE COLLATERAL

At the heart of every secured transaction sits the collateral itself. Should a dispute arise that calls for your analysis, there is no better place to start than identifying the collateral being fought over as precisely as you possibly can. First identify it in real terms: If the debtor is a manufacturer the subject collateral could be the stamping machine it uses to make the widgets, the raw materials that it whirls into the widgets, or the end-product widgets themselves. The debtor may have granted a security interest in the patent it holds, which allows it to make the product, or the accounts receivable it accumulates as the widgets make their way out of the plant and into the hands of the firm's contented customers. Collateral is real stuff; it is machinery or steel or a license to produce or the check delivered in exchange for something when it is sold. In any particular Article 9 dispute the parties may end up contesting a subtle point of law or the interpretation to be given to a complex set of facts, but what they're really arguing over is the right to get their hands on some particular piece or pieces of valuable personal property. Beware the temptation, if temptation you find it, to jump right to the metaphysical. Be sure in all instances that you get as good a handle as you possibly can on just exactly what property it is that the parties are arguing over and, hence, what you are talking about.

The next stage in your analysis should be to establish how the collateral that is at issue is to be characterized under the unique classification scheme established by Article 9. All collateral can and will fit within one *and only one* of a set of carefully defined types. Under the prerevision version of Article 9, any collateral would have had to fit within one of only a handful (ten, by most people's count) of types. The drafters of Revised Article 9 added to the classification scheme a good number of new and fairly arcane collateral types (see, for example, the definitions of *as-extracted collateral* in §9-102(a)(6) and *health care insurance receivables* in §9-102(a)(46)) the better to clarify the rules governing these sorts of things and the limited situations in which they are the subject of a transaction. For the purpose of this, an introductory survey of secured transactions, it will be sufficient if we focus our attention on a subset of all the possible types of collateral under Article 9, what can rightfully be thought of as the main or principal categories into which the collateral should fit in the great majority of cases. This will still leave us plenty to deal with.

Getting acquainted with the principal classes of collateral under Article 9 is all about careful reading and application of the definitions, all of which can be found in §9-102(a). Perhaps the easiest way to pull the pieces together initially is with a chart:

All cited definitions are found in §9-102(a)

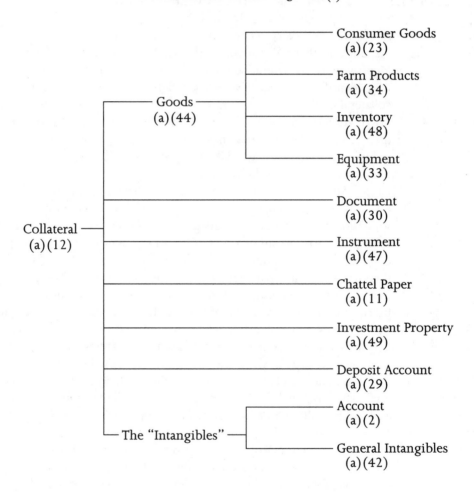

This chart could be refined and expanded still further if one had a mind to do so. In particular, as you will discover in the final example of this chapter, investment property as defined in §9-102(a)(49) actually covers a variety of means through which investments in corporate securities and the like can be held, each of which is in itself further defined in the Code either in Article 9 or in Article 8, which deals with Investment Securities.*

The examples that follow provide you with the opportunity to work through the various parts of this classification scheme. Before you head into the examples, you will want to take a first look at the various definitional sections referenced in the preceding chart. That will give you the general lay of the land. You will then, as you work through the individual instances, more than likely find it necessary to read and reread each of the definitions with the greatest of care. Help is also available in Comments 4 and 5 to §9-102.

Examples

1. The H.A.L. Corporation makes personal computers. At the end of a busy production cycle it has a large number of such computers stored in its warehouse facility. Were it to put up these computers as collateral in conjunction with a loan obtained from a major bank to further finance its operations, how would this collateral be classified?

2. Lucky Louie runs a retail store, Lucky Louie's World-O-Stuff, selling household appliances, electronics, and the like to the general public. Louie orders 40 computers from the H.A.L. Corporation. When they arrive he puts one on display and 38 others in his storeroom. The last he decides to set up in his office to use in keeping track of the operations of his business. If Louie were to use these computers along with other items in his stock as collateral to get a small business loan from a local bank, how would the computers be classified as collateral in his hands?

3. Louie sells one of the computers from his storeroom to Bess. Bess takes the computer home, where she sets it up in her den. She, her husband, and her children use it to do simple household accounting, play computer games, access the Internet, and browse the Web.
   a. How would this computer be classified as potential collateral as it now stands in the possession of Bess?
   b. Would your answer to (a) be the same if instead Bess had taken the computer home and set it up in the room in her home from which she runs a small business, telling her husband and kids to keep their hands off the machine?

---

* Finally, you will see in some parts of Article 9 references to "money" as collateral. I don't include it in the classification scheme because in practice it would have to be a fairly unusual situation in which someone would put up money as original collateral for a loan or to secure an obligation generally. Money is money, and those who have it don't usually have to borrow. In any event, and for the record, *money* is defined in §1-201(24) and §1R-201(b)(24) to mean cold hard cash.

c. Suppose that Bess had, as in part (b) above, placed the computer in room in her home, out of which she runs her business. She does use it in connection with that business. She also uses the computer to keep track of news and current affairs via the Web and to receive and answer e-mail, both relating to her business and personal. How should the computer be characterized under this set of facts?

d. Finally, suppose that Bess had initially bought the computer for her family's education and enjoyment and set it up in the den, as first assumed in (a). A couple of years later her family is getting cranky since the computer, being a few years old, does not have all of the latest multimedia, interconnective, and fancy features of the newer models. Bess buys a new computer for use in the den, and places the original two-year-old model in her office room, because it is perfectly adequate for doing the kinds of things she needs for her business. She purges the machine of the various games and programs that her children (and her husband) have loaded it with. She replaces these with a number of business-oriented applications, which she begins to use. At this point Bess decides to apply for a small business loan from a local bank. If the bank decides to give her the loan based partly on the fact that she is willing to put up collateral including the computer, how would this computer be classified for the purposes of this transaction?

4. Farmer MacDonald has a farm on which he grows a variety of crops, mainly cucumbers. And on this farm he has a tractor. He also buys at various times during the year and has on his property seeds, fertilizer and insecticide, crates in which to pack his produce, and of course fuel for the tractor. On his land there is also a shed in which he has a small setup (an oven, large pots, a canning machine, and a refrigerator), which he uses once his crop is in to turn some of his cucumbers into pickles which he sells as "Old MacDonald's Gourmet Gherkins" to a few stores in his area.

a. Should MacDonald apply for a loan from an area bank, he would want to use all of the valuable property on his farm as collateral. How would the bank classify each of the following: his growing crop, the crop once harvested, the tractor, seed, fertilizer and insecticide, crates, tractor fuel, pickle-packing paraphernalia, and the jars of pickles?

b. In addition, MacDonald keeps a half-dozen chickens in a coop next to his house. His children, the young MacDonalds, are responsible for taking care of these chickens and collecting the eggs for the family's own use. Classify the chickens.

5. Sparkle Plenty runs a small manufacturing facility producing tinsel of the type used to decorate Christmas trees and the like. It is a seasonal

business. Starting in January she makes large purchases and takes delivery of aluminum foil that she will later render into tinsel as well as the cardboard and cellophane wrapping that she will need, eventually, to package her product. She also stocks up on the fuel she'll need to run the two machines, a shredder and a packager, that are the heart of her operation. From March through August Sparkle works at converting the rolls of foil into tinsel and packaging it, first into individual boxes and then massing these boxes into larger crates suitable for shipment. In September she contracts to sell these crates to a few large Christmas supply wholesalers and arranges for their shipping. By the end of the month, if everything goes as planned, Sparkle's shop is empty save for the two machines waiting to do service the next year. Sparkle herself vacations the last three months of the year. Assume that she wishes to get a small business loan from a local bank. How should the bank classify all of the various equipment and supplies that she might put up as collateral: the machines and the fuel for the machines, the rolls of foil and packaging materials she buys, the tinsel as it is coming out of the shredder, and the tinsel as it is eventually boxed and crated?

6. Hartford Cogs and Widgets produces a large number of a particular item, its CyberCog 2100. Initially, upon production, it crates these cogs and stores them in its own warehouse adjacent to its factory.
   a. How would you classify these cogs, resting in Hartford's warehouse, as potential collateral?
   b. Eventually, Hartford contracts with one of its principal buyers for the sale of a number of these cogs. The sales contract calls for the buyer to pay Hartford in full for the merchandise within 90 days of its receipt of any shipment. The cogs are shipped off. How would you classify as potential collateral the amount now owed Hartford by this buyer?
   c. Assume that Hartford's production facilities are so active that it eventually runs out of space in its own warehouse to store the cogs and widgets it is turning out. It takes several truckloads of the CyberCog 2100 to Wally's Warehouse, one of the larger commercial warehouses in the area, where it arranges for their storage. Wally's Warehouse issues a negotiable warehouse receipt covering these cogs, which is given to Hartford. How do you classify this warehouse receipt? Would it make any difference if what it had received from Wally was a nonnegotiable warehouse receipt?

7. Lucky Louie, you'll remember, operates Lucky Louie's World-O-Stuff, a retail establishment selling household appliances, electronics, and the like to the general public. As sales are made, Louie takes payment in a

variety of forms. How would you classify each of the following of Louie's assets as potential collateral under Article 9?

   a. Checks he receives from customers, either as full or down payment for an item?

   b. Notes made payable "to the order of Lucky Louie" signed by the customers and calling for payment of an item's purchase price (with interest) over a series of months?

   c. Copies of a form "Retail Sales Installment Agreement," which he asks for from some customers who intend to pay over a period of months for larger purchases? The form sets out the periodic payments that the customer is to make and in addition states that "Buyer hereby grants to Lucky Louie a security interest in any and all items purchased under this agreement as security for Buyer's obligations to pay any amount due hereunder."

   d. In some instances Louie has his customers sign both this Retail Sales Installment Agreement and, in addition, promissory notes covering their payment obligation. Louie then staples each note to the corresponding Agreement. How would you classify the resultant packet of papers?

8. The Klavis Rent-a-Car company owns a fleet of cars that it leases to consumer and business users for periods ranging usually from one day to one year or, in some instances, a couple of years. How would you characterize the automobiles in Klavis' fleet? How would you characterize the written lease agreements that Klavis has in its files signed by each of its customers?

9. In 2006 Digger enters into an agreement with Landers, the owner of a large undeveloped piece of property bordering on his own. Under this agreement, which is to run for ten years, Digger gets the right to enter onto the land and prospect for minerals. Any minerals that he discovers he is entitled to remove from the land upon paying to Landers a 10% royalty. The agreement also gives Digger the option to buy the land outright in 2015 for a set price. In 2006 Digger comes upon what seems certain to be a particularly rich deposit of titanium ore situated right in the center of the land. There is no question that a major mining operation on the site will be well worth the time and money involved, but in order to do it efficiently Diggers will have to make a large investment in new mining equipment. He approaches a major bank in the area and enters into negotiation for a loan that will allow him to finance the operation. He offers as collateral his present right to take ore from the land as well as his option to purchase it eventually at what is now apparently an incredibly low price. As the bank's attorney contemplates what work will be necessary to properly document all aspects of this

loan, how should he or she classify for Article 9 purposes the collateral that Digger will be putting up?

10. Prudence Moneybucks, unlike some of her relatives, enjoys a very simple lifestyle. No flashy jewelry or expensive original artwork for Prudence, who lives comfortably but simply in a modest rental apartment. In taking stock of her assets, Prudence can look only to the following:

   a. Twenty shares in a small family-run corporation, Moneybucks Industries, Incorporated, which shares are represented by a share certificate she keeps in a desk drawer at her home (see §8-102(4)(a));

   b. Her interest in a mutual fund, The Rocksolid Investment Trust, from which she receives statements once a month (see §8-102(a)(18));

   c. An account she keeps with the stockbrokerage firm of James, Steven, Rogers & Company, a principal component of which is a hefty number of shares in the H.A.L. Corporation, one of the country's leading computer manufacturers (As to her account with the firm of JSR & Co., see §8-501(a). On what she would refer to as "her H.A.L. shares," see §8-102(a)(17).);

   d. A passbook savings account she has at Springfield State Bank;

   e. A ten-year certificate of deposit (a "CD") she bought for $50,000 in 2006 from Springfield State Bank. The CD entitles her to $50,000 plus interest in 2016, the full amount of which she now intends to "roll over" into another CD at that future date.

Should Prudence be looking to take out a personal loan and thinking of using any or all of the above as collateral, how would a lending institution classify — for the purposes of Article 9 — each of the pieces of her accumulated fortune?

Explanations

1. H.A.L. holds the computers it manufactures as inventory, not just in the ordinary household sense of the word but under the formal scheme of Article 9. The answer may seem obvious, but it's worth working our way to the result through the definitional route. First of all, computers would come under the definition of *goods* given in §9-102(a)(44). If they are to be used as collateral and a security interest attaches to them, then we expect they will be "movable at the time" that interest attaches. The word "movable" may seem an odd one to be used here, but the basic intention is to identify goods as tangible property (which has a concrete and discernable physical form) that isn't real property (land and the buildings on land, all of which is perfectly tangible and can be

quite substantial, but which we don't think of as moving from place to place). Recall that from the very outset, we saw, in §9-109(a)(1), that Article 9 applies to consensual security interests taken in personal property only, not to interests in real estate. The §9-102(a)(44) definition goes on to read into the definition of "goods" certain things that apparently have caused some confusion or question in the past and to read out a whole list of other types of Article 9 collateral — such as documents, instruments, and chattel paper — that we'll see get their own definitions elsewhere. All and all, goods are goods, and this definition does not seem to cause much trouble in day-to-day application.

Once we've established that a given piece of collateral is correctly characterized as goods, then it must fall within one *and only one* of the four categories of goods laid out in the other definitions of §9-102(a). Note the second paragraph of Comment 4a to that section:

> The classes of goods are mutually exclusive. For example, the same property cannot simultaneously be both equipment and inventory. In borderline cases — a physician's car or a farmer's truck that might be either consumer goods or equipment — the principal use to which the property is put is determinative. Goods can fall into different classes at different times. For example, a radio may be inventory in the hands of a dealer and consumer goods in the hands of a consumer.

We'll be following up on this last point in the next few examples. For the moment, note first that the classes of goods are meant to be mutually exclusive. At any given time in a particular debtor's hands goods must fall within one of the four classes set out in §9-102(a). Note further that the determination is to be made on the basis of the use, or in ambiguous cases the primary use, to which the goods are being put.

Looking through the categories of goods — consumer goods, inventory, farm products, and equipment — we have no trouble determining that the computers made by the H.A.L. Corporation and stored in its warehouse facilities are *inventory* in H.A.L.'s possession. Under (a)(48)(B) they are "held by a person [H.A.L.] for sale." That's clear enough, and we have no reason to fight over the easy ones.

2. The 39 computers Louie is holding for sale to his customers are inventory in his hands. The definitions we look to and the analysis are just as they were in the last question. The one computer displayed in his showroom and the 38 he has in storage are all "held by a person [now Louie] for sale." What of that other computer, the one he takes into this office to use in running the business? That, it turns out, is *equipment* under §9-102(a)(33). Equipment is, as you can see, the residual category of goods. If goods are not inventory, farm products,

or consumer goods, they must by a process of elimination be classified as equipment. The computer Louie is using in the office doesn't fall under the definition of inventory, or of farm products, or of consumer goods. Perforce, it is equipment. So these 40 computers, even though they might be exactly the same down to the last meg or ram, are not the same as potential collateral in the hands of our friend Louie. They are all goods, but the type of goods each is depends on how it is being used by the debtor.

3a. Bess holds this computer as *consumer goods*. See §9-102(a)(23). Goods are "consumer goods" if they are used or bought for use primarily for personal, family, or household purposes. That fits the situation perfectly. This one computer was bought by Bess and is being used as consumer goods.

3b. Change the use and you change the characterization of the goods; under this set of facts this particular computer is held by Bess as equipment under Article 9's way of characterizing things. It is certainly not inventory or farm products, nor under this set of facts could it be considered consumer goods.

This use of the term "equipment" as the default classification for all goods that don't fit into any other category can lead to results that may not jibe with how you use the word in everyday speech, all the more reason to be careful in applying the statutory definitions when the need arises. For an interesting case holding that 46 head of longhorn cattle were properly to be categorized under the circumstances as equipment, see *Morgan County Feeders, Inc. v. McCormick*, 836 P.2d 1051, 18 U.C.C.2d 632 (Colo. App. 1992). It turns out that the cattle had been purchased and held by the debtor, who apparently operated some sort of dude ranch, principally to be used by him on "recreational cattle drives" and not as rodeo calves or as feeder cattle. Given the situation, they were not inventory nor was anyone arguing they were farm products; they certainly were not consumer goods. The cattle were equipment and the rules applicable to equipment under Article 9 were applied to each and every one of them.

Another more recent reminder that equipment can come in all shapes and sizes is *Silver v. Wilson*, 50 U.C.C.2d 1196, 2003 Mich. App. LEXIS 1389, in which the Michigan Court of Appeals ruled that eleven paintings by various artists owned by a Mr. Mark M. Conti were not consumer goods but equipment. The trial court had classified four of the paintings as consumer goods, but this was held to be in error. The appellate court noted, "the testimony established that [all of] the paintings had been displayed in model homes, condominiums, and in various offices of Conti's company, but never in Conti's home," and that there had been no evidence that he ever displayed the paintings "in his own personal office or that there was any personal, familial, or household use" of the paintings in question.

3c. As the portion of Comment 4a to §9-102 quoted a couple of pages back says, "In borderline cases — a physician's car or a farmer's truck that might be either consumer goods or equipment — the principal use to which the product is put or to which the property is put is determinative." There is, as you would expect, no single test or criterion for which is the "principal" use in such situations. This is the kind of question that will necessarily have to be decided on a case-by-case basis. For an interesting recent case that tests these waters, see *Davenport v. Bates*, 2006 Tenn. App. LEXIS 790, 61 U.C.C.2d 542 (2006). In 2000 Davenport, a self-employed landscaper, bought a 1995 Chevrolet Corvette on credit from an auto dealership owned by Bates, granting the seller a security interest in the vehicle to ensure his payment. Later, following several years of late payments by Davenport and the eventual repossession of the car, one of several issues that arose in the course of litigation was whether the trial court had correctly characterized the Corvette as equipment, used by Davenport in the course of his landscaping business instead of as consumer goods. As the appellate court noted, at trial various witnesses gave lengthy testimony about the value of the Corvette and its condition, but there was only limited testimony relating to Davenport's use of the vehicle. At one point, Davenport himself had testified in response to a question by his counsel, that he had bought it and used it in his landscaping business, explaining further:

> Well, of course, I didn't haul dirt in it, it was a Corvette. I went and looked at jobs in it, went and collected money in it, and went and done [sic] proposals in it, things like that.

He also stated that one of his landscaping employees was paid to keep the car clean and that he had attempted to insure the vehicle under a commercial insurance policy covering his business. In front of the Court of Appeals of Tennessee he told a different story.

> Buyer [Davenport] now contends that his testimony, along with that of his witnesses, demonstrates that the Corvette was a collector's item, and thus, inherently for personal use. He refers to his testimony that he kept the Corvette in excellent condition and had it cleaned on a regular basis. He also notes that he referred to the car as his "baby" and said he loved the car. Also, he testified that he kept the car in a garage and did not drive it in the rain. According to the Buyer, this is "conclusive proof" that the vehicle was purchased for personal use.

The Appellate Court chose to disagree and upheld the trial court's conclusion that the Corvette was properly characterized as equipment and not consumer goods.

> In searching the extensive transcript of the testimony in this case," the court noted, "we are unable to locate a single reference to an occasion of Buyer driving the car for personal or family use. To the contrary, all of Buyer's testimony relates to his use of the car in his business. When a debtor would benefit if the collateral constituted "consumer goods," the debtor has the burden of proving the nature of the collateral. In borderline cases of classifying collateral, the principal use of the property is determinative. Buyer simply did not produce any evidence that the vehicle was "used or bought for use primarily for personal, family, or household purposes." [Citations omitted]

Davenport may have loved that car. I have no doubt he did. But, at least according to the courts of Tennessee, he loved what was his as equipment, not consumer goods.

3d. This part of the example points up a bit of potential ambiguity in the definitional scheme, here in the way consumer goods is defined. The definition directs the reader to look to the primary purpose for which the goods "are used or bought for use." Here the particular computer was bought for one use — as consumer goods — but over time has been converted to another use — as equipment — by the purchaser. So which is it? Do we look to the primary use for which the computer was originally purchased or the primary use to which it is later being put? *As of what moment in time* do we apply the goods-related definitions of §9-102(a)? The courts that have had to consider the issue have generally settled on the moment of attachment as the proper time for defining the nature of the goods. See, e.g., *In re Rex Group, Inc.*, 80 Bankr. 774, 5 U.C.C. 2d 712 (Bankr. E.D. Va. 1987). As the court there says:

> The test of the classification of goods under Va. Code Ann. §8.9-109 [the precursor to the definitions of the four types of goods now all to be found in §9-102(a)] is the owner's use of the goods. The generally accepted rule is that the debtor's stated intended use, at the time of attachment of the security interest, defines the nature of the goods for purposes of ascertaining the proper place for perfecting the security interest. [Under prior Article 9 the place for filing a financing statement, a topic we will get to later, was determined in large measure by the type of collateral involved. This is generally no longer true under present Article 9, but correct classification is still important for plenty of other reasons.] The relevant time to classify collateral for determining the requirement and consequences of perfection is the time surrounding the transaction that originally gave rise to the security interest. [Citations omitted]

This ruling makes sense. The proper characterization of the goods is important not just in the abstract. It makes a difference, as we will see, in how the secured party must deal with the goods to evaluate and to protect its position overall and in particular in any potential security interest it may take in the goods. Article 9 doesn't classify all goods just for the sake of it; it classifies all goods as possible collateral. Computers are just computers and cattle are just cattle until a potential secured party comes into the picture. It is then, as the moment of attachment draws near and may indeed take place, that the characterization of the goods *as collateral subject to an Article 9 security interest* becomes relevant. As we've previously seen, the moment of attachment is or at least should be a well-defined moment under the Code. It is as of that moment that a piece of property becomes collateral in the Article 9 sense, and it is as of that moment that its characterization as *what type* of collateral is best made.

4a. Let's take the pieces in order. The growing crop and the crop once harvested qualify as *farm products* under the definition of §9-102(a)(34), here part (A)(i), that includes "crops produced on trees, vines, and bushes." Cucumbers don't just appear out of the thin air, so there's no trouble here. The farmer's tractor is equipment, again by the process of elimination.

What of all of the following: the seed, the fertilizer, and insecticide, the crates, and the tractor fuel? These, it turns out, are also farm products under the full definition of §9-102(a)(34). Note that "farm products" includes not just crops and the like but, under part (C), "supplies used or produced in a farming operation." Seeds, insecticides, and the like, even the tractor fuel, all come within the scope of this aspect of farm products. You don't typically think of the fuel used up in a farmer's tractor, or the insecticide that is sprayed over the fields as a "product" of farming, but as you can see the definition of "farm products" is much broader than you'd initially imagine, and you always have to bear that in mind. So, for example, manure bought by a farmer to be used as fertilizer is considered a farm product. If the farmer's livestock provide manure that might eventually be used on that farm or sold off for use by others, that would be farm products, too, under part (D) (as long as it was still in its "as produced" state or close to it and hadn't been subjected to a manufacturing process). Get used to the idea that the term "farm products" covers a lot of things around the farm.

Of course not everything that a farmer has around the place qualifies as farm products. We've already seen that the tractor is equipment, not farm products. The difference is that the tractor, while it may be *used* around the farm isn't *used up* in the farming operations.

As we'll see in the next example, when we start talking about inventory, things that are to be treated as equipment, whether in the hands of a farmer or in anyone else's possession, tend to be those larger identifiable pieces of, well, equipment held for the long term; they are used around the place but not used up over the short term in the operation.

Finally, consider all of the pickle packing machinery that MacDonald has on his property and the jars of pickles themselves. The oven, the pots, the canning machine, and so on are equipment. The completed pickles, unlike the cucumbers as they come off the vine, would be, I'd think, inventory. "Farm products" includes "products of crops of livestock in their unmanufactured states" as long as these are still in the hands of the farmer. Once the stuff undergoes a transformation into a more sophisticated product, it ceases to be farm product and is considered inventory. See the third from the last paragraph of Comment 4a. Packing cucumbers into individual jars of spiced gherkins doesn't seem to me to be so "closely connected with farming" as the pasteurization of milk or the boiling of sap. It strikes me more like the "extensive canning operation" that takes the stuff out of the farm products category and into the realm of inventory. There's nothing wrong with this, of course. Farmers like MacDonald are entitled to have inventory (in the Article 9 sense) on their hands just like other people who hold goods for sale. There would be a problem, however, for a careless lender who agrees to a loan taking this as collateral who simply assumes the pickles are covered by the term "farm products" as used in its security agreement; should a controversy arise, the lender may find itself having no interest in the pickles when they are later classified by a court as inventory.

4b. These particular chickens are consumer goods. True, they happen to be the property of a happy farmer and his happy family, but they have been bought or at least are now being used "primarily for personal, family or household purposes." So they are consumer goods, just as much as the television set, the DVD player, and the dining room table in Farmer MacDonald's farmhouse.

5. The two machines that Sparkle uses in her operation are, of course, equipment. All the rest — the fuel, the raw materials, the packaging, the foil in the process of becoming tinsel, as well as the final product itself — is inventory. The Article 9 definition of "inventory" is broader than the conventional use of the word, so it's worth looking at in detail. Under §9-102(a)(48)(D), a debtor's inventory includes "raw materials, work in process, or materials used or consumed in a business." We tend to think of inventory as just the finished article, the product in its final state as it will be shipped out the door to some willing buyer.

But inventory under Article 9 encompasses much more. It includes not just the goods as they make their way through the production process but also the raw materials and all of the other stuff that will be "used or consumed" in the creation of the final product.

So Sparkle's inventory consists not only of the finished, packaged, and ready-to-go tinsel she'll eventually sell to her wholesaler customers, but much more as well, including, it would seem, any leftover aluminum foil scraps that don't make it into the final product and as such are byproducts of her operation. It may not be obvious at the moment, but there actually is a very good reason why all of this other stuff — that a layperson wouldn't think of as a manufacturer's "inventory" but that falls within Article 9's definition — gets lumped within this category. For one thing, if Article 9 didn't treat it as inventory, what exactly *would* it be, in the Article 9 sense, that is? It doesn't readily fit within any of the other categories of goods given in §9-102(a), nor does it seem to be "equipment," at least as we normally tend to use the word, so we'd need yet one more category and one more definition. We've plenty to deal with as it is. And there would then inevitably be the tricky question of exactly when, at what precise moment, this not-yet-inventory stuff went from being whatever else it was to being inventory. At exactly what moment does a whole mess of shredded aluminum foil make the magical transformation into becoming holiday tinsel? Under the Article 9 scheme and the definition of §9-102(a)(48), we don't have to put ourselves through such metaphysical speculation. Everything that Sparkle has around the shop and uses in her business is either going to be equipment or inventory. Those are the only two choices. How are we to distinguish this type of inventory from equipment? Fortunately for us, the relevant paragraph of Comment 4a concludes:

> Inventory also includes goods that are consumed in a business (e.g., fuel used in operation). In general, goods used in a business are equipment if they are fixed assets or have, as identifiable units, a relatively long period of use, but are inventory, even though not held for sale or lease, if they are used up or consumed in a short period of time in producing a product or providing a service.

The two machines Sparkle uses to work her magic and make simple aluminum foil into tinsel to delight all the girls and boys on Christmas morning are equipment. Everything else is inventory.

In addition to making our lives somewhat easier by limiting the number of classes of goods as it does, this expansive definition of inventory serves a more sophisticated function in the handling of affairs under Article 9. As we will encounter often in later material, it is not uncommon for a lender to take a security interest in collateral described simply as "all inventory now held or hereafter acquired." This general "floating lien" on inventory, as it is referred to, is not discouraged or looked upon with disfavor by Article 9. In fact, the Article is drawn to facilitate such dealings and to clarify how they work out if that is what the parties agree to. So if Sparkle wanted to borrow some money for operating funds from a bank using what she has on hand as collateral, she has two basic categories of stuff to deal with. She could offer a lender an interest in each or both of her two machines. Financing on the basis of equipment is surely an option, but as a practical matter her particular machines, old and highly specialized as they are, might not be worth that very much. More generally, a manufacturer will often borrow just to buy its equipment, so the equipment may already be subject to some other party's security interest. Sparkle's best bet is to offer up her inventory as collateral to secure operating funds from the bank. Here is a whole collection of valuable stuff sitting around her shop just begging to serve as collateral. The bank, after satisfying itself of her general creditworthiness and inquiring into a lot of other facts about her and about the proposed collateral, can agree to a loan taking an interest in all of her "inventory now held and hereafter acquired" without having to describe it in any greater detail. It can, as we will see, file once on her "inventory" in the correct place and not have to worry about constantly making revised or additional filings.

The possibility of a secured party's taking a general floating lien on all inventory taken together with the expansive definition of "inventory" we have been exploring makes life considerably easier for this type of lender. Its interest is in the total pool of inventory — as here broadly defined — and it doesn't have to worry about the fact that from day to day and even from moment to moment the exact makeup of that pool is shifting. Things move into inventory. Goods within inventory change from one kind of thing into another. Things may even move out of inventory, as we will see, with no great harm to the lender. From the lender's point of view the important thing is that the aggregate value of what is in the pool, in whatever form, from raw material to finished product, stays well above the amount of the outstanding obligation owed to it by the manufacturer.

This is obviously a significant simplification of the situation. As we proceed we'll see plenty of things to complicate the inventory financer's life. For the moment, however, it is important to focus on this one aspect of how Article 9 works, which makes inventory financing easier, and indeed without which it might not work very well at all. Look at Sparkle's business. It is to say the least highly seasonal, and I made it that way just to demonstrate this point most dramatically. Imagine that a local bank did make a loan to her taking a security interest in her "inventory now held or hereafter acquired." What goods exactly would it have subject to its interest at any one time? Toward the beginning of the year it would be mostly raw materials, packaging, and fuel. Starting in March, the pool of collateral would begin to consist less of this stuff and more of half-shredded tinsel (as work in process) and some finished product. By September the collateral would be almost all in the form of neat crates of completed tinsel.

During all of this time the form, the physical nature, of the collateral would have been changing, but not its basic attribute — as far as the bank is concerned — as a valuable business asset of Sparkle's subject to its security interest. In fact, if Sparkle's business is running at a profit, the one constant should be that the aggregate value of these assets has been steadily rising throughout the year. Simple aluminum foil bought in bulk, pedestrian cardboard packaging and fuel has been spun, by the magic of Sparkle's hand, into glimmering and highly expensive (given what's really in it) holiday tinsel for which people are willing, as the shopping days until Christmas dwindle down to a precious few, to pay plenty! Okay, so it may not be magic, but it is Sparkle's way of making money off of a legitimate consumer demand, and it is this money from which she is able to pay off her loan to the bank.

Note, by the way, that from the bank's point of view just about the worst thing that could happen is for Sparkle to borrow the money, buy all the raw materials, and then do nothing with them. Perhaps she just gets lazy or maybe she goes through a spiritual conversion of sorts and decides to give up her capitalist ways. The raw materials, and packaging and fuel, just sit there in the shop while Sparkle is off doing good work for others. The bank is now faced with the very likely prospect that Sparkle won't be making her loan payments as she's promised. And what of its security interest in the inventory? The bank is, of course, protected, but consider what it has to look forward to — taking the time and effort to repossess and try to resell if it can a whole lot of aluminum foil, some cardboard packaging (probably preprinted with Sparkle's name and logo on it) and a plentiful supply of the kind of fuel suitable to old tinsel-shredding machines. Happy holidays to the bank! We are faced with the realization that as a general matter the interests of the lender and the borrower are not in conflict but are very much in sync. It is in the interest of the lender, here the bank, that the borrower, here Sparkle, take advantage of the collateral in whatever way it knows best how to pull in income so that it can keep making its loan payments and make a profit as well (to encourage the borrower not to veer from the capitalist track). Nothing succeeds, to everyone's benefit, like success.

Finally, and to return to the more mundane matter of classifying the collateral, we have to appreciate how much easier the bank's lot is in this situation because it can describe the collateral, in the security agreement and in any filing it may make for the purposes of perfection, simply as inventory and leave it at that. The bank will not have to be running back and forth to the filing office during the year removing filings on "bulk aluminum foil" meanwhile adding filings on "work in process" or "tinsel as packaged." The single overarching floating lien on inventory can be treated, both in the documentation between the two parties in the security agreement and in notice to the world through their filing of record, by the use of the simple designation of "inventory" and left at that. Sparkle can get on with the business of making her tinsel, and the bank can minimize the paperwork with which it has to bother itself and Sparkle.

6a. There is nothing especially tricky here. These CyberCogs in Hartford's warehouse are goods under §9-102(a)(44) and inventory under (a)(48).

6b. The amount owed Hartford for the items sold is considered an *account* under §9-102(a)(2). The two classes of collateral — accounts and general intangibles — are sometimes referred to collectively as the "intangibles." This makes sense, as they are the only kinds of collateral that are (apart from deposit accounts and certain distinct forms of investment property with which we will deal in the last example), well, not tangible. They can be valuable enough certainly, but they have no physical presence, no material form. The owner of the intangible may keep on hand tangible evidence or a record of what it has — let's hope Hartford keeps some kind of listing of who owes it what — but that record is not in and of itself the thing of value. If Hartford's record of accounts was lost somehow (computer glitch?) or destroyed in a fire, it would be owed the money just the same. The intangibles have value as they are the right to receive value from others as that right would be enforced in a court of law.

The question occurs how to distinguish accounts from the other, the "general intangibles." The answer is found in the first sentence of §9-102(a)(2):

> "Account" . . . means a right to payment of a monetary obligation, whether or not earned by performance, (i) for property that has been or is to be sold, leased, licensed, assigned, or otherwise disposed of, (ii) for services rendered or to be rendered, . . .

and then on to a number of other ways in which an account may be generated, not all of which need concern us here. Note also in the final sentence to this definition that the term "account" does not extend to any "rights to payment evidenced by chattel paper or an instrument" or to deposit accounts or investment property. We'll see in a moment what such things as chattel paper, an instrument, a deposit account, and investment property are, but for now we can just satisfy ourselves that there's nothing like that in sight. Hartford has sold off some of the CyberCogs and gotten in return a bunch of accounts.

6c. The warehouse receipt is a *document* under §9-102(a)(30). You should look to §1-201 and its definition of "document of title." (Resist, if you can, the temptation to follow up on the reference in (a)(30) to subsection (2) of Section 7-201. It's a minor point that we can easily pass on, even if it does have to do with dealings in "distilled spirits.") Subsection 1-201(15) or §1R-201(b)(16) leads you to other definitions within that section and in particular to subsection 1-201(45) or §1R-201(b)(42) telling you a warehouse receipt is a "receipt issued by a person engaged in the business of storing goods for hire." There's a lot that could be said about documents of title, in fact it's the subject of an entire Article 7 of the Uniform Commercial Code, but happily for us it doesn't have to be said here. The crux of the matter as far as characterization of collateral under Article 9 is concerned is that a "document" is a document of title, a piece of paper of a special type. The two principal types are the warehouse receipt, which is issued, as we have seen, by a commercial entity engaged in the storage of other people's goods and which charges a fee for its services, and the bill of lading, which is issued by a commercial carrier on receipt of goods that it is to transport from one point to another in return for which it is to receive compensation. See §1-201(6) or §1R-201(b)(6).

What's important here, and what will sometimes cause unnecessary confusion if you aren't careful, is that a "document" for Article 9 purposes is not just any old document or piece of paper in the commonplace sense but in fact is one issued only by a special class of business entities, those that store goods (the warehouse receipt) or undertake the conveyance of goods (the bill of lading or some similar term depending on the means of transportation) as a commercial enterprise. When Hartford first put some of its product in its own warehouse, as in part (a) of this example, no document of title would have been involved. It was storing — true in a warehouse, but in *its own* warehouse — its own stuff and not paying another independent party for the service. If Hartford loaded a whole bunch of cogs or widgets onto *its own* trucks, no bill of lading or anything like that is involved. Only if it had taken the load of goods down to the local railroad yard, or put them into the hands of an independent trucking concern, would it have expected to get a bill of lading in return.

The warehouse receipt would still be classified as a document if it had been issued in a nonnegotiable form. "Documents" for the purposes of Article 9, and in contrast to "instruments" with which we deal in the next example, may be either negotiable or nonnegotiable documents of title.

7a. The checks are *instruments* under §9-102(a)(47). That definition gets long, but for our purposes it's sufficient to see that instruments include "negotiable instruments." At some time before your studies are complete, I hope you will have time to examine §3-104(a), which gives the U.C.C. definition of "negotiable instrument," for all that it's worth. It serves as the jumping-off point for the whole distinct area of commercial law studies, which you'll cover in your separate course (or part of a larger survey Commercial Law course) under the rubric of either Commercial Paper, Negotiable Instruments, or the increasingly common and more encompassing Payment Systems. On its own, and given just a quick once-over, the definition of §3-104(a) is hardly self-explanatory. Trust me, however, a check is a negotiable instrument under that section. (Or look at §3-104(f), puzzle over it for a bit, and then decide to trust me.)

7b. Notes of the type Lucky Louie is so lucky to be holding here are a second major type of collateral coming within the definition of instruments of §9-102(a)(47). Again you can look to §3-104(e) for verification that trusting me on such things isn't such a bad idea. You may wonder why these notes don't qualify as accounts as did the promises of payment Hartford Cogs and Widgets got from its buyers in part (b) of the previous example. The answer is that the definition of an account in §9-102(a)(2) specifically provides that the term does not include, among other things, "rights to payment evidenced by chattel paper or *an instrument*. . . ." Once Lucky Louie gets a signed negotiable instrument from his customer, it's just that: an instrument as potential collateral in his hands and not "merely" an account. How can you tell the difference? Well, that really is for the course covering negotiable instruments in more detail, but you should have noticed that the notes taken by Louie were more than just written I.O.U.s. They were writings signed by the customers promising to pay "to the order of Lucky Louie." That language, "to the order of," makes all the difference. It is, in the lingo of the commercial law, language of negotiability, and its presence on the writing (combined with a whole mess of other criteria, which is why §3-104 is so lengthy and the course on Payment Systems so enthralling) is what sets out negotiable instruments from other pieces of paper, even those that evidence somebody's promise to pay an amount of money in the future. Again, for our purposes we needn't get fancy. When we talk about a note we'll be talking about an Article 3 negotiable instrument, and an "instrument" for the purposes of Article 9.

7c. The form "Retail Sales Installment Agreement," once properly filled out and signed by the customer, becomes a single piece of *chattel paper*, as is defined in §9-102(a)(11). It is a record, in this case a writing, that evidences *both* (i) a monetary obligation, that is the customer's obligation to make his or her periodic payments to Louie, and (ii) a security interest in specific goods, in this case Louie's security interest in the goods sold. It's the combination of the two obligations — the promise of a party to pay money and the grant typically by the same party of a security interest — *both evidenced in the same record or records* that make for chattel paper. In this instance the one writing contains both parts and is itself chattel paper. In other instances it will be a set of writings normally physically held together, for example, stapled one to the other, that together evidence both a monetary obligation and a security interest in specific property. The packet is then considered to be a single piece of chattel paper. The term, as you might imagine, is not one dreamt up by the drafters of Article 9; the term and the practice of dealing in chattel paper as part of commercial financing long predate the Code.

7d. The packet of papers is, taken as a single entity, a piece of chattel paper. See the last sentence in §9-102(a)(11). The individual notes, for what it's worth, retain their character as negotiable instruments as far as the law of negotiable instruments is concerned. But now, wedded as they are to a security agreement and moving in tandem with it, they're part of a whole called chattel paper.

8. The cars in Klavis's fleet are inventory. See §9-102(a)(48)(A) and (B). Each of the written lease agreements is, as held by the Klavis company as potential collateral, a piece of chattel paper. Look again to §9-102(a)(11). Chattel paper includes those records or sets of records that evidence both an obligation to pay money, here the lessee's obligations to make their periodic payments, and "a lease of specific goods."

9. Both the present right that Digger has to take ore from the land and his option to purchase at a later date would constitute *general intangibles* under §9-102(a)(42). You get there by the process of elimination. What we're dealing with here are not accounts, chattel paper, deposit accounts, documents, goods, instruments, or investment property. Nor is Digger offering up as collateral any minerals to be extracted from the land, but rather the *right* to do his exploring and mining as well as the *right* to buy the property on certain terms. These rights are intangible, if potentially very valuable, and come within the meaning of "things in action" referenced in the (a)(42) definition. You can see that the drafters didn't even try to come up with a precise affirmative

definition of "general intangibles." It's a class delineated strictly in the negative sense. The class of general intangibles is the ultimate residual category in Article 9's classification scheme. If it is collateral under an Article 9 interest and it can't be fit into any of the other classes of collateral, it has to be a general intangible for lack of any other category into which it can be correctly cubbyholed.

10. The assets Prudence has at her disposal listed under (a), (b), and (c) are all examples of what Article 9 would classify as *investment property*. Look at §9-102(a)(49). "Investment property" means a security, whether certificated or uncertificated, securities entitlement, securities account, commodity contract, or commodity account. Being the type of cautious person she is, Prudence has steered clear of putting her money into commodities contracts — high-risk futures, options, and the like — and so we have to concern ourselves only with those types of investment property coming within the other parts of this definition. These sub-categories of investment property are defined through terms incorporated into the Code via a totally redrafted 1994 version of Article 8, the U.C.C. article covering so-called Investment Securities. Fortunately it is not necessary for us to work through all of the new Article 8 in any detail. You should be aware that, while it is true that people may invest in just about anything from gems to paintings to rare books, the "investment securities" with which Article 8 deals are restricted to those things which we in other circumstances might refer to as "corporate" securities, things like stocks and bonds issued by corporations. Article 8 is the part of the U.C.C. that deals with the rules on how investors can *hold, evidence their ownership of*, and when they so desire *transfer* such securities.

Central to this new version of Article 8 is a definitional scheme reflecting the different *forms* in which an individual investor can hold a corporate security. This variety is reflected in the various terms used in §9-102(a)(49), which we saw above, and in the variety of assets that Prudence has at her disposal to use as collateral.

Look first at (a), the 20 shares of Moneybucks Industries, Inc., that are represented by an actual paper share certificate which she has in her possession. Under §8-102(a)(4) you can see these shares would qualify as *certificated securities* under Article 8. They are represented by a certificate. If, as is probably the case, the certificate actually bears the name of Prudence as the owner of these shares, we could go further and say the shares were in *registered* form under §8-102(a)(13). Otherwise they would be in bearer form (§8-102(a)(2)). Either way we would say she held these shares in certificated form, and hence they would constitute a kind of investment property for Article 9 purposes.

Compare these 20 shares represented by an actual certificate to (b), Prudence's interest in the Rocksolid Investment Trust, a mutual fund. This interest might be characterized as consisting of so many "shares" of the fund, and there is nothing improper about using the term this way, but notice that there would be no certificate of any kind whatsoever evidencing Prudence's particular shares in the Trust. Her ownership of the shares would be evidenced by a recordation on the records of the Trust, which linked her name up with so many "shares" but by nothing more. Periodically she will get statements letting her know just how her account stands, but again these statements are not share certificates themselves. Prudence's investment in the mutual fund comes in the form of what Article 8 refers to as an *uncertificated* security under §8-102(a)(18).

What of Prudence's account with the brokerage firm of JSR & Co. and in particular the H.A.L. shares she has in that account? Under Article 8 terminology, Prudence is said to have agreed at one point to open a *securities account* with that firm. The definition of §8-501(a) is to this effect, even if the language is more technical and convoluted than we wish to deal with here. Prudence has opened an account with the firm and at one time apparently ordered her broker to buy some H.A.L. shares to add to the account. As you would imagine, when the brokerage executed this order it did not result in a share certificate issued by the H.A.L. corporation with Prudence's name on it. The transaction was presumably carried out by the people at JSR & Co., crediting her account as a bookkeeping matter with so many shares of H.A.L.; this transaction would be balanced in the brokerage's books by matching it with an order to sell the same number of shares some other customer had called in at about the same time. This was really more in the nature of an accounting type of transaction with a certain number of shares being added to one account (Prudence's) while at the same time the same number was deducted from the account of the seller. It was really just a paper transaction, or more likely one carried out through the computer system JSR & Co. has in place to facilitate just such orders from its customers with a minimum of muss and fuss.

Prudence's investment in a given number of shares in a publicly held company like H.A.L. is held in a form that Article 8 refers to as a *securities entitlement.* Look at §8-102(a)(17): A securities entitlement means "the rights and property interest of an entitlement holder [who would be Prudence under §8-102(a)(7)] with respect to a financial asset [the H.A.L. shares] specified in Part 5 [of Article 8]." There is no reason to try to master all that Part 5 of Article 8 has to say. From our perspective it is enough to recognize that Prudence's holding is what is referred to as an "indirect holding" of the shares. No certificate representing these shares has been issued by that corporation in

Prudence's name. That corporation will not keep any record of her holding on its books. She can be said to "own" or "hold" so many shares of this or that stock because of her arrangement with the brokerage, which would be termed a *securities intermediary* as in §8-102(a)(14)(ii). She is an *entitlement holder* (§8-102(a)(7)), entitled to issue *entitlement orders* (§8-102(a)(8)) to the brokerage — she can tell JSR & Co. to buy and sell for her account just such publicly traded securities.

Before we get lost in the depth of Article 8 and its flurry of definitions, let's return to the relatively simple proposition, which is all we need. Prudence's interest in "her H.A.L. corporation shares" is in the nature of a securities entitlement and as such, under §9-102(a)(49), is categorized as investment property for Article 9 purposes. Beyond that we can see that Prudence's entire account with JSR & Co., her broker, the entire basket of entitlements that she has collected, bought, traded in, and traded out over the years as it stands at any one time is a *securities account* and hence it, too — thought of as a whole and not just as the sum of its parts — can be correctly thought of as an item of investment property. Depending, of course, on how her various investment are doing, Prudence seems to have plenty of options about what to put up as collateral even if she hasn't surrounded herself with gems and furs.

Next we come to part (d) of this question, the savings account that Prudence prudently keeps with the Springfield State Bank. This asset would be classed as a *deposit account* under §9-102(a)(29).

Finally, what about the certificate of deposit issued by the bank? The answer, it will turn out, depends on *what type* of CD it is. Traditionally CD's (of the financial sort) were truly certificates, that is, pieces of paper issued by the bank that qualified as negotiable instruments. In effect they were, and still are, notes of the bank. See §3-104(j). If Prudence's CD is a certificated CD, then it is an Article 3 negotiable instrument and as such is an instrument for Article 9 purposes. See *Regions Bank v. Schmauch*, 354 S.C. 648, 582 S.E.2d 432, 51 U.C.C.2d 887 (Ct. App. 2003). Often today no tangible certificate is actually issued and the CD is evidenced only by an entry on the books of the bank and periodic statements to the holder. If Prudence's CD is such a uncertificated book-entry certificate of deposit, then it should be classified as a deposit account for Article 9 purposes. See *In re Verus Investment Management, LLC*, 344 Bankr. 536, 60 U.C.C.2d 60 (Bankr. N.D. Ohio 2006).

Perfection by Filing: When and What to File

INTRODUCTION TO THE MEANS OF PERFECTION

We begin by looking at §9-308(a):

> Except as otherwise provided in this section and Section 9-309 [with which we will deal in later chapters], a security interest is perfected if it has attached and all of the applicable requirements for perfection in Sections 9-310 through 9-316 have been satisfied. A security interest is perfected when it attaches if the applicable requirements are satisfied before the security interest attaches.

A few very important points practically leap off the page. First of all, a security interest cannot be perfected *unless* it has attached. Taking every step in the book meant to perfect an interest will be for nought if even one of the three criteria for attachment — recall §9-203 and what we did in Chapters 3 and 4 — is lacking. Second, notice that a security interest cannot be perfected *until* it has attached. For any number of reasons the exact moment as of which the secured party can lay claim to a *perfected* security interest can be crucial. That moment, the time of perfection, can, depending on the circumstances, be simultaneous with the time of attachment or it can come some time afterward. Perfection can never precede — even by so much as a second — attachment.

Subsection (c) of §9-308 is worth reading at this time as well:

> A security interest or agricultural lien is perfected continuously if it is originally perfected by one method under this article and is later perfected by another

method under this article, without an intermediate period when it is unperfected.

It will be important for the secured party that its interest not only be perfected but that it stay perfected, continuously perfected, as time marches on.*

All of which should more than arouse your interest in the basic question with which this part deals: How does a security interest become perfected under Article 9? What steps must or may be taken to do the deed? Fortunately, we are not talking here of a terribly long list of possibilities. There are basically four means by which an Article 9 security interest can be perfected. One of these, the acquisition of "control" as that term is more fully explicated in §§9-104 through 9-107, is a relatively new addition to the repertoire; it joined Article 9 only in 1994. More to the point, as it is applicable for our purposes only to the perfection of interests taken in collateral deemed to be investment property or a deposit account, we can set it to one side for the moment to return to it as a distinct topic in Chapter 11.

As a general matter — that is, as things stood before 1994 and as they still stand when the collateral is anything other than investment property or a deposit account — there are three ways to perfect a security interest under Article 9. These three means are perfection by filing, perfection by possession, and automatic perfection (by which we mean perfection automatically upon attachment without the taking of any other steps on the secured party's part). One way or another it has to be done or the secured party's interest cannot be said to have been perfected.

THE IMPORTANCE OF FILING

Look at §9-310(a), which tells us that unless one of a defined set of exceptions governs the case, "a financing statement must be filed to perfect all security interests" of the type governed by Article 9. Just to make sure no one misses the point, the drafters lead off their Comment 2 with the simple declaration that "Subsection (a) establishes a central Article 9 principle: Filing a financing statement is necessary for perfection of security interests and agricultural liens." In later chapters we will deal with the major exceptions to the principle that filing is the general mechanism for perfection of an Article 9 interest. These exceptions cover a lot of territory, but they by no means exhaust the possibilities. If perfection of a security interest is

---

* As the quoted language indicates, agricultural liens, which are governed by Article 9 even if they are not security interests, will also need to be perfected by the lien holder if they are to serve their purpose. See §9-308(b). As it turns out, perfection of an agricultural lien can be accomplished only through filing as required by §9-310(a).

important under Article 9, of which there can be no doubt, then filing when filing is required is key to the whole Article 9 enterprise.

Under Revised Article 9, filing is a *permissible* means of perfection of an interest in virtually any type of collateral, at least of the principal types we are dealing with. The only exceptions are that filing will not serve to perfect an interest in a deposit account or in money. See §9-312(b)(1) and (3).* In other situations, as we will discover, filing is the *only* possible means of perfecting a security interest. An interest in accounts or general intangibles, for instance, cannot be perfected by possession so that filing is in effect the exclusive way of perfecting on such collateral. In all other instances, even though an exception to the general filing requirement might be available to accord perfected status to the secured party's interest, filing is still generally permissible under the statute and often unquestionably advisable as a practical matter. Creating a satisfactory financing statement, getting it filed in the appropriate place or places, and paying the filing fees for each filing is not of course a cost-free undertaking. At the same time it is not the hardest thing in the world to accomplish, and the costs both in time and money can be relatively little compared to the extra protection a permissible, even if not absolutely indispensable, filing affords to the secured party. A general rule of practice goes something like this: When in doubt, file.

What exactly constitutes "filing" under Article 9? Look to §9-516(a):

> Except as otherwise provided in subsection (b), communication of a record to a filing office and tender of a filing fee or acceptance of the record by the filing office constitutes filing.

This seems straightforward enough. In particular, take heart in the fact that once the secured party prepares a proper financing statement and presents it to the filing officer along with the correct filing fee, his or her job is done. If the filing officer refuses to accept it for some unjustified reason, the secured party presumably has a right to have the filing accepted as offered. If nothing else, should a question of whether and, if so, exactly when the interest was perfected were later to arise, the time of a proper presentation once adequately proven would be the moment of "filing."†

---

* Even if filing is a potential means of perfection in a given situation, it does not always work out that filing or filing alone is the *best* way for the secured party to perfect its interest. As we will see in chapters yet to come, there are instances where an interest perfected only by filing is in effect "trumped" by the interest of another party who has perfected by other means. Filing in all instances is certainly better than doing nothing, but the careful secured party may, given the circumstances, want to do more, that is, obtain possession of the collateral or "control" over it. The reasons for this have to do with certain special priority rules of the type we will take up in great detail in Part III.

† Article 9, as we will see, limits the situations in which a filing office can rightfully refuse to accept a proffered filing. In the pragmatic sense, of course, it is often easier and far more

You might wonder what happens if the filing officer does accept a filing that is later misplaced, misfiled within the system, or otherwise mishandled through the fault of this office. Even the best, most well-run systems, depending as they do on fallible human beings and at times temperamental computer systems, can make mistakes now and then. The kind of mistakes that may and, we have to assume, do occur in filing offices can mislead and seriously harm totally innocent third parties who rely on these filing systems for important information. The answer under §9-517 is that the filing is deemed effective and the state or county that runs the filing system may be responsible for the loss once it is established that a filing was duly made, as called for in §9-516(a), but didn't make its way to the proper place in the filing system or index. In a number of states a procedure has been put into place by which a small portion of all filing fees is placed into a fund to cover just such losses.

There is another point to mention before we move on to consider in greater detail exactly what must be filed. Note §9-502(d): "A financing statement may be filed before a security agreement is made or a security interest otherwise attaches." So on the question of when exactly to file, the answer has to be something to the effect of, "as soon as possible." Actually, the better answer might be, "even a little sooner than that." Financing statements can be and often are filed prior to the lender's actually making the loan and obtaining a security agreement and in fact prior to the lender's having made a final decision for itself, much less any commitment to the eager borrower, that it will agree to the loan being applied for. For reasons that will become easily appreciated as we move through later material on priorities, it is common practice and in no way inappropriate for a *potential* lender to ask the person making application for a loan to authorize the filing of a financing statement (or however many are needed under the circumstances given the number of places that filing will have to be made) covering the property the applicant intends to offer up as collateral. The potential lender will then file these financing statements in all the proper places. Following up on this a short time later, the potential lender will have a search conducted at just these same filing offices to see what financing statements have been filed under the applicant's name. Obviously the lender wants to be sure that its filings have been received and become effective notice to the world. It expects to find them turning up under a properly

---

reasonable simply to comply with whatever the person behind the filing desk wants of you than to make a federal case, or a state case, or any kind of case for that matter out of the predicament. There may be instances, to be sure, where it makes sense to stand up for one's principles and one's refined reading of the Code, but most of the time you will be primarily interested and your client's interests will be best served by your just getting the darn thing filed in the sense of accepted by the filing clerk. This cannot be stated as a general rule of law or even of practice, only a personal opinion; when in doubt leave the righteous indignation and the test case litigation to others.

conducted search. Beyond that, this search would turn up any *other party's* filed financing statements, if any exist, that the potential lender has to be aware of.* It will be particularly concerned if this search turns up any financing statement possibly covering the same collateral it is looking to as security filed prior to its own financing statement. Even if there is no such prior filing, if there is anything on record that muddies the waters, this would be the time, before any money has been lent or credit commitment made, to deal with it and clear up the situation. If the result of the potential lender's search is that its financing statement is properly in place and that no other statement covering the same collateral predates it, the lender can now rest easy, or at least as easy as one ever can when handling this kind of affair.

Under the system of priorities created by Article 9 that we will take up in later chapters, this potential lender can now make its decision knowing that it will be "first" on this collateral should it now enter into a security agreement taking such an interest in them. The procedure of "prefiling," as it is referred to, and the later follow-up search have in effect held this one party's place at the very front of the line and there will be no need for a frantic rush to the filing office to protect any interest it may later take in the collateral. If for some reason it decides not to make the loan or to take an interest in this particular collateral, or if the applicant determines to take its business elsewhere, the potential lender will be obligated to terminate its financing statement, thus relinquishing its place at the head of the line. The prefiling will become a bit of not particularly interesting prehistory. The various players can move on to other things with no harm done and hopefully no hard feelings on anyone's part.

WHAT TO FILE

Here's a very straightforward answer to the question of what to file: To perfect through filing the secured party must file an *initial financing statement* meeting the criteria of §9-502(a).† Read that subsection. An initial financing

---

* The prospective lender naturally will have asked the applicant whether or not anything else is on file of which it should be aware and which it will want to take into account in making its lending decision. The point here, of course, is that the prudent lender does not and cannot afford to rely solely on information supplied by the applicant. It must and will make an independent appraisal of the situation.

† If you look to §9-311(a) and (b) you will see that in some instances a filing of a different sort, or notation on a certificate of title for those rare types of personal property covered by title laws, may be "equivalent to the filing of a financing statement under" Article 9. The alternative filing or certification of title systems that are here being invoked are of limited application, and we will not delve into their workings. In any event, the cardinal point still holds: A filing, some filing, either under Article 9 or some system that Article 9 deems to be its equivalent is the default mechanism for perfection under the Article.

statement is sufficient only if it provides (1) the name of the debtor, (2) the name of the secured party, and (3) indicates the collateral that it is meant to cover. Each of these criteria is then covered in more detail in follow-up sections: The names of the debtor and the secured party in §9-503 and what constitutes an "indication" of the collateral in §9-504.

If a record containing these three pieces of information is filed with the appropriate filing office and that office accepts it, then perfection by filing has been accomplished. As a practical matter, the conscientious filer will want to include, as a matter of course, in the initial financing statement some information beyond what is called for in §9-502(a). Look at §9-516(b). A filing office is not obligated to accept, and indeed is expected to reject, a record received by it for a variety of reasons. Subsection (b)(4) allows for refusal if the record does not provide the name and a mailing address for the secured party. Under subsection (b)(5), the initial financing statement must also, if it is to be assured of acceptance by the filing office as a matter of law, provide a mailing address for the debtor, indicate whether the debtor is an individual or an organization, and if it is an organization, provide additional information about its type, jurisdiction of organization, and give an organizational identification number if one is available. Note also that under §9-516(b)(3)(C) a filing office may rightfully reject a initial financing statement where the debtor is an individual if the submitted record does not indicate the debtor's last name. See Comment 6 for an example.

Look to §9-520:

A filing office shall refuse to accept a record for filing for a reason set forth in Section 9-516(b) and may refuse to accept a record for filing *only* for a reason set forth in Section 9-516(b).

The emphasis here is, of course, mine. But I have no doubt the drafters of Revised Article 9 would not object. See the first paragraph of Comment 2 to §9-520. A principal objective of the revision process was to standardize the operation of filing offices across the country. Under practices as they had developed under the original Article 9, what it took to get a financing statement accepted by a filing office all too often seemed to depend on what office, or even which person in that office, you were dealing with. Revised Article 9 contains, as its predecessor did not, a set of provisions intended to rein in the discretion of and in fact to mandate performance standards for filing offices that keep the Article 9 records.

One of the main problems that filers had to deal with under the old regime was that different states had over time come up with different standardized (at least for that state) forms — suggested or preferred, if not exactly absolutely required — for the initial financing statement when that statement was being filed, as almost all have been in the past, in writing. Some forms were big (that is, $8\frac{1}{2}''$ by $11''$ or something close to it), some were small (New York's turned out to be $7\frac{3}{8}''$ by $5\frac{3}{4}''$), and some were, well, somewhere in the middle, if not necessarily "just right." Each standardized form might call for pretty much the same information to be filled in by the filing party, but the various states' forms would differ not just in size but in format.* A potential filer, if he or she wanted to be prepared for all contingencies, had to not only be savvy about the particular predilections of the filing officers in each state, but also have on hand a whole collection of different blank forms representing something like a grand tour around the union.[†]

The revision drafters sought to bring some uniformity and clarity to the situation by adopting, as a part of the statute itself, a uniform form of the written financing statement. (Remember that the filing of an initial financing statement or of any other form contemplated under Article 9 is done by "communication of a record" under §9-516, and that a record need not necessarily be a writing. We will pick up on electronic filing in the next section.) See §9-521(a): "A filing office that accepts written records may not refuse to accept a written initial financing statement in the following form and format except for a reason set forth in Section 9-516(b)." Carefully look over the form given, headed simply "UCC Financing Statement," but which does bear the legend "Form UCC1" in small print at the bottom. Such a form (presumably meant to be on standard $8\frac{1}{2}''$ by $11''$ paper, while it may not appear so in your copy of the Code) properly filled in must be accepted by any filing office. (The second page, headed "UCC Financing Statement Addendum," is required only if the additional space or special information called for on that form, for example if the collateral is timber to be cut or as-extracted collateral, is required to correctly file in the particular case.)

Read Comment 2 to §9-521. The forms laid out in the section are, as you see, not to be made mandatory but filers are strongly "encouraged" to use them, "inasmuch as the forms are well designed and avoid the risk of rejection on the basis of form or format." In addition, as the comment points out, the uniform forms have "been designed to reduce error by both filers and filing officers." Look, for example, at box 1 of the basic financing statement form. It is the place where the filer is to fill in the name of the debtor, or of the first debtor if there are more than one. The filer is, by the nature of the form, forced to address the question of whether the debtor in question is an organization or an individual. If an organization, he or she is

---

* About the only bit of consistency under the prerevision filing system was that the initial financing statement came to be known as a "UCC1" form, even though that term appeared nowhere in Article 9. As we'll see, this designation has been picked up, if only in a small way, by the revision drafters.

† As a practical matter, what the diligent filer would often do, not just as a matter of convenience but for safety's sake, when called upon to file in a jurisdiction with which he or she was not used to dealing, would be to call upon a commercial filing service to actually take care of the mechanics of the filing in question, preparing the form and approaching the filing office in the remote or mysterious jurisdiction.

led to the final line of the box and to the requirement of additional information for an organizational debtor. If the debtor is an individual, the filer is practically forced to put the last name where the last name goes and the first name where the first name goes. This may seem obvious, but failing to get the name right in this fashion had been an all too frequent problem for filers under the old Article 9 and the forms that the states used or recommended under it. Recall §9-516(b)(3)(C). The drafters of Revised Article 9 do not claim in Comment 2 to §9-521 to have provided forms that will eliminate such errors — how could they? — but the hope and expectation is that such goofs will be "reduced" to an appreciable extent.*

Notice that, under §9-523(a), "[i]f a person that files a written record requests an acknowledgment of the filing," then the filing office is required to send to that person an acknowledgment of the filing showing the unique file number assigned to it along with the date and time of the filing. As you can imagine, this acknowledgment copy will be of great importance to the filer for any number of reasons, not the least of which is to serve as evidence that the filing was carried out, and it would be a sloppy filer who did not make such a request as a matter of course.

Two final questions remain. First of all, what is the consequence if a filing office mistakenly accepts a financing statement that it should have rejected under §§9-516 and 9-520(a)? The answer is given in §9-520(c) and Comment 3 to that section: A financing statement accepted for filing by the filing office that should have been rejected but still satisfies the requirements of §9-502(a) is effective. Second, we ask the converse question: What is the result if a filing office refuses to accept for filing a financing statement that it has no right to reject under §9-520(a)? Generally, the financing statement is effective to perfect even if not filed. See §9-516(d):

> A record that is communicated to the filing office with tender of the filing fee, but which the filing office refuses to accept for a reason other than one set forth in subsection (b), is effective as a filed record except as against a purchaser of the collateral which gives value in reasonable reliance upon the absence of the record from the files.

The exception set forth at the end of this subsection is far from trivial, even if its full ramifications are not such as you could be expected to appreciate at the moment. As a practical matter, as Comment 3 to §9-516 points out, the filing office that does reject a record presented for filing is required to give the filer prompt notice of its refusal to accept the record. Whatever the reason for rejection, and whether it be proper or improper on the filing office's part, a persistent filer should not rest until a financing statement

---

* I have heard people speak of the new standardized forms of §9-521 as "user-friendly" and, perhaps more accurately, "if not idiot-proof, at least idiot-resistant."

correct in all details has been accepted for filing and appears properly indexed in the filing office's records. Whether this goal has been achieved is something the filer himself or herself can and should check by doing a follow-up post-filing search of the records.

THE WAVE OF THE FUTURE — ELECTRONIC FILING

All that has been said so far on filing of the financing statement presupposes filing of a paper form. That's the way it has been done in the past, and in the majority of cases that is still probably the way it is being done today. Filing involves creation of a paper form meeting certain criteria and getting the actual form into the hands of someone at the filing office. Because the purpose of all this is to convey certain information to the filing office so that the information can be put on the public record, is there really any need for all this shuffling of paper back and forth? We live, after all, in the information age, and have become used to (or will have to become used to if we are not to be left behind) the notion that information can travel from point to point, often much more cheaply and efficiently, through electronic means than by the old horse-and-buggy postal system or even modern overnight delivery services. Type it into the computer, turn on the modem, and send it on its way.

As you might expect, the concept of electronic filing — transmission of the relevant information to the filing office by electronic means rather than through delivery of a paper form — is making its way into the Article 9 notice filing system. As this is being written, filing through electronic means is already a possibility in several jurisdictions. Others are at one stage or another of experimenting with the technology that will be necessary and the practices that will have to be put in place for the possibility of electronic filing to be made readily available and reliable. By the time you are reading this, it is safe to assume, electronic filing will be a possibility, if not necessarily a requirement or the general norm, in a significant number of jurisdictions.

The drafters of Revised Article 9 took special care to ensure that their end product did nothing to discourage paperless filings made possible by advancing technology. Notice that any filing is referred to in this latest, more modern version of the article, as a "record communicated" to the filing office, which would include but not be limited to a writing delivered in hand or by post. As the revision drafters state toward the beginning of Comment 4h to §9-101, in the course of summarizing the most important changes they have made,

> This Article is "medium-neutral"; that is, it makes clear that parties may file and otherwise communicate with a filing office by means of records communicated and stored in media other than paper.

The revision drafters obviously contemplated that electronic filing will become more commonplace as time goes on, and, in fact, give an incentive to electronic filing by providing for lower filing fees when the filing is other than in writing (§9-525(a)).

The basic concept behind electronic filing, no matter what form the particulars take is that a filer would "fill in" an electronic form, either at some kind of dedicated terminal, through use of specially prepared and provided computer software installed on his or her own computer, or perhaps via the Web. The information to be supplied would have to be essentially that called for by the paper forms given in §9-521. The filer would by such means make an electronic connection with a computer at the filing office to which it would transmit this information.

THE PRACTICALITIES OF THE PRESENT — SEARCHING THE FILES

However it is done, on paper or via the most advanced electronic means, filing is not an abstract proposition or a mere legal technicality. The files serve a very practical function. People search the files every day. The information that they turn up — and just as importantly the information that doesn't turn up in the course of a proper search — will influence business decisions in a very real way. You should resist all temptation to think of the Article 9 filing system as some kind of musty repository of aging legal documents generated at some past time but whose relevance is dwindling as the ink on them fades. The Article 9 filing system is by and large not past history; it is a *current* listing of, well, what's on file, what Article 9 security interests are or may be claimed in any one particular debtor's property.

The function of the filing system is to give effective *notice* of certain claims that may be made on the debtor's property. As you will see in the examples to follow, what counts for a proper filing has to take into account how a party interested in gaining this information would search for a filing and what types of errors have the potential to mislead the searcher so as to deprive him or her of effective notice. The criteria of what must go into the financing statement are given in §§9-502(a) and 9-516(b), and as we have seen, standardized forms have been developed to help the filer meet these criteria. Still, mistakes are made all too often. Look at §9-506(a):

> A financing statement substantially satisfying the requirements of this part is effective, even if it has minor errors or omissions, unless the errors or omissions make the financing statement seriously misleading.

The presence of this subsection can be of some comfort to the secured party whose filing contains a minor error, but for the moment the more important lesson to be drawn comes from considering the broader implication of this statement. A financing statement that contains errors that are more than "minor" and that have the potential to "seriously mislead" someone searching through the files, trusting that his or her search will reveal the proper information, is not just a bit of unfortunate business for which the careless filer will be expected one day to make some kind of token amends. The mistaken filing is purely ineffective; it is of no more consequence than if it had never been filed at all. If the secured party is expecting to claim perfected status on the basis of the filing, if he or she aspires to have some advantage when the going gets rough against a bankruptcy trustee or another party who might be making some claim of an interest in the same collateral, then the mistaken and misleading filing is of simply no use.

What kinds of errors in the form of a filing will cause it to be mistaken and fail in its function of giving notice?* To understand this we have to have some appreciation of how people actually conduct searches through the Article 9 filings in any of the various filing offices where they may be held. Of prime importance is the fact that the basic Article 9 scheme assumes that financing statements are filed or indexed in any office *according to the name of the debtor.* Similarly, that's the way a search will be done. The searcher will first want to see if there are any financing statements on file under the name of the particular person or legal entity — as debtor — in which he or she, the searcher, has an interest. If there are any such filings, the searcher will want to look at them to see, by the indication given therein of the collateral, just what property of the debtor is or may be subject to another's interest. Finally, the searcher should be able to take from the filing the basic information on how to get in touch, should he or she need or want to, with the party listed as the secured party claiming such an interest. Remember this: There are several criteria called for to make the financing statement sufficient and effective, but it is the *name of the debtor* with which the search begins. You will therefore want to give special attention to §§9-503 and 9-506(b) and (c) in addressing Examples 2 through 6 that follow.

Examples

In the following examples, you may assume that the financing statement has been filed, either in writing or electronically, in the correct place and on a form of a generalized type acceptable by that office. The issue is whether it meets the substantive requirements of Article 9 for a "sufficient" financing statement.

---

* We deal in this chapter with *what* information must be in the financing statement and how it must be presented. The following chapter deals with the equally important question of *where* the financing statement must be filed in order to be effective.

6. Perfection by Filing: When and What to File

1. Dexter Moneybucks arranges to borrow a sum of money from a business acquaintance named Sandy. He signs a security agreement prepared by Sandy under which he gives a security interest in a valuable painting in his art collection ("Wealth is Health") to Sandy to secure the loan. Dexter later learns that Sandy has filed a financing statement covering the painting with the appropriate filing office.

   a. Does Dexter have any cause for complaint that the financing statement was filed without his signature or his express consent that such a financing statement could be filed by Sandy? See Comment 3 to §9-502 and §9-509(a) and (b).

   b. Assuming the financing statement filed by Sandy meets the criteria of §9-502(a), could there later be any problem for Sandy because it nowhere discloses the exact nature of Dexter's obligation to Sandy or the amount of the loan given by her?

2. Isabelle Inkster runs her printing business as an unincorporated sole proprietorship under the name "Fineline Printing." She obtains a loan from her local bank that asks her to authorize the filing of an initial financing statement, which it then files and in which the name of the debtor is given as "Fineline Printing Company."

   a. Has the bank perfected by this filing?

   b. What if the financing statement gave the name of the debtor as "Inkster, Isabelle" and then gave the name "Fineline Printing" as the name of an additional debtor?

   c. Suppose instead that Isabelle had incorporated her business under the name "Fineline Printing, Incorporated." Under what name would you suggest the bank file to perfect its interest?

3. David Moneybucks secures a small personal loan from a firm called Household Lenders. He is more than happy to sign his name to a security agreement that that firm has prepared correctly describing the collateral. He sees no reason to bother the loan officer by pointing out that the agreement renders his name as "Bucks, David Money." Household Lenders files a financing statement giving "Bucks, David M." as the debtor's name. When Household Lenders files this statement, has it perfected? Would it make any difference if it could be shown that no one had ever searched the files in question for any possible security interests on any of David's property during any of the time in question?

4. The debtor's name was Rodger House. A financing statement giving the debtor's name as "Roger House" was filed by the secured party in the proper form with the office of the Secretary of State of Kansas, which was the proper filing office given the circumstances. Was the secured party's interest perfected by this filing?

5. The debtor's name was "Matasar Innovations Incorporated." A financing statement giving the debtor's name as "Matasar Innovations Corporation" is filed by a creditor of the firm. What argument can this creditor make that its interest should be deemed to have been perfected? Should this argument succeed?

6. The debtor's name, as he was later to give it in his petition for bankruptcy, was "Terrance J. Kinderknecht." The secured party, John Deere & Company, filed an initial financing statement prior to the bankruptcy with the state of Kansas giving the debtor's name as "Terry J. Kinderknecht." Was the security interest properly perfected by this filing?

7. Dan runs a small delivery service ("Dan's Vans") using a number of vans that he has had for some time and that he now owns outright. He decides that the volume of his business justifies his buying an additional van and arranges to borrow the money he needs to purchase this vehicle, a 2008 Chevy van, from a lender, Trucker's Credit Service. The security agreement he signs gives the Credit Service an interest in "one 2008 Chevrolet delivery van owned by Dan and used in his business/Serial #56Z798Q." The financing statement filed by the Credit service describes the collateral only as "Equipment — one Chevrolet cargo van."
   a. Is this financing statement sufficient to perfect the Credit Service's security interest under Article 9? See §9-504.
   b. What if the description had read "Equipment — one 2008 Chevrolet cargo van serial number 56Z789Q?" Recall the correct serial number is "56Z798Q." Does this defeat the Credit Service's argument for perfection of its interest?

8. The debtor's address is 123 Main Street in Smallville. The financing statement gives the address as "132 Main Street."
   a. In your opinion, is this financing statement fatally flawed? What if it could be shown that Smallville is the type of small town where any mail misaddressed in this way would be delivered to the debtor at his true address without any problems or hesitancy by the post office?
   b. What if the address were left out entirely?

9. In negotiating to obtain a loan, Debtor agrees to put up as collateral all of its property, including its machinery, equipment, furniture, fixtures, inventory, and accounts receivable. The financing statement it authorizes lists all of these where a description of the collateral is called for. Through an oversight, however, the security agreement signed by Debtor describes the collateral as only "all machinery, equipment, furniture, and fixtures" owned by Debtor. It omits to mention the inventory and accounts receivable. Are these last two types of collateral subject to the lender's perfected security interest?

Explanations

1a. As the comment to §9-502 indicates, one of the significant changes made by the revision of Article 9 is that the revised version contains no requirement that the debtor, here Dexter, sign the financing statement for it to be effective. Looking at the form for the initial financing statement in §9-521(a), you'll note that there isn't a space provided for the debtor's signature even if he or she should, for some strange reason, want to sign the thing.

The question under Revised Article 9 is not whether the debtor signed the financing statement but rather if the filer, in this case Sandy, was *authorized* to file the statement. The issue of under what conditions a party is entitled to file a record is dealt with by §9-509. Section 9-509(a)(1) states that a person may file an initial financing statement "if the debtor authorizes the filing in an authenticated record." Subsection (b)(1) further provides that,

> By authenticating . . . a security agreement, a debtor . . . authorizes the filing of an initial financing statement . . . covering the collateral described in the security agreement.

Dexter having signed the security agreement describing the collateral as the painting has *ipso facto* (as the drafters say in Comment 4 to this section) authorized Sandy's filing of this initial financing statement.

1b. Assuming the financing statement meets the requirements of §9-502(a) and §9-516(b), Sandy's interest would have been perfected by the filing. There is nothing in Article 9 that calls for the financing statement to disclose *more* than what is called for in those provisions, and in particular there is no requirement that an examination of the financing statement give even the most savvy searcher any indication of the nature or extent of any obligation which Dexter may have to Sandy the performance of which is being secured by this interest. You can look again at the form set forth in §9-521(a). There are certain boxes to be filed in with information, but just as assuredly there is no space calling for disclosure of this type of information.

Note also the beginning of Comment 2 to §9-502:

> This section adopts the system of "notice filing." What is required to be filed is not, as under pre-UCC chattel mortgage and conditional sales acts, the security agreement itself, but only a simple record providing a limited amount of information (financing statement). . . . The notice itself indicates merely that a person may have a security interest in the collateral indicated. Further inquiry from the parties concerned will be necessary to disclose the complete state of affairs. Section 9-210 [which you may want to glance over now] provides a statutory procedure under which the secured party, at the debtor's request, may be required to make disclosure.

However, in many cases, information may be forthcoming without the need to resort to the formalities of that section.

The notice on file is not meant to give the searcher, once he or she has found it, the full story of the "state of affairs" between the debtor and the secured party. For that the searcher will have to make "further inquiry," as the comment says, from the parties themselves. The parties may then, as they wish, disclose more information, or they can tell the inquirer to mind his or her own business. The "notice function" of the filing is met by its giving the searcher reason to know that something is up, or perhaps better stated that something *may* be up, with regard to this particular debtor and this particular collateral of which he or she, the searcher, has to take heed — a situation which he or she ignores at his or her own peril.

2a. No. The bank has not perfected by filing under this name. The Code is wonderfully helpful on this point. Subsection 9-503(a)(4)(A) states what is necessary here to provide the debtor's name. Inkster is running the business as an unincorporated sole proprietorship, hence it is *her individual* name that must be given as the name of the debtor. Note also that, under §9-503(c), a financing statement that provides only the debtor's trade name will not do. Remember, this is not just a minor problem for the bank. By making an "insufficient" filing, here by giving the name incorrectly, it has totally undercut any hopes it placed in the filing as a means of perfection. It is exactly as if it had never bothered to prepare the financing statement at all, or having prepared it never took the extra step of submitting it (with the correct fee) to the appropriate filing officer. The incorrect filing is, in effect, a nullity for all intents and purposes.

For a recent case illustrating how the secured party's filing under the debtor's trade name can only spell disaster, see In re *FV Steel & Wire Co.*, 310 Bankr. 390, 2004 Bankr. LEXIS 748 (E.D. Wisc. 2004). The filing in the case was made on May 10, 2001, so the court technically had to evaluate it under the pre-revision version of Article 9. The rule had always been that filing under a trade name except under rare conditions was not sufficient, so the result was the same as it would be under Revised Article 9. The bankruptcy judge ruling on the matter could not, however, resist the opportunity to discuss the adoption of the revised article. The secured party's financing statement, as she noted, had been filed within 60 days of the effective date of the Revised Article 9, under which it was conceded the filing would have been insufficient "as a matter of law." Furthermore, "[a] multitude of seminars and articles heralded the advent of Revised Article 9." After citing a goodly number of the articles on point, she continued: "One of the mantras espoused by the experts was the necessity of using the debtor's correct legal name, not a trade name or nickname" on the financing statement.

> In this heady atmosphere of the adoption of Revised Article 9, PSC [the secured party] and the Debtor entered into the Agreement and PSC filed its financing statement. PSC knew the Debtor's correct legal name. . . . Given the impending adoption of Revised Article 9, with the publicity about the importance of using the debtor's correct legal name, and PSC's knowledge of the true corporate name, PSC ignored the correct legal name and filed under the trade name at its own peril.

2b. Yes. The security interest is perfected. The debtor's name was given correctly as the name of the individual even if the financing statement gave a so-called trade name by separately listing "Fineline Printing" on another line. See §9-503(b)(1).

You should be aware that not only individuals run businesses under so-called trade names. Partnerships and corporations may do so as well, and §9-503 is just as clear that it is the partnership's or the corporation's actual name, not the trade name, under which the filing has to be made, even if the trade name is separately given as well.

2c. You would insist, not just suggest, that the debtor's name be given as that of the corporation, "Fineline Printing, Incorporated." That is the one way under §9-503(a)(1) that it may read if the filing is to be effective. As Comment 2 points out, the term "registered organization" is defined in §9-102(a)(70) to include a corporation.

3. Household Lenders does not perfect by filing this financing statement. True, it has attempted to put the individual's name in the "debtor's name" box on the form, but it has gotten the name wrong. David's last name is Moneybucks. They filed as if the person was someone with the last name of Bucks. This is out-and-out wrong, and the bank's interest is never perfected by this filing.

The mix-up here might seem to you not so terribly serious. After all, someone seeing the financing statement might easily put two and two together and, with the additional information that the address given for the debtor is where good old David lives, figure out that there's been some minor foul-up or typo here and nothing to make such a big deal over. But remember the fundamental fact about the filing system — a searcher going to the records searches for any financing statement that may be on file and indexed *under the debtor's correct name*. Furthermore, we have to assume that the searcher approaches the files with no predisposition to believe that there actually is, any more than that there isn't, any filing on the debtor's property. A knowledgeable searcher *searching under the correct name* whose search turns up no filing or filings indexed under the specific debtor's name will have no reason to question the result of his or her efforts. To say the very least, only some fraction of all the people in any community have authorized financing statements that have then been put on file.

The Article 9 filing system is not, you should know, a hall of records in which each member of the community, however defined, has a file kept, even if in many instances the file folder is only an empty one. If that were the case, then the searcher looking for the David Moneybucks file and finding nothing might notice that something is amiss. He or she might even think it important to hunt around the records until the apparently misfiled paper turns up. But, as I've said, that isn't the way the Article 9 records are kept. The *absence* of any filings under a particular name is a search result. It allows the searcher affirmatively to conclude that no filings under that name have been made. The fact that someone, in this case the hapless Household Lenders, attempted to place a filing covering some of David's property on record is simply irrelevant. There is no way for the searcher to know, from a search of the records — searching for filings made under the correct name — ever to become aware of that fact. Searching through Article 9 filings today is almost invariably done by a computerized search through an electronic database maintained by the filing office. As we will explore more fully in later examples, the test for whether a filing is under the correct debtor's name (under §9-506(c)) is whether a search under the correct name of the debtor and using what is referred to as the "standard search logic" of the filing office would disclose the filing. There seems to me no question that a computer search requesting any filings on a person whose last name is Moneybucks is not going to turn up a filing where the last name is given as Bucks. Computers are, as you know, quite literal when it comes to determining what strings of alphanumeric characters "match." The five-letter character string "Bucks" is not going to be picked out by the very picky, if wonderfully fast and efficient in other ways, computer as a match for "Moneybucks." No way. The filing is bad. It is ineffective. It does not serve to perfect the lender's security interest.

This result does not change even if it were to be shown without question that no one actually *did* search the files for any financing statements under David Moneybucks's name as debtor at any time. The "integrity of the notice filing system," as it's sometimes said, depends on the notices being filed under the correct name. True, as we will soon have cause to discuss more fully, §9-506(a) gives the filer a bit of help with the statement that "A financing statement substantially satisfying the requirements of this part is effective, even if it has minor errors or omissions, unless the errors or omissions make the financing statement seriously misleading." Household Lenders' filing, however, *was* misleading, and undoubtedly seriously so.

4. The facts, short and not-so-sweet at least as far as the lender is concerned, come directly from the recent and much-noted case of *Pankratz Implement Co. v. Citizens National Bank*, 281 Kan. 209, 130 P.3d 57, 59 U.C.C.2d 53 (2006). The answer is no; the misspelling of the debtor's name in this filing is sufficiently serious to render it ineffective to perfect. This might seem to you a particularly slight, and, we may assume, perfectly innocent, error on the filer's part. You look at §9-506(a) and its declaration that a financing statement "substantially satisfying" the requirements of the section is not to be considered ineffective because of "minor errors."

    Read on, however, to subsection (b) of that section:

    > Except as otherwise provided in subsection (c), a financing statement that fails to sufficiently provide the name of the debtor in accordance with Section 9-503(a) is seriously misleading.

    For reasons that we can now readily appreciate, mistakes in the name of the debtor are singled out for special attention. And what does subsection (c) have to say?

    > If a search of the records of a filing officer under the debtor's correct name, using the filing office's standard search logic, if any, would disclose a financing statement that fails sufficiently to provide the name of the debtor in accordance with Section 9-503(a), the name provided does not make the financing statement seriously misleading.

    It is hard to imagine any "standard search logic," or just about any logical search for that matter, designed to bring to light any financing statements carrying a certain debtor by his, her, or its name that would disclose a statement filed where the name was spelled incorrectly, if only by one letter, the lack of that one "d" in the debtor's first name. But the question did not have to be considered in the abstract, of course. It was conceded that a search in the files of the Kansas Secretary of State's office using that office's standard search logic under the correct name would not have disclosed the lender's filing under the misspelled debtor's name. That in effect decided the matter under the language of §9-506(b) and (c). The lender attempted to make the argument that a "diligent searcher" would have conducted a broader search, looking for example at likely misspellings of the correct name, common abbreviations which a filer might have resorted to of words in the name, and the like. This so-called "diligent searcher" test was in fact the generally received test developed by the courts under the pre-revision version of Article 9. But then that earlier version of the statute contained only the language which now is found in §9-506(a).

The revision drafters, as we have noted, added to this section subsections (b) and (c), and in doing so they meant to do away with what was undoubtedly a very vague test to say the least, by its nature never quite clear about what it called for a "diligent" searcher to contemplate and guard itself against in the way of likely filing errors. At the same time, the "diligent searcher" approach could be very forgiving, arguably too much so, of such errors on the filer's part.

The Supreme Court of Kansas discussed the change contemplated by the revision drafters in its *Pankratz* decision:

> Darrell W. Pierce, chair of the Article 9 Filing Project and member of the Article 9 Study Committee for the Permanent Editorial Board of the UCC, wrote that "case law that has served to protect filers at the expense of searchers by giving effect to filings not readily retrievable by a search will be overturned by Revised Article 9 . . . and, in doing so obviates the need for complicated search logics and multiple name searches." Pierce, *Revised Article 9 of the Uniform Commercial Code: Filing System Improvements and Their Rationale*, 31 UCC L.J. 16, 17 (1998).
>
> Harry Sigman sat on the Revised Article 9 Drafting Committee, and wrote that Article 9 "does not provide an absolute requirement of perfection. At the same time, it does not burden searchers with the obligation to dream up every potential error and name variation and perform searches under all possibilities. Revised Article 9 allows a searcher to rely on a single search conducted under the correct name of the debtor and penalizes filers only for errors that result in the nondisclosure of the financing statement in a search under the correct name." Sigman, *The Filing System Under Revised Article 9*, 73 Am. Bank. L.J. 61, 73 (1999).

After having cited a few other U.C.C. luminaries to the same effect, the court concluded that

> the primary purpose of the revision in the name requirement is to lessen the amount of fact-intensive, case-by-case determinations that have plagued earlier versions of the UCC, and to simplify the filing system as a whole. The object of the revisions was to shift the responsibility to the filer by requiring the not too heavy burden of using the legal name of the debtor, thereby relieving the searcher from conducting numerous searches using every conceivable name variation of the debtor. The effect is to provide more certainty in the commercial world and reduce litigation to determine whether an adequate search was done.

5. The debtor's name has not been rendered perfectly in the financing statement, but this may be one of the few instances where, even under the strict test of §9-506(c), this error may turn out not to be seriously misleading. Apparently, in most instances the "standard search logic" of the type that a filing office may adopt is programmed to ignore a list of what are often referred to as "noise words" such as "a," "and," "for," and "the." A standard search logic may — but the key

word here is *may* — also cull all or some symbols (such as &, periods, or commas) other than the 26 letters used in the English language and the ten numeric characters before it performs the task of checking whether or not two strings of characters match. Spaces may, or *may not*, be ignored. Some offices use search logics that strip off, and thus ignore for matching purposes, a lengthy set of words like "corporation," "incorporated," "limited," and the like as well as common abbreviations of such words — at least if they appear at the end of the name and not somewhere in the middle. Thus, a search under the correct name, "Matasar Innovations Incorporated," might well be expected to disclose the filing made under the name "Matasar Innovations Corporation." It would all depend, of course, on how the standard search logic of the particular filing office has been set up.

A problem that has to be noted with the new bright-line test of §9-506(c) is that the various filing offices around the country have not seen fit to adopt a single consistent standard search logic, and the search logics adopted at least initially by many of the states could legitimately be criticized as, let us say, less than ideal. This has led to some recent cases which, on first reading, do seem to be exceptionally harsh on the filing party. See, for example, In re Tyringham Holdings, Inc., 354 Bankr. 363, 61 U.C.C.2d 339 (E.D. Va. 2006), in which the court held that a filing under "Tyringham Holdings" was not sufficient where the debtor's name was "Tyringham Holdings, Inc." and the search logic in use in Virginia at the time of filing did not render these equivalent. See also Host America Corp. v. Coastline Financial, Inc., 2006 U.S. Dist. LEXIS 35727, 60 U.C.C.2d 120 (D. Utah 2006). In that case a filing had been made in Utah giving the debtor's name as "KWM Electronics Corporation." As it turned out, even after trial the parties could not agree as to exactly what the true name of the debtor was, either "K.W.M. Electronics Corporation" or the same but with spaces after each of the periods, but the court held this not to matter as there was no dispute that the true name did have periods in K.W.M., that the filing didn't, and that the periods — or the lack thereof — made a difference under the search logic in use at the filing office at the crucial time of filing. It is to be hoped that results such as these become fewer and fewer as the states adopt more "reasonable" or "intelligent" official search logics — whatever exactly that would mean — and then makes the exact rules under which its computerized system is working more readily available and comprehensible to all potential filers.

6. The secured party was filed under the debtor's nickname, not his full legal name. The answer, you would think, should be obvious. A search using the standard search logic (if the standard search logic was logical) under the correct legal name would *not* be expected regularly to bring up

the filing name under the nickname, as in fact it did not in the real situation on which the example is based. So the filing would obviously, under the rules as we've been studying them, not be valid. Note that it's just a coincidence in this situation that the proper name and the nickname even start with the same letter, as anyone named Antonio who's known to his friends as Tony could tell you.

It was therefore surprising, as it should be surprising to you, that the bankruptcy court judge who first confronted the question reached the conclusion that Deere's filing was valid. In re Kinderknecht, 300 Bankr. 47, 51 U.C.C.2d 1234 (Bankr. D. Kan. 2003). The judge's reasoning, such as it was, did not rely on any finding that a search under what he characterized as the debtor's "legal name," that is Terrance, would find a filing under his nickname, Terry. Rather the judge, stressing the fact that §§9-502(a), 9-503, and 9-506 all called for filing in the debtor's "name" or "individual name" and not his "legal name," did not require that only a filing in the legal name would do.

> Although a financing statement must include the name of the debtor, Part 5 offers no guidance on what constitutes the "the name of the individual debtor," i.e., whether the name of the debtor may be a nickname as opposed to a legal name. Nor do the sections indicate when the name of the debtor may be deemed sufficient.

The judge did note that the standard form found in §9-521(a) does ask for the debtor's "full legal name," but observing that since this is a suggested form only and not actually required of any filer, "[i]f filers are not bound to use the form, they are not bound to use the debtor's legal name in a financing statement." In short, the judge concluded that since "a commonly used nickname" may be a correct name for the debtor, if not the only one, a filing under such a nickname is sufficient to meet the requirements of Article 9.

Could this result possibly be right? The decision caused a good deal of criticism and consternation in the "Article 9 community" as soon as it became known. Would a diligent search now have to search under not just the legal name of a individual but under any other name under which he or she might be "commonly known"? Fortunately, the trustee in bankruptcy was allowed to make an expedited appeal directly to the Bankruptcy Appellate Panel for the Tenth Circuit, skipping the district court stage usual in such proceedings. The trustee was, in fact, supported in his argument for a reversal in an amicus brief submitted by the Secretary of State of Kansas, charged with maintaining the database used to track the filing of financing statements in Kansas and with promulgating the "standard search logic" for conducting searches of that database. In April of 2004, the Appellate Panel, examining both the literal wording and the overall intention of Part 5 of Revised Article 9, as well as the practical consequences of the bankruptcy court's conclusion, issued its ruling, which was a stern reversal.

> [W]e conclude that the bankruptcy court erred in holding that Deere's financing statements were sufficient and served to perfect its interests in the debtor's property. For the financing statement to be sufficient under Kansas law, the secured creditor must list an individual debtor by his or her legal name, not a nickname.

In re Kinderknecht, 308 Bankr. 71, 53 U.C.C.2d 167 (Bankr. App. 10th Cir. 2004). This Appellate Panel decision, which was relied upon by the courts in all of the cases cited earlier in discussion of Examples 4 and 5, is well worth reading, as a review of the "debtor's name" problem.

The eventual result of the Kinderknecht litigation — that filing under a nickname will not meet the requirements of the revised Article 9 — has more recently been adopted in two cases both of which found that the use of "Mike" was seriously misleading when the debtor's name was "Michael." See In re Berry, 2006 Bankr. LEXIS 2579, 61 U.C.C.2d 95 (Bankr. D. Kan. 2006), and In re Borden, 353 Bankr. 886, 61 U.C.C.2d 223 (Bankr. D. Neb. 2006).

The lessons to be gleaned from this and the three prior examples, lessons for the secured party, could not be clearer. First of all, make sure you know the *exact* name of the debtor you are dealing with. An individual debtor may tell you, "Just call me Liz," but is that her true first name? Might it be Elizabeth, or even Elisabeth? Or maybe her true first name is one to which she has taken a dislike and Liz is really her middle name. Liz can call herself what she likes, and in conversation with her you might as well address her as she wishes, but for the purpose of filing a financing statement and perfecting a valuable security interest, nothing but the correct legal name as called for by §9-503(a) will do. Second, of course, is to be sure that the correct name is given on the financing statement. Especially now that computers, which can be very literal and unforgiving beasts, are doing most of the searching, even the most seemingly minor error in rendering the name may render the entire filing "seriously misleading" and thus totally ineffective. The result will be no different than if no attempt at filing had been made at all. The interest will not be perfected by a seriously misleading filing.

7a. Exactly how precise and detailed the description of collateral has to be in the financing statement is not an easy question to answer. I tend to think that this description, "Equipment — one Chevrolet cargo van," if truly challenged in court, would probably not quite pass muster, but it's a close call. There wouldn't be any problem if the description were as it is in the security agreement. It doesn't tell us everything about the van one might want to know, but the serial number does about as good a job in describing it as could be expected in the space provided for on the standard initial financing statement form. Section 9-504(1) says that a financing statement sufficiently indicates the collateral that it covers "if the financing statement provides a description of the collateral pursuant to Section 9-108."

Recall that §9-108(a) instructs us that for Article 9 purposes a description of personal property is "sufficient, whether or not it is specific, if it reasonably identifies what is described." Comment 2 to this section seems to support finding a description such as we have here, even if the serial number of the van is missing, sufficient for the purposes of the financing statement. The "job assigned" to the description in the financing statement, after all, is only to meet the goal of a "notice filing" system. Anyone searching the records trying to determine whether Dan had granted any security interest in his new Chevy van, or any of his personal property for that matter, would come across this financing statement and would be put on notice that, at least possibly, something's up with respect to the particular van (#56Z789Q) in question.

The term that you hear sometimes in this regard is "inquiry notice," which suggests that once the searcher is given the kind of information from which he or she would know to inquire further, and in addition some indication of where to inquire, or whom to ask for more details, the description in the financing statement is sufficient for its purposes. In the situation as I've presented it, anyone coming upon this financing statement would, you could argue, have no trouble in contacting Dan or going over to his location and finding one and only one Chevrolet cargo van. Isn't this the end of the story? Well, no. First of all, Dan may have any number of other vans of this make. What then? Certainly the searcher could ask Dan to which one this particular filing applies, but how is the inquirer to know if he or she is getting the straight answer — or, for that matter, that Dan himself is able to keep such things straight, what with his business booming and all, and that his memory serves him correctly?

Courts can be sympathetic to the notion that the financing statement need not in and of itself tell all of the story, but they are understandably wary lest the concept of "inquiry notice" be expanded to the point where just about anything placed in the financing statement ("Certain personal property owned by debtor as agreed"?) seems to meet the bill leaving the searcher, entitled to at least some kind of reliable notice from what he or she finds in the hall of records, to go searching aimlessly. While it's hard to draw any hard and fast lines on an issue like this — other than that a careful filer so identifies the collateral that the issue never even arises — the courts seem to insist on at least enough information in the filing itself so that the searcher, if he or she does have to make further inquiry, will know pretty much for certain where to look and that his or her one further inquiry will definitively settle the question of exactly what property the filing is meant to cover, without having to rely on various individuals' suspect memories or later reconstructions of what should have been clear in the first place.

Consider, for example, a situation that comes up all too often. Through someone's foul-up no Schedule A is attached to the financing statement that describes the collateral in terms such as "all equipment of the debtor as listed in Schedule A attached hereto." Certainly it is true that someone coming upon this financing statement whose search is meant to uncover any security interests granted by the particular debtor in any or all of its equipment could, and would if he or she had any sense, not make a move until he or she had followed up, asking the debtor for a copy of this "Schedule A" among other things. Does this mean that the financing statement *minus* the schedule is sufficient under §9-502(a)? The courts usually say no. Perhaps this would squeak by if the relevant Schedule A had indeed been produced and was in existence at the time of the filing and there was some independent and trustworthy way to verify exactly what it said at the time and says to this day. If, however, as is all too often the case, the parties had never really made up a schedule but are offering now to tell the world what the schedule would comprise had they made up one, the answer is pretty surely that they should forget it. The filing doesn't describe the collateral sufficiently.

We return at the end to the situation with which we began: Dan and his vans. Recall that the filing in question described the one van subject to the creditor's interest only as "Equipment — one Chevrolet cargo van." We may know that a searcher coming upon this filing and making just the right inquiry of Dan could satisfy himself or herself without any elaborate time-consuming process and without having to rest on difficult speculation regarding exactly what Chevy van is being referred to, but there is nothing on the form itself that assures the viewer that this further inquiry would be not only warranted but productive and bring quick closure to the matter. Looked at from this perspective, I tend to think the description is probably not good enough, but as I said at the outset it could be a close call. I can imagine a court going either way on it. I certainly can imagine all the people at Trucker's Credit Service being more than a little upset with whoever it was who didn't take the extra effort to add to the filing the serial number or some other identifying information that in effect describes this van and this van only which would have avoided the whole problem right from the beginning.

7b. You might think that this description, being actually wrong and not just incomplete, might make things even tougher for Trucker's Credit Service, but there's probably nothing here that would invalidate the filing or jeopardize Trucker's Credit's perfection. Revisit §9-506(a). Unless Dan has a large number of vans and the serial numbers are nearly the same, this is almost certainly a "minor error" that would not be "seriously misleading."

You will want to compare this situation to the one given in Example 4, where the error at issue was one letter rendered incorrectly in the name of the debtor. You see how different the cases really are. It has to do with the important factor that financing statements must not only contain the name of the debtor along with some other information; they are filed and indexed by that name. One letter wrong in the way the debtor's name is given may easily be seriously misleading. A searcher checking for filings under the correct name for the debtor would *never even become aware* of the mistaken filing's existence. That's quite a different matter from a filing found containing a typo or slipup such as the one in our example in other information that the searcher could reasonably expect to see for what it is — if he or she notices it at all — and that should clear up any potential ambiguity and answer any questions. This is just the kind of situation for which §9-506(a) was included in Article 9. Look to Comment 2 to the section.

There will, of course, be cases in which the collateral description will be not only in error but "seriously misleading," rendering the filing insufficient. In the recent case of In re Pickle Logging, Inc., 286 Bankr. 181, 49 U.C.C.2d 971 (M.D. Ga 2002), an erroneous serial number given for a particular piece of equipment was found to render the financing statement seriously misleading and ineffective to perfect as to that piece of collateral. The debtor, Pickle Logging, Inc., had financed eight pieces of equipment with Deere Credit, Inc. One of the eight pieces, a 548G skidder serial number DW548GX568154, had been misidentified in both the security agreement and the financing statement as a 648G skidder, serial number DW648GX568154. The secured creditor argued that the serial number error was not "seriously misleading" as it was off by only one digit and that "a person of ordinary business prudence would be put on notice to inquire further about the 548G skidder despite the mislabeling." As it happens, however, there is such a thing as a 648G skidder and that, as an expert witness testified, a 548G skidder "is substantially different in appearance, performance, and price from a 648G skidder." The debtor, in fact, owned at least two 548G skidders and at least two 648G skidders. The court stated,

> The description [if inaccurate] merely needs to raise a red flag to a third party indicating that more investigation may be necessary to determine whether or not an item is subject to a security agreement. A party does not lose its secured status just because the description includes an inaccurate serial number. However if the serial number is inaccurate, there must be additional information that provides a "key" to the collateral's identity.
>
> Here, the description in the security agreement and the financing statement are identical. Both documents list a 648 skidder with the serial number DW648GX568154. There is nothing obviously wrong with the model number or the serial number. 648G is a model number for one type of skidder sold by [Deere & Co.]. The serial number listed for the disputed skidder is in accordance with other serial numbers issued by [Deere]. The insurance value listed on the security agreement for the disputed skidder is only $10,000 less than the 648G skidder, serial number DW648GX564990. With the $35,000 difference in insurance values between the 648G-4990 skidder and the 648G skidder, serial number DW648GX57391 skidder, a $10,000 difference in insurance values would not raise a red flag.

The court concluded that if just the model number or if just the serial number had been incorrect the result "may" have been different. "If the model number was not repeated in the serial number, then it would be apparent that something was wrong with one of the two numbers. . . . However, with both numbers reflecting a 648G skidder, there is nothing to indicate that there was a mistake." The court concluded that the skidder being misdescribed in both the security agreement and the financing statement, the trustee's rights in the one item were superior to that of Deere Credit.

8a. Given the circumstances, I would argue that the financing statement is effective if a wrong address is the only problem with it. Section 9-516(b)(5)(A) requires inclusion of "a mailing address for the debtor" and what we have here is technically wrong. This would be another instance where §9-506(a) could come into play to discourage, in the language of Comment 2, "a fanatical and impossibly refined" reading of the statutory requirement. The error could be considered "minor" and one that would not "seriously mislead" anyone. The situation would, of course, be different, if the address was so far off or if the city so large and filled with people of names like the debtor's that there was in fact a possibility of a reasonable misunderstanding about to whom exactly the filing was meant to refer. See, for instance, In re Grabowski, 277 Bankr. 388, 47 U.C.C.2d 1219 (Bankr. S.D. Ill. 2002).

8b. The complete absence of any address for the debtor would require the filing office to reject the filing under §9-516(b)(5). If, however, the filing were somehow accepted by the filing office in spite of this omission, the financing statement would be deemed "sufficient" under §9-502(a). See §9-520(c) and Comment 3 to this section.

9. This example is based on the well-known case of In re Martin Grinding & Machine Works, Inc., 793 F.2d 592, 1 U.C.C.2d 1329 (7th Cir. 1986), decided, of course, under the original version of Article 9. The court in that case held that the lender's security interest extended only to the property listed in the written security agreement and not to the inventory and accounts receivable. These last two types of possible collateral were, it was true, referred to in the financing statement (and in other loan documents as well), but, the court concluded,

> where the security agreement clearly grants a specific, unambiguous security interest, parol evidence cannot enlarge the security interest beyond that stated in the security agreement.

In deciding Martin Grinding, the Seventh Circuit had before it the task of interpreting the Code as adopted in Illinois; it was necessarily guided by prior decisions of the Illinois courts and by additional Official Commentary appended to the then-applicable Illinois version of §9-203. Significantly, as the court pointed out, that commentary bore the following warning to practitioners:

> [B]ear in mind that a difference in the description between the security agreement and the financing statement can lead to serious problems, if the difference involves omission of items of collateral from either document. The security agreement and the financing statement are double screens through which the secured parties' [sic] rights to the collateral are viewed, and his rights are to be measured by the narrower of the two.

And thus we have what has come to be referred to as the "Double Filter Rule" to guide us in an instance such as this, where there is an inconsistency between the description of collateral in the security agreement and the financing statement or other loan documents. The security interest can attach to no more than what is legitimately described in the security agreement. The other documents cannot extend the reach of attachment to anything else. And if the interest does not attach to any particular property, it certainly cannot subject that property to a perfected security interest, no matter what the financing statement may say. Other courts, themselves not bound by Official Illinois Commentary, have come to the same conclusion applying the prerevision Article. See, for example, In re Soden-Mardane Excavating, Inc., 178 Bankr. 631, 25 U.C.C.2d 1263 (M.D. Pa. 1994). I can think of no reason why the secured party could expect to fare any better under the recent revision. Once again we see, if we ever had any doubt, that getting the paperwork or electronic records right is fundamental to successful practice under Article 9.

CHAPTER 7

Perfection by Filing: Where to File

INTRODUCTION

Even the most meticulously and beautifully completed form of initial financing statement means little if it isn't filed in the proper place. It should go without saying that by "filing" we don't mean placing the financing statement tidily in just the right folder in our own internal office filing system, or keeping it stowed away in a vault with other company records. We know from §9-516(a) that,

> [e]xcept as otherwise provided in subsection (b) [which gives the filing office the right to refuse a submission under certain limited circumstances], communication of a record to a filing office and tender of the filing fee or acceptance of the record by the filing office constitutes filing.

What we need for our internal records, and for our peace of mind, is good and sufficient evidence that this *official filing* was carried out as it had to be. The evidence we really need will usually come in the form of an "acknowledgment" of acceptance of our filing that we may request and are entitled to receive (under §9-523(a) or (b)) from the filing office to which the filing has been physically delivered or electronically communicated.

So filing in the Article 9 sense of the word means filing with some "filing office" that will be an office run by or on behalf of the state either at the state's capitol or at a local level. Our concern and the subject of this chapter isn't finding *some* filing office somewhere willing to accept the form and the fee that comes with it. The trick is to find the right one. Filing with other than the correct office is of no good whatsoever. It will no more serve to perfect an interest than if no filing were made at all, anywhere. Only by filing in the correct office as called for under Article 9 will a filing be effective to perfect a security interest or an agricultural lien.

The problem of determining which office is the right office can be separated into two separate questions. First of all, to *what office* of the state, the central office or a local one, should the filing be presented? Second, in *which state* is the filing to be made? Before getting into further details, it really has to be pointed out that the Revised Article 9 makes the analysis of both of these two questions dramatically easier than what we would have encountered were we looking at secured transactions as governed by the old version of Article 9, and as practicing lawyers have had to contend with for decades prior to the adoption of Revised Article 9. A clearer and greatly simplified organization of the Article 9 filing system is without any question one of the truly significant, probably the most significant, of the changes brought about by the revision process. A high percentage of cases brought under prerevision Article 9 dealt with mistakes, or with what were argued to be mistakes, involving how and where a secured party had gone about filing a financing statement. The rules of Revised Article 9, which we will be examining in this chapter, greatly reduce the possibility of a secured party's filing in the wrong place within a jurisdiction or making a filing in the wrong jurisdiction.

Note, for starters, §9-501(a), which deals with the question of where within a state to file. Putting aside, as we should feel free to do, the question of transmitting utilities, "if the local law of this State governs perfection of a security interest or agricultural lien, then the filing office in which to file a financing statement to perfect the security interest or agricultural lien is," with some highly specialized exceptions given in subsection (a)(1), set forth in subsection (a)(2). Filling in the blanks in that subsection as the drafters asked the legislature of the state to do, the place for all filings other than those covered by (a)(1) will most often read simply "the office of the Secretary of State."

So the place for filing almost all financing statements within a state is at one central office run by the state. This is referred to as "central filing" to distinguish it from "local filing" at the county or town level, which was much more prevalent under the old Article 9. In fact, under that version of the article, different states were allowed to and did have different rules as to where an initial filing statement had to be filed in order to be effective. Some states' version of Article 9 called for central filing in all instances. Some states, however, required filing covering certain types of collateral locally and others at the state level. Still a third group of states required that identical filings under some (poorly defined) circumstances be made at both the local and the state level. Yes, it was a mess, but a mess that now has been effectively cleared away. See Comment 2 to §9-501. Revised Article 9 "dictates central filing for most situations, while retaining local filing for real-estate-related collateral and special filing provisions for transmitting utilities."*

Which brings us to the second question: In which *state* should the financing statement be filed? Note that §9-501 (a) says that the filing should be done in the state whose version of Article 9 we are consulting "if the local law of this State governs perfection of a security interest or agricultural lien." The question therefore becomes which state's law governs issues of perfection? Turn now to §9-301, noting that it is the first of a series of sections in Revised Article 9 (in Part 3, Subpart 1) providing us with the choice-of-law rules relating to perfection and priority. For our purposes, to determine which state's law governs the perfection of a security interest in most forms of collateral where perfection by filing is concerned, the general rule is found in §9-301(1):

> Except as otherwise provided in this section, while a debtor is located in a jurisdiction, the local law of that jurisdiction governs perfection, the effect of perfection or nonperfection, and the priority of a security interest in collateral.

As Comment 4 to this section explains,

> Paragraph (1) contains the general rule: the law governing perfection of security interests in both tangible and intangible collateral, whether perfected by filing or automatically [with which we'll deal in Chapters 9 and 10], is the law of the jurisdiction of the debtor's location as determined under Section 9-307.

As the comment goes on to discuss in the next paragraph — which I wouldn't suggest there is any reason for you to read unless you have a particular interest in how difficult things used to be in applying the pre-revision version of Article 9 — Paragraph (1) of Revised §9-301 "substantially simplifies the choice-of-law rules" from what they had been prior to

---

* Note that the only local filings now provided for under Revised Article 9, where the collateral is what the comment refers to as "real-estate-related collateral" — as-extracted collateral, timber to be cut, or goods that are or are to become fixtures — is, under subsection (a)(1), filing in the *real estate recording system* of the locality. Prior to the revision, counties or other localities in most of the states had to keep a separate recording system of U.C.C. Article 9 filings, a whole set of files separate from the real estate records. In fact, it was estimated that between the state and local recording systems, there were over 4,300 filing offices around the country where a secured party might conceivably file a financing statement. That number has now, as you can see, been drastically reduced, much to our relief. There will be one central Article 9 filing office in each state, as well as the one in the District of Columbia and those few other jurisdictions that operate under the Uniform Commercial Code (e.g., Guam and the U.S. Virgin Islands). We will deal with fixtures and the special case of the fixture filing in Chapter 15. Other than that, we can now justifiably consider questions of whether to file locally or at the state's cental filing office as relics of a bygone era.

the revision. The question of where to file to perfect a security interest has been reduced (with some exceptions given in §§9-303 through §§9-306, which need not concern us here) to the issue of in which jurisdiction the debtor is "located."*

Determining exactly where a debtor is located might seem at first something that could turn out to be far from easy, at least in some situations. Here, again, the drafters of Revised Article 9 have anticipated our possible problems. Turn now to §9-307. The general rules for determining a debtor's location are set out in subsection (b). As you can see:

1. A debtor who is an individual is located at the individual's principal residence;
2. A debtor that is an organization [on which see §1-201(28) or §1R-201(b)(25)] and has only one place of business is located at its place of business;
3. A debtor that is an organization and has more than one place of business is located at its chief executive office.

Section 9-307 does define the term "place of business" in subsection (a), but leaves undefined both "principal residence" and "chief executive office." The drafters do give us some help should these terms give us trouble in Comment 2, which is definitely worth a read at this point.

The general rules of subsection (b) for locating the debtor are subject to some exceptions (aren't there always exceptions?), only one of which we will need to consider. It is, however, a most important one. Under subsection (e), "A registered organization that is organized under the law of a State is located in that State." What exactly is a *registered organization?* See §9-102(a)(70).

With all this help served up by the revised version of Article 9 — help to us both as students now taking on the law of secured transactions for the first time and even more importantly as those who expect to put what we are learning into practice in the not-too-distant future — the question of where to file a financing statement in order to be sure of perfection, once one of the most devilishly tricky and maddening aspects of this subject, has become one of the most straightforward parts of the whole enterprise.[†] For which you will undoubtedly be most grateful as you work through the Examples that follow.

---

* You should note at this time that under §9-302, perfection of an agricultural lien is determined by the jurisdiction in which the farm products covered by the lien are located.
† You may start having some question at this point about what is going to happen if you get the filing correct initially, but then something changes. What happens, for example, if an individual debtor changes his or her principal place of residence or if a corporate debtor reincorporates under the laws of a different jurisdiction? In Chapter 12 we'll deal with such changes in an orderly fashion. This chapter is concerned only with what will be the correct place to file initially when perfection through the means of filing is first undertaken.

Examples

1. Sheila Ivories, who lives in an apartment in New York City, works in the field of certified public accounting. In need of some ready cash, she arranges for a loan from her bank, Downtown Federal, agreeing to give the bank a security interest in an expensive Steinmetz baby grand piano that she had inherited some years ago and that sits prominently in the living room of her New York apartment. Sheila signs a security agreement giving Downtown Federal a security interest in the piano to secure her repayment of the loan. The bank prepares a financing statement covering the piano naming itself as the secured party and "Ivories, Sheila" as the debtor.

   a. Where should the bank file the financing statement in order to perfect its interest?

   b. Would your answer be any different if Sheila was, instead of a CPA, a professional pianist who regularly used the piano for the purpose of practicing her art at home?

   c. What if the bank, Downtown Federal, was located in New Jersey?

   d. Suppose instead that the piano was located at a country house that Sheila owns in Litchfield County, Connecticut. Sheila visits her country home about two or three weekends a month, and it is there that she takes a break from her hectic life and plays the piano. Does this change your answer?

2. Barton Blackies also owns a piano, this time a concert grand Steinmetz, which he keeps in the penthouse apartment in Chicago where he lives throughout the year. Barton bought the piano several years ago with the intention of learning to play it, but has never gotten around to doing so. He decides it is time to sell the Steinmetz. He quickly finds a willing buyer, one Patricia Pedals. Barton assures Patricia that he owns the piano free and clear of any encumbrances, but Patricia is smart enough to know that she should check on her own to be sure that no party could claim a security interest in the piano that could affect the value of the piano should she buy it. Patricia is going to check the Article 9 filing system to see if any financing statement has been filed that might give its filer a perfected security interest in the piano. The question here is not where to file, but where to search. In what filing system, and for that matter under what name, should Patricia *search* in order to protect herself against any later surprises?

3. Dexter Moneybucks arranges for a loan from a friend, Sandra, agreeing to give Sandra a security interest in a valuable sculpture ("Free Market Figure") that is part of his extensive collection of classic and modern art strewn around a palatial home he owns in North Salem, New York. As it turns out, Dexter also owns a condo in Tampa, Florida, where he

spends most of the fall and winter months, returning to North Salem for the spring and summer. Where would you suggest Sandra file in order to assure herself that she has perfected her interest in the sculpture?

4. Dr. Tooth, a dentist, lives in a modest but comfortable home in Montclair, New Jersey. His dental practice is located in midtown Manhattan. Tooth arranges for a small business loan with the Gotham State Bank of New York in order to buy some new, more state-of-the-art dental equipment for his office, granting the bank an interest in "all of his equipment, now held or hereafter acquired."

   a. Where should Gotham State Bank file in order to perfect its security interest?

   b. Would your answer be any different if Dr. Tooth had two offices out of which he conducted his dental practice, one in midtown Manhattan and another in his hometown of Montclair, New Jersey?

5. Dr. Tooth of the previous example decides to go into partnership with two other dentists, Dr. Upper and Dr. Lower. They form a company under the name "Painless Partners" by signing a partnership agreement that states that the partnership is being formed under the laws of New York. The State of New York has no requirement that a partnership such as theirs file with the state in any way to be a duly formed partnership under its laws. The partnership operates a single dental office in midtown Manhattan. To set up this office, the partnership arranges for a small business loan with Gotham State Bank of New York, granting that bank a security interest in "all equipment now held or hereafter acquired" by the partnership.

   a. Where should the bank file a financing statement to perfect its security interest?

   b. Suppose that at the time the partnership was formed it was agreed among the three dentists that each would continue to do some dental work in a "satellite" office that might be set up near his or her home. Dr. Tooth has such an office in Montclair, New Jersey, where he keeps appointments on one or two days a week. Dr. Upper opens up a small office in the Bronx. Dr. Lower keeps an office she has near to her residence in Connecticut. Work done by any of the dentists, no matter at what office, is billed to the client as being the work of "Painless Partners," and all payments are to be made to the address of the midtown Manhattan office. All of the partnership's dealings with Gotham State Bank in obtaining the loan were carried out through its Manhattan office. Under this set of facts, where do you suggest the bank file?

6. General Gearmaker Incorporated is a corporation organized under the laws of the state of Delaware. Its production facilities are located in

Nevada and Oregon. It has sales offices in California, New York, New Jersey, Florida, and Connecticut. The corporate headquarters occupy all of a soaring skyscraper, the "GG Tower," in the heart of downtown Los Angeles. The corporation enters into a large-scale financing agreement with The Bank of the West, a bank organized under the laws of and operating in California. As part of the financing agreement, General Gear-makers grants to the bank a security interest in "all equipment, inventory, and accounts now held or hereafter acquired" by the corporation. Where is the bank going to have to file an initial financing statement in order to perfect this interest?

Explanations

1a. The bank should file with the New York Secretary of State to perfect its interest. Under §9-307(b)(1), the debtor who is an individual, as is Sheila, is "located" for the purposes of the choice-of-law rules of Article 9, "at the individual's principal residence." Sheila's principal residence, in fact the only residence we know of at this point, is in the state of New York. So that state's version of Article 9 governs the perfection of any security interest she grants in any of her personal property, and it is therefore in that state where the secured party, here Downtown Federal, must make its filing.

1b. The bank should still file in New York. The purpose for which she uses the piano, and the type of Article 9 collateral it is in her hands, now equipment instead of consumer goods, makes no difference and has no bearing on where the secured party must file. You might understandably wonder why I even asked the question. The fact is that under prerevision Article 9 in a majority of states the *type* of collateral—whether it was consumer goods, equipment, farms products, accounts, or what-have-you—did make a big difference in where a financing statement was to be filed within the state. For some types of collateral, filing was to be at the local level and for others at the central state filing office. The type of collateral could even make a difference in which state the financing statement was to be filed. The new, simplified filing rules of Revised Article 9 do away with all of that, and I couldn't resist pointing it out.

1c. Again, the filing should be with the Secretary of State of New York. The location of the *debtor* is what counts. The location of the secured party is irrelevant.

1d. For one last time, the place of proper filing remains the same, New York State. The location of the *collateral* need not be taken into account when determining where to file under the revised Article 9 (another change from how it sometimes worked out under the prerevision version). While the Code does not define "principal residence," it seems safe to say here that Sheila's Manhattan apartment is her principal residence, and her place in Connecticut that she uses on occasion doesn't change the fact.

2. Patricia should search in the files of the Secretary of State of Illinois for any filing under the name "Blackies, Barton." This is, of course, assuming that she has already done enough to convince herself that this is Barton's true legal name, that he indeed owns the piano in his individual capacity, and that his Chicago apartment would undoubtedly qualify as his principal residence. The point of this example is, when you come to think about it, an obvious one, but one that deserves to be made explicitly: *The correct place for a filer to file in order to perfect is the correct place for a searcher looking for any possible filings on the collateral to search.* This isn't, of course, just happenstance. If Patricia searches the Illinois state records under the proper name, she should come up with any financing statements filed by anyone else who might possibly claim a valid and perfected security interest in the piano. Need she search anywhere else? No. If, perchance, some secured party did in fact file on the piano but in the wrong place — which under our assumptions would be anywhere other than Illinois or under any other name — then that party's security interest would not have been perfected by the filing and is not something that Patricia need worry about. She is not expected to search all over the country just in case someone mistakenly filed in the wrong state any more than she is required to search under possible mistaken variants of Barton's correct name. Any mistaken filing, either in the wrong place or under the wrong name, will not serve to perfect the filer's interest. The problem of a mistaken filing is, naturally enough, the filer's, not Patricia's, if she has run a proper search.

3. The problem here, as you no doubt saw, is that there is a significant question about where Dexter has his "principal residence." Is it in New York or Florida? One possibility is to do a lot of investigation of Dexter's affairs (something about which he is not likely to be too enthused), as to where he is registered to vote, which state, if any, has issued him a driver's license, what he gives as his location for taxpaying purposes, and so on. All the factors might point to the same state, but it's perfectly possible that Dexter has been splitting his allegiance, so to speak, between the two states, without any regard for the fact that we have to figure out where his "principal residence" is for the purpose of this one transaction. Then we could have to do some research outside of the Uniform Commercial Code about how "principal residence" is determined in tough cases. This might give us a definitive answer, but then again it might not.

Let me offer a simpler solution. Wouldn't it be easier, a lot less time-consuming, and less costly for our client, if we recommended filing in both New York and Florida? One or the other would have to be the state of his principal residence, so either way we are covered. This eliminates not only time and effort but the risk that we may have counseled Sandra to file in the wrong state. This highlights an important practice point when working under Article 9: There is no penalty for overfiling, by which we mean filing, in addition to the correct place, in a jurisdiction or jurisdictions where a filing would turn out not to be required. Here, for example, filing in both New York and Florida, while it does require a bit more time and effort (and one more filing fee) than filing in one state, would almost certainly be easier than going through the complicated process of trying to determine exactly which one state had to be considered Barton's principal residence. Look at the final sentence of the second from last paragraph of Comment 2: In cases where a doubt arises [as to where the principal residence of an individual debtor is located] "prudence may dictate perfecting under the law of each possible jurisdiction."

So the rule of thumb, if not formally the rule of law, becomes, when in doubt in which state to file, file in any that could later be argued to have been the one place where filing was technically required. A corollary rule of thumb, picking up on the discussion of the prior example, and equally important in practice, goes like this: When there is reasonable doubt about where a proper filing on some collateral could have been made, the diligent searcher will search in all states where a proper filing *might* be located.

Consider, for example, someone who is interested in buying this particular artwork from Dexter or who may be willing to himself take it as collateral for a loan Dexter has asked from him. We'll call him Steve. Steve will, needless to say, want to check whether Dexter has granted any security interests in the sculpture because the price he would be willing to pay or the value of the sculpture as collateral will be directly affected, of course, by whether or not it is encumbered by any prior security interest. Steve will want to search the Article 9 records to see if any filing has been made on the sculpture. In which state should he check? He knows from §9-307(b)(1) that anyone claiming a security interest perfected by filing on the sculpture will have had to file a financing statement in the state of Dexter's "principal residence." He can see the artwork is located in New York at present, but he also knows that the location of the debtor, not the location of the collateral, is key to his search. Where does he determine Dexter's principal residence to be? Again, Steve could go through a long, costly, and highly risky analysis of which state is most likely to be considered Dexter's principal residence. Or he could take the simpler course of recognizing that there is some substantial doubt as to where Dexter's principal residence is located—New York or Florida—and himself search (or have a reliable search firm conduct the necessary search for him), looking for any filings under the name "Moneybucks, Dexter" in the records of *each* of those two states. If Steve's search comes up with no filing that covers the sculpture under that name in either state, then he can rest assured that no secured party has perfected on the sculpture, at least through the mechanism of filing. If he finds a relevant financing statement in either place, that would be enough to put him on notice that some party is at least possibly claiming a valid interest in the sculpture that could effect the value of what he may be buying or himself agreeing to take as collateral, and "prudence would dictate," as the comment drafters would say, that he get the matter cleared up with Dexter before he goes ahead with his purchase or loan.

4a. Gotham should file with the Secretary of State of New Jersey. Dr. Tooth operates his dental practice as a sole proprietorship, and so the debtor is him as an individual. That being so, as we have already seen in §9-307(b)(1), the correct place to file is in the state of the individual's principal residence. Dr. Tooth's principal residence is in New Jersey. The location of the collateral and of the secured party never enter into it.

4b. The answer remains the same. The place for filing is New Jersey as the location of Dr. Tooth's principal residence. The good doctor could have offices all over the country, but as long as he as an individual is the debtor, the one filing in New Jersey is all that is called for under the rules of Revised Article 9.

5a. The partnership is an "organization" under the Article 1 definition, but it is not a "registered organization" under §9-102(70). Since this organization has only one place of business, the rule is that given in §9-307(b)(2). The debtor is located at its sole place of business, here the office in Midtown Manhattan. Hence, the correct place to file is in the state of New York.

5b. The partnership is now an organization with more than one place of business. That means that under §9-307(b)(3), it is deemed to be located "at its chief executive office." As the fourth paragraph of Comment 2 states:

> This term "chief executive office" is not defined in this Section or elsewhere in the Uniform Commercial Code. "Chief executive office" means the place from which the debtor [here the partnership] manages the main part of its business operations or other affairs. This is the place where persons dealing with the debtor would normally look for credit information, and it is the appropriate place for filing.

Under the facts as given it would seem safe for Gotham Bank to conclude that the partnership's chief executive office is its midtown Manhattan dental office, and that therefore the appropriate place to file is in New York.

You can imagine that the decision as to exactly which place of business used by an organization would be rightfully considered its chief executive office may be at some times not as clear-cut as what we have here. What if the dental partnership was run out of three offices, one each in New York, New Jersey, and Connecticut, and each of these offices carried out the affairs of the partnership in essentially the same way? Nothing about the way the affairs of the partnership was run distinguished any one of the offices as somehow "chief" over the other two. The obvious solution here would be for the bank to file in each of the three states and let it go at that. Note the end of the paragraph of Comment 4 quoted earlier:

> With respect to most multi-state debtors, it will be simple to determine which of the debtor's offices is the "chief executive office." Even when a doubt arises, it would be rare that there could be more than two possibilities. A secured party in such a case may protect itself by perfecting under the law of each possible jurisdiction.

True, in this situation we have three possibilities, but that should not throw us, or the people at Gotham Bank, for a loop. Filing in three states, each of which is a candidate for the location of the partnership's chief executive office, is not terribly more difficult than filing in two. As a practical matter, I believe what the comment drafters were correctly trying to point out here is that when we come upon a debtor operating in several (be it more than two or more than three) states, it is likely that the debtor will be organized as a corporation or some other type of registered organization, and the issue of where the debtor's chief executive office is to be found goes away, as we will see in the final example.

You might be wondering at this point if Gotham Bank could make things a little easier for itself where there is some question of where the chief executive office of its organizational debtor is to be found by inserting in the security agreement that it gets the partners to sign some language to the effect that, "The parties hereto agree that the Chief Executive Office of Painless Partners is located at" the New York address of the partnership's office in that state. Would that justify the bank's then filing only in New York? The answer is no, and you should be able to appreciate why this is so. Think about the problem from the point of view of someone searching for any filings covering the property of the partnership. The searcher will have to search in the files of any state that could possibly be considered the location of the chief executive office of Painless Partners. The searcher would, for prudence's sake, have to search in all three states. He or she would not, of course, be privy to the private agreement between the partnership and Gotham Bank, and its rights and responsibilities could not be affected by that agreement. The carefully delineated rules of Article 9 set out what is necessary for a secured party to give, through filing, effective notice to others when it is or may be claiming a security interest in the property of the debtor. The secured party and the debtor have no power through private agreement to change or affect what will constitute proper notice to other, third parties.

Two recent cases both serve as good reminders of the important point made in the previous paragraph. Each was decided under the old Article 9's rules governing the correct place for filing, but there's no reason to suspect that the court's insistence that a filing in an incorrect place is simply ineffective and not to be "excused" for any reason would play out any differently under the new Article 9. In *Wetzell v. Equipment Dealers Credit Co.*, 274 Bankr. 825, 47 U.C.C.2d 778 (W.D. Ark. 2002), the secured party argued that its filing in the wrong county (this being in the days when filing at the county level was often required) did not render its interest unperfected, as it relied in good faith on information given to it by the debtor on his loan application. The address given by the debtor on the application turned out to be the address of his place of business, not his residence. Under the rules applicable at the time, the filing should have been made in the county of the debtor's residence. The secured party had filed in a different county based on the address it had been given. In a short opinion the bankruptcy court concluded that the lender's interest was unperfected and hence could be avoided by the trustee. Even assuming that the secured party had acted in good faith, no "good faith exception" could be asserted against the trustee in bankruptcy, the court determined, as the trustee can never be bound by "particular representations that may have been made [to the secured party] by the debtor." In *Fleet National Bank v. Whippany Venture I, LLC*, 307 Bankr. 762, 53 U.C.C.2d 125 (D. Del. 2004), the lender had filed in what was determined to be the wrong state. It argued the filing should still be deemed effective because it had relied on an opinion letter, written by counsel for the borrower and directed to it, which had rendered the opinion that the correct place to file was, well, what turned out to be the wrong place.

> As for the opinion letter of [debtor's] counsel, the [District] Court . . . agrees with the Bankruptcy Court that the opinion letter is not dispositive on the location of the issue of location for filing. As courts have recognized, a secured creditor is not excused from the filing requirements for perfecting a security interest as the result of a creditor's error in filing in the wrong jurisdiction, even where the creditor's error was based on its

> good faith reliance on the address provided by the debtor. . . . Indeed,
> public policy supports the Bankruptcy Court's conclusion that the correct
> location for filing should not turn on private representations of the parties,
> but on the public and objective information available to all creditors
> concerning where the debtor manages its business.

Or, as we could now add, information available to all creditors about where the debtor has his or her principal residence or, if a corporation, was incorporated. If the opinion letter in this case had been written by *the lender's* legal counsel and not the borrower's, do you think that would have made any difference? I can't see why, other than it would give the lender a different law firm to be upset with for rendering it what was — that is, what turned out to be — an erroneous opinion.

6. The Bank of the West must file in Delaware to perfect its interest. This is the important message of §9-307(e). The corporation is not just an organization, but is a registered organization under the definition of §9-102(70). Its location is, therefore, the state under whose laws it was organized, which is in this case Delaware.

   The rule under Revised Article 9 calling for filing on a corporate debtor in the state of its incorporation is a major change — and a tremendous simplification — from what was called for prior to the revision, where perfection in a multi-state situation such as this might have required the secured party to file in each of the numerous states mentioned. A truly complex deal could, under the filing provisions of the old Article 9, involve filing in just about every state imaginable. And recall that filing in the states was not uniform as it is under Revised Article 9; some states called for central filing only, some for local filing for some collateral and central filing for others, and some states had a system of "dual filing" that required duplicate filings under certain situations at both the local and state levels. Now, under Revised Article 9, a corporation like General Gearmaker can spread its tentacles throughout the country as it sees fit, but the rule for a secured party taking a security interest in any or all of its property remains the same. One filing in Delaware is all that is necessary. This, of course, simplifies matters to the same degree for searchers who are interested in finding whether interests may be claimed in any of the corporation's property. The searcher first determines that the corporation is organized under the laws of Delaware. He or she then searches for any financing statements that may have been filed with the Secretary of State in Delaware under the corporation's correct name. That's it. Three cheers for the revision drafters, who truly did clarify and greatly simplify the filing system that constitutes the very heart of Article 9 and that article's governance of secured transactions throughout this grand country of ours.

Perfection by Possession

INTRODUCTION

As you will recall, the starting point for our discussion of the means by which an Article 9 security interest may be perfected was §9-310(a), which states as a general rule that filing a financing statement is necessary to perfect a security interest. Subsection 9-310(b) does, however, recognize a series of exceptions to this general rule, listed as (b)(1) through (b)(10). In this chapter we explore how a security interest may be effectively perfected other than by filing through one of the exceptions, that of (b)(6) for a security interest "in collateral in the secured party's possession under Section 9-313." Perfection through the secured party's taking possession of the collateral — what was and is often still referred to colloquially as a "pledge" of the collateral — was undoubtedly the earliest technique devised for these purposes, the most primitive means of perfection if you will.* Primitive it may be, but in the right hands it works perfectly well even today (and anything that avoids a flurry of paperwork and having to deal with a layer or two of government filing clerks can't be dismissed lightly). Note Comment 2 to §9-313:

> As under the common law of pledge, no filing is required by this Article to perfect a security interest if the secured party takes possession of the collateral.

---

* You will also sometimes run into the terms "pawn" and "hypothecation" used as terms of art in connection with what we will now be able to refer to more generically, if not quite so colorfully, as simply "perfection by possession as provided for under Article 9."

And so it is to §9-313 that we now turn. As you work through the examples, be aware of a number of concerns to be addressed. For what types or classes of collateral is perfection by possession permissible under Article 9? Are there any types of collateral on which it is not possible to perfect by possession? At what moment does perfection by possession become effective and for how long does it last? And finally, of course, and not to get too philosophical about it, what exactly does it mean for the secured party to "possess" something for these purposes? A wealth of questions suggest themselves.

Examples

1. Stan and Delia, two lawyers, are members of a group that meets monthly for "a friendly (and, they have checked, perfectly legal) game of poker." At the end of one particular evening Stan has come out the big winner and Delia a big loser. Delia owes Stan $5,670 and, according to the custom of the group, is expected to come up with the cash by the end of the next day. Delia explains to Stan that she could, if pushed to do so, come up with the money in time but that it would cause her some embarrassment to do so. She asks if he will agree to hold off asking for payment for about a week, at which time she'd have no trouble meeting her obligation. Stan is understanding and has no real reason not to trust her, but is concerned. "How can I be sure," he asks, "I'll really get paid?" Delia takes from her purse a pair of earrings she had been wearing during the day. She says that they are real diamonds, easily worth much more than the amount Stan is due, and that she'd be willing to let him hold them for the week as collateral to assure that he gets his money. Stan looks at the earrings but confesses that he wouldn't have the slightest notion of whether they were indeed diamonds or merely cheap imitations. He cannot decide whether to give her the extra time to pay. Delia suggests that he take the earrings home with him. He can have them looked at by a jeweler the next day, and when he understands their worth he will, she is sure, agree to the arrangement she has suggested. "Okay," replies Stan, "I'll take them with me on that basis and let you know whether I can give you the extra time as soon as possible. But you'd better look into getting the money together, 'cause you know the rules."

   a. As they leave the game in the wee hours of the morning, Stan has the earrings in his pocket. Does he have a perfected security interest in them?

   b. At about 2 P.M. the next day Stan calls Delia and tells her that he has had someone who knows about such things appraise the earrings and that sure enough they are the real thing and quite valuable. He says that he will give her the extra week to come up with the money she owes him. To this she quickly agrees, thanking him for his generosity. Does Stan now have a security interest in the earrings? Is it a perfected interest?

2. Dexter Moneybucks, in need of some ready cash, asks his friend Susan if she will lend him $12,000. He promises to repay that amount with interest within a year and further offers to let Susan keep a valuable ruby ring of his "as collateral for the loan." Susan agrees. She gives Dexter a check for $12,000, and in exchange he hands over the ring. Nothing is in writing.

   a. Does Susan have a perfected security interest in the ring? If so, when did or when will perfection take place?

   b. Suppose that the original transaction took place in June. In the middle of December, Dexter contacts Susan and tells her that he has been invited to spend the holidays with his great-aunt. She is the person who gave him the ring, which has been in the Moneybucks family for generations, and would be upset to see that he wasn't wearing it. Dexter asks if he could have the ring back, "only for a short time." Susan agrees. Dexter comes and picks up the ring on December 22. He delivers it back to Susan in perfectly good condition on January 5. As of January 6, does Susan have a perfected security interest in the ring? If so, as of what time will the perfection be considered to have commenced?

   c. Would your answer to the previous part be different if Dexter had signed a receipt for the ring that he had given Susan acknowledging that "Susan continues to have a security interest in the ring" during the period he has "borrowed" it? What if in place of the ring Dexter has left with her an emerald stickpin (presumably an heirloom from some other branch of his family) during the holiday period?

3. Selma of Selma's Appliance City has a blockbuster "End of Summer Sale." While some of her customers pay by cash or credit card, others purchase on store credit. For smaller purchases Selma asks only that the customer sign a simple contract of sale calling on the customer to make final payment within 30 days from the date of purchase. She deals with larger sales in one of two ways — by having the customer sign either a note payable to the order of her business or a copy of her "Retail Installment Sales Agreement." The agreement makes no reference to a security interest, collateral, Article 9, or anything of the sort, stating only that the customer is to finish paying for his or her purchase in specified monthly payments over a number of months (in some cases up to 48) and further that "title to any appliance or appliances sold hereunder remains with Selma until full and final payment" by the customer. Selma's sale has been a huge success, but her inventory is woefully depleted. She needs cash and arranges a loan from a firm called Credit

Associates. She signs a security agreement giving Credit Associates a security interest in "all accounts, instruments, and chattel paper now held or at any time hereafter acquired" by her. At the time the loan funds are released to her, she turns over to Credit Associates all of the contracts, notes, and retail installment sales agreements which she has in her possession.

a. Does Credit Associates gain a perfected security interest in all of the collateral specified in its security agreement?

b. Would it change your answer to the previous question at all if what Selma delivered to the lender was instead a ledger listing all of her "accounts receivable" of the various types and indicating each to be "subject to the interest of Credit Associates"? What if the ledger were accompanied by photocopies of each of the contracts, notes, and retail installment sales agreements?

c. Selma's big sale is over, but she still continues to sell some of her merchandise. As each new customer signs either a simple contract, a note, or her retail installment sales agreement, is the particular signed piece of paper subject to Credit Associates' security agreement? If you conclude that the answer is yes, is the lender's interest perfected and, if so, when?

4. Leon has a valuable collection of Civil War guns and other relics that he keeps in a special room devoted to Civil War history at his home. He arranges a loan from First National Bank with the understanding that the bank will take the better part of his collection as collateral. Since the bank has no place readily available to store this collection, they agree that it shall be moved to the home of Leon's brother-in-law, one Norman, who will keep it safe on the bank's behalf. Norman signs a document acknowledging that he "holds said items as agent for First National Bank," attached to which is a detailed list of the items in the collection that have been transferred to his home. (In consideration of its valued customer Leon's strongly held belief that "there's no reason the whole world has to know about my financial affairs," the bank defers to his wishes that they not file a financing statement covering the collateral.)

a. Does the bank have a perfected interest in the collateral? See §9-313(c) and Comment 3.

b. Suppose instead that Leon's collection had for a long time been not at his home but in a local museum to which Leon had loaned the pieces so they could be more safely held and also displayed for the public to appreciate them. Each displayed piece is accompanied by a small label describing the item and bearing the words, "On Loan from the Collection of Leon." When Leon puts this collection up as collateral, First National sends a notice to the museum informing it that Leon has granted the bank a security interest in all of his property now in the possession of the museum. Is this sufficient for the bank to claim a perfected interest? See Comment 4.

5. Dan had among his assets a tangible certificate of deposit for $50,000 payable in the year 2012. In 2004 he negotiates a loan, to be fully paid off in the next four years, from First National Bank for $12,000. He pledges the certificate to First National, which keeps it in its files along with the rest of his loan documentation. In 2005 he approaches the bank asking for an additional loan of $5,000, which he proposes be secured by the same collateral. The bank declines to extend him any further credit. He then goes to Second Avenue Credit Associates, which is willing to lend him the money. A representative of First National delivers the certificate directly to Second Avenue, an authorized loan officer of which signs a paper stating that it, Second Avenue, "agrees that it acts as agent for First National Bank in holding" the certificate in question. In 2006, when Dan files a petition in bankruptcy, does First National Bank have a perfected security interest in the certificate? Does Second Avenue Credit Associates?

6. Several years ago Minnie started up a company, organized as Minimaker Corporation, to develop and market a new invention she had come upon. By 2008, the corporation is doing exceedingly well, but Minnie is ready for retirement. After a long period of negotiation, the terms are finally set for the purchase of the business by the large conglomerate Jumbo Incorporated. Jumbo is to get all of the shares in Minimaker Corporation, in exchange for which Minnie is to get a large number (the exact number having been fiercely negotiated) of shares in Jumbo. A few days before the closing of the deal is to take place, Jake, who is managing the acquisition for Jumbo Incorporated, becomes aware that Minnie has just received a letter from one Oscar stating that he was injured outside the premises of Minimaker and claiming damages "in an amount up to $100,000." Jake informs Minnie that he cannot go through with the deal unless she accepts fewer Jumbo shares to take into account this potential liability on the Minimaker Corporation's part. Minnie says that this is ridiculous. "This is obviously just a crackpot letter. We get 'em all the time. I'm sure we'll never hear from the guy again." Because she wants the deal to conclude as soon as possible, she says she is even willing to sign a document saying that she will reimburse Jumbo in cash for any amount it might eventually have to pay Oscar. Jake says that this would be a satisfactory solution but that he will need some additional security to back up her reimbursement promise. The two agree to an escrow arrangement. Lydia Lawyer, a prominent member of the local bar, is chosen by Jake to serve as the escrow agent. At the time of the closing of the purchase and sale of the Minimaker stock, Minnie delivers over to Lydia a certificate of deposit due in ten years for $100,000. Minnie, Jake (on behalf of his corporation), and Lydia (as "escrow

agent") sign an agreement. Under this agreement Lydia is directed to hold the certificate in escrow. Should Minimaker have to pay Oscar something, and if Minnie does not fulfill her reimbursement obligation within three months of notice to her, then Lydia is authorized to deliver the certificate over to Jumbo Incorporated. Should money be paid to Oscar and Minnie make good on her reimbursement promise, or if by the end of four years (which would be the statute of limitations on the type of action that Oscar is threatening) Oscar has not filed suit against the corporation, then Lydia is authorized to deliver the certificate back to Minnie. When Minnie files a petition in bankruptcy at the end of 2011, can Jumbo successfully claim a perfected security interest in the certificate of deposit?

Explanations

1a. No. It is important to remember the fundamental principle of §9-308(a): An interest is perfected "if it has attached and all of the applicable requirements for perfection . . . have been satisfied." No interest can be perfected *unless* and *until* it has attached. As they leave the game there isn't any security agreement. Stan has possession of the earrings for the purpose of inspection and nothing more. There is no attachment, which is of course equivalent to saying that there is as of that moment no security interest at all. If no security interest exists it certainly can't be perfected.

1b. Yes, he now has an interest, and yes, it is perfected. As soon as the two conclude their agreement over the telephone a security interest attaches. You should review §9-203(a) and (b). The three prerequisites to attachment are now met. Working through subsection (b), she has rights in the earrings, assuming they are hers, and value has been given by his extension of one week's worth of credit to her. Finally, there is a security agreement to satisfy (b)(3)(B). Recall, and reread in that subpart, that while a security agreement needs normally to be in writing, it is sufficient if "the collateral . . . is in the possession of the secured party under Section 9-313 pursuant to the debtor's security agreement." Their agreement here is oral and not terribly rich in detail, but it will do.

So the interest attaches at that moment in their call when agreement is reached. At that point the goods are also in the possession of the secured party. Under §9-313, goods are among the types of collateral in which a security interest may be perfected by the secured party's taking possession of the collateral. Delia has now agreed that Stan holds the earrings not just for inspection but as security for her obligation. The attached security interest is perfected by possession.

The obvious purpose of this question is to caution you once again never to forget that attachment is a prerequisite to perfection. In many instances you will be tempted to skip over the issue of attachment to get to perfection, but be careful. There are plenty of cases where the secured party's counsel must have spent all kinds of time and energy making sure perfection was just right, only to find that all of this effort (and all of his or her client's interest) is totally undercut when it is established that the claimed security interest never even attached.

2a. Yes. First of all, a security interest has attached. If you have any doubts about this, refer back to Example 3-1 (a), which contains this set of facts. There we asked only whether the security interest attached. The answer was yes. Now we venture further and ask whether the interest is perfected. Again we can answer yes. It is permissible under §9-313 to perfect an interest in goods by the secured party's taking possession of them. Here Susan has taken possession. So there is perfection. When did it take place, when was that all-important moment of perfection? Section 9-308(a) tells us that a security interest becomes perfected if it has attached and all applicable requirements for perfection [here under Section 9-313] have been satisfied. When she gave him the check (giving value for the purposes of attachment) and he handed over the ring (both making the oral security agreement sufficient for purposes of attachment and her "taking possession" for the purposes of perfection) the interest simultaneously attached and was perfected.

2b. Yes, because Susan is back in possession of the ring on January 6, she has a perfected security interest as of that date, but the perfection from then on will relate back only to the moment on January 5 when Dexter returned the ring to her, not to when she had first taken possession.
Section 9-313(d) is clear:

> If perfection of a security interest depends upon possession of the collateral by a secured party, perfection occurs no earlier than the time the secured party takes possession and continues only while the secured party retains possession.

There's nothing in Article 9 about the holiday season not counting or anything like that. Susan's interest was initially perfected in June. It then became unperfected when she surrendered possession back to Dexter on December 22. It became perfected for a second time when she regained possession some time on January 5.

You might wonder why it should really matter whether she was perfected during this period of nonpossession, but as we follow up on this hypothetical in later chapters, you will begin to see all the harm to Susan's position that could come during those few seemingly insignificant days. You will then have to wonder why in the world she would ever be so foolish to have let the thing out of her hands, even if Dexter is a friend and even if she was feeling the spirit of the season. For a case in which a bank (a bank!) let the pledgor take back possession of a diamond ring — and lived to rue the day — see In re Stewart, 74 Bankr. 350, 4 U.C.C.2d 271 (M.D. Ga. 1987).

2c. Neither of these variables changes the result at all. In fact the bank in the Stewart case just cited had gotten a signed writing from the pledgor, but, as the court rightly decided, it didn't help. If Susan takes the stickpin during the period the ring is out of her hands, she may have a perfected interest in that other bauble during the December 22 to January 5 period, but she loses that interest when she hands the stickpin back. And the analysis with respect to her interest in the ring remains the same.

You may wonder if there would be any way, short of Dexter's repaying what he owes Susan and getting the ring back for keeps, that she could let him have it back for the few weeks without losing her protected status. The answer is yes, but she will have to figure out some effective means of perfection other than simple possession to cover her during the interim. See §9-308(c). For her to be protected even when she returns the ring to him, she would have had to have filed an effective financing statement prior to her release of the ring.

3a. Selma has granted an interest in three types of collateral. She has turned over a bunch of papers to the secured party. The question is whether perfection by the means of possession is even possible for each type of collateral and then further whether "possession" has been transferred to Credit Associates. The first thing to do is to classify each piece of collateral using the definitional scheme of Article 9. The simple contract of sale signed by some of her customers is in itself just a piece of paper, a bit of evidence. The rights Selma gains under these contracts to be paid for goods sold constitute accounts under Article 9. The notes she gets from other customers are instruments. Finally, each retail sales installment agreement she gets is a piece of chattel paper. In fact, it is "tangible chattel paper" under the definition of §9-102(a)(78).

Look at the first sentence of §9-313(a):

> Except as otherwise provided in subsection (b) [which deals with goods, primarily motor vehicles, covered by certificates of title issued by the state], a secured party may perfect a security interest in negotiable documents, goods, instruments, money or tangible chattel paper by taking possession of the collateral.

The concluding sentence of this subsection tells us that a secured party may perfect an interest in a certificated security, the one tangible form of investment property, by taking delivery of the certificate under §8-301. So Credit Associates may and in this case has, by taking possession of the instruments and the tangible chattel paper, perfected on those pieces of collateral. Conspicuously *absent* from this sentence is any reference to deposit accounts, other forms of investment property, accounts, or general intangibles. These types of collateral are by their very nature intangible and as such can't really be "possessed" in a physical sense. *Under Article 9 it is not possible to perfect an interest in either accounts or general intangibles by possession.* So Credit Associates has not perfected on the accounts merely by taking possession of the contracts evidencing them.

3b. The ledger doesn't change the situation, except possibly for the worse if Credit Associates gets only photocopies of the instruments and chattel paper and not the real things. It may list the accounts, but it isn't the accounts themselves. So the secured party is not in possession of the accounts. You can convince yourself of this by noting that Selma could have produced two (or more) identical copies of the ledger with no great difficulty. Key to the concept of possession for our (or probably for any) purposes is that more than one person cannot have possession of the identical thing at the same time. But then accounts can't be "possessed" in the first place.

As we now know, instruments and chattel paper can be possessed and the possession can serve as a means to perfect, but they must be the real thing—not photocopies. As one court has recently pointed out, even the sharpest copies of this sort of thing "have no more binding legal effect than would a photocopy of, say, a ten dollar bill." *In re Equitable Financial Management, Inc.,* 164 Bankr. 53, 22 U.C.C.2d 1152 (W.D. Pa. 1994).

3c. Because Credit Associates has included an after-acquired property clause in its security agreement with Selma, its security interest attaches to any discrete account, instrument, or piece of chattel paper as soon as she acquires rights in it. If it is depending on possession as its sole means of perfection, however, any interest is not necessarily perfected at that time. Its interest in any newly generated instruments or chattel paper will become perfected only when it gets possession of the individual pieces. It can never, as we know, perfect its interest in accounts by possession. Contrast this result with what would be true if Credit Associates filed on the collateral—the accounts, instruments, and chattel paper—as a means of perfection.

4a. It seems very unlikely that a court looking on the situation at any time in the future would find First National to have perfected by taking possession through its "agent" Norman. As Comment 3 makes clear, a secured party may take possession through its agent, as long as that agent is not also an agent of the debtor or the debtor him or herself. Technically, Norman is not Leon's agent, just a brother-in-law. The comment goes on, however, to state that,

> [U]nder appropriate circumstances, a court may determine that a third person in possession is so closely connected to or controlled by the debtor that the debtor has retained effective possession, even though the third person may have agreed to take possession on behalf of the secured party.

We don't know the particulars of Norman's relationship with his brother-in-law, and he might justifiably take umbrage at the idea that he is under Leon's "control," but this does seem like a situation where the parties are trying to create the impression of perfection by possession in the secured party without having really to attain it. Perfection, either by possession or by any other legitimate means, is not just a matter of form or following a hollow legal technicality. There's some reason, some method behind all this. Perfection is to serve a purpose. And, I would argue, it doesn't look like this purpose is being well-served here, just because Norman is willing to sign a piece of paper denoting him an agent of the bank.

Which leads us naturally enough to a consideration of exactly what purpose is being served by the secured party's having to go through "all of the applicable requirements for perfection" (§9-308(a)) other than that it's the kind of thing which helps keeps lawyers occupied and off the streets. Why is Article 9 written, as we have seen, so that filing is considered the principal means of perfection? And why, other than that there is a long tradition behind it, should the taking of possession by the secured party exempt it (at least for most kinds of collateral) from having to make any filing?

The answer of course to both of these questions is that the purpose underlying the perfection requirements is the giving of *notice* to others that this particular bit of collateral is, or at least may be, subject to a valid security interest granted to another. Any third party that is considering either buying the property or allowing it to serve as collateral for its extension of credit will necessarily want to have a way of knowing whether it is already encumbered by an interest that would, or even arguably could, interfere with the value of the property for its intended use. If the property is of a type on which an Article 9 security interest can be perfected through filing, the prospective buyer or lender will be responsible (to itself) to check the appropriate records to see if any such interest has been recorded. This is of course the functional equivalent of the necessity in the real estate world of checking — not by asking the landowner who may be willing to say anything or merely befuddled by the whole exercise, but by recourse to the independently maintained and official records — whether there is a mortgage or other lien recorded on the property and possibly encumbering or diminishing the value of title to the property. In either case filing gives notice to the world at large of something going on which will be critical information for a prospective buyer or lender interested in the property.

In real estate transactions, of course, the prospective buyer or lender does more; it actually goes and takes a look at the property. Its mission is to check out exactly what shape the land and the buildings on it are in — whether toxic waste is spread knee-deep over the surface or termites have eaten their way up to the second floor. In our situation, where personal property is involved, the prospective buyer or lender will also want to see the property for himself or herself, but not just for the purpose of checking on its condition. Seeing the item of personal property *and* seeing that it is at the very moment still in the possession of the person claiming to be its owner will be absolutely essential — in addition of course to checking the appropriate public records — for assuring oneself that this particular property is indeed this person's to sell or use as collateral and furthermore that no other can claim a legitimate perfected security interest in it.

As we know, the style of filing on which the Article 9 system relies is of the type referred to as a "notice filing" system. The information placed on file need not and typically will not tell the whole story to anyone finding it through his or her search of the records. What it does do is let that person know that something's up, that someone does claim or at least may claim an interest, and that any such claim cannot be ignored. In exempting from the need for such a filing any interest that can be and is perfected by possession in the secured party, the drafters of Article 9 counted on the idea that a prospective purchaser or lender would not only search the records but demand to *see the collateral in the possession of the debtor.* If the debtor could not produce the collateral, then anyone with half a brain (and, of course, knowledge of the applicable law) would have effective notice, sufficiently equivalent to the type of notice it would get from any filing put on the public record, that the collateral may not be as unencumbered by the interests of others as the debtor may be asserting.

Return for a moment to the initial situation in Example 2. Dexter Moneybucks grants a security interest in his ruby ring to Susan and that interest is perfected not by a filing but by Susan's taking possession of the ring. Now suppose Dexter approaches another friend, Stuart, asking if he could borrow some money but offering to put up "that ruby ring I always wear" as collateral. Stuart would have to check in the appropriate place to see that there are no Article 9 filings under Dexter's name covering the ring. If he lends on that basis alone, however, he's probably going to end up regretting it. Didn't he notice that Dexter wasn't actually wearing the ring? Perhaps he did, and asked Dexter where the ring was. And then perhaps Dexter explained, "I don't wear it all the time now. I'm worried about flashing such a beauty on the streets these days." Or maybe, "It's at the jeweler's. I'm having it reset." Dexter may even offer to walk with Stuart over to the jeweler's shop so the two can view together the ring resting safe and snug in the store's window. In either case, Stuart, if he isn't completely dazzled by Dexter's willingness to do business with him and all the fast talk, had better hold on to his money until he gets a chance to see that the ring is back in Dexter's possession. Dexter's inability to come up with the ring on demand should serve as warning to Stuart, as sure as finding a filing in the records, that something is up even if he can't tell exactly what. The Article 9 means of perfection are meant only to give others this kind of fair warning, not every bit of detail. The reasonably prudent person can take it from there, and at the very least will not part with his or her money to buy or lend on the collateral until all of his or her questions are answered to his or her satisfaction. Let's hope for Stuart's sake that he is the kind of person who holds on to his money and knows the kinds of questions to ask.

The concept here being discussed is sometimes referred to as the "possession as notice" theory or principle. There is a problem here in that the word "possession" is never defined in Article 9, or anywhere else in the Code for that matter, and can be, at least at the margins, a difficult concept to define. I find it helps, at least in this instance, if we don't try to pin down the slippery concept of possession but to think of its use in §9-313 in a slightly different way. What counts as notice, and serves the function intended for it by the drafters of Article 9, is not really the possession by the secured party or its agent as much as the *lack of possession* by the debtor. If the situation is such that the debtor can no longer clearly demonstrate to another his or her "dominion and control" (in a phrase you'll often encounter in this context) over the article, the notice function of perfection would seem to have been met.

Return now briefly to the situation that started us down this road — Leon's guns being placed in the hands and at the home of his brother-in-law supposedly acting as agent for the bank. If the collection were put under the care of some true agent for the bank we would expect it to be difficult, if not impossible, for Leon to show off the guns to another person without that person becoming aware that the bank, or at least some other party, claimed an interest in them. The agent working under the bank's instructions would presumably be careful, even if he or she let Leon bring "a friend" along to look at the guns, to make clear that they were being held "to insure the rights of" another. In the case as I posited it, even if Norman isn't literally involved in some kind of scam with Leon or under Leon's control, does it seem reasonable that third parties would be given sufficient notice that Leon's collection might be encumbered in some way just because it's at his brother-in-law's place? I think not. Therefore, as I argued from the outset, I wouldn't see the bank's interest as being validly perfected in this situation.

4b. No. The key here is that the museum rightfully has possession of Leon's property but has not issued a document — that is something like a warehouse receipt — covering the collection. As Comment 4 states, this brings the situation within the rule of §9-313(c). That being the case,

> Notification of a third person does not suffice to perfect under Section 9-313(c). Rather, perfection does not occur unless the third person authenticates an acknowledgment that it holds possession of the collateral for the secured party's benefit.

The comment goes on to ask the reader to compare how Article 9 deals with the situation when a nonnegotiable document of title has been issued by a bailee holding goods, which brings the case within §9-312(d) where receipt of notification would be sufficient. In the case we have before us, however, the result is clear. Perfection of First National Bank's security interest in Leon's collection does not occur unless and until the museum authenticates a record "acknowledging that it holds possession of the collateral for [First National's] benefit."

5. It appears that both First and Second have perfected interests in the one certificate of deposit, each having perfected without filing via §§9-310(b)(6) and 9-313. To the very traditionally minded attorney, it would seem simply out of the question that the same collateral could be pledged simultaneously to two distinct lenders. The whole concept of the pledge was inextricably linked with the notion of possession taken and fiercely defended by the pledgee, and elementary physics tells us that one object cannot be in two places at the same time. Under Article 9, however, there seems nothing wrong or particularly troubling about what the parties — all of them — did here. First National initially perfected by taking actual possession and continued the perfection by having possession through Second Avenue, acting as its agent. Second has possession both as First's agent and acting on its own behalf to perfect. In a case on which this example is loosely based, the court held that each of the two secured parties held a perfected interest. In re Chapman, 5 U.C.C. 649 (Bankr. W.D. Mich. 1968). Chapman was decided, of course, under the old version of Article 9, but the more detailed treatment given to perfection by possession in current §9-313

undoubtedly supports its conclusion. The result makes sense if we focus not on the traditional mechanism of the pledge but on the underlying principle supporting perfecting by this means when filing is not made. Whatever else is true in the situation, not even a hint of dominion and control over the certificate of deposit has been left in Dan, and thus the notice function is well served.

6. The basic issue here — whether a security interest in collateral in the possession of an independent party acting as escrow agent under an enforceable escrow agreement can ever be deemed perfected by possession — is one that caused some difficulty for the courts under the prerevision version of Article 9. The first well-known case to have considered the issue, In re Dolly Madison Industries, Inc., 351 F. Supp. 1038, 11 U.C.C. 926 (E.D. Pa. 1972), aff'd, 480 F.2d 917 (3d Cir. 1973), spared no drama in declaring the simultaneous existence of an escrow and a pledge to be a "legal impossibility." The court reasoned that for a pledge to be effective dominion and control over the collateral had to reside in the secured party or its agent. The escrow agent was not an agent of the secured party alone; in fact it was legally bound to follow the escrow agreement, which included obligations to the debtor, and not solely instructions from the secured party as a classic agent of the secured party would. The Dolly Madison result seems to put form before substance. A second case decided not that long after got it better. In re Copeland, 531 F.2d 1195, 18 U.C.C. 833 (3d Cir. 1976), held that, for the purposes of perfection under Article 9, it is not necessary that possession be in the secured party or an agent under the sole control of the secured party. The escrow agent's possession,

> and the debtor's lack of possession clearly signaled future creditors that debtor's ownership of and interest in [the collateral] were not unrestricted. As an independent institutional entity, Wilmington Trust [the escrow agent] could not be regarded automatically as an instrumentality or agent of the debtor alone. There was consequently no danger that creditors would be misled by his possession.

In my hypothetical, the escrow agent isn't an institutional entity but a single individual, Lydia Lawyer. This should not make a difference. Lawyers are often called upon to hold property in escrow in just this kind of way to facilitate a closing or conclusion of a deal, and we expect them to carry out their obligations under the escrow agreement to the letter. Lydia, as a prominent member of the local bar, would not, we assume, risk losing her professional reputation and perhaps even her license by violating the escrow provisions.

If Copeland was a better result than Dolly Madison under old Article 9, as I believe it to be and as I think most commentators would agree, it is because it better relates to the underlying purpose behind the "possession as notice" concept. The court in *Dolly Madison*, looking more to the history of the pledge than to its present function, assumed that what was important was that the secured party end up having domination and control over the collateral. In *Copeland* the court focused instead on the negative; the escrow arrangement effectively precluded the debtor from asserting dominion and control over the collateral, which was enough to fulfill the notice function. This seems to be one of those rare instances when it makes more sense to focus on the negative rather than the positive. The drafters of Revised Article 9 come out squarely in favor of the *Copeland* approach. See the conclusion of Comment 3 to §9-313:

> In a typical escrow arrangement, where the escrowee holds possession of the collateral as agent for both the secured party and the debtor, the debtor's relationship to the escrowee is not such as to constitute retention of possession by the debtor.

One interesting case demonstrates the point well. *National Pawn Brokers Unlimited v. Osterman, Inc.*, 176 Wisc. 2d 418, 500 N.W.2d 407, 21 U.C.C.2d 1176 (Wisc. Ct. App. 1993), involved, as you might expect, something pawned. The stuff in question was jewelry originally purchased by the debtor, one Donald Pippin, from Osterman for $39,750.38. Unfortunately for Osterman, the checks he accepted as payment were drawn by Pippin on an account already closed. Osterman tracked down Pippin, who was charged with the crime of issuing a check for more than $500 with the intent that it never be paid, and later with criminal fraud as well. It became apparent that the necessary evidence, the jewelry itself, had been pawned by Pippin, and the police were requested to obtain a search warrant and then to search the pawnbroker's places of business. The police were able to seize the jewelry from the pawnbrokers and turn it over to the prosecution for use as evidence. After Pippin's conviction, both the pawnbroker and Osterman requested return of the jewelry. The circuit court ordered return to Osterman, and the pawnbroker appealed. The court of appeals determined that the relevant question was whether the pawnbroker had a perfected security interest that had priority over an interest claimed and perfected by Osterman only after the determination in the criminal case against Pippin. For the pawnbroker's interest to be perfected, the court had to determine first whether it had even attached as against the argument that Pippin as debtor never had "rights in the collateral" to begin with. The court held that a security interest granted by the scoundrel Pippin and in favor of the pawnbroker could attach, as you no doubt recall from the discussion of Example 3(c) in Chapter 4. Having attached, the interest was perfected when the pawnbroker took possession of the jewelry and, it was held, this perfection was not lost when the jewelry was turned over to the police.

> The notice function of possession by the secured creditor persuades us that the police seizure does not interrupt that possession under U.C.C. §9-305 [the precursor to current §9-313]. Third parties know the police make no claim to own the property they seize pursuant to a warrant.

More to the point, it's hard to imagine any way in which the seizure of the jewelry by the police could have led any disinterested third-party observer into a mistaken belief that Pippin had somehow regained unfettered dominion and control over the property. Pippin had other things to worry about, and we have to assume the police no more than the pawnbroker would not have allowed him to get his hands on or to start wearing the jewelry just for the sake of being nice.

Automatic Perfection: The Purchase-Money Security Interest in Consumer Goods

INTRODUCTION TO THE PMSI

In this chapter we run across for the first time reference to a security interest as not simply any old run-of-the-mill security interest, but as a *purchase-money security interest*, or, as it is often abbreviated, a PMSI. It should be emphasized that the purchase-money interest is first and foremost a security interest like all others — you should expect to find and be able to identify the obligation, the debtor, the secured party, and that particular collateral caught in the middle. The purchase-money interest has to play by Article 9 rules just like its more prosaic comrades. There will be instances, however, the first of which we deal with in the later part of this chapter, in which the PMSI does get a measure — often a rather hefty one — of special treatment under those very rules, so knowing whether a security interest you are dealing with qualifies as a PMSI is of no small importance to understanding some of the most elemental parts of the Article 9 scheme.

Look first at §9-103(b)(1), which tells us that a security interest is a purchase-money security interest "to the extent that the goods are purchase-money collateral with respect to that security interest." Subsection 9-103(a)(1) gives us a definition for "purchase-money collateral": It is collateral, either goods or software, that secures a purchase-money obligation incurred with respect to that collateral. We finally get to something more substantive, the basic principle that distinguishes the PMSI, in subsection (a)(2) and its definition of "purchase-money obligation," as

> an obligation of an obligor incurred as all or part of the price of the collateral or for value given to enable the debtor to acquire rights in or the use of the collateral if the value is in fact so used.

Note initially that it follows from these definitions that there is no way that a security interest can be a PMSI *unless* the collateral is either goods or software.

There are, when you get down to it, two paradigm situations in which a security interest will be validly characterized as a PMSI. In the first of these the obligation being secured is the debtor's obligation to pay to the seller from whom it has bought the collateral "the price" of the collateral itself. Consider the case of a seller who allows the buyer to purchase on credit, but as part of the exchange protects himself or herself by retaining a security interest in the goods sold. This interest will be held until the buyer finishes paying off the purchase price. If the collateral is consumer goods, this is simply the familiar situation of a consumer buyer having been extended credit by the seller directly to buy the car, the mobile home, the washing machine, or whatever. Somewhere among the papers signed by the eager buyer was an agreement that the seller would retain an interest in the goods being sold to ensure payment for them. When the debtor is a larger commercial entity, the collateral will typically be equipment or inventory purchased so that the debtor's business can function, and the secured party is the supplier of the goods. The supplier supplies on credit, but is careful to retain a security interest in the goods to secure its eventual payment for them. In either case the seller would have, under Article 9, a PMSI granted by the buyer to the seller to secure payment of the price of the goods bought.

The second type of PMSI is that granted to a third-party lender who has advanced funds to the debtor with which the debtor is to acquire the collateral and to whom is then owed, in the words of §9-103(a)(2), an obligation "for value given to enable the debtor to acquire rights in or the use of the collateral if the value is in fact so used." The lender could, of course, be anybody, even just a friend who is being very friendly. More often it will be some kind of financial institution that is helping to finance the debtor's acquisition of some item or items either for personal or business use. Friendship has nothing to do with it; some nonnegligible rate of interest is being charged in connection with the loan. As we shall see, if the loan proceeds are in fact used for the purchase intended, the lender will be able to claim a PMSI in the goods acquired with the money it has loaned and all the advantages that may bring.

AUTOMATIC PERFECTION FOR THE PMSI IN CONSUMER GOODS

Perfection of an Article 9 security interest, we know from §9-308(a), generally results from the combination of attachment and all other "applicable requirements for perfection." What is interesting is that in some situations as listed in §9-309, to which note §9-308(a) expressly defers, Article 9 calls for nothing more to be done, that no steps beyond those necessary for attachment need be taken, for the interest to be perfected. If the facts in a particular instance fit within one of these delineated situations we refer to the *automatic perfection* of the interest upon attachment. The moment of attachment is the moment of perfection without the secured party having to do any more. Sometimes — and of course in this and the following chapter, which deals with some other instances of automatic perfection, the emphasis will have to be how it is true only sometimes and the risk the secured party runs if it makes a mistaken judgment and the time is not now — it pays to do nothing.

There is no one central theme that binds together the instances where automatic perfection is allowed for under §9-309, rather a set of instances that have to be taken in turn. Each of these cases in this and the next chapter has to be considered on its own merits to determine what might have justified the drafters' decision to abandon in the particular instance the principal feature of the other methods of perfection — the notice given to third parties that something's afoot, that the debtor does not necessarily hold the property free and clear of any encumbrances. In these cases the balance is struck differently. Concern for the possibility of third parties not having notice of information that could be of value to them is now outweighed by other factors, presumably the inconvenience to the debtor and the secured party of having to take any additional steps to give that notice. This being so, we will naturally want to give some thought to how third parties, fully aware that the Code is not protecting them by insisting on a form of notice for their benefit, may act to protect themselves under the circumstances or learn to live with the additional risks inherent in the situation.

Undoubtedly the most important of the instances in which Article 9 provides for automatic perfection of a security interest, at least if we are to judge by the number of transactions affected, is that of §9-309(1), the automatic perfection of PMSIs taken in consumer goods other than goods covered under a state's certificate-of-title statute, the prime example of which would be automobiles. Important as this exemption is, we won't need too many examples to deal with it, but only because the two issues that come up repeatedly in the cases — whether the security interest was created and retains its character as a PMSI and whether the collateral under consideration qualifies as consumer goods — will have already been dealt with elsewhere. Whether a security interest is a PMSI is our first order of business in this chapter. Examples 1 through 7 below deal with issues of when a secured party can claim to be holding a PMSI — and how he or she may, through inadvertence or otherwise, fail to get or later lose this favored position. What allows us to categorize any particular collateral as consumer goods was covered in Chapter 5. The concluding examples of this chapter call for you to put the two pieces of the case of automatic perfection of the PMSI in consumer goods — the fact of the PMSI status and the further fact that it has been taken in something that qualifies as consumer goods — together.

Examples

1. Boris walks into the jewelry store owned by Susan. He sees a diamond stickpin that he likes. The price is $5,000. Since he is a valued customer who has bought many things from her, and since he has the air of a prosperous gentleman about him, Susan agrees to let him wear the piece out of the shop. Boris promises to bring her a cashier's check for the price within a week.

   a. Does Susan have a PMSI in the stickpin? Would it make any difference if Boris had given Susan a promissory note for the amount, due in one week?

   b. What if, in addition, Susan had asked Boris, before he left the shop, to sign a "Sales Agreement" that set forth Boris' payment obligation and included a clause saying that "Seller retains title to all merchandise pending full and final payment?" Does this change Susan's position?

2. Suppose that, as in the first part of the prior example, Boris is originally given the jewelry on the agreement that he'll deliver a cashier's check within the week, with no security for payment mentioned. A few days later he asks Susan if he can have a longer period to pay. She is willing to give him more time, but asks him to sign a security agreement giving her an interest in the stickpin as security for his obligation to pay her for it. Does she now have a PMSI?

3. Now assume that Boris and Susan did enter into installment sales and security agreements at the time of the sale. If Boris' payment schedule was to extend over a long period of time, it would be reasonable for Susan to charge some interest. The sales agreement would presumably spell out how much he'd have to make in monthly payments the total of which would include a "Finance Charge" above and beyond the original $5,000 cash price. Language on the security agreement form, signed by Boris, grants Susan a "security interest in the merchandise to secure the payment of all amounts, including interest, due to Seller." Does this jeopardize her PMSI status?

4. We'll let Susan get on to other things. Boris, however, isn't finished. He wants to buy more. In particular he sees a powerboat at Marty's Marina that he simply must have. The purchase price is $32,000. He goes to the Waterside National Bank and gets the bank's agreement to loan him $26,000, which he will use toward the purchase of the boat. They give him a check for the money, which, along with his personal check for $6,000, he delivers directly to Marty, endorsing the bank's check over to Marty to complete the purchase. As part of his loan agreement with the bank, it is given a security interest in the boat securing his obligation.

   a. Is the bank's interest a PMSI?

   b. Would your answer to this question change at all if Boris had initially put the money from the bank in his own checking account? There it sat, along with loads of other money that the wealthy Boris keeps in this account, for a month. Only then did he write out a check to the Marina for $32,000.

   c. What if instead Boris had cashed the bank's check and taken the resultant funds with him on a trip to Las Vegas? Say he won big. On his return from this trip he immediately took $26,000 in cash, along with his own check for $6,000, to the Marina to purchase the boat. Does the bank have a PMSI? Would your answer be any different if he had lost heavily in Las Vegas but still was able to come up with money for the boat? If he had just come out even? Why should *any* of this make any difference as long as he ends up borrowing $26,000 from the bank and shelling out $32,000 for the boat?

5. Suppose that when Boris initially entered into the agreement to buy the boat from Marty's Marina he had no intention of buying it on credit. He figured he would simply write one large check and own it outright. When the time came for him to close the deal he does pay by check, but he decides he wants to keep more cash on hand in his account. He then goes to the bank and arranges for the loan. The bank takes a security interest in the boat. Is it a PMSI?

6. One more question about Boris. Suppose that Boris' initial intention is to buy the boat on credit. In fact, Boris finds his standing with the bank so favorable, his credit so good, that he decides he might as well borrow as much as they are willing to let him have (at, of course, a healthy rate of interest for the bank). He arranges to borrow $50,000, signing a note for this amount and granting the bank a security interest in the boat he is to buy. The bank issues him a check for $32,000 payable to the marina, which he uses to get the boat. In addition, the bank issues him a series of traveler's checks worth $18,000, which he takes with him as he sails off on his boat for a long midwinter cruise to warmer climes. Boris leaves the picture, but the bank still has a question for us. Is there any reason to doubt that its security interest in the boat is a PMSI?

7. Assume that in 2005 Lucky Louie (of Lucky Louie's World-O-Stuff) sold a big-screen television set to Bess on credit. The purchase price was $1,200, which she agreed to pay, with finance charges, over four years. Louie took and properly perfected a PMSI in the TV. In 2007 Bess finds that she is having trouble making the monthly payments. She enters into a new agreement with Louie under which the amount still owed on the set, now down to $721.34, is to be paid off in a series of lower monthly payments over the next three years. So she will not own it free and clear until 2010. The new papers the two parties sign specify that Louie's security in the TV set will continue until the final payment under the new schedule is made.
    a. After the refinancing, is there any question that Louie's PMSI is still in good shape? Why? How, ultimately, do you think his security interest would and should be judged?
    b. Suppose instead that Bess' fortunes are quite different. In 2007 she finds herself well able to cover the monthly payments on the set. In fact she wants to buy more! She settles on an elaborate stereo system at Louie's that she intends to have. The two agree that the amount owed on the TV ($721.34) and the cost of the stereo ($2,495) will be "rolled over" into one new loan for $3,216.34, to be paid off over the next four years. The new agreement signed states that the amount owed to Louie is secured by both the TV set and the stereo and that both will be subject to the security interest until all amounts due have been paid up. Does Louie still have a PMSI in the television? Does he have a PMSI in the stereo?

8. Lucky Louie, of Lucky Louie's World-O-Stuff, sells a computer system on credit to one Bess. Bess signs a copy of Louie's retail installment sales agreement, a portion of which reads that "Buyer hereby grants to Louie as seller and secured party a security interest in all merchandise sold pursuant to this agreement." Bess takes the computer home, where she sets it up in her den. She, her husband, and her children use it to do simple household accounting, play computer games, access the Internet, and browse the Web. Louie, on his part, makes no filing with respect to the sale.
    a. Is Louie's security interest perfected under Article 9?
    b. Would your answer as to Louie's position be the same if instead Bess had taken the computer home and set it up in the room in her home from which she runs a small business, telling her husband and kids to keep their hands off the machine?

9. The wealthy Boris sees a powerboat at Marty's Marina that he simply must have. The purchase price is $32,000. He goes to the Waterside National Bank and gets its agreement to loan him $26,000, which he will use toward the purchase of the boat. They give him a check for the money,

which, along with his personal check for $6,000, he delivers directly to Marty, endorsing the bank's check over to Marty to complete the purchase. As part of his loan agreement with the bank, it is given a security interest in the boat securing his obligation. The bank makes no filing regarding this loan, but does check that its state has no certificate of title law covering boats of this sort. Is its security interest perfected under Article 9?

Explanations

1a. No. Susan does not have a PMSI in the stickpin. In fact, Susan doesn't have *any* security interest under Article 9. It is important to remember that, however different or special it may be in some respects, a PMSI is first and foremost just a security interest under Article 9 of the Code. Everything necessary to create an interest under that article must be present just as with any non-purchase-money interest. Under §9-203(b)(3)(A), no interest can attach unless there is some form of a security agreement between the parties meeting certain specifications. Under the facts as given here, there is no such agreement. A promissory note given by Boris wouldn't make any difference. Its language is only that of a promise to pay. It might give Susan some advantage if she has to sue for the money she is promised, but it wouldn't contain any language granting her a security interest in any particular item of property. Susan has sold the stickpin to Boris on unsecured credit.

1b. Now Susan does have a PMSI. The signed agreement makes all the difference. While the language speaks of her "retaining title" to the bauble, the legal effect is to create a security interest. See the end of the first paragraph of §1-201(37) or the penultimate sentence in §1R-201(b)(35). To be sure it qualifies as a PMSI, review the criteria of §9-103(a) and (b). The stickpin that Boris has purchased turns out to be purchase-money collateral and his obligation to pay Susan for it is "an obligation incurred as all or part of the price of the collateral."

2. Susan gets a written security agreement, so she does have a security interest. But is it a PMSI? You see the problem. The interest was taken by her *after* the sale had been completed. Analytically, it could be argued this is just her taking a security interest in a piece of his property, in this case a stickpin, to secure an antecedent debt that he happens to owe her. She had not insisted upon the security interest before giving him possession. Presumably, if he had not wanted to grant this interest in this particular piece of jewelry and she was getting worried about payment, he could have convinced her to take a security interest in some other valuable he owned. If to secure this obligation she had taken instead an

interest in another piece of his jewelry or one of his stable of thorough-breds, it clearly would not be a PMSI. Should the answer be different because it happens to be the same item for which the debt was originally incurred? A careful reading of §9-103(a) suggests Susan's interest is not a PMSI. See the concluding paragraph of Comment 3 to §9-103:

> The concept of "purchase-money security interest" requires a close nexus between the acquisition of collateral and the secured obligation. Thus, a security interest does not qualify as a purchase-money security interest if a debtor acquires property on unsecured credit and subsequently creates the security interest to secure the purchase price.

For a case that held to the same effect under the prerevision Article 9, see In re Carter, 169 Bankr. 227, 25 U.C.C.2d 239 (M.D. Ga. 1993).

Remember, even if Susan's interest is found not to be a PMSI, that doesn't mean it is not a perfectly good (albeit non-purchase-money) security interest under Article 9. But it's well she knows that from the outset, from the time she is granted the interest, so that she can properly evaluate what she has to do to perfect the interest and how her claim to the value of the stickpin will fare should Boris' fortunes turn sour, he fail to pay her what he owes her, and she end up duking it out with others also making claim to the same limited resources. If she would only be willing to take the interest if it will be first in line, she may have to do some checking of the files first, and in fact it may not be possible at all for her to go to the head of the line. But here, as we saw, Susan was initially willing to give unsecured credit to Boris. Now, at least she has some security, even if it isn't a purchase-money interest. If she does want more, is it wrong to ask her to take the extra steps that any other lender, loaning on the basis of this particular piece of collateral, would have to go through?

3. The fact that the amount secured includes a reasonable interest payment probably doesn't defeat her purchase-money status. The one reason we may have some doubt is that §9-103 requires that the interest secure all or part of "the price." The word "price" is not defined in the Code, but just the ordinary meaning suggests the price here is the $5,000. The language of the written agreement purports to secure more than that. The problem is sometimes referred to as that of "add on" clauses or "loading on" to the purchase obligation and trying to get it all covered by a PMSI. The question becomes, when does this loading on amount to an "overload" preventing purchase-money status? Under prerevision Article 9, as long as the amount beyond the cash price was not huge, and was really related to the cost of buying the item, the courts did not have much trouble finding the whole thing a PMSI. See, for example, In re McCall, 67 Bankr. 57, 1 U.C.C.2d 1323 (M.D. Ala. 1985), where the

court held that purchase-money status was not jeopardized by the fact that the interest secured what it called the "credit price," which included "finance, insurance, and other charges as part of the purchase price." If the finance charges were way out of proportion to the item's actual cash value, of course, it suggests that the transaction is really some kind of larger loan appended to the sale of an item, and presumably PMSI status, at least as to the entire amount owed, would be inappropriate. Revised Article 9 apparently adopts this approach. See Comment 3 to §9-103 as to what the terms "price" and "value given to enable" may include.

4a. Yes. This is a PMSI under §9-103. Check that all the criteria are met. The bank has given "value" to Boris. This value, the $26,000 check, was given to enable him "to acquire rights in . . . the collateral," and the check was "in fact so used." This is the classic situation of a financing agency lending money and taking in return a PMSI. It's all very straightforward.

4b. Now things are not quite so simple. The problem is that the money trail has gotten murky and there is at least a question about whether the $26,000 from the bank was "in fact" used to buy the boat. Ideally what the bank would like to be able to do is "trace" the money right into the hands of the Marina. Here the lending bank might be able to take advantage of some accounting methods (you may have heard of FIFO or LIFO and the like, but if not, don't worry) to make a case. If at all times the amount in Boris' account was well over $26,000, and there are no other complications, a court might well accept the tracing idea. The real problems surface in the part to follow.

4c. By now there's real reason to fear (on the bank's part) that the connection between the "value" given to Boris by the bank and the money used to buy the boat is simply too attenuated. The Code clearly requires that the value be "in fact" used to enable the debtor to acquire the item. The linkage between the loan and the purchase is crucial. Why should this be so? One answer, of course, is that the Code requires it, but that doesn't satisfy in and of itself. Going on a bit, the very fact that the PMSI is favored with a measure of special treatment, as we see in this chapter and as we will see in others to follow, has to be taken into consideration. If some particular creditor is going to get some type of advantage by being able to add the term "purchase-money" to his or her claim of a security interest, it does seem inappropriate for Boris, by wheeling and dealing, shifting money around, to favor one creditor over others in this way by deciding on his own and after the fact who gets a PMSI and who does not.

What could the lending bank have done to avoid this problem and protect its legitimate PMSI status? Presumably, on the loan application it will have asked for a statement about how the loan proceeds are to be used, but this won't be of any real help against other third parties if it later proves that Boris was lying or even that he simply changed his mind. The bank has to make sure this money is in fact used to buy the boat. What such lenders often do is make sure that the check they issue is not made out to the borrower alone. Here they could make the check payable directly to "Marty's Marina." Or they could make it payable jointly to Boris and Marty's Marina. Either way Boris could not get his hands on the money itself. He would have to use the bank's check to buy the boat or return it to the lender unnegotiated.

5. If the bank claims this to be a PMSI and it is challenged by another party, its claim probably wouldn't hold up. The value was given to Boris after he bought the boat. How could it be said that it was given "to enable" him to do something he already had done? Again, you can see how allowing the bank to take PMSI status here not only goes against the language of the Code but would allow Boris to borrow money from the bank, giving it not merely a secured interest in his boat, which he has every right to do, but giving the bank an especially favored *purchase-money* interest, which is presumably not his to do just because he wants to.

The courts that have faced this issue have usually found against the PMSI in such a situation. The best known case is *North Platte State Bank v. Production Credit Ass'n*, 189 Neb. 44, 200 N.W.2d 1, 10 U.C.C. 1336 (1972). There a rancher, Tucker, had entered into an oral agreement some time in November for the purchase of up to 100 head of cattle to add to his herd. Seventy-nine of the animals were delivered to his ranch on November 30. The court found that the transaction had involved an extension of open credit by the seller. Later, in January, Tucker paid the seller with money borrowed from the bank. The bank asked for and got from Tucker a security interest in these 79 head of cattle. The court held that what the bank did *not* get was a purchase-money interest. "The money advanced by the bank enabled Tucker to pay the price to Seller for the cows. But it was not used by Tucker to acquire any rights in the cows because he already had all the possible rights in the cows he could have with both possession and title." Read the case if you have a chance. The ruling was not just a matter of upholding technicalities for their own sake. Another secured party was involved which had really relied on inspection of the herd and of the records to gauge its own position. For the North Platte Bank to get a PMSI in this situation would have in effect caught this other party off guard with no way it could have been protected itself. For another case reaching the same conclusion with regard to a different agglomeration of cows, see *Valley Bank v. Estate of Rainsdon*, 117 Idaho 1085, 793 P.2d 1257, 12 U.C.C.2d 828 (1990). These two cases, were, of course, decided under the old Article 9, but there is no reason to think they would come out any differently today under §9-103.

6. Again, the bank may have real difficulty claiming purchase-money status in the boat, at least if the issue were eventually to arise in certain jurisdictions. The problem is how to treat an interest initially created in connection with a loan that seems in part to be a purchase-money loan and in part, well, something else. The direct one-to-one correspondence between the money advanced by the bank and the purchase of the single piece of collateral has been complicated by the advance of the additional $18,000, but has the purchase-money status that the bank would like to claim in the boat — after all, the boat was purchased entirely with money coming directly from the bank — been put in jeopardy? Many courts applying pre-revision Article 9 to such a question, under what came to be known as the "transformation" rule, answered yes. That is, they found an otherwise perfectly legitimate purchase-money interest to be "transformed" into a mere ordinary non-purchase-money interest by any tampering with the simple one-to-one loan-to-collateral formula. Here the bank has attempted to make the boat collateral for the funds borrowed to buy it *and* for other funds loaned as well. That is perfectly legitimate under Article 9, so the transformation rule goes, but what results is not a purchase-money interest on the boat for any purpose.

Similarly (and really a more likely scenario when you think about it), if the bank had agreed to loan enough money for the boat only if it could take an interest in the boat and, *in addition*, in some other property of Boris's, say, some shares of stock or another one of his valuable pieces of jewelry, under the transformation rule the bank could not claim a purchase-money interest in any of the property, even the boat bought directly with a check issued, the funds advanced, by the bank. Under the transformation rule, which was followed in a number of jurisdictions, the purchase-money status was "spoiled," as the courts were fond of saying, when anything gets too fancy or purchase-money dealing is mixed in with anything else. As one court expressed:

> A PMSI is spoiled if the creditor (1) secured the credit extended with collateral other than the assets of the debtor purchased with the proceeds of the creditor's loan and/or (2) had the assets the debtor bought with the proceeds of the creditor's loan stand as collateral to secure other debt the debtor simultaneously owed the creditor.

In re Brookwood Sand & Gravel, Inc., 174 Bankr. 309, 27 U.C.C.2d 593 (N.D. Ala. 1994). The hypothetical initially posed in the example would fall under the second part of this ruling so that, if the transformation rule were applied, the bank could not claim purchase-money status in the boat. My transformed hypothetical, where the bank takes an interest in the boat and some other collateral as well, would fall under the first part, and the bank's claimed PMSI in the boat would be "spoiled" just the same.

A number of courts, egged on by some commentators, took a different tack, in what has come to be known as the "dual status" rule or approach to such hybrid situations. Taking their cue from language in the prerevision section that defined the PMSI, stating that a security interest was to be considered a purchase-money interest "to the extent" that it met the test of that section, these courts held that, in effect, a given security interest can have "dual status" — that it can be part purchase-money and part not. The intriguing bit then becomes, of course, figuring out which part is which. In the case where the loan is secured by the collateral purchased with the proceeds as well as other previously owned collateral — by Boris's new boat and his emerald ring — the question doesn't seem too difficult to answer. We could say that the bank's interest in the boat is a PMSI and its interest in the ring, the additional collateral, is not. But then, if Boris defaults on his loan payments somewhere down the line, can the bank pick and choose which piece of collateral to go against? Does it always have to assert its interest in the two pieces of collateral in proportion to their original value, or can it say that Boris was first getting his piece of jewelry out from under the cloud of the security interest with his initial payments, and that it is left with a hale and hearty PMSI for the full value of the boat for as long as any money is due it?

Flipping back to the hypothetical as originally presented — that is, a loan of $50,000 to pay $32,000 for a boat with money left over for travel — if we wanted to apply the dual status rule, how would we do so? Can the bank claim that the first $18,000 it receives in payments (or really the first 18/50 of the payments including not just the $50,000 principal but the interest and other charges it has been promised) will all go to Boris's paying off the money lent in the form of travelers checks and that only the later payments are going toward paying for the boat? If that were the case, it could claim a PMSI to the full value of the boat even well into the game. Or should the security interest in the boat be viewed from the outset as part (32/50) PMSI and part (18/50) non-purchase-money interest?

Just because of such conundrums, some courts were willing to apply the "dual status" rule and rescue the lender from the fate of "transformation" only where some reasonable and comprehensible method of allocation of payments has been supplied by the parties in the contract itself, or in some instances by other state statute. Other courts went even further and apparently attempted their own judicial allocation, on some accounting basis or another, to determine how the various parts of the dual status were to be determined. Still other jurisdictions eschewed any attempt at overarching generalization and decided to take a case-by-case approach, which worked out pretty much as that suggests. A good overview of this territory under old Article 9 is given in In re McAllister, 267 Bankr. 614, 46 U.C.C.2d 1138 (N.D. Iowa).

The drafters of the Revision to Article 9 were well aware of this split of authority between the "transformation" and the "dual status" approach to such problems. In §9-103(e) through (f) they come down squarely on the side of the dual status advocates and decisions, at least when the transaction is not a "consumer-goods transaction" as that term is defined in §9-102(a)(24). See Comment 7. When it comes to consumer-goods transactions, such as Boris's in our hypothetical, the drafters decided, well, to make no decision. In fact, they didn't want to be seen as even venturing an opinion. Subsection 9-103(h) states:

> The limitation of the rules in subsections (e), (f), and (g) to transactions other than consumer-goods transactions is intended to leave to the court the determination of the proper rule in consumer-goods transactions. The court may not infer from that limitation the nature of the proper rule in consumer-goods transactions and may continue to apply established approaches.

The idea of firmly adopting the dual status approach for other than consumer-goods transactions but ducking the issue entirely when consumer purchases were involved was, depending on how you look at it, either the revision drafters' strong blow for consumer protection or merely a political compromise necessary if they were to get on with their work and come up with a product that could make it through all the states' legislatures. It certainly clears things up in the nonconsumer context. See, for example, the detailed rules on how payments made by a debtor are to be allocated between the purchase-money and the non-purchase-money parts of its "dual-status" obligation. The revision, however, gives us no firm answer — in fact, it firmly states that it wants us to make no inference at all — on how to deal with a consumer-transaction situation like the one Boris and Marty have placed themselves in.

If the problem of Boris and his boating exercise seems difficult, when this type of situation comes up in the actual cases it tends to be, if anything, much more complex and indeed sometimes verging on outright mind-boggling. The combined effect of future advances clauses, after-acquired property provisions (which working together set up intentionally or otherwise what is often referred to as "cross-collateralization"), refinancings, consolidations, and the like (things to be seen in the next example) certainly does muddy the PMSI waters, and you begin to feel some sympathy for the ardent advocates of the transformation approach. Remember, the transformation rule does not say that there is anything inherently wrong or unenforceable about any of these types of provisions, these comings and goings, only that their combined and cumulative effect is to lose the creditor the right to claim favored purchase-money status.

7a. Louie may indeed have lost purchase-money status with this refinancing. If this were not a consumer-goods transaction, then the rule would be clear. Section 9-103(f)(3) provides that in a transaction other than a consumer-goods transaction, a PMSI "does not lose its status as such" even if "the purchase-money obligation has been renewed, refinanced, consolidated, or restructured." This is in keeping with the revision's general adoption of the "dual-status" approach to such issues. But again, since our example involves a consumer-goods transaction, the rule, or rather the non-rule, of §9-103(h) leaves it to the court to make a determination applying "established approaches." The same choice that must be made between a "transformation" rule or a "dual status" rule, and the same split among the courts on which is the proper one to apply that we saw played out in the prior example prior to the revision of Article 9, has to be confronted here. In fact, if we were merely counting cases, the dispute seems to come up much more often in this kind of situation, a refinancing or a consolidation, than in transactions that are hybrids from the start as in the prior example.

The argument for the transformation rule here seems straightforward enough: Section 9-103 says a seller or a lender can have a PMSI when its extension of credit enables the debtor to become owner of the property. While that was initially true of Louie's loan in 2005, in 2007 Bess already owned the TV. His loan in 2007, complete with its own three-year payment schedule, wasn't instrumental in her gaining possession of anything new. This was in effect a loan by Louie that empowered her to pay off a prior debt, not to acquire anything she did not already have. So while the two, Bess and Louie, are perfectly free to agree that her obligation, incurred in 2007, will be secured by an interest in a piece of her property, what they cannot do (to the possible disadvantage of others) is put Louie in a position to claim his remains a purchase-money interest.

The contrary argument is, of course, that there seems no legitimate reason why Louie's interest should be "transformed," downgraded, or spoiled as to its purchase-money status just because he was willing to extend Bess a little more time to make payment on the TV set. He initially had a PMSI on the set. Who is actually prejudiced by his being able to claim one still? If there is such a party (and there usually isn't), let him or her come forward. Otherwise, so the thinking goes, leave Louie and Bess alone to do what's right between them.

7b. The situation here is referred to as a consolidation of debt, and, since this is a consumer-goods transaction, the problem of characterization remains. Louie started out with a PMSI in the TV. By lending to her so that she can also buy the stereo, in the course of which he gets to "cross-collateralize" the two loans he's made and the two articles he's sold, does he continue with that PMSI and get a PMSI in the stereo as well? Or has he "spoiled" the whole arrangement, from the purchase-money standpoint, so that he will have to settle for mere non-purchase-money standing on both items? At least here you begin to see more clearly the kind of concern that a court might have (in the way of consumer protection) about such arrangements. In 2007 Bess had paid approximately half of what she was to pay for the TV. In two more years it would have been hers free and clear of any security interest whatsoever. After the consolidation, which she might think to be all to her advantage, she will not own the TV free from Louie's interest for an additional four years. And for all that time the TV is now under the cloud of an interest supporting her obligation to pay not only for it, but for the stereo as well.

As a matter of fact, the reason why courts have found so much appeal in the transformation approach, and why it first arose and took hold in consumer refinancing and consolidation situations just like these, has less to do with the language or the intricacies of §9-103 than with one particular aspect of the Bankruptcy Code (you may or may not run into §522(f)(2) in your Secured Transactions studies) with which we have no reason to bother ourselves here. The decisions initially enunciating this approach almost certainly had more to do with the policy underlying that bankruptcy provision, and a determination of what best balanced the interests of the various parties in that situation and in light of that policy, than anything like a consideration of what "the drafters of Article 9" intended. Rules, holdings, and approaches, of course, begin to take on a life of their own in the law, and so we have many courts tenaciously adhering to the "transformation" rule for purchase-money interests — in its strictest reading a notion that any messing around with a strict one-to-one enabling loan-for-particular-collateral formula so compromises the pristine nature of the classic PMSI that it is transformed into a mere non-purchase-money interest, no matter what the context. Courts that hold steadfastly to this approach do so whether the muddying of the PMSI waters takes place at the time of the initial transaction (as in

Example 6) or through a later refinancing or consolidation of debt (as in this example).

Of course not all courts go this route. As I indicated in the discussion of the last example, some courts are willing to analyze the refinance or the consolidation situation under a "dual status" approach, at least where the parties themselves in their agreement or some state statute gives a credible allocation formula for separating out the purchase-money part of the transaction from the non-purchase-money component. Other courts may go even further, imposing some accounting methodology of their own to this end.

Basically there are no easy answers to problems such as these as they arise in consumer-goods transactions. Once such a transaction veers very far from the most simple one-to-one correspondence of the simple PMSI, either at inception or later on because of a renegotiation, the secured party runs the risk, at least in many jurisdictions, of losing some or all of its preferred purchase-money status. Research on the approach taken in the applicable jurisdiction and on how that approach would play on the facts of the particular transaction will be crucial, if not necessarily exceptionally thrilling or groundbreaking.

8a. Yes. Lucky Louie's interest is perfected, not because he's lucky but because of §9-309(1). Taking advantage of material we've already mastered, we confirm that his is a PMSI under §9-103, and that the computer system has been bought and is held by Bess as consumer goods under §9-102(a)(23). This being so, no filing is required for perfection, which means perfection comes automatically at the moment of attachment.

8b. Louie would not be so lucky under this scenario. He has still taken a PMSI, but here the computer system would be classified as equipment under §9-102(a)(33) because of the use for which it was bought. A filing would be necessary to perfect this interest.

An obvious question at this point is exactly how Louie is to deal with the predicament with which he's presented: He doesn't have to file if the goods are being purchased for "personal, family, or household" purposes, but he does have to file if the buyer has other uses in mind. One thing he can do, of course, is ask the buyer to declare his or her intended use of the goods when filling out whatever form Louie has developed as an application for credit or right on the retail installment sales agreement itself. Standard forms of this type often have a box to be marked if the buyer is obtaining the goods for "personal, family, or household" use. There would really be little reason for the buyer in most instances not to fill out this part of the form truthfully. Louie should also keep his eyes and ears open for what might be telltale signs that the customer is buying for other than consumer use. Certainly, if a customer comes along who wants to purchase something like a dozen computers along with the various wires, cables, and software that would link them together into a "multiuser fully integrated state-of-the-art network" system all the parts of which are to be delivered to an office address on Main Street, Louie should take the hint and deal with this as a sale of other than consumer goods.

In the example under discussion, Louie's sale of a single computer setup to Bess, he might take note of what choice Bess makes between the "Family Game and Educational" or the "Complete Home Office Start-Up" package of software, either of which she may have "free" with her purchase. At other times there will probably be no realistic chance of the retailer's verifying what use is going to be made of the item sold. A microwave oven intended for an employees' lunchroom looks no different from one to be used in a family kitchen. Apparently retailers such as Lucky Louie, at least when they are dealing with relatively low-ticket items, simply can't or don't want to mess around with getting the buyer to authorize that filing of a financing statement and then taking the time, trouble, and expense of filing. In doing so they are obviously running the risk of being caught with their interest unperfected from time to time, but it is evidently a risk they are willing to take and able to live with. In the end, it's a business decision for the individual seller. The lawyer's job is to explain the nature of the risk and what measures could be taken to eliminate or at least minimize the problem; from then on it is up to the client to make the decision with this information at hand.

The rule of §9-309(1) seems a potentially big "loophole" in the scheme central to Article 9 for providing third parties with notice of interests as they are taken, and it is certainly legitimate to ask what rationale there is for this exemption. Automatic perfection of PMSIs in consumer goods, it turns out, is nothing new. It was also the rule under the original Article 9, a comment to which reported that before the adoption of Article 9 many states had such an exemption to any filing requirements under prior analogous law and that it was the drafters' decision to "follow[] the policy of those jurisdictions." So history was partially on the drafters' side, both initially in the mid-twentieth century and recently as Article 9 was revised, but what more can be said than that? First of all, consider what benefit would be gained from having PMSIs in consumer goods all subject to the filing requirement just like any other Article 9 interests. The result would be effective notice to all third parties, at least those who bothered to look, of these interests. The drafters apparently concluded, and the general run of opinion seems to agree, that first of all there wouldn't be that many people who would bother to look for such filings even if they were technically available. Consumer goods, apart perhaps from the larger items like the automobile, typically depreciate in value fairly rapidly. People certainly do buy and sell used consumer goods, but most often only after the original purchaser has gotten some years use out of them, by which time they don't really amount to much. Also, just because they depreciate rapidly even in the hands of the most careful and responsible buyer, the credit offered to purchase such things typically has to be paid off within a shorter period of time. Retail sales installment loans covering consumer goods would rarely go beyond a year or two. So by the time of most sales of used consumer goods the security interest will have lapsed in any event.

What of parties who would be interested in taking a *non-purchase-money* security interest in consumer goods? What protection do they have in a world without notice? The answer is that they have little protection, but perhaps that is not such a bad thing. A lender other than the purchase-money lender, without whom the individual might not have been able to obtain the needed goods in the first place, that looks to take a security interest in an individual's personal or household possessions is not looked upon with any great favor in the commercial law. To be even more blunt about it, it's probably fair to say that he or she is viewed with a touch of suspicion. Recall, in fact, that Revised Article 9 specifically prohibits via §9-108(e)(2), as the prerevision version of the article did not, a lender from taking a security interest in collateral as broadly described as "all debtor's consumer goods." This would include not only all of the debtor's furniture and appliances, but his or her clothing and the pet canary, as well.

Certainly there are instances when a person has some consumer goods that are both valuable and not necessary for that person's day-to-day existence, just the kind of thing with which it makes sense to secure a loan. Just in this volume we have already seen how the Moneybucks clan seems to be repeatedly taking advantage of its valuable bits and pieces of jewelry and masterpieces of art, modern and otherwise, to serve as collateral for a loan. Lenders in such cases presumably will be aware that any relevant PMSI in this type of property would not necessarily be on file and have to take other steps and make further inquiries to get the knowledge they need to evaluate the collateral. The lack of notice, either through a public filing or by the collateral's having been taken out of the possession of the debtor, is something they can deal with.

Many, however, if not most attempts to get a non-purchase-money interest in a consumer's goods are not this type of situation. They are rather the kind of loan that goes to an individual who is not well-to-do and who in order to get the loan has had to sign an agreement giving the lender a security interest in something like, "Any and all furniture and household appliances now held by me or hereafter acquired." What, if anything, is the legitimate purpose of such a provision? The lender will claim he or she is just asking for a security interest in whatever the borrower has of value that can be put up as collateral. But, as we've already noted, the kinds of property that are covered in such a case are not usually of any great consequence. What real value do they have as collateral? The suspicion here is that the lender is interested more in having at his or her command a particularly chilling kind of threat over the borrower if he or she doesn't keep up with the required payments. "If you don't come up with that payment by tomorrow when it's due, we have the right to come and repossess the TV, the refrigerator, and the baby's crib, for that matter." And so they could. Seen in this light it's not hard to understand what might have at first seemed a striking lack of concern for the lender who would take a non-purchase-money interest in consumer goods. The Uniform Commercial Code does not prohibit such transactions (for which the Moneybucks are, we assume, forever grateful), but it doesn't exactly facilitate them either.

9. Whether or not the bank's interest is perfected without a filing is a question of what purpose Boris is buying the boat to serve. The bank's interest is a PMSI under §9-103. The question is whether the boat constitutes consumer goods. If Boris is buying the boat as a pleasure craft, then it is consumer goods and the bank's interest would be automatically perfected. If, on the other hand, he is buying it to use, for example, in running charter parties for profit, then the interest could be perfected only by filing. The bank as lender will probably question Boris about his intentions, but with a larger loan such as this it should and would probably err on the side of caution and file even if every indication is that he intends to use it only as consumer goods.

   Besides reminding you that a PMSI can be taken by a party other than the seller of the goods itself, this example highlights that some fairly expensive items can be classified perfectly appropriately as consumer goods under Article 9. The automatic perfection provision of §9-309(1) still applies, but the kind of cost-benefit analysis that the secured party will go through in order to determine whether to put all its eggs in this one basket instead of in addition filing on the interest may come out quite differently. The most common case of consumer goods sold on purchase-money credit is undoubtedly the personal automobile, and as you can see from §9-311(a)(2) and (b), to which §9-309(1) defers, a distinct regimen of vehicle registration typically calling for notation on the registration certificate itself of any outstanding security interests is in place in most states. This substitutes for, and potentially serves the same function of, filing under the

Article 9 system. Other big-ticket items, things for which there truly is a legitimate resale market, such as jewelry, artwork, and grand pianos, for example, are often not covered by any certificate-of-title law, however, and the seller or lender who takes a PMSI may be risking too much by relying solely on the automatic perfection provision of §9-309(1).

Automatic Perfection: Other Instances

10

INTRODUCTION

This chapter brings together a few other important situations where automatic perfection, either permanently or for at least some limited period of time, is possible under Article 9. Return first to §9-309, which lists a number of circumstances in which a security interest will be perfected upon attachment with the secured party having no obligation to do anything more to obtain perfection for his, her, or its security interest. In the prior chapter, we have already dealt with the case provided for in paragraph (1), the purchase-money interest in consumer goods. In Example 3 of this chapter, we will look into the instance covered by paragraph (2) of this section. The eleven other possibilities for automatic perfection upon attachment we will either deal with in later chapters or feel free to leave for another day entirely as, frankly, either not that important in the general scheme of things or at least well beyond the introductory scope of this book.

The first two examples deal with some special rules found in §9-312 concerning perfection when things like goods covered by a document of title or instruments are concerned. In some instances, as we will see, the article provides for what we might call *temporary automatic perfection* for a limited period of time, the purpose of which is to facilitate commercial dealings of one sort or another. These two examples do not exhaust the possibilities covered by §9-312, but for our purpose they will suffice.

Examples

1. Anticipating a coming surge in demand, Hartford Cogs and Widgets produces a large quantity of a particular item — its CyberCog 2100 — but has limited room in its own plant available for storage. In January it takes several truckloads of these cogs to Wally's Warehouse, one of the larger commercial warehouses in the area, where it arranges to store these cogs and receives in return a negotiable warehouse receipt. It then goes to its bank, Metalgrinders of New England, where it pledges the receipt in order to receive an extension on its line of credit (in order to get the cash to buy the materials from which it can make still more cogs and widgets).

   a. Does the bank have a perfected interest in the warehouse receipt? If so, how was perfection achieved?

   b. Does it have a perfected interest in the CyberCogs themselves? See §9-312(c).

   c. The cogs are resting securely in Wally's Warehouse. The negotiable warehouse receipt covering them is safe at the bank. All seems well until a trade journal reports that a serious flaw has begun to turn up in many of a particular type of computer chip that is key to the workings of Hartford's CyberCog 2100. On May 3, Hartford's Director of Quality Control goes to the bank, where she is given the warehouse receipt. She takes this receipt to the warehouse, where she surrenders it in exchange for the cogs themselves. She then takes the cogs back to Hartford's plant, where she has each one tested to see if it contains a faulty version of the chip in question. Fortunately, none of the Cyber-Cogs shows any signs of the problem. She has them repackaged as they originally were and then redelivers them to Wally's Warehouse. Upon turning them over she receives back in exchange the warehouse receipt. She redelivers this receipt to the bank on May 13. All is as it was; the cogs are in the warehouse, and the warehouse receipt is with the bank. Does the bank now have a perfected interest in both the receipt and the cogs themselves? More importantly, as of what date does the bank's perfection run? See §9-312(f).

   d. Would your answer to the previous part be the same if instead the warehouse receipt had not been redelivered to the bank until May 30?

   e. Subsection 9-312(f)(1) includes the possibility of the debtor's getting possession of the document or the goods it represents "for the purpose of ultimate sale or exchange." Suppose that there is no quality control problem. Rather, there is a potential buyer for all those CyberCogs. It is Hartford's Director for Sales who gets the warehouse receipt from the bank. He then sells the cogs in question (either by getting them out of the warehouse and selling them directly or by selling the warehouse receipt itself). What happens then, other than that the buyer has the cogs to do with as he or she wishes? Has Hartford pulled a fast one on the bank? In thinking about an answer to this part look not to any section or sections in the Code but to your own practical and business sense of what the parties are actually trying to accomplish here.

2. Selma of Selma's Appliance City has an arrangement with Friendly Factors and Lenders (FF&L), a company that makes loans to small businesses, taking as collateral their "accounts receivable" in various forms. In Selma's case, she makes larger sales to customers who in turn sign notes that allow them to pay for the items over a period of 36 or 48 months. Under her written agreement with FF&L, that firm will make available to her a line of credit equal to 60% of the sum total of all the notes which she turns over to them as collateral. Following a particularly busy week of sales, Selma contacts her account manager at FF&L and informs him that she has a total of $100,000 in new notes that she will be delivering to FF&L and that in order to take advantage of some good prices being offered by her suppliers she would like to draw on all credit available to her as soon as possible. Immediately after this phone call, the account manager gets the approval of his supervisor to increase Selma's available credit line by $60,000. Early the next day Selma calls her contact at FF&L in charge of funds dispersal and arranges for immediate wire transfer of a total of $58,345 to a number of her suppliers. This amount is released after a check of Selma's available balance. On Wednesday afternoon FF&L receives a package from Selma that she has sent via messenger. It contains a number of notes signed by various of Selma's customers, the face value of which totals $102,380.

   a. Does FF&L have a perfected security interest in these notes? If so, as of what moment did it obtain that perfection? See §9-312(e).

   b. One of Selma's customers who had signed a three-year note in 2007 tells her about one year later that he is interested in fully paying off his debt to her by exercising a prepayment option included in the terms of the note. Selma does a calculation and informs this customer that in order to prepay he has to come up with a certain amount in cash or its equivalent and present it to her on or prior to August 31, 2008. Selma is aware that should the customer pay off the note he will be expecting (and will be entitled to) its return on the spot. She then contacts FF&L, giving it the pertinent information to identify the note in question. That firm sends her the note by courier on August 15. Selma's customer never comes around to make the prepayment. She returns the note to FF&L, which receives it on September 1. Has the nature of FF&L's interest in this particular note changed in any way? See §9-312(g).

   c. Would your answer to the previous question be any different if FF&L did not receive the note back until September 15? Would it help FF&L in this instance if it had made an Article 9 filing covering "all notes" held by Selma, whenever acquired? See §9-312(a).

   d. Finally, suppose instead that the customer *does* come up with the money and on August 27 presents Selma with a certified check in the proper amount. He gives Selma the check and she gives him the note, which he immediately and joyfully rips into shreds. Selma, bemused, could care less. She has the certified check in hand. But what of FF&L? As a practical matter, what has happened to the value of its security interest and to its interests more generally? What steps should it take to protect itself in situations like this one?

3. Isabelle Inkster, the printer, does most of her work for local small businesses, schools, nonprofit agencies, and the like. Her normal procedure is to make delivery of a printing job along with an invoice for the price calling for payment within 60 days of delivery. When one of the machines she more regularly uses in her work, a small but vital component of many printing jobs, dies on her, she is in urgent need of a replacement. Luckily she quickly makes contact with another printer, Wilfred Smeers, who is in the process of closing up his shop and selling his equipment prior to retiring to Florida. Smeers has just the piece of equipment Inkster needs and is willing to sell it to her for $12,000 cash. Unfortunately, Inkster is short of cash. She tells Smeers that she has a number of large accounts coming due soon, including a payment of $20,000 from Downtown Urban Law School ("DULS") for all her work on an oversized glossy brochure that she delivered one month ago. It takes some talking, but Inkster is able to convince Smeers to let her have the machine right away, giving her one month to come up with the purchase price. What clinches the deal is that she agrees in writing that "Smeers shall have as collateral to assure my payment a security interest in the amounts now due me from Downtown Urban Law School." (Smeers reasons, quite sensibly, that any amount owed by a law school is as good as money in the bank.) Smeers makes no filing regarding his interest in the DULS debt. It turns out that at the time the total amount of accounts outstanding owed to Inkster for her printing work, including that owed by DULS, is approximately $50,000. Should a problem arise, what argument can be made on Smeers' behalf that his security interest in the DULS debt is perfected? Should the argument succeed? See §9-309(2).

Explanations

1a. Simply, yes. The warehouse receipt taken by Hartford is a negotiable document, and under §9-313(a) a negotiable document is a type of collateral upon which an interest can be perfected by possession. The bank has possession of the document, therefore it has a perfected interest in it. These cogs are goods and the bank could perfect an interest in them by possession — but first it would have to bargain for a security interest in the cogs themselves, which it does not appear to have done, and secondly it would actually have to take possession of them in some way, directly or indirectly. Where would the bank put all these truck-loads of cogs? The bank seems to be thinking only in terms of possession of the paper. Is this trouble for the bank? No, but for that we have to look to the next part of the example.

1b. The bank's interest in the goods themselves, the cogs, is perfected by virtue of §9-312(c)(1):

> While goods are in the possession of a bailee [Wally's Warehouse] that has issued a negotiable document covering the goods [the negotiable ware-house receipt issued by Wally], a security interest in the goods [those CyberCogs] may be perfected by perfecting a security interest in the document. . . .

The bank has perfected on the document by taking possession of it. The issuer has possession of the cogs, and so the bank has a perfected interest in not only the document but in the goods themselves. It is important that you recognize this rule is effective to perfect the bank's interest in the goods only when the document, be it a warehouse receipt or a bill of lading, is in *negotiable* form. Only when the document in question is a negotiable one is it possible to assert, as does Comment 7 to this section, that

> title to the goods is, so to say, locked up in the document. Accordingly, a security interest in goods covered by a negotiable document may be perfected by perfecting a security interest in the document.

This certainly is convenient for the parties. Hartford is able to take advantage of its large supply of cogs as collateral, and the bank is able to take that collateral and perfect its interest in it without having to bother with filing *and* without having to find some space on its own premises to take and hold possession of all of those cogs. A lender like Metalgrinders bank is presumably accustomed to keeping bits and pieces of paper well-protected and out of the hands of people who have no business fooling around with them. The bank would be very unlikely to have any interest in or expertise at taking possession and guarding a few truckloads of cogs. Hartford gets to use its bulky bunch of cogs as collateral by, as the comment says, "locking up" their value in a relatively slim and trim document.

As convenient as this system is for the debtor and the lender, does it impose too great a risk on others, that is, third parties who might be interested in either buying or themselves lending to Hartford on the basis of the cogs? Such third parties, it might seem, would not in this instance be protected by the kind of notice of Metalgrinders' interest that the Article 9 mechanisms for perfection are intended to provide. If you think it through, however, you will see that the fundamental notice function is satisfied here. Any third party who wants to assure itself that it has complete information on any security interests that are or may be claimed in the cogs—and who knows enough to realize that its investigation has to be by means independent of just asking the debtor to tell it "really truly" what the story is—will be able to protect itself. First it will check the relevant Article 9 public records to see whether any filing has been made covering any cogs or any warehouse receipts that could cover cogs under Hartford's name. Here, since the interest in the document has been perfected by possession only and the interest in the cogs themselves through this mechanism only, there will be no filings to give even the most diligent searcher of the records a hint of an interest by Metalgrinders or anyone else. That can't be the end of the story, however. The searcher has not found any filing on record, but it still has not seen the cogs themselves. How does he or she know they even exist, much less that they are the type, quantity, and quality of cogs that Hartford is saying they are? Remember that an adequate investigation requires not only searching the public records, the Article 9 system of filings, but also actually seeing the collateral in question in the possession, under the dominion and control, of the debtor claiming to own it.

So in our example, any third party inquiry will not stop at checking the filings, but will ask to see the cogs themselves. You can imagine what happens then. Hartford has to admit that they are not on its premises, but are instead at Wally's Warehouse. Nothing necessarily suspicious there. Goods are put in storage all the time. Then the inquirer will ask to see the warehouse receipt for them. Hartford does not have the receipt—it is out of harm's way in the bank's safe, we presume—and so will not be able to fulfill this perfectly reasonable request. Could Hartford's president work his way around this little problem by asking that the investigator accompany him down to Wally's Warehouse, where together they can get a chance to look at the cogs in question? The president can ask, and the investigator may agree to go along for the ride, but this isn't going to work. If Wally is holding the goods under a negotiable warehouse receipt therefor, he is under an obligation under the law relevant to negotiable documents and in jeopardy of taking on liability himself if he surrenders them up in any way to anyone, even the party who originally consigned them to the warehouse and whose name was placed on the receipt, who is not in actual possession of the document and a "person entitled" to delivery thereunder (see §7-403(4)). Wally may immediately recognize Hartford's president, like the fellow immensely, and wish him only the best, but if he knows his responsibilities and his potential liability under the law he is not going to let him have access to the cogs in storage any more than he would a stranger unless the president is holding and is willing to surrender the warehouse receipt in proper form. The negotiable warehouse receipt works to "lock up" title in the stuff itself, and by doing so allows for, among other things, the perfection of a security interest in the goods via possession of the receipt, exactly because the issuers of such receipts are professionals at what they do and take their responsibilities seriously.

1c. As of the redelivery of the receipt on May 13, the bank's interest in both the document and the cogs themselves is perfected. More importantly, the perfection runs from the moment in January when the bank originally got a perfected interest in the receipt. Under §9-312(e), in fact, this date would actually be the date of attachment if the bank gave new value at the time and if it got possession of the document within 20 days thereafter. We will deal with this subsection, allowing for a temporary period of automatic perfection on acquisition, in detail in the example that follows. What is interesting in this example is the workings of the so-called *release rule* of §9-312(f), allowing for a temporary period of automatic perfection running up to 20 days as collateral in the possession of a commercial bailee if released back into the hands of the debtor for certain purposes.

Reading §9-312(f) in a way directed to our story,

> A perfected security interest in a negotiable document . . . remains perfected for 20 days without filing if the secured party [the bank] makes available to the debtor [Hartford] the . . . documents representing the goods for the purpose of ultimate sale or exchange or for the purpose of loading, unloading, storing, shipping, transshipping, manufacturing, processing, or otherwise dealing with them in a manner preliminary to their sale or exchange.

While testing to ensure that the cogs won't blow a gasket is not mentioned explicitly in this list, it seems easily to come under the concept of "dealing with them in a manner preliminary to their sale or exchange." That being so, when the bank made available the receipt to Hartford on May 3, a 20-day clock began to run. During that time the bank's interest in the receipt continued to be perfected, even though it had surrendered possession back to the debtor itself. When the warehouse receipt returns to the possession of the bank ten days later, this period of automatic perfection has not lapsed and perfection by possession can be reasserted. Recall §9-308(c):

> A security interest . . . is perfected continuously if it is originally perfected by one method under this Article and is later perfected by another method under this article, without an intermediate period when it was unperfected.

So Metalgrinders' interest in the document is perfected now and, what is more, has been perfected continuously since January.

Be sure to note that this temporary automatic perfection when documents, instruments, or goods are surrendered back to the debtor "for limited use" as it is sometimes called (although you have to admit the list of potential purposes that fit the bill in §9-312(f) doesn't seem all that "limited") is applicable to goods only when they are initially perfected through placement into the hands of a bailee. It doesn't work when the perfection is based on possession directly by the secured party. In that situation, as we know from a prior chapter and we can check again in §9-313(d), perfection "continues only while the secured party retains possession."

The temporary automatic perfection made possible by subsection (f) of §9-312 is based partly in history (the prior Uniform Trust Receipts Act had a similar provision, as did prerevision Article 9), but survives mostly because of practicality. See Comment 9.

> There are a variety of legitimate reasons — many of them are described in subsections (f) and (g) — why certain types of collateral must be released temporarily to a debtor. No useful purpose would be served by cluttering the files with records of such exceedingly short term transactions.

You should have no difficulty appreciating the practicality of this solution at work here. If the bank could not temporarily hand over the warehouse receipt to Hartford for this purpose, it would have to come up with some other way for the testing to be done. Remember it is in the bank's interest as much as in the manufacturer's that the cogs be in good and undamaged condition and as valuable as both expect them to be. By and large the bank will regard its part in this financing arrangement as something to be taken care of at its offices. It wouldn't want to get involved with having to appoint an officer or agent to go to the warehouse, take possession of the cogs, and then stand guard over them for the ten days or so of testing at Hartford's facilities to be sure nothing untoward happens to them or to the bank's interest. The bank will have to be careful, as we will see in the next part of this example, to protect its interest, of course, but for the most part should be able to devise ways of doing so other than getting its hands dirty, actually messing around with cogs, or trooping down to warehouses.

The comment previously quoted speaks of "no useful purpose" to be served by requiring a filing in such a situation, but what of the unsuspecting third party who is now left with no notice, either through a filing or because the debtor has been deprived of actual possession of them, that this batch of cogs in Hartford's factory are subject to a security interest? Apparently, at least if we are to judge by what seems to be an almost complete absence of litigation in which this particular provision figures, parties potentially in the position to be misled by these temporary automatic perfection provisions are not tripped up to any significant degree. For one thing, these parties would tend to be professionals dealing in particular industries where such practices are common or at least well-understood and would presumably be savvy enough to know how to protect themselves against potential abuse. Note also that the comment speaks of the "exceedingly short term" nature of such transactions. Temporary automatic perfection can run for no more than 20 days. Other parties potentially drawn into a trap during the period can, if they are concerned, just wait for at least that time before they firm up any deal or release any funds. For that matter, in many instances it may be hard for a deal of any complexity to be concluded in 20 days even if all parties involved want things to be wrapped up as soon as possible. In commercial transactions, just like in most things in life, there are times when getting even the simplest thing accomplished takes longer than even the most pessimistic participant could have ever imagined.

1d. If the warehouse receipt is not received back by the bank until the 30th, which is more than 20 days after it was released back to the debtor, then the bank's interest is still reperfected as of May 30 but it would no longer relate back to the original date of perfection in January. Under §9-308(c), a party can claim continuous perfection only if there has been no "intermediate period" no matter how brief when the interest was unperfected. Here the interest would have been unperfected from May 24 through May 29, and that would be enough to defeat any claim the bank would have to continuous perfection dating from January.

What could the bank do to ensure against this happening? Of course it will get Hartford's promise that it will return the warehouse receipt within 20 days, and maybe with a few days to spare. If Hartford fails to keep this promise, the bank will be able to consider this failure a default by the borrower under the security agreement, and as we will see in the last part of this book, have all kinds of ways of making Hartford regret what it has done. So there will be pressure on Hartford as the debtor to get the warehouse receipt back to the bank with no question. The bank, of course, will do its part by keeping careful watch on the calendar and "reminding" Hartford with ample notice that the receipt is due back at the bank by such-and-such a date. One other thing that can make such a release less risky for the bank than may be first imagined is that this warehouse receipt is apt to be only one of many pieces of collateral subject to the bank's security interest. If the bank is careful not to release back to the debtor, Hartford, too much of this collateral at any one time, then it, the bank, can control the situation and take care that even if this one receipt is not returned it will have enough collateral safely under its control to protect against its being undercollateralized. And, as we will see, if the secured party has sufficient collateral under its control *and* is able to declare the debtor in default for its failure to do one thing or another required of it under the security agreement, well then the secured party has plenty of leverage to use against the debtor to get things back in order again.

If the bank does not have an interest in sufficient other collateral, it can, of course, refuse to release the warehouse receipt to Hartford, even for this limited purpose, until it completes filing a financing statement covering the receipt and the goods as well. This will take some time and energy, but it may be worth it for the bank and Hartford would have little choice but to go along. If an effective filing is in place prior to the release by the bank of the warehouse receipt, then under the principle enunciated in §9-308(c) the bank's interest will remain perfected and will be deemed continuously perfected from the initial perfection date in January. For a rare reported example of a lender's losing its perfected status on goods covered by a document of title (although not necessarily on the "identifiable cash proceeds" of these goods, a concept we have yet to encounter) through the interplay of §9-312(f) and §9-308(c), see In re Schwinn Cycling and Fitness, Inc., 2003 Bankr. LEXIS 1206, 51 U.C.C.2d 1224 (Bankr. D. Colo. 2003), as affirmed in part and reversed in part by 313 Bankr. 473, 54 U.C.C.2d 645 (D. Colo. 2004). The lender lost its perfected interest in the goods in question by its failure to file a financing statement within 20 days of its release to the debtor of the documents of title it had been holding covering goods, which were then quickly sold by the debtor in the ordinary course of its business, and which consequentially could not have been returned to the lender. The fact that the debtor had filed for bankruptcy within the 20-day temporary perfection period provided for in §9-312(f) was held not to have been a valid excuse for the lender's failure to file.

1e. Once this load of cogs has been sold, there will be no way, of course, for any warehouse receipt covering them exactly and still naming Hartford as the party entitled to retrieve them from the warehouse to be put back into the hands of Metalgrinders. From a purely technical angle, as we will see in chapters to come, whatever money Hartford got in exchange for the goods will be considered "proceeds" of the sale and the bank's security interest will attach to those proceeds automatically. Its interest may also remain in the cogs even though they are now in the hands of the buyer, but for the moment we need not worry about any of that. In fact, let's not worry about the proceeds aspect either. There will be time enough for that as we progress.

The aspect of this situation I'd ask you to consider for the moment is, strange enough to say, not a technical matter of Article 9 law. Just think about the business concerns of the parties involved here. Hartford has sold a few truckloads of its product. From its position, that can't be a bad thing. Hartford is in the business of not just making goods, but of selling them. An important thing to recognize is that this feature — that Hartford is actually able to sell to somebody the goods it produces — is welcome news not just for Hartford but for the Metalgrinders bank as well. Metalgrinders has loaned to a business expressly for the purpose of giving that business a chance to make the stuff that it can sell. Of course the bank has not done this just to be nice or as a charitable gesture. The bank's design in lending money as it does, the *raison d'être* behind the loan, is just that it expects to be repaid, with appropriate interest of course, by the borrower. It is in the bank's interest that Hartford be able to and does sell its product. If the people at Hartford Cogs and Widgets were some kind of cog-and-widget-fabricating fanatics who loved to make the things and store them in warehouses but who could not bear to part with them, the collateral to which the bank's interest would attach would undoubtedly keep increasing. But if Hartford would not or could not turn its products into cash or its equivalent — and the more realistic concern is, of course, that it will not be able to find willing buyers for one reason or another — then it is going to run out of funds fairly rapidly, and it won't be able to pay its debts, including most specifically the loan payments that Metalgrinders is expecting.

To make sense of the whole operation, from both the manufacturer's and the lender's side, you have to appreciate that the lender's principal concern is that it be paid on the loan in a regular and timely fashion. The security interest, and any rights it may have ultimately and as a last resort to take over and deal with the collateral directly, is a prudent measure as far as the lender is concerned. It probably would not have even considered making the loan, at least at the rate of interest that it did, without some kind of sufficient security. Don't make the mistake, however, of thinking of the lender as sitting around hoping or looking forward with anything but dread to its actually having to enforce its interest in the collateral. The security interest is a backup, a safety net if you will, that allows the lender to rest easier at night. It also works to gently prod and in some instances, we have to admit, to force the borrower into ensuring it gets its payments in on time rather than jeopardizing its position with the lender and running the risk of having its stuff repossessed. In the first instance, however, what the secured party wants is that the debtor meet whatever obligation it is that is being secured and the existence of the security interest remain firmly, but quietly, in the background.

In the situation before us, Metalgrinders wants to be repaid by Hartford. The bank's principal concern is that cash payments keep rolling in. It would not want its clean banker's garb soiled with cogs and the like. If the bank is to be paid, then Hartford, the manufacturer, must make some money, and the way it does that is by selling its product. In practical terms, what is expected here is either that Hartford will use some of this money to pay off all or a portion of the outstanding loan amount, in which case Hartford will be assured that the amount of the outstanding loan is sufficiently collateralized by the rest of the collateral that it still has covered by its security interest, or Hartford will use the money coming in to buy more raw materials from which to make more cogs or widgets, which it will then store and the receipts for which will be handed over to the bank, all within 20 days of course. The process calls for a continuously watchful eye on the part of the lender, to ensure that the total value of the collateral it has firmly under control is appropriate for the level of outstanding debt, but the lender is or at least should be experienced in this type of monitoring. And have no doubt that the need for this kind of effort on the bank's part is all figured into the cost of the loan and the rate of interest it is receiving, which is, after all, why the bank judges this whole set of affairs worthwhile.

We will see much more of this type of ongoing relationship in chapters to come, and of the Article 9 law that swings into play should something go wrong. For the moment, however, the significance of all this is more to emphasize that in the large majority of cases things don't go wrong, and that Article 9 has been drafted to allow for and indeed to encourage generalized lending and security arrangements that can have a good amount of flexibility built right in. In some examples with which we deal — for example, when one of the Moneybucks clan pledges a valuable piece of jewelry to a friend in order to obtain a loan, the jewelry to be returned upon a one-time full repayment — the security interest has the look and feel of a single one-shot contractual relationship. In other situations, however, such as the one in this example and the example that follows, it pays to think about the relationship between the secured party and the debtor as an ongoing affair. The exact amount of the money debt or other obligation owed to the secured party will, for perfectly legitimate business reasons, rise and fall over time, while at the same time the exact collection of collateral and its aggregate value will ebb and flow as well. The trick, one that should work to the mutual benefit of both parties, is for the two to be kept in the kind of rough coordination that gives the borrower the necessary flexibility to run its enterprise and the lender sufficient protection through the security interest mechanism. The borrower can make money doing whatever it does, the bank makes money doing what it does — lending money on interest — and, of course, the government takes its cut in taxes. But that, at least, is not our concern in this volume.

2a. Yes. FF&L has a perfected security interest in the notes in question. This interest attached as soon as Selma had possession of them, "rights in" the collateral for purposes of §9-203(b)(2). Furthermore, thanks to the unique rule of §9-312(e), FF&L's interest in the instruments was perfected

> without filing or the taking of possession for a period of 20 days from the time it attaches to the extent that it arises for new value given under an authenticated security agreement.

For a definition of "new value," see §9-102(a)(57). Here the lender gave new value when it committed itself to an *increase* in her authorized credit, so its interest was automatically perfected for a period of 20 days from that time. Within a few days, FF&L got actual possession of the notes and its perfection was continued through possession. Since there was no gap in perfection, its perfection on these notes will continue to date from the day of the phone call and credit authorization.

What is the value of a rule like this one? As I think you can appreciate, it allows for FF&L to extend credit on the basis of what it trusts is and will continue to be a good perfected security interest in the kind of collateral it has previously agreed in writing to accept without having to take the instruments in hand at the exact moment it lends. When you think about it, if this rule were not available in the situation, FF&L would have to wait until the notes made their way to its door before it could authorize any extension of credit based on them. That is a possible way to operate, but it does slow things down significantly.

Remember here that Selma, who is presumably a valued and trusted borrower, wanted to take advantage as quickly as possible of the credit that she knew would be available to her soon enough. Why make her wait? Note also that without this rule, if Selma did think it important to be able to use the notes she gets as collateral as soon as humanly possible — and in a business like hers every day may count in terms of making the most of the bargains available — she would have to limit her dealings to lenders located in her neighborhood, which right away cuts down on her options and her bargaining power as a borrower. In addition, she or an employee delivering notes to the lender would be inconvenienced and lose valuable time. The only alternative would be for her to arrange for a representative of the lender to be present on her premises as these loans are signed to take them into possession immediately. This sounds, in effect, like she will have to schedule something in the nature of a three-party closing, with the customer, herself, and someone from FF&L present each time a larger stereo system or refrigerator is sold. Closings of this type, or the analogous mechanism of an escrow arrangement, are in fact common in larger real estate transactions; all sane people complain or at least comment on the difficulty of simply "setting up" a closing at a time and place that is convenient to all, and on what always seems like the inordinate cost of having to have so many lawyers and agents gathered together in one place. I realize that I'm exaggerating a bit here, and there are certainly legitimate reasons why all the fuss may be necessary in other contexts, but I hope you appreciate the considerable benefit for Selma and FF&L—working in cooperation—that this rule of temporary automatic perfection makes possible.

You may have noticed, and worried on FF&L's behalf, that as I have outlined this system it works only because Selma *does* actually have the notes she tells them about in her phone call and *does* actually send them on to the lender within the 20 days. What if Selma were not playing strictly on the up-and-up? Twenty-one days pass, the borrower has taken advantage of the increased credit limit, and FF&L has not gotten possession of the notes. What then? Well, FF&L is obviously in some kind of trouble, but if it has been tending to its business carefully it shouldn't necessarily be left with a pure loss. Note that its agreement with the retailer calls for extension of credit only up to 60% of the value of the notes it is given as collateral. This percentage, in fact, might well vary over time with the lender's experience with the particular retailer and based on its evaluation of the lender's present trustworthiness and creditworthiness. If a particular package of notes doesn't arrive within a few days, FF&L will presumably start checking whether the notes in fact exist and, if so, where they could be. It might have, pursuant to the underlying written agreement with the retailer, the right to "freeze" its credit account until things are straightened out. In the event that the notes never arrive or should it turn out that they never even existed in the first place, FF&L will no doubt have the right to deem the retailer in default as to any and all parts of its outstanding loan. And, if it has been careful, FF&L will still have in its possession enough other collateral—notes delivered earlier—so that it won't necessarily face the problem of undercollateralization.

Again, as we saw in the prior example, the lender is not going to be happy at having to take measures against a defaulting borrower. It would much rather the borrower just keep doing the right thing by sending in those periodic payments. Even if the borrower does default, the lender's first reaction might well be not to try to bring the house down on the defaulter but to work with it to remedy the situation, to prop it up if you will. Still, as in the prior example, the lender's real protection is not in a single piece of collateral that sits in a vault waiting to be redeemed. The lender looks for its security to a pool of collateral the exact contents of which shift around with time—and trusting as well in its own ability to monitor the situation and stay one step ahead of any potential problems. As always, the costs of its having to be active to this degree on a daily basis in monitoring the loan will figure into the cost of the loan in terms of interest rates and other charges for the borrowing retailer.

2b. No. FF&L's interest remains intact, and its perfection still dates back to the initial date of attachment. Thanks to §9-313(g), the secured party's interest remained perfected for a period of 20 days without filing even as it delivered the instrument back to the debtor, Selma, for the purpose of collection. This 20-day period began on August 15 and still had a few days to go on September 1, when FF&L regained possession through which it could once again claim perfection. So FF&L's interest was continuously perfected, with no gaps at all, during the whole period in question. Under the principle of §9-308(c) it is deemed to have been perfected as of the first moment when perfection could legitimately be asserted.

Again you see the functioning of temporary automatic perfection in a situation like this to facilitate the parties' dealings. If the lender, FF&L, actually had to have physical possession right up to the moment when Selma's customer meant to pay off, it, FF&L, would end up needing to come up with some system comparable to the typical and terribly unwieldy multiparty (and multiple lawyer) real estate closing, with some representative of FF&L present and ready to hand over the note at only the right moment when it is assured of getting what it is due in return. This type of ceremony might make sense in the real estate situation, where typically large sums are on the line and the dealing is a singular occasion for those involved, but it would make the type of financing we are dealing with here much more expensive and cumbersome without, we have to assume, any compensating benefit for any of the various parties involved.

2c. If FF&L doesn't get back possession of the note until September 15, the situation is not the same. Since this is longer than 20 days after it delivered the particular note on August 15, the automatic perfection provided by the subsection lapsed. While FF&L's interest becomes reperfected when on September 15 it again has possession and can claim perfection on that basis, there has been a gap in perfection of a few days. That is enough to defeat any argument it might later want to make that its perfection on this note runs back to the original date.

Its new date of perfection is September 15, 2005, and no earlier. It may seem to you that it really doesn't make any difference as long as FF&L does get its interest back into a perfected state, and in an individual situation that may be true. As you will see later on, however, under scenarios of what has been happening or is to come the lender's position may be seriously hurt by its date of perfection having been moved forward in this way. For the moment it is sufficient to accept as given that it is better to be perfected than to be unperfected. Add to that the rule of thumb that all things being equal when it comes to perfection, the earlier the better.

Under the old version of Article 9, filing was not a possible means of perfection on instruments. The revision has changed this, as you can see in §9-312(a), so that it is now possible to perfect by filing on instruments. As Comment 2 points out:

> This rule represents an important change from former Article 9, under which the secured party's taking possession of an instrument was the only method of achieving long-term perfection. The rule is likely to be particularly useful in transactions involving large numbers of notes that a debtor uses as collateral but continues to collect from the makers.

That sounds like the situation we have here, in the arrangement Selma has entered into with FF&L. In fact, you might wonder why, if filing on instruments such as the notes Selma is given by her customers is now possible, FF&L bothers to go through the exercise of taking actual possession of them. Read on in Comment 2. Without going into all the details here, you can see that a security interest in instruments perfected only by filing "is subject to defeat by certain subsequent purchasers" who actually get possession of the note. So a general filing by FF&L covering the notes will be helpful, but helpful only to a degree. It will serve to bridge the gap of more than 20 days in our example, so that the secured party's perfection will relate back to when it originally perfected on the notes under the concept of continuous perfection. The filing may turn out not to be of much worth, however, if Selma never returns the note at all but sells it to some innocent purchaser and absconds with the funds.

So as a practical matter, a lender in the position of FF&L has to keep pretty close watch on exactly what date and on just which pieces of paper it has returned to the borrower and follow the situation closely. If it starts getting close to the 20-day deadline, a call to Selma from FF&L would be, to say the least, in order, just to remind her, of course, and to let her know that it will not take kindly to any foul-up even with respect to this one note. Be aware as well that FF&L's real protection comes from the fact it will presumably be sure to retain in its possession at any one time sufficient collateral so that, should there be a problem with Selma's performance of all of her duties under their underlying security agreement, including her agreement to account in one way or another for any notes sent to her for collection within a specified period set at no longer than 20 days, it will still have adequate collateral under its control to allow it to feel secure in its position.

2d. The situation is analogous to that which we explored in the prior example. The customer is happy in that he has actually been able to pay off his debt to Selma early. Selma is happy as she's gotten paid with a certified check, which should be as good as cash. At the same time, there is no reason for FF&L to feel threatened. Selma has taken in cash, and that's just what FF&L as one of her creditors likes to see. Its concern, of course, is that she doesn't do something foolish with the cash but that she use it to keep her business going and more specifically that she use it to meet her obligation under the loan agreement. She may do this by sending some amount of money to FF&L, based on the value of this particular note, which will be used to lessen the outstanding debt she has to FF&L. Or she might instead be entitled to return within a set period of time a comparable new note, signed by a different customer, but for which she would not expect to receive any additional extension of credit from FF&L. Again the important point is that neither Selma nor FF&L looks at the situation as static. They cannot afford to. From FF&L's perspective the critical concerns are that at any one time it have sufficient collateral on hand to cover the risks it is taking by lending to Selma *and* that it has reason to think that Selma's business is going along smoothly enough that she will be able to make any payments owed to it as they become due. The factor's primary interest will always be in her remaining a financially responsible and profitable ongoing enterprise — able to pay the kind of interest rates they charge and if all goes well wanting to borrow even more on the same terms.

3. Smeers will argue that his security interest in the $20,000 owed to Inkster by DULS is perfected, in spite of his having failed to file on it, due to the rule of automatic perfection laid out in §9-309(2). A filing is not necessary for perfection in which the interest is

> an assignment of accounts . . . which does not by itself or in conjunction with other assignments to the same assignee transfer a significant part of the assignor's outstanding accounts. . . .

The amount owed by DULS to Inkster is an account, and Smeers will claim that his situation fits well within this provision for automatic perfection. But does it? Notice first of all that while this paragraph uses the word "assigned" it is intended to cover both the grant of a security interest in an account as well as an outright sale. So Smeers is okay on that score. But does the single account assigned to him constitute only an "insignificant part" of all outstanding accounts of Inkster? Her total accounts outstanding are something like $50,000. The account assigned to him was for $20,000, which is 40% of the total. If the section is read literally and the test is a purely quantitative one, the question reduces to whether 40% of all outstanding accounts can ever constitute less than a "significant part" of the whole. While the courts have never come up with a bright line test for what is or is not a "significant part" in the quantitative sense, 40% will almost assuredly be more than ample. I had my example work out to 40%, as it turns out, just because it coincidentally was the actual figure in both of two fairly recent cases that interpreted this provision. See In re Klein Glass & Mirror, Inc., 155 Bankr. 718, 21 U.C.C.2d 372 (S.D. Tex. 1992), and In re Virgil Bros. Constr., Inc., 193 Bankr. 513, 29 U.C.C.2d 15 (Bankr. App. 9th Cir. 1996). In neither case did the court display any doubt that a full 40% of all the debtor's outstanding accounts is more than enough to go over the top when the prerevision precursor to what is now §9-309(2) was read in a purely quantitative sense, or as the lingo has developed by applying a "percentage test" to the issue. As the Ninth Circuit in Virgil Bros. Constr. conceded, courts that have followed the percentage test have not come up with a hard and fast rule, a single bright line of demarcation about how much is "significant." One earlier case had held 16% not to be a "significant part" of the whole, while another found 20% to be so. There's no reason to take from this that the line must be somewhere exactly between these two figures. Nothing so precise is likely to come out of repeated application of the percentage test, nor is there any particular reason to hope that it would. At the same time, it does seem by any reasonable reading of the language that 40% is more than enough to be a significant part of the whole. The Klein Glass & Mirror case so held, and Virgil Bros. Constr., citing Klein, upheld a decision of a lower bankruptcy court holding on the facts that 40% was a significant part of the debtor's accounts.

So it looks like Smeers will lose on the numbers alone. What arguments are left to him? Fortunately for Smeers there is something more to be said about §9-309(2). Smeers can point to language in the first paragraph of Comment 4:

> The purpose of paragraph (2) is to save from ex post facto invalidation casual or isolated assignments — assignments which no one would think of filing. Any person who regularly takes assignments of any debtor's accounts or payment intangibles should file.

From this language, which is basically the same as that appearing in a comment to the provision of former Article 9 that new §9-309(2) is meant to continue, Smeers could argue that the provision in question is not to be interpreted exclusively, or even primarily, with an eye to the amount or percentage of the account in which he took an interest, but rather by taking a look at the totality of the circumstances and whether his was a situation like the typical dealing in accounts, which would obviously call for filing in the minds of those involved. Since instead, he would argue, this was only a "casual" and "isolated" transaction between the parties — they'd never done any like it before, and didn't expect to do it again — which "no one would think of filing"; no filing was in fact required. Further, he would point out, he was about to retire after many years as a printer, nothing like a party who "regularly takes assignments" of other people's accounts.

Smeers may have some success with this argument, depending upon the jurisdiction in which he finds the issue is to be resolved. A number of courts in interpreting the precursor to §9-309(2) rejected the straight "percentage test" in favor of what is referred to as a "casual and isolated test," which, depending on how you read it, takes into account some or all of the various factors Smeers has going in his favor. This test doesn't just look at the numbers involved, but instead

> requires a court to examine the circumstances surrounding the transaction, including the status of the assignee, to determine whether the assignment was casual or isolated. . . . If a court finds that the transaction was not part of a regular course of commercial financing, it will not require filing. The underlying rationale behind the test appears to be the conclusion that it would not be unreasonable to require a secured creditor to file if he regularly takes assignments of a debtor's accounts, but it would be unreasonable if this was not a usual practice.

In re B. Hollis Knight Co., 605 F.2d 397, 27 U.C.C. 337 (8th Cir. 1979). This certainly seems to favor Smeers. There is no evidence that he regularly takes assignments of a debtor's accounts or that it was his usual practice to do so.

Even if a court is somewhat disposed toward the "casual and isolated test," the resolution in this instance isn't as evident as we might hope. The problem is that, even if a court is willing to abandon the "percentage test" as the only one, there still remains a question, or perhaps one should say some confusion, about how the two tests interact. Does a secured party have to establish that his case satisfies both of the tests in order to fit within the exception to the generalized filing requirement? In other words, is the "casual and isolated" transaction exempted from the filing requirement only when what is involved is in addition a relatively small part of the debtor's overall package of accounts? The Hollis Knight case quoted above suggests the answer is yes — the facts must pass muster under both tests. The court concluded both of the policies underlying the two tests appear to be valid limitations on the scope of what is now §9-309(2).

> The language of the section would not permit an assignee to escape the filing requirement if he received a large portion of an assignor's accounts whether or not the transaction was an isolated one.

So, if this were the end result, Smeers would get to make his argument based on the language in the commentary and it would get a level of respect, but in the end he would find himself unperfected as his interest covered 40%, clearly a significant part or a large portion of Inkster's outstanding accounts. Both of the recent cases cited earlier, Klein Glass & Mirror and Virgil Bros. Constr., give some attention to the secured party's argument based on the "casual and isolated test" but in the end come to this conclusion that once the percentage is as large as 40%, a filing has to be made to perfect, no matter what the other circumstances.

There is at least one case that can be read as holding that a secured party is protected and need not have filed if the situation meets either the "percentage test" or the "casual and isolated test." In re Wood, 67 Bankr. 321, 2 U.C.C.2d 1098 (W.D. N.Y. 1986). If that case controlled, then Smeers would have a much better chance, of course, but the bulk of case law, and particularly the two most recent cases cited, distinctly disapprove of allowing a "casual and isolated" trans-actor off the hook when the accounts in which the secured party takes an interest turn out to be a large portion of the debtor's accounts, even if the secured party had no way of judging the amount of the whole at the time he took the interest.

The cases discussed above were, of course, all decided under the prerevision version of Article 9. There is nothing in §9-309(2) or the commentary to it, however, to suggest the revision intended to make a difference in how this provision is to be read. From a planning perspective, of course, §9-309(2) doesn't present that much of a difficulty. As the comment says, it is meant to save from later problems someone who took assignment in one form or another of an account under circumstances where "no one would have thought" that filing was necessary. It follows, especially given the predisposition of any good commercial lawyer for always tending to err on the side of too much protection, that in any situation where the thought comes up that a filing might be necessary, a filing is necessary, or at least is highly advisable. You would have no one to blame but yourself if you fail to follow your better, more conservative instincts.

Perfection on Investment Property and Deposit Accounts

INTRODUCTION TO "INVESTMENT PROPERTY"

Up to this point we have been focusing on how a secured party may attach and then perfect on all sorts of different collateral, including ruby rings; crops; a merchant's inventory, equipment, and accounts; and so much more. There is one species of personal property, however, that can represent a large portion of an individual's or organization's wealth, and that that individual or organization owner might wish to put up as collateral to secure a loan or other obligation, from which we have pretty much steered clear up to now. I'm referring to all that value locked up in what we colloquially refer to as corporate securities or investments. A person can "invest" in various items — jewelry, art, rare coins, comic books — and can make, or lose, money depending on market fluctuation, but we tend to think of a person's "investments" more narrowly — as his or her holdings in corporate securities. While corporations with their wily investment advisors are always thinking up newer and more convoluted ways of structuring securities issues, for our purposes it will certainly serve to limit our focus to the most basic forms, by which I mean corporate stock (representing a slice of the ownership interest in the corporation itself) or bonds (reflecting some chunk of money borrowed and now owed by the corporation and paying the holder some rate of interest).

From its inception the Uniform Commercial Code contained an article (Article 8) dealing with such things, under the rubric of "Investment Securities." In addition, and in recognition that holders of such securities will often want to offer them up as collateral subject to a security interest of the Article 9 variety and that lenders may be more than willing to agree if the terms are right, the Code has always contained rules setting forth how a secured party could and should attach and then perfect on this form of personal property. The road has been, however, I think it only fair to say, a rocky one up until recently. Initially, in the 1962 Official Version of the U.C.C., the rules governing security interests in investment securities were to be found in Article 9, but these sections along with that very first version of Article 8 as a whole were pretty generally conceded not to be up to the task. In 1978 an amended version of Article 8 was approved and sent to the states. As part of this revision the key rules were moved out of Article 9 and into 8 itself. For a variety of reasons, the result was to prove not much more successful than what it replaced. In 1994 an entirely reconceptualized and rewritten version of Article 8 was approved by the bodies charged with certifying the Official Version of the Code (the A.L.I. and N.C.C.U.S.L., as you no doubt recall). As part of this project the rules governing security interests taken in investment securities were totally overhauled and then moved back into Article 9. These rules were then incorporated substantially unchanged into the latest Revised Article 9.

But that's all history. We are free to concern ourselves with the situation as it now stands, that is, as the law appears in Revised Article 9. The first thing to do is to recognize, as we did in considering Example 10 of Chapter 5, how the new Article 8 sets out a neat pattern and vocabulary for differentiating the *means* by which the owner of an investment security may be said to hold the security. The individual investor need not necessarily be bothered by all the technicalities of the U.C.C.; to consider the number of shares he or she holds in such-and-such a corporation is enough. For our purposes, however, we remember that an investment security of the type Article 8 deals with will always be held by the owner in one distinct form or another. While the investor may safely think of his or her interest as just so many shares of stock and concentrate on the economics of the situation, under Article 8, and now for the purposes of Article 9 we have to distinguish between shares or other investment securities as they are held, either as certificated securities (either in bearer or registered form), as uncertificated securities, or in the form of a security entitlement. In the latter case we have to be clear in our own minds just who is the "entitlement holder" and who the "securities intermediary."

To refresh your memory, take a look once again at the definition of "investment property" in §9-102(a)(49):

> "Investment property" means a security, whether certificated or uncertificated, security entitlement, securities account, commodity contract, or commodity account.

A security (defined in §8-102(a)(15)), both in certificated (§8-102(a)(4)) and uncertificated (§8-102(a)(18)) form, is something you can recognize from Article 8, as is the security entitlement (§8-102(a)(17)). The securities account is defined in Article 8 as well, in §8-501(a). The definition is a little long, given that the drafters had to deal with a variety of situations, but for our purposes it is enough to recognize that the securities account includes the kind of relationship that a typical investor as a customer of a particular brokerage firm has with that broker. The shares of this corporation or that held by the customer in the account are held in the form of securities entitlements, with the customer being the entitlement holder of those shares and the brokerage serving as the securities intermediary.

Don't worry about the references in the latter part of the definition of investment property and scattered about in Article 9 generally to commodity contracts and commodity accounts. Commodity contracts technically are not investment securities of any form whatsoever under Article 8, as they are not issued by a corporate or similar issuer; but since they may be the subject of an Article 9 security interest, §9-102(a)(15) defines them and then sets up a parallel set of rules governing security interests in them, and in the commodity accounts (§9-102(a)(14)), which is the commodities trading analogue to the securities account. We won't worry about commodities contracts or commodities accounts in what we do here; we have plenty to concern ourselves with as it is without adding on to our problems.*

The issues we now have to deal with in respect to that distinct type of collateral called investment property are in essence no different than those that we've already covered more generally. To be more specific, how does a secured party assure itself that it has properly attached and then perfected a security interest granted to it by the owner of a particular piece or pieces of investment property? The game is the same, even if the rules seem to have been changed a bit to reflect the new terrain.

TAKING "CONTROL"

When it comes to attachment and perfection of interests in investment property, all of the various concepts and methods we have already been dealing with will still be with us. For attachment, as we will soon see, we'll need to consider whether an agreement exists granting the security interest, whether value has been given by the secured party, and whether the debtor has rights in the collateral. There will be times when perfection will be in

---

* If for some reason of your own you do want to see more about commodities trading, Comment 6 to §9-102 might be of special interest to you and worth a read. As always, let prudence be your guide. And keep your hand on your wallet.

effect automatic upon attachment. In certain instances perfection might be attained by the secured party getting physical possession of the collateral. Filing will always be a possibility, if not necessarily the best way to go.

The 1994 amendments to Article 9 did not just introduce a new category of collateral, that of investment property, to the classification scheme. It also added, in conjunction with the rewritten version of Article 8, a new means of perfecting, one that at the time pertained to that category of collateral uniquely. As we will see in the examples to follow, an important method for perfecting an interest in investment property is to gain "control" over that property. Whether one has obtained control over a given piece of investment property collateral is not just something for you and I to have our personal opinions about. It is no vague allusion or merely a figure of speech. Whether or not one has gained *control* over a piece of investment property is the subject of some carefully crafted and highly sophisticated rules now to be found in §9-106 of Revised Article 9. Under subsection (a) of that section,

> A person has control of a certificated security, uncertificated security, or security entitlement as provided in Section 8-106.

So we look to §8-106. This is obviously a key section in the whole scheme of things, and you will be using it as you work through the examples to follow. The most important thing to note at the outset is that how and whether a person gains control in the §8-106 sense is a matter of *in what form* the security is held. So subsections (a) and (b) state the rules for determining how a purchaser gains control of a certificated security, in (a) when the security is in bearer form, in (b) when it is in registered form. Subsection (c) deals with gaining control of an uncertificated security and (d) with control over a security entitlement. You will end up needing the other subsections of §8-106 before the chapter is over, but I'll clue you into them as needed in the examples.

One thing may be unsettling to you as you take a first look over the obviously crucial §8-106. Each subsection speaks of how a "purchaser" has or gains control of a security in one form or another. In our studies we are not interested in how a buyer of securities takes from a seller of same, but in how a secured party takes and perfects an Article 9 security interest in such stuff. Fortunately, this is a potential mystery most easily cleared up.

---

* The concept of perfection obtained through "control," originally introduced in the Revision of 1994 as pertaining only to investment property, was thought by the later drafters of the entirely Revised Article 9 of 1999 to work so well that they extended the possibility to some other types of collateral. Note particularly §9-104 on control of deposit accounts, a section we will be using later in this chapter. Sections 9-105 and 9-107 deal with how one gains control over two very specialized types of collateral, electronic chattel paper and letter-of-credit rights, which we aren't concerning ourselves with in this volume.

The Code uses the term "purchaser" more broadly than might be common usage. Look at §1-201(32) or §1R-201(b)(29). "Purchase" as used throughout the U.C.C. includes "taking by . . . pledge, lien, security interest, . . . or any other voluntary transaction creating an interest in property." As we have seen from the earliest chapter, the creation of an Article 9 security interest is the grant via a voluntary transaction by the debtor of an "interest" in his, her, or its property to the secured party. True, it is not a grant of a full ownership interest, or title as we might be tempted to say, but it is a grant of a kind of interest, a security interest in the property. That is enough to make the transaction a purchase for the purposes of the U.C.C., Articles 8 and 9, and the secured party a "purchaser" able, if he, she, or it plays according to the rules, to gain "control" over the security as §8-106 uses the term.

For the sake of completeness it will be necessary to consider how one gains control, in the sense we are using that term, over that type of investment property that is referred to as a securities account. Remember that a securities account is a grab bag that may contain, or in the language of §8-501(a) "have credited to it" by the brokerage, a number of assorted securities, each held in the form of a securities entitlement, where the person whose account it is, the customer as we say, stands as the entitlement holder and the broker is the securities intermediary against whom the entitlement runs. We would hope, for the sake of the customer, the various entitlements that go into making this account haven't been chosen simply at random, but with care and expertise. (A little bit of luck never hurt, either.) The point here is simply that the account is not just the individual stocks and bonds that make it up but is in its wholeness a potential piece of collateral, a kind of investment property unto itself. Flip back to §9-106, now reading subsection (c): "A secured party having control of all security entitlements . . . carried in a securities account . . . has control over the securities account . . ."

The concept of control is obviously central to dealings in investment securities as governed by Article 8, and as we will see, to the attachment and perfection of security interests in investment property under Article 9. We will take time for the details in the examples to follow. The overarching principle, however, is well expressed in the single sentence that ends Comment 1 to §8-106:

> Obtaining "control" means that the purchaser [meaning, in the matters with which we'll be concerned, the secured party] has taken whatever steps are necessary, given the manner in which the securities are held, to place itself in a position where it can have the securities sold, without further action by the owner [who is for us the debtor].

Keep this in mind as you address the particulars.

ATTACHMENT AND PERFECTION ON INVESTMENT PROPERTY

Investment property may be a distinct class of collateral from those with which we have been dealing up to this point, but the basic scheme of analysis will remain the same. An Article 9 security interest in investment property is, just as has been any other security interest we've encountered so far, the product of a voluntary transaction. The debtor grants the interest to the secured party to support an underlying obligation. We now want to go down the same road we have previously taken for all the other types of collateral to consider what the secured party *may* do or in some instances *must* do to obtain perfection of any interest it claims.

As you would be no doubt the first to point out, the question of perfection cannot be answered without initially addressing that of attachment. The basic rule of §9-308(a), that "[a] security interest is perfected if it has attached and all of the applicable requirements for perfection . . . have been satisfied," applies no less to interests claimed in investment property than to those claimed in goods or instruments or documents. On attachment our guide remains §9-203 in which we will now want to give special attention to subsection (b)(3)(C) and (D) as well as subsection (h).

On perfection, we turn once again to §9-310. Among those instances allowing for perfection without a filing, listed in subsection (b), we find, number (7), which allows for perfection by possession of a certificated security. This is the only form of investment property that can be perfected upon by possession, which makes sense when you consider that it is the only form of investment property that has tangible form. In §9-310(b)(8) we find the general rule that filing is not necessary to perfect an interest in investment property "which is perfected by control under Section 9-314." That section, in subsection (a), which is all that need concern us, refers us back to §9-106, which as you'll recall in turn refers us to §8-106, at least when certificated securities, uncertificated securities, or security entitlements are involved.

ENTER THE DEPOSIT ACCOUNT

The prerevision version of Article 9 explicitly excluded from its scope any security interest that a creditor might originally try to take in a deposit account (for the definition of which see §9-102(a)(29)) held by the debtor. (There did remain the possibility that a secured party that had taken a security interest in some other form of allowable collateral would end up with an interest in a deposit account as "proceeds," a concept we will get to in Chapter 17.) A major change made by the recent revision is that security interests taken in deposit accounts as original collateral *do* now generally fall within the article's scope. See the beginning of Comment 4a to §9-101. The one exception, and a important one from the point of view of consumer rights advocates, is that, under §9-109(d)(13), Article 9 does not apply to "an assignment of a deposit account in a consumer transaction."

We therefore come to consider the questions of how a secured party wishing to take a security interest in a deposit account held by a nonconsumer, a commercial debtor, may do so. What is required to attach? How may or must the secured party perfect? Here the rules are somewhat different than we have found them for other types of collateral. In particular, a security interest in a deposit account may not be perfected by filing. See §9-312(b)(1). A security interest in a deposit account may be perfected only by control. This provision asks us to look at §9-314, whose section (a) refers us in this case to §9-104.

Take all these various definitions and directives (along with a few others that I'll signal to you as we move along), mix well, and apply to the examples concerning investment property and deposit accounts given below.

Examples

1. Prudence Moneybucks, unlike some of her relatives, enjoys a very simple lifestyle. No flashy jewelry or expensive original artwork for Prudence, who lives comfortably but simply in a modest rental apartment. In taking stock of her assets, Prudence can look only to the following:

   a. Twenty shares in a small family-run corporation (Moneybucks Industries, Incorporated) represented by a share certificate bearing her name as owner of the shares that she keeps in a desk drawer at home;

   b. Her interest in a mutual fund (The Rocksolid Investment Trust) from which she receives statements once a month;

   c. An account she keeps with the stockbrokerage firm of James, Steven, Rogers & Company, a principal component of which is a hefty number of shares in the H.A.L. Corporation, one of the country's leading computer manufacturers; and

   d. A savings account she has at Springfield State Bank.

   Prudence approaches the Wellington National Bank and discusses with a loan officer her desire to take out a sizable loan from the bank to engage in a new business venture. She offers all of the above as collateral. The bank agrees to grant the loan and before it hands over the check has her sign a security agreement listing each of the pieces of collateral. The bank files this financing statement in the appropriate place. Has it effectively attached on all of the collateral? Has it perfected?

2. Suppose instead that upon evaluation the bank determines that the value of the Moneybucks Industries shares alone is more than enough to serve

as collateral for the size of loan Prudence is requesting. Prudence, having no desire to encumber any more of her property than is necessary, gets the bank's agreement to grant the loan taking only these shares as collateral. She signs some loan papers, but none of them specifically make any reference to a security interest in the Moneybucks Industries shares or any other collateral. At the time she receives the loan funds from the bank, Prudence does, however, hand over to the loan officer the share certificate itself, which you recall she has been keeping in a desk drawer at home.

a. Under this set of facts, has the bank attached and perfected an Article 9 security interest on the twenty shares that Prudence has in Moneybucks Industries? See §9-203(b)(3)(C) and §9-313(a).

b. From what you can see is there any reason why the bank might not be in the best position possible if Prudence does nothing but hand over the certificate in this way? What more might you suggest the bank ask for to better protect its interests? See §9-328(5).

3. Assume now instead that the bank is willing to make the loan taking only Prudence's interest in The Rocksolid Investment Trust as collateral.

a. Prudence agrees that all but $100 of the present value of her account with the Trust will be transferred into another account to be opened with the Trust in the name of Wellington National Bank. There the money will sit until such time as she has repaid her loan to Wellington, when the then-value of the investment would be moved, on Wellington's instructions to the Trust, back into Prudence's account. If this arrangement is carried out by Prudence's giving the necessary transfer instructions to the Trust, does it serve to attach and perfect Wellington's claimed security interest in the value of what has been transferred into the Rocksolid account in its name?

b. Suppose Prudence and the bank try a simpler route. Prudence agrees in writing that Wellington may send a notice to Rocksolid asserting a security interest in Prudence's account with that investment trust. Wellington does send such a notice. The notice is received by Rocksolid. Has the bank effectively perfected via this route? Would it matter if Prudence co-signed the letter to Rocksolid and indicated that she gave her consent to the security interest claimed by the bank?

4. Now suppose that the Bank agrees to make the loan taking as collateral only the H.A.L. shares, which recall she holds in her account with the stockbrokerage firm of James, Steven, Rogers & Company.

a. Prudence directs her broker at JSR to transfer the number of H.A.L. shares that are credited to her account into an account which the Wellington bank coincidentally happens to have with JSR itself. JSR completes the transaction; that is, this number of shares are withdrawn from Prudence's account and an identical number credited to

Wellington's account. Assuming all other aspects of the loan agreement are in order, has the bank obtained a perfected security interest in the collateral in which it is interested by this procedure? Would it matter if the transfer were made instead to Wellington's account as a customer of another brokerage, say Smith Blarney?

b. Would it serve to perfect Wellington's interest if instead it simply sent a letter to JSR notifying the brokerage that it, Wellington National Bank, had obtained and was asserting a security interest from Prudence covering these shares in her account? What if the notice was signed not just by a representative of the bank but by Prudence as well? Assume all that and in addition that it could be shown without doubt that JSR had actually received this notice. Is this enough to perfect the bank's interest? If not, what more could possibly be done (and indeed would have to be done) to successfully perfect Wellington's interest in these shares?

5. Now suppose that the agreement between the bank and Prudence requires her to put up as collateral her entire account with JSR. She directs a notice to JSR informing it that it is to obey buy-and-sell instructions with respect to this account not from her but from a person (named in the notice) authorized to act on behalf of the Wellington National Bank as a party holding a security interest in the account.

a. This notice is received and its receipt acknowledged by JSR. Does this device serve to perfect the bank's interest in the account?

b. What if Prudence does not merely notify JSR of this arrangement but asks and receives the brokerage's agreement that it will obey orders from Wellington with respect to the account (instead of orders from Prudence herself)? Will this do the trick?

c. Would it change your answer to the previous part of this example if instead the agreement entered into by Prudence and JSR as her broker was that it would from that date forward recognize both Prudence and the authorized figure at Wellington as persons whose orders regarding the account were to be carried out? See §8-106(f).

6. Finally, with respect to Prudence's investment property, suppose that Prudence enters into an arrangement with JSR as her broker, allowing her to buy stocks "on margin." That is, the brokerage agrees that it will, on her instruction, buy stocks for her account (up to a certain limit) even if it has not received from her in cash the full purchase price of all the shares in her account. Under such a margin account agreement the brokerage JSR is itself advancing or loaning to Prudence the price of what she buys and has credited to her account beyond what she has actually delivered to JSR in cash or its equivalent to open or increase the account. The agreement states that JSR will have a security interest in any and all of the securities credited to her account to secure the obligation

to the brokerage that Prudence takes on by buying on margin. JSR makes no filing with respect to this claimed security interest, nor does it do anything else to put others on notice of it. Does JSR have to worry that it has not perfected on this interest? See §8-106(e) and Comment 6 to that section.

7. Now let us consider the amount that Prudence has tucked away in a savings account at the Springfield State Bank. Wellington determines that, in order to make a business loan of the type and size Prudence is requesting, it does want to take and perfect a security interest on this savings account along with the other collateral she has offered up. Prudence is willing that Wellington get such a security interest in the account. What special steps must Wellington take to assure itself that this interest is perfected?

Explanations

1. Yes, the bank's interest has attached, and yes, it is perfected *except* with respect to the savings account. Don't just take my word for it; check it out for yourself. First, as to attachment: What is necessary is that all of the three criteria of §9-203(b) have been met. Once the bank gives Prudence the loan proceeds or, in fact, once it makes a binding commitment to do so (remember the definition of Article 1), "value" has been given by the secured party to the debtor. We're assuming all along that Prudence has "rights in" all of the various pieces of collateral. So criteria (1) and (2) are met. What of subpart (3)? This requirement too has been met, since we are told that a written security agreement has been signed by Prudence. Hence, "the debtor has authenticated a security agreement that provides a description of the collateral."

    There are, as we now review, four ways that the criterion of §9-203(b)(3) can be met. Any one will do, and here we have a written security agreement signed by the debtor describing the collateral, so our inquiry can stop right there, at (3)(A). You might have been tempted to look to (3)(D), which assures us that its requirement is met when the collateral is investment property and the secured party has control pursuant to the debtor's security agreement, but you would have been going down a false road. As it will turn out in this initial example, the bank does *not* necessarily gain control over any of Prudence's investment property. Certainly it doesn't get it just by obtaining a written security agreement and filing a financing statement. The bank's never gaining control over the collateral here may or may not later give it grief. For the moment all that we need point out is that its not having control means that for its security interest to attach it had to have gotten a *written* security agreement signed (or otherwise authenticated) by Prudence describing the collateral, which it did. So the bank's security interest attached, and it did so at whatever time the last of the three criteria of §9-203(b) took place.

Now the question is whether Wellington bank's interest has been properly perfected as to the various pieces of collateral. Look to §9-312(a). The rule is simplicity itself: "A security interest in . . . investment property may be perfected by filing." So the bank's filing on Prudence's investment property — provided it meets the general requirements of §9-502(a) and it is filed in the correct place — makes a strong case for perfection by filing. The time of perfection was the latter of the time of filing or the moment of attachment.

You might well be wondering at this point why, if a filing is all it takes to perfect on investment property, there's really much more to be said on the subject of this chapter and why any more examples are necessary. And, come to think of it, why all this talk about the technicalities of "control" when filing serves to perfect? You'll have to be patient for the answer. In Chapter 19, where we get into the intricacies of the priority rules relating to investment property, we will see that perfection by filing is, well, not as perfect as you might at first imagine. There is no reason for you to worry about it at the moment, but we'll see that other parts of Article 9 introduced (in 1994) for the first time into the law of secured transaction the possibility that alternate *methods* of perfection, not just differences in timing, can lead to different results. Among other things we will come upon the rule that perfection by filing alone is easily trumped, if you will, by perfection claimed through control. All that is, as I say, for a later chapter. For now just rest assured that there is every reason in the world (and in the Code) for you to continue on to the following examples.

As to the last piece of collateral that Prudence is willing to give Wellington bank in order to get her business loan — that savings account in Springfield State Bank — Wellington's interest will have attached, but it will not have been perfected by, Wellington's filing. Subsection 9-312(b)(2) is clear: "[A] security interest in a deposit account may be perfected only by control under Section 9-314." We'll return in the concluding example to the question of what steps Wellington may, and indeed must, take to perfect its interest in the bank account.

2a. Yes. Thanks to the cited provisions the bank's interest has attached and is perfected by possession. Prudence's shares in this little, or probably not so little, family business are held in certificated form, and the piece of paper itself that she's been keeping safe at home is a "security certificate" (§8-102(a)(16)) in "registered form" (§8-102(a)(13)). The certificate has been "delivered" to the bank (§8-301(a)(1)) as the secured party pursuant to an agreement. True, the agreement that the bank holds the certificate as collateral is in oral, not written, form, but §9-203(b)(3)(C) does not call for an "authenticated" security agreement, so this doesn't defeat attachment. Furthermore, this delivery suffices for perfection of the security interest via the last sentence of §9-313(a).

2b. Notice that subsection (5) of §9-328 provides that a security interest in the shares attached and perfected in this way "has priority over a conflicting secured interest perfected by a method other than control." Although we have not yet defined "priority" in this case, obviously it is better to have it than to be subject to someone else's. If the bank's interest attached and perfected by the mere delivery of the certificate pursuant to agreement has priority over other conflicting interests perfected by means "other than control," you have to worry that if another party were somehow able to perfect on the same collateral via control, well, the bank runs the risk of someday coming in second in a contest where second is the functional equivalent of dead last.

In a situation such as this, it therefore stands to reason, the bank would do better to perfect by itself obtaining control. Fortunately, that is not a difficult thing to do if the bank knows the ropes. See §§9-106(a) and 8-106(b). The bank should make sure that when the certificate is handed over it is also endorsed over to it or in blank by an effective endorsement. On endorsement, you can look to §8-102(a)(11). Under §8-106(b)(2), the bank could also gain control by Prudence's having the shares actually transferred on the books of the Moneybucks corporation into the bank's name, but that hardly seems necessary here.

Once the bank takes delivery of this certificate properly endorsed, it has attached and perfected, and it no longer needs to rely on §9-313(a) to make its case. On attachment, note that under §9-203(a) criterion (3)(D) is met if the collateral is investment property and the secured party has control pursuant to agreement, whether or not the agreement is in writing. As to perfection, look at §9-314(a): "A security interest in investment property . . . may be perfected by control." What makes for control over investment property is covered in §9-106. All nice and neat.

3a. Yes. Prudence's interest, or "shares," in the mutual fund is an example of an "uncertificated security." Under §8-106(c)(1), a purchaser may obtain control over an uncertificated security by taking delivery of it. What would amount to delivery of an uncertificated security? Look at §8-301(b)(1). Here Prudence has caused Rocksolid, the issuer, to register Wellington, the secured party as purchaser, as the registered owner of all but $100 of her interest via a transfer of the rest. With Wellington having gained control, all of the requirements for attachment and in particular §9-203(b)(3)(D) will have been met. Further, control will mean perfection under §9-314(a). For a good example of a court's careful examination of the agreement entered into between a debtor, a lender, and the issuer of some uncertificated securities — and how that agreement was understood and put into effect by the parties — in order to determine whether the lender had gained control over the securities, see In re Pfautz, 264 Bankr. 551, 46 U.C.C.2d 236 (W.D. Miss. 2001).

You may be beginning to feel a bit nervous here on behalf of Prudence. The idea of giving control over investment property to the secured party as a means of perfection, introduced by the 1994 revisions, may be all well and good as an analytic matter, but it does seem to leave the secured party holding all the marbles, so to speak, and the debtor, the true owner of the property, only looking on from a distance. Control does really mean control; recall that according to the comment to §8-106, the secured party's gaining control means that it "has taken whatever steps are necessary . . . to place itself in a position where it can have the securities sold, without further action by the owner." It is important to remember, however, that whereas in this case the secured party has been given the *power* to deal with the securities as if they were its own — and in fact from all outward appearances the secured party appears to be the real owner — that is not the same thing as saying that it has the *right* to do whatever it wants with them. The secured party has had the securities transferred into its name, but it is holding them for safekeeping. Under its agreement with Prudence, as long as she keeps making payments on her loan and is in no other way in default in her obligations to the bank, Wellington will not have the right to sell or to fiddle around with the collateral. If it does so, it risks not only getting into trouble under the Code but ruining its reputation as well.

In a way you can analogize this situation to the pledge, or as we now more precisely say the security interest perfected by the secured party's taking possession of the collateral. When one of Prudence's relatives, Dexter, for example, uses a costly ruby ring for collateral and actually turns it over to the secured party to hold until his debt has been repaid he is in effect giving the lender control over the ring, if not in the technical sense of Article 8 or §9-106, both of which apply to investment property only. The lender is not the owner of the ring, and yet it does appear to be so for all intents and purposes. It has the power, if not the right, to sell it to a bona fide purchaser for value and make off (wrongly) with the proceeds. Dexter has to protect himself by making sure he is dealing with someone who is not about to do such a thing. Similarly, Prudence, by being cautious and dealing with a reputable bank, should minimize the actual risk of the situation. A different analogy, not to Dexter and the pledge of his ruby ring, but to the delivery of bearer certificates into the hands of the secured party, is offered up in the second paragraph of Comment 3 to §8-106.

3b. Wellington cannot and will not gain control simply by informing the issuer, the Rocksolid Investment Trust, of its interest. It doesn't matter that the trust receives the notice or even that Prudence indicates in writing her own consent to the arrangement. Read §8-106(c)(2). The secured party can gain control of an uncertificated security other than by having it actually transferred into its own name by an arrangement in which "*the issuer has agreed* that it will comply with instructions originated by the purchaser [the secured party] without further consent by the registered owner [the debtor]." So Wellington has to get Rocksolid's *agreement* that it will comply with its, Wellington's, instructions regarding the amounts in Prudence's account "without further consent" of Prudence.

A couple of things to point out: The issuer, here Rocksolid, may not enter into such an agreement without the registered owner's, here Prudence's, consent, as stated in the first part of the first sentence to §8-106(g), and, as stated in the second part of that sentence, it is under no obligation to enter into this agreement even if the registered owner directs it to do so. What happens then? Well, Wellington could open an account with Rocksolid and it and Prudence could use the mechanism of §8-106(c)(1) and the prior part of this example. Or, don't forget, if Rocksolid is under no obligation to enter into a so-called control agreement of the type contemplated by §8-106(c)(2), then Prudence is under no obligation to stick with Rocksolid. She could take her investment dollar elsewhere, to another mutual fund that *is* willing to enter into a control agreement when Prudence directs it to do so. This new fund (The Solid and Agreeable Investment Trust?) will, of course, have to make sure that the nature and terms of the agreement it enters into are fair to it. It will have its lawyers look over any document it signs, or may even itself have a standard form available that will meet Prudence's and Wellington's needs. Mutual funds and the like tend, to put it mildly, to compete for the business of people like Prudence. Rocksolid has to protect its own interests, and subsection (g) gives it the right to refuse Prudence's directive to sign a control agreement if it doesn't want to. Prudence, however, always has the right to take her business elsewhere, so if the request is reasonable — and there's nothing here to suggest otherwise — and if Rocksolid won't do it, then Prudence can find some other mutual fund that will. She might even get as a gift the mutual fund industry's equivalent of a free toaster for becoming a new investor somewhere else. I wouldn't worry about Prudence on this score.

4a. Transferring the H.A.L. shares to an account in the name of Wellington National Bank, whether an account at JSR or at some other brokerage, should meet the goals of Prudence and Wellington. That is, a security interest in her "securities entitlement" to this number of shares will have attached and been perfected with Wellington as the secured party. Our authority is now §8-106(d)(1). Wellington will have become the entitlement holder of the shares and hence have gained control over them. As before, with control subject to agreement comes attachment under §9-203(b)(3)(D) and perfection under §9-314(a). As a practical matter, the shares might be transferred into an account Wellington already has set up either with JSR or another securities intermediary, thereby increasing the number of H.A.L. shares credited to that account by 100, or into a new account opened by Wellington specifically for this purpose. Either accomplishes the same objective.

Note that JSR has no way of objecting to this procedure, nor should it. Prudence as the entitlement holder initially has the right to issue an "entitlement order" regarding these shares (or assets credited to her account) and JSR must comply (§8-507). The definition of entitlement order in §8-102(a)(8) makes clear that she can order the transfer of the shares (as one asset in her account) any which way she wants. See Examples 1 and 2 in Comment 4 to §8-106 which exhibit the same situation, but with Prudence taking the rather more mundane name of Debtor, H.A.L. stock as XYZ, Wellington Bank as Alpha Bank, and JSR as Able & Company.

4b. The mere sending of notice by Wellington, even if it is also signed by Prudence and even if it can be proven to have been received by the brokerage, will not suffice to give the bank control or to perfect the bank's interest. Under §8-106(d)(2), the bank could gain control of Prudence's entitlement to the 100 shares by getting JSR to agree "that it will comply with entitlement orders originated by the purchaser [here the secured party, Wellington] without further consent by the entitlement holder [who remains Prudence]."

See Example 3 in Comment 4 to §8-106. More generally, that comment makes clear that the agreement anticipated by subsection (d)(2) is not to be regarded as a mere formalism; the three parties to the agreement — the debtor, the secured party, and the securities intermediary — will each have details of their respective rights, responsibilities, and potential liabilities, which they will expect to see in the agreement before they would be willing to sign.

> This section specifies only the minimum requirements that such an arrangement must meet to confer "control"; the details of the arrangement can be specified by agreement. The arrangement might cover all of the positions in a particular account or subaccount, or only specified positions. There is no requirement that the control party's right to give entitlement orders be exclusive. The arrangement might provide that only the control party can give entitlement orders, or that either the entitlement holder or the control party can give entitlement orders. See subsection (f).

So JSR is not required to enter into any such agreement just because its customer, Prudence, directs it to do so. Of course, if it refuses to do so, and the terms of the agreement that it is being asked to entertain are reasonable, then Prudence should be able to find another broker more than willing to have her business who will enter into the requested agreement.

In addition, as in all true commercial agreements of any consequence, we would expect the parties coming to an agreement that all are willing to sign, and, if so, what is eventually bargained out will all depend on what's at stake for each party. In a simple, straightforward situation, all might be able to agree quite readily to a standard form control agreement that either the broker or the lender's attorney has written up for just such occasions. Other times the dealings will be far more complex, the bargaining more intense, and the ingenuity of the lawyers representing each of the three parties involved (the debtor, the lender, and the brokerage) really put to the test. At one symposium I attended dealing with the new Article 8 and perfection on investment property by the means of control, one panelist asked of another, "How likely is it that a major broker would be willing" to agree to such-and-such a provision? The answer in reply: "How big is the client?"

5a. By now the pattern should be obvious, and I won't belabor the point. If Wellington is to perfect by gaining control, here over the whole account, it requires the broker's active agreement to the arrangement. Notice to the broker of Wellington's intentions and even receipt of that notice is not enough to establish control.

5b. Yes. JSR's agreement to obey entitlement orders with respect to the account from Wellington instead of from Prudence, even though she remains the entitlement holder to all of the various financial assets in the account, will transfer control over the account as a whole to Wellington under §9-106(c). The account is a species of investment property, and under §9-314(a) as we have come to appreciate, a security interest in investment property can be perfected by control. See Comment 4 to §9-106.

5c. The answer remains the same; Wellington has gained control and hence perfection. Section 8-106(f) specifically states that a purchaser (here a secured party) has control,

> even if . . . the entitlement holder . . . retains the right to make substitutions for the . . . security entitlement, to originate . . . entitlement orders to the . . . securities intermediary, or otherwise to deal with the . . . security entitlement.

See also the second paragraph of Comment 7 to that section.

Earlier we concerned ourselves with whether the debtor's granting control to the secured party in the way the term is used here creates unreasonable risks for the debtor. We came to the conclusion that, as always, it depends on the situation and the trustworthiness of the secured party, who is expected to exercise its power over the securities only when it has the right to do so. Allowing the secured party to gain exclusive control over investment property should be in and of itself no more troubling than actually turning over full possession of other valuable property in the case of a pledge.

Now we have to wonder if the secured party, in gaining control in the technical sense but leaving power to continue dealing in the account and hence some measure of control in the practical sense in the hands of the debtor, is taking an unacceptable risk. After all, Prudence could, under this arrangement, start to make some particularly risky and in the long run bad investment decisions, the result of which would be to decrease significantly the value of the account. And the total value of the account, recall, is what Wellington is taking as collateral. Prudence may even be able, under the agreement, to sell and "cash out" some of the securities in the account. Where does this kind of dealing leave Wellington as a secured party?

The answer is that Wellington is like a lot of other secured parties who take an interest in collateral without taking possession, perfected for example only by filing, the result being that they leave the collateral in the hands and to some degree to the mercy of the debtor. When Wellington lends to a different party on the basis of, say, its machinery, it does the best it can by perfecting through filing, but the machinery itself has to be left with the debtor. The debtor will covenant in the security agreement to keep the machinery in good working order, to keep it insured, and certainly not to sell it without the bank's express permission, but there will be no way for Wellington to make sure that the debtor doesn't breach any of these covenants short of its putting a full-time employee (of the bank, that is) on the debtor's premises whose responsibility is to stare at the machine day and night, ensuring nothing untoward happens to it. Even if such a stalwart soul willing to work at minimum wage could be found, it is highly unlikely that the bank will think this a good use of its resources or of anyone's time. As we will see further in materials to follow, the bank will have to come up with ways to monitor to a *reasonable* extent given the circumstances in order to *reasonably* assure itself that the debtor is treating the collateral right, as it has promised to do.

Similarly, in the joint control over investment property type of relationship that we are contemplating here, the secured party may ask for and get agreement from the debtor to certain covenants about how she will deal with the account. Prudence may perhaps agree to make trades involving only some kind of "blue chip" sort of stocks. Or she may agree not to withdraw any cash from the account, or not to do so when it would bring the total value below a certain level. Wellington will be entitled, of course, as one granted control over the account, to periodic information about what's going on with it, so it has that means of monitoring. You can see why it would want JSR to agree to do some policing (similar in intent if not necessarily in style to the ever-vigilant guy or gal who stays up 24 hours a day staring at the machine collateral), say, not to obey certain entitlement orders from Prudence, but you can also see why JSR will be resistant to taking on too much responsibility along these lines. This is, of course, why the broker's actual agreement to the control arrangement and to its particular terms is necessary and why it is not placed under any legal obligation to agree at all.

Prudence and the Wellington bank cannot by their actions alone thrust upon JSR obligations and potential liability that it may not want to take on. These are the kinds of things that the three parties will have to work out. The broker may be willing to take on some responsibilities to block certain types of trades or instructions either by Prudence or by Wellington or both (it does, after all, have computers that may be able to be easily programmed to catch certain things), but only if its potential liability in case of some mistake due to its simple negligence is severely limited.

6. This is a particularly easy one to answer. The brokerage industry made sure it would be perfected when the 1994 revisions were under consideration. Under §8-106(e), since a security interest in the securities entitlements (Prudence's positions in the shares in her account) was granted by Prudence as entitlement holder to JSR as her own securities intermediary, JSR has control automatically. And control, of course, makes for attachment and perfection. As Comment 6 says, "A common transaction covered by this provision is a margin loan from a broker to

its customer." See also §9-309(10), which states that "a security in investment property created by a broker or securities intermediary" is automatically perfected upon attachment.

7.   Recall that, under §9-312(b)(1), "a security interest in a deposit account may be perfected only by control under Section 9-314." Under subsection (a) of §9-314, a security interest in a deposit account may be perfected by control, here under §9-104. Since in this case the secured party (Wellington) is not the bank in which the deposit account is maintained (which would be Springfield State), (a)(1) does not come into play. That provision is, as you can imagine, meant to give to a bank in which an account is held and that takes an interest in that account the same type of automatic attachment and perfection by control that a brokerage, as we saw in the previous example, will have for any security interest it takes in its own customer's securities held through the brokerage. Here Wellington will have to make sure it follows the dictates of either (2) or (3) of §9-104(a) in order to gain control over the account. One possibility is for it to enter into a tri-party agreement, either signed or otherwise authenticated by itself, Prudence, and Springfield State Bank, under which Springfield State agrees that "it will comply with instructions originated by the secured party [Wellington] directing disposition of the funds in the account without further consent by the debtor [Prudence]." The other possibility would be for Prudence to actually change the account into one held in the name of Wellington, so that Wellington as the secured party "becomes the bank's customer with respect to the deposit account." For a recent example of a lender's gaining perfection over a deposit account through control, see *Sonic Engineering, Inc. v. Konover Construction Co. South*, 51 U.C.C.2d 844, 2003 Conn. Super. LEXIS 2436.

In practice, the situations where a lender will want to take and perfect an interest in a deposit account are not likely to be like the situation we have before us here, where the borrower has some preexisting bank account rich with funds. If Prudence has that much in savings, wouldn't it make more sense for her to use that money to start up her business, decreasing the amount she'll have to borrow almost certainly at a higher rate of interest than what she has been earning even on the best savings account? More typically, a lender in a complex business arrangement will want the borrower to set up a special bank account, distinct from any other accounts the borrower may already have, intended to be the one account into which the borrower deposits all or a certain specified part of the proceeds it receives on the sale of its inventory or other collateral on which the lender will also have a security interest and out of which the borrower is expected to make its payments on the loan to the lender. An arrangement for a dedicated account such as this avoids, or at least minimizes, commingling of funds or the debtor's stashing away some or all of what it should be paying the lender in some other account over which the lender has no control and of which it may not even be aware. As you can imagine, commingling and diversion of funds owed to it are just the kinds of things that lenders want to prevent the borrower from even thinking about, much less carrying out. The lender's perfected security interest in a distinct account dedicated to the overall financing arrangement helps the lender keep a tighter rein on the situation.

The comments to §9-104, although they deal only with that particular section and the topic of control over deposit accounts, serve as a fairly good review of the notion of "control" more generally. You may want to read through these comments as a bit of review before you move on to the next chapter.

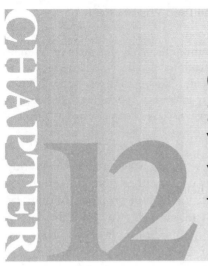

Changes in the Situation: When, Where, and What to Refile

DURATION AND CONTINUATION

Congratulations! You have just prepared an initial financing statement sufficient to meet the formal requisites of §9-502(a) and have filed this very statement in the proper state to give it effect. Good job. Pat yourself on the back, but don't think you can rest on your laurels forever. For one thing, when you get down to it all you did was what you were supposed to do, if perfection through filing was your objective, under Article 9. Still, given how often one sees situations where even these simple rules haven't been complied with giving rise to hotly contested cases that would have been avoided altogether if someone earlier on had just taken a little more care, the successful filing of an initial financing statement — while perhaps not on the level of finding a cure for the common cold — isn't anything to sneeze at.

What's more important here is that even the most brilliantly filed initial financing statement doesn't last forever. Your job for the moment has been done and done well. The filing is in place. For a variety of reasons, which I have tried to group together in this chapter, however, filings under the Article 9 system require a certain amount of upkeep as time goes by and as circumstances change.

Consider first the passage of time. Look at §9-515(a), which informs us that generally "a filed financing statement is effective for a period of five years after the date of filing." The one important exception to this rule is given in subsection (c):

The effectiveness of a filed financing statement lapses on the expiration of the period of its effectiveness unless before the lapse a continuation statement is

229

filed pursuant to subsection (d). Upon lapse, a financing statement ceases to be effective and any security interest or agricultural lien that was perfected by the financing statement becomes unperfected, unless the interest or agricultural lien is perfected otherwise. If the security interest or agricultural lien becomes unperfected upon lapse, it is deemed never to have been perfected as against a purchaser of the collateral for value.

So the very first thing you had better do, after you have finished celebrating the successful filing of this particular initial financing statement, and things have calmed down a bit, is to make a notation in your professional calendar reminding you at some time about four and one-half years from the date of filing to consider the status of the security interest on which you have just filed. If it is in your client's interest that the perfection through filing not lapse at the end of the five years, that will be the time, even if nothing has changed, when you are going to have to act or else have some explaining to do when a "lapse" occurs due to your lack of diligence.

What would you do as the five-year period begins to come to a close to prevent the filing's effect from lapsing as a matter of course? The language quoted above gives a great big clue. On your client's behalf you would make a new filing of a form referred to as a "continuation statement." Filing a continuation statement should not be a particularly difficult thing to handle, but evidence suggests that slipups occur in the process just as they do in the filing of the initial financing statement, so it is worthwhile to spend some time on the particulars.

The first two examples of this chapter deal with the consequences of a lapse in the effectiveness of a financing statement, when someone either chooses not to or through mistake does not effectively continue it through the filing of a continuation statement, as well as the principal issues that come up in determining whether a continuation statement has been properly filed.

MAKING AMENDMENTS

Section 9-512 allows for a person (the secured party or the debtor, though most often it would be the former) to make "amendments" to a financing statement. Note that subsection (a) comes in two distinct versions, the reason given in a Legislative Note following the text of the section. What is more interesting for our purposes is that under revised Article 9, this section on "amendments" includes within that term the continuation statement, which we have just considered, and the termination statement, which we'll get to soon enough. Under the prerevision version of Article 9 these types of later filings were dealt with as three distinct species. Under the revised article they are now technically all variants of one thing, the amendment filing, as we read in Comment 2:

> This section addresses changes to financing statements, including addition and deletion of collateral. Although termination statements, assignments, and continuation statements are types of amendments, this Article follows former Article 9 and contains separate sections containing additional provisions applicable to the particular types of amendments.

Look at the form set out in §9-521(b), which is strongly suggested although not absolutely required for the filing of an amendment of any sort. Box 1a is where the filer will fill in the file number of the initial financing statement to which the amendment relates, as is required under §9-512(a)(1). On the concept of the unique file number assigned to an initial financing statement by the filing office accepting it for filing, see §9-519(a) and (b).

Once the filer has filled in the correct file number, the §9-521(b) form can be made into a continuation statement by checking box 3. For a termination statement, the filer would check box 2, and so on. Later portions of the form allow for other types of amendments such as changes in the parties named or in the collateral description as given in the initial financing statement. In Example 3 below, I've put together at least one case in which an amendment of this sort will be called for.

CHANGES IN THE SITUATION

In a variety of situations, specific provisions of Article 9 call for the parties, specifically the secured party acting to protect its interest, to refile following some change in the circumstances surrounding the relationship and the secured transaction itself. There is obviously a core generalized concern that links these various situations — that the fundamental notice function of the Article 9 filing system not be compromised by changes transpiring in the outside world — but the various sections and subsections we will see here are not distinguished by any great consistency or at times even great clarity. We have to deal with each situation and each subsection on its own terms. As an initial listing of what is to come I offer the following:

> *Relocation of the Debtor:* The location of the debtor is, as we know, the key to knowing with which state the financing statement is to be filed. See §9-316(a)(2). If the debtor relocates to another jurisdiction the secured party is given four months to refile in the new jurisdiction.
>
> *Change in Name of the Debtor:* See §9-507(c). If the change of name has the effect of rendering the financing statement "seriously misleading," then, at least with respect to some later acquired collateral, the secured party had better file an

amendment to the financing statement giving the correct name within four months of the change in name.

Transfer of the Collateral to a Person Who Thereby Becomes a Debtor: In many instances, when the original debtor transfers all or a part of the collateral to another person that person will not be a debtor under Article 9 since he, she, or it will have taken the collateral free and clear of the secured party's interest. If, however, the transferee takes the collateral still subject to the secured party's interest then the transferee fits within the definition of "debtor" given in §9-102(a)(28)(A). If the transferee in such a situation is located within the same state as the transferor, no new filing is required. See §9-507(a). Under §9-316(a)(3), however, if the transferee is located in another state, the secured party is given one year to make a new filing in that state under the transferee's name.

Transfer of the Collateral to a "New Debtor": In some situations, a transferee will take the collateral not simply subject to the security interest but will actually agree to be bound by the security agreement or will be held bound to it under operation of law under the doctrine of "successor liability." Revised Article 9 refers to such a transferee as a *new debtor.* See §9-102(a)(56) and §9-203(d). Under §9-508(b), the transfer to a new debtor located in the same state as the original debtor is treated like the change in name of a debtor. If the name of the new debtor so differs from that of the original debtor as to make the initial filing "seriously misleading," then the secured party should make a new filing within four months of the transfer. See Comment 4 to §9-508.

We will have a chance to explore the intricacies of these rules in Examples 4 through 9.

TERMINATION

All good things, even an immaculately prepared and scrupulously filed and maintained financing statement, must come to an end. We have already seen that if the secured party doesn't act to continue a financing statement, the filing will naturally lapse at the end of five years. In many cases, however, the parties will want to terminate the filing earlier. See §9-513, as well as the concluding example of this chapter, on the Termination Statement.

Examples

1. As part of a loan agreement entered into in 2006, Dexter Moneybucks grants a security interest in his always valuable and by now legendary ruby ring to his friend Frank Furst. Furst files a financing statement correct in all respects in the proper place in March 2006. In 2008 Dexter is behind in the payments he owes for a bit of work done for (and on) him by a cosmetic surgeon, Sarah Second. Dexter promises to pay the

money as soon as he is able and to give Second a security interest in the ring to "back up" his obligation. Second checks the applicable Article 9 records and comes across Furst's filing. She recognizes that any interest granted to her by Dexter in the same collateral promises never to come in better than second to the interest claimed by Furst. Still, reasoning that it is better than nothing and seeing nothing else to do, she agrees to hold off suing Dexter for the money in return for which he signs a security agreement granting her an interest in the ring. Second files a financing statement covering the ring in the appropriate place in October 2008. Dexter files a petition in bankruptcy in November 2011.

a. Assuming Furst makes no filings subsequent to his initial filing in March 2006, does he have an interest that would be valid in the bankruptcy proceedings that are to come?

b. Would your answer be the same if in fact Furst had filed a proper continuation statement in February 2011?

c. Finally, suppose that Furst had not filed any continuation statement but had instead filed an entirely new initial financing statement covering the ring in the proper place in July 2011. What are the relative positions with respect to the one little, albeit valuable, ring that can be claimed by the trustee in bankruptcy, Furst, and Second under this set of facts?

2. The secured party files a properly completed and authorized financing statement in the proper place on August 1, 2006.

a. As of what date would the filing lapse if no continuation statement is completed and filed by the secured party?

b. Assume the secured party does have its wits about it and determines to file a continuation statement. What information must the continuation statement include? Is the secured party authorized to file this continuation statement? See §9-509(d).

c. If the secured party files a proper continuation statement in the proper place on June 1, 2011, to what date does the effectiveness of its filing now run?

d. If the secured party filed its continuation statement on September 15, 2011, what result? See §9-510(c).

e. What if instead the continuation statement were filed in the proper place on September 15, 2010, almost a full year before the effectiveness of the original filing was to lapse?

3. Dexter Moneybucks obtains a personal loan from Downtown Federal Bank in early 2007, putting up two original paintings from his sizable collection of modern art as collateral. He signs a financing statement adequately identifying the collateral ("Black Bear on Ebony" and

"Snowflakes on Copy Paper"), which financing statement is filed in the proper place by the bank on February 1, 2007.

  a. In 2008 Dexter has paid off approximately half of what he owes to the bank. Under his original arrangement with the bank it had agreed to relinquish its security interest in one of the two works when the outstanding loan amount was reduced to this level. An appropriate representative of the bank authorizes and files an amendment to the original filing which amends the description of the collateral to be only one painting ("Black Bear on Ebony"). This amendment is filed on June 18, 2008. The filing as amended now covers only this one work. As of when will it lapse if not properly continued? See §9-512(b).

  b. Suppose instead that in 2008 Dexter approaches the bank about borrowing even more money. The bank is willing, but only if Dexter adds to the collateral a third painting ("Ketchup on Red Flannel"). Dexter authorizes an amendment of the previously filed financing statement that extends the description of the collateral now to cover all three works. This amendment is filed on July 18, 2008. As of when will the filing as now amended lapse if a continuation statement is not filed? As of what date is the bank's security interest in this third painting (the red one) perfected? See §9-512(c).

4. Sheila Ivories is employed as a certified public accountant. In her spare time she enjoys playing the piano, so in 2006 she buys an expensive Steinmetz baby grand piano from a local piano store, which agrees to sell her the piano on credit. The store files an initial financing statement covering the piano in Colorado, where her home is located, on June 15, 2006. It then delivers the piano to her home. In early 2008 Sheila, throwing caution to the wind, quits her job as a CPA, and determines to earn her living by giving piano lessons out of her home. Does the piano store need to amend its original financing statement or refile in a different place to protect its interest?

5. Dr. Tooth is a dentist who lives in a suburb of Kansas City, Missouri. He runs his dental practice out of a single office located in the city itself. In 2006 he takes out a small business loan from First National Bank of Missouri in order to buy a state of the art dental chair and new X-ray equipment for his office. He grants the bank a security interest in "all of his equipment now held or hereafter acquired." The bank files an initial financing statement covering this collateral with the appropriate filing office in Missouri. In 2008 Dr. Tooth relocates his practice to an office in the same suburb in which he lives. He moves all of his previously owned equipment into this new office.

Explanations

1a. No. Furst filed a financing statement in March 2006. That means that by the end of March 2011 it must have lapsed according to §9-512(a) and (b), five years having passed and no continuation statement having been filed. Since Furst's interest is unperfected at the time of the bankruptcy in November 2011, it will turn out to be of no use to him in the bankruptcy, in which he will have to participate as a general unsecured creditor.

1b. Had Furst filed a continuation statement in February 2011, the effectiveness of the original filing would have continued into March 2016. Because we are told that the original filing was proper in all respects and filed in the appropriate place, it served to perfect Furst's security interest in the ruby ring. This perfection continues without abatement thanks to the properly filed continuation statement. Furst, holding a perfected security interest in the ring at the time of bankruptcy, will have an interest in the ring effective against the bankruptcy trustee. To the extent that the amount he is owed by Dexter is no greater than the value of the ring, he can expect to get full repayment at some time through the bankruptcy procedure, even if there might be some delay and headaches along the way.

    Note that Second will also have a perfected interest in the ring as of the time of the filing of the bankruptcy petition. Under the rules of priority we will soon take up in detail, however, Furst's interest will have priority over that of Second, so Second, as she feared, will be protected by her special interest in the ring and its value only to the extent that the bauble's value exceeds what is owed to Furst.

1c. Here Furst's initial filing lapsed as of some time in March 2011. He makes a second filing of a new initial financing statement in July 2011. This second filing will reperfect Furst as of July 2011. The bankruptcy occurs in November of that year. Both Furst and Second hold perfected security interests in the ring as of that date, so both will have interests good as against the bankruptcy trustee. Under the rules of priority, however, Second whose filing and perfection date from 2008 will now have priority over Furst, who can only rely on his filing and perfection in July 2011.

    You can look at this result as a kind of windfall for Second, who never expected to have a primary interest in the ring. Well, to be more precise, she never expected to have a primary interest unless Furst either voluntarily relinquished his interest in the ring (either because he had been fully paid off or otherwise) or slipped up in some way. Furst, by allowing his initial filing to lapse, did indeed foul up. He recovered somewhat by his later refiling, but only somewhat. You can look at this as a windfall for Second. You can also obviously look at this as the kind of thing that is liable to happen to someone such as Furst who doesn't carefully attend to his own affairs.

2a.   The effectiveness of the filing would automatically lapse under §9-515(a) and (b) at the expiration of five years, that is, on July 31, 2011, if no continuation statement is filed.

2b.   The continuation statement must identify the original statement by file number (§9-512(a)(1)) and indicate that the original statement is being continued. That is all that is required.

It seems clear beyond question that the *place* to file a continuation statement is in exactly the same place that the original financing statement had been filed. I can't imagine what a filing officer would do with a continuation statement that arrives at his or her office that does not correspond to any original filing held there. The considerate filing officer would probably send it back to whomever it came from suggesting to the filer that "There must be some mistake here." Another filing officer might just put it in a pile along with other mysterious items that have come in the mail and that he or she might get around to investigating some time in the future, or it might go directly into the trash.

Note that once the continuation statement is filed it becomes part and parcel of the *financing statement* as that term is defined in §9-102(a)(39):

> "Financing statement" means a record or records composed of an initial financing statement *and* any filed record relating to the initial financing statement.

One need not, indeed cannot, search separately for any continuation statement or other amending filing. If the filing office is properly doing its job, the diligent searcher looking for any financing statement under a given name in a given place should be able to come up with the complete package — the initial financing statement and in addition any amendments, continuation statements, or termination statements filed that relate to that initial financing statement — from which he or she, the searcher, will be put on notice of not only the fact that an initial financing statement had been filed, but of any other filing or filings from which he or she may judge the current status of the security interest.

Note also, getting back to the continuation statement in particular, that §9-515(d) specifically provides that, "Succeeding continuation statements may be filed in the same manner to continue the effectiveness of the financing statement."

2c. The original filing statement was filed on August 1, 2006 and would have lapsed of its own accord on July 31, 2011. A continuation statement is filed on June 1, 2011. This continues the effectiveness of the original statement "for a period of five years commencing on the day on which the financing statement would have become ineffective in the absence of the filing," which in this case would be through July 31, 2016.

2d. Subsection 9-515(d) is very explicit and precise that a continuation statement may be filed only during the period "within six months before the expiration of the five-year period specified in subsection (a)." This continuation statement, having been filed too late, is ineffective. The filing's effectiveness lapsed on July 1, 2011, and nothing has changed the situation. The secured party was unperfected, unless it happened to be perfected by some other means, from that date and continues unperfected into the future.

   Can the secured party make the argument that this late continuation statement should at least be treated like a new financing statement, thus reperfecting the interest starting all over again on September 15? It can make the argument, but it is unlikely to work. The financing statement called for in §9-502 is a very specific document containing distinctive information. The continuation statement doesn't have all that information on it. The continuation statement that comes in later refers to nothing on file other than a lapsed filing. It is a nullity. See §9-510(c).

2e. Here we have the opposite problem — a continuation statement that is filed too early rather than too late — but one that will turn out no less satisfactorily for the hapless or, in this case, perhaps overeager, secured party. The Code section says a continuation may be filed "only within" a given six-month period. This statement was not filed within the period and hence is not effective (§9-510(c)). This result may seem a bit formalistic and overly rigid, but if this type of so-called premature continuation statement were given effect, what is to prevent the secured party from simply filing an initial financing statement along with a continuation statement at the very outset, thus getting itself a 10-year period prior to an automatic lapse contrary to the general policy of Article 9? Or for that matter a 15-year period? The six-month period during which a continuation statement may be and indeed *must* be filed if it is to be effective is thought to be sufficiently generous that the secured party if it is on the ball should be able to file within that time. If it does not, however, it can expect to find little sympathy either in the Code or from the courts.

3a. Under the cited subsection the amendment does not extend the period of effectiveness of the original financing statement. It would still lapse on January 31, 2012 unless a proper continuation statement is filed.

3b. Once again because this is an amendment, the effectiveness of the original filing will not be extended. It will lapse at the end of five years, that is on January 31, 2012, unless an effective continuation statement is filed. As §9-512(c) makes clear, and as you would expect, the amendment is effective as to the third painting only from the date of its filing, July 18, 2008. Hence, if perfection in these paintings were based on the filings alone as is likely, perfection on the red one would date only from that date.

4. The store need neither amend nor refile if all that has happened is a change in the use or characterization of the collateral, which is all that we seem to have here. The original filing remains effective, which means that nothing need be done by the bank, other of course than to remind itself to file a continuation statement during the six months prior to June 14, 2011 if it wishes its perfection to stay intact.

5a. No. There has been a change in the location of the collateral, but (at least now, under the Revised Article 9) the location of the collateral plays no part in determining where the secured party is to file in order to perfect. The location of the debtor, here the residence of the individual debtor, is the key. There has been no change in the location of the debtor, so the original filing with the State of Missouri is still perfectly good.

5b. The answer is the same. Even though the collateral has now crossed the state line, the location of the debtor, Dr. Tooth remains the same. That being so, there is no need for the bank to refile.

6a. There is no need for the bank to refile. The "debtor's location" under the rules of §9-307 — and hence the place where the filing need be made — is still the same, the State of Missouri. There is no need for the bank to amend its filing to reflect the new address of the debtor, because that particular bit of information is not required for a financing statement to be "sufficient" under the criteria of §9-502. Also, it is hard to think that the change of the individual debtor's home address could render the financing statement "seriously misleading" so as to bring into play §9-506(a). Searches of the records kept at the office of the Missouri Secretary of State are carried out on the basis the *exact name* of the debtor, and there's certainly been no change in that. The reasonable searcher should be able to deal with the fact that the address of the individual may not now be what it once was. People move around all the time.

6b. Here, because the location of the debtor *has* changed, the governing rule is that found in §9-316(a)(2):

> A security interest perfected pursuant to the law of the jurisdiction designated in Section 9-301(1) [as was true here when the bank first

perfected under the laws of Missouri] . . . remains perfected until the earlier of . . . (2) the expiration of four months after a change of the debtor's location to another jurisdiction.

So the bank will have to protect its perfection on the collateral by filing an initial financing statement with the state of Kansas within four months of Dr. Tooth's move to his fancier digs in that state. Note that under §9-316(b), if the bank does make a filing in Kansas within the four-month grace period then its interest is deemed to be "continuously" perfected, meaning that the bank's date of perfection or filing, for the purposes of priority, remains the date when it first perfected or filed under the laws of Missouri back in the year 2006. If the bank were to file in Kansas more than four months after Dr. Tooth's relocation, it would then become perfected from the date of the Kansas filing but its date of perfection would not relate back to the time of the previous filing in Missouri.

A question you may be asking yourself is how the bank is to know that Dr. Tooth has moved his residence. Undoubtedly, the security agreement he signed will obligate him to give the bank notice at the very least if he intends to do so, but what if he should fail? The bank cannot simply rely on his doing as he promises in the security agreement. It has to be on the lookout so that it can catch such changes in location even if the debtor fails to report them, either because of some evil intent or just because a busy dentist in the midst of a move won't necessarily remember the obligations he took on in the fine print of some bank document signed a few years back. Presumably the bank is getting regular payments from Dr. Tooth on something like a monthly basis. People at the bank should be aware if the checks coming in start showing a different address. Certainly if the doctor has his principal checking account with the bank and sends in a request for a set of new blank checks with a different address preprinted on them it should send up a red flag that the people in the loan department can get to see and to which react. As in all manner of things, the bank can ask for and will no doubt get the debtor's promise that it will be informed of anything that may affect its interests, but as a practical matter it will have to set up practices and procedures that help it to catch such changes even if the debtor doesn't meet its obligation to give notice.

7. Yes, the bank most certainly needs to refile. The debtor has changed its name from "Harold's House of Fashions, Incorporated" to the more, well, distinctive "Monsieur Harold's House of Fashions, Incorporated." Harold may or may not have changed the name on the front of the store, but that is not the issue. Once the debtor is a corporation,

§9-503(a)(1) tells us from the outset that the debtor's name on the financing statement, and hence the name under which it will be indexed wherever it may be filed, is to be "the name of the debtor [here the corporation, which is a type of "registered organization"] indicated on the public record of the debtor's jurisdiction of organization [here California] which shows the debtor to have been organized."

Subsection 9-507(c) provides that:

> If a debtor so changes its name that a filed financing statement becomes seriously misleading under Section 9-506:
>
> > (1) the financing statement is effective to perfect a security interest in collateral acquired by the debtor before, or within four months after, the change; and
> >
> > (2) the financing statement is not effective to perfect a security interest in collateral acquired more than four months after the change, unless an amendment to the financing statement which renders the financing statement not seriously misleading is filed within four months after the change.

The bank's original filing in 2007 gave the name of the debtor, quite correctly, as "Harold's House of . . . ." Once the name of the corporation is legally changed it would be "seriously misleading" for anyone searching for filings where the debtor was a certain "Monsieur Harold's House of . . . ." The test for when a change in name makes a filing under the original name now "seriously misleading" must be, it stands to reason, the same as the test for whether a mistake in the rendering of the name in an original filing is not just a "minor error" but is rather "seriously misleading" for the purposes of §9-506, a question with which we dealt at some length in Chapter 6. In this case the answer isn't really in doubt: Any search conducted in the files of the California Secretary of State's office for filings under the debtor's name of "Monsieur Harold's House of Fashion" using that office's standard search logic is not going to bring to light the filing under the previous name. (I can't imagine any standard computerized search logic treating the word "monsieur" as an unimportant bit of static — such as the words "a" and "the" are often treated — which is ignored in testing whether two strings of alphanumeric characters are identical.)

Note that the change does not immediately render the old filing ineffective, nor does it even render it ineffective after the tolling of the four-month period. The danger to the secured party is only that *new* collateral acquired after the end of the four-month period, which it expects to have swept within the ambit of its perfected security interest through an after-acquired property clause, will fall outside its grasp unless a "new appropriate financing statement" is filed within the four months. Had Downtown Federal lent only on Harold's equipment and wasn't seriously concerned about taking an interest in after-acquired equipment, then this wouldn't matter much. Given that it has taken as collateral inventory, and in particular that it has included after-acquired inventory, however, the need for a refiling is obviously of a fairly high order. If Harold knows anything about fashion and if his House of Fashions is doing any kind of business, virtually the entire inventory will probably turn over within four or six months. Otherwise Harold is left stocking only last year's styles and last season's selections. So in a case like this the bank definitely will want to file an amendment correcting the debtor's name — and do so within four months of the change.

Having shown suitable concern for the interests of Downtown Federal, the secured party, under the change of name scenario, we now have to shift focus and ask what this means for others who might have some interest in the collateral, an interest of the type that would send them searching for any filings under the correct new name. Isn't it true that they could be misled by a system that makes the original filing still good as to any collateral that had been acquired by the debtor under its older name and even for four months following the change? The answer is yes, this does put the searcher under a disadvantage. If Downtown Federal doesn't refile it still has a perfected interest in all the equipment, which could be considerable, and whatever inventory Harold still has on hand acquired by him prior to his corporation's change in name. If it does choose to file it has in addition an interest in all that is acquired during the four months after the name change, so a searcher looking through the records during that four-month period and before Downtown Federal takes care of its refiling would have no way of knowing from the filing records alone what the full story was.

The answer is that the other interested party, the potential buyer or other lender, must protect itself by doing more than just looking through the filings. In particular, to minimize the problem we're dealing with here it must ask Harold not only the correct name of his corporation as of the moment but whether he has operated or granted a security interest in any of the property of concern under any other name at any time in the past. Just to be sure that it is getting an accurate picture it could search other records, including records of incorporation, to see if there have been any name changes in Harold's corporate past. If the debtor is an individual, the prospective purchaser or lender would presumably like to see some evidence of how the property came into the hands of the debtor. If the debtor is unable to present some record, such as a bill of sale, showing how he or she came upon the item, that may be of concern. If there is such a record, the astute observer would presumably quickly pick up on the fact that the property came into the hands of the debtor when he or she was using another name.

8a. No. As we will see in more detail in Chapter 16, under §9-507(a),

> A filed financing statement remains effective with respect to collateral that is sold, exchanged, leased, licensed, or otherwise disposed of and in which a security interest . . . continues, even if the secured party knows of or consents to the disposition.

As Comment 3 to this section explains,

> As a consequence of the disposition, the collateral may be owned by a person [here Smudge] other than the debtor against whom the financing statement was filed [Inkster]. Under subsection (a), the secured party remains perfected even if it does not correct the public record. For this reason, any person seeking to determine whether a debtor [such as Smudge] owns collateral free of security interests must inquire as to the debtor's source of title, and if circumstances seem to require it, search in the name of a former owner. . . . A disposition of collateral may result in loss of perfection for other reasons. See Section 9-316.

The "other reasons" to which this last sentence refers is the possibility that the new owner will be located in a jurisdiction other than that in which the original debtor was located. We do not have to worry about that here: Inkster, as an individual debtor, was located in the state of her residence, Connecticut. Smudge is located in the same state. Hence, the Journeyman company need not make any change to the public record to keep its interest perfected.

As the above-quoted comment reminds us, this result means that a searcher looking to determine if any or all of Smudge's equipment is encumbered by an Article 9 security interest will bear the risk of not becoming aware of Journeyman's interest in the Clarity Supreme in his possession if he or she relies on only a search of the files under Smudge's name. The searcher should as a matter of course not only consult the public records but inquire of the party in whose property he or she has an interest, here Smudge, how it came by this property. The diligent searcher will want to see some proof that Smudge indeed owns the particular machine (What's to say it isn't a bit of leased equipment which just happens now to be in Smudge's print shop?) and, beyond that, how he acquired it. This inquiry should give the searcher at least some clue that the Clarity Supreme, when it was purchased from Inkster, might have been subject to a security interest, which is still attached to the machine. The searcher will then consult the files with respect to any security interests that may have been granted by the seller, Inkster, and gain the information that the printing press was, and continues to be, subject to the Journeyman's company interest.

8b. The analysis remains the same. The Journeyman's company, as holder of the security interest, need not refile in order to protect its perfection. The location of the buyer, here a corporation, is once again Connecticut, the same as the location of the seller. The secured party need make no change to the public record to keep its position intact. As a practical matter, of course, once Journeyman's Press Corporation becomes aware of the transfer, it may want to take some action against Inkster — whose security agreement almost assuredly prohibited her from selling the collateral as she has done, or at least doing so without the express agreement of Journeyman's — or at the very least insist that Smudge allow it to file a new initial financing statement naming him as the debtor. While, as we have seen, it is not required by the rules of Article 9 given the circumstances of the case, it is probably a prudent thing for Journeyman's to do, setting the public record straight and obviating the possibility of any confusion or controversy in the future.

8c. The situation here is different. The purchaser is located (per §9-307(e)) in another state, Delaware. We therefore must consult §9-316(a)(3). A security interest perfected according to the laws of one jurisdiction (here Connecticut) remains perfected until the earliest of "the expiration of one year after a transfer of the collateral to a person that thereby becomes a debtor and is located in another jurisdiction." The Delaware corporation that bought the printing press has become a "debtor" as that term is defined in §9-102(a)(28)(A), even though it has not become an "obligor" under §9-102(a)(59). It is located in a different jurisdiction from the jurisdiction in which the interest was initially perfected. Journeyman's has one year to become aware of the facts of the transfer to the Delaware corporation and then perfect by filing in Delaware. If it fails to do so, its security interest lapses. See Example 4, as well as the text that precedes and follows it, in Comment 2 to §9-316.

9. Patty's corporation has become what Article 9 defines in §9-102(a)(56) as a *new debtor*, because it has "become bound as a debtor under §9-203(d) by a security agreement entered into by another person [that being Selma's corporation]." Note particularly paragraph (2) of §9-203(d). If Patty's newly formed corporation had been organized under the laws of some jurisdiction other than Idaho, and hence located for the purposes of Article 9 in that other jurisdiction, then the rule of §9-316(a)(2), which was explored in the last example, would come into play. But here the location of the new debtor is the same as that of the original debtor. Both are located in Idaho. The governing rule is found in §9-508. The name of the new debtor is significantly different

from that of the original debtor. Therefore, under subsection (b), if Best Bank of Boise wants its security interest to attach to collateral acquired by Patty's corporation more than four months after the transfer of the business from one sister to the other — and we have to assume it would given that a large portion of the collateral on which it is relying is the appliance store's ever-changing inventory and accounts — it will have to file an initial financing statement naming "Patty's Appliances Corporation" as the debtor with the Secretary of State of Idaho prior to the expiration of that four-month period.

10a. Look at §9-513(c). In the general case, by which I mean other than when the filing covers consumer goods, the secured party is not under any statutory duty to file a termination statement just because the underlying debt or obligation has been extinguished. It *is* under an obligation to provide the debtor with the termination statement it will need and want when the debtor makes written demand for such a termination statement. The *debtor* will then take or send the termination statement to the appropriate office, pay the necessary fee, and get the termination statement filed. The burden of actually filing the termination statement is put on the debtor not as punishment. Just the opposite. Because it is in the debtor's interest that the termination statement be well and truly filed, it makes sense that it undertake the filing itself. If it did not, but the responsibility were put instead on the secured party to do the filing, the debtor in its own interest would still have to check with the filing office to make sure the secured party did as it was supposed to.

The drafters were understandably concerned that a debtor who was a typical consumer might not know about when to demand or how to deal with the termination statement. In that situation, as you can see in §9-513(a) and (b), the secured party is required to file a termination statement within a specified period of time.

10b. The termination statement is simply added to the filings relating to the initial financing statement. The entire package of filings is (recall §9-102(a)(39)) still considered to be a "financing statement" located in that filing office and indexed under the name of the debtor. Under §9-519(g), this financing statement is to stay on record at the financing office for at least one year after the "effectiveness" of the financing statement lapses under §9-515. Note that filing of a termination statement does *not* mean that the initial financing statement has lapsed for these purposes. Lapse of the effectiveness of a filing occurs only at the end of the initial five-year period or, if a continuation statement has been filed, until the end of the extended period created by the continuation statement (§9-515(a) and (e)). So the initial financing statement filed by the secured party on August 1, 2006 — now with the related termination statement filed sometime in 2009 attached to it metaphorically if not literally — is to stay on file and remain retrievable through the index of the filing office at least through July 31, 2011.

Read Comment 6 to §9-519. As the second paragraph notes, under this rule of Revised Article 9, the filing of a termination statement does not require or even allow the filing office to immediately take the initial financing statement out of its records, as had been true under the old Article 9. So, in our example, someone doing a search under the debtor's name in the filing office of the state in which the debtor is located in, say, 2010, is going to come up with the information that a secured party did file on the debtor's property in 2006 and that a termination statement relating to this initial filing was filed in 2011. What is the value to the searcher of having this information available? The reason why the drafters of Revised Article 9 made this change is to give the searcher the opportunity and indeed place upon him or her the *responsibility* of, as the comment says, "determin[ing] the significance and effectiveness of the filed records." The searcher may make the decision to simply assume that the termination statement filed in 2011 was filed by someone with the right and authority to file it, or may want to make further inquiries with the secured party of record to ensure that this was not an unauthorized (or, as we sometimes say, a bogus) termination statement. Under the prior version of Article 9, the receipt of a bogus termination statement (which, note, the filing office would have no way of distinguishing from a valid and authorized one) would automatically result in the initial financing statement being wiped off of the public record. A subsequent searcher would have no way of knowing what had happened in the past, or even any clue that something might be amiss. Revised Article 9 in §9-519(g) seeks to remedy that situation. As long as an initial financing statement might be reflective of a still-valid security interest — that is until it would have to lapse automatically at the end of five years, or such longer period as it has been given life through the filing of one or more proper continuation statements — the initial financing statement, along with all filings made that purport to amend or modify it, stays on the public record. And then for at least one year more.

Priorities

Introduction to Priority and the Basic Priority Rules

INTRODUCTION TO PRIORITY MATTERS

A good place to begin this Part of the volume is subsection (a) of §9-201:

> Except as otherwise provided in [the Uniform Commercial Code] a security agreement is effective according to its terms between the parties, against purchasers of the collateral, and against creditors.

That the two parties to a security agreement, the debtor and the secured party, are able to enter into a contract that the state recognizes as enforceable will probably not strike you as particularly shocking, nor should it. All the same, it is nice to see it there in black and white. The particular remedies that Article 9 gives to an aggrieved party when there is a breach of the security agreement — meaning more specifically what the secured party has the right to do to enforce its interest when the debtor breaches in one way or another — will be the subject of the next and final part of this book. Before even getting into that, however, we have a whole additional and especially interesting set of concerns that we have to address.

Note that the crucial language of §9-201 quoted above does not just say that the security agreement is enforceable as between the two parties to that agreement. More intriguing, undoubtedly, is that it says that the agreement is "effective" as well "as against purchasers [a term of considerably broad scope as seen in its Article 1 definition] of the collateral, and against creditors." It is one thing for an agreement that rises to the level of a legally enforceable contract to be effective, to allocate rights and responsibilities, among the parties to that agreement. That is what standard contract law is all about. Here, however, is a statement that others *not party to the security agreement* may be "except as otherwise provided" in Article 9 bound by or at least subject to its terms. That is, as they say, quite another kettle of fish.

The story, or really the variety of stories, about how and why this can come about is what we now come to address, under the general rubric of the Article 9 "priority" rules. Problems there will be, and plenty of Examples and Explanations to aid you in sorting them out, but a few general guidelines about how to approach priority problems are in order to set you on your way into this material.

As a starting point, be sure you are perfectly clear exactly what piece or pieces of personal property the characters in the tale are fighting over. It may be a single ruby ring, the complete inventory of a business, a set of accounts, some shares of corporate stock, or any number of things. First, get this straight. You will observe that in the diagrams I use myself to help wrestle the stories, which can quickly become pretty complicated, into submission, I always put the property the parties are fighting over directly in the middle. That's not by accident or merely to enhance aesthetic appeal; I mean to represent as best as I can what the priorities problems are all about. You would be amazed how many people will, given the right set of circumstances, want to get their hands on a single beaten up 10-year-old Chevy or some such piece of property, but that is the way of the world when money is involved and there is not enough to go around.

Second, sort out the individual players, those who have or who assert they have some interest in that property. Identify what interest in or relationship with the property that party has or is asserting. We have already seen that when an Article 9 security interest is involved there will be at least one party who is the debtor (with some "rights in" the collateral) and another who is the secured party (with, by definition, a security interest in it). Priority problems get interesting because there are so many others who can come onto the scene so quickly. For one thing there may be more than one secured party with an interest in the identical collateral. We will also have to deal with various types of "lien creditors," including the all-important bankruptcy trustee; people who are buyers or other transferees of the stuff; those who assert an interest in the "proceeds" of any sale; and other characters. You'll see in my diagrams that I tend to scatter the players around the central property, the object of their desire, identifying them not just by name but by the role they have taken on. Sometimes it gets tough just finding enough room on a simple two-dimensional surface for everyone who wants to get into the act.

For those parties making a claim based on an Article 9 security interest, go through the process, which you should now consider routine, of assessing how the collateral is to be categorized, whether the claimed interest attached and if so, when, and whether it was ever perfected and if so, how and when. As to the parties claiming an interest via some other route, collect what data you have—names, places, dates, times, and any other relevant information—as to each of the players.

Finally you are ready to apply the various priority rules of Article 9 to the assorted claims and characters. What are those priorities rules? We begin in this chapter with the basics and move on from there.

THE BASIC RULES OF PRIORITY

There is not really much more that needs to be said in introduction to basic priority problems other than that they require some basic rules to sort them out and that Article 9 has just the rules you will need. You will find the indispensable rules in §9-317(a), abetted by the definition of "lien creditor" found at §9-102(a)(52), and in §9-322(a). There are, to be sure, exceptions to the basic rules given in these cited subsections, but we can wait on these for the moment as they will be covered in chapters to follow.

After this briefest of introductions, I give you the most crucial of examples and explanations. If you find yourself fuzzy on these after the first go-around, I'd advise you to slow down a bit and enjoy them at least one more time. There would be little sense in moving on to the following chapters if you were not perfectly secure in what you see here.

Examples

1. Donald arranges to borrow a sum of money from a business acquaintance named Sandy. On June 1, he signs a security agreement prepared by Sandy, under which he grants her a security interest in a valuable painting ("Still Life With Profit") in his art collection to secure the loan. Sandy prepares an initial financing statement correctly giving Donald's name and address, a description of the collateral, and her own name and address. She files this statement in the correct place on June 7. She later discovers that another creditor of Donald's, an interior decorator who had done significant work for Donald but whom Donald had never paid, had sued Donald and recovered a judgment against him. Frustrated by Donald's unwillingness to pay the judgment, the decorator had obtained an order of levy in her favor on several of his more valuable works of art, including the painting in question. The local sheriff had executed the levy on the artworks on June 6.

    a. Does the decorator or Sandy get paid first from the amount taken in when this painting is sold off?

      b. Assume instead that the decorator does not levy on the art, but is one of several creditors whose unpaid bills force Donald to file a petition in bankruptcy on June 6. What is Sandy's position in this circumstance? Would it make any difference to your analysis if it could be shown without contradiction that no one had made a search in the relevant filing office for any financing statements under Donald's name at any time between June 1 and June 7?

      c. How would you analyze the situation if, instead, Sandy had prepared an authorized financing statement from the outset and had filed it on June 1?

      d. Finally, suppose that Sandy did file on June 1. You are the trustee in bankruptcy. Can you think of any arguments you might consider that could at least potentially defeat Sandy's claim of an interest to which you would otherwise have to concede priority?

2. Debtor grants a security interest in certain collateral to creditor Able. Able never perfects on this interest. Subsequently, Debtor grants a security interest in the same collateral to Baker, who does effectively perfect her interest. Who has priority — Able or Baker?

3. Dexter Moneybucks, in need of some ready cash, asks his friend Susan if she can lend him $12,000. He promises to repay that amount with interest within a year and further offers to let Susan keep a valuable ruby ring of his "as collateral for the loan." Susan agrees. On July 1, she gives Dexter a check for $12,000, and in exchange he hands over the ring. Nothing is in writing. On December 26, Dexter files a petition in bankruptcy.

      a. Does Susan have a security interest in the ring that will be good as against the bankruptcy trustee?

      b. Suppose that in early December, Dexter had contacted Susan, telling her that he has been invited to spend the holidays with his great-aunt. This great-aunt is the very person who originally gave him the ring, which has been in the Moneybucks family for generations, and would be upset to see that he wasn't wearing it. Dexter asks if he could borrow the ring back, "only for a short time." Susan agrees. Dexter comes and picks up the ring on December 22. He delivers it back to Susan in perfectly good condition on January 5. Susan then discovers that Dexter had filed the petition in bankruptcy on December 26. What is her position under this set of facts?

4. This example starts out as the previous one. In July Susan lends Dexter $12,000, taking his valuable ruby ring in pledge. On December 22 she lets him take it back "temporarily" to wear for the holidays. On the afternoon of that day Dexter visits the offices of the Friendly Finance Company and arranges to borrow $15,000 from that company, giving it a security interest in the ring. Friendly Finance files a financing statement

covering the ring in the appropriate place on December 23. On January 2, Dexter returns to Friendly Finance, where he is told all is in order and is given a check for $15,000. Dexter returns the ring to Susan on January 5. Dexter now is able to hold off filing a petition in bankruptcy until April 1 of the same year.

    a. What are the relative priorities in the ring as between the three parties — Susan, Friendly Finance, and the bankruptcy trustee? How might the "loser" in the situation have protected itself against the outcome?

    b. Assume instead that Friendly Finance had not gotten around to filing its financing statement until January 7. All other facts remain the same. Now how do you evaluate the situation? And what advice would you give to the "losing" party as to how to conduct its business in the future?

5. (*The story here may seem a bit long, but it's worth it. What follows is a classic situation key to the whole nature of the Article 9 filing system and priority rules.*) Isabelle Inkster owns a small printing business including various pieces of printing equipment, all of which are fully paid for. In early November 2006 she speaks to a loan officer at her local bank, Downtown Federal, about getting a small business loan. The officer has her complete a loan application. He also has her authorize the bank's filing of a financing statement, which he fills in with a description of the collateral as "all Inkster's equipment, now owned or hereafter acquired." This officer tells Inkster that while he is favorably disposed, the bank's loan committee has been wary in recent years about making loans to businesses such as hers. He cannot assure her that the committee will approve the loan, and that it may take several months for her application to be processed, as the bank will have to check out her credit rating, get the collateral appraised, and collect other information. Only then will the loan be processed and a final decision made. The loan officer has the financing statement filed in the appropriate place on November 10. In December of that year Inkster approaches Traders Credit Association, a local lender that specializes in lending to small businesses, with whom she makes an application for a small business loan. The association is quick to approve her loan. She is asked to sign a security agreement giving Traders Credit an interest in "all of her equipment, now held or hereafter acquired." A financing statement covering this collateral is filed by Traders Credit in the correct place on December 13, and Inkster receives a check from this lender for $20,000 a week later. Later, on January 14, 2007, Inkster hears from the loan officer at Downtown Federal, who tells her to come to his office as soon as possible. There he hands her a letter from the bank stating that her loan application has been approved and that she is being offered an "InstaLoan" line of credit for $80,000 by the bank. The terms of the credit line are set forth in the letter. "All you have to do to have the money available to you," he explains, "is sign this security agreement and this

note." Inkster signs the bank's standard form of security agreement (describing the collateral as "all equipment now held or hereafter acquired) and the note for such a loan. The officer hands her a packet of materials explaining how she can "call on" the money now at her disposal, how she will be billed for payments and so on. The beginning of the year is a slow time in the printing business, so Inkster does not draw money from this credit line until some time in March. During the remainder of 2007 and into 2008 she keeps running a loan balance usually in the range of between $40,000 and $45,000 from this line of credit. She is always on time when it comes to paying the bank, as she is with her payments due to Traders Credit. In the middle of 2008 her business begins to flounder. On November 12 of that year she is forced to file a petition in bankruptcy court. The only things she has of value remaining to her name are the various pieces of printing equipment she has accumulated over the years. What is the relative priority in this equipment as between the three parties: Downtown Federal, Traders Credit, and the bankruptcy trustee who will be named?

6. First National Bank and Trust took a security interest in "all inventory, now held or hereafter acquired" of Harold's House of Fashion. The security agreement — signed in 2005 along with all the other relevant loan documents — provided that the collateral would secure not only the $65,000 lump sum loan made to Harold at the time, but also "all future advances of whatever kind later made to borrower by lender." First National properly filed on its interest in 2005. In March 2007, when the unpaid balance that Harold owed to First National has been worked down to $4,500, the bank agrees to lend Harold an additional $70,000 on the same collateral. Harold signs a new note for the additional amount but nothing else.

a. Does First National's security agreement or its filed financing statement need to be amended in any way or refiled in order to sufficiently protect the bank? See §9-204(c) and its Comments 5 and 7.

b. Suppose in addition that another lender, Second Avenue Credit Association, had lent Harold $40,000 in January of 2007 taking as security "all of Harold's inventory now held or hereafter acquired." It filed on the inventory in the proper place on January 15, 2007. Later in 2008, Harold files for bankruptcy. An optimistic but fairly reliable estimate of the value of the inventory which will be available in the bankruptcy is $75,000. During 2007, Harold has been paying interest to both First and Second, but has not paid off any principal amounts. As the final results of the bankruptcy proceedings unfold, which creditor, First National Bank or Second Avenue Credit, has priority on the inventory? How much should each expect to recover? See Comment 3 to §9-323.

7. In January Daniel finds that he has inherited an old violin from a distant relative. In need of cash to pay some unexpected bills, in February Daniel borrows money from the Friendly Finance Company. He gives Friendly Finance a security interest in the violin, which the lender duly perfects by filing on February 20. In March Daniel takes the violin to the shop of one Stella, who is expert in the repair and restoration of such instruments, and contracts to have it refurbished for a price of $500. Stella promises to have the work done within two months. Two months later Daniel goes to Stella's shop and asks to be given the violin. Stella tells him that she is willing to do so but only upon payment of her fee. Stella points out to Daniel that under a state statute she is entitled to "a lien" on the instrument to assure payment of any amounts due her in return for the work she has done on it. Assuming Stella does have this statutory right, is the interest she claims in the violin an Article 9 security interest? Is it a lien prior or subordinate in right to that of Friendly Finance? Recall §9-109(d)(2).

8. Farmer White arranges for a loan with which to pay her everyday operating expenses during the growing season from the Planters and Growers State Bank, granting the bank a security interest in "all crops now growing on her land, Whiteacre." She also purchases a large quantity of seed from Heartland Supplies, an agricultural supply company, to get her crop going, promising to pay for the seed when her crop has come in and been sold. A statute in the state gives "any supplier who furnishes crop production inputs [defined to include such things as seed] an agricultural input lien for the unpaid cost of the supplied inputs, which lien attaches to any crops grown using the furnished seed or other inputs." This agricultural-lien statute is silent on what priority, if any, should be given to a lien arising under its terms. When the crops come in, and when Farmer White fails to pay either of the creditors, both Planters and Growers State Bank and Heartland Supplies claim an interest in the crops. How do we determine which creditor's interest — the bank's or the supplier's — has priority over the others? See §922(g) and Comment 12.

Explanations

1a. The decorator will have priority, which means that she will be paid off first and, more importantly, stand a much better chance at being paid off fully when the painting is sold to cover Donald's debts. The first thing to do is to get all the facts straight. Some sort of diagram is usually helpful and often indispensable. Recall the simple diagram which I introduced in Chapter 1 for the prototype Article 9 secured transaction.

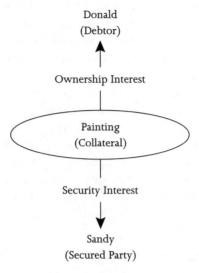

Now let's expand on this by adding whatever additional information we have about Sandy's dealings with Donald in particular.

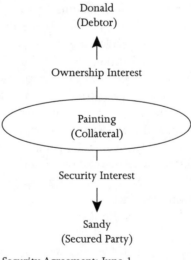

Security Agreement: June 1
Value Give: June 1
Rights in Painting: Long-standing
Filing: June 7

But wait, there's more! (Don't worry. Once we get the hang of things I won't be building up each diagram one step at a time — that'll be up to you—but cut right to a later or final version.) Let's add the *legal characterizations* of which we are now capable, having worked through earlier chapters, of the collateral and of the events as they transpired in this little scenario. In addition, it seems only fair to add the decorator and what we know about her position vis-à-vis the painting.

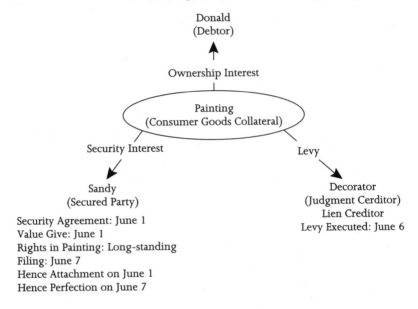

Now we are ready for some good old legal decision making, but it turns out that there is not much to it, and certainly nothing particularly tricky. We look to §9-317(a):

> A security interest or agricultural lien is subordinate to the rights of . . . (2) except as otherwise provided in subsection (e) [which we can check doesn't apply here], a person that becomes a lien creditor before the earlier of the time: (A) the security interest or agricultural lien is perfected; or (B) . . . a financing statement covering the collateral is filed.

The decorator happily points out to us that under §9-102(a)(52)(A), she is a "lien creditor," since she is a "creditor that has acquired a lien on the property involved by attachment, levy, or the like." She became a lien creditor under this definition on June 6 when the levy in her favor was executed. Sandy does have a perfected security interest, but it was perfected only on June 7. At the time the decorator became a lien creditor, Sandy's interest was unperfected and hence, under §9-317(a)(2) is subordinate to the decorator's rights. Given the facts of the situation, the decorator has priority in the painting over Sandy. For a recent case where the secured party *had* perfected prior to the judgment lien's coming into existence, and hence easily won the day, see *Chicago District Counsel of Carpenters Pension Fund v. Tessico Construction Co.*, 51 U.C.C.2d 268, 2003 U.S. Dist. LEXIS 9288 (N.D. Ill. 2003).

1b. The diagram of this situation is basically similar to the last one above, but now Sandy is trying to fend off not a disgruntled decorator but the bankruptcy trustee who will eventually be appointed in the course of the bankruptcy proceedings.

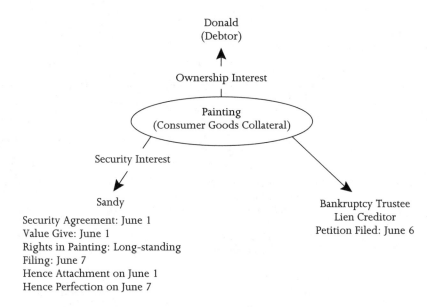

Donald
(Debtor)

Ownership Interest

Painting
(Consumer Goods Collateral)

Security Interest

Sandy

Security Agreement: June 1
Value Give: June 1
Rights in Painting: Long-standing
Filing: June 7
Hence Attachment on June 1
Hence Perfection on June 7

Bankruptcy Trustee
Lien Creditor
Petition Filed: June 6

For analysis, again we start with §9-317(a)(2) and then head straight to §9-102(a)(59)(C). Now we note that the definition of "lien creditor" also includes "a trustee in bankruptcy from the date of the filing of the petition." So it does not matter exactly when the specific individual who will serve as the trustee is actually selected and officially appointed. He or she will end up being a lien creditor as of June 6. And since, as we have already determined, Sandy's interest was unperfected until June 7, the trustee takes priority over Sandy's interest.

This result doesn't mean, to be sure, that Donald's debt to Sandy will not be given recognition in the bankruptcy at all. The debt isn't wiped out. It does mean, however, that Sandy's attempt to get a special position in the bankruptcy, to be recognized as a *secured* creditor, has all gone for naught because of her failure to file in time. The bankruptcy trustee will be able, under the so-called "strong-arm provision" of §544 of the Federal Bankruptcy Code will have the power to avoid Donald's security interest because it was not perfected as of the moment of the bankruptcy filing. Thus, the amount owed Sandy will simply be considered an *unsecured* debt of the debtor, Donald, for the purposes of the Bankruptcy proceeding, and will be added to what is probably a pile of other unsecured debts Donald owes as of the filing of the petition. Had Sandy had a valid *and perfected* security interest in the painting as of June 6 when the bankruptcy occurred, she would have had a good chance of eventually (when all the dust settled) coming out fully paid, as long as the value of the painting surpassed that which she was owed. As an unsecured creditor, she will be lucky to get five or ten cents on the dollar if Donald's bankruptcy is typical of how these things usually play out.

Look at the end of the initial paragraph of Comment 2 to §9-308:

> [I]n general, after perfection the secured party is protected against creditors and transferees of the debtor and, in particular, against any representative of creditors in insolvency proceedings instituted by or against the debtor.

The comment then goes on to remind us that "the time of perfection is when the security interest has attached and any necessary steps for perfection, such as the taking of possession or filing, have been taken." Unfortunately for Sandy in this example, she took the step of filing but just not in time. As to the question of whether it would make any difference if it could be shown beyond a shadow of a doubt that no one had made a search in the relevant filing office for any financing statements under Donald's name at any time between June 1 and June 7, the answer is a distinct "no." Section §9-317, and the priority rules in general, go by matters of timing strictly and not by examination of what parties "could have known," "should have known," "relied upon," or anything like that. You look at the date recorded on Sandy's financing statement as the date of filing and you look at the date of the bankruptcy petition's filing — and there you have it.

1c. If Sandy had filed a satisfactory financing statement in the appropriate filing office on June 1, then it would make all the difference in the world. Sandy would then have been perfected as of the moment the bankruptcy trustee comes into the picture as a "lien creditor" and hence her interest would not be subordinate to the trustee's claim on behalf of the estate. As we saw in the comment quoted above, the very idea of a perfected interest is that the perfected interest is "protected" against the bankruptcy trustee. There is no doubt about this general proposition, but it is a bit frustrating that you cannot find it laid out as clearly as you might wish in the text of Article 9 itself. Section §9-317 talks about what parties an unperfected security interest is subordinate to, but it never speaks in the affirmative of all the good that comes from having a perfected interest. It would be nice if it did, but it need not be any cause for concern. This is presumably just a situation where the drafters forgot to put into the statutory language something that was so obvious to them, something about which the language of Comment 2 to §9-308 quoted above certainly leaves no room to question.

1d. As trustee here you are not going to have any success railing against the basic rule of §9-317(a)(1). (You could, as academic and other commentators do from time to time, challenge the underlying justification for the basic principles of Article 9 allowing for secured credit and argue for a dismantling of the whole system. But you've got work to do, so you'll leave the public policy arguments and discussion of fundamental law reform for others.) If Sandy was well and truly perfected as of June 6, you will have to give her her due. But remember, this all depends on Sandy's claim to perfection, and perfection as of June 6, standing up to scrutiny, and you are not above taking a look at the arguments she uses and the facts she supplies to support her claimed secured position.

Let's be clear about one thing. The trustee, in attempting in good faith to defeat any claimed secured interest, is not being mean-spirited, devious, self-serving, or anything of the sort. The trustee represents the collective position of all of the unsecured creditors. If he or she can defeat a claim of priority that one creditor (arguing a perfected security interest in some particular property of the bankrupt's estate) is making, it brings the value of that property back into the pot (or more likely the relatively meager residue sitting in the very bottom of the pot) in which the unsecured creditors will share pro rata. The trustee has an obligation to challenge, if he or she in good faith can, vulnerable claims of priority which if left standing would only result in less for the unsecured creditors to share among themselves.

How might the trustee challenge and perhaps even defeat Sandy's or a like party's claimed perfected security interest? Well, for a start he or she might review the topics covered in earlier parts of this book. There he, she, or you will find a catalog of the kinds of arguments which may, given the facts of the situation, defeat a creditor's claim of a perfected security interest in particular collateral. I certainly don't intend to redo all of those chapters here, but just as a refresher, recall the following. For an interest to be perfected it must be attached and perfection can occur no earlier than attachment. Was Sandy's interest even attached as of June 6? Did a valid security agreement sufficiently describing the collateral and authenticated by Donald exist? Had value been given by Sandy to Donald by that date? Has Sandy effectively perfected? Remember: Sandy isn't going to volunteer information if some piece of the puzzle crucial to her asserted interest is missing; she might not even be aware of it herself. So the trustee has to check it out himself or herself. You may recall the case of In re Pickle Logging, Inc., 286 Bankr. 181, 49 U.C.C.2d 971 (M.D. Ga. 2002), which we looked at in Chapter 6. The court there held that the lender's filing of a financing statement did not perfect its interest because of material misleading error in its description of the collateral. The lender's security interest was therefore unperfected and could be avoided by the debtor-in-possession — a character in bankruptcy lingo who, as the court pointed out, has the same rights and powers as the bankruptcy trustee, including the "strong-arm" power to avoid unperfected security interests.

If Sandy's interest had attached as of June 6, were appropriate steps taken to perfect by that date? Sandy's claiming perfection through the mechanism of filing. Look at the financing statement. Are there any of the defects that would make it insufficient for the purposes of perfection under §9-502(a)? Was it filed in the proper place? If the trustee can successfully punch a hole in Sandy's claim of perfection as of July 6, he or she, and hence the group of unsecured creditors, wins. Remember too that the trustee's arguments along any of these lines are not going to have to depend on a showing that Sandy was acting fraudulently or with any kind of impure thoughts whatsoever, nor will they have to show any reliance on misinformation by the trustee or anyone else; if Sandy slipped up and failed to meet the technical requirements Article 9 lays out for obtaining perfected status, then Sandy is not branded a villain or a cheat, merely an unsecured creditor where she had not intended to be. And hence a bit of a sad sack.

As an aside before we move on to the next example, you might be surprised to find that this whole chapter has been written with reference to only a single real-life case. With all the stress I'm putting on the centrality of the basic, and later the not so basic, priority rules of Article 9, you would expect there to be a lot of litigation on the subject. Make no mistake about it: There are plenty of reported cases involving who has priority over whom in a particular bit of collateral. There are boatloads, large boatloads of cases where priority is what the parties are fighting over, and they aren't just litigating for the fun of it. (The drafters of Revised Article 9 saw as one of their primary objectives clarification and simplification of the rules relating to attachment and perfection. To the extent they have been successful in meeting this objective, they, and we, can hope to see the amount of litigation of this type greatly reduced in the future.) The point here, however, is that the priority battles are rarely if ever about the basic rules that apply once all the facts are in and who did what and when (in the Article 9 sense) has been sorted out. A typical case where priority is disputed quickly comes down to one or more issues of whether or not attachment was ever achieved, the characterization of the collateral, whether and when an interest was perfected, whether a filing was effective in form and filed in the proper place, and so on and so forth. Presumably, just about all of the issues, and a huge percentage of the cases real and hypothetical, of all the preceding chapters were (when you get down to it) of interest precisely because of how priorities would be determined based on the decisions there laid down. All we have done before was leading up to this. And so to Example 2.

2. This one's a snap, so easy in fact that you can see I just couldn't get up the steam to think of clever names for the parties. And we certainly don't need a diagram to map it out. Able's interest may have attached, but it isn't perfected. Baker's interest is perfected. Baker has priority. A perfected interest always prevails over an unperfected interest in the same collateral. This is unquestionably the result the drafters wanted and what they apparently mean to be saying in §9-317(a)(1). An unperfected interest, like Able's, "is subordinate to the rights of a person entitled to priority under Section 9-322." Take a look at §9-322(a)(2), which states the rule explicitly.

3a. Yes. Here is the diagram as I make it out.

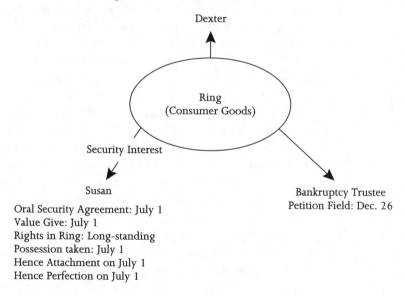

Dexter

Ring
(Consumer Goods)

Security Interest

Susan
Oral Security Agreement: July 1
Value Give: July 1
Rights in Ring: Long-standing
Possession taken: July 1
Hence Attachment on July 1
Hence Perfection on July 1

Bankruptcy Trustee
Petition Field: Dec. 26

Susan has a perfected security interest, one perfected by possession, as of July 1. Since her interest is perfected as of the date of the filing of the petition in bankruptcy, December 26, her interest is good as against the bankruptcy trustee. It is just another example of §9-317(a)(2) and the definition of §9-102(a)(52) in operation.

3b. It's the same old story, the story of Example 2(b) of Chapter 8, that is, but now with the moral to finish it off. You will recall that while Susan did gain a perfected security interest in the ring on July 1, she lost perfection when she relinquished possession of the ring (since possession was the sole means by which she would be able to claim perfection) on December 22. Since she was unperfected at the time of the filing of the bankruptcy petition, on December 26, she will lose out to the trustee. It matters not that she later gets the ring back in January; she's going to have to surrender it up to the trustee as he or she goes about collecting all of Dexter's possessions that rightfully belong in the bankruptcy estate. Susan will be able to file a claim against Dexter in bankruptcy for the money owed her, but only as an unsecured creditor.

4a. Our diagrams are getting a little more complicated, but then all the more useful:

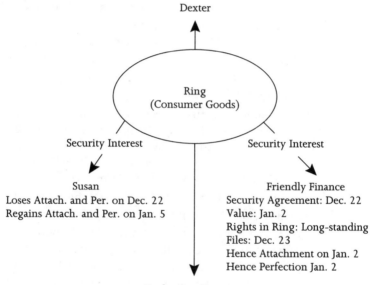

First look at each of the two lenders vis-à-vis the bankruptcy trustee. Susan, whatever might have happened around the holidays, *was* perfected as of April 1, so her interest is good as against the trustee. Friendly Finance was attached as of January 2 and since a filing was already in place was also perfected as of that date. So it too has an interest which will be good against the bankruptcy trustee. If, by some chance, the value of the ring is so great as to exceed the combined amounts owed to Susan and Friendly Finance, the excess will go to the bankruptcy trustee and can go toward paying off at least some percentage of Dexter's debts to his general unsecured creditors.

What's more likely to be the case, of course, is that the value of the ring will not cover Dexter's debt to both Susan and Friendly Finance. Both are perfected, but there may not be enough value in the ring to go around. That being so, it becomes more than a matter of academic interest as to which of the two of them has priority over the other. Now we go to §9-322, which deals with, as its caption indicates, Priorities Among Conflicting Security Interests in and Agricultural Liens on the Same Collateral. We want to focus now on the general rules as they are given in §9-322(a). In all cases not covered by one of the exceptions given in a later subsection dedicated to special occasions, "priority among conflicting security interests and agricultural liens in the same collateral" shall be determined by one of three basic rules. We've already seen (a)(2), the rule that a perfected interest always beats an unperfected one, in action. The rule of (a)(3) is really of little practical importance. If both interests are unperfected, then priority goes by date of attachment. But if both are unperfected, and we are in a bankruptcy situation, neither interest is worth anything special anyway and priority is nothing to worry about.

The more interesting and without a doubt the most important of the three basic priority rules is that set forth in §9-322(a)(1):

> Conflicting perfected security interests and agricultural liens rank according to priority in time of filing or perfection. Priority dates from the earlier of the time a filing covering the collateral is first made or the security interest or agricultural lien is first perfected, if there is no period thereafter when there is neither filing nor perfection.

So priority as between two perfected interests is determined by a first-in-time, first-in-right rule. But, and this is exceedingly important, the rule is *not* simply a first-to-perfect rule. A perfection can be beaten out by a prior filing, even if the filing party does not perfect until later. At the same time, the rule cannot be reduced to a simple first-to-file rule. A security interest can be perfected by some means totally apart from filing and still beat out a filed perfected interest.

Priority is determined under the critical (a)(1) by each contesting party's coming into the priority competition with a date which is the *earlier* of the date of its filing (if any) and its date of perfection. This date, which I sometimes refer to myself as its "priority date," is what counts, "if [of course] there is no period thereafter when there is neither filing nor perfection" on behalf of that party.

Rules of this type are usually easier to comprehend by seeing them in operation, so back to our example. Susan never filed, which is perfectly acceptable if she chooses to rely on possession to assert perfection, but it means her priority date is the date of perfection of her interest, which is January 5. (Note she cannot use December 22 when she first perfected, since there *was* a period between December 22 and January 5 when she was neither perfected nor filed on the collateral.) Friendly Finance filed on December 23. It was perfected on January 2. The earlier of these two dates is, I hardly need point out, December 23. Susan comes into the priority competition with a date of January 5. Friendly Finance can assert its priority date of December 23. The finance company's date is earlier, so it wins. The relative priorities of the three parties here, which all claim some interest in this one little ring, turn out to be Friendly Finance, then Susan, then the bankruptcy trustee.

A second question I asked you to consider in this part is how the loser — Susan as it turns out — could have protected herself against this outcome? We are not worried here about what the bankruptcy trustee could have done; the bankruptcy doesn't come into the picture until sometime after April 1. Of course, if the trustee saw any opportunity for establishing somehow that either of Susan or Friendly Finance's interests was not properly perfected, it would and should act on this opportunity.

The first thing we can think of is that Susan really made a mistake in surrendering possession back to Dexter the debtor. Kindhearted as this may have been, it allowed her perfection to lapse and for the other party, Friendly Finance, to come in ahead of her. Notice there's nothing improper or questionable about the finance company's behavior in the situation. It may very well have checked the Article 9 records in whatever office others would have filed financing statements on Dexter's property and it would have found no notice of Susan's possible interest. It could have seen the ruby ring right there in the hands of (indeed on the hand of) Dexter, so it had no constructive notice that another would be claiming an interest perfected by possession. Possession was in Dexter. Friendly Finance's victory here does not, of course, depend on its demonstrating that it actually did check the record and look at the ring in Dexter's possession. It may have failed to do either or both of these things, in which case it just lucks out that it itself is not caught in a sting. The fact remains, however, that Susan, by surrendering possession to the debtor, has only herself to blame when she loses out under the perfectly clear rule of §9-322(a)(1).

Suppose that Dexter was really pleading for use of the ring over the holidays and Susan really wanted to oblige — as long as she could protect her own interests. One thing she could have done would be to ask Dexter to then sign a security agreement and authorize the filing of a financing statement covering the ring. Susan would have filed the statement, making sure at the same time that there were no other filings covering the ring under Dexter's name, and once her filing was complete she could then have handed over the ring to Dexter in confidence. Her priority date would continue to be July 1, since right from that time until the bankruptcy the following April there would have been no period when her interest was neither filed nor perfected. Friendly Finance will now lose out to Susan, but that makes sense. It lent to Dexter and took a security interest in his ever-ready ruby ring at a time when a valid filing was in place covering the ring, giving it effective notice that there was someone who might claim an interest that would come in ahead of its own. Either it did not properly check the filings or it chose to ignore the information there on store and run what it should have known would be a heavy risk that its security interest would not amount to much if push came to shove. If, as we are assuming here, Susan did protect herself carefully, then her push would overcome Friendly Finance's ability to shove, and she would win.

4b. If Friendly Finance had taken its time about things and had not gotten around to filing until January 7, then this changes things dramatically. Both lenders, Susan and Friendly Finance, are still perfected as of the time of bankruptcy, so that stays the same. Now, however, application of §9-322(a)(1) leads to a victory for Susan. Her priority date remains the same, January 5, since it is the date on which she perfected, without her ever having filed at all. Friendly Finance now looks for the earliest date it can muster. It's interest wasn't perfected other than by filing, so the date of perfection is the same as the date of filing or January 7. January 5 comes before January 7, and so Susan's perfected interest has priority over Friendly Finance's perfected, but secondary, interest.

What advice would you give to Friendly Finance given this scenario to avoid its being stuck in the same way again? Well, as is fairly obvious, if you are going to perfect by filing, file as soon as possible. (Even, as we will explore in the following example, file a little earlier than that.) In this example at least we've seen that as the facts played out when the finance company filed on December 23 it had priority over Susan; when it delayed filing until January 7, it came in second to her. So earlier is better when it comes to filing, and not just because it keeps the clutter from accumulating on the top of your desk.

As a more general proposition, a lender like Friendly Finance should set up a system to assure itself that if it does lend its interest is going not only to be perfected but that it will not be "primed" by another perfected interest to which it will be subordinate. It can do this by making sure that at the time it releases the funds to the borrower (like Dexter) it has already filed a proper financing statement and furthermore has checked that no other financing statements are on file potentially covering the same collateral that come earlier in time than its own filing. Finally, as we know interests can be perfected by possession, it should make sure that as of the time it releases the funds the collateral is still in the possession of the debtor. They can't be shy about such things. Dexter, if he's going to put up the ring as collateral, has to come in and show them the ring. It wouldn't hurt if there was someone at Friendly Finance with enough knowledge about and experience with gems to give the ring the once over to make sure that it is indeed a real ruby and not a colored piece of glass. If the collateral is something that he would not or could not easily carry around with him, a grand piano say, the lender is going to have to take a trip over to Dexter's and have a look at the piece in Dexter's possession. If the person from Friendly Finance can't get a good look at the piano—Dexter insists the room's a mess and he'd be embarrassed to let anyone in there right now, or that the piano isn't around at the moment but is in the shop for repairs—well then that person just tells Dexter he's not going to get the loan proceeds, as friendly as you please.

This last bit of business should remind you of the discussion in Chapter 8, and particularly in the Explanation to Example 4(a), of why exactly possession by the secured party should be allowed to work to perfect a security interest and in that light of exactly what should count as "possession" for this purpose.

5. They say a good diagram is worth a heck of a lot of words, so let's first lay out the facts as we find them, and the basic legal characterization of events as we determine them to be.

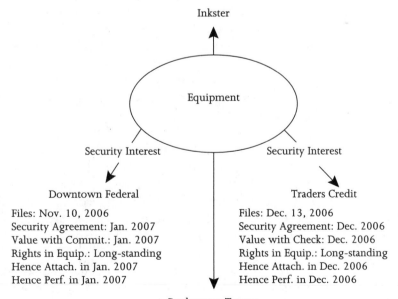

Inkster

Equipment

Security Interest   Security Interest

Downtown Federal

Files: Nov. 10, 2006
Security Agreement: Jan. 2007
Value with Commit.: Jan. 2007
Rights in Equip.: Long-standing
Hence Attach. in Jan. 2007
Hence Perf. in Jan. 2007

Traders Credit

Files: Dec. 13, 2006
Security Agreement: Dec. 2006
Value with Check: Dec. 2006
Rights in Equip.: Long-standing
Hence Attach. in Dec. 2006
Hence Perf. in Dec. 2006

Bankruptcy Trustee
Petition Filed: Nov. 2008

The first question we can ask is whether Downtown Federal's interest will take priority over any claim in the equipment made by the trustee. The answer is clearly yes; the bank's interest was perfected in January 2007 and was still perfected at the time of the filing of the petition in bankruptcy. A perfected interest is good against the trustee, hence, Downtown Federal comes out all right in that head-to-head competition. We next look at Traders Credit's interest. Again, since its interest was perfected here starting in December 2006 at the time of the bankruptcy, its interest will win out over the trustee.

The interesting question, of course, is then which of the two perfected security interests — Downtown Federal's or Traders Credit's — has priority over the other? You get the answer straight out of §9-322(a)(1) as we have already explored it in the last example. Downtown Federal claims priority based on its having filed on November 10, 2006, there being no period after that in which it had neither a valid filing or perfection. The earliest date Traders Credit can come up with is December 13, 2006, when it first filed. So even though Traders Credit's interest attached earlier and perfected earlier, the rules say that neither of these is the deciding factor; Downtown Federal's interest has priority over Traders Credit's under §9-322(a)(1).

This example is actually just Example 1 of Comment 4 to §9-322 gussied up with a bit more detail and my having attempted to supply the characters with the kind of motivation that makes them easier to play, and for you as audience to empathize with. The key here, as the comment goes on to explain after its example, is that Article 9 depends on "a notice-filing system under which filing may be made before the security interest attaches (see Section 9-502)." Yes, do see that section, in particular subsection (d). Downtown Federal has here taken advantage of the opportunity to "prefile," as it is sometimes said, meaning that it has filed a financing statement prior to lending the money, or to taking the security interest, prior even to determining whether it would enter into the deal at all.

What the bank did, if it was following standard practice in this kind of situation, was to get its filing of a financing statement authorized by the loan *applicant* as early as possible, and then file the statement in the appropriate place, again as soon as possible. A few days later it makes a search of the records in this same filing office checking to see what financing statements are on file under the name "Inkster, Isabelle." It is checking for two things. First of all it expects to find reference to its own financing statement, filed a few days before, coming up in the search results. This assures the bank that there has not been a slipup in its own filing or in how the filing officer handled the financing statement. True, if there was a mistake on the officer's part, and the bank has acknowledgment of its filing with the date and time recorded on it, it would later be able to establish the fact of its appropriate filing should it have to do so, in a legal proceeding for example. But who wants to go forward with a transaction with even the potential for this kind of difficulty hanging over his or her head? The bank wants to find that its notice filing has done what it was intended to do, that it would stand out big and bold to any reasonably diligent searcher. If for some reason it does not, now is the time, before the deal is finalized and any money changes hands, to tidy up any mistakes (on whoever's part) and head off any problems before they might occur.

So prefiling and then a follow-up search allow the filer to confirm that the filing has made it into the records as it should. Beyond this, however, the bank will be looking to see if there are any *other* filings on Inkster's equipment that might possibly give it pause. Frankly, just about any other filings covering or even tangentially mentioning her equipment would at least give pause, but what the bank is mainly concerned with is that the search turn up no *earlier* filings on the collateral it is being offered in connection with the loan. Any filing preceding its own would, we are now all too well aware, give the other filer a potential priority over Downtown Federal. Downtown Federal doesn't want that. Unless it is a very unusual lender, willing to take higher risks in conjunction naturally with its charging higher rates of interest and greater fees, it will be willing to lend to Inkster only if it can be confident that its security interest will have priority to the maximum extent possible over any other later comers.

So what the bank's prefiling and subsequent follow-up search on its own have allowed it to do is in effect take and hold for itself a place at the head of the line. Initially the filing is only this, a placeholder. It has not yet completed a loan transaction with Inkster and indeed it may never do so. If there does turn out to be some other filings on record which trouble Downtown Federal, the bank has the opportunity to insist that these be cleared away before it will close the deal. Remember that at the same time — that is, after Inkster's application in November through to the following January — the bank is carrying out the other steps it deems necessary and prudent to determine whether to loan to Inkster and on what terms. It has to undertake a credit check, get an independent appraisal of the collateral from someone knowledgeable about such stuff, get from her additional information about her financial status and future plans, run its own economic analysis of her ability to make payments, and so on and so forth. Anyone who has ever applied for a loan knows the potential lender has a lot of questions it wants answered.

Has First Federal done anything wrong or even questionable in asking Inkster to authorize a financing statement so early on, when it has not even agreed to lend her any money? No. We have already seen that as a technical matter Article 9 specifically allows for prefiling of the initial financing statement. That is why I always tried to be careful in the earlier chapters to say that a filed financing statement was notice that another *may* already hold or be claiming a security interest in the collateral described, not that anyone necessarily *does* at the moment have such an interest. Now we see the practical explanation of why the bank's having her agree to the filing of a financing statement so early on is not an unreasonable request. It is no more unreasonable than asking her to supply it with copies of recent tax returns, allow its appraiser to come into her print shop to look over the equipment, or authorize it to talk to her bank and other parties who would have special information pertaining to her creditworthiness. It is all part of the application process. Inkster is free to refuse to authorize filing of the financing statement, just as she is free to refuse the bank any of this requested information or authorization. Of course the bank for its part is free not to consider her application at all or to consider it in the most unfavorable light. Should the bank decide not to approve her application, or if she should decide for some other reason not to complete the transaction, then she will have the right to get a termination statement from Downtown Federal, which she herself can take to the filing office to ensure that the bank's placeholding filing is effectively terminated. All is then as it was.

In the instant case, of course, the bank does decide to loan to her and the placeholder filing becomes one that reflects an actual security interest granted and now perfected. But there was no need for the bank to do anything more at the filing office at the very moment the loan transaction with Inkster was finalized. Compare this with what you may be familiar with in the real estate situation, where there is no similar possibility for prefiling a mortgage in the land records. Some complex and highly ritualized process, either a closing or a formal escrow, has to be worked out by the parties so that all aspects of the entire transaction take place simultaneously and in an instant (at least conceptually, a typical closing can drag on for hours) *and* that all the important papers that have to go on the land records including the mortgage are filed at exactly that instant and in precisely the right order. In contrast, under the Article 9 scheme the potential lender can prefile, check that its place in line will be where it expects it to be and then carry out the rest of its investigation, decision making, and, if all goes well for the borrower, finalize the loan transaction in an orderly fashion as it sees fit. And all with papers passing by mail or messenger or in the comparable comfort of its offices.

What about Traders Credit? It comes out poorly in all of this, and it is only fair that we should give it a moment's consideration. True, it isn't really the "loser," but it does come in second to Downtown Federal. In what usually turns out to be a two person competition coming in second is a lot like losing. As a matter of fact we did determine that Traders Credit's interest was perfected, so it would still be good in the bankruptcy to the extent that there was any value in the collateral beyond what is necessary to pay off all that is owed to the bank. If after Downtown Federal is fully paid off out of the value of Inkster's equipment there is still something left over, then this would go to Traders Credit as a second, but still perfectly legitimate, perfected secured creditor. If the equipment is so valuable that Traders Credit can be fully paid off, then coming in second was not so bad after all. Of course, if her assets were really worth that much, why was Inkster in bankruptcy to begin with? It has to be the exceptionally rare situation where the secondary secured party comes out whole, or anywhere close to it, in a bankruptcy. It is at least possible that there will be something left over, in the value of the equipment, after Downtown Federal is fully satisfied. This residue will then go toward paying off a part of what is owed to Traders Credit. The rest of what that lender is owed is then counted as unsecured credit, and Traders Credit becomes a general creditor for this amount. As such it may get something, some small percentage on the dollar, of what it is still owed but for which it can claim no special security.

How did Traders Credit allow itself to get into this mess? The answer is fairly simple. Note that it lent to Inkster in December 2006. Had it checked under her name in the proper filing office, it would have found Downtown Federal's filing. This filing was made on November 10. The credit company's filing would be made on December 13. The people at Traders Credit would have had to know that they stood the very considerable risk that if they lent to Inkster, taking a security interest in her equipment, that their interest would be a secondary one and hence far less protective than what they presumably wanted. Perhaps they did check the record and determined to lend anyway, satisfied with taking a secondary interest. Well then, they certainly cannot complain if the risk they were willing to take came to pass. You have to assume, of course, that if they were willing to lend on such risky terms then they were charging a good deal more in interest. In the long run making such high-risk loans at higher rates may in fact allow for a profitable (if more nerve-jangling) business. What we do know is that it isn't the kind of business that a good steady downtown mainstream bank, like Downtown Federal, is going to be interested in taking up.

There may be one final aspect of this situation that you find troublesome and that deserves to be addressed: Is Inkster guilty of something wrong, illegal, or immoral in acting as she has, dealing with the two lenders apparently without telling each about the other and in fact borrowing substantial sums from each before her business goes under? The answer is almost assuredly, yes. In the security agreements she eventually signed with both there would presumably be some place where she warranted that she has not granted nor will she ever grant a competing security interest in the described collateral to anyone else, that she hasn't authorized any financing statements relating to the collateral other than that giving the particular lender as secured party, that the equipment is not now nor will she ever allow it to become "encumbered" in any other way, and so on and so forth. You know how the warranty or covenant provisions of standard form documents tend to be wordy. Inkster, by signing the forms and giving such assurances to each of the two lenders, may have been consciously trying to mislead. It is also quite possible that she didn't even read all the fine print and had no idea exactly what she was "warranting." Remember that from her point of view the important point was that she was regularly making the called-for loan payments to each of the two, so it may not even have occurred to her that anything was amiss. If two lenders are willing to approve your loan application and give you money, what is so wrong about that?

The fact is of course that, whatever you conclude about the morality of what she's done, both of the lenders have a good solid case for breach of contract against Inkster — based now not on the fact that they aren't being repaid, but on the fact that she has breached a warranty in the security agreement she signed. The security agreement is, we continually remind ourselves, first and foremost a legally binding contract between the debtor and the secured party. The problem for Downtown Federal and for Traders Credit is not in establishing that she is in breach of contract, but in figuring out something to do about it. For Downtown Federal, as it turns out, this isn't really a problem. It wins in the priority dispute, and while it would have liked not to even have been faced with the challenge, just as it would have been much happier never having to get involved in one of its loan customer's bankruptcy proceedings at all, it should come out whole. Its principal grief is that it has been dragged into participating in the bankruptcy proceedings when it would have much preferred just to keep collecting the loan payments on a regular basis. There is also the possibility, of course, that the value of the equipment will have sunk to a point where it does not fully cover the outstanding amount of Inkster's debt to it; but this is a problem that it always faces in secured lending, and not one that was necessarily exacerbated by the involvement of Traders Credit.

Traders Credit, on the other hand, stands to lose big. As we have already discovered, it really has itself to blame if it did not check the records carefully before loaning to Inkster. Can it shift this loss back to Inkster by suing her for breach of the warranties she made in the security agreement? What would that accomplish? Traders Credit could win its case and get a judgment equal to the amount they were adversely affected by either her guile or her innocent failure to follow through on the terms of a contract she signed, but it would be a judgment against a party *who is already in bankruptcy*. The chances of the lender collecting on this are the same as its chances of collecting on the debt that it now finds to be unsecured. It's all thrown into the same pot with Inkster's other debts to general or unsecured creditors, which means that the chances of Traders Credit getting very much out of that pot are slim.

The moral of the story as far as Traders Credit is concerned is that if it would have been satisfied in the first place to lend money to Inkster relying on the direct protection of standard contract principles alone, then it could have dispensed with all the Article 9 nonsense to begin with. It could have lent to her in return for her contract promise to repay, and when repayment was not forthcoming brought a traditional breach of contract action. Apparently Traders Credit didn't think this type of transaction would give it enough security. The motivation for its insistence on an Article 9 security interest in some valuable collateral (and for that matter your motivation for studying Secured Transactions to begin with) is that it is often important to get some protection, some security, beyond that offered by contract law alone.

Once that was so it was up to Traders Credit to make sure that the security interest was a good one. It had to protect itself at the loan origination stage by conducting its own investigation — checking the crucial facts out for itself and then making its own determination of how things stood. Easy as it would be, Traders Credit is only doing itself a disservice, to put it mildly, if it relies upon information given it by the loan applicant without doing its own independent investigation. Traders Credit, like any party thinking of going into a secured transaction as the secured party, has a duty *to itself* to make sure that things are in order and satisfactory from its end and if not to back off from the deal. This isn't because all borrowers are bad actors intending to take the lender for a ride, although there are some of those. More typically the debtor is a hardworking upstanding type who has no interest in hurting anybody. When his or her financial affairs turn sour, however, the debtor, however embarrassed or apologetic, is simply not in the position to do much other than to offer those apologies and to try to pick up the pieces of his or her own life as best as possible. The fact is, however, as Traders Credit is about to learn, that you can't get blood out of a stone.

6a. No amendment of either the security agreement or the financing statement, or any refiling, is necessary in March 2007. Section 9-204(c) specifically authorizes the inclusion of such "future advances" clauses as was here in the original security agreement. Comment 5 explains the operation of such provisions. Comment 7 explicitly states that, "There is no need to refer to after-acquired property or future advances . . . in the financing statement. See Section 9-502, Comment 2." The original financing statement, filed in 2005, says all that it needs to say, so there is no need for an amendment much less a refiling of any kind.

6b. We really don't need a diagram here, because it's all in the numbers. First filed first so it obviously has initial priority. Second, however, would like to make the argument that at the time it lent the $40,000 and filed its own financing statement Harold's debt to First was only about $4,500. It, that is, Second would acknowledge that First deserves to first be paid this $4,500, leaving $70,500 of value in the inventory still to be divvied up. Second would then claim that it was the next in line and should get the next bite of the apple, that is, it should get its $40,000. This would leave $30,500, which First would then get and which would go toward repaying the $70,000 it lent after Second made its loan. First, however, would end up with $29,500 of the amount owed to it by the hapless Harold unsecured. It might get some small percentage of this repaid, as it would go into the pool of general unsecured obligations, but First couldn't expect ever to see much of it.

First would understandably take a different view of the situation, and in this it would be supported by §9-323(a), although it is awfully hard, I have to admit, to get the result directly from the statutory language. First would do better by drawing the attention of Second and anybody else who would listen to what is stated in Comment 3 to this section:

> Upon a proper reading of the first-to-file-or-perfect rule of Section 9-322(a)(1) . . . , it is abundantly clear that the time when an advance is made plays no role in determining priorities among conflicting security interests except when a financing statement was not filed and the advance is the giving of value as the last step for attachment and perfection [which First will rightly point out was not the case here, as it filed long ago]. Thus a secured party [such as Second] takes subject to all advances secured by a competing security interest having priority under Section 9-322(a)(1). This result generally obtains regardless of how the competing interest is perfected and regardless of whether the advances are made "pursuant to commitment" (Section 9-102).

Example 1, which follows soon after this language, demonstrates this result in action.

As does, of course, our own example. Under §9-322(a)(1), First both filed and perfected before Second did either, so it has priority over Second, and §9-323 (a) now adds the happy news for First that this priority is good *with respect to the future advances* just as much as it is with respect to the initial advance. So First, which is now owed $74,500, gets all of this off the top, so to speak, out of the $75,000 the inventory is worth. Second gets the remaining $500. The rest of the amount it is owed by Harold, $39,500, is unsecured and will be recovered, if at all, only at some small fraction on the dollar.

You certainly have a right to wonder what calls for this outcome, or at the very least what Second could have done to avoid its seemingly harsh results. Answering the latter of these questions goes a long way toward giving the answer to the first. Second could have protected itself, once again, by checking in the relevant filing office or offices to see if anyone else had filed under Harold's correct name on the same collateral in which it was interested. It would have found First's filing. What then? Remember that the form of financing statement does not give any indication of what obligation Harold might be securing by his grant of a security interest in his inventory to First. It says nothing about how much, if *anything*, Harold actually owes to First. Second could then ask Harold, who would say truthfully that at this point he only owes First something like $4,500. First could even, with Harold's approval, confirm this information. What it would not do is represent to Second that it will never under any circumstances make further advances to Harold to be secured by this same collateral. And it certainly would not agree to ignore the rule of §9-323(a) should it ever find itself in need of invoking that particular provision.

There's an important lesson here: Once a party such as Second searches and does find a financing statement covering property that it itself is thinking of taking as collateral, it has to *assume* that the value of the property is in effect "used up" as far as it might be concerned by the claim of the prior party. True, it may be that the debtor does not now have, and in fact may never have, a significant obligation to the prior filer, which is secured by the particular property. The secondary party, however, once it knows this filing is in place and would always be there antedating any filing it might make, is in no position to assume (except in some situations that we will later observe that take it out of the basic rule of §9-317(a)(1)) other than that in a priority conflict with the earlier filer, it will always come in second — and that coming in second in this type of competition could easily mean its security interest would be worthless.

What is a party such as Second to do? Well, as we have already noted, first it should check the files. Once it finds the prior filing on the same collateral, it cannot ignore the situation or merely hope for the best, unless it enjoys living dangerously and leaving a lot to luck. Second together with Harold could approach First and ask that it agree in writing to subordinate all interest in the collateral beyond the value of $4,500 to an interest to be taken by Second. First might agree to this, but it would probably think it a lot of bother given the relatively small amount of money Harold now owes it. And, of course, it would then not lend him the additional money in March 2007, if it knows what is good for it.

A solution that is probably more likely to work out is for Second to agree to loan Harold something like $4,500 more than he has initially applied for, with the understanding that the extra money would be used to pay off First and get it out of the picture. Harold pays off First, First provides a termination statement, which Second makes sure is properly filed, and then Second can file its own statement making it the only one (and hence the first from that day forward) filing on Harold's inventory.

This leads to the question of why, in January 2007, Harold did not just go to First and borrow the $40,000 he then needed directly from that lender. It certainly would have made life, and this part of the example, a lot simpler. One possibility is that First would not have been willing to extend him any additional credit, or to lend on the same terms as he was able to get from Second. This could have been because of some concern First had about Harold's business as of that time, or business conditions generally, or perhaps it was just thinking of getting out of the practice of making that kind of small business loan entirely. In any event, if Harold did not have a binding commitment from First that he could borrow more, he might have been stuck, save for Second's willingness to lend him $40,000 at the time. The trick, as we can see, is for Second to know what it is getting into and to agree to in effect refinance all of the debt that Harold is securing with his inventory. Harold's protection, if he goes to First and First says no when others would in fact be willing to lend to him, is not in any guarantee from First that it would always be willing to lend to him whatever he wants to borrow. He is not going to get any commitment like that, not from a lender like First, or any sane lender for that matter. What protects Harold in the situation is that his agreement with First should and almost assuredly would contain a provision allowing him the right of prepayment of all amounts due, perhaps with some "penalties" or special charges, when he desires and is able to do so. Note in this regard Harold's right under §9-210(a)(4) to verification from First of a calculation of "the aggregate amount of unpaid obligations secured by collateral as of a specified date." This statement is Harold's way of knowing exactly how much cash or its equivalent he has to come up with on a given date fully to pay off First and get it to terminate its financing statement as of that date.

Once again the question occurs, as the example is originally laid out, whether Harold may bear some accountability for misrepresentations made or vital information withheld from First, from Second, or perhaps from both. And once again the answer is probably yes, but in a practical sense it really doesn't matter much. First may be upset that Harold took on more debt than they were aware of. The increased amounts he ended up having to pay to the two lenders combined each month may have partially been responsible for his falling into bankruptcy. But at least as far as First is involved, when the bankruptcy did occur its loan was sufficiently collateralized, if just barely. Second is the real loser here, and it really has itself to blame if it didn't check the records or regard what it found there with due solemnity. Whatever money it ends up short Second may try to get out of Harold based on his misrepresentations or failure to disclose, if any, but Harold is now bankrupt. That doesn't mean that any questionable behavior he may have engaged in earlier on is forgiven or forgotten; it does mean that an attempt by any party wronged in this way to get financial recompense from him for his misdeeds is extremely unlikely to amount to anything.

7. As we can see in §9-109(d)(2) — and as we did see in Example 10 of Chapter 1 — Stella's right, what is traditionally referred to as a mechanics lien, is not an Article 9 security interest. Friendly Finance, on the other hand, does have an Article 9 interest, attached and perfected. How do the two stack up? As a general matter, Article 9 does not give rules relating to how interests asserted under it compete with other non-Article 9 interests. For some reason, however, as §9-109(d)(2) and its Comment 10 helpfully point out to us, there is an exception to this general policy when it comes to mechanics liens and it is to be found in §9-333. Under subsection (b) of that section, as long as the violin is still in Stella's possession her lien "has priority over [Friendly Finance's] perfected security interest in the goods unless the lien is created by a statute that expressly provides otherwise." So we'd have to look at the distinct state statute on which Stella is making her claim of a lien. Unless it "provides otherwise," her interest takes priority over that of Friendly Finance. For a recent decision, one rendered in the understandably much more complex case of a multi-million-dollar bankruptcy, discussing in great detail both statutory and common law artisans' liens, see In re S. M. Acquisitions Co., 296 Bankr. 452, 51 U.C.C.2d 867 (Bankr. N.D. Ill. 2003), affirmed by 2005 U.S. Dist. LEXIS 19850 (N.D. Ill. 2005). The claimant argued, unsuccessfully as it turned out, that it had such a lien for more than $2 million enforceable against the bankrupt's estate.

8. Now that agricultural liens have been brought within the scope of Revised Article 9, as they were not in the old version of the article, the method of establishing their priority is simplicity itself. Since the agricultural lien statute is, as we are told, silent on priority, we need not refer to any law outside of Article 9. The key is our old friend §9-322(a). Under Article 9 both a security interest and an agricultural lien can be perfected by filing. So we ask whether either, neither, or both of the two creditors did protect itself through filing. If neither perfected, then we look to (a)(3) and the victory goes to the one whose interest attached first. If only one perfected, then it wins under (a)(2). If, as we would hope, both had properly perfected their interests, then the rule is the first-to-file-or-perfect rule of (a)(1), which in this instance reduces itself to a first-to-file rule, since both would have had to perfect by filing. The introduction to §9-322(a) leaves no doubt that priority among "conflicting security interests *and* agricultural liens in the same collateral is determined" by the rules of that subsection.

Note that if, in another situation, the agricultural-lien statute in question *does* purport to grant priority to a lien created under its provisions, this could change the result because of §9-322(g). So when in doubt, the route for our analysis is clear; we have to check the statute under which the supplier is claiming an agricultural lien and take it from there.

CHAPTER 14

Priority and the PMSI

INTRODUCTION

The basic rules of the last chapter go a long way toward answering most questions of priority under Article 9. We know it is better to hold a perfected rather than unperfected interest. In addition, it is to the secured party's advantage to be first and not second, much less third or fourth. As you might expect, however, there are exceptions and special cases to make it more interesting. Paramount among these special cases is that of the exceptional treatment, which may, if specified conditions are met, be afforded the purchase-money security interest, or, as we are now used to calling it, the PMSI. We saw one such instance, that of §9-309(1), relating to the PMSI in Chapter 9. That special rule, allowing the secured party to attain perfection automatically without having to file or take any other action on some (but by no means all) PMSIs, was an important part of the secured transactions scheme; but be careful, it is not the situation on which we are about to focus.

The rule of §9-309(1) had to do with perfection. We are now in the world of priorities and about to see that a PMSI may gain, under the right set of circumstances and no matter how perfected, a kind of "superpriority" and jump to the head of the line in front of other perfected interests or be good against lien creditors, which, under the general rules of the prior chapter (that is, the rules of §§9-317(a) and 9-322(a)), would normally have it beat. The PMSI holder will find some extra-special help in §9-324. You should glance over subsections (a) and (b) now, and then use them in analyzing the following examples. Along the way you will stop, I have no fear, to consider why, other than the fact that the drafters drafted these particular provisions into Article 9 and they stuck, the PMSI gets such special treatment, and why (if that is so) the criteria of these subsections are set out as they are.*

Examples

1. Isabelle Inkster, the printer, gives a security interest in all of her equipment "now held or hereafter acquired" to Downtown Federal Bank in June 2006. The bank makes a proper filing on this collateral at the time. In May 2008 Inkster is at a trade show where she is taken by a new kind of binding machine, The BindAll 2400, manufactured by the Bindy Corporation. The Bindy representative says that the machine can be hers for only $13,595 and that his firm is ready to sell it to her on "easy credit terms." Inkster signs a sales order on the spot. The Bindy representative promises to personally deliver the machine to her later in the week. On May 14 he arrives at her business with the machine. He delivers it into her printing shop and helps her set it in place. She gives him a check for $1,360 representing the down payment and signs a note prepared by the firm under which she will pay the remainder of the price, at a defined rate of interest, in monthly installments over the next two years. Inkster also signs a security agreement by which the Bindy Corporation gets a security interest in the particular machine, which is properly identified in the paper. A financing statement is filed by the Bindy Corporation in the proper office on May 20.

   a. Suppose that a petition in bankruptcy had been filed by Inkster on May 17. Does Downtown Federal have a security interest in the BindAll 2400 machine that will be good against the bankruptcy trustee? Does the Bindy Corporation have an interest that will be good in the bankruptcy?

   b. If you conclude in (a) above that both creditors have an interest that will be good in the bankruptcy, which one will have priority?

2. Change the facts in the prior example to the following: Bindy is responsible, under the contract of sale, not simply for the delivery of the machine but for its assembly, installation, and testing. The Bindy

---

* The special priority rules for the PMSI have been carried over from the original Article 9 to the revision substantially unchanged — with one exception, which I point out for your information, since you may be reading cases decided under the pre-revision version and coming across the difference. The "grace period" for filing of the PMSI, which we will encounter in the examples and, as you will see, now runs for 20 days, was a period of only 10 days under the original Article 9.

representative first showed up at Inkster's place of business with the machine on May 8. As he is setting it up he realizes that one small but crucial part of the machine is missing. Rather than lug the whole thing away, it is agreed that he will leave the mostly assembled if inoperable machine where it is. On May 14 he returns with the needed part and completes installation and testing of the machine. The filing now takes place on May 30. Under this new set of facts, what is your analysis of the situation?

3. Coincidentally, the following also just happens to be true about Inkster and her printing business. In early April 2007 a sales representative from the Digipress Corporation pays her a visit. The representative anxiously hopes that Inkster considers buying its newest model, the Digipress 2500, for her business. When Inkster proves a hard sell, the representative makes an offer: "Why don't you try it free and under no obligation for three months? I can have one delivered to you and up and running by the day after tomorrow at the latest. If at the end of the trial you don't want it, fine. We'll take it back. If you want it, I'll make sure you get it at a good price." Inkster readily agrees, and on April 20 the press is delivered to her place of business. The press is quickly set up, and Inkster is instructed in its basic features. Over the next three months she uses it often and concludes that it would be a good addition to her business. When the Digipress salesperson pays her a visit on July 8, Inkster tells him she is indeed interested in buying the machine, but that she doesn't have the cash available to make the purchase price. The salesperson says this is no problem and that all she will have to pay as a down payment is $200. He whips out of his briefcase a sales agreement that has already been filled in with Inkster's name as buyer and the press already in her offices identified with appropriate detail as the item being sold. She signs this agreement and also signs a security agreement giving Digipress a security interest in the press, as well as a note for the purchase price minus $200. She gives the salesperson a check for $200. He gives her copies of all the papers she has signed and takes off. Digipress files a financing statement covering the press in the appropriate place on July 12, 2007. Recall that a bankruptcy petition covering Inkster's business is filed on May 17, 2008. Recall as well the part Downtown Federal has been playing in Inkster's affairs. In the bankruptcy proceeding, will Digipress have a perfected security interest? If so, does it or Downtown Federal have priority in the Digipress 2500?

4. In June 2007, Harold of Harold's House of Fashion is able to obtain a loan for his business from Downtown Federal Bank. As part of the loan transaction he signs a security agreement giving Downtown Federal an interest in "all inventory of Harold's House of Fashion, now held or hereafter acquired." Downtown Federal files a financing statement

describing the collateral in the same manner and correct in all other respects in the proper place on June 12, 2007. In early August 2008, Harold is visited by a representative of Coates and Co., a manufacturer of quality women's and men's leather coats and jackets. This representative very much wants Harold to add the Coates line of outerwear to his stock, and says that her company would be willing to deliver a large selection of its product line to Harold in time for the fall sales season and would not demand immediate payment in cash. Coates would be willing to deliver this merchandise to Harold on specified credit terms that seem reasonable to Harold. He agrees to the purchase. He signs a purchase order produced by the Coates representative and also signs a security agreement granting Coates and Co. a security interest in all of its line of merchandise to be delivered to him under the plan. Coates and Co. files a financing statement covering "all Coates and Co. clothing held by Harold as inventory, now or in the future," which is correct in all other detail. Coates files this financing statement in the appropriate place on August 6. On the same date it sends off a notice to Downtown Federal indicating what has transpired and that it claims a security interest in the merchandise that it plans to deliver to Harold's. Downtown Federal receives this notice on August 9. Harold receives a large shipment of Coates and Co. merchandise on August 12. Who — Downtown Federal or Coates and Co. — has priority of interest in the large quantity of men's and women's apparel, manufactured by Coates and Co., now sitting in Harold's store?

5. Boris arranges to buy a yacht from Marty's Marina, the total price of which is $30,000. Marty insists on a down payment of one-third of the price but is willing to extend credit for the remainder as a loan, as he is given a security interest in the yacht itself to secure payment of the amount. Boris finds he is not able to come up with $10,000 in cash to make the down payment. He goes to a friend, Sacha, who agrees to lend him that amount of money for the express purpose of using it as the down payment to purchase the yacht. Boris is to repay Sacha within a year. He signs a security agreement granting Sacha a security interest in the yacht to secure this debt. Sacha gives Boris a check for $10,000 made out to Marty's Marina. Boris takes this check and gives it to Marty. He then signs a note payable in specified installments to Marty for the remaining $20,000 as well as a security agreement granting the marina a security interest in the yacht being sold to secure Boris's payments as due under the note. Boris gets his yacht. Both Sacha and Marty have a security interest in the yacht. The question is this: Which of the two lenders' security interests — Sacha's or Marty's — would have priority over the other? See §9-324(g).

Explanations

1a. First let's get the situation straight. It starts out simply enough, so that as of early May 2008 it looks like this:

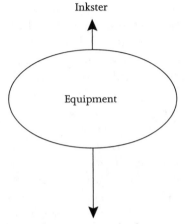

Downtown Federal
Attached and Perfected (by filing) in 2006

By the end of the month two things have happened: The Bindy Corporation has sold Inkster a machine (the BindAll 2400) on secured credit, and Inkster has gone bankrupt. This certainly makes for a more interesting picture, if not one that is all that rosy what with the bankruptcy:

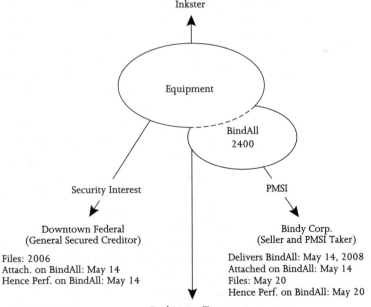

285

Now let's deal with the questions asked in turn. First of all, does Downtown Federal have a security interest in the BindAll 2400 that will be good as against the bankruptcy trustee? The answer is yes. From June 2006, the bank had a security interest in all of Inkster's equipment, including that after-acquired. Such an after-acquired property clause is perfectly valid under §9-204(a). Its interest in the new machine attached when the last of the three criteria of §9-203(b) occurred. This would be sometime no later than May 14 by which time Inkster had possession as a purchaser and hence "rights in" the binder. Downtown Federal's security interest in the BindAll machine was perfected as soon as it attached, given that the bank already had a filing in place covering just such collateral. Recall the last line of §9-308(a). So Downtown Federal has a perfected security interest in the machine as of May 14. The petition in bankruptcy was filed May 17. By the basic rule of §9-317(a)(2), and by all that is holy under the fundamental rules of priority so diligently attended to in the last chapter, the bank's interest will be good as against the bankruptcy trustee. It was an Article 9 security interest in the particular collateral perfected at the time of the filing of the bankruptcy petition.

Now what of the Bindy Corporation's interest? First convince yourself (if you need any convincing) that this is an Article 9 security interest, and in fact is a PMSI under §9-103, as a security interest retained by the seller to secure Inkster's payment of the price of the goods. It attached on May 14, when Bindy got a signed security agreement and gave the value, and Inkster got rights in this beauty of a binder. Was Bindy's interest ever perfected, and if so, when? Yes, it was perfected by filing, the filing taking place on May 20. This would at first blush seem to spell trouble for the Bindy Corporation when it comes to the bankruptcy, since the filing of its financing statement and hence perfection were a few days *after* the filing of the bankruptcy petition. All is not lost, however. Section §9-317(a)(2), at which we have been looking, begins with the phrase "except as otherwise provided in subsection (e)," so we naturally enough cast our eyes down the page to that subsection. It says,

> Except as otherwise provided in Sections 9-320 and 9-321 [about which we need not be concerned here], if a person files a financing statement with respect to a purchase-money security interest before or within 20 days after the debtor receives delivery of the collateral, the security interest takes priority over the rights of a buyer, lessee, or lien creditor which arise between the time the security interest attaches and the time of filing.

Well, that's handy for Bindy. Remember that the bankruptcy trustee, under §9-102(a)(52)(C), is considered a lien creditor whose rights arise as of the date of the filing of the petition. That would be May 17.

Bindy's interest — a PMSI — attached on May 14 and was perfected by filing on May 20. The importance of May 14 for these purposes, however, is that it was the date on which "the debtor [Inkster] receive[d] delivery of the collateral." Bindy did file on this PMSI within 20 days of May 14, and hence it takes priority over the bankruptcy trustee, whose position is that of a lien creditor. What rationale there might be for giving the PMSI holder this 20-day grace period to complete its filing will be discussed after we've looked into the next part of the puzzle in part (b).

It is worth pointing out that the 20-day grace period allowed the PMSI holder is good for exactly 20 days and no more. The PMSI holder should not and cannot expect a court to grant any further "grace" for even a day. See the recent case of In re Lockridge, 303 Bankr. 449, 2003 Bankr. LEXIS 1922 (D.Ariz. 2003), where the good graces of §9-317(e) were of no help to a retail seller of recreational vehicles and trailers that had taken a PMSI in a trailer sold to a customer but had not perfected that interest until 25 days (!) after the buyer took possession. From the opinion, it appears that the fatal delay was most likely due to the fact that the buyer's title clerk had taken an eight-day vacation during the middle of August 2002, and things, important things in the world of secured transactions, must have gotten backed up during his or her absence.

1b. So Downtown Federal and Bindy both have interests that beat that of the bankruptcy trustee representing the whole mass of general unsecured creditors. The trustee comes in third. The question is who — the bank or the Bindy Corporation — comes in first. In the last chapter we saw that the general rule on priority between two perfected security interests in the same collateral is given in §9-322(a)(1). If that were the operative rule governing this situation, the bank would have to win. Its priority is based on the date back in 2006 when it filed, which was well before Bindy Corporation either filed or perfected (or even existed for all we know). But again we are looking at a situation that is not governed by the general rule. Subsection (f) of §9-322 provides that the general rules of (a) are subject to, among other things, "other provisions of this part." As Comment 2 notes, among the rules that override subsection (a) are those applicable to purchase-money interests given in §9-324. Look now at §9-324(a):

> Except as provided in subsection (g) [which you can check does not apply here], a perfected purchase-money security interest in goods other than inventory or livestock has priority over a conflicting security interest in the same goods . . . if the purchase-money security interest is perfected when the debtor receives possession of the collateral or within 20 days thereafter.

This suits Bindy's situation to a tee. It took a PMSI in a piece of what would be classified as equipment, not inventory and certainly not livestock, in the hands of the debtor. Hence it could gain priority over the conflicting interest in the same collateral held by Downtown Federal if its, Bindy's, PMSI were perfected at the time the debtor received possession of the collateral, which would be May 14, *or within 20 days thereafter.* Bindy's interest was not perfected on May 14, but it was perfected by filing within 20 days of that date, and hence under §9-324(a) its interest has priority over that of Downtown Federal.

It is more than appropriate to ask why exactly the creditor who takes a PMSI is given such favored treatment under the Code. Not only is it given a grace period to file, as we saw in part (a) and as we will consider soon enough, but here we see it gains a kind of superpriority: It is able to jump to the head of the line, provided of course the criterion of §9-324(a) of perfection no later than the end of this grace period is met. Why exactly should the PMSI get such a big boost up? One answer of course is that the drafters of Article 9 got to write the rules and they could write them any which way they chose, but this is hardly satisfactory. I could go on to report that even before the adoption of the original Article 9, prior law usually gave the PMSI a preference roughly like what we are seeing here, but we can do better than that.

Imagine what the situation would be like if a party, such as Bindy, here trying to make a sale and more than willing to do so on credit provided it could retain a PMSI in what it sells, could not avoid the effects of the general rule of §9-322(a)(1). The initial general creditor, which thought to include a standard after-acquired property clause in its security agreement, Downtown Federal in our example, would always trump any later lender who took an interest in any equipment. What if a debtor such as Inkster was interested in buying some additional equipment? She could always do so for cash of course, but in many cases that is hardly realistic. She could ask the seller to let her purchase on general unsecured credit, but except for fairly small items it is unreasonable to expect the seller to go along with this. The seller or the financial agency lending money for the express purpose of allowing Inkster to purchase the new equipment would be extending a good deal of value and would have to get some kind of security to back it up. That is exactly where the PMSI comes in. Of what real value is the PMSI, however, if it will always come in second, when interests conflict, to that of the general secured lender? You can't take much security from obtaining a security interest, even an Article 9 security interest, in property if it is by its very nature a secondary interest right from the start.

Inkster does, of course, have another way of obtaining the new equipment. She could go back to the bank, the general creditor, and ask that it extend her additional funds, which would allow her to obtain the new equipment outright. In many instances this is not only an option but a perfectly fine way, from Inkster's point of view, of handling the situation. There are circumstances, however, when her trying to get additional loan funds from the general lender is less than ideal. For one thing, the bank may simply refuse. It has its own way of calculating the maximum amount of credit that it will extend to Inkster. This depends not just on the total package of collateral that she will be putting up, but on how much cash the bank sees her business generating, what debt service (that is total loan payments) it thinks her operation can reasonably support, and so on. So for perfectly good reasons Downtown Federal could say, in effect, that it did not think her purchase of the new binder was worth the risk it entailed and that it would not finance any further expansion on her part. The wise business people at Downtown Federal may well be right in their appraisal of the situation, but you have to remember that because it is Inkster's business we are talking about here, she understandably might feel annoyed, to put it mildly, to think that "her bankers" are telling her exactly how to run her business, including what new equipment she may or may not acquire.

There is a second problem that comes up if the rules were so rigid as to allow the initial general lender to in effect monopolize the situation, by which I mean take up the position as the only possible party who would agree to lend to Inkster on a secured basis. The bank, having this power by dint of the way the rules of priority ran, would be under little or no compulsion to give her a particularly good rate of interest on this additional loan. The Bindy Corporation, remember, as a seller might well be willing to give an especially favorable rate of interest to buyers of its products, if nothing else than as a way of making sales in the first place. Inkster would like to take Bindy up on this offer, but if she cannot assure it of a good first-in-line security interest even in the very item that it is selling to her, there is no way that Bindy can allow it to happen.

So what we have come to is that the rule of §9-324(a), as well as the similar results under prior law, is a way of in effect making sure that a debtor such as Inkster is not entirely under the thumb of the general secured creditor with the after-acquired property clause. If she wants to go to another lender to refinance her business, then she is going to have to get Downtown Federal's loan paid off and its security interest lifted. If, however, all she wants to do is to buy a particular piece of property, giving the seller or another lending institution advancing her the purchase price a PMSI in that one piece of property only, the rule of §9-324(a) allows it to happen with amazingly little fuss.

Now let's look at the other side of the story. Is there anything inherently unfair to *Downtown Federal* about allowing another party to come in later in time and yet gain priority over it as is the case here? Not generally. Look again at the two diagrams above, which I very carefully crafted to show the bank's position both before and after Inkster took the BindAll 2400 aboard. Prior to this transaction the collateral on which the bank has a first interest is indicated by the larger oval. After the transaction this pool of collateral is not lessened in any way. There is in fact a bit of a lump or bump representing the newly acquired binder that reminds us that the acquisition of this one new piece of equipment has actually increased the total value of the collateral subject to the bank's interest. True, the area within the collateral space bounded by the solid line no longer has the neat simple geometric profile that it had before. The total collateral pool is beginning to look a bit more like the makings of a cartoon figure, but that shouldn't distract us from the reality of the situation; the addition of the BindAll 2400 binding machine increased the total value of all equipment subject to Downtown Federal's interest. Of course because of §9-324(a), the bank's interest in the newly acquired machine (that lump hanging down to the side) is not a primary interest. The Bindy Corporation has the first priority in that. The bank, however, still has top priority in all the rest of the equipment that was there before the delivery of the binder. The oval representing the collateral on which it has first priority has not gotten any smaller. So after Inkster's acquisition of the binder in this manner, giving a PMSI to the seller, the bank still has a first priority in as much collateral as it had prior to the binder's arrival — and its lot has increased at least somewhat by its acquiring at no cost to it a secondary interest in the newly acquired piece of equipment.

Now we have reason to feel that along with there being a legitimate rationale for allowing the debtor to give a first interest to a PMSI holder superior to the interest of the general secured lender, even if it comes into the picture later in the game, there is generally no harm done to the general lender claiming only on the basis of its after-acquired property clause if this outcome is allowed. There are a couple of situations, however, where the general lender could, for reasons not now evident, be hurt by a simple rule as in §9-324(a). Putting aside the problems associated with livestock, our concern has to do with the special dynamics in play when the PMSI is taken in newly arriving inventory. But then you have already noticed that subsection (a) of §9-324 specifically applies only to cases where a PMSI is taken "in collateral other than inventory." When a PMSI in inventory is involved, the rule gets a little more complicated, as we'll see soon enough in Example 4.

A final point that I have left hanging but to which I now want to return is this: Why does the PMSI taker get not only this special rule on priority but a 20-day grace period to take advantage of it? This same grace period also graces, if you will, the PMSI in §9-317(e), where the competition is not with another secured party but with the bankruptcy trustee himself or herself. The answer is one of practicality. The party taking a PMSI is typically a seller. Sellers have to be able to deal with impulse purchases. A potential buyer comes into the seller's store. Something catches his or her eye right away, the seller offers reasonable payment terms based on a secured credit arrangement, the buyer signs all the necessary forms (including one authorizing the filing of a financing statement) and walks out of the store with the purchase under his or her arm. The credit seller, unlike the general lender such as a bank or credit agency, is not in a position to say, "Fine, it's yours on those terms. Now sign these papers. Then return in a week or two and if everything is in order, you can have the goods." That's just not the way to make a sale.

The example we have here, where Bindy delivers the machine to Inkster's location, is somewhat different, but the principle still applies. Notice that Inkster is willing to sign a sales order form at the trade show, but if the Bindy representative tried to get too much more paperwork accomplished then and there he couldn't really tend to any other interested customers. When the man from Bindy shows up later with the machine, he is then able to get the necessary papers including one authorizing the filing of a financing statement signed. He is also able to drop off the goods right then and there. Were the situation to be such that in order to protect the company's interest he would have to get authorization to file a financing statement, file that statement, check after a few days that it has been correctly indexed, and so on — all before he could go out to Inkster's again and actually deliver the machine — this would add to the complication of his life more than a little.

So the result is a kind of compromise. The party taking the PMSI has 20 days to get to the proper filing office and get its financing statement on record. This does impose, to be sure, some measure of risk on others. During this lag time they could diligently check the records and not be given notice of an interest that would later be found to come in ahead of theirs. In all practicality, however, if another lender were asked by Inkster to lend to her based on collateral, which just happens to be a brand new piece of machinery resting on her plant floor, this other lender would have to be fairly dense not to wonder what was going on. At the very least, if it is such a new piece, Inkster should be able to show the prospective lender the bill of sale indicating how, when, and from whom she obtained it. Inkster would be able to provide a bill of sale from the Bindy Corporation indicating that she had bought the piece, but unless something was seriously amiss it would not read anything like "Paid in Full." If nothing else, the wary prospective lender could just put its decision off for at least 20 days (and what non-purchase-money loan transaction doesn't end up taking at least an extra couple of weeks just as a matter of course?) and then check the filings once again. By that time Bindy would have filed its financing statement — or by failing to do so have forfeited any chance of relying on §9-324(a) to its advantage.

2. Your analysis of this situation depends, as you see, on what you determine to be the time "the debtor receives delivery of the collateral" for the purposes of §9-317(e) or when "the debtor receives possession of the collateral" for application of §9-324(a). The pre-revision version of Article 9 used the word "possession" in both instances, and I can find nothing to indicate that the revision's change to the word "delivery" in §9-317(e) was meant to work any change on the existing rule. I have to believe the time of delivery and the time when the debtor takes possession for the purposes of these two provisions are essentially the same, at least for a situation like we have here. Since, as we will see, the revision drafters did include some helpful commentary on how to deal with issues that may arise, as they do in this and the following example, of exactly when the debtor "receives possession" for the purposes of §9-324(a), I'll confine the following discussion to how that language is to be interpreted. Presumably whenever it is that the debtor "receives possession" for the purposes of §9-324(a) is also when it "receives delivery" for §9-317(e), as least as far as we need be concerned.

If Bindy is to have the advantage of each of those two subsections, as the holder of a PMSI, it would have the phrase understood so that Inkster did not have "possession of" the BindAll 2400 until May 14, when it was up and running. Its filing of May 30 would then have come within 20 days of the date of possession and the results here would be no different than they were in the prior example: Bindy's interest would be good against the trustee in bankruptcy and would have priority over Downtown Federal's perfected but non-PMSI interest.

Both the trustee and the bank, however, would argue that Inkster had possession as of May 8. Bindy, the PMSI holder having filed on May 30, it did not make the 20-day deadline of §9-317(e) or §9-324(a). There's no crime in this. Bindy doesn't get thrown into jail. It does, however, get thrown into §9-317(a)(2) and §9-322(a)(1). Under the first provision it would have an interest that would not survive into bankruptcy. Under the latter, even if it had filed its financing statement prior to the bankruptcy petition's filing, its interest would be secondary to that of Downtown Federal's. In other words, if we change the facts one more time so that the date of Inkster's possession is held to be May 8, with Bindy filing still on May 30, and the bankruptcy petition not coming in until, say, June 17, then both Downtown Federal and Bindy would indeed have perfected security interests that would be good in the bankruptcy. Bindy's could in fact still lay claim to being a PMSI, but it would not be a PMSI entitled to the special priority over the earlier filer potentially available to it under §9-324(a). The conflict between the two perfected interests would therefore be decided under the rule of §9-322(a)(1)(a), which would give the win to Downtown Federal.

So the question remains, and it is by no means a merely academic one, as many cases attest, as decided under the original Article 9 of when the debtor is deemed to have "possession" of the collateral for the purposes of these special provisions. The answer is not free from issue. One early and fairly well-known case, In re *Automated Bookbinding Services, Inc.*, 336 F. Supp. 1128, 10 U.C.C. 209 (D. Md. 1972), rev'd, 471 F.2d 546, 11 U.C.C. 897 (4th Cir. 1972), involved a complex piece of bookbinding machinery, the contract for the sale of which anticipated not only that it would be delivered in a number of crates but that the seller was responsible for assembly and installation as well as training an employee of the debtor to operate the thing. The district court determined that "possession" for Article 9 purposes would not be in the debtor, and the (then applicable) 10-day clock start to run, until the seller had performed all of its obligations under the sales contract. The circuit court rejected this result and moved the date of possession up to that time when the last of the bookbinder parts was delivered to and hence under the control of the debtor.

In the same vein, In re *Vermont Knitting Co., Inc.*, 98 Bankr. 184, 8 U.C.C.2d 516 (D. Vt. 1989), found that "possession" for these purposes occurred once "all material components" of a piece of machinery had arrived on the debtor's premises, even though it had not yet been set up for use. The court, citing the *American Heritage Dictionary*, reasoned that the essence of possession is control. "To possess, a transitive verb, means to gain or exert influence or control, dominate; to cause to own (or) hold something such as property." It continued:

> The facts show Knitting [the debtor] had the machines and their computers within its control on July 19, 1986 [by which time all material components had been delivered]. If Universal [the seller and secured creditor] wanted to repossess the machines for any reason after July 19, 1986, they would have needed Knitting's permission to do so.

These cases, and this approach, would seem to bode well for Bindy in the facts as we now have them. The last component, that one little but crucial piece, is not delivered until May 14, and Bindy does file within 20 days of that date.

Other cases, however, show concern less with the fact of actual control over the property than with what is sometimes referred to as the "ostensible ownership" of it. Whose stuff would it appear to be to an outside disinterested observer? In a case that discusses at length the various complexities of the time of possession question, *Citizens Nat'l Bank of Denton v. Cockrell*, 850 S.W.2d 462, 36 Tex. Sup. J. 640, 19 U.C.C.2d 1205 (1993), the Supreme Court of Texas noted:

> "[P]ossession" in [this section] is interpreted in light of the impression conveyed to an observer not involved in the transaction, not according to the private limitations contained in the contract between the buyer and seller.

This test is not necessarily in conflict with drawing the line more mechanically at the time of delivery of all the component pieces; in some, perhaps most, instances the result would be the same. You can imagine situations, however, and we will in a later example have chance to examine at least one, where the two approaches do not necessarily lead to the same result.

The drafters of Revised Article 9, aware of this controversy, dealt with it not in the language of the Article itself, but in a comment to §9-324. Look at the second paragraph of Comment 3:

> Normally, there will be no question when "the debtor receives possession of the collateral" for purposes of subsection (a). However, sometimes a debtor buys goods and takes possession of them in stages, and then assembly and testing are completed (by the seller or debtor-buyer) at the debtor's location. Under those circumstances, the buyer "takes possession" within the meaning of subsection (a) when, after an inspection of the portion of the goods in the debtor's possession, it would be apparent to a potential lender to the debtor that the debtor has acquired an interest in the goods taken as a whole.

In other words the revision drafters take the correct approach to such a question to be in effect "the ostensible ownership" test as articulated in *Citizen's National Bank of Denton* and reject the earlier cases such as *In re Automated Bookbinding* and *In re Vermont Knitting*.

For a recent case that follows the lead of that portion of Comment 3 quoted directly above, see *In re Piknik Products Co., Inc.*, 346 Bankr. 863, 60 U.C.C.2d 791 (M.D. Ala. 2006). This case involved the sale, for a price of $369,865 "exclusive of certain miscellaneous costs such as taxes, permits, and freight," of certain equipment, specifically a "Juicy Juice System," to be delivered to the buyer's plant in Montgomery, Alabama. The buyer paid 35% of the price as a down payment and the majority of the system was delivered and bolted to the floor sometime in July 2005. The seller, which claimed to have reserved a PMSI in the system to secure full payment, did not file to perfect its interest. In 2006 it was making the argument in effect that the beginning of the 20-day grace period of which it wished to take advantage had not yet come to pass as the Juicy Juice System had yet to become "fully operational." The court rejected this contention, quoting from Comment 3 to §9-324 followed by its determination that,

> Here, the majority of the Juicy Juice System was delivered to Piknik's Montgomery, Alabama facility around July 2005. The equipment comprising the system was actually bolted to the facility floor. Under these circumstances, it is clear that a potential lender would conclude that Piknik had acquired an interest in the Juicy Juice System.

In conclusion the court commented,

> The result here appears harsh. The court sympathizes with Crouch [the seller]. Crouch sold Piknik equipment worth more than $350,000 in May 2005 for which it was paid only $129,452.75. A mere four months later, Pitnik filed a petition in Chapter 11, and Crouch now finds itself in the possession of an unsecured creditor with little hope of receiving any distribution on its claim. Yet, Crouch failed to properly perfect a lien as provided by law, and this court's sympathy must give way to that reality.

As far as Bindy is concerned, if a court were to follow the lead of this comment it probably would not be found to have filed in time to gain the special priority for its purchase-money security interest. The mostly assembled and installed machine resting on Inkster's production floor, even if missing a crucial part and not operational, would most likely be found enough to give a third-party the reasonable impression that Inkster had, in the words of the comment, "acquired rights in the goods taken as a whole" as of May 8. Its filing more than 20 days later serves to perfect as of the filing date but does not result in Bindy's having the special priority provided for in §9-324(a).

3. Digipress should not have any problems with the Trustee in Bankruptcy. Its PMSI in the press attached on July 8 and it filed on July 12, 2007. So it was perfected prior to the petition's being filed in 2008. Hence, under the basic rule of §9-317(a), its interest survives into the bankruptcy. We don't even have to worry about whether it could take advantage of the rule of §9-317(e), since Digipress doesn't need any special help here.

    The same cannot be said of Digipress in its priority conflict with Downtown Federal. As we have already seen, Downtown Federal's interest based on its after-acquired property clause and having been filed upon in 2006 would easily have priority over the interest granted to Digipress in 2007 under the default rule of §9-322(a)(1). Digipress, of course, would want to invoke §9-324(a), but the question is whether the facts of the case fit that subsection's crucial timing criterion. Once again the question, as in the prior example, is the correct interpretation to be given to the phrase "when the debtor receives possession of the collateral," but the problem is a different one. Inkster, Downtown Federal would argue, clearly had "possession" of the press from April 20, 2008. It was all in her shop and up and pressing, and she was using it in her business. Digipress filed on July 12. There is no way, Downtown Federal would insist, that you can find Digipress's interest to have been "perfected when the debtor receive[d] possession of the collateral or within 20 days thereafter." Hence, the situation does not come within §9-324(a), but is governed by §9-322(a)(1) where Downtown Federal has priority.

This does seem initially to make a lot of sense. One early case, however, interpreted the grace period criterion of the precursor section to §9-324(a) as meaning that the period begins to run when an individual such as Inkster in this case has possession of the collateral *as a debtor* under an Article 9 security agreement. See *Brodie Hotel Supply, Inc. v. United States*, 431 F.2d 1316, 8 U.C.C. 113 (9th Cir. 1970). The reasoning here is that the press isn't "collateral" and Inkster isn't a "debtor," the precise words that are used in the provision, until July 8, the date on which a security agreement is concluded. Digipress filed on July 12, within 20 days, and hence can take advantage of the special rule of §9-324(a) for claiming priority over Downtown Federal.

Some cases decided under the original version of Article 9 followed the *Brodie Hotel Supply* case's reasoning and approach. Others, perhaps a majority, confronted with the same basic issue, did not. Once again, the drafters of Revised Article 9 give their opinion in Comment 3 to §9-324. They agree with the court in *Brodie*.

> A similar issue [similar to what we dealt with in the prior example] concerning the time when "the debtor receives possession" arises when a person acquires possession of the goods under a transaction that is not governed by this Article and then later agrees to buy the goods on secured credit. . . . [T]he 20-day period in subsection (a) does not commence until the goods become "collateral" (defined in Section 9-102), i.e., until they are subject to a security interest.

In our example, while Inkster had possession of the press as of April 20, she had possession under an agreement with Digipress that she would try it out. This is not a transaction, as of April 20, which is subject to Article 9. Later, on July 8, she *does* enter into an Article 9 transaction when she agrees to purchase the press and grants Digipress, the seller, a PMSI in it. Only then does the press become "collateral" subject to a security interest, and only then — at least if we are to follow the lead of the drafters of this commentary — does the 20-day clock of §9-324(a) begin to run. Digipress filed on July 12, well within 20 days of the eighth, and hence has an interest that beats out not only the bankruptcy trustee but also Downtown Federal's.

4. This calls for application of §9-324(b). As I make it out the final diagram looks like this:

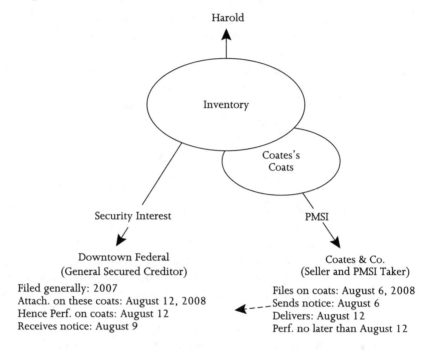

Once again there really is no issue that Downtown Federal has a perfected interest in the new Coates & Co. merchandise by virtue of its after-acquired property clause, and perfected no later than August 12, 2008, when the coats arrive in Harold's store. Downtown Federal can also claim priority on all the inventory including these coats based on a filing of 2007, so it will have priority over Coates and its interest unless that company can take advantage of §9-324(b).

Taking advantage of that subsection means nothing more or less than meeting all its criteria. Here it seems that Coates & Co. should be able to establish that it has done so. As far as (1) is concerned, Coates perfected by filing no later than August 12. The precise moment of perfection would presumably depend on when the particular coats that were going to be delivered to Harold's were "identified" to the contract as that term is used in §2-501. At that moment the interest would attach and, the filing having been made on August 6, the latter of these two dates would be the moment of perfection. In any event, it has to be sometime before the actual delivery into the "possession" of Harold on August 12.

Criterion (2) requires that the PMSI party give notice in writing to the holders of certain conflicting interests. Which parties with conflicting interests are entitled to such notice? For that we look to subsection (c). In this case there is no question that Downtown Federal, the holder of the interest with which Coates will be conflicting, did file and meets the subcriterion (c)(1) as its filing was prior in time to that of Coates. So Coates had to send Downtown Federal a notice in writing. How does it know of Downtown Federal's conflicting interest? Because it checked the filings prior to delivering the coats to Harold's of course. And how does it know where to send the notice which it must send to the bank? Recall Downtown Federal's initial financing statement — the one Coates got a chance to see — is required to include the address of the secured party if it is not to be rejected by the filing office, so Coates sends the notice to that address.

As to what must be in the notice, see (b)(4). It must state that Coates "has or expects to acquire a purchase-money security interest in" some of Harold's inventory and describe the inventory. I haven't given you the complete text of the notice Coates sends to Downtown Federal, but it appears that it said what it had to.

Which leaves us with (b)(3). It is necessary that "the holder of the conflicting interest [here Downtown Federal] receives the notification [sent by Coates and Co.] within five years before the debtor [Harold] receives possession of the inventory." Here Downtown Federal did receive the notice and received it on August 9, which is easily "within five years before" August 12 of the same year, the date on which Harold received his first shipment from Coates and Co. Note that Coates and Co., if things are going well, may make additional deliveries to Harold without having to send a new notice each time, at least for a period of five years from August 6, 2008. After that, Coates and Co. would be required to send a new notice to Downtown Federal to assure itself of special PMSI priority in that part of Harold's inventory that it claims an interest in. Recall that anyone claiming perfection through filing has to file a continuation statement five years after the initial filing, so there is no reason not to put the same requirement on the notice here.

The justification for the special treatment of the PMSI in this subsection, the balancing of interests, is basically the same as we saw in the first example with respect to the PMSI in collateral other than inventory. The debtor needs the chance to borrow on a secured basis from others, and the general financer is not necessarily hurt as long as the pool of collateral on which it retains priority status is not diminished. The obvious question at this point is why there are these extra procedural hurdles placed in the way of the party taking a PMSI in inventory, if it is to get special treatment under §9-324(b), that we did not see when we considered the PMSI taken in collateral other than inventory as governed by §9-324(a)? Why is there no 20-day grace period? (Note that the party taking a PMSI in inventory does get the advantage of this grace period against lien creditors such as the bankruptcy trustee because of how §9-317(e) is worded. It does not, however, get the grace period against conflicting security interests.) And why the notice requirement of §9-324(b)? The rationale appears in a portion of Comment 4:

> The arrangement between an inventory secured party [here Downtown Federal] and its debtor [Harold] typically requires the secured party to make periodic advances against incoming inventory or periodic releases of old inventory as new inventory is received. A fraudulent debtor may apply to the secured party for advances even though it has already given a purchase-money security interest in the inventory to another secured party. For this reason, subsections (b)(2) through (4) [which gives similar treatment to the purchase-money secured party who delivers new live-stock] and (c) impose a second condition for the purchase-money security interest's achieving priority: the purchase-money secured party must give notification to the holder of a conflicting security interest who filed against the same item or type of inventory before the purchase-money secured party filed. . . . The notification requirement protects the non-purchase-money inventory secured party in such a situation: if the inventory secured party has received notification, it presumably will not make an advance; if it has not received notification . . . , any advance the inventory secured party may make ordinarily will have priority under Section 9-322. Inasmuch as an arrangement for periodic advances against incoming goods is unusual outside the inventory field, subsection (a) does not contain a notification requirement.

The general idea is important, and it is one that we will see more in what is to come. The party who loans on "inventory, now held or hereafter acquired" is usually taking what we colloquially refer to as a "floating lien" on the collateral, in this case inventory. The precise nature of what is within the net of its security interest, the inventory, is expected to change from day to day if not from minute to minute. When Harold sells an item out of his House of Fashion, his inventory is decreased to that degree. As new deliveries are made by his suppliers, the inventory grows. The inventory of a debtor as defined in Article 9 is not a static assembly of property, nor would the parties want it to be. Certainly Harold doesn't want his inventory to stay languishing on the shelves unloved but more importantly unpur-chased. He wants goods to move in and out of the store as quickly as his cash registers allow. Equally important is the fact that Downtown

Federal, as the general inventory financer, does not want the inventory pool to remain stuck as one set of items any more than Harold does. True, it might make Downtown Federal's concerns in some respects a little more manageable if Harold's House of Fashion just never sold anything or brought in new merchandise. But this is supposed to be a retail establishment, remember, not a museum. Downtown Federal wants Harold's business to do well, if for no other reason than because Harold will only be able to make his periodic loan payments to the bank if he can sell (and sell at a sufficiently high level). And he has to keep taking in new merchandise if he is to keep his shelves and racks full and customers interested.

So the general inventory financer taking a floating lien on the inventory has a special problem. It has to take precautionary steps and periodically monitor the situation to assure itself that the sum total of Harold's stock that comes within its security interest is sufficiently great to support the amount of loan that Harold has outstanding. Harold, from his perspective, does not want a single loan in one lump sum. During slow periods he will want to keep low the amount of debt he owes to the bank, to keep to a minimum his interest charges. When a busy season is approaching, he will want to, or at least may have to, borrow more from the bank in order to get his inventory to a proper level. It is, as you can imagine, just his skill in making these kinds of balancing decisions that can account for his success or failure as a retailer. The arrangement between Harold and the bank will typically provide for his having a "line of credit" up to a certain amount on which he can draw.

The bank, on its part, has to make sure that the inventory on which it is relying as collateral is all that it seems to be, because it bases to a large extent the maximum credit it will extend Harold on the collateral's value. Downtown Federal may ask Harold to show it papers, invoices, and the like — it may even make some random visits to his store — so that it can evaluate the inventory on its own. Imagine the situation if the inventory appraiser who works for the bank were to come into Harold's not knowing that the large quantity of obviously valuable Coates & Co. apparel that Harold has mixed in with all the other goods he sells was in fact not subject to Downtown Federal's first priority security interest. The bank could find itself tricked, whether deliberately or otherwise, into extending more credit than it would agree to it if knew the full story. That is what the notice provision in subsection (b) is all about, as the Comment seeks to explain.

5. First of all, it is important to note that both Sacha and Marty have PMSIs in the yacht, as you can confirm for yourself by returning to §9-103.

Sacha's security interest secures an obligation undertaken by Boris to repay the "value given to enable" him to acquire rights in the collateral, the yacht, since the value was "in fact so used" when it was turned over to Marty to take care of the down payment. Sacha's loan was what is often referred to as an *enabling loan*, given by a person other than the seller that helps the buyer make the purchase. Marty's interest is also a purchase-money interest, since it was an interest taken by the seller of the collateral to secure an obligation by the buyer to pay "all or part of the price of the collateral" due to the seller.

Under §9-324(g), a provision added to Article 9 in the recent revision, Marty's interest will have priority over Sacha's under subpart (g)(1). As Comment 13 states:

> New subsection (g) governs priority among multiple purchase-money security interests in the same collateral. It grants priority to purchase-money security interests securing the price of the collateral (i.e., created in favor of the seller) over purchase-money security interests that secure enabling loans.

What if Boris was able to buy the yacht by convincing two friends to make enabling loans? Say he borrows $10,000 from Sacha and $20,000 from Natasha? He is then able to buy the yacht in effect for cash from Marty's Marina, which is paid the entire price at the time of the purchase. He grants to each of the two lenders, Sacha and Natasha, a PMSI in the yacht to secure repayment of what he owes them. Which of them has priority? The answer is, once again, given in §9-324(g), only now in subpart (2). Since (g)(1) does not come into play here, there being no security interest granted to the seller of the collateral, "Section 9-322(a) applies to the qualifying security interests." So Sacha and Natasha are left to compete under the first-to-file-or-perfect rule of §9-322(a)(1). It's all going to be a matter of timing, of who did what when. See the concluding sentence of Comment 13 to §9-324.

15

Fixtures

WHAT *ARE* FIXTURES?

From early on in our consideration of Article 9 the term "fixtures" has been turning up with disturbing regularity. Indeed, we quite quickly found in §9-109(a)(1) the articulation that "this Article," meaning Article 9, of course, applies to "a transaction, regardless of its form, that creates a security interest in personal property *or fixtures* by contract." Each time we have come across such a reference, we've allowed ourselves simply to ignore the word, the concept, the very idea of fixtures until a later time. That time has come. This chapter is about fixtures.

So what exactly *are* fixtures? From the outset we are faced with a question the answer to which is far from clear. The drafters in §9-102 (a)(41) took a stab at a definition by writing that

> "Fixtures" means goods that have become so related to particular real property that an interest in them arises under real property law.

So fixtures are goods, but goods that under the circumstances have become so attached to a particular bit of real estate that our friends from another related but distinct legal discipline, Real Estate Transactions, feel they may justifiably start taking a special interest in them. This gives us at least a clue: Goods qualify as fixtures (or do not so qualify) based on their relationship (or lack thereof) to a specific piece of real estate.

It helps at this point to step back and consider the various ways that goods can relate to real estate. Goods are tangible personal property, so they must at any given time be someplace. And yet the very fact that they occupy a space, that they can be found within the borders of some particular slice of real estate, does not make them fixtures. Every tangible object has to be someplace. Comment 3 to §9-334 does a fairly good job of setting out the lay of the land, at least initially, with the following:

> [T]his section recognizes three categories of goods: (1) those that retain their chattel character entirely and are not part of the real property; (2) ordinary building materials which have become an integral part of the real property and cannot retain their chattel character for purposes of finance; and (3) an intermediate class that has become real property for certain purposes, but as to which chattel financing may be preserved.

This third and "intermediate class" constitutes what we call fixtures.

It therefore seems that the best, or at least a passable, way to approach the subject is to look at what goods fall within the first and second categories referred to in this comment. Imagine a piece of furniture, say an overstuffed leather sofa, brought into and kept in a particular building. The piece may have been specially designed and built for the exact room in which it is now located. I will even accept for the sake of argument that all who see it just have to blurt out to the proud owner, "It just fits so perfectly there, I can't even imagine it anywhere else!" Be that as it may, this is still just a piece of furniture that happens to be at a particular place at the time. We can imagine it being taken from the room and the real estate involved at any time by the commonplace act of a gang of movers coming, picking it up and toting it away. The furniture is hence of the first category referred to in the comment, something that "retain[s] its chattel character entirely and [is] not part of the real property." For financing purposes it is "pure goods"; it may be subject to an Article 9 security interest, but will not become subject to any real property interest just because it happens to be located on some real property at any given moment.

Consider now a large quantity of nails or cans of paint. Sitting in the manufacturer's warehouse or on the shelves of the retail home improvement center, they are, no doubt, goods. Suppose, however, they are delivered to a buyer who incorporates them into a building on her premises. The nails are hammered into the walls as they go up. The paint is spread over the surface of those walls. These are then transformed into the second of the classes set out in the comment, "ordinary building materials which have become an integral part of the real property and cannot retain their chattel character for purposes of finance." See the sentence of §9-334(a): A security interest does not exist under this article in ordinary building materials incorporated into an improvement on land." If the buyer of the nails or the paint had bought them on credit and granted an Article 9 security interest in them, there is nothing inherently wrong with this. There may not be, however, much right with it either, at least as far as the Article 9 secured party is concerned; as soon as the ordinary building materials are incorporated into the structure, the Article 9 security interest ceases to have any effect. The nails and the paint have become part of the building. If there is anyone who may gain it is a party who has taken a security interest, now not an Article 9 security interest but a security interest in the *real property* in question of the type we traditionally call a mortgage. The real property subject to the mortgage has, by the well-thought out addition of some nails and paint, presumably become more valuable at least to some degree. The real property security interest holder, the mortgagee, finds that the value of the collateral subject to its interest has increased. Congratulations to the mortgagee and condolences to the Article 9 secured party — to the extent it did not understand the rules of the game and expected to continue to have a special interest in the nails and/or the paint.

The one thing that these two categories, sometimes referred to as "pure goods" (the first) and "pure realty" (the second), have in common is that they do not pose the possibility of a conflict between an Article 9 secured party and a real property mortgagee. The real estate mortgagee would not think of claiming an interest in so-called pure goods. Article 9, as we have just seen, says that the Article 9 secured party cannot claim any security interest and hence has no fight to pick with any mortgagee of the property into which the "pure realty" has become assimilated. But then there is that third category, which we call fixtures. Fixtures are goods that become real estate "for certain purposes, but as to that chattel financing may be preserved." What distinguishes fixtures is that they may be simultaneously subject to an Article 9 security interest *and* to rightful claims made by the real property financer, the mortgagee. This not only distinguishes fixtures but makes them terribly difficult to deal with, as you can imagine. It is why we have been holding off on the topic until this point. It is why they get a section, §9-334, and a chapter all their own.

As the above examples should have convinced you, in the large majority of cases when goods do not fall under the category of fixtures there really is not much doubt about it. Furniture that comes into the building and could leave it again with no difficulty and without leaving a trace will not be fixtures. Ordinary building materials that are so incorporated into the structure as to bond with it, literally and not just metaphorically, will not be fixtures either. As you would expect, however, not every case is as clearcut. There are bound to be grey areas. Unfortunately for us, §9-334 and the Uniform Commercial Code have said "hands off" when it comes to possibly articulating a way to decide the hard cases. We harken back to the definition of §9-102(a)(41) with which we began, now to take note that the test for whether goods are fixtures for purposes of Article 9 is whether "they

305

become so related to particular real property that an interest in them arises *under real property law.*"

Real property law is not dealt with in the Code. It is a matter of local law, to be found in state case law and statutes. It is studied not in Commercial Transactions or Secured Transactions courses, but in Property and Land Transactions. Article 9 defers, to put it politely, to the local law of real property transactions for a determination in any instance of whether a particular bit of goods, some stuff having more than a passing relationship with a certain piece of real property, has passed over the line of demarcation and become a fixture. All would be well, or at least a good deal more satisfactory, if that line were well drawn under real property law. What I can claim to know with confidence of the finer points of real property law you could put on an exceptionally tiny plot of land on the wrong side of the tracks in the less exclusive part of town, but I do know this: There is no consistent, uniform, and readily workable test *under the law of real property* for when goods are to be dealt with as fixtures.

Many of the states have over the course of time adopted, under their law of real property, tests or sets of factors or language thought to be helpful for determining when a fixture is a fixture, some tending to emphasize one aspect of the circumstance over the other, but at core there is probably less difference in substance than in how the answers are expressed. One factor that, at least in the earlier round of cases, seemed to be central was "intent." Was it ever intended that the goods in question would become fixtures so allied with the land that ownership of them would thereafter pass with the title to that particular real property as time went on? The problems with a test based or centering on intent should be obvious. Precisely whose intent counts? Is it the intent of the party who first brought the goods on the land and affixed them thereto? Or is it the joint intent of the parties to the original transaction, the seller and buyer of the goods? In any event—and this is an aspect of the inquiry that holds particular fascination for us, studying as we are, the how, when, and whether of *third parties* being affected by security interests in property created by contracts to which they were never invited to consent—should the mutually held intention of even these two noble figures, the seller and the buyer, affect the characterization when it comes to the rights and potential risks of others who had nothing to do with creating the situation?

You will still see references to and some consideration of intention in cases discussing whether or not particular property qualifies as a fixture under current law, but the focus of the investigation is usually elsewhere. One element that often plays a key part is the degree to which and the method by which the goods have been attached or affixed to the structure. Something bolted down to the floor or strapped to the walls is not necessarily a fixture. On the other hand, if the thing has been so embedded into the architecture that severing it would cause material, if not necessarily structural, damage, it is more likely to be classified as a fixture. Other factors that can play a role are the degree to which the goods themselves are particularly appropriate for or have been adapted to use in that specific space and also how integral they are to the use for which the space was either originally erected or later reconfigured.

Think, for example, of the rows of seats in a theater or movie house. They certainly qualify as more than just furniture. At the same time we are all aware of instances when such seating has been replaced with new seating. Rows of seating of this kind do seem a good example of fixtures. Removing them is possible and will not cause structural damage to the theater. At the same time the theater owners will probably not be able to take them out and replace them with others without having to repair the underlying floor, or make alterations or improvements. You cannot just take out one set of seating and plop another set down in its place as you would when you replace one dining room table with another. Also, if seating is removed, only a large open area with a gently sloping floor facing a stage or screen exists. Something's missing. The theater seating had its meaning and was fulfilling its destiny, if you will, only as it was present in this or some comparable space. At the same time the space the seats occupied was either originally constructed or later adapted in a way that just cries out for seating of this sort. The goods and the structure bear some kind of special relationship, and that relationship goes a long way toward allowing us to identify them as fixtures.

A bit of language that you often see in the cases and that may be helpful in thinking about this problem comes from the American Law of Property. It says,

> Under the modern cases [this was written in 1952, but still seems to hold true] no more precise definition is possible than this: a fixture is a former chattel which, while retaining its separate physical identity, is so connected with the real estate that a disinterested observer would consider it part thereof.

The theater seating example seems to me to fit this definition of "fixture" nicely.

Moving closer to home, imagine that you were looking to buy a house and were taken by a real estate agent to see one that had just been placed on the market at a given asking price. As you wander through the house you note a particularly nice dining room table and some artwork on the walls that you find attractive. You may admire these pieces, but it's unlikely you would assume that they would "go with" the house under a standard purchase and sale of realty. You might be able to convince the present owner to sell them at the same time he or she sold you the house, but it would have to be a side deal for the sale of some personal property (governed by Article 2 of the U.C.C. and not local land law), and you certainly would not expect the price to be included in what you have been told the owner is asking for the house itself. The furniture and the artwork are not fixtures, no matter how beautifully they look in the particular setting. You assume, barring some contrary information, that the owner plans to take them along when he or she moves out.

As you pass through the house you also notice the wallpaper on the kitchen walls and the exposed wooden beams making for such a distinctive ceiling in the family room. You expect that if you bought the house the wallpaper would still be there when you moved in and the beams would still be holding up the family room ceiling. These are not fixtures, of course, but are what we have seen termed "ordinary building materials" and hence "pure realty." They have been so incorporated into the structure that they have become part of it. Looking back to the language from the American Law of Property, this wallpaper and these wooden beams have not retained a "separate physical identity." They are at one with the house. If you buy the house you get them, not as fixtures that pass with the real property but as part of the real property itself.

Finally, let's go down to the basement. There you see a water heater attached to and running as part of the plumbing system. You may think to ask about the water heater's capacity and about how old it is, but I doubt you would think to inquire, "And does this come with the property?" The water heater *does* still have a separate physical identity that remains intact. If you buy the house you might choose to have it removed and replaced with a newer or larger unit. Still, it is connected with the house in a way that the furniture and artwork are not, and by tradition water heaters, unlike dining room tables and paintings on the walls, stay in a house when it is sold to another. The water heater, however unglamorous, would be a fixture.

Water heaters, wall-to-wall carpeting, boilers, and larger appliances are the kinds of things that typically will be fixtures in a residential setting. For a case relying upon the undisputed characterization of a completely new kitchen consisting of "new countertops, cabinets, sinks, disposal unit, dishwasher, oven, cooktop and hood," installed and financed by Sears, Roebuck and Company, as a fixture under the definition now found in §9-102(a)(41), see *Maplewood Bank & Trust v. Sears, Roebuck & Co.*, 265 N.J. Super. 25, 625 A.2d 537, 21 U.C.C.2d 171 (1993), aff'd, 135 N.J. 97, 638 A.2d 140, 22 U.C.C.2d 1209 (1994). To add a bit of glamour to what seems to be turning into an awfully humdrum subject, see *In re Flores de New Mexico, Inc.*, 151 Bankr. 571, 20 U.C.C.2d 1353 (D.N.M. 1993), in which a company's prize rose bushes, some 60,000 of them valued at $100,000, were held to be fixtures relating to the 28 acres of land on which they were located.*

---

* To add just one more complexity to the situation, a few states still adhere to an earlier notion referred to as the "assembled industrial plant doctrine," under which all personal

By now you are presumably well ahead of me and will not be surprised at the following bit of advice: When in doubt, the prudent lawyer advising at the transaction stage gives serious consideration to dealing with the situation to cover each of the reasonable possibilities, figuring that a bit of extra precaution at this point could save a lot of grief in days to come. He or she takes comfort that this is not a situation where it is necessary to follow only one course of action; here, in fact, a bit of overkill might be the wisest course. Comment 3 to §9-334 concludes with the following:

> Because the question whether goods have become fixtures often is a difficult one under applicable real-property law, a secured party may make a fixture filing [a special type of filing we will get to in a moment] as a precaution [in addition to making a regular filing on the goods, assuming them not to be fixtures, as we have previously discussed]. Courts should not infer from a fixture filing that the secured party concedes that the goods are or will become fixtures.

WHAT TO DO IF IT *IS* A FIXTURE

Assuming for the moment that we know a fixture when we see one, the next issue is, not surprisingly, what difference it makes that the goods in question fall within the category. Looking back to §9-109(a)(1), the crucial scope provision of Article 9, we now take time to linger over that aspect of the provision that says that the article applies "to a transaction, regardless of its form, that creates a security interest in personal property *or fixtures* by contract." We then check in with §9-334(a), which leads off with, "A security interest under this article may be created in goods which are fixtures or may continue in goods which become fixtures."

---

property taken into an industrial plant for permanent use and necessary to the operation of that plant become fixtures regardless of whether they are physically attached to the plant or not (in the words of an earlier case, "whether fast or loose"). See, e.g., In re Griffin, 182 Bankr. 8, 26 U.C.C.2d 670 (M.D. Pa. 1995), reaffirming the continued vitality of this doctrine in Pennsylvania. See also ATC Partnership v. Town of Windham, 268 Conn. 463, 845 A.2d 389 (2004).

One particular type of big ticket item which may or may not be a fixture and which in the past seemed to end up the subject of litigation with some regularity is the mobile home or prefabricated modular building brought onto a piece of land with the intention of its being left there for some indefinite period of time. If one lender holds a real estate mortgage on the land and another has taken a PMSI in this kind of somewhat movable building, who has priority in the building? The revision of Article 9 did what it could to clarify the situation, or at least some situations, by introducing definitions of "manufactured home" and "manufactured-home transaction" in §9-102(a)(53) and (54) as well as a special rule governing priority when such a transaction has occurred in §9-334(b)(4). See In re Bennett, 2002 Bankr. LEXIS 1793 (D. Neb. 2002), and in re Hoggard, 330 Bankr. 595, 59 U.C.C.2d 1056 (W.D. Mich. 2005).

At the same time, and what makes our life all that much more interesting, under subsection (2), "This article does not prevent creation of an encumbrance upon fixtures pursuant to real property law." Real property law, you can be sure, is not shy of rules about who gets ownership of or who can take security interests in fixtures. The general rule is that one who buys outright a piece of real property (the details of which transaction are of course covered by real property law and nothing in the U.C.C.) gets all the fixtures attached to the property unless a contrary agreement is made by the vendor and the vendee. Recall the water heater in that house you were thinking of purchasing just a few pages earlier. In addition, any real estate lender that takes its security in the form of a real property mortgage will claim an interest in the land, any buildings on the land, and on top of that any fixtures annexed to the land or the buildings. The typical real property mortgage includes some language giving the mortgagee an interest even in fixtures later brought onto the land.* Even if there is no such language, the common law of real property would generally give the mortgagee an interest in any after-acquired fixtures.

So fixtures don't so much lead a double life as lead a single life subject to tugs in two directions. Security interests in personal property, those with which we are concerning ourselves in this volume, can and do attach to fixtures. At the same time these same fixtures may be subject to real property interests that we ignore at our peril. Fixtures have to be dealt with distinctly and very carefully. For one thing, perfection in fixtures takes on a special nature, with the requirement of the so-called "fixture filing." In addition, the rules of priority, dealing as they must with competing *real property* interests and not just other Article 9 interests and the bankruptcy trustee, take on a whole new level of complexity.

THE FIXTURE FILING

Perfection on a fixture is done through the proper filing of a *fixture filing*, defined in §9-102(a)(40) as "the filing of a financing statement covering goods that are or are to become fixtures and satisfying Section 9-502(a) and (b)." So a fixture filing is first of all a financing statement. It must exhibit and be correct in all of the respects that we have previously considered for the

---

* So the mortgage deed will grant the lender an interest in the real property "together with the tenements, hereditaments, and appurtenances, thereunto belonging, or in anywise appertaining," which any educated individual can tell means to cover fixtures including those after-acquired. See, if you're so inclined, *K & L Distributors, Inc. v. Kelly Electric, Inc.*, 908 P.2d 429, 30 U.C.C.2d 965 (Alaska 1995).

run-of-the-mill nonfixture financing statement, the general requirements of §9-502(a). In addition, however, under subsection (b), it must

(1) indicate that it covers fixtures;
(2) indicate that it is to be filed in the real property records of the filing office;
(3) provide a description of the real property to which the collateral relates; and
(4) if the debtor does not have an interest of record in the real property, provide the name of the record owner of the real property.

On what will count as an adequate description of the land, see Comment 5.

> The proper test is that a description of the real property must be sufficient so that the [fixture filing] will fit into the real-property search system and be found by a real-property searcher.

This also explains, of course, why the name of "a record owner" of the land is necessary if the debtor does not himself, herself, or itself have such an interest.

The contents of a fixture filing are meant to "fit into the real-property search system" and it is into that system that the filing has to go. Look back at the "where to file" rules of §9-501, now focusing on subsection (a)(1)(B). When the financing statement is being filed as a fixture filing, the correct office at which to file is not the central filing office for the state. It is "the office designated for the filing or recording of a mortgage on the related real property." This will most typically be an office found not in the state capitol but locally, at the county seat of the county in which the land is located. The fixture filing, just like any other financing statement, will not be valid to perfect on the collateral unless the filing is correct as to both form and place of filing. At least here we do not have to worry about any multistate problems, unless of course the real property in question straddles the border between two states. The state under whose laws the fixture filing is to be filed is the state in which the land is located.

The point of all of this is not hard to pick up. The fixture filing is to "fit into" the real property records. Its purpose is to give notice to a person searching those records — as one searches in those records, not by the name of the secured party but by the record owner of the land and the description of the particular piece of land itself — that a security interest in the fixture or fixtures in question may be claimed under the rules of Article 9 by the secured party. The purpose of the fixture filing requirement is to give constructive notice to those interested in the real property and the fixtures which may be attached to it. It is also important to note that a searcher who mistakenly takes the collateral to be pure goods and not fixtures will not become aware of the interest since he or she will be searching in the ordinary Article 9 filing system where nothing will come up, even for the most diligent searcher.

PRIORITIES IN FIXTURES

With all this fuss about whether or not a particular bit of chattel gets classified as a fixture affixed to a specific piece of real property, and then the added complication of the fixture filing, well, there must be some payoff somewhere. The payoff, if that is the way you think about these things, is that we are now ready to take on the special priority rules relating to fixtures set out in §9-334. Look first at subsection (c), which states the general rule:

> In cases not governed by subsections (d) through (h), a security interest in fixtures is subordinate to the conflicting interest of an encumbrancer or owner of the related real property other than the debtor.

This tells us two things. First of all, and unfortunately not terribly obvious from the statutory language itself, when a question comes up about the relative priority of one party's interest in a fixture and another party's conflicting interest in the same stuff where that other party's interest is not claimed under real property law — when he or she is not an encumbrancer or owner of the real property concerned — then §9-334 has nothing to say on which of the conflicting parties gets the priority nod. See Comment 2. This section is meant to exclusively govern priority disputes that arise when one disputant is claiming an Article 9 security interest and the other is claiming its interest through the applicable local law of real property. If the Article 9 claimant is coming up against another Article 9 security interest holder, a lien creditor or (most importantly) a trustee in bankruptcy who is claiming only in such a capacity, then we're out of §9-334 and back into the other sections and rules of priority we have already covered.

Of course the quoted language of subsection (c) has its other more affirmative aspect as well, and this it states with perfect clarity. If one party claims an interest in a fixture under Article 9 and another through a real property interest, either as an owner or the holder of a valid mortgage on the property to which the fixture is affixed — well then, unless the Article 9 claimant can point to some exception found somewhere in §9-334 itself, he or she is going to come in second in the priority competition.

All hope is not lost for someone taking an Article 9 interest in a fixture, however. The principal exceptions to the default rule of subsection (c) are to be found in subsections (d) and (e). Subsection (e)(1) states a straightforward first-to-file rule, where the filings to be considered are those duly recorded in the land records covering the real property involved. Subsection (d) even carries forward the general principle we have already encountered in Article 9 of giving a kind of "superpriority" to purchase-money security interests that are perfected according to the rules laid down.

The examples that follow will help you work through these basic priority concepts.* We will finish up with a couple of examples which, as I've labeled them, take us out of the realm of fixtures and §9-334 altogether. Article 9 covers the phenomena it denotes "accessions" in §9-335 and "commingling" in §9-336. These concepts and their attendant sections are among the least referenced in all of Article 9 discussion, litigation and practice. You see they didn't even make it into the title of this chapter. Still, I thought I'd give at least one example apiece trying to give you the flavor of each, should you care to partake.

Examples

1. Dexter Moneybucks lives on a large estate in one of the most fashionable parts of the county. What is more, having inherited it from his father (the Moneybucks who actually started out with nothing and earned all the money by his diligence, intelligence, and the sweat of his brow), Dexter owns the property free and clear of any mortgage or other encumbrance. The dining room of Dexter's mansion is dominated by a large and terribly valuable crystal chandelier reputed once to have been owned by Ludwig of Bavaria. In 2006 Dexter arranges to obtain a loan from the National Bank of Redono Beach, granting the bank a security interest in the chandelier (which the bank has of course had appraised by an expert) as collateral. The bank prepares an initial financing statement carefully describing the chandelier as the collateral, which financing statement it files with the Secretary of State of the state in which Dexter's home is located. In 2008 Dexter files a petition in bankruptcy.

   a. Will the bank's interest be good as against the bankruptcy trustee?

   b. Suppose that sometime in 2007 Dexter had sold his estate in a perfectly unexceptional residential real estate transaction to one Donald Trumph, a new wealthy kid on the block. What then would be the value of the Redono Beach bank's interest in the chandelier in the course of Dexter's bankruptcy proceedings?

---

* In an effort to keep this chapter to a reasonable length and lest we get distracted from the most generally applicable rules, we will not be covering, through the Examples, every aspect of §9-334. Subsection (e)(2) gives a special rule of priority where the fixtures are "readily removable" factory or office machines or replacements of domestic appliances that are consumer goods. If you can't control your curiosity about what's going on here, consult Comment 8. Similarly, if subsection (h)'s special rule of priority where a "construction mortgage" is involved becomes important to you, you have Comment 11 to serve as your guide. The rule of subsection (f) shouldn't cause any problem even on a first reading. It means what it says.

    c. Would your answer to part (b) above be any different if the bank had initially filed a proper fixture filing, correct as to all particulars, in the real property records of the county where the home is located?

    d. Suppose that instead of selling the house to Trumph in 2007, Dexter had borrowed money from the Highflyers Fiduciary Trust Society giving that lender a standard real estate mortgage on his land, which mortgage was duly filed. What would be the relative priority of the Redono Beach Bank and Highflyers Trust in the chandelier assuming, first, that the bank had filed only a standard initial financing statement, and, second, that it had filed a fixture filing back in 2006?

2. Professor Frock owns a perfectly respectable, if not terribly lavish, house in a decent part of town. Needless to say, the good professor was able to purchase this house only through applying for and obtaining at the time of purchase in 1986 a long-term real estate mortgage from Blackacre Bank. The mortgage document granting the bank its interest was properly filed immediately after the deed into Frock on the land records covering the house in question. In the middle of the winter of 2007, Frock's furnace gives out. He is told that he will need to replace it with a completely new furnace. He arranges to buy one from Boiler Brothers of Brooklyn (BBB), a heating contractor. The price, including installation, is $12,867. Since Frock does not have this kind of money readily at hand, he enters into an installment purchase agreement with BBB, under which he will pay for the furnace over four years, making monthly payments calculated based on the purchase price and an appropriate rate of interest. He signs a security agreement giving BBB a security interest in the furnace. Prior to delivery and installation of the furnace, BBB files this fixture filing in the proper land records covering Frock's simple (if perfectly respectable) home.

    a. Who has priority in the furnace — Blackacre Bank or BBB?

    b. Would your answer to part (a) above be any different if BBB had installed the furnace on January 13, 2007, and not filed the fixture filing until January 30?

3. Debtor operates a manufacturing business on some land that it owns and that is subject to a real estate mortgage held by Blackacre Bank, which is properly on file in the land records. Debtor later grants a non-PMSI in a valuable industrial fixture, an integrated widget painting, drying, and annealing assembly, residing in the factory to a second lender, Manufacturers Bank for Industry, which files a fixture filing on the machinery in the correct place. In the course of a major refinancing of its land, Debtor obtains a release of the mortgage it had granted to Blackacre and grants a new mortgage to the new lender, Whiteacre Bank. The release and new mortgage are correctly placed on record.

    a. Which institution has priority over the widget processing assemblage as a fixture — Manufacturers Bank or Whiteacre Bank?

    b. What would be the result if the land refinancing had involved not Blackacre's release of its mortgage but its assignment of the mortgage to the new lender, Whiteacre?

4. Let us return now to Dexter Moneybucks in his palatial estate with the crystal chandelier hanging high over the dining room. Assume that Dexter first gives an Article 9 security interest in this fancy bit of lighting to the National Bank of Redono Beach in 2006, which the bank perfects through a proper fixture filing at the time, in connection with a loan to be paid off by him in monthly installments over the course of the next three years. Dexter then borrows money in 2007 from the Highflyers Fiduciary Trust Society giving that lender a standard real estate mortgage on his land, which mortgage is immediately filed. In 2008 Dexter, for some reason or another, stops making his payments as due to the Redono Beach bank. What remedy does that bank have? See §9-604 (c) and (d).

5. *On Accessions and §9-335:* The Acme Corporation is engaged in the business of construction and repair of roads, bridges, and the like. Among its various pieces of equipment, all subject to a valid and properly perfected Article 9 security interest held by the Roadrunner State Bank, is an 80-foot crane. When the main engine that powers the crane becomes too old to operate efficiently any more, Acme has a new engine installed. It buys this engine for $80,000 from the Coyote Corporation, which agrees to take payment over a four-year period on the installment basis if it is given a security interest in the engine. Acme signs a security agreement granting Coyote such an interest. Coyote files a financing statement in the proper place for filing of an interest in Roadrunner's equipment. Which lender has priority of interest in the newly installed engine sitting in the crane — Roadrunner or Coyote? See subsections (a) through (c).

6. *On Commingling and §9-336:* Commodore Crunchy and Company, Incorporated, makes granola cereal. Apricot Inc. sells Commodore Crunchy a large supply of dried fruits and berries on credit, retaining a purchase-money security interest in what it delivers. Apricot files a proper financing statement. Bran Corporation sells Commodore Crunchy carloads of bran, oats, and wheat with which it deals similarly. Finally, Caraway Seeds and Nuts makes an industrial size delivery of, well, seeds and nuts, on the same terms. The cereal manufacturer goes into operation and blends all of these various ingredients into its own patented brand of Commodore Crunchy granola cereal. Large bins of it are sitting in its plant when the bottom drops out of the granola market and Commodore Crunchy is forced to file a petition in bankruptcy. What rights do each of Apricot, Bran, and Caraway have in the granola?

Explanations

1a. We're assuming throughout this example that a chandelier like this is a fixture, and indeed a pretty impressive one at that. For a case that so holds, see *Equibank v. I.R.S.*, 749 F.2d 1176 (5th Cir. 1985). That being said, we cannot help but note that the bank did not perfect its interest in the chandelier via a fixture filing. This mistake will cause it problems in later parts of this example, but its regular nonfixture perfection, as if this magnificent fixture were just another piece of Dexter's consumer goods, will at least be sufficient to protect its interest against a bankruptcy trustee. Recall that the general principle of §9-334(c) subordinates an interest in fixtures not otherwise exempted to "a conflicting interest of an encumbrancer or owner of the related real property," but the bankruptcy trustee is neither. Once the bankruptcy petition is filed, the trustee comes tromping in via the bankruptcy law in the guise of a kind of lien creditor, a notion we've seen reflected in the definition of §9-102(a)(52).

Look also to §9-334(e)(3). The bankruptcy trustee will gain as part of the bankruptcy experience a lien on the real estate in which the chandelier hangs. That lien, however, is effective no earlier than the date of the filing of the petition. And (e)(3) says that "a perfected security interest in fixtures has priority over a conflicting interest of an encumbrancer [which now the trustee gets to be]" when "the conflicting interest is a lien on the real property obtained by legal or equitable proceedings *after* the security interest [in the fixture] was perfected *by any method* permitted in this Article." The bank can argue that it did perfect, even if not by the fixture filing method, and that it did so prior to the bankruptcy trustee's conflicting interest in the real property came into being. It, the bank that is, has priority in the fixture ahead of the bankruptcy trustee.

That this result is what the drafters of §9-334 (and its precursor, §9-313 of pre-revision Article 9) intended and hoped would come of their language in (4)(d) is told to us in a bit of Code drafting history. In part of the "Official Reasons for the 1972 Change" in the Official Text of Article 9 (the "old" Article 9) can be found the following:

> This requirement for filing in real estate records applies only if the priority advantages of Section 9-313 [now §9-334] are desired. If the secured party is not concerned about priority against real estate parties, he can file for a fixture as an ordinary chattel, in the chattel records, omitting the filing in the real estate records, and he will have a security interest perfected against everyone but real estate parties. . . . For the question of the effect of the debtor's bankruptcy, see Comment 4(c) to Section 9-313.

The comment referred to stated that

> [E]ven a prior filing in the chattel records protects the priority of a fixture security interest against a subsequent judgment lien. . . . It is hoped that this rule will have the effect of preserving a fixture security interest so filed against invalidation by the bankruptcy trustee.

Why the drafters spoke of a "hope" and not an out-and-out commandment here has to do, as the later language of the comment makes clear, with the fact that they had to deal with the then-operative federal Bankruptcy Act as they found it and were in no position to redraft, improve, or make definitive interpretations of that Act. Later development in the federal law of bankruptcy leaves no doubt that the revision drafters of 1972 were not hoping in vain. A filing on a fixture as if it were a simple piece of personal property will serve to perfect and protect against the bankruptcy trustee, now under §9-334. It will not, however, have any effect on "real estate parties," as the commentators referred to them, which is what will cause the National Bank of Redono Beach so much grief in what is to come.

1b. The bank's security interest in the chandelier would almost certainly disappear. When Trumph buys the property he gets, unless there is some contrary agreement with the seller, all of the fixtures. The real property records will reflect first of all the ownership of Dexter up to the point of sale and then the transfer of all his right, title, and interest in the land, its buildings, and the fixtures attached thereto into the name of Trumph as record owner. This is only fair and reasonable. Trumph, when he is looking over the property, will have seen the chandelier and reasonably enough, knowing a fixture when he sees one, will have assumed that it came with the property. In buying the real property he will have had a complete search of the *real property records* conducted, to alert him to any potential problems in Dexter's claim of good title or any encumbrances that he, that is, Trumph, as buyer might later be subject to. Since the Redono Beach bank did not file in the real property records, Trumph and his people will have no notice whatsoever of the bank's interest and he will hence buy free from it. Dexter's obligation to repay his loan to the bank remains, of course, but any leverage the bank thought to gain by its taking an Article 9 security interest in this piece of Dexter's property has been lost.

1c. If the bank had instead filed a fixture filing covering the chandelier correctly in 2006, the answer would indeed be different. Under §9-334(e)(1), an interest perfected in this way would have priority over the conflicting interest of an owner of the real property where, as here, the security interest "is perfected by a fixture filing before the interest of the . . . owner is of record. . . ." The remainder of this sub-part need not detain us now. As Comment 6 makes clear:

> Subsection (e)(1) . . . contains the usual priority rule of conveyancing, that is, the first to file or record prevails. In order to achieve priority under this rule, however, the security interest must be perfected as a "fixture filing" (defined in Section 9-102), i.e., a filing for record in the real property records and indexed therein, so that it will be found in a real-property search.

If the deed into Trumph is recorded in the real property records after the fixture filing, then Trumph takes subject to the bank's interest in the chandelier.

This result, too, makes perfect sense. Since the fixture filing is on file in the real property records prior to the closing at which Trumph takes title and makes the land his, he has to be perfectly well aware of the bank's interest and of this particular encumbrance on the property. Trumph, once his initial check of the real property records reveals this encumbrance, can, of course, deal with it in a variety of ways. He can insist, in his dealing with Dexter, that Dexter clear the encumbrance from the record prior to his, Trumph's, taking title. Dexter, if he's that interested in selling off the old homestead, may have to scrounge up some money, pay off Redono Beach in exchange for a termination statement, and then file the termination statement in the real property records to wipe the fixture filing off the books. If Dexter doesn't have that kind of cash available, the parties may have to work out a way that the real property closing will include a diversion of some of the purchase price being paid by Trumph directly to the Redono Beach bank, which will then and there hand over its termination statement.

Another possibility is that Trumph, reasoning that he is going to keep the chandelier in place anyway, will just agree to buy the property *subject to* Redono Beach's security interest in the chandelier. Trumph will then make sure, of course, that the amount he pays Dexter for the property is that much less, since as a practical matter it will be up to him to continue making payments to the bank to assure that the chandelier is not repossessed. This is the same as the instance under real property law of a party buying a piece of property "subject to" an already existing mortgage, only here we have an already existing and effective fixture security interest that the buyer will be taking subject to.

1d. If the Redono Beach bank had filed only a standard nonfixture financing statement on the chandelier, its interest would be subordinate to the mortgage taken out by Dexter later in time but filed on the land records without any prior filing on the chandelier appearing there. This is just the same as part (b) of this example, only the party Redono Beach is conflicting with is a real property "encumbrancer" and not an "owner." All throughout §9-334 you can see the two are treated equivalently, as "real property interests" with whom the fixture financing party has to contend on real property terms.

If the bank had made a fixture filing on the chandelier in 2006, then this filing would precede the real property mortgage recorded by Highflyers Fiduciary Trust in the very same records the following year. This is, as you can see, analogous to part (c) of this example, only again where the conflict is with a later encumbrance instead of a change in ownership. And the answer is no different. All the action is taking place in the real estate system and on the real estate records, and the general rule applies: Priority goes by a classic real property first-to-file rule.

2a. We are all understandably pleased that the good professor does not have to freeze through the winter, but the question here is something else: Between Blackacre Bank and BBB, who has priority in the new furnace installed in January 2007? The general rule, as we've just seen, is that which governs land transactions generally. The first party on record has priority. Blackacre's mortgage document no doubt is drafted to cover fixtures that later become affixed to the property (similar to the standard "after-acquired property" clause in an Article 9 security agreement), so its interest would indeed extend to the new furnace. BBB, however, can point to the special rule for purchase-money security interests in fixtures, which is to be found in §9-334(d). A perfected security interest in a fixture has priority over a conflicting interest of an encumbrancer like Blackacre if the debtor has an interest of record in or is in possession of the real property, and:

(1) the security interest is a purchase-money security interest;
(2) the interest of the encumbrancer or owner arises before the goods become fixtures; and
(3) the security interest is perfected by a fixture filing before the goods become fixtures or within 20 days thereafter.

All of the criteria are easily met here. Frock the debtor has an interest of record in the property. BBB's interest is a PMSI under §9-103. The interest of the encumbrancer, Blackacre Bank, arose back in 1986, well before the new furnace became a fixture attached to Frock's modest residence. Finally, and most important, BBB's security interest in the furnace was perfected by a fixture filing before the furnace became a fixture.

The justification for this exception for the PMSI, allowing it to gain priority over an interest that would otherwise have priority over it, is presumably the same as that for the other rules we have already looked at in Chapter 14 and embodied in §9-324(a). Frock has to borrow money from *someone* in order to keep his house from freezing. BBB will sell to him on credit only if it can be sure that its interest will be first in line with respect to what it is selling and not subordinate to that of the general mortgage lender. If BBB could not gain a primary interest under a rule like this, Frock would have little alternative but to go to Blackacre and ask for an extension of additional credit backed by the same mortgage the bank already has in the home. Blackacre might be willing to make the further advance, but it might not. If nothing else, its mortgage lending department is not set up to respond quickly to requests for what are for it relatively minor sums. Allowing the PMSI interest to come out ahead in this way does no great harm to Blackacre and will even be doing it some good when four years hence BBB has been paid off and the house on which the bank holds a mortgage has been upgraded by a newer, working furnace. See Comment 7 to §9-334.

2b. The result should be no different if the new furnace had been installed and taken its rightful place as a fixture on January 13 and the fixture filing had not been made until January 30. The language of §9-334(d), quoted above, requires only that "the security interest [be] perfected by a fixture filing before the goods become fixtures or within 20 days thereafter." This, again, is parallel to the treatment of the PMSI of §9-324(a) as well as §9-317(e) and comes with the same explanation. If the people at BBB were able to install a new furnace on a moment's notice and do the paperwork as a follow-up, by which time Professor Frock is back in a heated house, so much the better.

3a. Manufacturers Bank would have priority over Whiteacre in this fixture. It is a straightforward application of the first-to-file rule of §9-334(e)(1). You look through the land records and what you find is a fixture filing entered by Manufacturers followed by a mortgage granted to Whiteacre. So, in the crucial words of this paragraph, "the security interest [in the fixture] is perfected by a fixture filing before the interest of the encumbrancer [Whiteacre]." There is, it must be admitted, some language following this that we will get to in the second part of this example, but it does not come into play here. There is here no "predecessor in title of the encumbrancer" in that Whiteacre took a new, never-before-used mortgage from Debtor.

3b. The situation here is different. While the first document on the land records referencing Whiteacre, the assignment to it of Blackacre's mortgage of record, comes *after* the fixture filing recorded by Manufacturers, the additional language of §9-334(e)(1) does in this instance make a difference. Note that the full language of that paragraph includes two distinct criteria, both of which must be met — they are joined with an "and" — before the perfected interest in the fixture can take priority over a conflicting interest claimed by an encumbrancer. The first criterion, that Manufacturers' fixture filing has come before Whiteacre's interest in the land is of record, is met. The second criterion, however, now comes into play. In this instance it is not true that "the security interest [of Manufacturers] has priority over any conflicting interest of a predecessor in title [herein Blackacre] of the encumbrancer [Whiteacre]."

Look to the ending of Comment 6:

> The condition in subsection (e)(1)(B), that the security interest must have had priority over any conflicting interest of a predecessor in title of the conflicting encumbrancer or owner, appears to limit the first-in-time principle. However, this apparent limitation is nothing other than an expression of the usual rule that a person must be entitled to transfer what he has. Thus, if the fixture security interest is subordinate to a mortgage, it is subordinate to an interest of an assignee of the mortgage, even though the assignment is a later recorded instrument. Similarly if the fixture security interest is subordinate to the rights of an owner, it is subordinate to a subsequent grantee of the owner and likewise subordinate to a subsequent mortgagee of the owner.

So here, Blackacre holding a mortgage that is prior in time and hence prior in right to Manufacturers' security interest in the particular fixture is able to assign that mortgage in all its fullness, including its position superior to Manufacturers' interest, to another party, the party in this case being Whiteacre.

4. The bank's remedy is laid out in §9-604 with reference to all of the secured party's usual rights and remedies under Part 6 of Article 9, which unfortunately we haven't taken up yet. The basic idea, however, is not hard to grasp. The secured party, on the debtor's default, may "repossess," as we will say, the collateral. Under the present case, that means it may "remove his collateral from the real property." What makes the problem in the case of fixtures somewhat different is that they are not just sitting in or on the real estate but are to some degree attached to it. So it has to be assumed that their removal might take a little more effort, and have some greater effect on the real estate, than would the repossession of "pure chattel" collateral.

The law prior to Article 9 sometimes limited the ability of the secured party to reclaim its collateral upon default, when, for example, "material injury to the freehold" would have resulted. Subsection 9-604 is, as you can read, not so limiting. In the particular instance, since Dexter is the debtor, there is no obligation to "reimburse" him for the cost of repair of any physical injury occasioned by the removal, much less for any diminution of the value of his estate because of the removal of the chandelier. It would have to agree to reimburse Highflyers but then only for the cost of repair or any physical injury. Apparently the Redono Beach bank can just go in and take the thing, making sure not to do damage to any other part of the property, the surrounding ceiling and so on. We'd advise, I guess, that they make sure not to leave any exposed wires flapping around. Perhaps they could replace the chandelier with a simple bare bulb or some minimal lighting fixture purchased from the local home supply center correctly wired into place, at least leaving Dexter some light to dine by.

5. First we have to determine that the new engine is indeed an "accession," as the word is used in §9-335. See the definition in §9-102 (a)(1). The term is used to denote goods that are "physically united with other goods in such a manner that the identity of the original goods is not lost." You can see the analogy to fixtures, which are goods installed in or affixed to real property, and as with fixtures it is not always so clear what is considered an accession. If the goods become so integral a part of the larger whole (a new coat of paint for the crane, perhaps?) then they could not be accessions, nor would they be if they remained sufficiently independent and just happened to be lying around or loosely attached (the tool box kept on board). There are, in fact, unlike in the circumstance of fixtures, very few cases that have had to wrestle with the issue. About the only example of an accession — and one that everyone seems certain of — is the "new motor in the old car" kind of thing (see Example 1 in Comment 3), and not coincidentally that is what has turned up in our hypothetical.

So at least we know we are dealing with an accession. Which lender — Roadrunner State Bank, which has an Article 9 interest in the crane as a whole, or Coyote Corporation, which has taken a PMSI in the newly installed engine, takes priority with respect to that engine? This depends on a number of factors. First of all, does Roadrunner have a security interest in the new engine? The answer is probably yes. The description of its collateral in the security agreement it got Acme to sign would, if properly drawn up, cover not just the crane as it was at the time of attachment, but "any accessions, additions, or improvements" to the crane as time went on. See Comment 5. So Roadrunner's interest in the new engine will be perfected as of the time it becomes an accession to the crane as a whole. As to Coyote's interest, it is a purchase-money interest retained by it as seller. Coyote is presumably not claiming a security interest in the entire crane, only in the new engine that it has provided. Subsection (d) of §9-335 says that question of priority in accessions generally are to be considered by looking to other provisions of "this part," by which is meant Part 3 of Article 9. In particular we have to look back to §9-322, which gives the general rules when security interests in the same collateral are in conflict, and §9-324 on the special priority that a purchase-money security interest may achieve. As long as Coyote perfected its interest in the engine "when the debtor receive[d] possession of the collateral [the new engine] or within 20 days thereafter," then under §9-324(a) that wily corporation would have priority in the engine itself. If it failed to perfect within the grace period, or if for some reason its interest were not considered a purchase-money security interest, then Roadrunner would have priority under the first-in-time rule of §9-322(a)(1). See Comment 6 and its Example 3, which basically parallels the question we have before us.

6. Look at §9-336(a). What we have here is a classic case of commingled goods, or at least what would rank as a classic case if commingling played any significant part in the workings of Article 9. In reality the cases where the term, much less the issue here presented, has come up are few and far between. It seems pretty clear to me that lending parties do just about anything they can to avoid the whole issue from the start. We'll soon see why when we examine how the problem works out here.

Each of the three suppliers, Apricot, Bran, and Caraway, would seem to be able to take advantage of the rules of subsections (b) through (d). Each had a perfected security interest in the particular ingredients it delivered, and subsequently all that stuff was "physically united with other goods in such a manner" that its individual identity was "lost in the product or mass." That seems pretty obvious unless you have some weird belief about how easy it is to disassemble granola once it is all mixed up. The result under §9-336 for each is that its security interest continues into the granola and is automatically perfected.

Under subsection (f)(2) since more than one security interest, in this case at least three, attaches to the granola via this route, and the interest of each in the granola is perfected, "the security interests rank equally in proportion to value of the collateral at the time it was commingled." This may or may not be an easy calculation (see, if you dare, the various examples in the comments to this section), but it isn't one with which lawyers who practice in this area of law could possibly enjoy becoming involved. This part of §9-336 appears to be the only place in all of Article 9 where conflicting interests in the same collateral (here those bins of granola) are not dealt with strictly as a matter of priority with one party coming out ahead or having priority and the other losing out and being subordinated to the first. As we've already spent a great deal of time discovering, Article 9 law is keyed to the notion of priority and a strict ranking of interests. Here we have the possibility of a "share-and-share-alike" approach, or more precisely a share according to some formula you can fight over. It is not that Article 9 lawyers don't normally extol the virtues of sharing; it's just that they aren't accustomed to thinking this way when it comes to Article 9 security interests.

Sales and Other Transfers of Collateral

LOSING INTERESTS

Looking back over the preceding chapters, you can see that we spent a good deal of time considering how the debtor's property may be burdened with security interests, oftentimes interests piled on interests, but not much on dealing with how it may be set free of them. A security interest may attach to the collateral, we know, at the inception of the debtor's and secured party's relationship, or it may attach later on as the result of an "after-acquired property" provision. More than one secured party can have at the very same time a security interest in the very same property. Interest follows on interest, allowing for complex questions as each scrambles for priority one over the other.

Is the collateral never to break free from all these potential competitors and their claims to a piece of its future? If interests can be "attached" to property, it stands to reason that they can "unattach" as well, but how and when? Article 9 does not provide any specific word or words to define the moment when a particular security interest, held by a given secured party in some distinct collateral of the debtor, is over and done with. We do not speak of an interest "unattaching" any more than we would refer to the moment of "unperfection." We have to invent our own language for the magic moment when the secured party's interest ceases to have its hold on the collateral. The semantic issue, however, is not the real crux of the problem. More fundamental is considering how, when, and whether a security interest — which is, remember, a legal construct, an interest held by one person in the property of another, not a tangible object with physical dimensions — ceases to exist.

One way that this type of interest comes to an end and naturally self-destructs is for the debtor to fully and finally make good on all of its obligations to the secured party. As Article 1 tells us, security interest is an interest in the property of another "which secures payment or performance of an obligation," and it must follow that when there is no longer any underlying obligation outstanding the security interest will perforce simply vanish into the vapor. There need be no great ceremony involved, nor does Article 9 call for any. If, of course, the security interest had not only attached to the collateral but been perfected by some action of the secured party, then the debtor will expect and have every right to a reversal of that action so that there will no longer be the appearance to the outside world that the secured party may be claiming an interest it no longer has. If the collateral is the subject of a pledge, that is the interest having been perfected by possession in the secured party, the debtor will want to regain possession. If the interest was perfected by a filing, then a termination statement, as provided for in §9-513 is in order. We may then say, choosing what language we wish, that the interest has terminated, or that the collateral has been released from the interest, or that the collateral is out of hock. The whole affair is over, done with, history.

Another possibility is that the secured party, even if the debtor's underlying obligation has not fully been met, may allow or acquiesce to a release of its interest in the collateral — either in advance should certain conditions be met or on the spot as the mood (and good business judgment) takes it. The secured party can agree to a full release or to a partial release of the collateral to which its interest has attached and may do so for no consideration or in return for some concession on the debtor's part. An Article 9 security interest is a creature of contract, and there is nothing to prevent the parties to that contract from altering its terms, the result of which will be relinquishment of any or all claims of interest that the secured party was initially granted or has come to hold in the collateral.

In this chapter we consider a distinct way in which a piece of collateral may, should the conditions be right, shake itself free of the security interests that bind it. It will turn out that should the debtor sell or otherwise transfer the collateral to another there is the possibility that the collateral will come into the hands of the new owner "free of" or "unencumbered by" a security interest that had prior to the transfer been attached to it. When, how, and why this may come about is a story, or a compilation of stories, of no small significance to the entire Article 9 saga.

BUYERS AND OTHER TRANSFEREES

You no doubt noticed that the end of the preceding section emphasized that the transferee *may* take free of a security interest, that it was a *possibility* only. That is because, as the Code makes clear, the starting assumption is that the sale or other transfer of a bit of property will not do anything to affect the interest, which will, as a general rule, go along for the ride. Recall §9-201(a):

> Except as otherwise provided in [the Uniform Commercial Code], a security agreement is effective according to its terms between the parties, *against purchasers of the collateral*, and against creditors.

Now note §9-315(a), which repeats the refrain:

> Except as otherwise provided in this article . . .
>
> (1) a security interest or agricultural lien continues in collateral notwithstanding sale, lease, license, exchange, or other disposition thereof unless the secured party authorized the disposition free of the security interest or agricultural lien; and
> (2) a security interest attaches to any identifiable proceeds of the collateral.

The second part of this subsection, referring to "identifiable proceeds," will take up our attention in the chapter to follow. For the moment, we concentrate on what precedes it. As the language makes clear and as Comment 2 drives home,

> Subsection (a)(1) . . . contains the general rule that a security interest survives disposition of the collateral. In these cases, the secured party may repossess the collateral from the transferee or, in an appropriate case, may maintain an action for conversion. The secured party may claim both any proceeds [as we will discover in the next chapter] and the original collateral but, of course, may have only one satisfaction.

Things don't look so sweet for the buyer or other transferee. We start with the assumption that he or she takes title to whatever is being transferred, but only as that title is encumbered by any and all security interests that at the moment of transfer are attached to it. The transferee gets the property, but has to accept it, warts and all. This really should not surprise us. It is only one more example of the basic principle, central to so much of commercial law, that the transferor of property can generally not transfer any interest or title better than what he or she has to begin with.

The sections at which we have just looked talk in terms of not just sale of the collateral, but of disposition or transfer in general. In practical terms, however, the more interesting problems come up when the debtor doesn't just give the collateral away but also gets something back in the bargain, when the collateral is sold to some buyer who pays a price for what it gets. The buyer, who has, after all, now coughed up something of value in exchange for getting the stuff, may reasonably expect to take it free and clear of all encumbrances. If the buyer does not take it free of the security interest but ends up holding it subject to that interest, he or she at least should know that this is the case and discount what is paid accordingly. So the core question in most instances becomes whether the collateral in the hands of a buyer, not just any transferee, remains subject to or is free from a security interest that just prior to the sale was enforceable against the collateral as it stood in the hands of the seller.

A diagram for the world we are about to enter looks something like this:

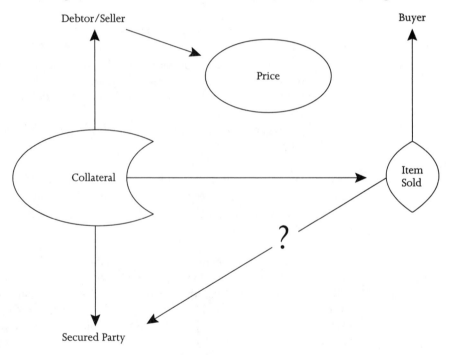

I recognize, of course, that in many instances the debtor will be selling off all of the collateral and not just some lesser chunk of it, as would appear from this picture, in which case the debtor-seller is left holding nothing in the way of collateral but presumably a greater amount of that stuff, which for the moment I merely labeled the "price." I've chosen to draw a more general picture, but the principle and the main issue remain the same. Whether the debtor sells off just some or gets rid of all of the collateral, the issue is whether that which the buyer gets is free of or still subject to the security interest the secured party had prior to the sale enforceable against the seller.

It is worth mentioning here, if only to leave the richness of detail for further discussion in the chapter to follow, that what I have labeled the "price" in the diagram above, as a conventional term when we think of this as a purchase and sale, will take on the special role of what is defined and then dealt with as "proceeds" when viewed through the lens of secured transactions and Article 9. We will deal with the proceeds aspect of this situation in the next chapter.

For the moment, we stare at the diagram and we find one big question: When will the secured party's interest remain attached to, or fall away from, the collateral after the sale? We return to the language of §§9-201(a) and 9-315(a) with which we started. The default assumption is that the security interest remains enforceable, that it carries on unaffected by the sale or other transfer. If that were the end of the story, this would be the end of the chapter. Notice, however, that each of these subsections suggests something more need be considered. Section 9-201 starts out with the tantalizing phrase "Except as otherwise provided in the Uniform Commercial Code, . . ." In §9-315(a) we see the similar "Except as otherwise provided in this article . . . ," and also a reference to the case where "the secured party authorized the disposition free of the security interest. . . ." Something's out there, in Article 9 itself, that will allow the buyer to take free of the interest consistent with the language and underlying policies of and reflecting regular day-to-day practice under the Secured Transactions article of the Uniform Commercial Code.

Before heading into some examples, take a look at two parts of Article 9. Subsection 9-317(b) sets the standard for when a transferee can take free of an *unperfected* security interest. That's all well and good, but if the secured party has been tending carefully to its business, it will have perfected and §9-317 becomes irrelevant. Look then to §9-320(a) and (b). Here we have a set of rules that allows for situations in which the buyer of goods (and notice only that class of collateral) can take free and clear of even a *perfected* interest. Now that's something to talk about. And talk about it we shall.

Examples

1. Selma of Selma's Appliance City grants a security interest in "all inventory now held or hereafter acquired" to Credit Associates in late 2007. That firm files a financing statement in the appropriate place at the time. In 2008 Selma is approached by someone from the Springfield Youth Center, a local charity, asking if she could make a donation to their cause. Instead of making a donation in cash, Selma takes an expensive microwave oven out of her storeroom and has it delivered to the Youth Center, accounting for it mentally and in the books of her business as a charitable contribution.

    a. The Youth Center now owns the microwave oven, but does it own it unencumbered or is it still subject to Credit Associates' security interest and, hence, to being repossessed by the creditor should Selma default in her payment obligations or go into bankruptcy?

    b. Would your answer be any different if you were to discover that Credit Associates had not filed effectively and hence had never perfected its interest?

2. Assume as we did in the previous question that Selma had granted a floating lien in her inventory to Credit Associates and that the lender had properly perfected on the interest at the time. In 2008, Prof. Flock goes into Selma's and buys a washer-dryer combination for his home. Flock being no charity case, Selma insists that he pay the full price she has set out for the item, which he does. The appliances are delivered to him in June 2008. In November of that year Selma is forced into bankruptcy.

    a. Will Credit Associates be able to assert any interest in the washer-dryer combination now resting in Flock's house?

    b. Would it make any difference to your answer to (a) above if it could be shown that Flock, as an expert in commercial law, knew or should have known that the inventory of a retail store such as Selma's would normally be subject to a floating lien of the type involved here?

    c. What if it could be shown that in the particular instance Flock was actually aware of Credit Associates' interest, his hobby being to browse the UCC filings of his state during his off hours?

3. Another individual, Jane Doe, goes into Selma's in October 2008 and buys a stereo system at, as Selma advertises, a "giving it away" price. Doe, who has been doing comparison shopping, does note that the price for this system at Selma's is significantly below what she has read is the "suggested retail price" of the item, and is in fact a bit lower than she's seen at other similar stores. Does Doe hold the stereo free of any interest that could be claimed by Credit Associates?

4. On November 13 another individual, Robert Roe, is offered a stereo system similar to the one bought by Jane Doe. Selma says that he, Roe, can have the item at a price that is one-half of what Doe had been charged the month before, but only if he takes her up on the offer immediately and pays her in cash. Roe goes for the deal and takes possession of the stereo. Selma's petition in bankruptcy is filed on November 17. Is the item Roe purchased free and clear of any interest that may be claimed by Credit Associates during the course of the bankruptcy proceedings?

5. Isabelle Inkster, the printer, had done a printing job for Selma for which she was supposed to be paid in August 2007. Selma keeps putting off Inkster's demands for payment. Finally, in early November Selma

suggests that she take her payment in property instead of in cash. Inkster agrees to and does take a particular make and model of vacuum cleaner and an air conditioning unit in lieu of payment. Does Inkster hold these items free and clear of any claim to them that can be made by Credit Associates?

6. Sam, of Smiling Sam's Autorama, grants a security interest in all of his "equipment" to a local bank, First National of Shelbyville. The bank properly files on the equipment in 2007. In June 2008, Sam decides to redecorate his showroom and office to give them a "new look." He sells his antique desk for $13,500 to Lydia Lawyer, who is setting up a practice in the community.
   a. Does First National continue to have a security interest in the desk after the sale to Lydia is complete?
   b. Would your answer to (a) above be any different if Lydia had bought the desk not for her office but for her home? (Lydia, you should be aware, tries to keep her professional life from encroaching on her personal time and never takes work home from the office. Her desk at home is strictly for keeping track of her personal correspondence and other nonprofessional matters.)
   c. Would your answer to (b) remain the same if for some reason First National had failed to file on the desk?

7. Suppose that Sam, of the previous example, also sells in the course of his redecoration the set of leather chairs and a sofa that have been in his office to a friend, Max, for a total of $10,000. Max borrows the money to buy this furniture from Happy Home Finance ("HHF"), which is careful to carry out the transaction so that it obtains a PMSI, granted to it by Max, in the items he is purchasing. HHF is careful to perfect this interest on the same day it dispenses the funds to Max. It now appears that two separate parties, First National Bank of Shelbyville ("FNB") and HHF each has a valid and perfected interest in the furniture now in Max's possession. The question naturally arises: Which secured party's interest has priority? See §9-325.

8. Andrew bought an expensive computer system from a retail store, Computermania. He bought the system on credit, agreeing to pay for it with a system of monthly installments over the next two years. The sales agreement he signed gave the store "a security interest in any and all computer equipment or supplies being purchased by buyer under this plan." The store never made any filing with respect to this purchase. Andrew took the system home, where he used it to do his personal accounting, keep track of his extensive comic book collection, and play computer games. About a year later Andrew grew tired of this particular computer, which he saw as outmoded, slow, and unreliable. He sold

the system to his next-door neighbor, who planned to use it for playing games only, for $1,000 cash. He also stopped making payments to Computermania. When that store comes to declare Andrew in default on his obligation to it, will it be able to assert any interest in the particular computer to help it find relief?

9. In 2007 Sheila Ivories buys an expensive baby grand Steinmetz piano for the purpose of giving piano lessons out of her home. She buys it from an authorized Steinmetz dealer, which agrees to sell her the piano on credit. The dealership makes sure that it obtains a properly attached and perfected PMSI in the piano before it delivers it to Ivories' address. Ivories initially pays $2,000 down toward the $20,000 price of the piano and agrees to pay the remainder in installments of $400 a month. Within a couple of months of this purchase, she realizes that she can no longer keep up the stressful life of a full-time piano teacher and decides to quit it all. She puts an ad in the local paper offering to sell the "barely used" piano. Her ad brings a response from one Sharpie, a dealer in used pianos. He comes to take a look at the instrument and offers to buy it from her. She informs him that it is not completely paid for, but he assures her that this is something he can take care of. "I know the dealership," he assures her, "so I'll work it out with them." He gives her $2,400 and takes the piano back to his own store. There it soon catches the eye of one Emily, an innocent, who buys the piano for $19,780 using a certified check. Sharpie never makes any contact with the Steinmetz dealership from which Ivories had originally bought the piano. Ivories stops making payment to the dealership, and in fact leaves town for the quieter life of a shepardess in Bohemia. When the dealership stops receiving payments from Ivories it tries to contact her but finds that her telephone has been disconnected. It goes to her home but only to find that she, and the piano, are no longer there. Through sources it discovers that this particular piano now is sitting in Emily's apartment. Is the dealership's security interest in the piano still effective, so that if need be it can repossess the piano from Emily?

10. Farmer Jane T. Kirk borrows money in early 2007 from Enterprise State Bank, granting the bank an interest in "all crops now growing or to be grown" on her farm. The bank does all of its paperwork well, so there is no doubt that its interest has attached and been properly perfected. When her cucumber crop comes in during the summer of 2008 she sells it in its entirety to Peter Piper and Company, a pickle packing concern. The cucumbers are loaded onto Peter Piper's trucks and carted away.

    a. Does Peter Piper take the cucumber crop free and clear of Enterprise State Bank's security interest?

    b. Would your answer to (a) be any different if it turned out that by some mistake Enterprise had never correctly perfected its interest?

Explanations

1a. The Youth Center has its microwave oven, but it owns it subject to a security interest held by Credit Associates as the secured party. There's no way around it. Recall that §9-315(a) is quite insistent that a security interest "continues in collateral notwithstanding sale, lease, license, exchange, or other disposition thereof" unless the secured party has authorized the disposition or where some express exception to the rule is provided for elsewhere in Article 9. Selma was very generous; hers was a disposition by way of gift. There is no legal or ethical reason why she should not give away her property, but she can only give what she has — a microwave oven subject to a security interest. She conveys title to the oven to the charity, but only as it is encumbered by the then existing security interest.

There is always the possibility, of course, that a contribution of this sort on Selma's part but free from the security interest was "authorized" by Credit Associates in the security agreement, but it is highly unlikely. The typical inventory financing agreement will if anything be very explicit in having the debtor, Selma in this case, agree not to dispose of any of the collateral except by sale to what we will later refer to as a buyer in the ordinary course. Maybe there is some exception in the agreement signed by Selma with Credit Associates for minor donations such as we have here, but I'd doubt it. More than likely Selma is in fact in breach of her contractual arrangement with the lender for having acted as she has. The lender may not count it as a very serious breach, but it would probably be an occasion of "default" as we will later start using that term.

If Selma wanted to be sure that the Youth Center got the microwave free of the security interest and any slight tarnish that it would necessarily bring to her gift, she could of course ask for Credit Associates' written authorization for this disposition prior to the donation. If all is going well between Selma and her lender, it is unlikely that they would refuse. Then again, they might not really want to be bothered with such a minor matter.

If Selma does not have authorization from Credit Associates for this disposition free from its security interest, given either in the security agreement or later on, is there any provision of Article 9 that will strip the interest from the microwave as a matter of law? The answer is no. Since Credit Associates has perfected, we have to look to §9-320, but there is nothing relevant to the situation there. As Comment 2 first states, "This section states when buyers of goods take free of a security interest even though perfected." The Youth Center is a donee, not a buyer, and that's the end of the story.

1b.   If Credit Associates' interest had attached to the inventory including this one microwave but had never been properly perfected the result would not be any different. We look to §9-317(b). It states that in general a buyer of goods takes free of a security interest "if the buyer gives value and receives delivery of the collateral without knowledge of the security interest . . . and before it is perfected." We can assume that the Youth Center had no knowledge of the security interest, but the fact is that it is not a buyer of the goods. It did not give value. So the charitable donee does not come within the protection of §9-317(b) even if Credit Associates' interest had never been perfected. It holds the microwave oven subject to the unperfected security interest.

2a.   Credit Associates will not be able to get its hands on Flock's washer-dryer. The good professor is the quintessential example of the *buyer in ordinary course* as that term is defined in §1-201(9) or §1R-201(b)(9). He is a person who

> buys goods in good faith, without knowledge that the sale violates rights of another person in the goods, and in the ordinary course from a person, other than a pawnbroker, in the business of selling goods of that kind. A person buys goods in the ordinary course if the sale to the person comports with the usual or customary practices in the kind of business in which the seller is engaged or with the seller's own usual or customary practices.

We're taking it for granted that Selma is not a pawnbroker.

At this point you might object to the fact that Flock seemingly doesn't buy that many washer-dryer combinations as part of his daily routine. Is it appropriate to say that this purchase was in the "ordinary course" of his affairs? He might be a first-time buyer of such an item and may never buy one again. The answer is to appreciate that the term "ordinary course" as used in this definition is meant to connote that the sale was of a kind, and carried out in a manner, that was in the ordinary course *of the seller's business* and not of the buyer's life. We will get to situations soon enough where this criterion is not met, but from all we can tell here Flock was just one of many customers who descended on Selma's Appliance City one particular day and who bought from her in the most routine and ordinary manner. No big deal! This is the kind of transaction that Selma makes all the time. It was in the ordinary course of her business.

Judging Prof. Flock to be a buyer in the ordinary course of business is important not just because it would justify his adding BOCB (as "buyer in the ordinary course of business" is often abbreviated) to the various credentials following his name. It has relevance to the situation because of the all-important rule of §9-320(a):

> Except as otherwise provided in subsection (e) [a very unusual situation with which we need not be concerned here], a buyer in the ordinary course of business, other than a person buying farm products from a person engaged in farming operations, takes free of a security interest created by the buyer's seller, even if the security interest is perfected and the buyer knows of its existence.

This suits Flock's situation to a tee. He is a BOCB, has not come anywhere near any farm products, and is concerned about the possible effect on him of a security interest created by his seller, the one and only Selma. Subsection 9-320(a) will put his mind at ease. When he bought his washer-dryer combination, he took it free of Credit Associates' security interest, even though that interest was perfected at the time.

2b. The answer remains the same. Flock may have reason to suspect that what he is buying is subject to a security interest granted by his seller to a lender, but the language of §9-320(a) allows him, as we will see in discussing the next part of the example, to take free and clear even if he actually *knows* for sure of the existence of the interest. So let's go on to that next part.

2c. Our analysis here remains the same. If he is a buyer in the ordinary course of stuff other than farm products then he buys it free of any security interest created by his seller even if that interest is perfected at the time of sale and even if he actually "knows of [the security interest's] existence."

Your one concern at this point may be whether Flock can still legitimately be considered Prof. Flock, BOCB, that is, a buyer in the ordinary course of business, given that he now knows of Credit Associates' interest in the property he is buying. After all, looking back at the Article 1 definition, one criterion for a buyer to qualify as a BOCB is that he or she have no knowledge that the sale to him or her would "violate rights of another person in the goods." Has Flock not run afoul of this part of the definition? The fact is that he has not. Flock may be aware, as he was in (b), that a retailer like Selma might well have her inventory subject to a lender's security interest and he may even know about it for sure, as he does here, including the name of the lender. That is not the same as his being aware or even having any reason to believe that a sale of the item to him on the terms including the price to which he was subjected would be in *violation* of any such third party's security interest in the inventory. Here Flock is aware of the security interest but has no knowledge that the sale to him would be in violation of the agreement Selma would have entered into with Credit Associates. He can still take free and clear of the interest even if perfected.

Look back to §9-320 and the third comment to that section. The end of the first paragraph of the comment takes note of the distinction we have been addressing:

> The buyer in the ordinary course of business is defined as one who buys "in good faith, without knowledge that the sale violates the rights of another person and in the ordinary course." Subsection (a) provides that such a buyer takes free of a security interest, even though perfected, and even though the buyer knows the security interest exists. Reading the definition together with the rule of law results in the buyer's taking free if the buyer merely knows that a security interest covers the goods but taking subject if the buyer knows, in addition, that the sale violates a term in an agreement [the seller has entered into] with the secured party.

What makes the difference, as Flock, a master of commercial law, would well understand, is that a party like Credit Associates that lends on a retailer's inventory would normally have no objection to the debtor's selling off pieces of that inventory free of its interest as long, that is, as the buyers were just the type of person like the Flocks of this world — people who qualify as buyers in the ordinary course of the retailer's business. In fact the security agreement between Selma and Credit Associates would most likely carry a specific authorization that Selma may make such sales, but such sales only, without asking for further clearance from the lender.

Why would Credit Associates be so willing to allow Selma to strip it of its security interest in even a single piece of her inventory when that interest is what, after all, secures her obligation to make good on her loan obligations? Why would it not insist on keeping its hooks firmly lodged in every last bit of collateral that it could? On the surface that might seem to make sense, but we would be wrong to stop at the surface.

Underlying this whole arrangement is the fact that Selma has borrowed money from Credit Associates. What that august firm wants first and foremost is that she make payments on her debt to it as they become due, something they realize she can only do if her business generates enough cash or its equivalent sufficient to cover her loan payments along with her other expenses, and, if all is going to continue running smoothly over the long haul, a bit of profit. How can and does Selma's business generate cash? By selling off day after day and piece by piece individual items from her inventory. Each sale she makes yields what we will end up calling the proceeds of that sale. How will Selma make these sales and rake in the resulting proceeds unless she is able to deliver what she sells to the individual buyers *free and clear* of any security interest? Ordinary buyers are not about to pay a price that they view as a fair market value for any of Selma's wares unless they can be assured that they are getting not just physical possession of the item and the right to its use but full and unencumbered title to it, unsullied by any lien or interest of another type that might have been created in the past.

So that's the way the system works. Credit Associates loans money to Selma so that she can purchase inventory, so that she has stuff to sell to Flock and other buyers like him, so that these buyers will hand over the price for their purchases to Selma, who will then have money with which to pay back Credit Associates. The trick, of course, at least as far as Credit Associates is concerned, is that it get repaid not just the principal it lent but a reasonable rate of interest as well. Commercial lenders such as Credit Associates are all about loaning money at an interest rate. This entire security arrangement is, remember, no matter how much energy we seem to be spending on it, just part of the background that gives the lender greater assurance that the cash payments keep flowing its way as they are supposed to. It won't hurt either, as we will explore more fully in the next chapter, that while Credit Associates will be stripped of its security interest in the goods sold by Selma out of her inventory to BOCBs it will automatically get an interest in the proceeds of these sales in the process. If Selma's business is really running as it should, the value of the proceeds can be expected to exceed (at least to some degree) the value of the goods she sells; that's what it takes to run a profitable retail establishment. So in the end Credit Associates can think of itself as having agreed to give up its interest in inventory collateral only to gain an interest in the proceeds as collateral, which are of greater value. That's hardly a sacrifice on the lender's part.

One final point before we allow Flock to get back to doing his washing and drying. You might have been tempted in analyzing this situation to call upon subsection (b) of §9-320. It is, after all, captioned "Buyer of Consumer Goods," and Flock, unless he runs a launderette on the side, seems to be buying this amazing combination that both washes and dries clothes just for his own personal use. As it turns out, §9-320(b) does not apply here. What that particular subsection is meant to deal with is the case when goods that are consumer goods *in the hands of the seller* are then sold to another. Selma held the washer and dryer combination as inventory and not as consumer goods and thus we are justified in consulting §9-320(a) only. We will get to use §9-320(b) in a later example (Example 7 to be precise), but it is only a red herring here.

3.   There's no reason to think that Jane Doe is not a buyer in the ordinary course and hence under §9-320(a) someone who takes free of any interest that could be claimed by Credit Associates. She may have gotten a good deal, but there is nothing here to suggest that Selma, whatever her protestation, has not sold at a price that works for her as well. There is nothing here to call into question Doe's good faith or to give her reason to believe, much less actual knowledge, that the sale of the stereo to her on these terms is in violation of any third party's rights whatsoever.

4.   Credit Associates will argue that Robert Roe cannot claim protection under §9-320(a) because he does not qualify as a buyer in the ordinary course. Its argument seems strong, certainly as compared to any argument it might try to make against the very differently situated Jane Doe of the previous example. Was Roe (in buying) acting in good faith? The term "good faith" is defined for the purposes of Article 9 in §9-102(a)(43) (or §1R-201(b)(20)) as requiring "honesty in fact and the observance of reasonable commercial standards of fair dealing." As you see it, is there anything dishonest or outside the bounds of reasonable commercial standards of fair dealing in buying something for "a steal" when the opportunity comes along? When the seller demands an immediate response and payment only in cash? Your answer may depend on what more we can find out about Roe. Did he have reason to know that the price for which he was being offered the stereo was indeed so far below the item's market value that there just had to be something fishy going on here? If we judge the situation to be one in which Roe has real reason to suspect that someone, even if not Selma, who is the one who has suggested it, is being cheated out of something by this deal — if we see him as responding to it so eagerly because of a bit of larceny in his own heart — then Credit Associates' argument might carry the day. If, on the other hand, Roe has no reason to suspect that he is getting anything other than a good deal at a fair, if to him very desirable, price, he should prevail.

Prior to the recent revision of Article 9, the question of a buyer's good faith would have been addressed by the "subjective" standard, which you can see articulated in §1-201(19) of the original version of Article 1. Under that standard, a party will be found to have acted in good faith as long as he or she demonstrated "honesty in fact in the conduct or the transaction involved." The subjective standard allows, at least in theory, for the honest but terribly naïve buyer to legitimately claim that he or she had been acting in good faith, even if a more experienced person would have had reason to question whether what the seller was willing to take in payment did not in some way suggest something was, let us say, unusual about the proposed transaction. The revised Article 9 adopted what is generally referred to as the "objective" standard of good faith, as we read in §9-102(a)(43). (If you don't find it there, it's because your copy of the Code incorporates the revised version of Article 1, in which case look at §1R-201(b)(20).) This requires a party's acting not only honestly, but in observance of "reasonable commercial standards of fair dealing." So now, Roe's naïveté alone presumably would not serve as protection should his good faith be called into question.

As a practical matter, the distinction between the subjective and the objective measures of good faith, at least when the buyer under scrutiny is the single retail customer such as the Does and Roes of this world, probably does not matter that much. In those cases decided under pre-revision Article 9 in which a buyer was held not to have been a BOCB it was usually by a pretty hefty margin where a number of factors, not just an indecently low price, came into play and where it was not just a question of how naive a person can be before he or she should reasonably suspect that the deal is not on the up and up.

In *International Harvester Co. v. Glendenning*, 505 S.W.2d 320, 14 U.C.C. 837 (Tex. Civ. App. 1974), for example, Don Glendenning, the buyer in question, had purchased three new tractors from a farm equipment dealership, worth something on the order of $22,500, with a cash outlay of only $16,000. Evidence made clear, however, that this was more than just an incredibly lucky day for Glendenning. It turns out he was a sophisticated customer, well-versed in the ways of commercial finance. He had every reason to know that what he was paying was far below the fair market value of the three tractors. In addition he had agreed at the seller's request to sign a retail order form that indicated that in addition to the $16,000 cash he had actually paid for his purchase he had traded in four used tractors recorded as worth $8,700 but that existed only in the minds of the seller and buyer. At trial the buyer,

> admitted that he knew that the information contained in the printed form concerning trade-ins and total consideration [which had been given as the $16,000 plus the $8,700 supposed value of the trade-ins] for the sale of the three tractors was false; that he knew of this falsification when he signed the order form; and that he also knew that such a falsification would mislead any creditors relying on the document, such as a dealer, a manufacturer or a bank lending money with the equipment [that he was buying] as collateral.

A few days after the transaction a representative of International Harvester, which not only manufactured the equipment but more importantly for these purposes had lent on it as part of its overall financing arrangement with the seller-dealership involved, suspicious about the whole affair, called Glendenning and was falsely told by him that the four trade-in tractors did exist. The buyer testified that he knew he had lied to the International Harvester representative "and that such oral misrepresentation or lie was dishonest." In spite of all of this a Texas jury somehow found that the buyer had acted in "good faith" as defined by the Code. On appeal the jury's determination was overturned, the Court of Civil Appeals concluding,

> The complete picture revealed by all of the material testimony in this case reveals a definite pattern of lies, deceit, dishonesty and bad faith. We find no competent evidence in this record to support the jury's [determination that Glendenning had acted in good faith] and therefore [this determination] should have been set aside and disregarded by the trial judge.

Glendenning was not a buyer in the ordinary course of business, his argument of good faith as a buyer being not only questionable but downright impossible to take seriously.

In *First National Bank and Trust Co. of El Dorado v. Ford Motor Credit Co.*, 231 Kan. 431, 646 P.2d 1057, 34 U.C.C. 746 (1982), the principals of a corporation that owned and operated a Ford dealership sold themselves some cars. In purchasing the cars, however, they neglected actually to turn over to the company the cash down payments called for, they never transferred title into their own names as owners, and they never removed the cars from the lot but allowed them to remain among the dealership's stock of new cars available for sale. Such buying was held, unremarkably, not to be buying in the ordinary course. The BOCB of a new car would, we have to assume, normally be expected to pay the down payment and would expect in turn to actually take title and possession of the car, to drive it away.

5. No. Inkster is not a BOCB of the vacuum or the air-conditioner. This has nothing to do with any lack of good faith on her part or suspected larceny in her heart. Look again at the definition of the BOCB in Article 1:

> A buyer in ordinary course of business may buy for cash, by exchange of other property, or on secured or unsecured credit, and may acquire goods . . . under a pre-existing contract for sale. . . . [The term] does not include a person that acquires goods in a transfer in bulk or as security for or in total or partial satisfaction of a money debt.

You have got it right if you realize that Inkster's problem under the circumstances is not that her acquisition of the appliances will be considered a transfer in bulk or a taking as security. She has, however, taken the goods in satisfaction of a money debt owed her. She therefore cannot, in spite of all the good intentions in the world, be a BOCB.

This result makes sense if you recall the reasons we saw why Article 9 allows for the BOCB to take free of the secured party's interest. The "buying" part of the BOCB means that the transaction will generate for the seller some compensating new value in cash or as we have just read "by exchange of other property." In the ordinary sale Selma will have lost the odd vacuum or an air conditioner, but she will have gotten compensation for whatever it is that has made its way out of the lender's collateral pool, usually cash or at least some equivalent that will help her pay off her debt to Credit Associates and that will be in addition identifiable proceeds in which that lender will automatically have a resultant security interest of proportional value. When Selma exchanges the particular vacuum or air conditioner for release of a preexisting debt owed to Inkster, nothing new comes into Selma's pot that serves this function. This is not an ordinary sale by Selma, and Inkster is not a buyer in the ordinary course of such sale. As such she takes the goods subject to Credit Associates' security interest in them.

6a. Yes. First National's interest continues on as the desk travels into Lydia's office. Recall that this is in fact the general rule — the security interest is effective not only between the initial parties to the transaction creating it, here Sam and the bank, but also "against purchasers of the collateral" under §9-201(a). The bank's interest here has been perfected, so it can also point to §9-315(a)(1) to the same effect. The real question is whether Lydia can claim the benefit of some part of §9-320, which sets out the only ways a perfected interest can be stripped from an item upon sale, and the answer is no. Her one chance is §9-320(a), because she definitely does not come within the scope of subsection (b). Sam did not hold the desk as consumer goods and Lydia is not buying for her personal use either.

Why can't Lydia claim to be a BOCB, a buyer in the ordinary course of business, and hence gain the protection of §9-320(a)? The answer lies in the definition of the BOCB, which we have already looked at a few times. Now we pay special attention to that language of the Article 1 definition which requires that the buyer be buying from "a person . . . in the business of selling goods of that kind." Sam is in the business of selling autos. People who buy autos from his inventory can, if they meet the other criteria of the definition, claim BOCB status. Sam is not in the business of selling desks, antique or otherwise. Lydia is buying an item of Sam's equipment and as such could never qualify as a BOCB. It turns out that no one can ever even hope to qualify as a BOCB unless he or she is buying items that constitute inventory, as that term is carefully defined in §9-102(a)(48), in the hands of his or her seller.

So Lydia takes the desk subject to First National's security interest. If Sam defaults on his loan, Lydia may be faced with a bank representative seeking, with every legal right, to repossess the desk. How could she have avoided this situation? Well, Lydia, as a lawyer, should have thought back to her Secured Transactions course and recognized that since she was buying a piece of Sam's equipment she would necessarily be taking it subject to any security interest that might be perfected on it. She could have checked the Article 9 filings in the appropriate filing office and found there proper notice of First National's interest. At this point she might have turned sour on the whole deal, or she could have asked Sam to provide her with the bank's written authorization for the sale of the desk to her free and clear of its interest. There is still that possibility under the language of §9-315(a)(1). Will the bank authorize the disposition? Perhaps yes; perhaps no. It will presumably do so only after making a current evaluation of what collateral comes within the scope of its security interest in all of Sam's equipment, how this compares to the amount Sam has outstanding on his loan, and how this balance would be affected if the desk were to leave the picture. Sam may have to pay down the outstanding amount he owes First National to get it to release its claim on the desk and authorize sale to Lydia free from its interest. Lydia, however, cannot afford to simply ignore the problem — or what she learned in her Secured Transactions course.

6b. Unfortunately for Lydia the situation is no brighter here. She still cannot take advantage of §9-320(a), as she is not a BOCB, or §9-320(b), because, while she may be buying for her own personal use, the desk was not held by Sam, the seller, as consumer goods. She is still buying a piece of Sam's equipment, and hand in hand with such an action comes the need to check those Article 9 filings and treat what you find there seriously.

6c. If the bank had not filed or its filing were for some reason ineffective (for instance, because it had misspelled even slightly the name of the debtor or had filed in the wrong place), then its interest would not be perfected. Does Lydia take free and clear of an *unperfected* interest? For that we look to §9-317(b). Lydia, it turns out, is not subject to First National's attached but unperfected interest as long as she "gives value and receives delivery of the collateral without knowledge of the security interest and before it is perfected." "Knowledge" is defined in §1-201(25) or §1R-202(b) as actual knowledge, so unless Lydia really knows of First National's interest (in which case she would be a fool to touch the desk without getting the whole matter cleared up) she should be in the free and clear. She has paid $13,500 for the desk, which easily constitutes giving value.

Notice that §9-317(b) doesn't distinctly mention good faith. True, under §1-203 or §1R-304, "Every contract or duty within this

Act imposes an obligation of good faith in its performance or enforcement," and Lydia's purchase of the desk is a transaction governed by Article 2 of the U.C.C., but none of this should cause Lydia any trouble as long as she paid a fair market price for a desk of this type. If, in another situation, a buyer were to pay what was recognizably to him only a fraction of the item's worth, then §9-317(b) would not necessarily allow him to claim protection from the secured party's later claim. The purpose of this part of §9-317 is to protect the party who has traditionally been referred to as the "good faith purchaser for value" or the "bona fide purchaser for value." Neither of those terms is used by Article 9 exactly, but it is doubtful that someone acting not in good faith (or not "bona fide" in this respect) would find much sympathy from any court should a question of interpretation of §9-317(b) ever arise.

So if the interest is not perfected, Lydia, acting in good faith, would be able to take free of First National's interest. Again, you should be able to see the sense in this. Lydia is interested in buying something that she knows to be classed among Sam's equipment. She checks the Article 9 filings in the appropriate place and under his correct name, and finds no record, is given no notice, of First National's interest. She has done all she is called upon to do to check whether her purchase could potentially run afoul of some secured party's claimed interest, and she has found nothing to suggest that it would. She is paying a fair market price. Lydia beats First National hands down.

Subsection 9-317(b) does not always give a victory to the buyer, of course, just because the seller's lender failed to perfect its interest. For a case in which the buyer of some equipment did not take free of an unperfected security interest created by its seller under §9-317(b) because, as the court found on the facts, it had actual knowledge of the security interest by the time it accepted delivery of the collateral, some three snow-making machines, pursuant to the contract of sale, see *Snow Machines, Inc. v. South Slope Development Corp.*, 300 App.Div.2d 906, 754 N.Y.S.2d 383, 50 U.C.C.2d 613 (2002).

7. The parties have, by their actions, presented us with a classic case of what is referred to as the "double debtor problem." Notice the problem rears its head not simply because we have two security interests in the same collateral — we've seen plenty of such situations in Chapters 13 and 14 — but because the two competing interests were granted by two distinct debtors. Sam granted an interest in the furniture as part of his equipment to FNB. Max granted an interest, a PMSI in fact, to HHF, when he borrowed money from that lender to buy the furniture from Sam. So which interest comes out ahead? FNB might

first point to §9-322(a)(1), claiming that it should have priority because of the first-to-file-or-perfect rule that governs competition between two perfected interests in the same collateral. HHF will counter with §9-324(a), arguing that it was careful to perfect its PMSI in this collateral, which is neither inventory or livestock in the hands of its debtor, Max, so as to gain the special priority that it gains under that subsection. Matters might end here if it weren't for §9-325. This section, added as its commentary tells us, to Revised Article 9, settles the question and settles it in FNB's favor. The story is told in a careful reading of §9-325(a). That subsection does begin with the invocation that it is applicable "[e]xcept as otherwise provided in subsection (b)," but you can check that in our situation at least, subsection (b) isn't a problem for FNB. Its competitor, HHF, is claiming a priority "solely under" §9-324. So subsection (a) applies.

We can now read that subsection as it covers the particular problem we are looking at:

> A security interest created by a debtor [here Max] is subordinate to a security interest in the same collateral created by another person [here Sam] if:

> (1) the debtor [Max] acquired the collateral subject to the security interest created by the other person [Sam];

> (2) the security interest created by the other person [Sam] was perfected when the debtor [Max] acquired the collateral; and

> (3) there is no period thereafter when the security interest [created by Sam in favor of FNB] is unperfected.

Quickly checking each of these three criteria, we see that we can say (1) Max did acquire subject to FNB's interest, (2) FNB's interest was perfected when Max acquired the stuff, and (3) there has been no period when FNB's interest has been unperfected. So FNB comes out ahead thanks to §9-325. You can check that this fact pattern is basically the same as that found in Example 1 in Comment 3 to this section.

8. No. Finally we have a case that truly fits under §9-320(b). The neighbor has bought the computer from Andrew, who was holding it as consumer goods, and takes it free from Computermania's security interest even though perfected if he or she bought without knowledge of the security interest, for value, and for his or her own personal, family, or household purpose. There is no reason to think that the neighbor had actual knowledge of the store's retained security interest, and he or she gave $1,000, which counts as value in anybody's book.

Computermania, when it comes to repossess, would have no right to do so, assuming that it could even figure out in whose possession the computer is. Andrew might well tell the store what he's done, and the store could hunt down the neighbor, but it could not take possession of the computer. It is now free of any interest that Computermania would want to claim in it.

Notice that this result stems from the fact that the store took a PMSI in the computer it was selling to Andrew and then relied solely on the automatic perfection rule of §9-309(1) to perfect its interest. Had the store decided, as it well might on larger big-ticket items, not to rely solely on this means of perfection but had gotten Andrew to authorize a financing statement and then filed in the correct place for recording on Andrew's property, the neighbor would not find protection in §9-320(b) by virtue of the concluding portion of that subsection. The store saved some time and expense in not filing on the computer, and consequently the possibility that Andrew could sell it free and clear to another consumer is a risk it took.

9. Yes. It turns out that Emily paid the full market value of the piano but holds it subject to a security interest that can still be claimed on it by the Steinmetz dealership. How has this happened? Look first at the sale of the piano from Ivories to Sharpie. The dealership's security interest does not lapse as a result of this sale. Sharpie would not qualify as a BOCB, and hence §9-320(a) does not come into play, because Ivories is not in the business of selling pianos. Nor does this sale qualify as a consumer-to-consumer transaction under §9-320(b), as Sharpie is not himself buying it for his own personal, family, or household purposes. So the security interest is still in place as the piano sits in Sharpie's store. What of the sale from Sharpie to Emily? We can see right away that it is not a consumer-to-consumer sale, but why can't Emily claim and take advantage of her BOCB status? The answer is that while Emily is indeed a BOCB, a careful reading of §9-320(a) reveals her problem: The buyer in the ordinary course gets the chance under that provision to take free "of a security interest *created by the buyer's seller*." The security interest with which Emily now is contending, however, was *not* created by her seller, Sharpie, but by another, Ivories, who is by now long gone and with her sheep.

How could this happen to the innocent Emily? I hope by now you have figured out that Sharpie is a bit of, well, a disreputable character and that he has pulled a scam on Emily. He purchased the piano from Ivories for $2,400 and immediately turned around and sold it to Emily for $19,780. That's more than just a healthy profit; it's the result of Sharpie having sold to Emily what he gave her to believe was a piano not subject to any encumbrance when in fact it was still under the thumb of the dealership's security interest. What is Emily to do? Well, if she can still find Sharpie she can sue him under §2-312(1), the warranty of good title in the sale of goods. You can look to that section. Unfortunately, if I had to guess I'd say that by the time Emily gets wind of the problem, Sharpie will not be easy to find; dishonest characters such as Sharpie are awfully hard to locate by the time their dishonest deeds come to light.

We naturally ask if there is anything that Emily could have done to spare herself this loss. Notice that she had no obvious reason to think of herself as other than a buyer in the ordinary course of something that the seller owned and had a right to sell. Had Emily thought to check if anyone claimed an interest in any property held by Sharpie she would have found no financing statements, or certainly no financing statements referring to the piano. If she had thought to ask him to produce some evidence of his ownership of the piano and how he came by it, for example, a bill of sale signed by the previous owner and marked "Paid in Full," he would not have been able to produce any document. Or maybe he could have. If someone is willing to do to the innocent Emily what Sharpie has apparently done, there is no reason to think he would shy away from doctoring up some documents and forging a signature or two.

The outcome seems awfully unfair to poor Emily, but you do have to consider the dealership's side of the story. It has done nothing wrong here, and were it not able to foreclose on the piano it would itself be out a considerable amount of money. The real villain here, the one it appears who has gotten away with something like $17,380 in ill-gotten gains, is Sharpie. The dealership never had anything to do with Sharpie. As between the two unsuspecting parties, the dealership and Emily, one of whom must bear the loss of Sharpie's misbehavior, the outcome is that Emily — who at least did personally deal with and had some opportunity to take the measure of the man — must bear the loss. It is a hard result, but one that cannot be avoided unless Sharpie reenters the picture as an atoned, apologetic man and coughs up the $17,380 to set things right.

10a. Peter Piper may be a buyer in the ordinary course of business, but even so he will not take free and clear of the bank's security interest. Look again at §9-320(a). It allows the buyer to take free if it is a BOCB "other than a person buying farm products from a person engaged in farming operations." At least as far as Article 9 is concerned, this buyer, not having the advantage of §9-320(a), will take subject to the security interest under §9-315(a)(1) "unless the secured party authorized the disposition free of the security interest." It is extremely doubtful that Enterprise authorized anything of the sort in the security agreement. If anything, a typical security agreement covering farm products in a situation such as this would be very explicit in requiring the lender's written agreement to any disposition of the whole or any substantial portion of the crop. Farmer Kirk is going to have to get such a written authorization from the bank for any such sale, as a savvy buyer of farm products like Peter Piper should realize. Even if Piper is not provided with a written authorization from the bank allowing for the sale to him free of its security interest, he may still get the cucumbers free and clear, but not because of anything we see in Article 9. A federal statute, the Food Security Act of 1985, 7 U.S.C. §1631, may disencumber the cucumbers sold here of the bank's interest. I will not go into the workings of the FSA here, which, as a matter of fact, can operate differently in different states, but if you want to know more about it you might want to check out — other than the statute itself — the recent decisions in *Farm Credit Midsouth, PCA v. Farm Fresh Catfish Co.*, 371 F.3d 450 (8th Cir. 2004), and *Consolidated Nutrition, L.C. v. IBP, Inc.*, 2003 S.D. 107, 669 N.W. 2d 126, 51 U.C.C.2d 329 (2002).

10b. If the bank had mistakenly failed to perfect, the situation is covered by §9-317(b), and the result would likely be different. Peter Piper would be able to take free of the bank's interest to the extent that he "gives value and receives delivery of the collateral without knowledge of the security interest and before it is perfected." Just another example of how important it is for a secured party to take steps to perfect and carry them out correctly to protect its most basic interests.

Proceeds

CHAPTER

INTRODUCTION

In the last chapter we found reason on numerous occasions to refer to the general rule of §9-315(a)(1). We start this chapter by looking again to that section, but stressing now subsection (a)(2):

> Except as otherwise provided in this article . . . a security interest attaches to any identifiable proceeds of collateral.

If the debtor transfers the collateral in a transaction other than one of sale or exchange — in other words, if he gives the stuff away, hopefully with the approval of the secured party — there will be no proceeds generated. In all other cases the debtor who disposes of the collateral gets something in return. The term *proceeds* is defined in §9-102(a)(64). For our purposes it will be sufficient to concentrate on part (A) of that definition: Proceeds include "whatever is acquired upon the sale, lease, license, exchange, or other disposition of collateral." Note that the term "collateral," as defined in §9-102(a)(12), itself includes "proceeds to which a security interest attaches." The result is that if identifiable proceeds are themselves disposed of in exchange for something else, that something else is itself proceeds of the original collateral and not just of the first batch of proceeds. To put it briefly: Proceeds of proceeds are proceeds.

Recall the key diagram of the previous chapter. I reproduce it here but with a bit of a twist:

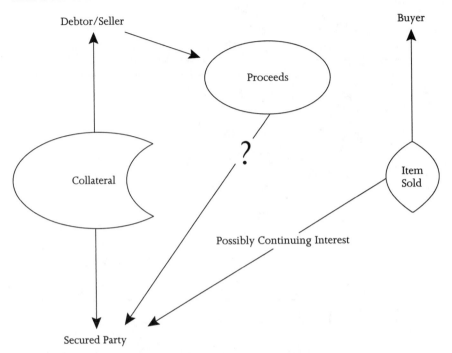

As now seems justified, I have replaced the commonplace term "price" for what the debtor who sells collateral gets from the buyer with the more precise "proceeds." Also, as you can see, the focus of our questioning has shifted. The secured party may or may not retain an interest in the item sold, as it is now property of the buyer. That question was what the last chapter was all about. We now turn our attention to the secured party's relationship to the proceeds of the sale. What exactly will constitute "proceeds"? If, as our reading of §9-315(a)(2) above already has made clear, the secured party's security interest automatically *attaches* to the proceeds as they become proceeds, will that interest need to be separately *perfected*? If so, when, where, and how? What are the priority rules when we are considering conflicting interests not in the original collateral but now the proceeds resulting from sale of the collateral, or even the proceeds that result from the sale or other disposition of what are already proceeds?

Examples

1. Dexter Moneybucks, as debtor, and his friend Sarah, as secured party, enter into a security agreement in which a certain valuable lithograph in Dexter's collection ("Hypothetical Living") is the collateral. The simple

written agreement makes no mention of "proceeds" or anything of the sort.

  a. Should Dexter sell the lithograph, will Sarah be able to claim a security interest in whatever he gets from the buyer? See §9-203(f).

  b. Suppose that this lithograph is stolen from Dexter's home. Fortunately, Dexter has insurance covering the theft of his property. After investigation the insurance company gives him $24,000 to cover this loss. Does Sarah have a valid security interest in this money? Look to §9-102(a)(64)(E).

  c. Suppose that Dexter takes the check he has received from the insurance company and immediately signs it over to an art dealer with whom he regularly deals in order to obtain one of the few remaining copies of this same lithograph. Can Sarah claim a security interest in this new copy? Would it make any difference if instead he had used the check to purchase a statuette by a different artist?

2. Selma of the famous Selma's Appliance City has granted a security interest in all of her inventory to Credit Associates. Selma sells some items to her customers for cash or (when accompanied by a proper ID) a check. She is also willing to sell on credit. In some instances she asks for payment in a lump sum within a month of the sale, while in others she is agreeable to the customer's making a series of monthly payments. For larger items she may ask the customer to sign a note for the balance due after a cash down payment has been made. In still other instances she has the customer sign her form of Retail Sales Installment Agreement in which the buyer promises to make a series of payments and further agrees that Selma will retain a security interest in the items being sold to secure payment.

  a. As each item is sold out of her inventory, does Credit Associates get a security interest in what Selma receives in return? How would you classify each mode of payment she is willing to take? Which of these are "cash proceeds" and which are "noncash proceeds?" See §9-102(a)(9) and (58).

  b. As payments, either in cash or by check, arrive at Selma's from her credit customers, does Credit Associates have an interest in these later payments? See §9-102(a)(64)(B).

  c. Selma deposits the cash and the checks that she receives in an account she has at a local bank. Does Credit Associates have an interest in this account?

3. Tony of Tony's Trailer Town sells a new mobile home to a customer. In exchange, he takes a used mobile home as a trade-in, a check for $2,000 representing the down payment, and a promissory note signed by the customer payable to Tony. Assume that Wellington Bank and Trust ("WBT") has a continuing interest in "all inventory now held or

hereafter acquired" by Tony and that a financing statement covering this interest has been filed in the proper place.

    a. Does WBT's interest continue in the new mobile home once it is delivered to the customer?

    b. Does WBT have an interest in any proceeds of the sale? What are these and how would they be classified?

    c. Does WBT need to take any action as it becomes aware of the sale to assure itself of the best possible position regarding these proceeds? See §9-315(c) and (d), and §9-330(d).

    d. Assume that instead of getting a check for $2,000 Tony took from the customer, who happened to be an artisan whose work was well-known and much prized, a handmade desk and chair combination that Tony puts in his office. How does this change your analysis of the situation?

    e. Finally, assume instead the following: Tony gets the $2,000 check as a down payment. He goes directly to a nearby furniture store where he negotiates the check over to the owner in exchange for $2,000 worth of office furniture, a desk, and a chair. This furniture is delivered to his Trailer Town, where it is put in Tony's office. What's the situation here as far as WBT's interest goes?

4. Delmore Debtor owns a valuable construction crane. First National Bank has a security interest in the crane, perfected by filing. Second Avenue Lenders also has a security interest in this very same crane, also perfected by filing. First filed before Second. Debtor exchanges the crane for a backhoe and a tractor. Does either First or Second have an interest in all that Debtor obtains in exchange? Does either of the lenders have priority over the other in the backhoe and the tractor? See §9-322(b)(1).

5. Isabelle Inkster, the printer, gives a security interest in all of her equipment "now held or hereafter acquired" to Downtown Federal Bank in June 2006, and the bank properly perfects by filing at that time. In May 2008 she obtains an additional piece of equipment, the BindAll 2400, directly from its manufacturer, the Bindy Corporation. She buys the BindAll on credit, granting the Bindy Corporation a security interest in it at the time of purchase and to secure her future payments for the machine. Bindy files on the machine prior to making delivery to Inkster. In 2009, in need of cash, she sells the BindAll 2400 to another printer. Does either Downtown Federal or the Bindy Corporation have a security interest in the money she receives for the machine? If both have an interest, which firm has priority? Consult §9-324(a).

6. Sam of Sam's Autorama has granted a floating lien in all of his inventory to Samstown National Bank, which has properly perfected by filing in the appropriate place. He later agrees to buy a single highly unusual

customized VW minibus, said to have once been used by the Monkees on tour, from its current owner, Davy. Sam agrees to buy this "truly priceless" item for $23,000, but only if Davy will extend him credit. He gives Davy $1,000 in cash and signs a note for the rest. He also signs a security agreement and authorizes the filing of a financing statement prepared by Davy's lawyer. This lawyer makes sure that the statement is filed and that a proper notice under §9-324(b) is given to Samstown National Bank to assure that her client's interest in the VW will have priority over that of the bank. To Sam's surprise he quickly finds a buyer for the VW, one Mickey. Mickey agrees to pay with a $4,000 down payment, an installment note made payable to the order of Sam for $20,000, and a trade-in Sam values at $7,800. Can Samstown National Bank and/or Davy claim an interest in the cash, the note, or the trade-in, all now in Sam's possession? If both have a legitimate claim, who has priority as to each item? You will need to consult §9-324(b) just as Davy's lawyer did earlier.

Explanations

1a. Yes. Under §9-203(f), "The attachment of a security interest in collateral gives the secured party the rights to proceeds provided by Section 9-315. . . ." Subsection §9-315(a)(2), as we saw in the introduction, gives the secured party, Sarah, rights in any "identifiable proceeds" received by the debtor, Dexter, upon his sale or other disposition of the collateral. Note this is true whether or not Sarah also continues to have a security interest in the original collateral, the painting, or whether that interest was stripped away at the time of sale by operation of law or by her authorization.

1b. Yes, Sarah can claim an interest in the $24,000 insurance recovery as identifiable proceeds of this "disposition" of the painting. That insurance payments of this sort may be proceeds is directly provided for in the full definition of proceeds. You may recall that an insurance policy itself or money due under a policy generally cannot be collateral under Article 9, but when you look once again at §9-109(d)(8) you see that there is an express exception "with respect to proceeds." So Sarah can and does have an Article 9 security interest in the insurance recovery claimed by her as proceeds.

1c. Yes, Sarah can make a claim to a valid security interest in this new copy of the lithograph. The insurance company check constituted proceeds subject to her interest. It was disposed of or exchanged for this new piece of art, which is therefore proceeds of the proceeds. As we saw in the introduction to this chapter, proceeds of proceeds are themselves proceeds of the original collateral. And proceeds of those proceeds, which were proceeds of proceeds, would be proceeds as well. You get the point. Sarah has the right to any "identifiable proceeds" received by Dexter upon the sale or disposition of the original collateral, and it does not matter how many transformations the proceeds go through as long as they are still suitably "identifiable" or traceable back to the original stuff.

Similarly, if Dexter had used the insurance check to buy a statuette by a different artist, as long as the money trail remained clear, this statuette as proceeds of proceeds would be proceeds itself and hence subject under §9-315(a)(2) to Sarah's security interest as a matter of law.

As a practical matter, of course, it often quite quickly becomes difficult to follow the wandering trail of proceeds as values get mixed up and funds commingled. No reasonable secured party just sits back and waits around once he or she is aware of the disposition of the original collateral to see where the bouncing ball will land. There is also the possibility that what still technically qualifies as proceeds may fall into the hands of an innocent party who has given value for them in good faith and from whose hands the secured party might not be allowed to repossess. The secured party must monitor the situation carefully and get on the case quickly once a disposition of the collateral is made by the debtor. Still, the principle that proceeds of proceeds are proceeds is an important one to keep in mind and not merely a bit of wordplay.

2a. Selma certainly is flexible in how she's willing to make a sale. Credit Associates will indeed have a security interest in each and every type or form of payment she receives from a customer at the time of sale. Let us count the ways:

> She receives cash for some sales. This is "money," as you are no doubt aware.

> She receives checks, which are negotiable instruments under Article 3 of the U.C.C. and "instruments" for Article 9 purposes.

> She extends unsecured credit to some buyers, the result of which is her immediate holding of "accounts" as that term is defined in §9-102(a)(2).

> She asks for and receives a note, that is also an "instrument" under Article 9.

> Finally, her Retail Sales Installment Agreement, duly signed by the buyer, is a piece of chattel paper.

The cash and checks, as well as any bank accounts into which she might eventually deposit cash or checks she receives, will constitute "cash proceeds" under §9-102(a)(9). All other receivables — the accounts, the notes, and the chattel paper — will be "non cash proceeds."

2b. Yes. As money trickles in from the customers as they make good on their accounts, pay monies due under their notes, or make good on the obligations to pay evidenced by the chattel paper — these "collections" are themselves proceeds and hence subject to Credit Associates' interest. The cited part of the definition of proceeds expressly states that the term covers "whatever is collected on . . . collateral."

2c. Yes. The proceeds are now in the form of a deposit account, and Credit Associates now has an interest in that account. The problem for Credit Associates here would be if this account consisted not just of proceeds from the sale of goods on which it held an interest, the inventory, but also of other income of Selma's, her tax refund, birthday gifts, and so on. Credit Associates will in all likelihood have gotten Selma's agreement to open and maintain a separate and distinct "proceeds account" at a bank, if not of its choosing, at least one of which it approves. The security agreement will contain Selma's covenant to deposit all cash proceeds in this account and limitations on the purposes for which she can make withdrawals from the account. If Credit Associates has not thought to so protect itself, or if Selma gets sloppy and does not strictly observe her responsibilities with respect to the proceeds account, the lender can be put in quite a bind should Selma's business go sour and it has to repossess proceeds that have been mixed up and mingled with other funds, or perhaps even spirited away before it can get its hands on them. For two recent cases that demonstrate how difficult it can be for a secured party to successfully trace and "identify" specific cash proceeds, see *Van Diest Supply Co. v. Shelby County State Bank*, 425 F.3d 437, 59 U.C.C.2d 1089 (7th Cir. 2005), and *Metropolitan National Bank v. La Sher Oil Co.*, 81 Ark. App. 269, 101 S.W.3d 252, 51 U.C.C.2d 213 (2003).

Can you see why it would be wise for Credit Associates of this example, if possible, to not only require Selma's setting up of such a distinct bank account into which all cash proceeds should be quickly deposited, but also to take a security interest in this account, which it would then perfect by gaining "control" over the account and then regularly monitoring what funds come into and are dispersed from this account?

3a. No. This is just a review question of what we saw in the previous chapter. The buyer was presumably a buyer in the ordinary course and under §9-315(a)(1) would take free and clear of WBT's interest. That is all the more reason why the following parts regarding the proceeds element of the transaction are so important.

3b. Yes, WBT gets an interest automatically under §9-315(a)(2) in the proceeds of the sales. These are the trade-in that becomes part of his inventory, the check that is an instrument but also cash proceeds, and the note that is an instrument but of the noncash variety.

3c. The problem for WBT is not whether its security interest continues into these proceeds but whether this interest will be *perfected* over time. Attachment of the resulting interest is automatic because of the way §9-315(a)(2) is worded, but perfection is a much more complicated story under §9-315(c) and (d).

Note first of all that there is an automatic 20-day period of perfection on any proceeds. So WBT has at least some time to become aware of the sale and to take any additional action to protect itself if that turns out to be necessary. After the end of the 20 days, however, perfection in the proceeds lapses unless one of the criteria (d)(1) through (3) is met. Look first at (d)(3), which just says the obvious: If WBT separately perfects on any or all of the proceeds, then it is perfected, and its perfection is continuous from whatever earlier date there was first perfection on the original collateral. So under this provision if you take new steps to perfect on the proceeds you are quite reasonably perfected on them. The question is whether you do in fact need to take any additional actions at all to continue perfection into the proceeds.

Look now to (d)(2). It says that no new action need be taken to prevent the automatic perfection in proceeds from lapsing at the end of the 20-day period if "the proceeds are identifiable cash proceeds." If for some reason Tony still has the check for more than 20 days after the sale, or if by this time he has deposited it in a proper proceeds account, then the check or its value of $2,000 in the account will be "identifiable cash proceeds." Since WBT initially filed, and thereby perfected, on the inventory, it need do no more to keep its interest in the check or its value perfected.

What of the other noncash proceeds, the trade-in, and the note? By the end of the 20 days WBT will have to perfect on these unless it can fit within the provision (d)(1). This paragraph automatically continues the perfection in noncash proceeds beyond the 20-day limit if

A. a filed financing statement covers the original collateral;
B. the proceeds are collateral in which a security interest may be perfected by filing in the office in which the financing statement has been filed; and
C. the proceeds are not acquired with cash proceeds.

We will get to the curious condition of part (C) in a later part of this example. For the moment, focus on parts (A) and (B).

It is true that a filed financing statement naming WBT as the secured party and covering the inventory continues on file in the office appropriate for a filing covering inventory. The trade-in is another part of his inventory. Should WBT have to file on it, the place to file would be the same office where the original filing was made. Notice that this does not depend on the original filing's covering, in its description of the collateral, the trade-in. The fact that the *place* where a filing to perfect on it would go is the same *place* as the filing on the original collateral already resides is enough to satisfy this provision.

WBT would also have its interest in the note continuously perfected beyond the 20-day limit without its having to take any other action. Once again we check that there is a financing statement covering the original collateral, the new trailer in Tony's inventory, filed by WBT. So (d)(1)(A) is satisfied. True, that financing statement may not refer to "any instruments received as proceeds" or anything like that, but the criterion of (d)(1)(B) is still met. The office in which a secured party *may* file on instruments in Tony's possession if its intent is to perfect on those notes would be the same office where one would file on his inventory, in the state of Tony's location. So criterion (B) is met, not by WBT's making any additional filing on the notes, but because the *place* of the original filing covering the inventory *is the same place* where WBT would file on the notes if it chose to. We look at this type of situation — where the concern for the secured party is continued perfection on noncash proceeds of a type not identified as collateral in the financing statement — in more detail in the next part of the example.

Since, as we've just seen, WBT's security interest in the note taken as proceeds is automatically perfected for the 20-day period and without WBT's having to take any additional steps, we are tempted to take that as the end of the story. As you will be aware, however, if you have already studied Article 3 of the Code and its treatment of negotiable instruments, such pieces of paper can and do pass from hand to hand under a distinct set of rules that often give the transferee greater rights in the instrument than his or her transferor had. It's a long (and compelling) story, which is why I assume you will include in your studies of commercial law a thorough going-over of Article 3, if you have not already done so. For the moment, we see this principle reflected in §9-330(d), which provides that in general

> a purchaser of an instrument has priority over a security interest in the instrument perfected by a method other than possession if the purchaser gives value and takes possession of the instrument in good faith and without knowledge that the purchase violates the rights of a secured party.

The note now in Tony's possession is an instrument. Were he to sell it off to another party who took possession and who had no actual knowledge that this violated Tony's security agreement with WBT (as it almost certainly would if WBT has drafted the security agreement carefully), then that party would have taken the note free and clear of WBT's interest. As a practical matter, WBT is going to want to do what it can to prevent the note from getting into the hands of a purchaser who can claim the priority afforded by this subsection. It will want to establish a system under which it either gets possession of the notes that come into Tony's Trailer Town as quickly as possible, thus perfecting through possession, or somehow marks the notes with an indication (often referred to as a "legend") that they are subject to a security agreement that prohibits their transfer to other parties so that no one could purchase the notes without the kind of knowledge that would prevent it from being able to rely on §9-330(d) to claim priority over WBT.

One way of dealing with this problem — where the debtor's sales of collateral typically result in its taking as payment notes or chattel paper — that is not uncommon in an arrangement like the one between WBT and Tony is that the secured party, here WBT, will itself buy the notes or chattel paper taken as proceeds. As soon as Tony sells a trailer, he would be obligated to turn the note generated by the sale over to WBT. The bank would then either pay him in cash the present value of the note based on a calculated amount previously agreed to or, more likely, would credit this amount to that which Tony owes WBT — remember this whole thing started out and still depends on a loan made by WBT to Tony — thus lowering Tony's outstanding debt.

3d. The desk and chair taken by Tony certainly constitute proceeds, so WBT automatically has an interest in them. The issue is whether WBT needs to take some distinct new action to perfect on the furniture within 20 days of the sale of the trailer for its perfection on the furniture proceeds to continue beyond the 20-day automatic grace period of §9-315. It turns out that WBT will be perfected even if it does nothing else or file anything anywhere. Again, it's a question of reading §9-315(d) carefully. The original filing still in place presumably lists only inventory as the collateral. The proceeds with which we are now concerned would be classed as equipment. The filing now in place does not by its terms cover the proceeds, but that is *not* the test. If WBT were to file on the furniture, *where* would it file? Under §9-501(a)(2) the place for filing on equipment is the same place as one would file on inventory. That being so the perfection that WBT has in the furniture does not lapse at the end of the 20 days, *even though* they never file on the furniture and *even though* the financing statement they have in place does not purport to cover equipment.

Is there any sense to this rule working out this way, or is it just a bit of twisted business thrown in by the drafters to make sure we don't get too complacent in reading the Code? It seems to me that there is a rationale to be offered for WBT's not having to refile under this situation. Imagine that a third party took a real shining to the desk and chair in Tony's office and wanted to buy them. This third party would naturally want to make sure that Tony truly owned the pieces and that they were free of all encumbrances before he would be willing to buy them. (Remember he would not take free and clear as a buyer in the ordinary course of business as he is contemplating buying some of Tony's equipment, not anything out of Tony's inventory.) Our potential buyer cannot, however much he might want to, simply take Tony's word for the fact that the expensive desk and chair combination are his to sell and free of all liens. For all he knows Tony rents all his office furniture and is thinking of selling him a rental piece before he, Tony, leaves town without a trace. So our third party has to protect himself by making his own independent inquiries. First of all, needless to say, he checks the Article 9 filings in the place where he would expect to find any filings covering Tony's equipment. He will *not*, as a matter of fact, find any such filings covering equipment, but he will come across WBT's filing on the inventory. Our third party is now aware at least that Tony's inventory is subject to a security interest held by WBT. The next thing the potential buyer of the desk would check is whether Tony truly owned the piece. He would ask for some proof of ownership, something like a bill of sale from a store or a previous owner. However, Tony would be hard-pressed to produce any such proof, because he took the piece in partial exchange for one of the trailers he sold; or if he could it would presumably read something like, "in partial consideration of a trailer sold." Our wary and well-informed party now has to apply some logic. Tony's inventory is subject to a security interest. The desk apparently comes under the category of proceeds from the sale of inventory, and hence an interest in it would be claimed by the inventory financer WBT. The potential buyer has constructive notice, once he puts all the pieces together and assuming he knows the rule of §9-315(a)(2), that WBT can rightfully claim an interest in the furniture. The notice function of perfection being met, there is no reason to ask WBT to burden the filing system with yet one more piece of paper just to give further notice of what an intelligent third party can already make him or herself aware.

The example I have provided is, admittedly, a bit far-fetched. But at least it explains why §9-315(d)(1) is written as it is, calling only for the place of filing to be correct as to the proceeds and not that the filing itself in all its detail, including its description of the collateral, be so.

3e. In this situation WBT would lose its perfected status on the furniture unless it made a separate filing covering it within the 20-day period or amended its prior filing to include things such as the furniture under the description of the collateral. This situation calls for us to look at the last part of §9-315(d)(1), the criterion that, in addition to what we have already seen in parts (A) and (B), subsection (d)(1) provides for continued perfection on proceeds without the need to file on them only if "(C) the proceeds are not acquired with cash proceeds." The furniture under this set of facts was acquired with the check, a piece of cash proceeds, and hence it is not enough that the financing statement that one would file to cover it would be filed in the same place that WBT's existing filing currently resides. The description of the collateral in WBT's actual existing financing statement covers only inventory. Therefore this furniture does not come within the description. Normally if the stuff had not been acquired using cash proceeds this would not matter, but the furniture having been acquired with cash proceeds changes the rules of the game. WBT must amend its original filing quickly so that the collateral description covers the desk and chair in particular or equipment in general so as to fall within §9-315(d)(3).

What could possibly be the sense of this last twist? Imagine once again a third party just dying to get her hands on this particular desk and chair combination. She checks the filings on Tony and finds only that his inventory is encumbered by WBT's security interest. Worrying that the furniture might possibly be proceeds from a sale of one of his trailers, she asks to see some proof that it is not. In this situation Tony could easily satisfy her with a "Bill of Sale — Paid in Full" from the furniture store where he acquired the set. The potential purchaser has no notice that WBT would possibly be in a position to claim an interest in this furniture as proceeds of proceeds. The buyer buys paying full price and has every right to rely on the situation as she sees it that neither WBT nor anyone else for that matter claims any security interest in it through any route.

4. Both First and Second can claim an interest in the backhoe and the tractor as proceeds from the sale or exchange of the crane by Debtor. The only interesting question is what their relative priorities in these new pieces are, and the answer is not hard to come by. Under §9-322(b)(1), "For the purposes of subsection(a)(1), the time of filing or perfection as to a security interest in collateral is also the time of filing or perfection as to a security interest in proceeds." First was first in time as to the original collateral and hence it is first in time as to the proceeds. First has priority over Second, via §9-322(a)(1), in the proceeds just as it did in the original collateral.

5. Downtown Federal initially has an interest in the BindAll 2400 by virtue of its original security agreement and the after-acquired clause it contained. This interest attached and was perfected when Inkster

acquired the machine in May 2008. The Bindy Corporation takes a PMSI in the machine it sells to Inkster, attached and perfected in May 2008 as well. To review, even though under the general rule of §9-322(a)(1) Downtown Federal, having filed a full two years before Bindy either filed or perfected, would have had priority in the machine, Bindy (if it handled the sale and filing correctly) could have priority because of the exceptional treatment granted to the PMSI holder in §9-324(a).

Now, however, the BindAll 2400 is sold. Cash proceeds are generated. Since both Downtown Federal and Bindy had a security interest in the machine sold they also have a security interest in the proceeds thanks again to §9-315(a)(2). The question now is, who has priority over whom? We consult §9-324(a) to find that the party who takes a PMSI in collateral other than inventory has priority not only on the original collateral but, with one exception that need not concern us here, also a perfected security interest in its *identifiable proceeds* if the PMSI is perfected at the time the debtor received the original collateral or within 20 days thereafter. Assuming that Bindy met this requirement when it initially delivered the machine in 2008, it now has priority over Downtown Federal in any and all proceeds, and proceeds of whatever type, that Inkster gets when she sells it off.

6. Davy has priority in this VW, as it is inventory on Sam's lot, over the general inventory financer, Samstown National Bank, due to the special rule of §9-324(b). Does this priority carry over into the proceeds of Sam's sale to Mickey? The answer, it turns out, depends on what type of proceeds are concerned. Unlike subsection (a), which continues the PMSI holder's priority in collateral other than inventory over into all proceeds, subsection (b) says that the party who takes a PMSI gets special priority status in the proceeds in only two situations, if the proceeds are chattel paper or an instrument, "if so provided in Section 9-330," and if the proceeds are "identifiable cash proceeds . . . received on or before the delivery of the inventory to the buyer." Davy could not claim priority in the trade-in. He *could* claim priority in the note since it is an instrument constituting proceeds of the original collateral, at least as long as the note does not come into the hands of a purchaser who "gives value [for the instrument] and takes possession of the instrument in good faith and without knowledge that the purchase violates the rights of the secured party." Recall §9-330(d). Assuming Sam received the $4,000 down payment prior to his delivery of the van to Mickey, Davy also has priority in that money, as long as it remains "identifiable cash proceeds."

One of a whole series of problems dealing with who gets what when "cash proceeds," a particularly slippery type of collateral, are involved that we don't get into in these examples, but of which you should be aware, is that proceeds such as cash and checks are often quickly deposited into a bank account by the debtor. Recall that under revised Article 9 it is possible that such an account could, as a deposit account, be itself subject to a security interest held by some other party. What happens then? The governing rules are given in §9-327, to which you will have noted §9-324(a) and (b) both defer. You may want to follow up on this situation by looking at subsection (1) of §9-327 and the first paragraph of Comment 3 to that section. Or what if the debtor writes a check out of a dedicated proceeds account in violation of his agreement with the lender as to how that account can be used — say a check to repay a personal loan or a different creditor? The person who receives the check cashes it. Does the lender's security interest continue into the cash now in this person's hands? See §9-332.

Chattel Paper and Account Financing

INTRODUCTION

This chapter deals with the special problems presented where the debtor is some kind of retail establishment — for example, a store or a car dealership — and the proceeds it receives when it sells merchandise out of its inventory are other than identifiable cash proceeds. Many retailers must, if they are to make their sales, extend some measure of credit to buyers of expensive or even moderately priced items.

Assume to start that the retailer has entered into a loan agreement with either a bank, a finance company, or even with the supplier of its principal product (as will often be the case, for instance, with a car dealership) putting up as collateral "all inventory now held or hereafter acquired." As individual pieces are sold out of the retailer's inventory to individual customers, the inventory financer's security interest in each piece falls away under the rule of §9-320(a), the result of another sale by the retailer to a buyer in the ordinary course of its business. We allow that buyer and his or her purchase to leave our diagram, which now trims down to what we see in the figure on the following page.

The inventory financer, of course, gains by virtue of §9-315(a)(2) an interest in the proceeds of the sales made by the debtor.

That portion of the proceeds that are cash proceeds should, under the retailer's basic contract with the inventory financer, be used in large measure to pay down the debt owed to that financer or to purchase new items of inventory so that the total inventory collateral in which the financer has an interest remains at about the same level as before the sale. Consider, however, that portion of the proceeds that is not cash or the equivalent of a check that can be immediately turned into cash. The debtor may tend to group all of the amounts it is owed by those customers to whom it sells on credit under the collective term "accounts receivable." We can go further than this, however, and classify what the retailer receives upon making a credit sale into three distinct types of Article 9 collateral:

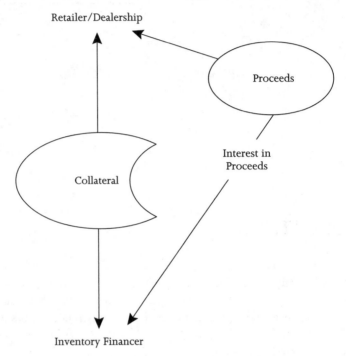

(i)   accounts — under §9-102(a)(2) those rights to payment for goods sold that are *not evidenced by chattel paper or an instrument*

(ii)   chattel paper — as defined in §9-102(a)(11), which could take the form of a Retail Sales Installment Agreement with or without the buyer's payment obligation being evidenced by an accompanying note made part of the paper

(iii)   instruments — under §9-102(a)(47) negotiable instruments of the type governed by Article 3 of the U.C.C., in particular notes *not made a part of chattel paper.*

All three of these forms of proceeds may be happily welcomed into the hands of the selling retailer or dealership, but some bad news comes with the good. The good news is that each represents money owed the seller that should eventually make its way into the seller's coffers. The bad news is that the money is not there yet. It is to be paid in the future. And then, of course, there are all the risks normally associated with selling on credit. In particular the credit buyer may for one reason or another not pay the full amount actually due on his account or his note or his installment payment agreement. The buyer may not even pay a penny of what he or she owes. It has been known to happen.

From the retailer's standpoint there can be a particular problem with the fact that these "accounts receivable" are just that — receivable in the future, not cash in hand. True, most individuals would prefer having actual cash money in their pockets over the promise of cash to flow in over time. For the retailer, however, this can cause a unique difficulty; he or she has given up pieces of inventory in the present for these rights to payment sometime in the future. Inventory has been depleted and the retailer's shelves or the dealer's lot needs to be restocked. Where is the seller going to get the money to buy more stuff that he or she can then sell and in so doing turn into still more accounts receivable? The wheels of commerce have to keep turning and turning; they cannot take a break waiting for money to trickle in over the next weeks, months, or years.

You can appreciate this situation if you consider, for example, the retailer who does a substantial proportion of her business during the end-of-year holiday season and on terms of the "You Pay Nothing Until March" variety. Come the beginning of January and her storeroom is low on just the products that she will, after all, want to continue selling in her "After Christmas" and, later, "Valentine's Day Extra Special" sales. Where is the money going to come from for her to restock?

The retailer does of course have something valuable on hand, her whole pile of accounts receivable in whatever form. It is natural for her, and a perfectly reasonable business exercise, to either sell off these receivables or to use them in turn as collateral for a loan that will tide her over until the amounts owed by her end-of-year buyers start flowing in.

The practice of a retailer's or dealership's selling off or using as collateral its accounts receivable is in fact a very common one in the commercial world. It predated the adoption of Article 9, and that article was in turn drafted with an eye to the problems that could come up under this system of so-called receivables financing. Note in fact, as we saw from the very first chapter and our reading of §9-109(a)(3), that "the sale of accounts, chattel paper, payment intangibles, or promissory notes" and not just their subjugation to a security interest falls directly within the defined scope of Article 9.

We had a look at what happens when the proceeds are in the form of a negotiable instrument not integrated into and made part of chattel paper in Example 3c of the last chapter. In particular we looked at §9-330(d), which provides that in general a purchaser of an instrument — who could be either an outright buyer or someone taking a security interest in the instrument by dint of the broad definition of purchaser in Article 1 — stands to take priority over the inventory financer claiming an interest in the instrument as proceeds "if the purchaser gives value and takes possession of the instrument in good faith and without knowledge that the purchase violates the rights of the secured party." In this chapter we look at some trickier matters involving the sale or subjection to a security interest where the proceeds consist of accounts or chattel paper.

TAKING AN INTEREST IN ACCOUNTS OR CHATTEL PAPER

When the retailer's accounts receivable are in the form of accounts or chattel paper, it has the same two options that it had with pure instruments to turn these assets — valuable in themselves but not the same as cash on hand with which it can pay its current debts or restock its inventory — into something of more immediate value. The retailer can either sell its accounts and chattel paper outright to someone other than the inventory financer or it can arrange for a loan from this distinct entity in which it puts up the accounts and chattel paper as collateral. While these two transactions, the outright sale and the grant of a security interest in accounts and chattel paper, will function somewhat differently in the economic or business sense, they are alike in one very important respect for our purposes. Recall that the *sale* of accounts or chattel paper comes within the scope of Article 9, under §9-109(a)(3), just as would a grant of a security interest in such collateral.*

Assume that the retailer, in order to better its present cash position, does either sell its accounts and chattel paper or make use of them as collateral, selling them to or borrowing from a distinct entity that we will refer to as the "Accounts Receivable Financer." The diagram with which we started out this chapter can now be elaborated upon. Those accounts and pieces of chattel paper that were previously identified solely as proceeds in the hands of the retailer, subject to the inventory financer's security interest in them as proceeds, now have a second party claiming an interest, either as an owner or as a secured party under a distinct security agreement, in them.

---

* To remind yourself of how the sale versus the use as collateral of accounts and chattel paper will differ in terms of their financial consequences, if not in their treatment under Article 9 for purposes of priority and the like, you may want to review Example 7 of Chapter 1 and the explanation thereto.

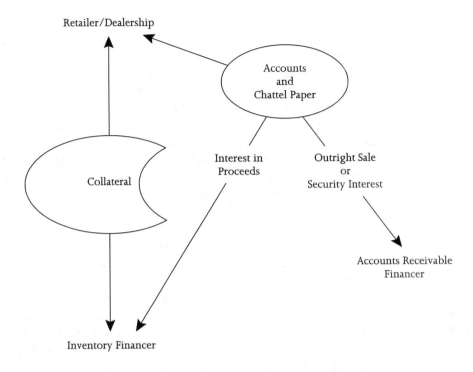

This diagram not so subtly sets up the basic conflict with which we now have to contend. Two parties are claiming an interest in the same valuable goods, here the accounts or chattel paper generated by the retailer's business. As must always be the case when two self-interested parties — there is no reason to suspect uncommon greed here, just a healthy interest in getting what one is due — are contending over the same assets, the issue is one of priority: If the two are not going to be made to share equally, and we know that is definitely not the way of the world when it comes to Article 9, whose interest has priority over the other's? As we will see in the examples to follow, when the stuff at issue is correctly classified as accounts, the precepts of priority are as we have already experienced them. No special rules apply. Dealings in chattel paper were, however, prior to the adoption of Article 9 a different and a more complex story, and the drafters of the article thought it important not to undercut commercial practice and expectations and so kept that story alive. Their rendition of the special rules affecting those who deal in chattel paper is given, if not in a particularly stirring narrative form, in §9-330 (a) through (c), which you should look over now before you venture into the examples.

Examples

1. Dr. Tooth the dentist is, of course, not a retailer, but his practice of polishing and grinding his patients' teeth does generate accounts, the "right to payment of a monetary obligation for . . . services rendered" not evidenced by an instrument or chattel paper, as he is willing to do dental work on the understanding that he will be later paid for his services. A visit to the dentist and a consideration of his accounts will help set the stage for what is to follow. Imagine that Tooth, when he set up his dental practice, was able to obtain a long-term loan from the Shelbyville Bank and Trust. He offers as security for the loan the equipment in his office, but the bank insists that they also include in the covered collateral "all accounts now held or hereafter generated in respect to the debtor's dental practice." Tooth signs a security agreement including this language in the description of the collateral, and the bank files a financing statement in the correct place that describes the collateral as "all equipment and accounts of debtor, now held or hereafter acquired." A couple of years later the good dentist borrows some money from a local credit union in order to partially remodel his waiting room. He signs a security agreement giving the bank a security interest in "all accounts now held or hereafter acquired" by him. The credit union files a proper financing statement covering these accounts in the appropriate place. Which lender, the Shelbyville Bank or the credit union, has priority of interest in the accounts generated by Dr. Tooth's business?

2. Laura runs a business called Laura's Lawn Supply, from which she sells seeds, fertilizer, and the like, and lawnmowers. She is willing to make sales below a certain amount on a "pay within 30 days basis." The customer walks out of the store with his or her purchase (lawn supplies and smaller hand or gas-powered mowers) having signed only a bill of sale and an agreement to pay the price within 30 days from the date of sale. When Laura sells the larger riding mowers, however, she gets the purchaser to make a down payment and to sign a Retail Sales Installment Contract for the remainder of the price. This contract calls for the purchaser to make installment payments, calculated to include a reasonable amount of interest, over the next 12 months, and also grants Laura a security interest in the item being sold to secure payment of the price. In 2006, Laura takes out a small business loan from the Shelbyville Bank and Trust, granting that bank a security interest in among other things "all accounts and chattel paper now held or hereafter acquired" by her. The bank files a financing statement covering the accounts and chattel paper in the appropriate place. Later, in 2007, when Laura's business is going through a rough period, she obtains a short-term loan from Friendly Factors Inc., to which she also grants an interest in her accounts and

chattel paper. Friendly Factors files a financing statement covering this collateral in the appropriate place.

a. Under this scenario, which lender, the Shelbyville Bank or Friendly Factors, will have priority over the accounts and chattel paper?

b. Suppose instead that Friendly Factors had taken possession of the various Retail Sales Installment Agreements signed by Laura's customers. Does this change your analysis of the situation?

c. Suppose instead that, rather than simply lending on the Retail Sales Installment Agreements, Friendly Factors had bought them outright, taken possession of the agreements, and notified the individual customers that they should make their remaining monthly payments directly to them, Friendly Factors. Does Friendly Factors have anything to fear from Shelbyville Bank and Trust because of its earlier filing of a financing statement covering the chattel paper?

d. Now, just to make things really interesting, consider the following scenario: Friendly Factors buys the installment agreements but does not itself want to have to worry about collecting from the individual customers. It files a financing statement covering the chattel paper in the appropriate place, but it leaves the individual agreements in Laura's possession. Later, when Laura finds her business is not generating the cash she needs to meet even her basic expenses, Laura sells some of these same installment agreements to Second Factors of Springfield, which is also in the business of buying and lending on retailers' accounts and chattel paper. Second Factors takes possession of the agreements. Later, when Laura files a petition in bankruptcy, which party — Friendly Factors or Second Factors — will have priority of interest in the agreements now in the possession of Second Factors?

3. Selma of Selma's Appliance City obtains a loan from Wellington Bank & Trust (WBT), granting the bank a security interest in "all inventory, accounts, or chattel paper now held by Selma or hereafter acquired by her." WBT files an effective financing statement covering this collateral in the appropriate place. Under the terms of the loan, Selma has made available to her a line of credit on which she may call as she sees fit up to an amount determined as "50% of the cost of all her saleable inventory plus 80% of the amount of all receivables of whatever form held by her and not in default more than 30 days." When Selma sells smaller items on credit she asks her customers to sign only a simple agreement in which they promise to pay for their purchases 30 days after receipt. When larger items, such as major household appliances, are involved, Selma has the customers sign copies of her Retail Sales Installment Agreement, under which the customer agrees to make installment payments as specified and which grants to Selma a security

interest in the item or items being purchased to secure their payment of the installments as due. As part of her agreement with WBT, Selma is obligated to stamp each Installment Agreement she has signed by a customer with an indication that it is, "Subject to an Interest Granted to Wellington Bank and Trust." When Selma's business is going through a slow period she finds herself in need of more funds to pay her rent and meet her payroll. She takes a number of the Retail Installment Sales Agreements that she has been keeping in her filing cabinet to an office of Friendly Factors, which is willing to pay her $40,000 in exchange for these agreements. When Friendly Factors buys these agreements from Selma, does it take them free from or subject to WBT's interest in them?

4. Tony of Tony's Trailer Town is an authorized dealer in Tyro brand trailers, manufactured by the Tyro Corporation. He buys his stock of inventory directly from that corporation, granting it a security interest in "all inventory now held or hereafter acquired." Tyro files an effective financing statement covering this collateral in the appropriate place. Tony sells a new mobile home to a customer, Leo, in exchange for which he takes a down payment of $2,000 along with a promissory note for the remainder of the purchase price signed by Leo and payable to Tony. Tony also gets Leo to sign a security agreement granting him a security interest in the mobile home being sold securing payment on the note. Tony then attaches this security agreement to the note and sells the two as a package to Friendly Factors. He endorses the note to Friendly Factors and executes an assignment of his security interest to the firm as well. All this paper he turns over to Friendly Factors in exchange for a check representing a suitably discounted value for the secured note. Should Tony go into bankruptcy, which party, Tyro or Friendly Factors, has priority of interest in the note and accompanying security interest both signed by Leo?

Explanations

1. The bank will have priority. It first filed on the accounts as a means of perfection. Indeed, this is the only means of perfecting on accounts, as they are intangibles and not susceptible to perfection through possession by the secured party. The credit union comes along and takes a perfectly valid security interest in the same accounts and also files on them, but its filing follows and will always follow (if the bank is careful to file continuations statements as needed) that of the bank. So the bank's interest will have priority over that of the credit union's. The credit union, of course, could have avoided this grief, if grief it be, by checking for any filing under Dr. Tooth's name in the correct filing office before it made this loan based on the accounts as collateral.

There's nothing particularly novel in this tale of Dr. Tooth and his accounts. I just wanted the chance to make certain we are clear that accounts as collateral are subject to the Article 9's general first-in-time as first-in-right principle, with which we are now familiar, no different from most other forms of collateral. We will soon have a chance to contrast this with the special treatment given chattel paper. One difference will be that chattel paper, unlike accounts, may be perfected upon either by filing or by the secured party's taking of possession. So that complicates things right away. More interesting still is the fact that the party who takes possession of chattel paper in certain defined circumstances will have an opportunity to gain priority over one who has filed earlier or otherwise gained perfection on chattel paper as proceeds as a matter of law. This eligibility of the party taking chattel paper to gain a kind of super-priority — what you will sometimes hear spoken of colloquially as "special chattel paper treatment" — is the subject of the examples that follow.

2a. The bank, which filed first on both the accounts and the Installment Sales Contracts, which constitute tangible chattel paper, has priority over both types of collateral. Section 9-330, to which we turn in the next part of this example, gives potential superpriority and works its special magic on behalf of the purchaser of chattel paper only when that purchaser actually takes possession of such tangible chattel paper. Possession for this purpose is, let it be emphasized, true possession, not just a token or a symbolic gesture. See, for instance, In re New Mexico Ice Machine Co., Inc., 32 U.C.C. 1647, 1981 Bankr. LEXIS 5207 (D.N.M. 1981), holding that a secured party had not taken possession through obtaining copies of chattel paper when the originals remained in a prior secured party's hands.

2b. The story with respect to the accounts is no different. The bank's filing precedes that of the factor and so it has priority in the accounts. With respect to the chattel paper, however, we now have to consider §9-330(b):

> A purchaser of chattel paper has priority over a security interest in the chattel paper which is claimed other than merely as proceeds of inventory subject to a security interest [which is not the case here, as Friendly Factors is not claiming an interest in the chattel paper "merely as proceeds" but as original collateral] if the purchaser gives new value and takes possession of the chattel paper . . . in good faith, in the ordinary course of the purchaser's business, and without knowledge that the purchase violates the rights of the secured party.

We have to check whether each of the various criteria has been met by Friendly Factors so that it can take advantage of this provision. First of all, is Friendly Factors a "purchaser" of the chattel paper? Yes. Recall the broad definitions of "purchase" and "purchaser" in Article 1. Someone who takes a security interest in property is a purchaser under the Code. Did Friendly Factors give "new value"? Yes. See §9-102(a)(57). If Friendly Factors actually gave "new" money to Laura when it made the loan (and did not for instance simply use it to pay off another loan which Laura had taken out earlier) then it gave new value. New money came into Laura's business through the transaction. Did the factor take possession? Yes, fortunately (and cleverly) for it, it did. Was Friendly Factors acting in good faith in purchasing the chattel paper as it did? Good faith, as defined in §9-102(a)(43), will always be dependent on the facts of the particular case, but there is nothing in this scenario, at least if Friendly Factors paid at a reasonable market rate for this type of consumer paper, to suggest that it was acting other than in good faith.

Did Friendly Factors give new value and take possession "in the ordinary course of [its] business?" Again the answer is yes. This would always be a question of fact, of course, but we are assuming that Friendly Factors is just the type of commercial actor that typically and in the ordinary course of its business either buys or takes as collateral chattel paper. That's what makes it a "factor" in reality and not just in name.

Lastly we ask whether the factor acted in taking the chattel paper "without knowledge that the purchase violates the rights of the secured party." You may have some doubt about this. After all, the bank does have a security interest in the paper, and a financing statement giving public notice of this interest is on file in the proper place. The language of §9-330(b), however, makes the test whether the purchaser had "knowledge" and not mere "notice." Looking to §1-201(25) or §1R-202(b), we see that a party has "knowledge" of a fact only when it has *actual* knowledge of it. On behalf of the bank you might want to argue that the factor, before it lent on this collateral, had an obligation to check the relevant U.C.C. filing records where it would have found the bank's financing statement and hence gained "actual knowledge" of the bank's interest. Comment 6 to §9-330, however, tells us that this argument on the bank's behalf should not be successful.

> In contrast to a junior secured party in accounts, who may be required in some special circumstances to undertake a search under the "good faith" requirement, . . . , a purchaser of chattel paper under this section is not required as a matter of good faith to make a search in order to determine the existence of prior security interests.

Furthermore, even if the factor had made a search of the records and thus become aware of the bank's filing, it would not from this alone be barred from relying on §9-330(b). As the comment continues:

> There may be circumstances where the purchaser undertakes a search nevertheless [that is, even though it is not required to do so to demonstrate good faith] either on its own volition or because other considerations

make it advisable to do so, e.g., where the purchaser is also purchasing accounts. Without more, a purchaser of chattel paper who has seen a financing statement covering the chattel paper or who knows that the chattel paper is encumbered with a security interest does not have knowledge that its purchase *violates* the secured party's rights.

As the comment goes on to suggest, if the bank truly wants to insure that no purchaser can take possession of the chattel paper free of its interest, the customary method is for the bank to insist that each piece of chattel paper, as soon as it is received by Laura, immediately be "legended" with a clear indication on the paper itself that it is subject to the bank's interest and that purchase by another would violate the bank's interest. This would prevent anyone else, such as Friendly Factors, from coming into possession without the kind of knowledge that would give it the advantage of §9-330(b).

2c. No. Recall that under §9-109(a)(3) a sale of chattel paper is governed by Article 9. Here Friendly Factors has actually bought the chattel paper, and that certainly qualifies as a "purchase" for purposes of the Code and §9-330. The economics of the transaction between Laura and Friendly Factors are different. When in (b) Factors makes a loan, Laura gets a present sum of cash and is responsible for making whatever payments she has promised Factors eventually to pay off the loan. The chattel paper serves as collateral just as we have become used to thinking of collateral; whatever its ultimate value, given exactly how much the individual customers end up paying or failing to pay on their individual installment contracts is a risk that Laura still carries. In the sale of chattel paper, as in this part of the example, Laura gets her sum of money as payment and from then on the risk that it will generate a greater or lesser flow of cash as the customers make good or fall behind on their promised payments has been transferred to Friendly Factors.

The Article 9 analysis, and in particular the workings of §9-330(b), remains the same, however. Friendly Factors is a purchaser giving new value and taking possession of the chattel paper in the ordinary course of its business. Its interest, here an ownership interest and not "just" a security interest, will prevail over that of Shelbyville Bank and Trust as long as it took the paper without knowledge that its taking of the specific paper was in violation of the secured party's rights. And as above, the factor in buying in the ordinary course of its business should not be held to have any duty to search the Article 9 records or make other inquiries which might reveal the bank's security interest.

2d. It might strike you as strange that Friendly Factors would actually buy the chattel paper and yet leave it in the hands of Laura the seller; this is, however, an arrangement that is apparently not unheard of in the highly specialized world of those dealing with chattel paper. Note that the special chattel paper treatment granted in §9-330 is reserved for those who buy or loan on this type of collateral "in the ordinary course" of their businesses. Dealing in chattel paper is not for the novice or the amateur.

Friendly Factors here may be a professional, but it has apparently been willing to take a significant risk by leaving the chattel paper in the hands of the seller in such a way that she can effectively, even if no doubt in breach of her agreement with Friendly Factors, sell some part of what she has already sold once again to another party who will be able to claim the advantage of §9-330(b). You can check that Second Factors meets all the criteria of that subpart. It therefore has priority over the "security interest" of Friendly Factors, which was perfected only by filing. You might want to make the argument on behalf of Friendly Factors that its interest was something more than a "security interest," but look at the definition of §1-201(37) or §1R-201(b)(35), the second sentence of which states, "The term also includes any interest of . . . a buyer of accounts [or] chattel paper that is subject to Article 9." So there goes that argument.

So if Laura goes bankrupt, Second wins out over Friendly even though Friendly was first. Is there any way Friendly Factors could have saved itself from this rude shock other than by its actually taking physical possession of the installment contracts and holding on for dear life? Remember, the buyer or lender on chattel paper that does not want to take possession can always protect its interest by stamping or noting on the paper the fact that it has been assigned to it. A well-placed notation — placed directly on the paper itself — will serve to give notice that the *specific paper* is indeed subject to the rights of another, which rights would be violated by further transfer. That renders §9-330(a) and (b) of no help to those who take later on.

3. If Selma has placed the appropriate notation on each of these Installment Sales Agreement forms, as she was bound to do under her arrangement with WBT, then Friendly Factors will not be able to make an argument under §9-330 that it bought this chattel paper free and clear of WBT's interest. If, by any chance, Selma has "neglected" to stamp the necessary legend on the paper she sells to Friendly Factors, then that firm should be able to establish that it took the paper free and clear of WBT's interest. The important issue here is whether this case is governed by subsection (a) or (b) of §9-330. Subsection (a) covers those cases where the purchasers of chattel paper are contesting priority with someone having an interest

"which is claimed merely as proceeds of inventory subject to a security interest." Subsection (b) covers all other situations.

The question then becomes whether the interest here being claimed by WBT in the chattel paper, which is after all generated by Selma through her sale of inventory, is an interest claimed "*merely as proceeds*," whatever is meant by that phrase as used in §9-330(a). The answer will turn out to be that WBT's interest is not *merely* this, and hence Friendly Factors will not take free and clear of WBT's interest only if it has actual knowledge that it is taking the paper in violation of that interest under the test of §9-330(b), which we have previously examined. The issue of what exactly the term "merely as proceeds" means in this subpart is certainly not clear from the context, nor is there any reason to think it would be at all obvious to anyone not familiar with the ways in which chattel paper is dealt with by those comfortable in trading in such stuff in the ordinary course of their business. Read the first paragraph of Comment 3. The Permanent Editorial Board for the U.C.C., in its Commentary No. 8, which you should have available to you in an appendix to your copy of the Code, deals with this as its Issue I. The Commentary is lengthy, but it boils down to a distinction to be made — one that we will make in the course of this and the following example — between two types of inventory secured financing. The Commentary decides to denote these "type A" and "type B," but the letters are not what is significant. As it turns out, I've decided to deal first with Selma and her appliance store — an example of what the Commentary designates as "type B" inventory financing. As you will see when you look at the Commentary, I have actually written into the contract between WBT and Selma just the type of "availability loan" provision that the Board uses as exemplary of this situation.

The crux of the matter is that in a situation such as ours here, the Board's type B financing, the lender takes an interest in the receivables, including all chattel paper generated by the business as *original* collateral and not just as proceeds. That is, it makes its lending decision based not only on the value of the inventory but on the distinct and separately accounted for value of the receivables Selma has in her store of goodies at any given time. You can see that from the way the maximum amount that she can have outstanding on her loan at any one time is calculated. A diagram representing the situation we have here would not mirror that of the figure that appears on page 367, where the "Collateral" and the "Accounts and Chattel Paper" were viewed as distinct and detached pools of assets, with the Inventory Financer's interest in the latter an interest in proceeds merely, but look more like the following:

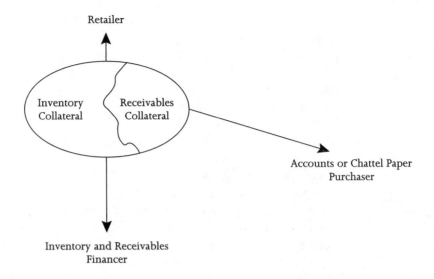

Here the bank is lending on a pool of assets made up in varying proportions of inventory and receivables. Right before the Christmas rush the amount of inventory might easily predominate. After the frantic holiday season ends, Selma might have little left on her shelves and in her storeroom, but she would have a pile of accounts and chattel paper to her credit. The bank would not think of dealing with each sale of a toaster or even a stereo system as a distinct event of which it would have to take notice. What matters is that the total value of the collateral pool, as measured by the key formula set forth in its agreement with Selma, stays at a certain level. In this "type B" inventory financing, any party who purchases chattel paper from the debtor will not be able to rely on §9-330(a), but will find itself subject to the rules as laid down in subsection (b). We can contrast this to the treatment of what the Commentary refers to as "type A" inventory financing as we will see it in operation in the following example.

4.   Friendly Factors will have priority over Tyro because this is a case where that inventory financer, which, as will often be true of such dealerships, is also the supplier of the inventory, will be claiming an interest in a particular piece or particular pieces of chattel paper generated by Tony's sales "merely as proceeds of inventory." Look again to the P.E.B. Commentary No. 8, but now to its discussion of what it refers to as "type A" inventory financing. This is the situation, as the Commentary states, involving the debtor's selling of "automobiles and other large pieces of equipment in which the financing is primarily item by item (each item of inventory secures a precise amount loaned against that item . . .), with a requirement that the associated inventory debt be paid off when

the item is sold, or after a maximum period (usually 90 days subject to renewal), whichever first occurs." As the Commentary then goes on to state, "the Board believes that a type A inventory financer will frequently have only a 'mere proceeds interest' in the chattel paper which is generated when items of inventory subject to its security interest are sold."

The arrangement is for Tyro to deliver individual trailers to Tony's on credit, making it possible for his dealership to have a decent supply and variety of Tyro products on hand. Each trailer delivered will be individually accounted for, its serial number and other pertinent information recorded, on both Tony's and Tyro's books. Tony will be under an obligation when any individual trailer is sold to report as much to Tyro and to use the proceeds of the sale to pay down the debt it owes to the supplier on account of that one item of inventory (while still having enough left over to cover Tony's overhead and allow for a little profit as well, of course).

Tony may be pulling a fast one when he sells the trailer at market value to Leo, keeps the chattel paper for himself, fails to legend it, and then sells that to another, Friendly Factors, for cash. The factor according to the rule of §9-330(a) does not have to worry whether Tony is acting within his rights in selling the chattel paper as he does, and certainly doesn't have to worry whether Tony uses the cash he is paid for the chattel paper to pay his debt to Tyro. It is that firm, the Tyro Corporation, which in entering into this kind of relationship has to be aware of the risk it is taking. It will have to regularly monitor the situation as it stands at Tony's. Are the trailers that it, Tyro, has recorded as delivering to Tony and that it has no notice of Tony's having yet sold truly still on the lot? If not, something is amiss. If Tony reports a trailer sold, he should at the same time be able to account to Tyro for the proceeds he has received, be they in the form of cash, a trade-in, or, as we have here, chattel paper. If the proceeds are not all in order, and if Tony's pay-down of its debt to Tyro is not properly forthcoming, then again something is not right and Tyro has to be in a position to swing into action. It cannot rest secure merely in the knowledge that Tony has signed a valid security agreement and that it has itself filed a proper financing statement in the correct place. Each trailer must be in place on Tony's lot, and any purported proceeds properly accounted for.

Priorities in Investment Property and Deposit Accounts

INTRODUCTION

We have already seen how the Article 9 rules regarding attachment and perfection in that type of collateral now denoted "investment property" were given a basic overhaul in 1994 in conjunction with the introduction of an entirely new version of Article 8 dealing with Investment Securities. Along with the new Article 8, the 1994 upgrade added provisions to Article 9 to deal with the issues of attachment, perfection, and priority of security interests in investment property. The rules established by these provisions were carried forward with only some modification into the most recent revision of Article 9. We dealt with attachment and perfection — and in particular the possibility of perfecting on such collateral by means of control, as set forth in §9-106 — in Chapter 11. We now follow up by considering the distinct rules established for determining the priority of interests in this class of collateral. Fortunately, the rules are not hidden anywhere. See §9-328. You will be needing various parts of this section, as well as what you learned in Chapter 11 about how a party takes control of a security or a securities account, to work through the initial examples of this chapter.

We also saw in Chapter 11 that it is now possible, under newly Revised Article 9, for a party to take and perfect a security interest in a deposit account as just another form of Article 9 collateral. Recall, however, that the deposit account is unique in that perfection on such an item can be perfected only by control. There still remains, however, the potential for a priority conflict since it is possible, as we now know, for someone to be claiming an interest in the money in a deposit account as proceeds of some other collateral in which it had an initial interest. We'll look at this problem, as governed by §9-327, in the final example of this chapter.

The priority rules relating to investment property and deposit accounts are unusual not just because they pop up in distinct sections of Article 9. They are based upon some ideas very different from anything we have dealt with up until this point. Priority under Article 9 as a general matter depends upon the concept of perfection, and perfection for one purpose, being good as against the bankruptcy trustee, has been good for its other purpose, defeating later purchasers or those who took securities interests later in time, as well. As to perfection in investment property, as we are soon to see, these two functions have to be seen as distinct. If all the secured party cares about is having its interest still valuable should a bankruptcy occur, we may question the wisdom of such a laid-back approach, but at least the secured party can have its way with little fuss. If survival into bankruptcy is the interest taker's sole objective, then it will be sufficient for it to perfect by filing. If, however, the secured party is concerned with getting the full benefit of its security interest and as much protection of it as the Code will allow, filing will not be a reasonable alternative.

This leads us to the more fundamental difference that we'll see in the rules of §§9-327 and 9-328. The general rules of Article 9 rely principally on the timing of the parties' actions in determining who has priority over whom. Article 9 priority, as we have been studying, has been, with a few carefully carved out exceptions for the PMSI, a matter of first-in-time being first-in-right. With respect to investment property and deposit accounts the rules introduce the notion that the manner of perfection, not the timing, is what counts. Note the following from Comment 2 to §9-328:

> Paragraph (1) states the most important general rule — that a secured party who gains control has priority over a secured party who does not obtain control.

In Comment 3, the point is driven home.

> The control priority rule does not turn on either temporal sequence or awareness of conflicting security interests. Rather, it is a structural rule, based on the principle that a lender should be able to rely on the collateral without question if the lender has taken the necessary steps to assure itself that it is in a position where it can foreclose on the collateral without further action by the debtor. . . . A secured party who is unwilling to run the risk that the debtor has granted or will grant a conflicting control security interest should not make a loan without obtaining control of the collateral.

As should be obvious from the above, if you yourself don't feel in control of the concept of "control" as a means of perfecting on investment property, then you should brush up on §9-106 and the crucial §8-106 to which it refers before moving on.

Examples

1. Prudence Moneybucks decides to go into business producing and marketing one of her favorite recipes (which other members of the family have always assured her is unlike anything they have ever tasted) under the name Prudence's Power Pudding. She approaches Wellington Bank & Trust and discusses with a loan officer her desire to take out a sizable personal loan from the bank in order to engage in this new business venture. She offers to put up as collateral the following:

   (i) Twenty shares in a small family-run corporation (Moneybucks Industries, Incorporated) represented by a share certificate bearing her name as owner of the shares, which she keeps in a desk drawer at home;

   (ii) Her interest in a mutual fund (The Rocksolid Investment Trust) from which she receives statements once a month; and

   (iii) An account she keeps with the stockbrokerage firm of James, Steven, Rogers & Company ("JSR & Co.").

   The bank agrees to grant the loan and before it hands over the check has her sign both a security agreement and authorize a financing statement listing each of the pieces of collateral. The bank files this financing statement in the appropriate place. Unfortunately, the public is not as enamored of the pudding as Prudence had expected and the venture is a decided failure. Prudence is forced to declare bankruptcy.

   a. Is Wellington Bank & Trust's interest in the various pieces of collateral going to be good against the bankruptcy trustee?

   b. Assume that in addition Prudence had, prior to declaring bankruptcy, in an effort to shore up her business, borrowed more money, but now from DeJohn Financial Associates. DeJohn also takes a security interest in all of Prudence's investments and files its own financing statement in the correct place. DeJohn's filing is made after Wellington's. In the bankruptcy proceedings, will DeJohn's interest be effective against the bankruptcy trustee? If you determine that both Wellington Bank & Trust's and DeJohn Financial Associates' interests will survive into the bankruptcy, which of the two will have priority in the collateral?

2. Assume as in the previous question that Prudence gives a security interest to Wellington Bank & Trust in collateral including her shares in Moneybucks Industries, Incorporated, and that the bank perfects by a filing. When she realizes that she will need more money to properly market her product, she is able to get a loan from a friend, Frank. As security she hands over to Frank the certificate (which, recall, she has been keeping in

the drawer of her desk) representing her interest as a shareholder in Moneybucks Industries, Incorporated, which she endorses in blank.

    a. When Prudence declares bankruptcy, will Frank's interest in the Moneybucks Industries shares continue to be effective? How will it rank relative to any interest that the Wellington bank may claim in the same shares?

    b. Would it make any difference to your answer if when Prudence gave Frank the share certificate she had failed to endorse it? See §9-328(5).

3. Continue to assume that the Wellington bank has taken an interest in and filed to perfect on all the collateral Prudence had to offer in Example 1, but add the fact that Prudence then took out a second loan—from Ryerson Bank of New Haven. This bank gets Prudence's agreement along with that of The Rocksolid Investment Trust that the mutual fund will recognize any purchase or sale instructions with respect to Prudence's interest in the fund not only from her but also from a person identified in the agreement as authorized to act on behalf of the Ryerson Bank as a party holding a security interest in Prudence's account. Between the two creditors, Wellington and Ryerson, which will have priority in the value of Prudence's Rocksolid account?

4. Assume now that Wellington Bank never entered the picture. When she decides to jump into big-time pudding production Prudence turns first to Ryerson Bank for a loan and grants it an interest in her account with the JSR & Co. stockbrokerage house. Before the bank releases any money to Prudence it asks for her signature as well as that of an authorized party at JSR & Co. on a control agreement under which the brokerage agrees to follow orders respecting the account made by the bank as if they were orders of Prudence. Later, when she is in need of additional funds, Prudence gets a second loan—from Wilkes Bank and Trust, which *also* gets a control agreement signed by both Prudence and JSR & Co. covering the exact same account. When Prudence goes into bankruptcy, do Ryerson and/or Wilkes have a perfected security interest that will be good as against the trustee in bankruptcy? If both have continuing valid interests, which will have priority?

5. Now suppose that at the time Prudence is forced to declare bankruptcy it turns out that some of the corporate stocks in her account with JSR & Co. are held "on margin," that is she has, under a margin loan arrangement provided by the brokerage, borrowed money from it in order to purchase the shares. In order to secure her obligation to repay this loan she has as part of her customer agreement granted JSR & Co. a security interest in all of the shares in her account. How does the brokerage firm's security interest stack up against others who may be claiming an interest in the value of the account in the course of the bankruptcy proceedings? See §9-328(3).

6. In order to set up a new auto dealership, Sam of Sam's Autorama is able to obtain a small business loan from Merchant's Credit Association. This lender takes a security interest in Sam's equipment and also on a savings account at Samstown National Bank into which Sam has been regularly making deposits in anticipation of opening his business. Merchant's Credit perfects its interest in the equipment by filing in the proper place. It perfects its interest in the savings account by entering into a control agreement with Sam and Samstown National Bank. When Sam gets a check from Merchant's Credit, representing the amount he is borrowing from that lender, he dutifully deposits the check into the savings account. From time to time, as he goes about procuring the equipment he will need to run his Autorama, he withdraws amounts from this account to pay for his purchases. Sam is simultaneously working out the details of an agreement under which he will become an authorized dealer in Zephyr automobiles. The Zephyr Motors Corporation agrees to deliver autos to Sam on the condition that it retain a security interest in all of his "inventory, now held or hereafter acquired." Sam also agrees that upon sale of any Zephyr to a consumer he will forward a certain portion of the proceeds directly to Zephyr within two days. Sam carries through with this obligation for several years. When his business starts to run into difficulty, however, he sells a couple of cars for cash but does not forward any of the proceeds to the car manufacturer. Instead he takes the checks (totaling $45,000) that he has been given for these cars and deposits them into his savings account. Before he can do anything with this money, Sam is forced to declare bankruptcy. Which creditor, Merchant's Credit or the Zephyr Motors Corporation, has priority in the $45,000?

Explanations

1a. Yes. Recall that §9-312(a) allows for a security interest in investment property to be perfected by filing. So Wellington's interest is perfected at the time of the filing of the petition in bankruptcy. We are back to the basic rule of §9-317(a): If the interest is perfected when the bankruptcy proceedings commence that security interest is going to be good as against the bankruptcy trustee.

1b. DeJohn's interest, having been perfected by a filing, is, like Wellington's, going to be effective as against the bankruptcy trustee. So now we have two security interests in investment property, both of which are perfected. We look to §9-328 to determine which has priority over the other. Both parties have perfected, but only by filing. Neither has perfected by "control" as that term is used in the investment property context. The priority issue does not fall within any of the parts (1) through (6) of §9-328, so we are left with the residual rule of (7). Priority between two security interests in investment property both perfected only by filing reverts to the rules of §9-322. In this case it means that under subsection (a)(1), the first to file will have priority over a party that files later. Wellington has priority over DeJohn.

What we now can see is that if all a secured party such as Wellington is interested in is in being able to prevail over the bankruptcy trustee should a bankruptcy occur and over parties who perfect by filing subsequent to its own filing, then perfection on investment property through a simple filing meets these objectives. The real lesson, however, as we see in the later examples, is that perfection by filing on investment property meets these limited objectives only and that a secured party that relies on filing as its sole means of perfection in investment property is basically running a huge risk. Wellington in this example comes out with its interest intact and with priority, but that may be more a matter of luck than of anything else. Perfection by filing in investment property is permissible and it works, if no other party takes "control" of the situation.

2a. Friend Frank, having taken delivery of the certificated security endorsed in blank, has control over the shares under §8-106(b)(1). Now we look to §9-328(1):

> A security interest held by a secured party having control over investment property under Section 9-106 [here Frank] has priority over a security interest held by a secured party that does not have control over the investment property [here the hapless Wellington bank].

Wellington has perfected, but only by filing. Its interest is automatically, and easily, trumped by Frank, who, whether he knew it or not, took "control" in the technical sense in which that term is used when speaking of investment property in Articles 8 and 9. Frank's interest in the Moneybucks Industries shares has priority over Wellington's.

2b. Frank's taking delivery of a certificated security but without its being endorsed over to him or in blank means that he does not have control. He does, however, have §9-328(5) on his side. Under §9-313(a), a secured party may perfect a security interest in certificated securities by taking delivery. So Frank's interest will survive into the bankruptcy. Beyond that, his interest has, simply because he took delivery of the certificate pursuant to a security agreement, "priority over a conflicting security interest perfected by a method other than control." Wellington's interest is perfected, it's true, but by filing and not by control. So Frank still prevails over Wellington.

3. Ryerson Bank will have priority over Wellington Bank. Ryerson gained perfection over this uncertificated security by its gaining control pursuant to §8-106(c)(2). Once again, as Wellington is beginning to appreciate, a secured party who perfects via control beats one who perfects but does not have control. Wellington is perfected, but has no control. Wellington comes in second to Ryerson.

4. Both Ryerson and Wilkes have perfected by control. Each has a control agreement entered into with both Prudence and the broker. But which has priority? Look to §9-328(2). Except for situations not here part of the picture, "security interests held by secured parties each of whom has control rank according to priority of time." Ryerson has priority over Wilkes.

   Notice that the one way Wilkes could have come out ahead of Ryerson is if it, that is Wilkes, had taken control by actually having the securities account turned into an account in its name and not merely entered into a control agreement with Prudence and the brokerage under which the account holder remains Prudence. This follows from §9-328(2)(B)(i), because then Wilkes's interest would be the first in time to be perfected by control in this particular manner.

   What is more interesting is to consider the situation of Ryerson and Wilkes. How did it come to pass that both were able to get a valid control agreement worked out with JSR & Co.? Unless one of the two lenders was itself incredibly sloppy in its handling of the situation, this will almost assuredly be some kind of slip-up on the broker's part. Ryerson Bank, when it entered into the control agreement with Prudence and JSR & Co., would have asked for a covenant on the broker's part that it had not previously entered into any similar agreement with anyone else and furthermore that it would not enter into any such agreement with anyone else in the future, a so-called no further encumbrances provision. Wilkes Bank and Trust would have presumably asked for and received the same kind of assurances from the broker. What's the good of having control if someone else can have it as well?

   So the most likely scenario here is that the brokerage fouled up by entering into two control agreements covering the same account when it had promised not to let this happen. If in the course of Prudence's bankruptcy, the obligations to both banks cannot be fully satisfied by the value of the account, each of the banks will know where to turn for satisfaction. Ryerson can hold JSR & Co. in breach of contract for its having entered into the subsequent agreement with Wilkes, and Wilkes can go against the broker for its failure to disclose earlier that there already was a control agreement covering the account. Of course it is probably also true that because she signed both agreements and made similar covenants, Prudence will be in breach as to each bank, but remember that she's bankrupt and no one is going to get any more out of her.

The brokerage, of course, can avoid being liable to any lender who takes a security interest in any account it holds for a client by refusing to include this type of covenant in any control agreement it signs. The problem with this is that the savvy lender will not agree to loan without such an assurance. The brokerage may just have to take the consequences if it cannot keep its own records straight. Another way it might minimize the possibility of any conflict, and one that might satisfy the first lender (here Ryerson) even more is for the lender to take control of Prudence's account by having all of the securities in the account actually transferred into an account in the lender's (Ryerson's) name. Recall that under §8-106(d)(1), a purchaser of (which includes someone taking a security interest in) a securities entitlement can gain control by "the purchaser becoming the entitlement holder." Once Prudence's account is in effect transferred into Ryerson Bank's name, it would be hard to see how Wilkes could somehow get any interest in it, much less control over it.

5. This one is easy. Under the cited provision,

> A security interest held by a securities intermediary [JSR & Co.] in a securities entitlement or a securities account maintained with the securities intermediary [here by Prudence] has priority over a conflicting security interest held by another secured party.

The margin loan gets paid off first.

6. Merchant's Credit will have priority over the savings account and any money in it. Look at §9-327(1): "A security interest held by a secured party having control of the deposit account under Section 9-104 has priority over a conflicting security interest held by a secured party that does not have control." Merchant's Credit has control. Zephyr does have a security interest in at least $45,000 held in the account — its interest coming from the fact that this amount constitutes identifiable cash proceeds received by the debtor, Sam, on disposition of some of his inventory — and its interest is automatically perfected under §9-315(d)(2). The car company's interest, however, has not been perfected by control and, hence, comes in second to the interest held by Merchant's Credit. As a practical matter, the way an inventory financer such as Zephyr tries to minimize, even if it cannot entirely eliminate, the problem we see here is for it to insist that the debtor establish a special "proceeds account" into which the debtor will

immediately deposit any cash proceeds and over which the inventory financer itself will have initially secured control. The inventory financer regularly monitors this account, just as it monitors the inventory in the hands of the debtor, with an eye to catching any improper diversion of the proceeds into an account or other form of proceeds in which it does not have priority of interest.

PART IV

Default and Enforcement

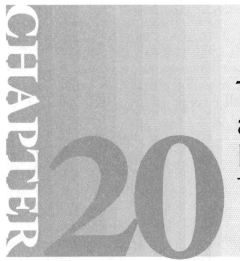

The Event of Default and the Process of Repossession

INTRODUCTION TO ENFORCEMENT

"The rights of a secured party to enforce its security interest in collateral after the debtor's default," as the first sentence of the second comment to the first section of Part 6 of Article 9 pointedly reminds us, "are an important feature of a secured transaction." To be sure, no security interest will have been negotiated and agreed to, then attached, perfected and carefully tended to by the secured party with any *hope* on his or her part that the interest will ever actually have to be enforced, any more than a party signs a simple contract with the *hope* that a breach of contract action will be forthcoming. Still, enforcement of the security interest, the topic of Part 6 of Article 9 and of the concluding chapters of this book, is crucial to this grand scheme. If your typical Article 9 security interest were to turn out to be unenforceable just when enforcement was needed, there would be very little reason for any of what has gone before. The possibility of calling on the muscle of the security interest in those rare instances when that is really called for, its *enforceability*, is what gives the whole enterprise its meaning; it's what puts the "security" in the security interest.

From the very beginning we have assumed that any security interest has been playing in effect a supporting role. The security interest is put in place to back up an obligation owed by the debtor to the secured party. The secured party's chances of actually seeing that obligation met by the debtor are enhanced by the existence of the security interest. The debtor will be working toward fulfillment of its obligation not just because it fears something like a breach of contract action should it breach, but that it will in addition and perhaps much more dramatically lose possession and eventual ownership of some valuable piece of property if it fails to hold up its end of the bargain. The secured party's expectations out of the whole affair are that the debtor will meet its underlying obligation, making cash payments when due, performing a service as promised, or whatever. The secured party wants the debtor to succeed. It wants the debt to be paid or the services rendered. The "rights of " the secured party in the event of default including the right of repossession, as we will study, may be "an important feature" of the secured transaction, but you should guard against any mis-conception that default, repossession, and possible resale of the collateral represent the natural healthy outcome of the secured transaction experience. In the best of cases, in fact in any case that rates as even passable or fair, the security interest is never actually enforced in this sense nor should there have even been any point along the way where the subject came up in either the debtor's or the secured party's mind.

Enforcement in the sense we will be talking about it here — default and its consequences — is a sign of something having gone seriously wrong. The debtor has not met its obligation. This is hardly a moment the secured party will have been looking forward to with anything but dread. It, that is the secured party, may be left with no other alternative but to go down the repossession road, but this is rarely a pleasant prospect for the secured party even to have to contemplate.

The purpose of a security interest from a creditor's or lender's point of view is that it adds a little to its peace of mind. Should anything go wrong, there is someplace else the secured party can turn to get what it is due and salvage what it can out of what is often a pretty dismal situation. The creditor has been prudent and done as it should in demanding a security interest to back up the debtor's obligation and in tending to the details of acquiring and protecting that interest as we have described, just in the way a prudent homeowner will want to have a fire insurance policy covering his or her property and take care that the premiums are paid as called for. The secured party that finds itself facing the gloomy prospect of having actually to enforce its security interest through repossession and all that goes with it can feel justifiably pleased that its prudence has paid off, but it is no more to be envied than the homeowner who comes home to find his residence burnt down to the ground, even if the place was well-insured against just such a catastrophe. For the secured party, declaring a default and moving if necessary on to the stage of repossession and possible resale, is in the position of someone trying to put together the pieces as best as may be done of something that he or she would have much preferred had never shattered in the first place.

THE INSTANCES OF "DEFAULT"

Section 9-601(a), the introductory subsection of Part 6, starts out simply enough:

> After default, a secured party has the rights provided in this part and, except as otherwise provided in Section 9-602, those provided by agreement of the parties.

So it is a "default" by the debtor that triggers the whole scheme of a secured party's rights and remedies under this concluding Part of Article 9. This being the case you might reasonably expect to find a definition or explication of exactly what constitutes a "default" on the debtor's part somewhere in this section, but as a matter of fact there is none to be found here or anywhere else in the Code for that matter. Look at Comment 3 to §9-601. "Under subsection (a) the secured parties' rights arise '[a]fter default.' . . . [T]his Article leaves to the agreement of the parties the circumstances giving rise to a default." The Article 9 security interest, as we have seen from the very outset, is a creature of contract. It arises out of the agreement of two parties, the debtor and the secured party. While there is no statutory requirement that this agreement always be evidenced by a writing, for all practical purposes it is rare when there is not just an agreement in fact but a document, a *written* security agreement, which once having been signed by the two parties creates the Article 9 security interest and which binds them together to play out their respective roles — not for all times and all purposes, but as far as the particular transaction goes — as the debtor and the secured party of an Article 9 secured transaction.

Not all written security agreements are alike. Some, probably the vast majority, are relatively straightforward form contracts drafted initially by the secured party, typically a seller or a commercial lender, and used by it whenever the need comes up. The debtor is expected to see that the few pertinent facts unique to the situation have been correctly entered into the blanks (generally the description of the collateral and that his or her name has been spelled correctly) and sign the thing as is. In the rare deal, where the stakes are higher and the debtor has some real bargaining power over details, the exact language of the written agreement will be the subject of bargaining, bickering, and compromise between lawyers representing the two parties to the transaction. In any event, it is the written security agreement that spells out the terms and conditions under which the parties will live out their unique tale of debtor and security party under Article 9.

You should expect to find in even the simplest form security agreement some paragraph or section labeled "Default" or "Events of Default," for example. It is here, in the agreement of the parties, that we find laid out precisely what events will constitute defaults, thus enabling the secured party if it so chooses to spring into action and exercise its rights and remedies under Part 6. Even in the simplest agreement this list of events can quickly become a long one. These security agreements are, after all, drafted by lawyers, almost always lawyers for the secured party, and these lawyers will be by their nature (and quite rightly in view of their roles) worried about all kinds of things that might happen in the future to somehow upset the situation or lead to anxiety from the secured party's perspective. If such a possibility comes to mind — even a remote one — it is likely to be added to the list of events of default for that security agreement, and quite often for every security agreement the lawyer drafts from that day forward.

The principal event of default — one that you would certainly expect to find on a basic list — is, of course, the debtor's failure to make good on its obligation. The debtor will be in default if he or she fails to make a payment when due or provide a service as promised. This, however, will rarely exhaust the possibilities. The agreement will typically set out any number of other events or conditions that will make less likely the possibility that the debtor will be able to perform in the future or that will impair the value of the collateral on which the security interest rests. The exact list of events set forth in the "Events of Default" section of any particular security agreement would, of course, depend on the circumstances, but you might expect to see some of the following occurrences:

- The making of any false or misleading statements or the provision of any false information by the debtor in connection with the making of the agreement.
- The collateral being lost, stolen, damaged, or destroyed.
- The failure of the debtor to keep the collateral insured as agreed or failure to keep it in good repair.
- A grant by the debtor of a security interest in the same collateral to any other party.
- Any levy upon or seizure of the collateral or subjection of it to any other judicial process.
- Failure of the debtor to make available to the secured party for inspection its books and records or the collateral itself when and as required by the agreement.
- Failure of the debtor to notify the secured party as required by the agreement of any change in its name, organizational structure, place of doing business, or location of the collateral.
- Death, dissolution, termination of existence, insolvency, or business failure of the debtor.

Notice that some of the things listed here are not examples of what we ordinarily think of as a failure or a default on anybody's part. Certainly the debtor's death, in the case of an individual, does not strike us as an event for which we would normally consider him or her to be at fault or in any way accountable. The secured party may have been among the people closest to the debtor in life and genuinely grieving. The debtor's demise does, however, still rank as the kind of occurrence that could give the reasonable secured party justifiable concern about whether the debtor's obligation can or will now be met.

The listing of those specific events such as was given above that will constitute a default would seem to cover just about everything imaginable, but on the theory that the unimaginable might just possibly happen, the security agreement will often contain one final bit of language, what is often referred to as a "general insecurity clause." It will usually read something to the effect that included among the events of default under the agreement will be all those specific instances of the type already enumerated and,

> any other change in the condition or affairs, financial or otherwise, of the Debtor or any guarantor or surety of the liability secured by this agreement which in the opinion of the Secured Party impairs the value of the collateral or imperils the prospect of the Debtor's full performance or satisfaction of its obligations secured by this agreement.

That certainly ought to cover it.

A likely question at this point is whether such a clause, giving the secured party what seems like close to unfettered discretion to determine when in its opinion the debtor is in default, should be considered enforceable at all. The answer is that such clauses are legitimate provided that we read them in the context of the general obligation of good faith, which, as we know, governs all contracts and duties subject to the Code via §1-203 or §1R-304. "Good faith" for the purpose of Article 9 is defined in §9-102(a)(43) to mean "honesty in fact and the observance of reasonable commercial standards of fair dealing."* Should a secured party rely too

---

* If you find this language missing or replaced by the cryptic note "Reserved" when you look at §9-102(a)(43) in your copy of Article 9, it is nothing to worry about. The editors of your statutory supplement have presumably replaced the original version of Article 1 with the new, revised version, and also made minor corresponding changes in the other articles as well. In §1R-201(b)(20) the term "good faith" is given this so-called objective definition to be applied throughout the entire Code (except in Article 5, for reasons that certainly need not concern us here). The editors therefore deleted what became a redundancy in the definition section of Article 9. Note, however, that if a particular jurisdiction has not yet adopted the revised Article 1 — or is one of those handful of jurisdiction which have adopted the revised version of Article 1 in general but which have chosen to retain the older subjective definition of "good faith" nonetheless — that state's version of Article 9 would still carry the objective definition in §9-102(a)(43). So one way or another this is the definition of good faith that applies in any case or controversy governed by revised Article 9.

Note also the language of §1-208 or §1R-309 quoted in the next section, which touches on this matter.

quickly or too cavalierly on a general insecurity clause, declare a default, and take some impetuous action it could find itself regretting the move. We have to remember, of course, that the sensible secured party is rarely looking for reasons to declare a default and move into the next stage of enforcement just on a whim or because it has nothing better to do with its time.

The general insecurity clause, the workings of which we will explore more fully in Example 1, is not meant to be the basis for the secured party's playing fast and loose with the affairs of the debtor, and the rational secured party does not see it that way. It is drafted into the agreement to cover the unexpected, those difficult to predict, define, or articulate, events that may occur in the course of a longer-term commercial relationship. It is probably the exceedingly rare situation where the secured party ever has to look to the general insecurity clause to meet its legitimate needs. Thought of in this way its main function may be in helping the secured party drafting a standard form of security agreement keep its list of specific articulated instances of default from growing even longer, more verbose, and convoluted. Certainly if in any given transaction an occurrence unique to that situation that would seriously affect the value of the security interest comes to mind when the security agreement is being negotiated, it would be better for both parties if it were dealt with from the outset directly through some additional specially crafted language added to the enumerated instances of default.

ON ACCELERATION

Many security agreements also contain what is generally referred to as an "acceleration clause." Such a provision states something to the effect that

> In the event of any default by the Debtor, and notwithstanding any time or credit allowed under any contract or instrument evidencing the Debtor's obligations, all obligations secured by this agreement shall be at the option of the Secured Party and without notice or demand immediately due and payable in full.

Again, you may wonder whether such a clause should be valid. The way it reads, if the debtor misses one payment or fails in some other respect to fulfill an obligation under the agreement the *entire* amount it has borrowed is then immediately due at the discretion of the lender. And this is indeed the way it works. Any doubts about the validity or enforceability of such an acceleration clause can be laid to rest by turning to §1-208 or §1R-309:

> A term providing that one party . . . may accelerate payment or performance . . . "at will" or "when the party deems itself insecure" or words of similar

import, means that the party has power to do so only if that party in good faith believes that the prospect of payment or performance is impaired. The burden of establishing lack of good faith is on the party against whom the power has been exercised.

You should also read the first paragraph of the Official Comment to this section. An acceleration clause read as this section dictates and tempered by the obligation of good faith is not to be considered void as against public policy or to render the contract illusory or too indefinite for enforcement.* We will explore the workings of such a clause in Example 2 to follow.

ON NOTICE

This security agreement's listing of specific instances of default, the general insecurity clause, if there is one, and the possibility of acceleration are still only part of the story. One question that can arise, and that the carefully drafted security agreement should take into account, is whether the secured party is under any obligation to notify the debtor that he or she is considered to be in default prior to taking any remedial action and particularly prior to attempting to repossess the collateral. In a way it seems only fair that the debtor be given the chance to rectify the situation before the secured party takes any definitive action. As a practical matter, however, any such general requirement of notice to the debtor that it is considered in default and stands to soon suffer the consequences could work a considerable hardship on the secured party. First of all it is only fair to note that when a debtor is in default he or she should know as much. After all, the debtor signed the security agreement and should have knowledge of its terms. In the most typical instance of default, when the debtor has failed to make payment of money when due, the debtor is perfectly well aware that he or she is behind in payment. True, there are times when even the most conscientious of us may misplace a bill or send in a payment a day or two, even a week or two, late. A single late or missed payment, however, is rarely, if ever, going to even suggest to the secured party that it go through the hassle of repossession. The typical situation where the secured party does even consider starting the repossession process is one where the debtor has been habitually late or is seriously behind in payments, and that is the kind of thing of which

---

* You should also be aware that many states have passed their own form of consumer protection legislation that may, to some degree, prohibit the inclusion of or rein in the creditor's power to invoke either a general insecurity clause or an acceleration provision, at least when the wording of the agreement would seem to allow for the creditor's acting arbitrarily or without good cause.

the debtor cannot reasonably claim to be unaware or of which it needs have any right to notice.

Beyond this, if the secured party were required to give notice that it has had enough of late payments and the like and was about to declare a default and that it stood ready to "assert its rights" under the security agreement, this would simply serve as a red flag for the debtor that his or her property was about to be repossessed. Repossession, as we will soon see, is not exactly a game of great subtlety. If the secured party were required to signal its moves ahead of time, it would be the rare case where the collateral would be available for self-help repossession just when that process is most called for, and allowed for, under Article 9. With a little bit of warning the debtor can be expected to lock his or her car — as you might expect, the greatest number of repossessions or at least those that end up in controversy and make their way into the cases have to do with consumers who have not been paying on their auto loans and the like — in the garage or stash it away someplace where the secured party, acting through a professional repossession firm, will not be able to get its hands on it. Self-help repossession works best, and is indeed intended to work best, when the secured party can take advantage of a bit of surprise. It is not a game that you would expect to be played well if one party were required to signal all of its moves even a bit ahead of time.

Given our understanding of the situation, you can see why the secured party will typically have drafted into the agreement the provision that any event of the type we have seen listed will *automatically* constitute a default "without notice or demand" to the debtor and give it, the secured party, the right to immediately act as it is entitled to pursuant to the security agreement and under Part 6.

THE SECURED PARTY'S OPTIONS ON DEFAULT

It is important to note from the outset that the fact of an event's being considered a default by the debtor does not *require* that the secured party take any action when it comes about or that the whole intricate security arrangement set up by the debtor and the secured party must necessarily come tumbling down. An event that can be characterized as a default under the security agreement gives the secured party the opportunity, if it so chooses, but not the obligation to pursue its rights and remedies under Part 6.

It is probably fair to say that most often following an event of default the secured party, while it may use the occasion to nudge the debtor into compliance, does not seize upon the opportunity to declare a default, repossess the collateral, or anything of the sort. The opportunity is there, but the secured party will rarely want to take on the headache of going the enforcement route unless there seems to be no other workable alternative. At the same time, should the secured party simply let it pass and not even comment on the debtor's failure, it may find itself unable to rely upon the episode to justify actions later taken or worse yet to have "waived" in some way (that a court will later inform it of) its right to insist on full performance to the letter of the security agreement for the future. At the very least, a secured party that becomes aware of an occurrence that constitutes a default under the terms of the security agreement will want to make known to the debtor its displeasure and its "firm anticipation" that the default will be remedied as quickly as possible and not repeated in the future.

In some instances the happening of a default will call for a bit more on the part of the secured party. A debtor who is having trouble making payments as they become due because of a business downturn or other financial problems may be in the technical sense very much at the mercy of the secured party, but often it will seem at least to the secured party the other way around. The secured party may have the right to declare a default and indeed thanks to its acceleration clause to call for immediate repayment of the entire outstanding balance of the loan or other obligation, but what would be the point? If the debtor is having trouble making its monthly payments as things stand, it certainly is not going to be able to come up with the entire principal in cash. At the same time, while the secured party may have the right to repossess the collateral, this is often a terribly unattractive alternative. Repossession, resale, and so forth is, as we will see, laden with problems for the secured party, not the least of which is that it will then have the collateral in its possession often without the slightest idea of what to do with it or even a good place to put it. Beyond this, having taken the collateral out of the hands of the debtor makes it even less likely that it, the debtor, will be able to keep its business going at all. Once the widgetmaking machinery has been repossessed, the widgetmaker is pretty much out of business. And the absence of any incoming cash further decreases the chances that the secured party will get paid off in the long run. In a large number of situations it will be best for all concerned, the secured party as well as the debtor (not to mention the debtor's employees, other creditors, family, and friends), for the secured party and the debtor to work out some kind of extension of the time for repayment or a decreased but more manageable monthly payment amount. The secured party will often, and probably in the majority of cases, find it a better route to try to keep the debtor on his or her feet and operating under a debt burden that it can handle rather than doing anything that would bring the debtor's whole empire crashing down.

Even should the secured party find that in its own self-interest it has to do something, we should remember that repossession of the collateral is not necessarily the only or the best option. Note §9-601(a)(1): The secured party may upon default, "reduce a claim to judgment." That is, the secured party may simply ignore for the moment the fact that it is a secured party and, relying on its primary role as a contract obligee, sue for the full amount it is now due. The contract action should not be that difficult to win, and the secured party will now be a judgment creditor for the full amount owed it. If, even after repossession and resale of the collateral, the secured party would be left being owed a substantial amount, which it would have to pursue as a deficiency, there is often good reason for it to bring a contract action as soon as possible while still leaving the collateral in the possession of the debtor.

There remains for the secured party the option upon default — best conceived of as a last resort rather than any great cause for celebration — of repossessing the collateral and at least assuring itself of some measure of recovery under that route. The concluding examples of this chapter deal with the secured party's rights and responsibilities in taking possession, which are laid out, albeit in remarkably little detail, in §9-609. The secured party can repossess without judicial process, taking advantage of so-called self-help repossession, as it is referred to, but is limited, as we will have to consider, by the requirement that this be done only when possible without a "breach of the peace." The secured party may also proceed by action, that is through the use of the courts and if necessary the local sheriff, to get possession of the collateral. What constitutes breach of the peace, repossession through legal action, as well as other aspects of §9-609 are covered in the examples.

IF THE SECURED PARTY FOULS UP

The central premise of the default provisions of Article 9 is that, unlike what would be true when a real estate mortgagee makes the decision to foreclose on its interest and repossess land subject to its mortgage, the Article 9 secured party is free if it can to carry out each of the steps necessary to enforce its interest and obtain remedy without resort to the courts. Section §9-609 specifically authorizes repossession upon default without the secured party's having to get any court order supporting the move. In the following chapter we will see that the secured party who has obtained possession is then free to dispose of the collateral through purely private means. Just as there is no general requirement that a court authorize or supervise repossession, there is normally no judicial involvement in the later sale or disposition of the collateral or the allocation of the proceeds of that sale.

Enforcement is basically a private matter under Article 9. The secured party decides what steps it wants to take and when to take them. If all goes according to plan, as far as the secured party is concerned no court need ever be drawn into the picture. This is obviously an attractive feature of the Article 9 scheme for the lender, but it is not without a downside. The good news for the secured party is clear; any time you can avoid having to go through potentially lengthy and almost assuredly costly legal proceedings simply in order to secure what is rightfully yours with no question, so much the better. But there is bad news, as well. In the course of enforcement the debtor is not without protection. The debtor's protection resides in its right to insist that the secured party as it carries out its self-determined plan of enforcement does not overstep the bounds laid down in the security agreement and by Article 9 itself.

Should the secured party err — either when it wrongly declares a default, by gaining possession of the collateral through improper means, or, as we will see in the later chapters, by failing to observe the correct procedures regarding the disposition of the collateral and application of the proceeds — the debtor can be expected to call the secured party out for the mistake. The secured party does not have to go into court to get its remedy, but should it foul up in some way the debtor will then have the option of commencing an action. And the secured party, which has been acting on its own and without court approval or supervision will not, unlike in the case of the real estate foreclosure and sale that is carried out under public authority and the court's watchful eye, be able to point to a court's prior approval of anything that it has done.

The secured party under Article 9 gets to enforce its interest as it sees fit. It acts on its own, but it therefore necessarily acts at its peril. Should it later be brought into court by the debtor and its actions be found to have fallen below what is required of it by the Code, it will find itself wide open to a variety of sanctions. It is important in working and thinking through Part 6 of Article 9 to concentrate not only on what the secured party may do to enforce its interest but also what it may not and further on what jeopardy it faces if it is later deemed by a judge or jury to have gone beyond the bounds of its proper authority.

Sections 9-625 through 9-627 deal with the secured party's liability for failing to comply with the rules within which it must play under Article 9, but its provisions will more typically be relevant if the secured party slips up in how it handles the situation once a repossession has taken place. When the problem is a wrongful repossession, either because not warranted at the time because no default had yet occurred or thanks to a self-help repossession that fails to go exactly according to plan, the secured party's potential accountability arises more typically under the most basic common law of the state, which usually doesn't look kindly on a party's taking something which is not rightfully its to take. The debtor may be successful with a breach of contract suit, if it wants to stand on its rights under the security agreement or underlying contract of obligation, or it may assert the tort of conversion when it is deprived of its property wrongfully. If a breach of the peace does occur during an effort to repossession, the secured party can be liable under the common law for that as well, and in the odd case when things really get out of hand for physical assault on the person of the debtor, his or her spouse, children, or other relations, or just about anyone who gets caught up in the excitement of the moment.

In practice, of course, where the goods are consumer goods (and a healthy majority of repossessions involve consumers' autos, trucks, and the like) and even when there are not it is rarely the secured party or even one of its regular employees who actually carries out the repossession. It has to be the rare banker, not to mention the commercial lawyer, who spends his or her day driving around in a tow truck looking for cars whose owners have fallen behind in payment. This bit of business is typically left to the repossession professional, or "repo man," who goes about his business with a cool efficiency, if not necessarily the greatest of finesse.* The repo man usually is hired by the secured party as an independent contractor, but this doesn't mean the secured party is off the hook if something goes wrong in the course of the repossession. A series of decisions under prior Article 9 made it clear that the secured party's obligation to ensure that repossession is carried out correctly and without a breach of the peace is a so-called non-delegable duty, that is, one that cannot be abdicated simply by arranging to have it performed by an independent contractor. See, for example, *DeMary v. Rieker*, 302 N.J. Super. 208, 645 A.2d 294, 33 U.C.C.2d 315 (1997). The drafters of the revision give their blessing to this result in the sentence concluding the first paragraph of Comment 3 to §9-609.

This pattern of Article 9 enforcement and its underlying philosophy can be the source of both comfort and sorrow for the secured party faced with a default by its debtor. The secured party is free to act on its own; it does not need to apply to a court or any other legal agency for relief. If it knows what it wants to do and how to go about it, the secured party can avoid dealing with lawyers altogether. The potential for sorrow flows from the fact that should it slip up, the debtor is then in the position of looking to the court for relief, and often in a situation well-suited to presenting himself or herself as the beleaguered consumer or small business owner much harassed and put upon by the cold impersonal institutional lender. The lender is, of course, owed what is due it and is given rights and remedies under Article 9, but woe to the secured party that appears to be overreaching or stepping over the line in the pursuit of what it probably could otherwise rightfully have had just for the asking.

---

* There are apparently some women who have entered the ranks of the repossession profession, although they are still fairly few and far between. The extent to which this will change in the coming years in anybody's guess and not something I would even care to speculate upon.

Examples

1. Cosmo Grafix negotiates a small business loan from a local bank, the Smallville Bank and Trust, for the purpose of setting up a computer graphics and design firm. To obtain the loan he uses as collateral "all of his equipment now held or hereafter acquired." One term of the security agreement that is presented to him by the bank for signature specifies that among the instances of default will be, in addition to a long list of specific events, "any other act, condition or event which in the sole opinion of Lender renders the value of the collateral or the prospects of Debtor's full performance hereunder less likely." Do you believe the bank would be justified in holding Grafix in default and taking steps to enforce its interest, including possible repossession of his equipment, in any of the following situations?

   a. The bank officer who initially approved the loan begins to wonder whether or not she had done the right thing and looks at all of the information on Grafix's application once again. The officer concludes that she should not have allowed the loan to be approved as it had. She wants to call a default and threaten repossession, if for no other reason than to get Grafix's agreement to a set of terms somewhat more favorable to the bank.

   b. The economy of the area in which Grafix and the bank are located begins to suffer a severe recession. Local business papers begin regularly to report how the economy's downturn is seriously affecting small businesses such as Grafix's. The bank's loan committee initiates a much more stringent policy on lending to small businesses such as his, which for all intents and purposes takes the bank out of the business of lending to such borrowers at least until the economy turns around. Would the bank be justified here in deeming itself "insecure" and invoking the quoted clause?

   c. The loan officer at the bank hears from reliable sources that the downturn of the economy has begun to affect Grafix's business. Several of his larger clients have canceled orders or asked him to cut back on the work he was doing for them. In addition, the reliable sources report that Grafix has had trouble meeting some of his other financial obligations, such as the rent on his office space, and has been in negotiation with his landlord hoping to get some concession from the landlord on the amount of his rent.

   d. The loan officer becomes aware that while Grafix's business appears to be strong, Cosmo himself is increasingly spending more and more time in another city scouting out possible locations for a second office. He leaves the day-to-day operation of his present office in the care of his niece, Cosima, who is not as proficient or experienced in computers and computer graphics as her uncle.

2. Professor Flack buys a beautiful sailboat from Marty of Marty's Marina. His agreement with Marty calls for payment in monthly installments of $1,000 over a five-year period and grants Marty a security interest in the boat to secure payment of the purchase price. One term of the agreement provides that "Upon any default by Debtor and at the option of the Secured Party, all obligations secured by this agreement shall immediately become due and payable in full without notice or demand." Professor Flack makes the first couple of payments on the boat, but during the summer takes a three-month cruise, during which time he forgets to make arrangement for monthly payments to Marty. He returns home to find a notice from Marty stating that because Flack has failed to make his June and July payments, Marty considers him to be in default as to their agreement and demanding immediate payment of all $58,000 that remains to be paid on the boat. Flack quickly contacts Marty and offers to "catch up" with his $3,000 in payments for the missed summer months and promising that "this will never happen again." Is Marty obligated to accede to Flack's proposal?

3. Sam of Sam's Autorama is an authorized dealer in Aspen automobiles. He sells a particularly luxurious model, the Aspen 2400E&E, to one Dr. Jerry Morgan under a retail sales installment payment plan that calls for the doctor to make monthly payments for the car over a period of four years. Each payment is due on the first of the month. From the very beginning, Morgan has difficulty keeping up with his payment schedule. In fact, of the first 14 monthly payments, only one is delivered to Sam on time, the others from at least a few days to, in one case, over a month late. While Sam contacts Morgan a couple of times to inquire about late payments, at no time does he refuse any of the delinquent payments or suggest that he intends to insist upon strict compliance with the terms of the contract. Finally, when the 15th payment is a week overdue, Sam decides that he has had enough of Morgan and has the car repossessed from a public street. Can you think of any argument on behalf of Dr. Morgan that would allow him to claim that Sam acted wrongly in repossessing as and when he did? Do you think this argument should succeed? Is your assessment of the situation affected by the fact that among the terms of the retail sales installment agreement signed by Morgan was one that read as follows?

> Waiver of or any acquiescence in any default of the Debtor, or failure of the Secured Party to insist upon strict compliance by the Debtor of any of its obligations hereunder, shall not constitute a waiver of any subsequent or other default or failure.

4. Sam sells another new Aspen automobile to one Andrew. During the second year of the four-year payment period, Andrew is several times

late in making his scheduled monthly payments. A couple of times the checks that Andrew sends in payment bounce, and Sam has to contact Andrew and arrange for payment to be resubmitted. Each time something like this happens Sam is quick to send a notice to Andrew insisting that he expects buyers to make regular and timely payment, as called for in their contracts, and that he considers the failure to do so a default. Finally, when a check from Andrew bounces for the second month in a row, Sam decides to take action. He contacts a repossession agent, one Rocky Fieldston, who operates a one-person operation out of his own tow truck. Sam instructs Fieldston to take possession of Andrew's car on Sam's behalf, giving Fieldston a description of the car and its license plate number. Fieldston adds Andrew's car to a list of those he has been contracted (by Sam and others in the area) to repossess. While cruising the city, Fieldston comes across Andrew's car parked on a public street. After verifying that it is Andrew's car, Fieldston hitches the car to the back of the tow truck and takes it away, delivering it to Sam's Autorama. When Andrew returns to his parking spot he finds his car is gone. Two days later he receives at his home a notice from Sam to the effect that his car has been repossessed by the dealer and that he, Sam, intends "to proceed in accordance with all of the rights and remedies granted me under our contract and by law under the circumstances."

a. Does Article 9 give Andrew any grounds for objecting to the manner or timing of the repossession? Does Andrew have any argument based on the fact that he was never given any formal notice that Sam considered him under default as of the time when the car was taken? What of the fact that he was given no notice that Sam intended for the car to be repossessed?

b. Suppose Andrew could show that one month previously he had written Sam acknowledging and apologizing for the fact that he had sometimes been "a bit remiss" in making timely payment but that "In no event should you repossess my car. Should you feel yourself aggrieved in the future by what you believe to be any default on my part, I insist that you contact me first before taking any action against the car." Does this help Andrew's case?

c. Assume instead that Andrew had never written any objection of any kind, but that he returns to his parking spot just as Fieldston is starting to hitch the car to the tow truck. Andrew never directly approaches the repo man, always staying on the adjacent sidewalk. He does, however, repeatedly declare in a loud voice, "My good man, stop that this instant! I feel bound to protest your taking my car." Fieldston hears all this, but calmly goes about his task. As he drives away in the truck, with the car in tow, he calls out to Andrew, "Take it up with Sam." Does Andrew have any relief in this situation?

d. Now suppose that Andrew comes upon the scene and does not just register his objection orally. He confronts Fieldston and tries to pull him away from the car. Fieldston merely brushes him aside as he coolly goes about his work. Andrew then decides to sit on the hood of the car, but Fieldston makes sure to drive off slowly and Andrew hops off as the car is towed away. Andrew is not physically hurt in any of this, but of course he doesn't have his car. Does he have any rights against Sam under this scenario?

e. Finally, consider this scenario: Fieldston finds and is able to tow away the car before Andrew comes on the scene. Fieldston has parked his truck with the car still in tow in a parking lot while he goes to make a call to Sam to report his success. Andrew, who has returned to his parking place only to find his car gone, has seen it being towed away and by running has caught up with Fieldston. He approaches the truck and tries to release the car from the towing bar. When this fails he decides to hop on the hood of the tow truck and refuses to get off when "requested" to by Fieldston. "Not until you release my car," insists Andrew. Fieldston calls in the police who arrive on the scene to find Andrew still perched on the hood of the truck refusing to remove himself unless and until he gets his car back. You make the call. Is Andrew within his rights in acting as he does? If not, what problem does he now face?

5. Sam sells yet another of his stock of Aspen autos to one Johanna. When Johanna falls behind in payments Sam forwards the pertinent information to Rocky Fieldston, the repo man, asking that he make a repossession of Johanna's car. Late one night Fieldston drives by Johanna's home and sees the car parked in Johanna's driveway. He backs his truck (quietly) into the driveway, hitches up the car, and tows it away. Johanna is not aware of what has happened until the next morning.

a. Does Johanna have any right to object to this manner of repossession?

b. What would be the situation if instead Fieldston had found the car in Johanna's garage and towed it away from there? Would it make a difference if the garage door had been left open during the night or if it had been closed and Fieldston had (quietly) opened the door in order to find and take the car? What if the garage door had not only been closed but locked and Fieldston had (quite easily and perfectly quietly) broken the lock in order to take the car?

c. Suppose that when Fieldston takes Johanna's car, no matter where or when, and drops it off at Sam's Autorama, Johanna's valuable set of golf clubs are in the trunk. Sam does not bother to check the trunk, or if he does he just ignores what he finds there. Can you think of an argument for Johanna which will give her at least some leverage against Sam? What would you advise Sam to do as a matter of course when a repossessed auto is returned to his Autorama to minimize any difficulties he might later have because of other property, like the golf clubs, which the cars' buyers may have stowed in their cars?

6. When Dexter Moneybucks was in need of some cash he negotiated a loan of $7,000, which he promised to repay within a year from a friend and fellow art collector, Sarah. As collateral he gave Sarah a security interest in a small statuette ("A Hypothetical Figure") that is a part of his art collection and that sits on his mantelpiece. When the year is up, Dexter has not repaid Sarah what he owes her nor does he show any signs of being willing and able to do so. Sarah pays a visit to Dexter and demands repayment. When Dexter tells her he is unable to pay, Sarah walks over to the mantelpiece and takes hold of the statuette, intending to put it into her spacious shoulder bag. Dexter makes no move to physically confront Sarah or to bar her from leaving but he most strenuously objects, "Oh, no you don't. Sue me if you want, but that piece stays here."

   a. Were Sarah to ignore his objection and take the piece with her, would her repossession be an effective one under §9-609?

   b. Suppose, after some further heated conversation, Dexter were to say, "All right, you can take the thing if you really want it. But if you do it's only on the condition that there's no more bugging me for money. I'll consider us even." How would you advise Sarah to proceed?

   c. Finally, suppose that when Sarah comes to call Dexter simply refuses to let her in. What option or options are now open to Sarah?

7. Hartford Cogs and Widgets buys a large number of specifically designed and configured handheld computers (the "Phaser" system) to be used by its nationwide force of sale representatives from the computer maker, Sisko Enterprises. Hartford agrees to pay for the computers over a period of time, granting Sisko a purchase-money security interest in all of the computers to secure its payment of the price. Hartford soon runs into business difficulties and begins falling behind in its payment to Sisko. Sisko determines that it would like to repossess all of the Phasers, since with only minor adaption they could be made usable by another of its customers. Does Sisko have to hire repossession agents all over the county to take possession of the Phasers one-by-one from each of Hartford's sales reps, or is there another way for it to proceed? See §9-609(c).

8. Hartford Cogs and Widgets purchases a large, complex, and expensive piece of widgetmaking machinery (the "Voyager System") from its manufacturer, Janeway Machine Tools, Incorporated. Hartford arranges to pay Janeway for the complete system in monthly installments over a period of five years, granting the seller a purchase-money security interest at time of purchase. Various parts and subsystems of the complete

Voyager are delivered to one of Hartford's plants over a period of weeks in January 2006 and assembled at the plant. In February 2008, Hartford runs into financial difficulties and stops paying Janeway. That firm eventually decides to take back possession of the system so that it may resell it to another widgetmaker. Hartford does not object, because it sees no way of making payment on the system and is having to scale back its production in any event. Can you suggest any way that Janeway may proceed other than by actually disassembling the whole system, carting it away from Hartford's plant and then putting the pieces in storage? See §9-609(a)(2).

Explanations

1a. If the bank did declare a default by invoking the general insecurity clause in this situation it would almost certainly be found, if Grafix were to challenge the action as we hope he would, to have acted improperly. The justification for allowing such clauses and recognizing their enforceability in appropriate instances is that circumstances unforeseen at the time of the initial agreement and not more specifically dealt with by the security agreement may arise that justify the secured party's *increased* insecurity. Here, nothing new has come up. There is no change in the circumstances from what they were at the time of the bank's initial determination to lend on these terms. Recall that the relevant provision in Article 1 legitimates clauses such as we have here as long as they are construed to mean "that [the secured party] shall have power to [accelerate at will when it deems itself insecure] only if [it] in good faith believes that the prospect of payment or performance is impaired." The word "impaired" in this section, and for that matter the use of the phrase "less likely" in the security agreement as drafted and offered up by the Smallville bank, suggests quite strongly that reliance on the clause is appropriate only if something new comes up that changes, meaningfully if not radically, the lender's chances of being repaid from what it would have evaluated them to be at the time of its initial decision to take the risks inherent in its granting this particular loan.

The lender should, and I have little reason to doubt would, be held by most any court to have acted beyond its rights if it were to invoke the general insecurity clause simply because it later regrets its initial decision to lend to the debtor on the terms already agreed to. The situation I have posited here, where the bank may well want not merely to invoke the clause in order to "undo" the relationship but in effect as a way of insisting on a renegotiation, would even call into question whether it was acting in good faith, as is required under

§1-208 or §1R-309 and more generally under §1-203 and §1R-304. Look again at the definition of "good faith" found in §9-102(a)(43) or the revised version of Article 1.

1b. While you can more readily appreciate the bank's increased insecurity in this case, it is unlikely that a court would approve of the bank's reliance on the general insecurity clause based on changes in general economic conditions alone. The risks that the economy will at times turn sweet or sour (either on some naturally occurring cycle or for reasons that no one, and certainly not any trained expert economist, has any way of explaining) are intrinsic to any of the loan arrangements entered into by Smallville Bank and Trust. A general insecurity clause is presumably appropriate for use not only when there has been some change in circumstance from the time when the loan was initially entered into but where the triggering event is a change in the circumstances of the *particular* borrower's business or state of affairs which renders the lender's prospects of payment or performance on this *particular* loan less likely. To read the clause otherwise is to read it out of the context, a listing of "defaults" by the borrower, in which it appears.

1c. The bank would be on much safer ground if it looked to its general insecurity clause under this set of facts. Of course, it had better be sure that its sources are reliable. In fact the bank stands a hefty risk of being found to have acted precipitously if it were to immediately attempt to repossess, for example, or invoke a companion acceleration clause and call the entire debt without even contacting Grafix and asking him what was going on. On the other hand, if things really are as the reliable sources report them to be, the bank may have to act quickly to protect its position. Should Grafix run into real trouble with his landlord there is the possibility that he could find himself locked out of his business premises. Of as much concern to the bank is that its collateral, the equipment, will probably still be locked up inside the place and the landlord might be asserting some kind of statutory or common law landlord's lien on whatever the tenant leaves behind. The bank wants to be repaid or if that is not possible at least have a clear path to the collateral. It certainly does not want to lock horns with the landlord much less all those other unsatisfied creditors who will be knocking on Grafix's door, only to find nobody minding the shop.

The bank is in a difficult situation here and not even the most careful reading of the Code or of the signed documents it has on hand will eliminate all doubt about what actions it may or may not take and what risks it might be incurring if it is later found to have acted improperly. That, however, is all too often the lot of the lender when the borrower seems to be teetering on the brink of real disaster. If you act too quickly or take too drastic a course, you might later be held to have violated the borrower's rights with real damages flowing. If you wait until you are perfectly sure of what to do, it may be too late to do much except get in line after (or in a tussle with) other creditors and similar parties trying to sort out the mess left in the wake of the borrower's accumulated defaults or a petition in bankruptcy. A general insecurity clause, if properly applied and not just thought of as a way for an anxious lender to go off half-cocked without having to worry about the consequences, may give the secured party a little more room to maneuver when things get dicey, but it is by no means a cure-all.

1d. This conceivably could be an instance where the insecurity clause could be properly invoked, but it would have to be a pretty gutsy lender who would rely on this information alone to invoke it. The interesting aspect of this hypothetical is really the moral that if the Smallville bank's initial determination to lend to Grafix's business rested to any great extent on the continued personal involvement of Grafix, Cosmo, that is, on a day-to-day basis, it would have made sense for the bank to include some special, more particularized language in one of the other default provisions to take care of this possibility. A clause could be added saying, for instance, that not only Cosmo's death but his permanent disability or his failure to continue working for the business on a full-time basis would in and of themselves be events of default. The added time and trouble of getting something like this agreed to as part of the security agreement, even if it meant the bank's going beyond its standard off-the-shelf form agreement, would have been well worth the effort. That way, should Cosmo start to wander away from the business putting its continued health in jeopardy the bank would have something much more concrete to go on. Just as important, by including language directed at this possibility in the agreement, and by drawing Cosmo's attention to it at the time the loan is initiated, he will be aware what is expected of him by the lender and will presumably be less likely to roam.

2. No. Marty may choose to forgive, even if he should never totally forget, Flack's tendency to be absentminded, but he certainly is under no obligation to do so. Acceleration clauses such as that found in Marty's agreement are pretty much routine in such circumstances, and the courts in general have no problem with them. After all, if Marty could legitimately hold Flack in default, but only for $3,000, what good would it really do him? Repossession of the boat would only mean that he would have to sell it off, take his expenses plus $3,000, and, as we will see, hand over all the surplus from the sale to Flack. Flack would have, in effect, turned Marty's sale of a sailboat, from which he expected to make an appropriate profit, into something equivalent to a five-month rental of a new boat for $5,000 plus change. And all the

effort and aggravation would be on Marty, not Flack. If Marty were not allowed to accelerate the full amount due and did not repossess then he could now sue only for $3,000 and keep suing for similar smaller amounts for each month or so that Flack "forgot" to pay. Considering how much aggravation it is to bring a law suit, the result (again assuming acceleration were prohibited) would be that Flack could pretty much pay on whatever schedule he pleased as long as he did not get too egregiously behind. That is simply not fair to the seller, Marty. The practical value of the secured party's right to repossess upon default is obviously very much intertwined with the accompanying right that it assures itself of in the agreement to accelerate the debt on the event of default so that the threat of repossession is meaningful.

3. Dr. Morgan appears for real, but trying to get back his 1984 Porsche, in *Mercedes-Benz Credit Corporation v. Morgan*, 312 Ark. 225, 850 S.W.2d 297, 20 U.C.C.2d 705 (1993). The Arkansas Supreme Court determined that a jury that had found for Morgan on a theory of conversion could properly have concluded that MBCC the lender had waived its right to repossess when one more payment was late, "based on its having repeatedly accepted late payments," and further that "in order to reinstate its right under the parties' contract, MBCC was required to give Morgan notice that MBCC expected strict compliance in future dealings. "If," the Arkansas Supreme Court concluded, "MBCC failed to give such notice in these circumstances, it would then not have had the right to declare a default and repossess its collateral."

Most courts would probably agree with this waiver resulting from a course of performance analysis in general terms. The interesting question arises when one brings into the picture the "nonwaiver" type of provision that we have in our hypothetical agreement and that our seller Sam would reasonably want to take advantage of in such a case. Note the following language from Comment 3 to §9-601:

> This Article does not determine whether a secured party's post-default conduct can constitute a waiver of default in the face of an agreement stating that such conduct shall not constitute a waiver. Rather, it leaves to the parties' agreement, as supplemented by law other than this Article, the determination whether a default has occurred or has been waived. See Section 1-103.

Such nonwaiver clauses are fairly standard in security agreements. As a matter of fact, there was such a clause in the contract between the real-life Dr. Morgan and the Mercedes-Benz Credit Corporation, but the Arkansas Supreme Court relegated it to a footnote because MBCC had apparently failed to present any argument as to its effect in the course of the litigation. The Arkansas Supreme Court's note did, however, recognize a split of authority as to whether such a clause would have any effect on the purported waiver. There is a good review of the issue, and a lineup of the cases that hold each way, to be found in *Moe v. John Deere Company*, 516 N.W.2d 332, 25 U.C.C.2d 997 (S. Dak. 1994). In *Moe*, the Supreme Court of South Dakota aligned itself with what it characterized as a majority of states adhering to a rule that in effect requires a secured party that has repeatedly accepted late payments to give notice that it intended to require strict compliance for the future before it can claim a subsequent late payment to be a default *even in the face of* a contractual "nonwaiver" clause. The court in *Moe* reasoned:

> Adopting the rule that a creditor must give pre-possession [sic] notice upon modification of a contract results in both the debtor and the creditor being protected. The debtor would be protected from surprise and from a damaging repossession by being forewarned that late payments would no longer be acceptable. Likewise, the creditor would be protected utilizing the device of "one letter." The creditor can totally preserve its remedies so that if the account continues in default, repossession could be pursued as provided in the contract without further demand or notice.

The same result is seen more recently in *Davenport v. Bates*, 2006 Tenn. App. LEXIS 790, 61 U.C.C.2d 542.

For a case that holds to the contrary, see *Monarch Coaches, Inc. v. ITT Industrial Credit*, 818 F.2d 11, 3 U.C.C.2d 1274 (7th Cir. 1987), in which Judge Posner pointed to cases holding nonwaiver clauses enforceable under Illinois law that governed the contract in question, and further explained:

> By assuring that a lender will not be penalized for his forbearance, a no-waiver clause is, ex ante (before the fact — i.e., before default), in the interest of debtors as well as creditors, for it makes the creditor likelier to accept late payments rather than declaring a default. There is no possible injustice in enforcing the clause against Monarch [the debtor].

Of course, as Judge Posner earlier pointed out, Monarch, the continually late debtor in the situation before him, was "a corporation, not a confused consumer" who when it failed to make payments due in May and June, "must have known that it was in default." Could the same be said of the Dr. Morgans and the Moes of this world? Even if not, is there good reason for giving the "confused consumer" an argument that in effect nullifies a term of a contract he or she has signed which argument is not available to others?

4a. Under §9-609(a)(1) the secured party has the right upon default to take possession of the collateral. Andrew here certainly has no argument that Sam waived that right by any acts on his part. Subsection (b)(2) tells us that the secured party may proceed under subsection (a) "without judicial process, if it proceeds without breach of the peace." The term "breach of the peace" is obviously key here. It is a term of art, the use of which long predated the enactment of the Uniform Commercial Code. It is nowhere defined — or even "explained" (see Comment 3) — in Article 9 or anywhere else in the Code, but has to be understood through a look at the cases as they have piled up over time and what the courts will and will not allow the repossessing party to do in taking possession before it has crossed the line and committed a "breach of the peace." There is no simple or single formula for determining when a breach of the peace has occurred, but for starters it is probably fair to say that there will not be a breach of the peace if in repossessing the collateral the secured party or its representative does not enter into any private structure or proceed in the face of opposition to its actions which threatens violence or physical confrontation.

We will test out this crude characterization — which must be a pretty crudely understood concept given the forces at play — in the varying situations presented in this and the following examples. We start out with an easy case: The car has been repossessed from a parking spot on a public street without any interference from the debtor, indeed without his even being aware of the event until some time later. This is the classic example of a good, healthy repossession without even a hint of a breach of the peace. Would they all be so simple for Fieldston, the repo man, to accomplish and for us to evaluate.

Andrew may well be upset about what has happened, but he has no ground for legal objection. Sam was acting, through Fieldston, as he had a right to under §9-609(a)(1). Andrew has no right to insist on any notice stating that he is in default under the security agreement. The agreement will undoubtedly provide that nonpayment is an instance of default in and of itself with no necessity of notice or demand for payment by Sam. Andrew is expected to know when payments are due under the contract he signed and that his failure to make a timely payment is a default on his part.

Nor is Andrew entitled to any notice that Sam, the secured party, intends to act on his rights under the agreement and §9-609(a)(1) to repossess the auto. Andrew is likewise expected to know that repossession can be a consequence of default. If Article 9 had been drafted to give a debtor the right to some forewarning that a repossession was being contemplated, this would have just about eliminated the chances of the debtor's being able successfully to carry out a self-help repossession, the possibility of which is a central feature of the article. Given notice that the collateral was about to be repossessed, it wouldn't take much intelligence on the debtor's part to realize that he or she should hide it (or protect it day and night sitting nearby with a shotgun in hand), and any attempt to repossess on the secured party's part would be pretty much futile, or lead to just the breach of the peace situations which §9-609(b)(2) attempts to avoid.

4b. Andrew's prior objection to any repossession of the car makes no difference. Sam had the *right* to possession of the auto once Andrew was in default, by virtue of §9-609(a)(1). He did not need to get the debtor's permission to exercise this right. The "debtor's objection" is sometimes articulated as the reason why a repossession was improper, but this will not be or at least it should not be meant to suggest that the secured party needs the debtor's permission to repossess. Rather, as we will see in the latter parts of this example, the contemporaneous objection of the debtor may, if it rises to a certain level and if it is expressed in the right way, make it impossible for the secured party to repossess without committing a breach of the peace. The fact that Sam had received a letter from Andrew a month or so in the past expressing his, Andrew's, hope that Sam will not repossess does not turn a perfectly peaceful, short and sweet, repossession (a good repo man can apparently tow off an ordinary automobile in less than a minute) into one that was accomplished only through a breach of the peace.

4c. Andrew will probably not be able to establish that a breach of the peace occurred in this situation. True, he objected as the repossession was taking place, but in such a gentlemanly and restrained manner that there never seemed to be any likelihood that violence was about to follow. In *Chrysler Credit Corporation v. Koontz*, 277 Ill. App. 3d 1078, 661 N.E.2d 1171, 29 U.C.C.2d 1 (1996), the debtor, who had rushed outside in his underwear hollering "Don't take it," to the repossessor in the process of taking his car from in front of his home, tried to argue that this "unequivocal oral protest" to the taking of his vehicle was in and of itself enough to make its seizure under the circumstances a breach of the peace. The Appellate Court acknowledged that the phrase " 'breach of the peace' has never had a precise meaning in relation to specific conduct" and must be applied according to the circumstances. That actual violence occurs is not necessary; "Threats and epithets directed at another may or may not constitute a breach of the peace, depending upon the likelihood that a disturbance will follow." It concluded:

> [T]he term "breach of the peace" connotes conduct which incites or is likely to incite immediate public turbulence, or which leads to or is likely to lead to an immediate loss of public order or tranquility. The probability of violence at the time of or immediately prior to the repossession is sufficient.

As to Koontz, the court held,

> In this case Koontz himself testified that he only yelled, "Don't take it," and that the repossessor made no verbal or physical response. He also testified that although he was close enough to the repossessor to run

over and get into a fight, he elected not to because he was in his underwear. Furthermore there was no evidence in the record that Koontz implied violence at the time or immediately prior to the repossession by holding a weapon, clenching a fist, or even vehemently arguing toe-to-toe with the repossessor so that a reasonable repossessor would understand that violence was likely to ensue if he continued with the vehicle repossession.

The evidence supported the trial court's determination that Chrysler Credit Corporation, acting through a repossession agent, had been able to take the car without a breach of the peace. Andrew's demeanor in our hypothetical, even if he does have all of his clothes on, seems pretty much like that of Koontz and hence he would probably have no grounds for objecting to the taking of his car by Fieldston on behalf of Sam.

4d. Even though nobody was actually hurt here, Andrew can rightly argue that his somewhat uncouth response to the situation did transform the otherwise tranquil city street into the site of a breach of the peace. Look again at the language of the court in the *Koontz* case above. As the hypothetical now stands, there has been some measure of confrontation, and potential violence and possible injury, even if Andrew was the one possibly bringing it on himself. Fieldston, as a "reasonable repossessor," could have understood that violence was likely to ensue, if not inevitable, if he continued with the repossession — which meant he should have stopped right there. His failure to do so makes him — and through him, Sam — liable for wrongful repossession, the various potential consequences of which we have only begun to consider, and possibly the tort of conversion.

Not all debtors who physically get involved in an attempted repossession are as lucky as Andrew is in our hypothetical. In *Callaway v. Whittenton*, 892 So. 2d 852, 52 U.C.C.2d 525 (Ala. 2003), the Alabama Supreme Court was recently confronted with a case in which the trial judge had ruled as a matter of law that the repossession had not involved a breach of the peace preventing the wrongful-repossession claim from even going to the jury. The parties, not surprisingly, differed on exactly what happened when Whittenton came to the home of Joy and Christopher Callaway on November 6, 2000, to repossess their Tracker SUV. The Supreme Court acknowledged that the account according to the Callaways themselves was "not altogether consistent." Among their allegations, however, were that

> Christopher grabbed the roll bar of the Tracker as Whittenton began to drive away. Christopher banged on Whittenton's truck and yelled to get Whittenton's attention. Then, as Whittenson was driving down the driveway, the Tracker hit a pothole, and Christopher lost his balance. While he

was trying to regain his balance, the rear tire on the driver's side of the Tracker ran over Christopher's foot. Christopher then grabbed the roll bar on the Tracker again so that it would not roll over him. Whittenton continued driving, dragging Christopher down the driveway and 60-100 feet down Highway 10. One of the vehicles ran over the family's cat.

The Supreme Court held that, viewing the evidence in the light most favorable to the Callaways, they had presented sufficient evidence from which a jury could have concluded that a breach of the peace had occurred and that their wrongful-repossession claim should not have been summarily dismissed at trial.

4e. Andrew has objected to the repossession, and certainly forcefully, but he has done so too late, after the repossession was completed. Objection after the repossession has been successfully accomplished without any confrontation with, or impropriety on the part of, the repossessor is not turned into one involving breach of the peace by this kind of altercation after it is over and done with, even if as here the time that has passed is not that great. The situation here is Andrew himself engaging in some peace-disturbing behavior and, had he been successful in getting the car away from Fieldston, it would have been Andrew who was converting property now rightfully Sam's (in Fieldston's care) and not his anymore.

For a case in point you might want to look at *James v. Ford Motor Credit Company*, 842 F. Supp. 1202, 24 U.C.C.2d 363 (D. Minn. 1994). On June 29, 1992, one Robert Klave, an employee of the firm of Special Agents Consultants, acting on behalf of Ford, removed the plaintiff's, Stephanie Ann James's, car from a parking lot with no incident. Approximately one hour later and several miles from the parking lot, James saw Klave, who had already reported his repossession of the car to Ford and been instructed to deliver it to Minneapolis AutoAuction, inside the car. According to the report of the case, she "entered the car and an altercation ensued." Klave was able to drive the car away and into another parking lot "where the struggle continued inside the car, then outside the car and finally inside the car again." James apparently gained the advantage and was able to drive the car home. Klave reported the incident to the police, accusing James of assault, theft, and damage to property. He reported the car as stolen. On July 8, 1992, James was spotted by the Minneapolis police driving the car and was arrested. Klave was then able to repossess the car again. James sued Klave, Special Agents, and Ford on a variety of theories. For our purposes it is sufficient to relate that the district court held that Klave's initial taking of the car — before he had the pleasure of meeting Ms. James — was lawful and not accompanied by any breach of the peace. "Once a repossession agent has gained sufficient dominion over collateral to control it, the repossession has been completed." Thereafter,

> James' protest was to no avail. It would be unjust to hold that the violence caused by James in a public place after the repossession was complete could somehow dispossess [the repossessing secured party] of their present right of possession.

In our hypothetical, Andrew's behavior was not quite as dramatic as Ms. James's, but it was no more appropriate. His car has been lawfully repossessed. The later breach of the peace was of his own making and something for which he will be responsible once the police can get him down from the hood of the tow truck.

5a. We know that the repossession would have been perfectly fine had Fieldston taken the car from the public street in front of Johanna's house. Is the situation any different once he goes onto her property and takes it from her driveway? The cases seem to be in agreement that if this is all he has done, if there has been no altercation and he has not acted in the face of a contemporaneously expressed objection to his being on the land, then this is still all right and no breach of the peace has occurred. See, for example, *Giles v. First Virginia Credit Services, Inc.*, 149 N.C. App. 89, 560 S.E.2d 557, 46 U.C.C.2d 913 (2002), where the plaintiff's auto was easily taken from their driveway around 4 A.M. without incident. Mr. and Mrs. Giles were awakened not by the sounds of the repossession agents doing their job, but by a call from a neighbor who had, roused by the noise, observed the goings-on from a distance, and called to tell them that their car was apparently being stolen. Neither of the plaintiffs were even awake to see the car being repossessed. As the court also noted, there had been no contact, much less a confrontation, between them and the repossession agents, nor between the agents and the neighbor, who did put up a shout, but from a distance.

5b. The situation would be quite different if Fieldston had entered into an enclosed structure on Johanna's property, certainly if he had broken into the locked garage and even if he had not. While there is no perfect consistency in the cases, the majority appear to hold that there is a breach of the peace once the repossessor has entered into the debtor's home or garage without express permission, even if there is no direct confrontation between the repossessor and anyone on the property. Compare *Pantoja-Cahue v. Ford Motor Credit Company*, 375 Ill. App. 3d 49, 872 N.E. 2d 1039 (breaking into a locked garage to repossess a car may be found to constitute a breach of the peace) with *Raffa v. Dania Bank*, 321 So. 2d 83, 18 U.C.C. 263 (Fla.App. 1975) (no breach of the peace occurred in repossession of a car left with keys in its ignition parked partially under carport and it was undisputed that no door, "not even one to a garage," on the debtor's premises was opened, much less broken, to repossess the car). It should not be difficult for you to come up with your own ingenious fact patterns that fall somewhere neatly in between these two extremes, so I leave you to it.

5c. Section 9-609(a)(1) gives Sam, the secured party, upon default the right to take the collateral. It does not give him the right to take any other of the debtor Johanna's property. He has no right to take and hold onto her golf clubs. The best thing Sam can do here is to get the golf clubs back to Johanna as quickly as possible, either by offering to drop them back at her home or to make them available for her to pick up at her convenience. In *Clark v. Auto Recovery Bureau Conn., Inc.*, 889 F. Supp. 543, 27 U.C.C.2d 649 (D. Conn. 1994), the district court held that the repossessor had in fact committed conversion of several items of the debtor's personal property when it took possession of the car in which they were at the time. It awarded compensatory damages, however, only for the one item the temporary loss of which caused the debtor measurable damage, a costume that her son was to wear in a school play that had to be replaced on short notice at a cost of $50. Other than that, the court held, it would not award any additional compensation for "claimed emotional distress, embarrassment and inconvenience" arising out of the debtor's temporary loss of an umbrella, a raincoat, and a purse containing $150, all of which were returned to her.

6a. If Sarah were to take the statuette over Dexter's express objection, it would likely be ruled an improper repossession involving a breach of the peace. While it might be hard to imagine the situation escalating into one of violence or the threat of violence (although it is awfully hard to rule anything out with these characters), if you put together the two factors — that this would be a taking from within the debtor's residence and that the debtor has made an express and unequivocal objection to the repossession — it would be best for Sarah not to take the statuette even if she thought she could get away with it, without Dexter's actually barring the door. She would have the collateral in her possession, true, but Dexter could later argue an improper repossession and Sarah would be subject to all the woes of the secured party who has overstepped the line in taking possession on her own under §9-609(b)(2). Dexter has given her permission to enter his residence, not permission to repossess. Even if he were initially to give her permission to take the piece but then before she left the apartment were to change his mind and object to the repossession, Sarah would be wise to lay off. Even where the debtor initially gives permission to the repossession, the rule seems to be that the debtor can revoke that permission any time before the repossession has been completed.

6b. Sarah should not take the statuette if these are the terms Dexter is holding out. He would later be able to claim that he never gave permission to a §9-609 repossession, which would allow Sarah, as we will see in the coming chapter, to resell the piece and still hold him liable for any deficiency, but was offering to enter into an accord and satisfaction, the end result of which would be that she would have the artwork but would have forsaken any chance to a deficiency judgment should the piece be worth less than what Dexter now owes her. Unless Sarah is quite sure that the statuette is valuable enough to make this result attractive to her, she had better put it back on the mantlepiece and pursue her other options.

6c. The right to effectuate a self-help repossession under §9-609(b)(2) is a valuable, but not invariably practicable, one for the secured party. Here Dexter has made the choice an easy one as he has out-and-out barred the door. Look now to §9-609(b)(1): In taking possession the secured party may proceed "pursuant to judicial process." So one option open to Sarah at this point is to bring an action against Dexter to get possession of the piece. The exact terminology for the type of action that Sarah will have to pursue will differ from state to state, but the end result should be the same. Dexter will be ordered to surrender the goods. If by this time Dexter still doesn't see why he has to hand it over, Sarah will be able, after filing an affidavit or a copy of the judgment and probably having to post bond, to get the local sheriff to seize the property. The sheriff, of course, will insist on a fee for his or her services, but this should get the job done. Repossession by action involves, as you can see, a good deal more time and effort for the secured party as well as additional expense. Occasionally, as when Dexter bars the door, it might be the only way to proceed. In other circumstances, where self-help repossession is possible but threatens to become tricky and runs the secured party the risk of making some mistake in carrying it out, it is the wiser course even if not the only one.

For a case that makes Sarah's possible difficulty in getting possession of the one statuette Dexter is holding on to seem like a day in the park, see *Christie's Inc. v. Davis*, 247 F.Supp.2d 414, 49 U.C.C.2d 684 (S.D.N.Y. 2002). The world-renowned auction house had made loans totaling up to $15,495,000 to the Davises secured by collateral the court summarized as "hundreds of pieces of fine and decorative art and antique furniture, most of which the Davises kept in their house in Greenwich, Connecticut." The security agreement specifically provided that in the event of a default, the lender could repossess collateral whose "low estimated value" (a term carefully defined in the loan documents) was twice the amount of indebtedness, but no more. Even though the debtors had repaid some on the money borrowed, they conceded they were in default. Still, making a variety of arguments, they refused to allow repossession of any of the collateral. The court granted what it acknowledged to be a rare summary judgment in favor of a plaintiff, despite the Davises limited opportunity for discovery. Christie's was awarded a judgment of $6,873,044, the minimum amount the Davises admitted to be due. The Davises were also ordered to "make available" to Christie's items of the collateral, to be selected by it in accordance with the loan documents, having an aggregate "low estimated value" of $13,746,088. The court further directed the parties

> to meet and confer regarding a mutually satisfactory disposition of the remaining disputes in this case, in order to avoid causing more attorney's fees to accrue by protracting the litigation through further efforts by [the Davises] to avoid their clear obligations.

Note that under §9-615(a)(1) once the secured party does get possession of the goods and decides to resell, the reasonable expenses of retaking the goods will be assessed against the debtor when the proceeds of the resale are divided up. This, of course, argues for the rational debtor's acquiescing in a simple, straightforward self-help repossession as often as possible. If the car is going to be repossessed eventually anyway, there's no reason to make the lender go to the extra expense of having to hire a repossession firm, the cost of which will only come out of your pocket. Of course, as we have already seen in a number of examples, the average debtor and the reasonable debtor may not always be one and the same.

Sarah has another option open to her besides getting a court's and the sheriff's assistance in repossessing the piece. If she believes that its eventual resale value would in any event not be great enough to cover both the costs involved with repossession and the full debt owed to her, she might determine that she would in any event have to sue Dexter for a deficiency judgment. If she is going to have to sue him anyway, why wait? Look to §9-601(a)(1): Upon default, the secured party "may reduce [her] claim to judgment" as an alternative to foreclosing on the collateral. Sarah can just sue Dexter for the money now owed her under their loan agreement, the underlying obligation, ignoring at least initially the security interest in one particular piece of his accumulated assets. Remember, the security interest, while it has been throughout this volume (and will continue to be as we wind down) the principal focus of our interest, is still only a backup to the underlying obligation. When it comes down to it, the dispute between Dexter and Sarah is now over the $7,000 plus interest, which he has borrowed and failed to repay in a timely fashion. Sarah probably has no great interest in the statuette in and of itself; she may even hate it.

Her purpose is to get the money owed her, and what is to say that a direct suit on the underlying obligation is not the best way of going about that?

If Sarah does bring suit on the repayment obligation and obtains a judgment in her favor, then she may proceed as would any other judgment creditor. If Dexter doesn't respond to the judgment and come up with the cash, she may be forced to levy against his property, which would include not only the particular statuette on which she has a security interest but other of his possessions. Notice that by going this route Sarah does not relinquish the special position she has in the one piece of his property, the Hypothetical Figure, on which she had previously taken a security interest. Under §9-601(e), the lien of any levy that she would have by virtue of the general levy would, with respect to this particular piece, relate back to the earlier of the date of perfection or making a filing relating to the security interest. This will help her — at least in regard to this one bit of Dexter's property — if she is by this time scrambling to get her share of Dexter's fortune and in competition with other of his creditors or a trustee in bankruptcy. See also Comment 6 to this section.

7. Under §9-609(c) Sisko can "require the debtor to assemble the collateral and make it available to [it] at a place to be designated by [it] which is reasonably convenient to both parties."

8. Janeway has the right, under the cited provision, to render the Voyager "unusable," let us say by removing the all-important warp core from inside the assembled system, and then may dispose of the collateral on Hartford's premises. This would mean showing it to potential buyers at this location, holding an auction there, and so on. The assembly could then be transferred directly from Hartford's plant to the eventual buyer's place of business. See Comment 6 to §9-609.

21

The Foreclosure Sale

DISPOSITION OF THE COLLATERAL

Assume the debtor is in default under the terms of the security agreement. Assume furthermore that the secured party is in possession of the collateral, either because it had initially perfected by possession and been sure to hold on tight or because it had repossessed as provided for under §9-609. Where, exactly, does this leave the secured party? Well, as we have postulated it has possession of the collateral, the car, the equipment, the chattel paper, or whatever. The secured party will rarely find any great pleasure in its possession of the collateral just for its own sake; it is unlikely itself to have need of yet another used car or widgetmaking machine. If anything, having to take physical possession of the collateral is something of a pain. The secured party now has to find some place to keep the thing, to take responsibility for it, to make sure it is well protected and maintained. Most importantly, now that the collateral is in the secured party's hands, it will be for the secured party to decide what happens next. It cannot just let things ride. Not only will it start running up enormous storage fees if it fails to take some action regarding the collateral, it stands to run into problems under the rules of Part 6 of Article 9 if it does not do something and, as we will see, if it does not do what is called for exactly as required.

So, the secured party has the headache of actually having the collateral in hand. What it doesn't have is the money it is owed by the debtor, or satisfaction of whatever other nonmonetary obligation of the debtor was being secured by the security interest in the collateral to begin with. The trick for the secured party is to turn the one, the collateral on hand, into the other, the money it is owed or the monetary equivalent of the debtor's failure to meet its obligation whatever that may have been. In theory this should not be that difficult a trick to carry off. In practice, as we will see in this and the succeeding and concluding chapter, it is a routine full of potential pitfalls for the secured party where one false step can leave it in serious trouble or at least holding the decidedly short end of the stick.

Initial reading of §9-610(a) seems to, and indeed does, give the secured party wide latitude in what it may do following the debtor's default with any collateral it has had or has then taken into its possession.

> After default, a secured party may sell, lease, license, or otherwise dispose of any or all of the collateral in its present condition or following any commercially reasonable preparation or processing.

In addition, the concluding sentence of subsection (c) provides that:

> [A] secured party may dispose of collateral by public or private proceedings, by one or more contracts, as a unit or in parcels, and at any time and place and on any terms.*

We will leave for later discussion the introductory part of this sentence, as well as the sentence that proceeds it, with their invocation of the requirement that all be done in a "commercially reasonable" manner. As you might imagine, however, it is this qualification that will so concern the secured party in what is to come.

From what we have read so far, at least, it appears that the secured party is given a great deal of freedom as to how it may dispose of the collateral it has on hand. That is, indeed, the idea. The purpose of the disposition is to generate funds in exchange for the collateral, and it is in everyone's interest that the secured party get as high an amount as it reasonably can for what it is selling. This is highlighted by our knowing what is to become of the

---

* The distinction between what would be a public sale and what a private one is not made explicit in this section, or anywhere else in Article 9 for that matter. It has always been taken for granted, however, that what is meant by the distinction is that a "public" sale is one by auction and anything else is a private disposition. See Comment 4 to §2-706 where this reading of the terms is made explicit in an analogous Code context. For an auction to be a "public" sale, of course, it must be an auction truly open to the public. The courts have held that a so-called "dealers-only" auction, open only to dealers in the particular type of goods involved — which is actually a fairly common way that repossessed used cars and large equipment are sold off, and in many respects a perfectly commercial reasonable way to do so — is not public in character. See, for example, *Beard v. Ford Motor Credit Co.*, 41 Ark. App. 174, 850 S.W.2d 23, 20 U.C.C.2d 1158 (1993). Thus the notice which is required of the secured party if the collateral is sold off in such a matter is that called for when a private disposition is contemplated, not a public one. *In re Downing*, 286 Bankr. 900, 49 U.C.C.2d 697 (W.D. Mo. 2002).

proceeds of the sale or other disposition of collateral under §9-610. Look to the end of §9-615(a). The proceeds are applied in the following order:

(a) to the reasonable expenses incurred in the secured party's repossession and sale (including "to the extent provided for in the agreement and not prohibited by law," its reasonable legal expenses);

(b) to the satisfaction of the indebtedness secured by the security interest under which the disposition is made — that is, paying the secured party what it is owed on the underlying obligation;

(c) to the satisfaction of any security interest of lesser priority provided the holder of the interest has made an authenticated demand.

If the proceeds of the sale cover at least all of (a) and (b), then the secured party comes out whole, even if it has gone through a lot of aggravation to do so.

The next important bit of business to consult is §9-615(d). After having applied the proceeds of disposition as provided for in subsection (a), the secured party is obligated to account for and pay over any surplus to the debtor. If there is no surplus but instead the proceeds of disposition do not fully cover the debtor's obligation, then the debtor-obligor is still liable for any deficiency.*

The price the secured party is able to obtain for the collateral on disposition, as well as how much it first shells out in the way of expenses, thus is of no small importance to the debtor as well. Should that price be greater than the sum of (a), (b), and (c) above, we say there is a *surplus*. As a practical matter it is the rare sale or other disposition that generates a surplus; if the goods are worth that much it would be unlikely that the debtor would have let the situation get to this point where they had to be repossessed and sold, and a sale, whether public or private under this kind of "distress sale" conditions, is unlikely to bring top dollar. Still, a surplus is a possibility, and if there is a surplus it belongs to the debtor.

A much more typical outcome is that the sale, even if carried out as well as can be expected of the secured party, will not generate enough cash to cover all of (b), the indebtedness owed it by the debtor. In this case we say there is still a *deficiency* and §9-615(d)(1) makes clear that unless the secured party has previously agreed to forsake any chance of recovering the deficiency, the obligor (whom we'll assume for our purposes is identical to the

---

* Subsection (e) just makes explicit that an out-and-out sale of accounts, chattel paper, payment intangibles, or promissory notes, which sale is governed by Article 9, is what it is. The buyer in such a situation gets to keep any surplus and cannot sue for any deficiency. It paid a price to become the true owner of the stuff and got exactly what it paid for, no more and no less.

debtor) is fully liable for the amount. The debtor may, of course, pay this amount once informed of it just to be rid of the matter, but if it does not the secured party will be forced to bring an action on the debt unpaid (the amount owed minus what it has recovered from sale or other disposition of the collateral above and beyond its expenses of repossession and disposition) and obtain a deficiency judgment.

PROTECTING THE DEBTOR'S INTERESTS

The secured party runs the show that is the §9-610 sale; that much is clear. The debtor, however, is not altogether out of the picture, nor can it afford to be. It may have lost possession of the collateral, but it will not have lost interest in what becomes of it and particularly in what price it commands on sale. The higher the price the collateral fetches on sale, whether public or private, the better off the debtor is. Every extra dollar that the sale brings in means to the debtor either one more dollar in surplus due it — in those rare instances where the proceeds of the sale are great enough to fully cover both the secured party's reasonable expenses and the obligation owed it and still leave a surplus for distribution to the debtor — or more typically one less dollar in what it, the debtor, will still be obligated for as a deficiency. If the secured party were to run the foreclosure sale without regard for the fact that it is in effect selling for the benefit of both it and the debtor, or if it were to sell for just any old price that met its criterion for what would be good enough, the interests of the debtor could be seriously undermined.

The drafters of Article 9 were perfectly aware of this predicament. They chose to address it not by insisting that the disposition of the collateral be carried out in any one particular specified and carefully defined manner. Instead, as we have already seen, they gave the secured party the right to run the show and furthermore gave it broad discretion to do so in whatever way it thought it stood to realize the best take on sale. The debtor's role is basically a passive one. In rare instances, where it can be established that the secured party is "not proceeding in accordance with the provisions of" Article 9, the debtor may under §9-625(a) go into court for an order providing it relief. Much more typically, however, the debtor just stands aside and observes the procedures and the outcome of the sale. After the disposition of the collateral, if it can establish any failure on the part of the secured party on how it went about disposition, then it will take advantage of the fact — either insisting through an action for a greater surplus than it has been offered or (again, much more usually) defending against the level of deficiency being sought by the secured party on the grounds that the collateral was not disposed of properly and hence did not realize as much as it could and should.

The debtor is given three principal means of protection under the terms of Article 9, to which it may later turn in this way. Note first of all the first sentence of §9-610(b), to which I promised we would return. The secured party is given significant leeway in how it goes about the sale, but the debtor has a right to expect that

> Every aspect of a disposition of collateral, including the method, manner, time, place, and other terms, must be commercially reasonable.

True, as you can see in §9-627(a), the secured party cannot be faulted and held to have failed in its obligation to make what may be termed a "commercially reasonable sale" merely because the result was not the absolutely best price that could possibly have been achieved. As a practical matter, however, the courts have not been slow (and indeed may often be too quick in the opinion of some observers) to look to what appears, in the light of all circumstances and with the benefit of hindsight, at a low price as in and of itself a strong indication that something just must have been wrong in the way the secured party went about its task of selling for the benefit of both.

In addition to its right to insist on a sale commercially reasonable "in all aspects," the debtor has another, more technical procedural protection built into Article 9. Look over §§9-611 through 9-614, which provide for a type of notice to be given to the debtor (and certain other interested parties) of the pertinent information about any proposed disposition of the collateral by the secured party. Section 9-611(b) requires that "a secured party that disposes of collateral under Section 9-610 shall send to the persons specified in subsection (c) a reasonably authenticated notification of disposition." Section 9-612 deals with the timeliness of this *notice of disposition*. The two following sections lay out the requirements as to the content and form of the notice, §9-613 dealing with what the secured party must do to satisfy this requirement when the context is other than a consumer-goods transaction and §9-614 dealing with the special case of the consumer-goods transactions. The theory behind the notice requirement is fairly clear. For one thing, as we will see in the next chapter, prior to the time of disposition the debtor will have the right if it can rustle up the cash to redeem the collateral. It is only fair that the debtor know when its chance to do so will pass. Even if the debtor is not able itself to redeem the collateral, it may have special information about prospective buyers who would be particularly interested in bidding on the property, about advertising methods most likely to lure those bidders who could appreciate its true worth, and so on. At the very least, if the sale is to be by public auction, the debtor should know when and where the auction is to take place so that it can send someone to observe the proceedings to make sure everything is on the up-and-up.

A third means of protection of the debtor is to be found in §9-615(f). As Comment 6 to this section states,

> Subsection (f) provides a special method for calculating a deficiency or surplus when the secured party, a person related to the secured party (defined in Section 9-102), or a secondary obligor acquires the collateral at a foreclosure disposition. It recognizes that when the foreclosing secured party or a related party is the transferee of the collateral, the secured party sometimes lacks the incentive to maximize the proceeds of disposition. As a consequence, the disposition may comply with the procedural requirements of this Article . . . but nevertheless fetch a low price.

That is, to put it in the starkest terms, the secured party understandably may be concerned only that the collateral fetch — and that it or the party close to it need pay — enough to make sure the obligation it has secured is fully covered. Paying any more for the collateral is "only" to the benefit of the defaulting debtor. It will increase any surplus to which that debtor is entitled or decrease the amount of deficiency it need pay. As the comment goes on to describe, and as you should read for yourself, "Subsection (f) adjusts for this lack of incentive," by incorporating a special rule for calculation of any surplus or deficiency when the disposition has been made to the secured party or a person related to the secured party.

In the §9-610 disposition, the secured party runs the game and the debtor stands on the sidelines. The debtor will keep careful watch, however, for if it spots any infractions of the rules by which the game is to be played — any way in which the secured party falls short of the generalized "commercial reasonableness" requirement, any failure by the secured party to give notice to the proper parties with technical precision, or any disposition bringing into play §9-615(f) — it may well be able to use this valuable information to its later advantage in claiming that it is owed a greater surplus or owes less of a deficiency or perhaps none at all. To muddle my metaphor only slightly, the secured party plays the sale game when and how it thinks appropriate and on its home turf. The debtor plays a very cautious defense, watching and waiting to see if the secured party should stumble or fumble.

WHEN THE SECURED PARTY FUMBLES THE BALL

As we have already noted, if the debtor believes that the secured party is not proceeding along the lines laid down for it under any of the sections of Part 6 of Article 9, it has, under §9-625(a), the right to get a court order ordering a disposition or restraining one "on appropriate terms and conditions."

Reading further into this subsection (b) we find that in addition if a disposition has already occurred any party including the debtor which feels its rights have been violated, has a right to recover from the secured party any "loss caused by a failure to comply with the provisions of" Article 9. In addition, under subsection (c), if the collateral is consumer goods, the debtor has the right to recover a statutory measure of punitive damages, which we will have the chance to consider in Example 1 below.

It might initially seem sufficient to the case that the debtor, or any other party entitled to notice of the disposition under the terms of §9-611, who is not properly notified or who has cause to argue that the secured party has not otherwise proceeded according to the Part 6 rules of the game, should be able to recover in the general case for a "loss caused" by the secured party's failure to comply. In reality, however, it may be very difficult, if not impossible, for the wronged party trying to establish any measure of loss, or even the very fact of a loss caused by the secured party's slip-up, to meet the burden of proof on the issue. Who is to say what the value would have been of a notification that was never sent or that had not contained misinformation? How can you quantify how much more the collateral would have brought in at sale had the secured party not failed in one aspect or another to proceed in a commercially reasonable manner in its disposition?

These problems are particularly troubling when the disposition of the collateral has failed to bring in enough money sufficient to fully satisfy the debt owed to the secured party, who then proceeds against the debtor for a deficiency judgment. If the measure of the deficiency judgment is going to be the debt owed reduced by what the collateral brought in on sale, what particular incentive is there for the secured party to get the best price possible? The difference between what the secured party *did* actually bring in on sale and any greater amount that it *might have* brought simply ends up coming out of the debtor's pocket if a deficiency judgment is sought. Of course, the debtor is often in no position to pay a deficiency judgment of any size whatsoever, so there is good reason for the secured party to do the best it is able to get what money it can be sure of through a proper sale or other disposition of the collateral. Still, should it slack off in some way it will be the debtor, not the secured party, that would have to make up the difference, and the courts have been particularly sensitive to this possibility when a deficiency judgment is sought.

The prerevision version of Article 9 contained nothing that addressed this issue directly. Over time, courts came up with at least three distinct rules relating to how a secured party's failure to give notice as required or to dispose of the collateral in a commercially reasonable manner might affect such proceedings.

The "Set-Off" Rule: In a few jurisdictions (fewer than a half-dozen) the rule evolved that the secured party-creditor was entitled to its deficiency subject only to a setoff for any amounts that the debtor could prove resulted from the improper sale. Because the Article already provided for the debtor's right to recover "any loss caused by [the secured party's] failure to comply with the provisions of" its rules on disposition, adoption of the "set-off" rule was really just the same as relegating the aggrieved debtor to this statutory remedy alone. The secured party, which has misbehaved, is not otherwise penalized or caused to forfeit any part of its deficiency.

The "Rebuttable Presumption" Rule: This became the most widely followed rule, having been expressly adopted in something like 26 jurisdictions. The presumption underlying this rule is that the collateral was worth, at the time of sale, and thus sold for, an amount equal to the outstanding debt owed by the debtor to the secured party at the time of default. This presumption arises if either the secured party is not able to prove that it met the criteria of Part 6 or the debtor is affirmatively able to prove that it did not. Once the presumption, in effect that the deficiency is zero, is in place, the *secured party must meet the burden* of proving that the collateral was worth less than the debt and by what measure if it is to collect any deficiency. Since proof of actual value of repossessed goods is often an extremely difficult if not impossible task, this rule puts a heavy burden on the secured party which fails to make a proper disposition, which otherwise would have had to prove no more to gain a deficiency beyond what it had obtained at sale and the outstanding balance of the debt at the time of default.

The "Absolute Bar" Rule: This rule found favor in only a handful of states, but in those its importance could not be minimized. The rule was that a secured party which failed to follow to the letter the dictates of Article 9's default provisions was *absolutely barred* from recovering any deficiency judgment whatsoever. If this works a penalty on the secured party, whose failure may in actuality have caused loss nowhere near the potential deficiency, so be it. There is no getting around the fact that such a bar can work a significant penalty on a secured party, even one which has been proceeding on good faith, but that is the way that it operates.

The drafters of Revised Article 9 were well aware of this split of authority and addressed the issue directly in §9-626. Subsection (a) basically adopts the rebuttable presumption rule for any transaction "other than a consumer transaction." See Comment 2. That still leaves the question of which rules govern when the transaction is a consumer transaction. The drafters chose — or were convinced by consumer advocates who have an understandable fondness for the absolute bar rule if they can get a court to apply it on behalf of their consumer clients — to take no position on how this problem was to be addressed in the consumer context. Or rather they took the firm position that they were to be understood as having nothing to say on the matter. Read §9-626(b):

The limitation of the rules in subsection (a) to transactions other than consumer transactions is intended to leave to the court the determination of the proper rules in consumer transactions. The court may not infer from that limitation the nature of the proper rule in consumer transactions and may continue to apply established approaches.

See also Comment 4 to this section.

Between the statutory remedies for the debtor aggrieved by an improper disposition, as laid out in §§9-625 and 9-626, and these extra added rules generated by courts applicable to potential deficiency actions, at least when a consumer transaction is concerned, it is apparent that the secured party has plenty to worry about as it goes about disposing of collateral once it has gotten its hands on the stuff.

Examples

1. Sam of Sam's Autorama is an authorized dealer in Aspen automobiles. He sells a particular new Aspen to Andrew, who intends to use the car for his personal everyday driving. The cash price of this particular model would be $16,000, but since Andrew does not have that kind of cash he purchases on Sam's Retail Sales Installment Plan agreeing to make 48 monthly payments of $384.95 each. Almost immediately Andrew falls behind in his payments. Sam has the car repossessed and returned to his lot. A week after the repossession, Andrew receives an official looking letter from Sam indicating what has happened and that he, Sam, has himself "repurchased the vehicle in question for $12,350. Because the outstanding amount you owed on said vehicle was $16,167.79 (42 payments still due of $384.95 each), I expect payment of a deficiency of $3,817.49."

   a. Andrew comes to your office, tells you this story and shows you the letter from Sam. He asks whether he has to pay the amount Sam is demanding. What aspects of the Article 9 do you consult and how do you counsel Andrew?

   b. Would the situation be any different if Andrew had bought the car not for his personal use but so that he could use it in his job as a traveling salesman?

   c. Suppose instead that the story told to you by Andrew is as follows: Soon after the repossession he received a notice from Sam officially notifying him of the repossession and that he, Sam, intended to place the car on his used car lot for resale within a week. Three weeks later Andrew receives a second notice from Sam informing him that the car has been sold to one Jessica for $14,000. It also states that Sam's cost of repossessing the auto was $300 and that he spent $175 for minor repairs and cleaning prior to putting the car back on his used car lot. Sam claims a deficiency of $2,642.79 ($16,167.79 due him minus $13,525 he netted from the resale). Do you see any arguments for Andrew in this situation that he is not responsible for the deficiency?

2. Coincidentally, Sam sells an identical model Aspen auto to Johanna on the same terms as he sold to Andrew in the previous example. Johanna, however, makes her regular payments for more than three years before suffering a financial crisis and failing to pay for several months in a row. Sam repossesses and sends Johanna a notice that he intends to resell the auto from his used auto lot at some time after one week following minor repair and cleaning. He is able to sell this car to one Bobbie for $12,345 (remember, it is a few years older). Again his costs are $300 for the repossession and $175 for getting the car into shape for putting out on the lot. At the time of repossession, Johanna had made all but seven of her monthly payments of $384.95 each.

   a. Is Johanna due any money from Sam under these facts?

   b. Would it make any difference to your answer if among the terms of the Retail Installment Agreement originally signed by Johanna was one that said, "Buyer hereby waives right to any surplus which may be otherwise due Buyer in the event of a repossession and eventual resale of the automobile being sold pursuant to this Agreement?" See §9-602(5).

3. The Wellington Bank & Trust agrees to make a substantial loan to Prudence Moneybucks. Among the collateral that Prudence puts up for the loan is a block of 10,000 shares in the publicly traded corporation H.A.L. Industries that she carries in her account with JSR & Co., the brokerage firm through which she handles her investments. Wellington's security interest in these shares is perfected by Prudence having them transferred into a special account that Wellington opens up with JSR & Co. expressly for this purpose. Prudence defaults on her loan. Without giving her any notice, Wellington Bank orders JSR & Co. to sell these shares on a day when they are trading at $14 a share. Prudence receives a letter from Wellington informing her of what they have done and that the $140,000 realized from this sale is being applied to lower the outstanding balance of her loan. By the time she receives this letter, Prudence notes that H.A.L. shares, the value of which has been steadily increasing over the past few weeks, are now trading for $16.75. Has Prudence any grounds for objecting to Wellington's actions or for arguing that she should be credited with a greater amount in reduction of her outstanding loan balance?

4. When Dexter Moneybucks was in need of some cash he negotiated a loan of $7,000, which he promised to repay within a year from a friend, Sarah. As collateral he gave Sarah a security interest in a small statuette that is part of his art collection and that sits on his mantelpiece. When the year is up, Dexter has not repaid Sarah what he owes her nor does he show any signs of being willing and able to do so. He objects to her repossession of the piece and Sarah is forced to obtain

a court order and then use the services of the local sheriff to eventually gain possession of it. At this point she places a telephone call to Dexter. She tells him that unless he pays her all that he now owes (including an additional $350 in repossession expenses she has had to lay out) she will "sometime next week" look for a way to resell the piece and get her money that way. Dexter's only response is that Sarah "shouldn't do anything until you hear from me." In fact, Sarah waits a couple of weeks. She then goes to an art gallery in her town and asks the owner, "How much would you give me for this thing?" The owner looks the piece over, tells her that it is in fact a valuable piece by a well-known artist, and offers to buy it on the spot for $10,000. Sarah says, "Sold!" and walks out of the gallery with a check for this amount in her pocket. A few days later, when the gallery owner's check has cleared, she sends Dexter a check for $2,650, representing the surplus to which she figures he is entitled. Does Dexter have any way of objecting to the way Sarah has disposed of the collateral or the amount he has been sent by her?

5. Suppose the facts are initially as they were in the prior example except for the fact that Sarah is not only a friend of Dexter's, but is herself a collector of fine art. In March, some time after the sheriff has come and taken away the statuette, Dexter receives a letter from Sarah's lawyer saying that the piece is to be sold "at a public auction" to be held at his office (the exact address of which is given) at noon on Monday, April 6, 2008. Also, Dexter sees in the local newspaper, the Shelbyville Tattler, dated March 30, a small notice giving the time and place of the auction, and picturing and correctly identifying the piece to be sold. Dexter does not go to the lawyer's office at the time and date specified, but later receives a letter telling him that the auction took place as scheduled and that the piece was sold for $7,600. Sarah, in satisfaction of her interest, has received $7,000 (the $7,600 minus the $350 repossession fee and the $250 it cost to conduct the auction), leaving exactly zero as a surplus for Dexter. Dexter later learns that the only bidder present at the auction was Sarah and that she was the one to purchase the piece with her initial bid of exactly $7,600. Does Dexter have any way of objecting to the procedure used or the result of the disposition of the collateral?

6. In 2006 Hartford Cogs and Widgets negotiates a general operating loan from the National Bank of Connecticut, giving as collateral "all of Debtor's equipment now held or hereafter acquired." Hartford properly perfects by filing in the appropriate place. In 2007 Hartford buys a special cog polishing machine from the firm of Spiffy and Sons, agreeing to pay for this particular piece over the following 10 years and granting the seller a purchase-money security interest that Spiffy is careful to deal with so that its security interest in the polisher has priority over that

of the bank. In 2008, Hartford, desperate for funds, is somehow able to negotiate a short-term (and high-interest) loan from Lastditch Financial Services, granting that firm an interest in "all of its equipment." Lastditch makes a proper filing in the appropriate place. In 2009, Hartford fails to make several consecutive payments to the National Bank of Connecticut, which repossesses all of the equipment. It decides the way to realize the best value on the collateral is through entering into private sales on the various pieces of equipment arranged for it by a firm that specializes in finding suitable buyers for industrial machinery of just this type.

a. Are Spiffy and Sons and Lastditch entitled to notice of the potential sale of the cog polisher? See §9-611(c).

b. Assuming that a sale is eventually carried out in proper observance of all of the Article 9 requirements for a good sale, what does the buyer of the cog polisher get? That is, will its ownership of this piece of equipment be encumbered by a security interest claimed by any of the National Bank of Connecticut, Spiffy and Sons, or Lastditch? See §9-617.

7. Dexter Moneybucks is for one last time (at least as far as we are to know) in need of ready cash. He finds himself with nothing of value — no jewels, no works of art — that can serve as collateral for the small short-term loan he needs to get him through "the rough patch" he is going through. He is able to convince a friend, one Lucky, to loan him a gaudy but valuable emerald brooch that Lucky had long ago inherited from his mother and that he has, from the time he received it, kept in a drawer in his home. Dexter and Lucky take the brooch down to the Friendly Finance Company, where Dexter completes the forms necessary to finalize a loan from that firm. Lucky shows the finance company proof of his ownership of the brooch and signs a security agreement that grants the lender a security interest in the item backing up Dexter's obligation to repay his loan. The brooch is left in the possession of Friendly Finance, which puts it away in a safe. Suppose that Dexter were later to fail to repay Friendly Finance the amount he has borrowed. The lender determines that it will sell the piece of jewelry (Lucky's mother's brooch) to a well-known jewelry auction house, which should be able to get top dollar for the piece.

a. To whom is Friendly Finance obligated to give notice of this public sale?

b. Should the price for which the brooch is sold at auction exceed the amount due Friendly Finance plus the reasonable expenses of the sale, to whom is the surplus due?

c. On the other hand, if the price the brooch takes at auction does not cover both the expenses of sale and what Friendly Finance is owed, to whom should that firm look to make up the deficiency?

Explanations

1a. Sam has made at least two mistakes following his repossession. First of all, he has not given Andrew, the debtor, any notice whatsoever of the "time after which" a private sale was to be made. See the notice requirement if a private sale is intended in §9-613(1)(E). Here Andrew didn't hear about the sale until after the fact.

Failure to give proper notice in and of itself would make this a fatally flawed sale. In addition, however, we note that Sam has sold the repossessed auto to himself. Look to §9-610(c). The secured party is generally free to purchase at a *public sale*, but may not normally buy through a private sale. The secured party is allowed to purchase privately only where "the collateral is of a kind that is customarily sold on a recognized market or the subject of widely distributed standard price quotations." This phrase is meant to cover such things as publicly traded investment securities and certain commodities that are "going at" an established price in a defined market on any given day. The secured party is allowed to buy the collateral through a private sale only when its fair market value at the time of sale can be well-determined without real dispute, because it is the kind of stuff for which an objectively determined market value at any given time can be established through recourse to publicly available figures. Sam might want to argue that he consulted something such as a used car dealer's "red book," which lists values for various makes and models of used cars depending on their age, but this is not the same thing. While such books serve as a sort of convenient guide to the typical or likely price of a car of that description, we know that individual cars will still fetch higher or lower prices in the marketplace based on their individual condition, their special features, how well the features operate and so forth. For a case holding under the precursor section to what is now found in §9-610(c)(2) that Sam's reliance on such a "red book" value would not justify his buying at that price at a private sale, see *Chrysler Credit Corp. v. H & H Chrysler-Plymouth-Dodge, Inc.*, 927 F.2d 270, 14 U.C.C.2d 377 (6th Cir. 1991).

Sam, having failed to proceed in accordance with the rules of Part 6 of Article 9, is liable under §9-625(b) to Andrew for the loss caused by his failure to do so. Andrew might have trouble establishing how much if at all he was harmed by Sam's behavior, but, luckily for him, because the collateral was consumer goods he can take advantage of §9-625(c)(2):

> [I]f the collateral is consumer goods, [the debtor may recover] in any event an amount not less than . . . the time price differential plus 10 percent of the cash price.

Under the circumstances this comes out to be $2,477.60 (the difference between the 48 payments of $384.95 and the cash price of $16,000) plus $1,600 (10% of the cash price), or a total of $4,077.60. This would seem to more than cover any deficiency Sam is arguing for, although perhaps not quite if Sam is allowed to throw in the cost of repossession and the (presumably low) cost of sale.

As a matter of fact, it always strikes me that there are so few cases reported where a consumer debtor takes an award based on this formula given in §9-625(c)(2). Perhaps this is because consumers are not well aware of its availability. Or perhaps it is that those who regularly sell to consumers, and regularly are forced to repossess, know enough about how to carry out the relatively easy-to-follow notification and other resale requirements that the chances of their making the kind of mistakes Sam has made here, and hence subjecting themselves to the statutory penalty available to the wronged consumer buyer, are slim.

Note, in addition, that should Sam bring a deficiency action against Andrew, Andrew could insist that the deficiency be calculated based not on the $12,350 Sam has received (from himself) for the repossessed auto, but on "what would have been realized in a disposition complying with [Part 6 of Article 9] to a transferee other than the secured party [or] a person related to the secured party." This is because the disposition of the collateral was made as a sale to the secured party himself, one situation that triggers the rule of §9-615(f). Finally, since this is a consumer transaction, Andrew could also hope that the court might adopt the so-called absolute bar rule and hold that he was not responsible for *any* deficiency under the circumstances where Sam, the secured party, has failed to properly follow the dictates of Article 9 on disposition of the collateral after repossession. Recall what we saw in the introduction and the rule (or rather the non-rule) of §9-626(b). For evidence that the absolute bar rule is still alive and well under the Revised Article 9 when consumer transactions are involved, see In re Downing, 286 Bankr. 900, 49 U.C.C.2d 697 (W.D. Mo. 2002), and Coxall v. Clover Commercial Corp., 4 Misc.3d 654, 781 N.Y.S.2d 567, 54 U.C.C.2d 5 (Civ.Ct. City of N.Y. 2004).

1b. If Andrew had bought the auto not as a consumer good but rather as a piece of equipment for his business, the situation would be different in several aspects. Andrew now has no right to gain statutory damages under §9-625(c), as this is no longer a consumer goods transaction. All §9-625(b) has to offer Andrew is that for all of Sam's mistakes he, Andrew, that is, has a right to recover for any loss he can prove was caused by Sam's failure to act as he should have. Can Andrew prove that if he had gotten proper notice that a private sale was intended at some time in the future and that if someone other than Sam had eventually bought the car it would have gone for more than $12,350 *plus* Sam's expenses in "retaking, holding, preparing for sale or lease, selling" and the like *plus* Sam's "reasonable attorney's fees and legal expenses," as are no doubt provided for in the security agreement? Perhaps Andrew will be able to prove as much, but it will not be easy.

If he is sued for a deficiency, Andrew could still call on the rule of §9-615(f), but again he has the problem of proving what proceeds "would have been realized" in a commercially reasonable sale to someone other than the secured party or a person related to the secured party. In any suit for a deficiency brought by Sam, Andrew could not expect to get the benefit of the absolute bar rule, as this is not a consumer transaction. He would, however, be able to assert without question the rebuttable presumption rule by virtue of §9-624(3)(b) and (4). The deficiency he would be expected to pay would be zero, unless Sam can prove that "the amount of proceeds that would have been realized had the noncomplying secured party [that's Sam] proceeded in accordance with the provisions of [Part 6 of Article 9] relating to collection, enforcement, disposition, or acceptance" is less than the sum of Andrew's outstanding obligation plus Sam's expenses and attorney fees. Sam having failed to give proper notice, the burden is now on him, if he wants to be awarded any deficiency, to prove what *would* have been received for the auto had notice been given correctly.

1c. Andrew may be able to argue that this has not been a proper disposition of the car, but there is no obvious way for him to do so given the facts as we now have them. Sam's notice is timely under §9-612. We would have to check, of course, that it meets the content and form requirements for a private sale of either §9-613 or §9-614 depending on whether or not this was a consumer transaction. If the notice requirements have been met, Andrew's only recourse would be to show that some other aspect of the sale failed to meet the standard of "commercial reasonableness."

2a. Yes. Johanna is due a surplus. The $12,345 proceeds of the sale are to be applied first, under §9-615(a) to the expenses of repossession and sale, which here come to $475. That leaves $11,870. The debt still owed by Johanna to Sam equals the seven payments of $384.95 each not yet made, for a total of $2,694.65, which Sam gets. Since there are no junior security interests of which we are aware, the remainder of $9,175.35 is distributed by Sam, who has it in his possession as the reseller, back to Johanna as the surplus due her.

2b. Under §9-602(5), the secured party's right to a surplus under §9-615(d)(2) may not be waived or varied. This term in the security agreement would be unenforceable and of no effect. Johanna has a right to what is hers, and Article 9 does not allow her to contract it away. You should take this opportunity to look at the other parts of §9-602 that constrain the degree to which the parties, even if they should both want to, may vary or deny one or the other of them the rights and remedies provided for in Article 9.

3. Assuming that she was indisputably in default, Prudence does not appear to have any valid argument to be made with the way Wellington Bank disposed of the shares. The usual necessity for notice of an intended sale called for under §9-611 is dispensed with, in subsection (d), when the collateral "is of a type customarily sold on a recognized market," which certainly is true for stock of publicly held and traded companies like the H.A.L. Industries of this world.

Prudence may be upset that Wellington called for the sale on a day when the shares were selling for only $14, in light of their later rise in value, but that should avail her nothing. It is in the very nature of the stock market that a sale made at any time for the then trading price might in retrospect seem to have been a poor decision, but then of course it was equally likely that the value of H.A.L. shares could have plummeted right after the sale by Wellington, or just stayed at the $14 per share level. It is and should be hard to argue that the sale of any publicly traded security was made in a commercially unreasonable manner just because it would have yielded more had the seller waited a bit longer. On a true market like that on which shares of public companies are traded, remember, the traders are evenly distributed between those who believe the stock can be expected to rise in value and those who are of the mind that it is due for a fall. And all of them "commercially reasonable," every one.

The Article 9 drafters attempted to deal with this problem — that it is all too easy for a decision to seem awfully flawed in hindsight — in §9-627(a):

> The fact that a greater amount could have been obtained by a [disposition] at a different time or in a different method from that selected by the secured party is not of itself sufficient to preclude the secured party from establishing that the [disposition] was made in a commercially reasonable manner.

So in any instance of a sale, public or private, a debtor challenging the "commercial reasonableness" of "an aspect" of the disposition must do more than find some way of showing that the collateral could have fetched more if sold to some other party, or at another time, or in a different way.

Wellington Bank & Trust is in a particularly good position, thanks to what we see in §9-627(b): A disposition is deemed to have been made in a commercially reasonable manner if it is made "in the usual manner on any recognized market" or "at the price current in any recognized market at the time of the disposition." Either would seem to apply without any real doubt to the bank's selling of the shares on the stock market. See Comment 4. The bank disposed of shares of stock worth $14 each for $14. That amount gets credited to Prudence's debt. She cannot ask for more.

4. Sarah has disposed of the collateral through a private sale to an art gallery in her town. Dexter cannot object that she has done so, even when he asked her not to, as this is within her rights under §9-610. The issues that arise are whether he has any grounds for objecting to how the sale was carried out. If so, he could argue that a proper sale would have brought in a higher price for the piece of art and hence generated a greater surplus for him. Dexter's potential attacks on the manner of disposition go along two lines: Was there proper notice to him as called for in §9-611, and further was "every aspect of [the] disposition including the method, manner, time, place and other terms" commercially reasonable given the nature of the thing being sold per §9-610(b)?

As to notice, in the case of a private disposition, §9-613(1)(A) calls for certain information to be given by the secured party to the debtor. Sarah here gave notice of the manner in which she intended to dispose of the piece, but it was oral notice only. Is oral notice sufficient for the purposes of §9-611? The answer is not entirely clear from the text. The language calls for "reasonable authenticated notification" not "reasonable written notification." We know (from §9-102(a)(7)) that only a writing or some other record (§9-102(a)(69)) can be authenticated as that word is now used in Article 9. A telephone call, at least one that is not recorded by the agreement of the parties, would presumably not be an authenticated notice for the purposes of §9-611. In this regard it is interesting to look at In re Ott, 278 Bankr. 154, 48 U.C.C.2d 1234 (N.D. Ohio 2002) which held oral notice insufficient to meet the requirements of Article 9. The case was decided under the old Article 9, the language of which did not literally require a written notice but which did call for the notice being "sent" to the debtor, a word which seemingly implied a written notice was necessary. The court held that under the pre-revision Article 9 written notice was not required as a matter of law but that for an oral notice to be sufficient "a debtor, although not having to participate in the sale process, must be given every opportunity to do so. This, at the very least, requires that the debtor be imparted, as is provided for in the statute, with knowledge as to the time and place of the forthcoming sale of the collateral." While this case was decided under pre-revision Article 9, its basic reasoning seems sound. The debtor will normally, I believe, be entitled to a record, whether it be a writing or some other type of communication, giving him or her all of the information called for in either §9-613 or §9-614, depending on which is applicable. I would argue strenuously on behalf of Dexter that Sarah's phone call to him does not fit the bill.

Under pre-revision Article 9, cases where the debtor argued an improper disposition on the basis of a notice defective in some way, allowing him or her to invoke the precursor section to §9-625 or perhaps one of the various rules limiting his or her liability for a deficiency, were plentiful. And, it seems, the debtors won a fair number of these. Sometimes it seemed the court sided perhaps a bit too quickly with the debtor in finding insufficient notice where it was hard to discern any real prejudice to the debtor. In other situations the results seem justified even to the most skeptical observer because the failure of notice really did cut into the protection it is intended to afford the debtor.

A good part of the problem was that the original version of Article 9 did little to specify what was required in the way of notice to the debtor, stating only that "reasonable notification" was to be given. No wonder a lot of argument and litigation ensued. The revision drafters tried to minimize (even if they would never be able to eliminate) such controversies by giving the secured party planning a disposition clear instruction as to whom (§9-611), when (§9-612), and in what form (§§9-613 and 9-614) the notification of disposition is to be given. Trying to ensure that the debtor gives and, of course, the debtor receives, proper notice of an intended disposition should work to both parties' advantage.

Without proper notice that a sale is intended, the debtor — who will often after all have the greatest familiarity with the collateral, how it might be sold most successfully, where potential buyers are lurking, and so on — does not have the opportunity to bring this information to the attention of the secured party so that it can be used to the benefit of both. Dexter in our example might have in mind another art collector who he believes has always craved this particular artwork and from whom he thinks it would fetch top dollar. Without effective notice of how much time he has to look into the matter and bring it to Sarah's attention, he is put at a disadvantage and might not be able to make the connection. Of course, as we have already noted, in this instance Dexter did get the word, even if it was only through a telephone call. But then he did tell Sarah to refrain from doing anything until she "heard" from him. While he has no right to insist she defer indefinitely, the fact that she ignored him entirely may go to whether the sale was carried out in a "commercially reasonable" manner, the important criterion of §9-615(b), which we'll look at next.

Dexter can also challenge Sarah's disposition on the ground that it was not "commercially reasonable" in every respect "including the method, manner, time, place and other terms of the disposition." Sarah did take it to an art gallery, but then to only one, and apparently, the one most convenient for her. And then she took the first offer made her by the owner. Is this the way to sell a valuable work of art? Dexter might assert that any work like this should be sold at auction, that a private sale will by its nature be inappropriate to a work of art. Or he may argue that if Sarah were selling a piece like this strictly for her own account she would have taken it to more than one gallery, or would have searched out which gallery even if it was not one in her community specialized in works of this artist. Or perhaps she would have, had it been a sale from which she expected to reap the entire reward, placed an advertisement about the piece in a particular art collector's magazine.

Just as there will still be numerous, even if we hope fewer, cases where the debtor, usually in the context of resisting a claim for a deficiency, argues that he or she did not receive proper notice under §9-611, there will be many in which the argument is that the disposition failed to be commercially reasonable in one respect or another. The secured party is given, as we have already seen, some aid in the language of §9-627(a) to the effect, "The fact that a greater amount could have been obtained by a [disposition] at a different time or in a different method from that selected by the secured party is not of itself sufficient to preclude the secured party from establishing that the sale was made in a commercially reasonable manner," but sometimes it does seem that what later appears to a court as an "insufficient" or "unreasonable" price may spell trouble for the secured party. In practice, of course, while even under §9-627(a) the fact that the secured party did not get a better price on disposition does not in *itself* prove that the sale did not meet the test of commercial reasonableness, if the debtor can point out *why* or *how* the secured party failed to get an offer at the better price, or worse yet that it did and passed it up, the secured party will have a tough time of it. See, for instance, *Automotive Finance Corp. v. Smart Auto Centers, Inc.*, 334 F.3d 685, 51 U.C.C.2d 297 (7th Cir. 2003), where the debtor's argument that the secured party had failed to dispose of them in a commercial reasonable manner appeared based on little more, at least as the appellate court saw it, than on the assertion that the secured party "didn't get enough money for the vehicles." The argument was easily disposed of by the circuit court in a paragraph. The deficiency judgment obtained by the secured party at the district court level, based on the difference between what the debtor owed and what the secured party *actually did get* in exchange for the vehicles was upheld. And, it should be noted, the secured party was given the opportunity to submit a statement of the attorneys fees it incurred it connection with the appeal.

5. Here Sarah has chosen to dispose of the piece through a public sale or auction. We first ask, on behalf of Dexter, whether he received appropriate notice. Barring other facts of which we are not aware, it seems Sarah's notice was good here. The purpose behind this notification requirement, of course, is to give the debtor the opportunity to attend the auction if he or she chooses, to bid on the item if that is possible or more probably to alert those who he believes might want it and be willing to bid up the price to the fact the auction will take place, and generally to ensure that the auction is carried out as it should be. Here Dexter passes on the opportunity to attend, but that is his decision. He has been given proper notice of the time and the place.

A second question is whether the auction sale was carried out in a commercially reasonable manner. Again Dexter can question whether an auction of an artwork such as this would not normally — and reasonably — be conducted through a specialized art auction house and not at a lawyer's office. He can also take issue with how the auction was advertised to the public. Would it not be reasonable to advertise the auction sale of a piece by a well-known artist in some place other than just in the Shelbyville Tattler?

A distinct concern that is presented by this situation is that, as it turned out, the auction was not a very exciting one. It took place at the offices of Sarah's lawyer, Sarah was the only bidder in attendance, and (surprise) she got the piece for a bid just equal to what she is owed by Dexter, leaving him with no right to any surplus. Does the fact that the secured party buys at the public sale necessarily invalid the result? No. Subsection 9-610(c)(1) specifically provides that, "A secured party may purchase collateral at a public disposition."

Normally, we know, the secured party may not buy at a private sale, and so it is not uncommon for this type of "public sale," in which the secured party is, for all intents and purposes, the only bidder to be conducted. Nor, would you be surprised to learn, is it common at such an auction for the secured party to buy at a price no greater than what he or she is owed by the debtor. Why pay more for the collateral when all that it will mean is that this amount will have to be accounted for to the debtor as a surplus? In fact, many times the secured party will "bid in" and take the collateral at a price below what he or she is owed and then, based on this price, sue the debtor for a deficiency. There is nothing inherently wrong or sleazy about this type of operation. Frankly, there are times when it would be difficult to rustle up any true outside parties with even the slightest interest in buying the collateral at whatever price. The secured party will feel in effect forced to buy it so that a disposition can be made and, following that, a final accounting, be it for a surplus or, more likely, a deficiency. The secured party wants to dispose of the collateral in some way, and as we have seen a private sale to itself is barred in most instances by the language of the Code. So this type of intimate auction at a private office is sometimes the best way to deal with the situation. On the other hand, there are certainly situations when this kind of one-person auction result is inherently unfair to the debtor. See, for example, *AAR Aircraft & Engine Group, Inc. v. Edwards*, 272 F.3d 468, 46 U.C.C.2d 1 (7th Cir. 2001). Edwards had been the chairman and principal shareholder of Kiwi Airlines. As such, he acted as a personal guarantor (what the revised Article 9 would recognize as a "secondary obligor") when his company bought an airplane engine priced at $1,325,000 from AAR on credit, the engine itself serving as collateral. When Kiwi defaulted after having paid only $325,000 on the debt, AAR sued Edwards on his guarantee and got a summary judgment for $1 million, the district court having ruled that Edwards effectively waived in his written guarantee any right to deduct from his obligation any amount recovered on the collateral put up by Kiwi and also waived the right to question the "commercial reasonableness" of any disposition of the collateral by the secured party if it did occur. As it turned out, AAR also repossessed the engine, after which it then, in the words of Judge Evans of the Seventh Circuit,

> 'bought' it back at an auction for $250,000 — some $750,000 less than its estimated value — when no one else appeared and entered a bid. Therefore, when the district court entered summary judgment for AAR, it got both a $1 million damage award against Edwards plus the engine, which was worth roughly the same amount. So it got, in essence, double what it had coming. Edwards, apparently no meshuggener [Yiddish for "crazy person", as the judge apparently assumes all readers of the Federal Reporter would know], senses that something is not quite right with this deal so he appeals.

Edwards was indeed wise, or at least not crazy, to appeal. The Seventh Circuit ruled that he should have been given the right to question the commercial reasonableness of the sale and, if the sale were found to be unreasonable, have the benefit of the rebuttable presumption rule.

The *AAR* case was decided under the pre-revision version of Article 9, but it illustrates well the type of situation of which the revision drafters were well aware and which explains their addition to

Article 9 of the new §9-615(f), a new rule which addresses the problem directly.

If the person who buys or otherwise takes the collateral in a disposition is the secured party itself, a person "related to the secured party" as that term is defined in §9-102(a)(63), or a "secondary obligor" (who is a type of character with whom we have not had to deal in our introductory survey of Article 9), then any surplus or, more typically, deficiency is calculated using not the amount actually paid for the collateral but "the amount of proceeds that would have been realized in a disposition complying with [Part 6] to a transferee other than" the inside party. In our hypothetical, how Dexter will be able to establish what amount such a disinterested arm's-length sale would have generated is, of course, a difficult problem of proof. But at least §9-615(f) now gives him the chance to directly make his case that the painting would have gone for a larger price without his having to first establish some failure in the notice given to him by Sarah or in the way she carried out the sale.

6a. Yes. The "notification date" under §9-611(a) of National Bank of Connecticut's notice will be sometime in 2009. It is required to give notification not only to the debtor but under §9-611(3)(B) "any other secured party . . . that, 10 days before the notification date, held a security interest in . . . the collateral perfected by the filing of a financing statement," that meets certain requirements that are in effect to ensure that the foreclosing party will have the opportunity through a search of the records to know of the other filed interests. Both the firm of Spiffy and Sons and Lastditch Financial Services have presumably filed in the correct place far more than ten days prior to the notification date. They are therefore entitled to receive a notification from the Connecticut bank of what it intends to do. See Comment 4 to §9-611 for more discussion of this question — who is entitled to notice of a planned disposition — and how Article 9's answer to the question has changed over time.

6b. Under §9-617(a), the purchaser for value at the sale takes all the rights the debtor had in the goods, free from the security interest of the secured party making the sale of and any security interest subordinate thereto. So in this case the good faith purchaser for value of the polisher would be getting it free from the bank's interest and that of Lastditch, but not free of Spiffy's interest superior to that of the bank. This means that the purchaser will have to do its homework before it buys on sale about what interests exist in the goods, but that is no different than the situation of anyone buying a product not as a buyer in the ordinary course of business who is taking something that conceivably might be subject to one (or more) security interests. The buyer in this case would presumably be willing to pay only up to the value of the polisher minus what is still owed Spiffy on it. It could then arrange to pay off Spiffy with the rest of the money, which that company would probably be more than happy to accept, and own the thing outright.

7a. Friendly Finance is responsible for giving notification of the sale to Lucky. This is because Lucky is actually the "debtor" in this situation (see §9-102(a)(28)(A)), even though he is not the "obligor" (§9-102(a)(59)). The obligor is, of course, Dexter, but the notification given by the secured party who intends to dispose of the collateral upon default is, under §9-611(c)(1) owed to the debtor, not the obligor. The principal obligor, the borrower him- or herself, is not necessarily entitled to notification of disposition if he or she has no rights in the collateral itself, as Dexter here has no rights to Lucky's brooch. See the example given at the end of Comment 3 to §9-611. We have to assume, however, that Lucky will let Dexter know of what's going on — that Lucky's brooch is about to be sold off to satisfy Dexter's debt — that is, if Lucky can find Dexter at this point. Lucky was indeed a good friend to Dexter when Dexter was in need. Let us hope for his sake that Lucky does not live to regret his act of kindness.

7b. As we have already seen in §9-615(d)(1), Lucky as the debtor would be entitled to any surplus.

7c. Subsection §9-615(d)(2) makes clear it is the obligor, here Dexter, who is liable for any deficiency. Lucky is not, in our hypothetical, an obligor, and is hence not responsible for any deficiency. Dexter is responsible for the deficiency. And, more than likely, he has some explaining to do to Lucky.

CHAPTER 22

Strict Foreclosure and the Right of Redemption

INTRODUCTION

Assume a default has occurred and the secured party has repossessed the collateral. The previous chapter dealt with what will generally or normally be expected to follow: The secured party arranges for and carries out a disposition of the collateral, either by private or public sale. If the amount received from the sale is enough to pay off the debtor's obligations and cover the secured party's reasonable expenses as well, and there is still some left over, then the debtor is to receive the surplus. If what is taken from the sale does not cover the secured obligation, the secured party has the right to go against the debtor for a deficiency judgment and collect what it can of this judgment just as it would any other money judgment rendered by a court. Repossession and resale is the most typical tale of enforcement under Part 6 of Article 9. This chapter deals with two other possible ways the enforcement scenario may draw to a close, in either case at the instigation of one or the other of the parties.

Under §9-620 the secured party and debtor may agree to the secured party's retaining the collateral "in full or partial satisfaction of the obligation it secures." This procedure, generally referred to as that of *strict foreclosure*, is, except for those instances falling within the ambit of §9-620(e) where the collateral is consumer goods and at least 60 percent of the price or loan secured by those goods has already been paid by the consumer debtor, an option open to the secured party at its discretion. The secured party must, of course, get the debtor's consent to its retention of the collateral in full or partial satisfaction of what it is owed. The important question of what constitutes consent for these purposes is dealt with in subsection (c) of §9-620. Consent of the debtor may be given in an authenticated record "agree[ing] to the terms of the acceptance [of the collateral by the secured party to satisfy, either entirely or partially, the obligation] in a record authenticated after default." Note that, in addition, when acceptance by the secured party in full satisfaction is contemplated, under the workings of §9-620(c)(2), the secured party may also obtain the debtor's consent to the strict foreclosure by a procedure under which the debtor is sent a proposal indicating what the secured party intends to do and the debtor does not object to the proposal within a specified period of time. We will explore the workings of the strict foreclosure story in Examples 1 through 5 below.

The debtor's *right to redeem* the collateral is found in §9-623. Prior to the secured party's disposition of the collateral under §9-610 or before a strict foreclosure has been agreed to by the parties, the debtor always has the right to get the collateral back, provided of course he or she can come up with and tender the cash to "fulfill[ ] all obligations secured by the collateral" as well as the reasonable expenses already incurred by the secured party. Examples 6 and 7 put the right to redemption to the test.

Examples

1. In 2006 Isabelle Inkster, the printer, purchases a new printing press from its manufacturer, the Pressman Corporation. She buys on credit, agreeing to pay for the press in monthly installments over a four-year period and granting the seller a security interest in the press to secure her payment of the price. In 2008 Inkster's business is not doing well and she fails to make several payments to Pressman. Invoking an acceleration clause in the security agreement, Pressman declares her to be in default and makes a demand for all that remains due of the full purchase price of the press. Seeing no way to come up with this amount of cash, Inkster makes no objection when a representative of Pressman comes to repossess the machine in March. On April 11 Pressman mails to Inkster a notice proposing that it retain possession of the press in full satisfaction of her debt.

   a. Inkster, just happy to be out from under this debt and believing that the used press would be unlikely to fetch more on resale than what she currently owes Pressman, makes no response to this proposal. What consequences flow from this proposal and Inkster's lack of response?

   b. Suppose instead that Inkster judges the resale value of the press to be significantly in excess of what she still owes Pressman. She responds in writing to Pressman that she does not agree to its proposal, this notice being received by Pressman on April 23. What is the status of the parties under this set of facts? Whose move is it?

c. Finally, suppose that Inkster does write to object to Pressman's proposal, but that her written objection is not received by that firm until May 11. What would be the result now?

2. As it turns out, in 2006 Isabelle Inkster, the printer, also bought a new binding machine from its manufacturer, the Bindall Corporation, under an agreement to pay the purchase price ($60,000) over three years and granting the seller a security interest in the machine to secure payment of the price. In 2008, when her business begins to run into financial difficulty, she realizes she can no longer afford payment on the binding machine, and in fact stops making payments to Bindall. That company considers the situation and determines, since the market for this type of binder, especially in a used condition, is particularly poor, that the current value of the machine does not come up to what it is still owed by Inkster. It agrees to take the binder off her hands, but only if she agrees that Bindall's retention of the machine will only partially fulfill her obligation. Inkster agrees in writing that Bindall can repossess the machine and retain it in satisfaction of all but $10,000 of her outstanding debt. Bindall does come and take the machine in accordance with this agreement. What is the result here?

3. Professor Flack acknowledges he is tired of bicycling to work and decides to treat himself to an expensive new luxury Aspen auto from Sam's Autorama. He signs a note agreeing to pay for his purchase in equal monthly installments over a four-year period. He also signs a security agreement giving Sam a security interest in the car to cover his payment obligation. After only a couple of months, Flack begins to fall behind in making his payments and soon he has missed three months in a row. He also is surprised to discover how much he must pay to properly insure this model of car, as he is committed to do under the terms of the security agreement, as well as how expensive are the other costs of upkeep. Flack realizes he is in over his head and does not object when Sam sends a repossession agent to take back the car. On December 1 Flack receives a notice from Sam, who proposes to retain the car in full satisfaction of all amounts owed to him by Flack. Flack makes no response to this notice.

a. What is the status of the transaction as it now stands?

b. Suppose instead that for the first three years of the four-year payment period Flack dutifully makes each monthly payment as due, keeps the car properly insured and meets all of his other responsibilities under the security agreement. At this point Flack suffers a financial setback when sales of the books that he writes, which had previously generated plenty of extra disposable income for him, inexplicably fall off. He is struggling financially and finds that he cannot meet his payments on the car. As soon as Flack misses a payment, Sam declares him in default and accelerates the debt. The car is repossessed. Flack receives written notice from Sam proposing that he, Sam, retain the car in full satisfaction of what would be the eight remaining payments he is still owed by Flack. Flack, still stunned by the fact that his books are not selling as well as they had, decides not to object to Sam's proposal. The auto is gone, but so are his monthly payment obligations. Flack returns to his bicycle and thinks nothing more of it. When he later relates this story to you, what is your response?

4. Andrew purchases a new pickup truck from Sam of Sam's Autorama, which he will use in his delivery business, on Sam's Retail Sales Installment Plan, agreeing to make 48 equal monthly payments of $384.95 each. After almost three years of payments, Andrew begins to fall seriously behind. He is in default and Sam has the truck repossessed and returned to his lot. Andrew waits to hear from Sam about what is to happen next, but he hears nothing. Eventually he assumes that Sam has just decided to keep the truck in satisfaction of his remaining debt. About three months later he is passing the Autorama and decides to have a look in. He notices that the pickup is sitting on a back lot, with no "For Sale" sign in the window. Sam explains to Andrew that he still has not decided what to do with the particular truck. "That's a very interesting model, but it isn't the kind that suits everyone's needs. I had it on the sales lot for a while but no one seemed interested, so I thought I'd just let it lie for a while until maybe things change." Andrew returns home and writes Sam a letter indicating that in view of the time that has passed and Sam's apparent disinclination to do anything to dispose of the truck, he, Andrew, considers their dealings at an end. "You," he writes Sam, "have the vehicle and can do what you want with it. I consider myself free of any obligation to you to make further payment or to meet any deficiency you may eventually encounter." Sam quickly responds to this letter with one of his own. "It is not for you to say when and how I dispose of your repossessed vehicle. I'm in the business of selling cars and trucks and I'll decide when the time is right. In the meantime I reserve the right to hold you to your payment obligation and to your obligation to pay any deficiency which may result from an eventual resale. I'll keep you informed." Andrew comes to you for advice. Who has the better argument here, him or Sam? See §9-620(b).

5. Recall the case from Example 1 in which Isabelle Inkster, the printer, purchased a new printing press from its manufacturer, Pressman Corporation, on credit and granted the seller a purchase-money security interest. When her business is in difficulty in 2008, Inkster fails to make several payments to Pressman and the machine is repossessed. On April 11 Pressman mails to Inkster a notice proposing that it retain possession of the press in full satisfaction of her outstanding debt, which

is in the neighborhood of $46,000. Inkster has no firsthand experience with the market in used printing presses but estimates that the used press would be unlikely to fetch more than at most $50,000 on resale. She therefore makes no response to Pressman's proposal. Inkster later sees in an industry publication that in fact this particular type of press is in short supply and that even used ones are in great demand. She is able to find out that by early June, Pressman had been able to resell the press repossessed from her to an eager buyer for $87,500. Can you think of any argument on her behalf against Pressman that would enable her to share in some of this money? Do you expect the argument would succeed?

6. Delia buys a car for her personal use from Sam of Sam's Autorama. When she falls behind in her payments Sam has the auto repossessed from a parking lot while Delia is doing some shopping. Sam sends her a notice telling her what has happened and informing her of his intention to resell the vehicle applying any proceeds towards the total amount she now owes him. Delia sends Sam a letter in which she offers to immediately deliver to Sam a certified check for all that she owes him along with his "reasonable expenses incurred to date" in connection with the car and its repossession. Sam chooses to ignore her offer and resells the car in accordance with §9-610.
   a. Does Delia have any remedy against Sam, assuming that the §9-610 sale was carried out in full compliance with that section?
   b. Assume that Sam could point to a provision in the written security agreement Delia had originally signed that states that "Buyer agrees to waive any right to redeem upon default or repossession the goods being purchased pursuant to this agreement." Would this make any difference to your answer to part (a) above? See §9-624(c).

7. Professor Flack's books are selling very well and he seems to have more money than he knows what to do with. Not only does he stow his bicycle and buy a luxury car, but he also buys a beautiful sailboat (which he christens "The Aspen Exemplar") from Marty of Marty's Marina. His agreement with Marty calls for payment in monthly installments of $1,000 over a five-year period and grants Marty a security interest in the boat to secure payment of the purchase price. Professor Flack may be rolling in dough, but he is still a bit forgetful. After one year of dutifully making payments to Marty, he forgets to make two payments in a row. Marty repossesses the boat and under a term of the security agreement invokes his right to accelerate all the debt due by Flack under the purchase agreement. He so informs Flack.
   a. Flack offers to immediately give Marty a cashier's check for the $2,000, representing the two missed payments, plus any additional amount for the reasonable expenses Marty has incurred so far in relation to the repossession. Is Marty obligated to accept Flack's offer?

b. What if instead Flack offered to give Marty a check equal in value to all of the remaining payments he is contracted to make plus Marty's reasonable expenses? Will Flack then have the right to get back possession of his beloved boat?

Explanations

1a. Since the press in question is definitely not a consumer good and since a full strict foreclosure is what the secured party is seeking, we look to §9-620(c)(2). The secured party, here Pressman, may and in fact did propose after default its retention of the collateral in full satisfaction of Inkster's obligation. The proposal was sent to Inkster in writing and no other parties appear to need notification. Inkster's failure to object makes it a done deal. Pressman may and does retain the collateral in satisfaction of Inkster's debt. She owes the company nothing further; the Pressman Corporation is once again owner of the (now slightly used) press. See §9-621(a).

1b. Here, Inkster *does* object to Pressman's proposal. She does so in writing within 20 days of Pressman's notice being sent. The result is that Pressman will have to proceed with a §9-610 disposition and thereafter either account to Inkster for a surplus or sue her for a deficiency. We, along with the Pressman Corporation and Inkster, are back to consulting the previous chapter.

1c. If Inkster objects in writing but her objection is too late, as it is in this part of the example, then under §9-620(c)(2) Inkster would be deemed to have "consented" to Pressman's proposal. Pressman has effectively strictly foreclosed on the press.

2. This is what is referred to as a *partial* strict foreclosure. The revised version of Article 9 specifically authorizes (as the prerevision version did not) an agreement of this type except when the collateral is consumer goods (§9-620(g)). Inkster consented to the partial strict foreclosure by authenticating a record of the agreement after she was in default, so she has effectively consented under §9-620(c)(1) to the arrangement. Bindall takes the machine and retains it under the terms agreed to. Inkster now owes Bindall $10,000, but no more.

3a. Flack is, for all his apparent worldliness, still a consumer buyer. He goes into default and the car is repossessed when he has made only something like two of the 48 required payments. The situation here does not fall within the special rule for consumers who have paid 60 percent of the price, which we will look at in §9-620(e). It belongs in subsection(c)(2), which we have already considered. Sam has proposed in writing his retention of the car in full satisfaction of all Flack would otherwise owe, and Flack has not responded. A strict foreclosure has occurred.

3b. Under this set of circumstances, Flack has paid 40 of the 48 equal installments, which would make up more than 60 percent of the purchase price. Now, under §9-620(e), Sam *must* upon repossession dispose of the collateral and in fact he must do it within 90 days of the repossession (§9-620(f)). If he fails to do so, Flack may at his option either recover in conversion the value of the car, as used of course, or may recover the statutory damages allowed him in §9-625(c)(2) for the secured party's failure to comply with the provisions of Part 6.

4. Andrew has bought a piece of equipment, not a consumer good, so he cannot argue under §9-620(e) that Sam is obliged to dispose of the truck within any given period of time. What Andrew is in effect proposing in his letter is that Sam keep the truck in a strict foreclosure, but that does not work under the statute. Under subsection (b)(1) §9-620, a strict foreclosure cannot occur unless the *secured party*, here Sam, also consents. Can Sam just leave Andrew hanging like this, never knowing for sure whether he may be pursued for a deficiency at some indefinite time in the future?

A possible answer to Andrew's dilemma might be found in §9-625(a), where it is said that

> If it is established that the secured party is not proceeding in accordance with the provisions of this article, a court may order . . . disposition of collateral on appropriate terms and conditions.

The problem is that Part 6 in general sets out no time limit within which the repossessing secured party must dispose of the goods. Presumably if Andrew can "establish" that not selling it as soon as possible is necessarily "commercially unreasonable" he would have a chance to get a court to order Sam to dispose of the truck. But doesn't Sam have a point that there are times when holding onto goods for a while might actually be the commercially reasonable thing to do?

5. The answer here seems pretty straightforward. Inkster defaulted and Pressman repossessed. Pressman then made an offer of a strict foreclosure under §9-620(c)(2), which Inkster received but to which she did not respond. There being no objection, the strict foreclosure has occurred. Inkster has had her opportunity to evaluate the situation and has decided what route to take. The fact that Pressman Corporation in effect takes back title to the press for $46,000 and is able to quickly resell it for $87,500 is great for the company, but on what basis can

Inkster now object or complain? Had she objected to the original proposal and forced a §9-610 disposition she might well have received a hefty surplus, but those are the breaks, aren't they? Inkster could try to argue that Pressman was in effect later disposing of the repossessed collateral, giving her a right to share in the proceeds, but there does not seem much support for that. Inkster might want to argue that Pressman's proposal was not made in good faith, but I think it is doubtful that would be successful. See Comment 11 to §9-620, particularly its concluding sentence.

6a. Under §9-623, Delia has the right any time prior to the completion of a §9-610 disposition by Sam (or to the completion of a strict foreclosure carried out pursuant to §9-620) to redeem the collateral by tendering fulfillment of all obligations secured by the collateral as well as the secured party's expenses to date. Comment 2 to §9-623 says that

> A tender of fulfillment obviously means more than a new promise to perform an existing promise. It requires payment in full of all monetary obligations then due and performance in full of all other obligations then matured.

Delia has not actually sent over the certified check for the full amount, but she has offered to do so immediately. Sam cannot simply refuse to listen to her and by so doing refuse her the right of redemption. His failure to do so would, at the least, subject him to the secured party's liability for failure to comply with Part 6 as set forth in §9-625(c), which in the case of a consumer buyer such as Delia is at a minimum the amount as calculated under paragraph (2) of that subsection. Notice that the result here would not be the same if Delia's offer had been only to send him a check "soon" or "when she could." Nor could she exercise the right to redeem by offering to give him what she owes "over time." See the comment quoted in the preceding paragraph and *Automotive Finance Corp. v. Smart Auto Center, Inc.*, 334 F.3d 685, 51 U.C.C.2d 297 (7th Cir. 2003).

6b. The debtor may waive the right of redemption under §9-624(c) only by "an agreement to that effect entered into and authenticated *after default*." Delia has not done so here. A term such as Sam has drafted into his security agreement, signed by Delia prior to default, will have no effect and cannot deprive her of her right of redemption.

7a. No. Flack has a right to redeem the collateral, but Marty almost certainly put into his standard form of security agreement the right to accelerate all payments due on a single default. As a result, as Comment 2 to §9-623 makes clear, "If the entire balance of a secured obligation has been accelerated, it would be necessary to tender the entire balance." Flack will have to do better than this to get his boat back.

7b. Flack is the unusual consumer in that he seems to have enough money so he *can* do better. He tenders everything due on the boat plus Marty's expenses and is therefore entitled to redeem the boat. We can leave things there. Marty is fully paid. And what about Flack? We last encounter him on the deck of his beloved boat, sailing serenely into the sunset.

Table of U.C.C. Sections

Index